MUSIC VIDEO:
A Consumer's Guide

MUSIC VIDEO:
A Consumer's Guide

by
Michael Shore

edited by
Patricia Romanowski

A SARAH LAZIN BOOK

BALLANTINE BOOKS • NEW YORK

 Published in the United States by Ballantine Books, a division of Random House, Inc., New York, and simultaneously in Canada by Random House of Canada Limited, Toronto.

Library of Congress Catalog Card Number: 86-91561

ISBN: 0-345-33346-2

Text design by Gene Siegel

Cover design by Richard Aquan

Manufactured in the United States of America

First Edition: April 1987

10 9 8 7 6 5 4 3 2 1

To the women in my life—my wife, Susan, my mother, Joyce, and my sister, Robin. Also to the women in my professional life: Sarah Lazin, for her guidance, class, and professionalism; and Patty Romanowski, whose Elvis Movie reviews make me laugh and cry every time I read them, and who just plain did an all-around ace job.

Acknowledgments

For all their time, energy, and assistance in providing review copies of videos and information on those programs, the following people at home video distribution companies have my deepest thanks:

Sherry Goldsher-Marsh and Barbara Davis at A&M Video; Jackie Sharp at Independent World Video; Joe Rees at Target Video; Loretta Reed and Jim Gullo at Media Home Entertainment; E. Fritz Friedman and Marilu Eagles at RCA/Columbia Pictures Home Video; Robin Sloane at Elektra Video; Curt Creager at Atlantic Video; Amy Alter at CBS/Fox Video; Lynn Singer and E. J. Levine at I.V.E.; Cathy Mantegna at Vestron Video; Pam Ostroff and Sandy Leggett at Embassy Home Entertainment; Jane Ayer, Lisa Shipp, and Barbi Glass at MCA Home Video; Linda Anderson at MPI; Stefanie Shulman and Joan Axelrod at MGM/UA Home Entertainment; Dianne Kramer at Nina Stern Public Relations for Paramount Home Video; Dana Kornbluth at Bender Communications for Karl-Lorimar Home Video; Danny Kopels at Continental Video; Andy Tannen and Margaret Durante at Ruder, Finn and Rotman Public Relations for Thorn-EMI/HBO-Cannon Video; Mike Finnegan at Warner Home Video; Susan Silverman and Greg Sage at Warner-Reprise Video; Paul Tashjian at V.I.E.W. Video; Michael Shamburg and Ann Thompson at Of Factory US; Rob Wallis and Paul Segal at DCI Music Video; Happy Traum at Homespun Tapes; Beth Lewis at Private Music; Deborah Roth and Rob Patterson at Hot Licks Productions; Mark Freed at Star Licks; Michelle Zieminski at Ken Baker Public Relations for Pacific Arts; Victoria Rose at Howard Bloom Public Relations, and Jody Miller at JLM Public Relations, for Sony Video Software; John O'Donnell, Meg Murphy, and Julia Byrd at Sony Video Software; Mary Kincaid and Sandy Davidson at Walt Disney Home Video; Ron Rich at Pioneer Artists; Howard Wuelfing at JEM/Passport; Ted Ewing at Blackhawk Films; Bruce Ricker at Rhapsody Films; Dr. S. M. Markle at the University of Illinois at Chicago Instructional Research Lab; and Les Blank at Flower Films.

Extra-special beyond-the-call-of-duty thanks to the *real* Mr. Home Music Video, Greg Neutra of Playings Hard to Get.

Also, special thanks to Tim Sommer for his help and input, and to Doug Herzog and Stuart Cohn for their helpful understanding.

Thank-yous, even extra-special super-duper thank-yous, hardly seem enough for my editors, Patricia Romanowski and, at Ballantine, Risa Kessler; my packager, Sarah Lazin, and her assistant, Stephanie Franklin, and Kaija Berzins, Holly George, Janis Bultman, Tom Merrick, and Philip Bashe. But since I can't think of anything else to offer, extra-special super-duper thank-yous will just have to do.

Last but not least, extra-*extra*-special super-duper thanks to my parents, Joyce and Lester Shore, and to my wife, Susan Flinker, and her family, for putting up with me while I worked my way through this opus.

Michael Shore

Contents

PREFACE

Though music video has single-handedly revolutionized several other industries, as an art form and an industry on its own, it's still relatively young. So when Michael Shore first embarked on his quest—to see and review every music-video program released or available in the United States—the task seemed large enough. Of course, as is always the case when you set out to track down popular culture, you encounter the demands and limitations of the marketplace and time. While in a better world than this, institutions and businesses would make available to the public all art in all forms, we all live in this one, so we do our best.

We began by obtaining every catalog published by home music-video distributors, manufacturers, and outlets—both industry giants and independents. From this list were chosen those videos that (a) qualified as music videos under our criteria, and (b) fell within the scope of this book.

First, what is a music video? For our purposes, it is programming available through sale or rental for home viewing that is either a popular-music product (such as a clips compilation, a historical series, or a performance video) or a film that either contains a great deal of popular music, shows a clear "rock video" influence, or is in some way relevant and of interest to the music-video fan. With the growing importance of video as a promotional medium for feature films and the power of hit movies to spin off hit singles and soundtrack albums, picking out most feature films was not difficult—*Flashdance* and *Footloose* are examples of this category. The majority of feature films included are documentaries about performers or films in which they star or play some significant role. Among the programs we considered worthy of inclusion, though technically outside this description, were the instructional programs in which a famous or eminently qualified musician demonstrates how to play an instrument. History always seems to repeat itself, especially in rock 'n' roll. If just seeing the Beatles or Elvis Presley for a few minutes on television changed generations, there's no telling what getting these "private lessons" from other stars could do for the rockers of tomorrow. We would guess the answer is a lot, thus their inclusion.

Falling in less clearly demarcated terrain are those films that are important, but whose qualifications are less clear-cut. In some cases, we relied on our own judgment and our emotional response to such films as *Breathless* or *Zabriskie Point.* In others, we tried to evaluate an artist's general popularity and the degree to which an artist or group's work in a particular film reflected on their careers as musicians. Under these guidelines, *How I Won the War* (co-starring

John Lennon) or *Caveman* (co-starring Ringo Starr) wouldn't warrant inclusion simply because each featured a member of the Beatles, but Paul McCartney's *Give My Regards to Broad Street* would. There are also those film performances that—for better and/or worse—have become so inextricably woven into a star's legacy that they cannot be ignored—Mick Jagger's role in *Performance* and Elvis Presley's movies are examples of these.

As far as genres are concerned, *Music Video: A Consumer's Guide* includes every major popular music style—rock, pop, avant-garde, jazz, country, MOR (middle-of-road), gospel, and blues. Classical music is specifically excluded, since classical music fans and critics evaluate those works using specific and distinct criteria which neither the author nor I felt qualified to tackle. Also out of this guide's range are most musicals. Yes, you could argue that *West Side Story* is a music video, and it certainly has inspired more than its share of video clips, but these films have been catalogued and evaluated elsewhere. Also excluded are bootleg tapes, which exist in such small numbers that very few people might ever see them or have access to them, ourselves included.

After sorting out choices by genre and form, we next sought to obtain every available program for review, either through the manufacturer or distributor directly, or by renting it from local (i.e., New York City and its eastern suburbs) video stores and public libraries. For the most part, distributors were quite happy to cooperate and supplied most of the programs. But there were a few independent distributors who either could not or would not provide review copies. Generally, these were the smaller organizations that simply did not provide review copies to anyone for any reason. Some, however, simply declined to make their product available for review either because the idea didn't appeal to them or because they didn't see any financial benefit in it. We hope this book's success will prove them wrong, so that we can better serve readers in the future with a truly complete listing.

In most cases, distributors just didn't have copies on hand, or the program had been released years before and/or was now off the shelves ("moratoriumed," as they say). When a tape wasn't available through the usual channels, regardless of the reason for its unavailability, we investigated our other sources, though that created a different problem. Most rental outlets stock only the most popular titles, and those few public libraries that do have pop-music titles in their circulating catalogues stick to the standards (such as the Beatles). Interestingly, these secondary sources turned up some nice surprises, such as a tape on the black female gospel group Sweet Honey in the Rock.

After more than a year and half of tracking titles down, and with the deadline looming, we had to set a cutoff date, after which we would add no more new releases. For this edition that date was September 1, 1986, though we tried to squeeze in as many major titles as we could after that. Sadly, in that time, several important programs eluded our efforts, and because of the high retail price (as compared with audiotapes and records, for example), purchase of all of the "missing" titles was not a viable option. Ninety percent of the time, however, the tapes were just not to be had at any price.

Once we got the programs, each and every one was viewed from beginning to end. Though I personally reviewed a small number of these tapes, Michael Shore saw them also and we conferred on the reviews and the ratings for all the programs included. Our format calls for basic information: title, artist(s) featured, distributor, date of release, running time, producer, director, the source of the music, and the selections included. Where information—such as the director's name—is missing, it's because either it did not appear on the program or on the packaging or because there were such serious discrepancies between the two that we opted to delete it. The problem of discrepancies in programming information is quite serious, though, judging from our shared experience in documenting popular recordings, not surprising. Misspellings, mention on the outside sleeve of a song not included in the program, or, worse yet, no listing of titles either on the package or in the credits, were common problems. In feature films, for example, the credits were meant to be read from a theater screen and not a relatively tiny television set. In these instances, we brought our familiarity with the music to bear and identified as many as we could. Where possible, independent fact checkers tracked the titles through soundtrack albums, the Phonolog, or Joel Whitburn's Record Research books, which are derived from the *Billboard* charts. In every case, the form, content, spelling, and punctuation of song titles, album titles, and proper names used in these and a few other standard music reference works (including Leonard Feather's *Encyclopedia of Jazz, The Rolling Stone Encyclopedia of Rock & Roll,* David Ehrenstein and Bill Reed's *Rock on Film*) prevailed. When possible, we referred to the actual records themselves. Those cases in which not all titles are identified or identifiable with a reasonable degree of accuracy are listed as "selections included," meaning there were others besides those listed here.

When running time was not given on the package, we watched the clock and noted these instances with the word "approximately."

We included information on the audio recordings under the section titled "Music From." In the cases of soundtracks or videocassettes based on a particular album, the title was obvious. In other cases, we used this category to guide viewers who, for example, might like what they hear on a Scorpions tape and want to get the records. In many cases you will note that just a label or the act's name is given. Here, the music on the tape comes from a wide range of recordings, or it contains music this artist may not have recorded, or did record but is now not widely available. Again, these records are listed as a guide to viewers; they are often selective and not intended to be definitive.

Our original plan to note every format a program was available in was scrapped after we recognized the sheer impossibility of accurately presenting this information. With Beta production in decline in some companies and others introducing a growing array of forms—VHS, stereo, 8-millimeter, VHS Stereo, Beta Stereo, Beta Hi-Fi, VHS Hi-Fi, videodisc—and in anticipation of unforeseen other permutations, we decided to note only videodisc releases, feeling that these would be of particular interest to consumers. Unless a review indicates that a program is available only on videodisc, you can assume that it is more than likely out on VHS and perhaps Beta as well. At any rate, check with your local video store, or use the addresses at the back of this book and write to the distributor to request information on that particular program or on the distributor's whole catalog.

You will also find in the Appendix the addresses of independent or mail-order video outlets, many of whose tapes are reviewed here. We encourage anyone with a particular interest to write for materials from these companies. As the home music-video universe expands, the range and quality of titles will only increase; though, with the "franchisization" of the local video rental outlet, those music programs that don't sell millions of copies will be passed over. We believe that these alternative outlets—which carry most of the blues, avant-garde, and more artistically adventurous programs—are making a significant contribution to video and music in general, and we urge you to support their efforts. And don't overlook your local public library, some of which are amassing impressive music catalogs and in some cases making them available to you for very negligible fees or even for free.

Because we intend this book to function as a viewer's resource and music lover's reference, we have strived to make it as accurate and complete as possible. As large as this book is, it is the cornerstone of a reference work we hope to update many times in the future. Readers with further information to offer—or a particular artist or tape we've omitted that they feel should be included in future editions—can write to Michael Shore, c/o Sarah Lazin Books, 302 West 12th Street, apt. 11B, New York, New York 10014. Although every letter will be read and considered, we cannot guarantee a personal response, nor can we be responsible for materials, such as tapes and catalogues.

—Patricia Romanowski

About the Ratings

Each videocassette or videodisc reviewed here is rated, using a star rating system, with five stars indicating the highest-quality, best, most worthwhile programs; and no stars, half a star, or one star indicating the lowest quality, worst, least worthwhile programs. Along the way, there are also ratings that include half-stars—a three-and-a-half-star designation, for example—and in rare cases, a dual rating, which might give a performance video four stars for a great show, but only two stars because of poor direction. The dual ratings are used only when we believed that the single rating would mislead readers.

Despite the hours of attention, thought, and discussion we have devoted to the ratings system—in fact, I was quite pro-rating; my editor and collaborator, who had experience with other rated guides, was totally opposed—we recognize that at a certain point any such system is subjective. We looked carefully at how other consumer guides used their ratings and exactly what we hoped our ratings would accomplish. In the final analysis, we decided that the reader should consider the star ratings as an important part—but only a *part*—of the entire review. A case in point would be a tape such as *Xanadu*, which is, admittedly, not a great movie, but, as we note in the review, is an innocent, happy little spectacle that would be appropriate for children who like rock 'n' roll. Readers intent on building their own music video library, or who may be purchasing tapes sight unseen from mail-order sources or importers, may use the ratings to help them decide on one tape out of several available from one artist. Still we urge you always to read the accompanying review copy for the final word.

As stated in the introduction, we bring to this book the basic belief that, from a purely historical point of view, each tape has some value merely by dint of its existence. For this reason, there is no program reviewed here that is rated with no stars, although in our system that rating exists theoretically. Now, that doesn't mean that we don't think some are a waste of your time, a waste of an artist or a director's talent, or an insult to the music presented—and those programs certainly exist. We have strived to be objective and not, for example, to downgrade all tapes by an artist simply because we may not think that artist's music is worthy. A tape by Bananarama, to name just one such act, is not automatically given a low rating because it is by Bananarama. By the same token, a tape by or about a rock great, such as John Lennon, doesn't automatically rate extra points because of its subject. On the other hand, a so-so tape, like an otherwise intolerable 1950s rock movie or an otherwise boring film such as *No Nukes,* might be rated higher if it includes rare or vintage performances that may be unavailable elsewhere.

We also recognize the fact that viewers have their own criteria for their own "ratings." Our only presumption about readers is that they know what they're looking for. The goal of this book is to help them find it. A Beatles fan, for example, may be such a completist that he or she would want to own everything any Beatle ever did, while an audiophile might choose to pass over *The Concert for Bangladesh* and someone who loves videos for their visual potential might exclude from his collection *Let It Be* or *Magical Mystery Tour.* The hard-core historian would want to see all of them, while the casual fan or someone building a respectable but not exhaustive collection might be satisfied with *The Compleat Beatles.* These considerations are discussed in the reviews but do not come into play in the ratings. For example, *Magical Mystery Tour* is not downgraded because we expect something better or more from the Beatles, or because this film isn't as good or as historically important as *A Hard Day's Night* or *Let It Be*.

You may note a seemingly undue preponderance of titles rated with two and half stars, which in our system translates roughly as "fair to good." For the most part, these titles have both good and bad aspects, and an absolute final verdict could go either way. So, rather than take a purely subjective final step in the ratings, we've tried to indicate in the review what these good and bad points are. Also not considered in the ratings are any problems (discrepancies, errors, etc.) on the packaging. Unfortunately, in the home-video industry these kinds of problems are common and beyond the control of a program's stars, directors, or producers. These problems are noted but do not affect the ratings. If they did, many programs would unfairly suffer for problems that really do not affect viewer enjoyment.

With all of that said, here is the basic guide to the star rating system. (Half-star ratings indicate that a program falls on the cusp between the two full ratings.)

—Michael Shore

★★★★★ Excellent and recommendable without qualification to *all* viewers. This program's music, performance, direction, sound, visuals—essentially everything about it—makes it a must-see for any music video fan and a must-have for any serious collector.

★★★★ Excellent and highly recommended to everyone, but *particularly* to fans of the artist or genre featured, though basically worthwhile for all.

★★★ Good and recommendable to both fans and nonfans of the genre or star of the program, and/or makes good enough use of the medium to warrant consideration from others, especially music video fans and scholars.

★★ Fair and recommendable only to fans and completists interested in the star or genre. Others may be disappointed.

★ Poor. Only hard-core fans, completists, masochists, or the insatiably curious need bother. Others *will* be very disappointed.

INTRODUCTION

Music Video: A Consumer's Guide is intended to be the most comprehensive, informative consumer guide to the vast variety of popular home music-video programs available. Here you will find roughly 800 entries, each with production information, in-depth reviews, and convenient star ratings to guide you in selecting from the various rock, pop, country, jazz, blues, ambient, ethnic, and avant-garde titles.

The reasons for compiling such a guide are many, and some are quite surprising. In 1983, when I wrote *The Rolling Stone Book of Rock Video,* music video seemed a medium that even in its infancy held infinite possibilities. As I researched the history of music and film all the way back to the turn of the century, I found a number of little-known video visionaries whose work was ahead of its time or its technology.

Today, with the technology readily available, the choices open to those with access to only broadcast (e.g., *Friday Night Videos*) and cable television (e.g., MTV, VH-1) are quite limited. As always seems to be true of any medium with vast commercial impact, there were contemporary artists whose work was overlooked because it didn't fit the MTV mold. In 1983, artists and directors spoke glowingly of the future, when they would create video works independent of any music release. At the same time, others were bemoaning the advent of the so-called "video act," the performer or group whose phenomenal popularity derived not from musical talent nor any ability other than that of looking good on the screen.

To a certain extent, each of these things has occurred, either more or less, depending on how you look at it. While there have been "video bands," the use of video promotion by acts outside rock 'n' roll has proven that bad taste isn't synonymous with rock: a Ronnie Milsap or Amy Grant video can be just as tasteless and dumb as the lowliest heavy metal or the shallowest power-pop clip. And besides, it's hard to argue against video, when the new medium can be held responsible for the newfound popularity of a Cyndi Lauper or the rekindled career of a Tina Turner. The large number of full-length video works has yet to materialize, though rock video's style and attitude have so dramatically influenced television, movies, commercials and Madison Avenue, and fashion that it's almost as if rock video has permeated every visual art in the culture. A grand statement, yes, but one not totally without merit.

If you picked up this book expecting to find yet another "rock book," you will no doubt be surprised at the wide array of artists and genres covered, many of which you may never see unless you view the cassette in your home. And, believe it or not, between a third and half of these programs were available before MTV went on the air in 1981 and changed the course of rock history. Even then, before all of the music network's impact was clear, some movers and shakers in the new home-video industry—most prominently John O'Donnell of Sony Video Software—were trumpeting the imminent home music-video revolution.

Even though music titles have been outsold and outrented by feature films and interactive/how-to programs (such as Jane Fonda's best-selling workout tapes), industry observers generally believe that music is and will continue to constitute a vital segment of the home-video software market. This is due in part to the built-in, inherently "repeatable" nature of music itself and thus music programs—which is something feature films decidedly lack—and partly due to the advances in video hardware. The technological improvement can be seen on two fronts. At the high end of the VCR cost spectrum, there have been the introductions of Beta and VHS Hi-Fi stereo sound, both of which finally allow videocassettes to sound virtually as good as anything else ever has, including laser videodiscs—provided, of course, you connect the VCR to your stereo. The tradeoff, however, and the reason VCRs and videocassettes far outsell videodisc players and the discs themselves is that despite their superior sound and picture quality, discs can only be watched, not recorded on. At the lower end of the price spectrum was the introduction of a variety of low-cost VCRs in 1985, a sort of replay of the early sixties when cheap portable record players sparked a massive sales boom in rock records.

Indeed, between 1985 and the fall of 1986, VCR sales were spiraling. Nearly a million units sold per month, and America's VCR-owning population nearly doubled in less than two years. Overall sales and rentals of video programs naturally increased commensurately. Industry observers were predicting that, with the post-'60s audience—weaned on rock and TV—now buying most of those fast-selling VCRs, music titles would account for at least a quarter of the total software market. In anticipation of that time, marketing techniques were becoming increasingly sophisticated. For example, CBS/Fox Video's *The Ultimate Ozzy,* a concert program shot early in Ozzy Osbourne's extended 1986 U.S. tour, was released midway into the tour, rather than after it—an ingenious move that will most certainly be copied by other acts who aim to boost record and concert ticket sales, not to mention home-video sales.

Of course, with more and more software distributors rushing to take advantage of this newly expanding market, there will be more programs released at greater frequency. It can be hard to keep up—in the six to eight months between the day I write and the day this book hits the shelves, dozens more tapes will be available. But fear not: if you watched a tape a day, every day, it would take you at least two and a half years to see all of these, and by then a revised edition should be on its way. And, of course, you can keep track of what's out there through the various video magazines available, the video review columns that are now common in most daily newspapers, and by writing to distributors for information on releases or by talking to your local video-rental store owner. Bear in mind, though, that the industry is still in its early years, and things do change, such as distributors (U2's *Under a Blood Red Sky,* first released by MCA, is now distributed by RCA/Columbia). Also, sometimes a previously available tape will be pulled out of circulation for a period of time, only to return the next year or so. Others may go out of print forever. But if enough people write to the last known distributor, who knows what could happen?

The summer of 1986 seemed like an especially good time to lay the foundation for a critical guide to home music-video programs. Despite the rampant optimism sparked by those phenomenal hardware sales, there were some downbeat signals being sounded then, too. Most notably, industry leader Sony had finally begun to pull back from its usual avalanche-of-titles release schedules. For several years prior to that, Sony had developed one of the biggest and broadest catalogues of music titles of any software distributor. Like record companies in the fat sixties and early seventies, Sony had read the music explosion and the tremendous hardware sales as a sign that the public would want to check out everything from avant-garde theater pieces to MOR clips compilations. Despite the novelty of home music videos, consumers proved disappointingly consistent in their tastes. No matter how innovative, provocative, or artistically valid the lesser-known title, consumers weren't interested. They wanted the big names, the familiar faces. Not surprisingly, Michael Jackson, Prince, David Bowie, and Madonna were at the top of the video sales and rentals charts, not Jesse Rae's *Rusha* nor the *Danspak* collections.

But, as independent film and record companies proved long ago, our pluralistic society also includes a large and constantly expanding marketplace for these experimental and decidedly non-mainstream works. In this light, Sony's withdrawal from this segment of the marketplace doesn't portend dire days for the industry, only its maturity into specialization, as new distributors and mail-order houses are stepping in to fill the gap. We've tried to include as many as possible of these lesser-known tapes, simply because they are often released with little or no fanfare. Of the many such tapes I've viewed, I can say without qualification that in terms of quality and long-term replayability, a large percentage of these are exceptional and deserve the widest audience possible.

You may well wonder "Why should I rent a tape of, say, Tina Turner in concert, when I could see it on HBO?" Or, "What's the point of watching *The Song Remains the Same* or *This Is Spinal Tap* at home if I have seen it, or could see it, at the local movie decaplex?" There are the standard arguments—home viewing is convenient, repeatable, and totally viewer-controlled. And, generally speaking, the quality of the tape you rent is probably superior in sound, at least, to the one you make by copying a program from the television. But, further, you often get extras on home-video programs that you don't see elsewhere—perhaps a brief interview with your favorite star, or an additional video tacked on at the end, or just the packaging and the attendant information.

But those are the practical, most obvious considerations. This book is based on my personal belief that music video is an art form that offers the viewer ways to experience music that were heretofore impossible. Unlike the mass-oriented public spectacles in which much of popular music, particularly rock and country music, are entrenched, home video is a private, personal, and intimate experience. Here again are practical considerations. The fan too young to attend a concert on his or her own, the homebound, the harried, people who just don't like crowds or who live far from major venues can all benefit. Of course, that's not to say that seeing the tape of a concert is just like being there—it's not. But by the same token, when one sees David Bowie live, it's impossible to stop the action and see your favorite song performed again; in a movie theater, you can't yell at the projectionist screening *Quadrophenia* to rewind it and slo-mo or stop the action so you can tell if the swimmer off Brighton Beach really is Keith Moon. With home video, you can talk to your friends about what you're seeing. If you own a tape or are lucky enough to have a wide selection of rental tapes available through stores or public libraries, you can watch as often as you want, or at least with more frequency than if a film were to play at the local theater or your favorite rock star were to appear in your town. And best of all, there's no need to suffer through a rash of wimpy power-pop clips and commercials while you're waiting for your favorite Iron Maiden tape.

Music video also offers amazing educational possibilities. There's no question that music with visuals is easier for some people, especially kids, to get into than music alone. A family viewing night might pit Mom and Dad's *Woodstock* against Grandpa's favorite Duke Ellington tape and Junior's Judas Priest compilation. As I discuss later, home viewing changed more than a couple of my own preconceptions about performers and genres. The immediacy of the home-video experience makes this possible. You might have heard Elvis Presley's records a million times, read every word written about him, and even seen him in concert a couple of times. Yet it's only when you pop in that tape and see him as he was in 1956 on Ed Sullivan that you are as close as possible to having actually been there yourself. You don't have to read about what someone else thought about what they saw that night; you can see for yourself. All of this alters the viewer's perception of the program in question, making the home video experience unique. Thus, no matter what some video critics may say about the disadvantages of watching certain theatrical films on the smaller home video TV screen, the fact remains that seeing something on home video makes possible some perceptual insights that can be obtained nowhere else.

Another way in which home video is unique is that it's virtually the only outlet for a great deal of material that never gets appropriate distribution through theaters or on television and which couldn't be seen otherwise and would never find its audience (and vice versa) were it not for home video. Rock-history programs such as the *Ready Steady Go* series come immediately to mind in this regard, as do the instructional music video tapes that are born of and tailored to the medium. And, again, there are the lesser-known independent releases that could appeal to fans seeking an alternative to what's around or in addition to what they've got or seen already. For example, Beatles fans should at least know that there exists an independently released mail-order tape called *The Beatles Video Scrapbook* that compares well with the better-known, but not necessarily better, *Compleat Beatles.* You can find Bessie Smith and Duke Ellington in their 1920s prime, Miles Davis at his peak in the 1950s (with John Coltrane, yet), the undeservedly overlooked documentary *Chicago Blues,* and the infotainment program *The Other Side of Nashville.*

There is also the chance to see feature-length films that are no longer shown in movie theaters but which may appear on television in expurgated forms. To cite another example, folkloric documentarian Les Blank's delightful films on various American ethnic subcultures, their music and life-styles, often play small repertory theaters and art houses in major metropolitan or college areas only. Or take Target Video's hardcore punk tapes. The vast array of alternatives grows weekly.

Home music video could very conceivably allow popular music, and especially rock music, history to be rewritten. Music video allows us to experience such legendary figures as Elvis Presley, Bob Dylan, the Beatles, and the Rolling Stones through the medium and in the environment the majority of earlier fans did—in the living room or den, sitting in front of the tube. You don't need rock critic intermediaries to tell you what your mom or dad saw in Miles Davis, the Beatles, Duke Ellington; you can see for yourself. For artists outside rock and mainstream country, the home-video experience allows us to see them, and, although the medium is vastly different, the important thing is that we *do* see them. For example, without Bessie Smith's *St. Louis Blues* on home videocassette, what are the chances that you or your children would ever see this stunning piece of work? Furthermore, in many cases we see these people as artists, far beyond the reaches of myth-mongering and clichés. On the vintage historical tapes, the performers—Marvin Gaye, Bessie Smith, the Beatles, Elvis, and everyone else—remain in their prime forever.

The home video viewing environment, and the plasticity of the viewing experience, could also present many a challenge to one's established tastes—a personal revisionism, if you will. It happened to me with surprising frequency as I sat through virtually every one of these tapes. Things I remembered fondly from years before didn't look so good, and things I thought I hated held up better than I'd dreamed. Along the way I found myself pleasantly shocked to be genuinely entertained by Paul Anka and Liberace, among others, and came to the happy realization that these guys aren't simply the two-dimensional shlockmeisters that my rock generation peers and I always dismissed them as. After recovering from this realization, I watched the programs again and unself-consciously enjoyed them, as my parents might. I found this a rather uplifting experience and not a crushing betrayal to my hard-bitten rock and pop music aesthetics.

In another instance, regarding music I thought I knew well enough to loathe, I got another pleasant shock. Watching the British heavy-metal band Judas Priest's *Fuel for Life* clips compilation, I was take aback by the lyrics of "Robbing the Bank," a song whose video had rarely if ever been broadcast. I found Priest's stock rising, when while viewing and cogitating on the Clash's *Rude Boy* and *This Is Video Clash,* the latter's stock began dipping. Comparing the legitimate punk outlook of Priest's clip to the Clash's idiotic romanticism in "Bank Robber," I had to conclude that the critically beloved Clash could be wrong, and the wrongly maligned Priest right. Countless such surprises await you; all you have to do is look and listen. Many standard assumptions—all Elvis movies stink, everything the Beatles did was amazing, kids raised on rock will never get into jazz, *American Bandstand* was square, *The Monkees* was silly kid stuff, big-band swing is for old fogies, the blues is too depressing, who cares about Patsy Cline?, and so on—can easily go by the boards.

There are downsides to many home music-video titles. Some of them are rip-offs, some are merely uneven and/or disappointing, and many contain erroneous or misleading information on the packages that is controverted by the tape or disc inside. We try to be as forthright and accurate as possible in such cases, telling you which titles fall into this camp, and why and how, and to what degree.

If we accept the old cliché and assume that a picture is indeed worth a thousand words, that puts the value of home video tapes somewhere in the vicinity of a thousand books. Seeing—and hearing—is believing. And enjoying.

—Michael Shore

Abbreviations of Video Distributors

A&M (A&M Video)
Carmine Appice Enterprises
Atlantic (Atlantic Video)
Blackhawk (Blackhawk Films)
CBS/Fox (CBS/Fox Home Video)
Continental (Continental Video)
DCI (DCI Music Video)
Disney (Walt Disney Home Video)
Elektra (Elektra Home Video)
Embassy
Factory (Factory Records U.S.)
Factory/Ikon (Factory Records U.S.)
Flower (Flower Films)
HarmonyVision/Vestron (see Vestron)
HBO/Cannon (HBO/Cannon Video)
Homespun (Homespun Tapes)
Hot Licks (Hot Licks Productions)
Independent (Independent World Video)
Instant Replay
I.V.E. (International Video Entertainment)
JEM/Passport
Karl/Lorimar (Karl/Lorimar Home Video)
Magnum (Magnum Entertainment)
MCA (MCA Home Video)
Media (Media Home Entertainment)
MGM/UA (MGM/UA Home Video)
Monterey/IVE (*see* IVE)
MPI (MPI Home Video)
Pacific Arts (Pacific Arts Video Record)
Paramount (Paramount Home Video)
Pioneer (Pioneer Artists)
Private (Private Music)
Ralph (Ralph Records Video)
RCA/Columbia (RCA/Columbia Pictures Home Video)
Republic (Republic Pictures Home Video)

Rhapsody (Rhapsody Films)
Sony
Spotlite (Spotlite Video)
Star Licks
Stevenson (Stevenson Productions)
Target (Target Video)
University of Illinois at Chicago
USA (USA Home Video)
USA/IVE
Vestron (Vestron Video)
Video and the Arts
Video Yesteryear
V.I.E.W. (Video International Entertainment World Video)
Warner Home Video
Warner-Reprise (Warner-Reprise Video)

The home-video industry continues to undergo change at a rapid pace, with mergers, buyouts, and name changes making absolute accuracy in this area impossible, given the time constraints and time lag of book publishing. This list reflects the state of the industry, circa autumn 1986.

A

☐ ABBA
ABBA
★★½

Monterey/IVE, 1980, 60 minutes
MUSIC FROM: Various Abba albums, including *Greatest Hits, Volume 1ABBA* (Atlantic, 1976); *Greatest Hits, Volume 2ABBA* (Atlantic, 1979); *The Singles, the First Ten Years* (Atlantic, 1982).
SELECTIONS: "Gimme Gimme Gimme (A Man after Midnight)," "Knowing Me, Knowing You," "Take a Chance on Me," "Money, Money, Money," "The Name of the Game," "Eagle," "Voulez-Vous," "On and On and On," "One Man, One Woman," "Summer Night City," "Dancing Queen," "Does Your Mother Know," "The Winner Takes It All."

☐ ABBA
ABBA AGAIN
★★

Monterey/IVE, 1983, 35 minutes
MUSIC FROM: Super Trouper (Atlantic, 1980); Frida: *Something's Going On* (Atlantic, 1982).
SELECTIONS: Abba: *"Super Trouper,"* "Happy New Year," "Head Over Heels," "When All Is Said and Done," "The Day Before You Came," "Under Attack"; Agnetha Faltskog: "The Heat Is On"; Frida: "I Know There's Something Going On."

Abba (the name is an acronym for the first names of members Björn Ulvaeus, Benny Andersson, Anni-Frid "Frida" Lyngstad-Fredriksson-Andersson, and Agnetha "Anna" Fältskog) was a Swedish pop factory that ruled the European charts through the '70s and dented the American Top 40 with some regularity as well. The group has always been deservedly notorious for the high levels of sugary pablum in their ever-smiling pop. Still, their densely layered, sunny melodic and bouncing approach has also resulted in some marvelously mindless pop gems: "Dancing Queen," "Knowing Me, Knowing You," "The Name of the Game," and "Take a Chance on Me." Since all of those smashes are included on *ABBA*—a collection of pre-MTV performance videos that are mildly intriguing for their primitive production values—that's the program to get, though there's really nothing to recommend the video if you already have the records. Unless you really, really *like* the sight of those smilin' Swedes lip-synching.

ABBA Again features somewhat more advanced and conceptual videos—but much, much weaker music. The *Super Trouper* LP (named, believe it or not, for a type of spotlight used at many concerts, rather than for any kind of dependably game showbiz performer) was one of the band's last after they ran out of musical steam and finally gave up (maybe it's better that they named it after the spotlight). Of minor interest: Agnetha's solo video, "The Heat Is On," featuring typically Abba music but a conceptual scenario that's steamier than usual, with close-ups of fingers caressing sweaty skin and Agnetha acting smilingly saucy à la Olivia Newton-John in "Physical" (that's okay—ONJ owes Abba a debt, too); and Frida's post-breakup (she was married to Andersson; Björn and Anna were also wed) solo clip "I Know There's Something Going On," a brilliantly stark song production from Genesis drummer Phil Collins smothered by a prosaic video that's too long on dull, confusing exposition and too short on paranoid atmosphere to match the sound.

☐ ABC
MANTRAP
★½

RCA/Columbia, 1983, 58 minutes
PRODUCED BY: Michael Hamlyn
DIRECTED BY: Julien Temple

MUSIC FROM: The Lexicon of Love (Polygram, 1982).

SELECTIONS: "Show Me," "Many Happy Returns," "The Look of Love," "4 Ever 2 Gether," "All of My Heart," "Mantrap (Main Theme)," "Poison Arrow," "Tears Are Not Enough."

Also available on Pioneer Stereo Laser videodisc.

This comparatively early attempt at long-form conceptual rock video falls halfway between a promotional video clip and a rock-musical movie—and flat on its face. A misguided attempt to marry post–New Romantic British band ABC's lavishly romantic musical mélange of David Bowie, Roxy Music, Motown, and disco to a half-baked Cold War espionage plot, *Mantrap* is at least notable for being one of rock video *auteur* Julien Temple's few big flops and for being an ambitious, pioneering stab at a new genre. ABC lead singer Martin Fry may be able to rise it all now and then (mainly in "The Look of Love" and "Poison Arrow"), but ultimately *Mantrap* is an embarrassment. There's some nice scenery of London, Paris, and Vienna here and there, just as there's the occasional decent song; otherwise, it's a moronic story (the stupidity of which is only accentuated by the "ambiguous" ending) acted so woodenly (by the band *and* the "real actors" involved) it's hard to believe. The best thing about it—aside from its admitted pioneer status—is Temple's brilliant use of his excellent "Poison Arrow" promo clip as a Martin Fry nightmare sequence. Unfortunately, that's about the *only* good thing in *Mantrap.*

□ AC/DC
LET THERE BE ROCK

★★★★½

Warner Home Video, 1982, 98 minutes

PRODUCED BY: High Speed Films

DIRECTED BY: Eric Dionysius and Eric Mistler

MUSIC FROM: High Voltage (Atco, 1976); *Let There Be Rock* (Atco, 1977); *Powerage* (Atlantic, 1978); *If You Want Blood You've Got It* (Atlantic, 1978); *Highway to Hell* (Atlantic, 1979).

SELECTIONS: "Live Wire," "Shot Down in Flames," "Hell Ain't a Bad Place to Be," "Sun City," "Walk over You," "Bad Boy Boogie," "The Jack," "Highway to Hell," "Girls Got Rhythm," "High Voltage," "Whole Lotta Rosie," "Rocker," "Let There Be Rock."

□ AC/DC
FLY ON THE WALL

★★½

Atlantic, 1985, 28 minutes

DIRECTED BY: Brian Ward

MUSIC FROM: Fly on the Wall (Atlantic, 1985).

SELECTIONS: "Fly on the Wall," "Danger," "Sink the Pink," "Stand Up," "Shake Your Foundations."

AC/DC is one of the world's best rock bands. Certainly, at least, they are the most delightfully, deliriously riff-happy and least ludicrously silly band in heavy metal: no Gothic/pulp-comic/leather-spandex crap for these Aussies, just heads down and plow through some great, crunching, meaty hard rock. And Angus Young, the amazing endlessly gyrating adorable short (5′4″) guitarist, is a classic rock 'n' roll stage act (*à la* Elvis's hip swivel, Chuck Berry's duckwalk . . .) all by himself. *Let There Be Rock* is a fairly typical on-the-road rockumentary capturing AC/DC in Belgium and Paris circa 1980, but it's exceptional *because it captures AC/DC*—and in doing so, is as straight-up as the band's music. As a bonus, it catches an earlier edition of the band, led by late lead singer Bon Scott, whose proto–Johnny Rotten whine and exuberant, unpredictable rowdiness were more interesting than the endurance-test screaming and longshoreman's lurch of his replacement, Brian Johnson. And there's plenty of Angus doing his wondrous riff-as-animus psycho-dramatic thing, including an incredible ride through the audience that's really one of the sweetest moments in rock filmdom.

By contrast, the later *Fly on the Wall* came *after* the rock-video revolution—so it's got a "concept" (the "amusing" goings-on amongst the peripheral scene-makers as AC/DC play in a seedy pool-hall/club) that keeps getting in the way of the band, thinking it's funny the whole time (occasionally it does raise a chuckle or two) when in fact AC/DC just playing would be more entertaining. Really, a classically misguided move: the added junk will only annoy AC/DC fans, and is nowhere near good enough to attract new ones.

□ ADAM AND THE ANTS
PRINCE CHARMING REVUE

★½/★★★★

CBS/Fox, 1982, 76 minutes

PRODUCED BY: Mike Mansfield

DIRECTED BY: Mike Mansfield

MUSIC FROM: Dirk Wears White Sox (Do-It U.K., 1979); *Kings of the Wild Frontier* (Epic, 1980); *Prince Charming* (Epic, 1981).

SELECTIONS: "Picasso and the Planet of the Apes," "5 Guns West," "That Voodoo," "Sex to Sex," "Scorpios," "Antmusic," "Dirk Wears White Sox," "Prince Charming," "The Human Beings," "Ants Invasion," "Killer in the Home," "Mohawk," "Dog Eat Dog," "Jolly Roger," "Los Rancheros," "Christian Dior," "Kings of the Wild Frontier," "AntRap," "(You're So) Physical," "Stand and Deliver."

Let me explain the split rating: this is both one of the worst pieces of garbage ever, *and* one of the funniest rock video tapes ever released. The garbage part: Adam Ant (né Stuart Goddard) tried hard and was good-looking beneath the Indian warpaint, but with his inane pirate shtick and "Antmusic for Sexpeople" rap he was just a no-talent hype who deservedly went under in short order; the Ants (whose guitarist, Marco Pirroni, looks old enough to be Adam's dad) manage exactly *two* of their typical fusions of Ennio Morricone and double-drummer Burundi beat that are listenable, "Antmusic" and "Dog Eat Dog." And neither is as good here as on album.

Now we come to the unbelievably hysterical part: the Ants *do* sound live, or at least *semi*-live—as in maybe a few bits of live percussion were overdubbed onto lip-synched studio tracks. Whatever, Adam's up there yelping in his thin sub-Bowie voice and gyrating clumsily in his excuse for dancing, as if he's really doing it for a rabid live crowd. But while we do hear applause between songs, we *never* see a single cutaway to the audience. Obviously there was none there while Adam and the Ants went through their pathetic paces for this program. But it's hilarious to see the way that producer/director Mike Mansfield (or *some* diabolical genius) tries to cover that: the dubbed-in applause is not the usual few-seconds-of-white-noise canned stuff; here we get applause *with* shouts and hoots and hollers, and it *dies down* slowly too, just like *real* applause. Wonder what concert it was taken from? Between guffaws, you'll notice Adam dutifully throwing the nonexistent crowd some ain't-I-great? reaction shots. If Spinal Tap had devolved into a lousy new wave band, this would be their home video.

□ BRYAN ADAMS
RECKLESS

★★★

A&M, 1985, 30 minutes

DIRECTED BY: Steve Barron

MUSIC FROM: Reckless (A&M, 1985); *Cuts Like a Knife* (A&M, 1983).

SELECTIONS: "This Time," "Summer of '69," "Somebody," "Heaven," "Kids Wanna Rock," "Run to You."

Adams creates good sing-along radio fodder from his Springsteen/Tom Petty influences, but he lacks the charisma to carry off an extended video by himself. Thankfully, director Steve Barron not only does a beautiful job directing the clips in this compilation, but also takes the care to weave a modestly affecting, remarkably uncontrived unrequited-love motif through the program. Along with the simple, shallow pleasures of Adams's music, this makes *Reckless* an eminently enjoyable video you don't have to think too deeply about. Particularly noteworthy is famed movie cinematographer Vilmos Zsigmond's energetically mobile black-and-white camerawork in "This Time."

☐ **VARIOUS ARTISTS**
AFTER HOURS
★★★★

Rhapsody, 1985, 27 minutes
DIRECTED BY: Shepherd Traube
MUSIC FROM: Television show *After Hours* (1961); various albums by various artists.
SELECTIONS: Roy Eldridge with others: "Sunday"; Coleman Hawkins with others: "Lover Man (Oh, Where Can You Be)"; several other songs by vocalist Carol Stevens.

Though self-conscious, campy, and dated, this 1961 television approximation of a late-night jazz-club jam session is also, somehow, a very fond and vivid evocation of a jazz era gone by. It takes place in the "After Hours Club," a TV art director's conception of a smoke-filled jazz joint, complete with the atmospheric touches of a scantily clad cigarette girl and a dancing headwaiter. This may or may not be what jazz clubs were really like in the '50s, but it's certainly a surprisingly cool example of what TV was like in the so-called "Golden Age." The late William B. Williams, who was Sammy Davis, Jr.'s surpassingly obsequious second banana on the immortally awful talk show *Sammy and Company,* provides the narration in his soft, golden-voiced DJ tones, telling us at the outset that what we're about to see could happen only "in the wee small hours of the New York dawn." The musical high points come quickly, and they are very high indeed: the great trumpeter Roy Eldridge blows the lid off of "Sunday," while the renowned drummer Cozy Cole whacks out a big, post–rock 'n' roll beat behind him, and the awe-inspiring Coleman Hawkins takes a gratifyingly extended series of poignant, pithy choruses on "Lover Man." Williams then murmurs that "other jazz greats will drop by—they always do." However, the rest of the program wastes its time on a thoroughly unremarkably chanteuse named Carol Stevens. Still, the footage of Eldridge and Hawkins is absolutely invaluable, and is enough on its own to make this most recommendable. And the nostalgia value of the '50s-hipsterism on display in *After Hours* has its own ephemeral attractions, too. (Available by mail order from Rhapsody Films.)

☐ **AIR SUPPLY**
LIVE IN HAWAII
★★★

RCA/Columbia, 1983, 75 minutes
PRODUCED BY: Danny O'Donovan
DIRECTED BY: Mike Mansfield
MUSIC FROM: Various Air Supply albums (RCA, 1980–83).
SELECTIONS: "I Can't Get Excited," "Chances," "Lost in Love," "Every Woman in the World," "Don't Turn Me Away," "Now and Forever," "Here I Am," "Sweet Dreams," "Even the Nights Are Better," "One Step Closer," "Late Again," "I Want to Give It All," "All Out of Love," "I've Got Your Love," "The One That You Love," "This Heart Belongs to Me."
Also available on Pioneer Stereo Laser videodisc.

The terminally mushy Australian soft-pop duo—one of the few modern music bands with the dubious distinction of having been profiled on *Lifestyles of the Rich and Famous*—purvey their relentlessly romantic pablum in the suitably paradisical setting of the Blaisdell Arena in Hawaii. Actually, boring as Graham Russell (the tall blond one) and Russell Hitchcock (his Dudley Moore–ish partner) are onstage, the show itself is quite a sight, with a lavish Australian-desert stage set and state-of-the-art laser lighting effects. Of course, I could never have the heart to recommend this to *anyone* but the staunchest Air Supply fan. Though I suppose if you had any enemies you wanted to kill by putting them to sleep, this would be as good a weapon as any.

□ ALABAMA
GREATEST VIDEO HITS

★★½

RCA/Columbia, 1986, 37 minutes
PRODUCED BY: RCA Video Productions
DIRECTED BY: Marc Ball and David Hogan
MUSIC FROM: Various albums by Alabama, including *Greatest Hits* (RCA, 1986).
SELECTIONS: Forty-Hour Week (for a Livin')," "The Closer You Get," "Mountain Music," "There's No Way," "(There's a) Fire in the Night," "Dixieland Delight," "Feels So Right," "I'm Not That Way Anymore," "Can't Keep a Good Man Down."

Fans of Alabama—and, since Alabama became one of countrypolitan music's most successful exemplars in the '80s, they are legion—will probably enjoy this compilation of their video clips. Others are advised to stay far, far away, for Alabama's whitebread, lowest-common-denominator sound will either serve as an unduly expensive sleeping pill or kill diabetics at ten paces. For anyone interested, however, it's worth noting that this is an exceptionally mediocre collection of video clips. "Forty-Hour Week (for a Livin')" looks almost exactly like one of those "Miller's Made the American Way" rah-rah commercials; so does "(There's a) Fire in the Night," in fact, with the four band members in the woods round a campfire, engaging in the usual male-bonding shtick—until the leggy bimbos in gossamer gowns start floating through in slo-mo, taking everything down to the level of clichéd rock video sexism. In "The Closer You Get," which is basically a performance-oriented clip, the on-camera instrumental work is distinctly out of synch with the audio track. For a band as successful as Alabama, such low-quality work is surprising, almost shocking. Speaking of which, one has to wonder just what the Bible-thumping, PMRC-applauding fans in Alabama's audience might think of such satanically tempting videos as "(There's a) Fire in the Night."

□ THE ALARM
SPIRIT OF '86

★★★½

MCA, 1986, 90 minutes
PRODUCED BY: Jay Boberg and Ian Wilson
DIRECTED BY: C. D. Taylor
MUSIC FROM: Declaration (IRS, 1984); *Strength* (IRS, 1985).
SELECTIONS: "Declaration," "Marching On," "Howling Wind," "Knife Edge," "Blaze of Glory," "Absolute Reality," "Where Were You When the Storm Broke," "Walk Forever by My Side," "68 Guns," "Spirit of '76," "Strength," "The Stand," "Knockin' on Heaven's Door."

Welsh post-punk rockers the Alarm perform with fire and urgency in this April 1986 concert on a sunny day outdoors at UCLA, which was simulcast on MTV and around the world. With song titles like "Marching On," "Blaze of Glory," "68 Guns," and "Spirit of '76," it's not hard to see what the Alarm are all about. In fact, with their folkish (they started out as a predominately acoustic band, but by this show were almost totally electric), storm-the-barricades anthems, the Alarm are sort of a minor-league Clash. They're "rebels" who never outgrow those quotation marks nor transcend the prescribed limitations of the "political rock" label to make truly dangerous and seditious music. But then, how many bands really do? No matter what, the Alarm seems earnest and they do demonstrate that they've got the stuff to someday move beyond that rebel pose, especially with such rousing fare as their hit single "The Stand." Veteran music video maker C. D. Taylor's direction is perfectly appropriate and exceptionally exciting, with strategically placed cameras putting the viewer right into the first row as vocalist Mike Peters shakes hands with the highly responsive throng, as well as providing some medium- and long-range angles on the outdoor panorama that are more interesting and entertaining than usual.

□ ALICE COOPER
THE NIGHTMARE (formerly WELCOME TO MY NIGHTMARE)
★

Warner Home Video, 1983, 66 minutes
PRODUCED BY: Carolyn Pfeiffer, Jorn Winther
DIRECTED BY: Jorn Winther
MUSIC FROM: Welcome to My Nightmare (Warner Bros., 1975); *Greatest Hits* (Warner Bros., 1974).
SELECTIONS: "Welcome to My Nightmare," "Devils Food," "Some Folks," "Only Women Bleed," "Cold Ethyl," "The Black Widow," "Years Ago," "Department of Youth," "Steven," "The Awakening," "Ballad of Dwight Fry," "Escape."

A nightmare, indeed. This is the April 1975 TV special that sealed Cooper's crossover from rock's Grand Guignol cult antihero to mainstream camp figure and signaled his imminent decline. Sure, most of the set-pieces can't help but have anticipated music video clips to a degree, but the execution is strictly from prime-time hunger: guest star Vincent Price's warhorse act is Shakespeare compared to the truly horrifying costumes and dancing. The presence of the same crack band that backed Lou Reed's *Rock 'n' Roll Animal* comeback (here minus second guitarist Steve Hunter) can't save this Halloween trifle from hollow lameness. Such Cooper classics as "Only Women Bleed" and "Ballad of Dwight Fry" manage to hold up on their own merit—barely.

□ ALICE COOPER (WITH THE TUBES, NAZARETH, SHA-NA-NA)
ALICE COOPER AND FRIENDS
★

Media, 1978, 52 minutes
PRODUCED BY: David Forest
DIRECTED BY: Martin Morris
MUSIC FROM: Various albums by various artists.
SELECTIONS: Alice Cooper: "School's Out," "Who I Really Am," "Under My Wheels," "Billion Dollar Babies," "You and Me," "Only Women Bleed," "Lace and Whiskey," "I Love the Dead"; Nazareth: "Love Is Just Physical," "Love Hurts," "Better to Have Loved and Lost"; Sha-Na-Na: "Yakety Yak," "Jailhouse Rock," "Leader of the Pack," "Blue Moon"; The Tubes: "Love Will Keep Us Together," "This Town."

Mediocre rockumentary of a mediocre 1977 all-day rock festival in Anaheim, California, originally shot for syndicated TV. Alice Cooper was just about to throw in the towel on this phase of his shlock-shock-rock career, and it looks it. Also on hand are Nazareth, a completely unremarkable Scottish heavy-metal band, and Sha-Na-Na, as execrable as ever. Compared to the rest of this sorry lineup, the Tubes stand out with so-so satires of the Captain and Tennille on "Love Will Keep Us Together" and Frank Sinatra on "This Town." Actually, the most entertaining thing is the copy on the cassette cover: above the title, it reads, "A concert of the most contemporary music ever!" At least *that's* so bad it's funny.

□ THE ALLMAN BROTHERS BAND

BROTHERS OF THE ROAD

★★½

RCA/Columbia, 1983, 113 minutes

PRODUCED BY: Amy Polan, Len Dell'Amico

DIRECTED BY: Len Dell'Amico

MUSIC FROM: Brothers of the Road (Arista, 1981); *At Fillmore East* (Capricorn, 1971); *Eat a Peach* (Capricorn, 1972); *Brothers and Sisters* (Capricorn, 1973); *The Road Goes On Forever* (Capricorn, 1975); *Wipe the Windows—Check the Oil—Dollar Gas* (Capricorn, 1976).

SELECTIONS: "Pony Boy," "Jessica," "You Don't Love Me," "Blue Sky," "Never Knew How Much (I Needed You)," "Statesboro Blues," "Whipping Post," Hotel Jam: "Let Me Ride"/"Danny Blue"/"The Preacher," Studio Jam: "Melissa"/"Come and Go Blues," "Can't Take It with You," "Crazy Love," "In Memory of Elizabeth Reed," "One Way Out," "Southbound," "The Judgment," "Ramblin Man."

Also available on Pioneer Stereo Laser videodisc.

As the first and best Southern twin-guitar boogie-rockers, the Allman Brothers Band has a double-edged sword of a legacy: on one hand, their own catalogue is something to be proud of; on the other, their early and well-deserved success inspired a mudslide of boring, trite, soundalike Southern twin-guitar boogie-rock bands. But that's nothing compared to what had happened to the band by the time *Brothers of the Road* was shot: the deaths of guitarist Duane Allman, bassist Berry Oakley, and Oakley's replacement Lamar Williams, and the much-publicized health and drug problems of Gregg Allman had all taken their toll, leaving the once-redoubtable Allmans in less than prime condition. This version includes original members Gregg Allman (organ, piano, vocals), Dickey Betts (guitar, vocals), and drummer Butch Trucks, plus recent additions Dan Toler (guitar) and Mike Lawler (bass). This edition is probably most notable as the first with only one drummer, original member J. J. Johansen having left the year before.

Brothers of the Road features footage from several sources: the first seven songs (through "Whipping Post," that is) were shot at an outdoor concert at the University of Florida in Gainesville where the band sounds as good as could be expected before a heartily partisan crowd. There's an okay "Hotel Jam" shot on the road, with Betts and Toler on acoustic guitars; a better, electric studio jam on two of the Allmans' lovelier older numbers, "Melissa" and "Come and Go Blues"; and the last half, starting with "Can't Take It with You," is from a concert at New Jersey's Capitol Theater. Betts's trademark sweet-toned lead guitar is in fine form, but Gregg Allman's heavy-lidded, slack-jawed appearance and marble-mouthed vocals are simply off-putting, and on the whole, *this* version of the Allman Brothers Band just barely manages to do justice to its material. It's all shot passably, but there's nothing to write home about. Long-time fans should rightfully curse the fact that the band wasn't filmed earlier in its career—say, around 1971 or 1972, when they were making records like *At Fillmore East* and *Eat a Peach.*

☐ **VARIOUS ARTISTS**

ALL-STAR SWING FESTIVAL

★★½

Vestron, 1986, 52 minutes
PRODUCED BY: Bernard Rothman and Jack Wohl
DIRECTED BY: Grey Lockwood
MUSIC FROM: Various albums by various artists.
SELECTIONS: Ella Fitzgerald with the Count Basie Orchestra: "Lady Be Good"; Duke Ellington and His Orchestra: "C Jam Blues," "It Don't Mean a Thing If It Ain't Got That Swing"; Ella Fitzgerald: "Goody Goody," "Body and Soul"; Dave Brubeck Quartet featuring Paul Desmond: "Take Five"; Count Basie Orchestra: "Jumpin' at the Woodside"; Joe Williams with the Count Basie Orchestra: "Well Alright, Okay, You Win"; Benny Goodman Quartet: "Avalon," "Moonglow," "Ding Dong Daddy from Dumas"; Doc Severinsen, Earl "Fatha" Hines, Barney Bigard, Arvell Shaw, Barrett Deems, Tyree Glenn, Bobby Hackett, Max Kaminsky, Dizzy Gillespie, Ella Fitzgerald: "Tribute to Louis Armstrong"; Duke Ellington/Count Basie Orchestra: "Things Ain't What They Used to Be."

If you look again at the lineup for this 1972 TV special, shot at New York's Lincoln Center, you'll see that for once, a program with the term "all-star" in the title really lives up to that billing. However, this program's luster is tarnished quite a bit by the restrictions that seem inevitably to come into play when jazz meets television: not just the rather tacky and predictable direction and production—but, even worse, there's a certain ineffably perfunctory, freeze-dried quality to the performances themselves, which is exacerbated by the brevity of most of those performances. On the other hand, there *are* some fine moments. For one thing, how bad could Ella Fitzgerald, Count Basie, and Duke Ellington be under *any* circumstances? Right, and they all sound fine, even though they trot out such warhorses as Ella's "Goody Goody," Basie's "Jumpin' at the Woodside" (which, to the credit of the song itself as well as Basie and his band, still sounds like the thrilling, full-bodied essence of swing itself), and Ellington's "C Jam Blues." The real highlight, however, is a first-time-on-TV, last-time-ever reunion of the original Benny Goodman Quartet, with pianist Teddy Wilson, drummer Gene Krupa, and Lionel Hampton on vibes. In their day, they revolutionized jazz (then popular dance music, period) with their delicate, small-group sound. Here, even though they, too, play half-forgotten Swing Era chestnuts, they just sound great, swinging especially hard on their mini-set closing "Ding Dong Daddy from Dumas."

All of *All-Star Swing Festival*'s problems are compacted into, and epitomized by, the finale, a tribute to Louis Armstrong that, while obviously well intended, crams so many players onstage—some of whom, like ex-Ellington clarinetist Barney Bigard, bassist Arvell Shaw, drummer Barrett Deems, and trombonist Tyree Glenn, had been members of Armstrong's 1950s–1960s All-Stars—that none of them ever really get a chance to express themselves fully, much less shine. Some of them, such as the incomparable pianist Earl "Fatha" Hines (who played with Armstrong in the '20s, when Louis was in his fullest glory), aren't even heard at all—and in the case of Hines that's an especially unpardonable sin.

After this rather frustrating exercise, stifferoo host Doc Severinsen (wearing a tuxedo coat that's tacky even by *his* standards—it looks like a salon full of cubist painters threw up on it) appears on camera to say, "Well, folks, we've had a *very* groovy time here this evening . . . " And yet, just as you finally get through wincing in agony, you'll catch a lovely moment: as the various all-stars of the evening parade back onstage while Basie and Ellington lead an amalgamated big band in the sweetly swinging strains of "Things Ain't What They Used to Be," Dizzy Gillespie executes an impromptu, and of course quite swinging, foxtrot with Ella Fitzgerald. That's the way it goes with *All-Star Swing Festival*: one has to be rather patient to find these small, rewarding moments. And, unless you're a traditional-swing completist or have a really burning need to experience the Goodman Quartet on video, it's hard to recommend *All-Star Swing Festival* wholeheartedly.

☐ **VARIOUS ARTISTS**
ALWAYS FOR PLEASURE
★★★★½

Flower Films, 1979, 58 minutes
PRODUCED BY: Les Blank
DIRECTED BY: Les Blank
MUSIC FROM: The Wild Tchoupitoulas (Island, 1976); Professor Longhair: *Crawfish Fiesta* (Alligator, 1980); *The Best of Frankie Ford* (Ace, 1961).
SELECTIONS: Frankie Ford: "Sea Cruise"; Olympia Brass Band: "Nearer My God to Thee," "Just a Closer Walk with Thee"; Doc Paulin's Dixieland Jazz Band: "Li'l Liza Jane"; Art Ryder's Electric Street Band: "They All Aks'd for You"; Dixie Band: "Four Leaf Clover"; the Hawkettes: "Mardi Gras Mambo"; Nkaw Kaw Brass Band: "Brass Song"; Congo Bereji: "Congo Bereji"; the Wild Tchoupitoulas: "Hell Out the Way," "Indian Red," "Meet de Boys on the Battlefront"; Professor Longhair: "Big Chief"; Kid Thomas and His Preservation Hall Jazz Band: "Panama."

Always for Pleasure is one of documentary filmmaker Les Blank's best, at least in part because it deals with New Orleans and the Mardi Gras—the city whose mystique centers on its ability to make partying a transcendant art form—and its Ultimate Party. This is one colorful, piquant subject for Blank, and he tackles it with gusto: he celebrates along with the participants in joyfully subjective fashion, marching right along with funky Dixieland parades, getting down with the homespun ceremonial spectacle of the aptly named Wild Tchoupitoulas; he intercuts such orgiastic footage with informative celebrations of the behind-the-scenes craft that goes into making such a theatrical spectacle of oneself. We learn that it takes the Wild Tchoupitoulas a year to create their brilliant, intricately beaded and feathered costumes. In fact, these guys are a club that exists solely to prepare for and celebrate the Mardi Gras. Renowned R&B shouter Irma Thomas discloses a Creole gumbo recipe. And, in the film's most haunting moment, blues belter "Blue Lu" Baker unexpectedly injects a dark creepiness into the festivities, with an evocative childhood reminiscence of getting frighteningly lost amidst the surreal funhouse of music and marching.

Always for Pleasure covers other, smaller and lesser-known New Orleans celebrations, which also have the same spicy aroma and rollicking, sensual spirit. Throughout, the music is irrepressible and irresistible, from the solemn marches of the Olympia Brass Band to the various genuine Dixieland bands, with the highlights including Professor Longhair's proto-rock 'n' roll blues/jazz/Caribe stew, and the Wild Tchoupitoulas with their tribal, Afro-antiphonal stomps. Surely, *Always for Pleasure* has to qualify as *the* next best thing to being in the Crescent City. (Available by mail order from Flower Films.)

☐ **VARIOUS ARTISTS**
AMERICAN GRAFFITI
★★★★★

MCA, 1984 (originally released in 1973), 112 minutes

PRODUCED BY: Francis Ford Coppola
DIRECTED BY: George Lucas
MUSIC FROM: American Graffiti motion picture soundtrack (MCA, 1973).
SELECTIONS: Bill Haley and the Comets: "Rock Around the Clock"; the Crests: "Sixteen Candles"; Frankie Lymon and the Teenagers: "Why Do Fools Fall in Love"; Del Shannon: "Runaway"; Buddy Holly: "Maybe Baby," "That'll Be the Day"; the Platters: "Smoke Gets in Your Eyes," "The Great Pretender," "Only You (and You Alone)"; the Flamingos: "I Only Have Eyes for You"; the Beach Boys: "Surfin' Safari, " "All Summer Long"; the Diamonds: "Little Darlin' "; Joey Dee and the Starliters: "The Peppermint Twist"; the Regents: "Barbara Anne"; the Monotones: "Book of Love"; Lee Dorsey: "Ya Ya"; Fats Domino: "Ain't That a Shame"; Chuck Berry: "Johnny B. Goode"; the Big Bopper: "Chantilly Lace"; the Silhouettes: "Get a Job"; Bobby Freeman: "Do You Wanna Dance"; Johnny Burnette: "You're Sixteen"; the Skyliners: "Since I Don't Have You"; Sonny Till the Orioles: "Crying in the Chapel"; Shep and the Limelites: "Daddy's Home"; the Cleftones: "Heart and Soul"; the Crows: "Gee"; the Five Satins: "To the Aisle"; the Dell-Vikings: "Come Go with Me"; Buddy Knox: "Party Doll"; the Clovers: "Love Potion No. 9"; Booker T and the MGs: "Green Onions"; Flash Cadillac and the Continental Kids: "At the Hop," "She's So Fine," "The Stroll," "See You in September," "Louie Louie."
Also available on Pioneer Laser videodisc.

American Graffiti follows four boys through one night, circa 1962 or so, in a rural California valley town. Of the four, two (played by Ron Howard and Richard Dreyfuss) are leaving for college the next day, one (Charles Morton Smith) is a nerdy loser, and the fourth (Paul LeMat) is the town hot-rod king. It may not sound like much, but it's so beautifully written, directed, and acted (with a cast that also includes Cindy Williams, Mackenzie Phillips, Candy Clark, and others) that *American Graffiti* transcends every "teen movie" cliché and stands, over a decade later, as an understatedly brilliant classic. The film's characters exist in a discrete universe peopled only by other kids and centered on the radio, specifically Wolfman Jack's radio program, with its hits, callers, and dedications. The Wolfman himself appears as the local god, a man of mystery about whom the kids spin their own mythology. But the real story is about growing up and making decisions. Part of the film's power is its ability to convey the experiences that transform each character as they occur—outside the realm of the adult world, just as kids live them.

The film's soundtrack is a must-have for any record collection. The music is so deftly used here that the period's rock culture becomes a symbolic character on its own. Included are many classics and some less well remembered tunes that deserve to be better known, such as "Heart and Soul" and "Since I Don't Have You." Flash Cadillac and the Continental Kids appear in a sock-hop scene and run through a few of the era's hits. All the rest of the music comes to the film's characters—and us—over the car radio. Even if you've seen this before, it holds up extremely well after repeat viewings and may even be worth owning. During his stint as a movie usher, your author, Michael Shore, saw this more than a thousand times and claims not only never to have been bored but to have found something new with each viewing. A must-see. —P.R.

□ PAUL ANKA
AN EVENING WITH PAUL ANKA
★★★★

USA/IVE, 1986, 87 minutes
PRODUCED BY: Don Spielvogel
DIRECTED BY: Joshua White
MUSIC FROM: Various *Paul Anka* albums.

SELECTIONS: "Take Me Down," "Let Me Try Again," "(You're) Having My Baby," "I've Waited for You All My Life," "I Don't Want to Run Your Life," "Let Me Try Again," "Times of Your Life," Medley: "Diana"/"Put Your Head on My Shoulder"/"Puppy Love"/"A Steel Guitar and a Glass of Wine"/"Lonely Boy"/"You Are My Destiny"/"Love Me Warm and Tender"/"It's Time to Cry"/"Eso Beso (That Kiss)"/"My Home Town"/"(All of a Sudden) My Heart Sings," "It Doesn't Matter Anymore," "My Way," "New York, New York," "Hold Me til the Mornin' Comes," "Jubilation," "The Bitch Is Back," "What'd I Say"/"Whole Lot of Shaking Going On"/"Jambalaya"/"Oh, Lonesome Me"/"Bye Bye Blackbird"/"Mack the Knife"/"I'm So Excited," "Anytime (I'll Be There)."

I'll bet Martin Short—who once did a smashing Anka on *SCTV*'s "Sammy Maudlin's 23rd Anniversary Special"—owns and loves this well-shot concert tape from New Haven, Connecticut's Palace Theater in 1985. And, after sitting through it, I can see why. To my great surprise, I was gradually won over by a masterful demonstration of textbook crowd-pleasing by a genuine heck of an entuhtainuh, a deserved giant in the business, and by the business of course I mean the industry. (This Paul Shaffer reference is intentional: Anka, a Canadian who affects a New York accent, is revealed here as the obvious model for Shaffer's hip parodies of showbiz smarm.)

It's hard to pinpoint exactly when I was converted. It starts out with Paul silhouetted and fog-enshrouded in the wings; he's announced, strides out from a side door between the front row of the middle-aged-to-elderly audience and the lip of the stage, gladly accepting handshakes and kisses from the crowd. He takes the stage, his crack band starts cooking—and he sings *horribly,* like a caricature of a bad Sinatra imitator with a head cold. With what appears to be a hideously forced singing-skull smile, that stiff-backed, bantam-rooster strut of his, and those clipped inflections trying unsuccessfully to hide the subtle traces of his Canadian accent, he seems *almost* as good as Short's impression of him.

But then he starts strutting his stuff. He cruises the front of the stage, crooning, and improvises such interpolations as, "I see a lady there in the front row . . . With a camera in her hand . . . Lemme go on over and give you a picture to remember, honey . . ." And he actually yanks her out of the front row, holds her camera at arm's length, and snaps a photo of her being kissed by Paul Anka! Forget the treacly nausea of "(You're) Having My Baby." Check out the maniacal, somebody-*stop*-this-guy selflessness of "I Don't Want to Run Your Life" and the nigh-existentially maudlin "Let Me Try Again." There's a big screen that rolls down over the stage for a nostalgia/home-movies montage to go with Paul's Kodak-film commercial jingle, "Times of Your Life." He goes on a meet-the-people hand-clasping foray through the audience during his '50s medley, making certain that he "personally touches" what seems like *everyone* in the crowd.

And then he dedicates "It Doesn't Matter Anymore" to Buddy Holly ("May you rest in peace, Buddy" he says while casting his eyes heavenward)—for whom he wrote it, believe it or not. (Considering its title, it is ironic that it was the first Holly single released after his tragic death). Maybe the Holly connection subliminally influenced me, but this is far and away the best song Anka has to offer here. And by this time, I was stunned into grinning submission by the sheer surreal intensity of it all. After the all-time classic "My Way," Paul lets a guy from the audience sing a chorus of "New York, New York." And then he lights into a rocking little version of Elton John's "The Bitch Is Back"! To put the capper on it, during his second extended medley, Anka does a breathless bossa-nova take on "Mack the Knife" that's unique.

Really. No, *really.* Paul Anka is *that good*—certainly several cuts above what the cynic might expect. You could enjoy this in an ironic, campy frame of mind. Or, you could look and listen a little harder, and note that Anka is so genuinely, *desperately* eager to entertain, despite his manifest vocal limitations, that his particular brand of shlock is transcending itself even as you sit there shaking your head in disbelief.

□ CARMINE APPICE
THE CARMINE APPICE DRUM CLINIC
★★½

Carmine Appice Enterprises, 1985, 40 minutes

PRODUCED BY: Carmine Appice

MUSIC FROM: Carmine Appice Drum Clinic.

SELECTIONS: Not listed.

Appice is a respected "heavy" drummer whose credits go back to '60s psychedelic sludgemongers Vanilla Fudge and also include Jeff Beck, Rod Stewart, and Ozzy Osbourne. Here, his clinic revolves around hard rock and jazz-rock fusion techniques, and the stuff he covers is not for beginners. His teaching, which seems just a bit perfunctory, also competes with a rambunctious impulse to self-congratulation. He alternates explanations and demonstrations of practice routines and tricks of the trade with ostensibly rehearsed-to-seem-spontaneous answers to all-about-Carmine questions. The inquiring audience, as well as the players Appice jams with on a few fusion workouts, are all off-camera the whole time. Weird. But if you like his drumming and its musical contexts, you may like this. (Available by mail order from Carmine Appice Enterprises.)

□ CARMINE APPICE
DRUM MASTER CLASS
★★★★

Hot Licks, 1986, 60 minutes

PRODUCED BY: Arlen Roth

DIRECTED BY: Mark Kaplan

MUSIC FROM: Various demonstrations and performances by Carmine Appice.

SELECTIONS: Substitution patterns, accents, time signature feels, hi-hat figures, advanced stick-twirling, double-bass patterns, soloing, various other patterns and licks.

Drum Master Class does a much better job than *Drum Clinic* (which Hot Licks also distributes) of showing Appice as the hardworking, much-traveled instructor, author of how-to-drum books, and clinic leader that he is. The direction, using three cameras (one just for Appice's feet, which are often engaged in double-bass drum figures), is infinitely better, and Appice's routines are better suited to instruction, whereas those in *Drum Clinic* are more demonstrations or would offer usable tips only to fairly accomplished players. As in other Hot Licks videos, split-screens are used to show what both Appice's hands and feet are doing at the same time. And as with all instructional home videos, you can always rewind and replay whatever throws you at first. (Available by mail order from Hot Licks Productions.)

□ APRIL WINE
LIVE IN LONDON
★★½

HBO/Cannon, 1981, 60 minutes

DIRECTED BY: Derek Burbidge

MUSIC FROM: The Whole World's Goin' Crazy (London, 1976); *Live at the El Macambo* (London, 1977); *First Glance*

(Capitol, 1979); *Harder . . . Faster* (Capitol, 1980); *Nature of the Beast* (Capitol, 1981).

SELECTIONS: "Big City Girls," "Crash and Burn," "Tellin' Me Lies," "Future Tense," "Caught in the Crossfire," "Sign of the Gypsy Queen," "Just Between You and Me," "Bad Boys," "One More Time," "All Over Town," "Wanna Rock," "Ladies Man," "I Like to Rock," "Roller."

Also available on Pioneer Stereo Laser videodisc.

□ APRIL WINE

APRIL WINE VIDEO 45

★½

Sony, 1985, 15 minutes

PRODUCED BY: Picture Music International

DIRECTED BY: Stephen Gelber, Martin Kahan, Derek Burbidge

MUSIC FROM: Sons of the Pioneers (Capitol, 1984).

SELECTIONS: "Sons of the Pioneers," "This Could Be the Right One," "Tell Me Why," "Enough Is Enough."

By the time of *Live in London*'s January 1981 show at Hammersmith Odeon, this veteran Canadian hard-rock band's constant touring—not to mention the poppier, sub–Guess Who style being used by guitarist and leader Myles Goodwyn, by then the only original member left—had finally begun to pay off. April Wine were nearing a peak in popularity outside the Great White North, a peak they were about to reach with their first gold album, *Nature of the Beast.* Here, before a receptive audience, they cover both their earlier, no-frills sub-heavy metal boogie and their then-current AOR-formula hard pop. April Wine's fans will love it, and some hard-rock aficionados might like it, too. But anyone else will probably find the music as uninspired and uninspiring as director Derek Burbidge must have; his diffident camera work and ineffectual use of occasional slo-mo, video-game graphics and other bits of techno-psychedelia, suggests he was bored silly by his subject. Of course, these lackluster visuals don't help, even if you are an April Wine fan. Things aren't much more exciting on *Video 45,* a collection of moribund concept and performance videos to accompany some mechanically punched-out, thoroughly uninspired performances (including one that made Lennon-McCartney's "Tell Me Why" sound mediocre!). *Yawn.*

□ JOAN ARMATRADING

TRACK RECORD

★★★½

A&M, 1986, 91 minutes

PRODUCED BY: Don Hawkins

DIRECTED BY: Ray Argall, Tom Schwalm, Steve Barron, Chris Ashbrook, various unidentified others

MUSIC FROM: Show Some Emotion (A&M, 1977); *To the Limit* (A&M, 1978); *How Cruel* (A&M, 1979); *Steppin' Out* (A&M, 1979); *Me, Myself, I* (A&M, 1980); *Walk Under Ladders* (A&M, 1981); *The Key* (A&M, 1983); *Secret Secrets* (A&M, 1985); *Track Record* (A&M, 1986).

SELECTIONS: "Temptation," "Kind Words (and a Real Good Heart)," "Rosie," "Steppin' Out," "Call Me Names," "To the Limit," "Bottom to the Top," "Down to Zero," "Love and Affection," "Heaven," "Drop the Pilot," "I'm Lucky," "Walk Under Ladders," "Show Some Emotion," "Me, Myself, I," "Willow," "Frustration."

Critical favorite Joan Armatrading's probingly intelligent and emotional funk-inflected folk-rock has never been as popular as it deserves to be. She's an exceptional artist whose work has long and consistently displayed a thoughtfulness and maturity as distinctive as her deep, pliant voice. Unfortunately, in an understandable attempt to gain a wider pop audience, Armatrading's recordings have gradually added increasing layers of extra (and esthetically unnecessary) rock textures over the years—often obscuring her voice in the mix and obliterating the vivid intimacy that made her minor hits "Down to Zero," and "Show Some Affection" so special.

Even more unfortunate, perhaps, is the surprise this nicely produced and variegated profile-of-the-artist program holds in store. *Track Record* contains video clips spanning 1977 to 1986 (nicely illustrating the changes in her sound—and the competence of her backing band, no matter how much some of their arrangements might get in the way of her voice and lyrics), a profile of Armatrading by the Australian version of *60 Minutes,* a hefty chunk of her 1983 concert in Sydney (which closes with a moving audience singalong on "Willow"), and, most intriguingly, extended footage of her visit to St. Kitts, the Caribbean island of her birth, on the occasion of its independence from England. Armatrading moved to England with her family when she was three—something which provides a fascinating parallel to St. Kitts's independence festivities, since in her interviews and actions she makes it clear that she's on a search for roots that she can't even remember having. As she mingles with the locals, visits the house where she was born, checks out local calypso bands and steel drum orchestras, and attends the Independence Day ceremony (at which the Queen of England is also present, as the Union Jack is lowered and the flag of St. Kitts is raised), she seems just another tourist. Ah, such irony: she's a British stranger in her own homeland while that homeland is finally escaping British rule. Talk about "you can't go home again"! More irony: we see Armatrading at a reggae sound-system party with the local dreadlocked Rastas, and then she tells her interviewer that, if anything, Jamaican reggae and not the locally prevalent Caribbean calypso influenced her music—yet she then adds that she doesn't think she plays reggae very well. On the same theme, the Australian interview points out that while Armatrading is black, her audiences are almost unanimously white.

So what's the big surprise, you're wondering? Just this: from her music, one would suspect that Armatrading is an interesting person with something to say—yet she comes across as really rather normal and even a little *dull*. Which is not to say the program itself is dull. She *is* a fine artist, and if anything, *Track Record* lives up to its title in a punny sort of way by reminding us that we should judge the art and not the artist. In fact, she herself claims that she *doesn't* write all her songs from a deeply *personal* point of view in the self-absorbed folkie manner, but rather uses experiences she's gleaned from others—because, as she says, no *one* person can be interesting enough to write dozens of songs about. In a way, Joan Armatrading's very dullness is kind of, um, interesting.

☐ **VARIOUS ARTISTS**
THE ARMS CONCERT, PART ONE
★★★

Media, 1984, 60 minutes
PRODUCED BY: Glyn Johns
DIRECTED BY: Stanley Dorfman
SELECTIONS: Eric Clapton: "Everybody Oughta Make a Change," "Rita Mae," "Lay Down Sally," "Rambling on My Mind," "Cocaine"; Andy Fairweather-Low: "Man Smart, Woman Smarter"; Steve Winwood: "Road Runner," "Slowdown Sundown," "Take Me to the River," "Gimme Some Loving."

☐ **VARIOUS ARTISTS**
THE ARMS CONCERT, PART TWO
★★★½

Media, 1984, 60 minutes

PRODUCED BY: Glyn Johns
DIRECTED BY: Stanley Dorfman
SELECTIONS: Jeff Beck: "Star Cycle," "The Pump," "Led Boots," "Goodbye Pork Pie Hat," "Hi Ho Silver Lining"; Jimmy Page: "Who's to Blame," "City Sirens," "Stairway to Heaven"; Eric Clapton: "Tulsa Time," "Layla"; Ronnie Lane and Ensemble: "Goodnight Irene."

These two tapes document the 1984 British benefit show for former Faces bassist Ronnie Lane's Appeal for Action for Research into Multiple Sclerosis (ARMS). The all-star ensemble includes Rolling Stones Charlie Watts and Bill Wyman, the Who's Kenney Jones, underrated veteran Brit-rock critics' fave Andy Fairweather-Low, and Elton John's onetime percussionist, Ray Cooper. The footage of MS victim Lane talking about the fundraiser and how touched he was that British rock royalty pitched in to help is kept to the point and at a minimum, evoking just enough poignancy and avoiding mawkishness. Part Two rates an edge over Part One musically, because guitar heroes Clapton, Beck, and Page each take turns at center stage. Clapton presents the Derek and the Dominos classic "Layla," Beck is in his full fusion-jazz chops-mongering glory, and Page somewhat shakily pulls off an erratic, yet eerily effective solo set, which includes an instrumental version of the Led Zeppelin classic "Stairway to Heaven." The grand finale, with Lane tottering out, shaky but determined, to join all the stars in "Goodnight Irene," makes for a nicely understated, moving coda. Steve Winwood's set is the highlight of Part One.

□ LOUIS ARMSTRONG AND HIS ALL STARS

GOODYEAR JAZZ CONCERT WITH LOUIS ARMSTRONG

★★½

Video Yesteryear, 1980, 27 minutes
MUSIC FROM: TV concert special (1961).
SELECTIONS: Not listed.

Grainy kinescope of Louis and his All Stars, who feature trombonist Trummy Young in this edition, playing their spirited New Orleans Dixieland jazz for a TV special circa 1961.

□ HORACEE ARNOLD AND ED SOPH

THE DRUMSET: A MUSICAL APPROACH

★★★½

DCI, 1985, 120 minutes
PRODUCED BY: Rob Wallis, Paul Siegel, and Steve Ross
DIRECTED BY: Steve Ross
SELECTIONS: Not listed.

Originally produced for Yamaha Drums, this two-hour tape has two accomplished, veteran jazz-based drummers: Horacee Arnold, whose expertise has been in more experimental modern jazz; and Ed Soph, a more mainstream studio pro who's played on thousands of sessions for records, TV shows, and commercial jingles. Together they cover a history of the modern drum set's development and a parallel history of the way drumming styles have developed through the course of the twentieth century. They also discuss and illustrate the fundamentals of jazz, rock, and funk drumming, and go deeper into concepts and techniques such as hand/foot coordination, solos, and fills, playing with a rhythm section (here composed of some NYC studio all-stars).

□ THE ART ENSEMBLE OF CHICAGO

LIVE FROM THE JAZZ SHOWCASE

★★★★

University of Illinois at Chicago, 1982, 52 minutes
PRODUCED BY: Dr. Susan Markle

DIRECTED BY: William J. Mahin
MUSIC FROM: Various Art Ensemble of Chicago albums (1969–82).
SELECTIONS: "We-Bop," "Promenade: On the Cote Bamako," "Bedouin Village," "New York Is Full of Lonely People," "New Orleans," "Funky AECO," "Theme (Odwalla)."

Superb concert shoot of the small-ensemble version of Sun Ra's big band: five master musicians (trumpeter Lester Bowie, reedmen Joseph Jarman and Roscoe Mitchell, bassist Malachi Favors, drummer Famoudou Don Moye) who merge a kaleidoscope of jazz-related Afro-American musics with an outlandish sense of theater to create a surreal, mytho-poetic hybrid. Live in Chicago in November 1981, the Art Ensemble are *not* one of your typical "no visual appeal" jazz bands: they wear face paint and/or masks and tribal garb (except the underdressed Mitchell, and Bowie—who sports a doctor's lab coat), and play amidst a gleaming jungle of saxophones, flutes, cymbals, gongs, bells, drums, ad infinitum. The music floats free as the wind through a seamless set, from aleatoric tone clusters to terse bebop, from delicate lyricism to dissonant majesty to the two hard-swinging closing numbers (in which Mitchell marvelously resurrects the long-forgotten bass saxophone for maximum, and literal, gutbucket effect). In fact, the music is as theatrical as the Art Ensemble's visual presentation. This is truly a band tailor-made for video, yet the University of Illinois production is not content to sit back with the usual long-shots mixed with close-ups. Director Mahin artfully mixes all sorts of good camera angles, many of which capture more than one musician at a time. He accepts the challenge of keeping up with all that is going on aurally and visually, and does a darned good job of it, enhancing an already great performance. (Available by mail order from the University of Illinois at Chicago.)

□ ARTISTS UNITED AGAINST APARTHEID
SUN CITY
★★★★★

Karl/Lorimar, 1985, 45 minutes
PRODUCED BY: Hart Perry, Steve Lawrence, Vinnie Longobardo
DIRECTED BY: Kevin Godley and Lol Creme, Jonathan Demme, Hart Perry.
MUSIC FROM: Sun City (Manhattan, 1985); *Liner Notes* TV special (MTV, 1985).
SELECTIONS: "Sun City," "No More Apartheid," "The Struggle Continues," "Silver and Gold."

This is a superb documentary about Steven Van Zandt's righteously urgent, cross-racial, multistylistic "Sun City" single and video and the *Sun City* album. The project brought together a passionate ad hoc coalition of artists—from Pat Benatar to Ruben Blades, from Miles Davis to Bruce Springsteen, from Peter Gabriel to Run-D.M.C.—to protest apartheid in South Africa.

It opens with the vicious thrill of the incendiary "Sun City" video itself (directed by Godley and Creme, Jonathan Demme, and Hart Perry), and includes material from MTV's *Liner Notes* special on the making of the video, as well as footage on the making of the album and on the situation in South Africa that inspired it. There are so many memorable moments along the way: Daryl Hall calling Rod Stewart and Queen "jerks" for playing the Sun City Resort; Miles Davis in his hoarse, ghostly whisper, grimacing, "South Africa makes me *ill* . . . when I think about it, I can't even play"—and then playing as gorgeously as only he can anyway; rare footage of South African freedom fighters Nelson and Winnie Mandela speaking on camera; Van Zandt astutely observing (keeping in mind the single's color- and category-blind roster) that his record's eclecticism is aimed at "breaking down our own apartheid here, too"; and so much more. Long after apartheid is finally abolished, this will remain an artifact of one of rock's prouder moments.

□ ASHFORD AND SIMPSON
THE ASHFORD AND SIMPSON VIDEO

★★★

HBO/Cannon, 1982, 56 minutes
PRODUCED BY: Keefco
DIRECTED BY: Keith "Keef" MacMillan
MUSIC FROM: Street Opera (Warner Bros., 1982); *Performance* (Warner Bros., 1981); *Musical Affair* (Warner Bros., 1980); *Stay Free* (Warner Bros., 1979); and other Ashford and Simpson albums.
SELECTIONS: "I Need Your Light," "Nobody Knows," Medley: "Landlord"/ "Clouds"/"The Boss"/"Mighty Mighty Love," "Street Opera, Part 1 (Working Man)," "Street Opera, Part 2 (Who Will They Look to)," "Street Opera, Part 3 (Street Corner)," "Street Opera, Part 4 (Times Will Be Good Again)," "Working Man (Reprise)," "Love It Away," "Found a Cure," "I'll Take the Whole World On," Medley: "You're All I Need to Get By"/ "Ain't Nothin' like the Real Thing"/"Ain't No Mountain High Enough"/"Is It Still Good to Ya."
Also available on Pioneer Stereo Laser videodisc.

□ ASHFORD AND SIMPSON
ASHFORD AND SIMPSON VIDEO 45

★★★

Sony, 1984, 21 minutes
PRODUCED BY: Picture Music International
DIRECTED BY: Keef, Mark Robinson, Simon Milne
MUSIC FROM: High-Rise (Capitol, 1983); *Street Opera* (Capitol, 1982).
SELECTIONS: "It's Much Deeper," "High-Rise," "Street Opera."
Also available on Pioneer 8-inch Stereo Laser videodisc.

Nickolas Ashford and Valerie Simpson, the veteran Tamla/Motown husband-and-wife songwriting team, wrote such classics as Marvin Gaye and Tammi Terrell's "Ain't No Mountain High Enough" and Diana Ross's "Reach Out and Touch (Somebody's Hand)" before finally becoming performers themselves in the early '70s. Here, they're caught in a straightforwardly shot, slick but satisfying London concert in the spring of 1982. Nick and Val perform with a solid band, before a flashing neon backdrop and a city-street set for the two medleys from the *Street Opera* album. There's another medley, of hits they penned for others (including "Ain't No Mountain") and themselves (including "Is It Still Good to Ya," one of their biggest) to close the show. Ashford and Simpson are not unattractive and are undeniably very talented. But what will separate their real fans from others here is the unbounded ardor with which Nick and Val sing, to each other at least as much as their audience. They're so intensely passionate it's embarrassing.

Video 45 brackets one excellent video clip with two that are just okay. The latter are "It's Much Deeper," an uninspired mélange of romantic images, and "Street Opera," an extended street-set performance that's very similar to the one staged in *The Ashford and Simpson Video.* Mark Robinson's "High-Rise," however, is one of the better narrative black-pop mini-movies in recent memory: Val's a piano player at boyfriend Nick's little dive of a club; she dreams of making it big, with Nick lending quiet background support all along—until she makes it to the penthouse suite of her new record label, where she meets the president, who (no surprise) is Nick. Val wakes from her dream to find herself in the same old dive and gazes at Nick with a resigned, bittersweet half-smile—perhaps realizing that their love already makes them fairly rich and successful, yet at the same time longing for that big dream to come true. A bit corny, yes, but Robinson handles it with genuinely impressive dramatic momentum and production values, and he gets fine performances out of the principals, especially Val.

□ ASIA
ASIA IN ASIA
★★½

Vestron, 1984, 60 minutes
DIRECTED BY: David Mallet
MUSIC FROM: Asia (Atco, 1983).
SELECTIONS: "Time Again," "The Heat Goes On," "Here Comes the Feeling," "Eye to Eye," "Only Time Will Tell," "Open Your Eyes," "The Smile Has Left Your Eyes," "Wildest Dreams," "Heat of the Moment," "Sole Survivor."
Also available on Pioneer Stereo Laser videodisc.

Asia was an AOR elephant's graveyard for progressive-rock dinosaurs Steve Howe (former guitarist with Yes), Carl Palmer (former drummer with Emerson, Lake and), and John Wetton (former bassist with King Crimson, Uriah Heep, and U.K.), along with comparative young gun Geoff Downes (former keyboardist with the Buggles and latter-day Yes). This 1983 MTV concert special from the Budokan Arena in Japan finds Asia in typically bombastic form, weighing down turgid, blandly formulaic four-minute FM rockers with the fussy embellishments of eight-minute art-rock suites. Definitely for serious fans only. Of historical interest: Wetton left shortly before this gig and was replaced by Palmer's old ELP cohort, Greg Lake (who looks even more bloated than Asia's music, which is really saying something). This is the *only* live show Lake ever played with Asia.

□ ATLANTIC STARR
AS THE BAND TURNS . . . THE VIDEO
★★★★

A&M, 1986, 15 minutes
PRODUCED BY: Len Fico, Tina Silvey, Masai Enterprises
DIRECTED BY: Fritz Goode, Jane Simpson
MUSIC FROM: As the Band Turns (A&M, 1985).
SELECTIONS: "Secret Lovers," "Freak-a-Ristic," "If Your Heart Isn't in It."

These three video clips, all from the popular R&B band's gold LP *As the Band Turns,* complement Atlantic Starr's smoothly savvy black pop with intelligent, mature scenarios that epitomize the general difference between the coldly arrogant sexism of so many white rock videos, and the softer, sweeter romanticism of most "urban contemporary" (as in black pop and dance music) clips.

"Secret Lovers" starts as vocalist Barbara Weathers introduces the ballad live onstage with a good-naturedly sassy rap, before the two-timing story is fleshed out with illustrative conceptual scenes (with Weathers, vocalist Wayne Lewis, and guitarist David Lewis as the points of the love triangle) intercut with the live rendition. "Freak-a-Ristic" is one of those wild party scene clips, in which Wayne Lewis is seduced by the stunning lady of the title. Here especially, in a setting that would invite repulsive sexist machoisms were a white rock band being filmed, the absence of same in favor of affectionate comedy and choreography is a pleasure to observe. Best of all is "If Your Heart Isn't in It," a Pirandellian scenario with the band in a screening room watching themselves (and reacting with sharply conflicting emotions) in a '40s-style movie that continues the story of "Secret Lovers." It's beautifully produced and directed by Tina Silvey and Jane Simpson, respectively. (Simpson has directed fashion videos for designer Norma Kamali, one of which was used with added performance scenes for Chaka Khan's "I Feel for You" clip.)

Atlantic Starr's fans will find satisfaction aplenty here. And for anyone who's weary of rock-video overload, a program like this may seem like a refreshing relief.

☐ VARIOUS ARTISTS (INXS, EUROGLIDERS, MEN AT WORK, OTHERS)

AUSTRALIA NOW

★★½

Media, 1985, 60 minutes

PRODUCED BY: Pom Oliver and Peter Clifton

DIRECTED BY: Peter Clifton

MUSIC FROM: Various albums by various artists.

SELECTIONS: Mondo Rock: "No Time"; INXS: "Stay Young," "The Loved One"; Australian Crawl: "Errol," "Shut Down"; Mental as Anything: "I Didn't Mean to Be Mean," "Got Hit"; Split Enz: "Six Months in a Leaky Boat"; Eurogliders: "Waiting for You"; Men at Work: "Be Good Johnny," "Down Under," "Who Can It Be Now?"; Angel City: "Eat City"; Icehouse: "Great Southern Land"; unidentified Aborigines: "Songs of the Bamyili"; No Fixed Address: "We Have Survived"; Cold Chisel: "Star Hotel"; Midnight Oil: "Lucky Country"; the Little Heroes: "One Perfect Day"; Moving Pictures: "What About Me?"; Goanna: "Solid Rock."

Seventeen bands parade through this meagerly produced 1983 video missive from the Oz-Rock Chamber of Commerce. While the selection of bands is extensive and, one supposes, fairly comprehensive, the music is very uneven, and the visuals are uniformly uninspired and low-budget. Highlights include: Midnight Oil's lurching juggernaut of politicized rock; Mental as Anything's clever, witty, scruffily likable pub rock; Split Enz, INXS, and Men at Work, the three best-known bands included; and the only real discovery here, Angel City, who look new wave but actually play a strangely satisfying, fractured sort of Foghat-style boogie with a saxophonist spitting and snarling atonally over it all. A section on Australian Aborigine music—with face-painted natives playing evocative *dijeridoo* (a long, blown wooden tube) music, and Aborigine reggae band No Fixed Address—would have been a major highlight, had it lasted longer than its paltry two minutes of screen time. Throughout, travelogue footage and brief snippets of interviews with some of the performers are intercut with the performances. The only other points of interest here are: the Monitors' opening "What Should We Be Singing in the '80s?" being lip-synched by two little girls in Kiss makeup (strange); some fairly riveting teen-riot footage from *somewhere* intercut for who knows what reason with the concert performance of "Star Hotel" by Cold Chisel, whose lead singer Jimmy Barnes would later find some Stateside solo success; and the only really actively abhorrent moment on this whole good-to-dull program, Moving Pictures' "What About Me?"—a singularly obnoxious pomp-rock melodrama, as its title suggests.

☐ AVERAGE WHITE BAND

SHINE

★★

Media, 1984, 30 minutes

DIRECTED BY: Mike Mansfield

MUSIC FROM: Shine (Ariola, 1980).

SELECTIONS: "Let's Go Round Again," "If Love Only Lasts for One Night," "Whatcha Gonna Do for Me,"

"Shine," "For Your Love," "Catch Me," "Into the Night."

By the time this was shot on AWB's 1980 European tour, the band had long since sunk into a predictably slick disco/funk/pop formula (they'd actually peaked some seven years earlier with the *AWB* LP). Their performance is pleasant and competent and all that, but there are no thrills. There *are* some production frills—special video effects (like a rotating digital-video cube with the band performing on each side, which reminds me of a disco-era mirrored ball)—to try to alleviate the visual boredom, but there's not much you can do in a case like this. For fans only.

B

☐ **VARIOUS ARTISTS**
B.C. ROCK
★★★

Vestron, 1985, 82 minutes
PRODUCED BY: Jenny Gerard, Picha, and Michel Gast
DIRECTED BY: Picha
MUSIC FROM: The movie *B.C. Rock* (1984).
SELECTIONS: Alan Brewer: "Where I Belong"; Clarence Clemons: "Feline Blues"; Alan Brewer and Rick Derringer: "Afraid of the Night"; Genesis: "Afterglow"; Hall and Oates: "Alley Katz"; Kevin Kelly: "Ant Battle"; Anna Pepper: "Friends"; Leo Sayer: "Eating," "Taking the Brake Off," "Shake the Hand," "It Hurts Every Time But We Love It"; Steel Breeze: "This Time Round," "Step by Step"; Triumph: "Empty Inside"; Rick Wakeman: "Flyin'," "Steamhole Dance."

This R-rated animated feature film with rock score is definitely *not* for kids. It's a ribald (at times downright obscene), irreverent sort of Stone Age *Alice in Wonderland* by way of Cheech and Chong (make that Stone*d* Age), following a bumbling but gifted Cro-Magnon named Stuey through prehistory as he discovers fire, the wheel, and sex, meeting all manner of characters along the way (a jive-rapping pterodactyl; an uppity dragonlike dinosaur who farts fire instead of breathing it; an effete boar—get it?—with a James Mason–like voice). Picha's animation is crude and caricature-ish but distinctive; the voices are endearingly hip and funny; and the script is as witty as one might expect from onetime *National Lampoon* editor and *Spinal Tap* costar Tony Hendra. But don't see it to hear the rock soundtrack. It's mostly bland and anonymous, with Genesis's "Afterglow" and Hall and Oates's "Alley Katz" the only recognizable tunes (and neither is anywhere near the best of what either band has to offer).

☐ **BANANARAMA**
ANDTHAT'SNOTALL . . .
★★★

Sony, 1986, 35 minutes
PRODUCED BY: James Ewart
DIRECTED BY: Jonathan Gershfield, others
MUSIC FROM: Deep See Skiving (London, 1983); *Bananarama* (London, 1984); *The Wild Life* motion picture soundtrack (Polygram, 1984).
SELECTIONS: "Robert De Niro's Waiting," "He Was Really Sayin' Somethin'," "Shy Boy (Don't It Make You Feel Good)," "Cheers Then," "Na Na Hey Hey Kiss Him Goodbye," "Cruel Summer," "Rough Justice," "State I'm In," "Hot Line to Heaven," "The Wild Life."

Bananarama consists of three blonde British babes named Sarah, Siobhan, and Keren, whose voices mesh pleasantly enough on record. But on video, at least, they are in fact *babes*—for to call them women or ladies would be to somehow deny the cherubic, cloying cuteness they seem so strenuously bent on projecting. In fact, it's this relentlessly willful naïveté that is both their chief draw and their undoing. On the one hand, Bananarama come off as sweet, innocent, endearingly wholesome; on the other, they come off *so* damned sweet, innocent, and endearingly wholesome you long to reach into your TV and squash them. Trouble is, the three are, from time to time, placed in some potentially provocative, if ostensibly frolicsome, video scenarios that muck about with some intriguing subtexts: politics of media in "Rough Justice," and macho sexism in "Na Na Hey Hey Kiss Him Goodbye," for instance. But whatever's going on around them, they still play it determinedly vapid, vacuous, and fatuously cheery. If you're in a really strange frame of mind, I suppose you could read that as some sort of transcendent irreverence. Anyway, this is still an entertainingly put-together program, with its self-parodying, hyperbolic-history-of between-clips matter, and, besides, lots of people like blonde British bubbleheads.

□ THE BAND, OTHERS
THE LAST WALTZ
★★★★★

CBS/Fox, 1983, 117 minutes
PRODUCED BY: Robbie Robertson
DIRECTED BY: Martin Scorcese
MUSIC FROM: The Last Waltz motion picture soundtrack (Asylum, 1978).
SELECTIONS: The Band: "Don't Do It," "Up On Cripple Creek," "The Shape I'm In," "It Makes No Difference," "Stage Fright," "The Weight" (with the Staple Singers), "The Night They Drove Old Dixie Down," "Chest Fever," "Ophelia," "The Last Waltz"; Ronnie Hawkins: "Who Do Ya Love"; Dr. John: "Such a Night"; Neil Young: "Helpless"; Neil Diamond: "Come Dry Your Eyes"; Joni Mitchell: "Coyote"; Paul Butterfield: "Mystery Train"; Muddy Waters: "Mannish Boy"; Eric Clapton: "Further On Up the Road"; Emmylou Harris: "Evangeline"; Van Morrison: "Caravan"; Bob Dylan: "Forever Young," "Baby Let Me Follow You Down"; Dylan, Ringo Starr, Ron Wood, the Band, et al.: "I Shall Be Released."

□ THE BAND
THE BAND REUNION
★★★

Media, 1984, 87 minutes
PRODUCED BY: Jack McAndrew
DIRECTED BY: Mike Watt
MUSIC FROM: Various Band albums (Capitol, 1968–78).
SELECTIONS: "Rag Mama Rag," "Up on Cripple Creek," "The Shape I'm In," "It Makes No Difference," "Milk Cow Boogie," "The Weight," "King Harvest," "Long Black Veil," "W. S. Walcott's Medicine Show," "Mystery Train," "Ophelia," "Don't Start Me Talkin'," "Java Blues," "Chest Fever," "Going Back to Memphis," "In a Blaze of Glory," "Willie and the Hand Jive."

The Last Waltz is a superb documentary on the Band's Thanksgiving 1976 farewell show at Winterland in San Francisco, where they were joined by a list of guest performers as eclectic and impressive as the Band's music itself. Highlights include Muddy Waters's ageless raunch, Neil Young's lunatic eyes, Robbie Robertson's guitar duel with Eric Clapton on "Further On Up the Road" (Robbie wins going away), Bob Dylan rocking out on "Baby Let Me Follow You Down," and best of all, Van Morrison's "Caravan"—by far the most outgoing, down-to-earth, crowd-pleasing performance we've even seen, or are ever likely to see, from this mightily gifted but usually introverted, highly temperamental performer. Also noteworthy are the studio-mounted tunes shot with the Band, the Staple Singers, and Emmylou Harris. Director Martin Scorcese carefully storyboarded both the live and studio shoots, and his care was well worth it. This most meticulous of rock concert films is also among the most beautiful, both visually and aurally, and of course it only helps that Scorcese picked a subject so worthy of such attention. The interview segments—where an awkwardly self-conscious Scorcese manages an uneasy conversational truce with the coolly self-conscious Band, who appear terminally road-weary except for the perpetually down-to-earth Levon Helm—can't hold up too well in the wake of *This Is Spinal Tap,* but that's just carping in light of the glittering whole.

Seven years after that swan song, the Band—*minus* Robertson, and with the addition of four musicians from drummer Helm's backing band the Cate

Brothers—staged a "reunion" tour, which wound up with the Vancouver show caught here. It's great to see musicians of this caliber together again, and it's hard to argue with songs like "Rag Mama Rag," "Up On Cripple Creek," "The Shape I'm In," and "The Weight." But just as surely, things ain't quite the same without Robertson, and all those extra Cate Brothers just end up getting in the way. Overall, a bit of a disappointment—but mainly because this is merely *good* compared to the nonpareil *Last Waltz.* The same comparison holds true for the competent but uninspired direction here, if not for the scattered interview snippets.

□ BAND AID
"DO THEY KNOW IT'S CHRISTMAS?" THE STORY OF THE OFFICIAL BAND AID VIDEO
★★★★

Vestron, 1984, 30 minutes
PRODUCED BY: Nigel Dick and Band Aid Trust
DIRECTED BY: Dave Bridges and Rob Wright
MUSIC FROM: "Do They Know It's Christmas?" by Band Aid (single) (Polygram, 1984).
SELECTIONS: "Do They Know It's Christmas?"

This documentary on the first African famine benefit single to kick off the charity rock craze of 1985 has all the ingredients: a galaxy of British pop and new wave stars arriving, mixing (music, and with each other), recording separately and together, talking about the cause and the event, and the official video itself as a finale . . . But, unlike *We Are the World: The Video Event,* there's no sanctimonious voiceover narration. There probably wasn't time for one, since Band Aid organizer Bob Geldof wanted the tape released as quickly as possible, the better to speed relief to Africa. Geldof personifies the dour urgency that permeates this entire program, offering such a welcome contrast to the comparative Hollywood hype of *We Are the World* (early on, Geldof comes right out and calls the African famine crisis a political "crime," rather than a natural disaster). Sting and the ever-lovable Boy George provide articulate, sensitive commentary later on. Throughout, there's a gritty immediacy to the production. And, beyond the good-cause level, it's fascinating to watch singers like Paul Young and U2's Bono Vox, or a drummer like Phil Collins, performing their parts solo, wearing headphones: we hear them loud and clear, but the accompanying music is distant background.

□ BUDDY BARNES (WITH GUEST SYLVIA SYMS)
LIVE FROM STUDIO B
★★★

Sony, 1984, 30 minutes
PRODUCED BY: Doug Breitbart
DIRECTED BY: Paul Shavelson
SELECTIONS: "I've Been to Town," "Don't Fight It, It's Chemistry," "Colors of My Life," "Penny By Penny," "My Ship," "Pick Yourself Up," "Long Before I Knew You," "Guess I'll Hang My Tears Out to Dry."

Barnes is a very well respected Manhattan-based cabaret and saloon singer/pianist in the mold of Bobby Short or Hugh Shannon, with a lovely, sweet tenor voice and a rather genteel, tenderly passionate warble in his phrasing. His bass and guitar rhythm section in this straightforwardly intimate, low-key concert video (his audience sits on folding chairs in what appears to be an actual studio) is joined by renowned veteran trad-jazz cornetist Ruby Braff, who adds sweet-and-low obligatos to Barnes's tasteful, accomplished crooning. Sylvia Syms—

one of those singers who, like Billie Holiday and Mabel Mercer, Frank Sinatra has always said taught him how to sing—joins Barnes for "My Ship," "Pick Yourself Up," "Long Before I Knew You," and "Guess I'll Hang My Tears Out to Dry," singing with her customary graceful poise and dignity, and trading hornlike scat-sung phrases with Braff. The concertlike, non-supper-club setting may be a bit disorienting, but for fans of the genre this is a solidly satisfying, if unspectacular, little program.

□ COUNT BASIE AND HIS ORCHESTRA
LIVE AT THE HOLLYWOOD PALLADIUM

★★½

Media, 1984, 42 minutes
PRODUCED BY: Hurst–Longo Productions/Syntar Productions
MUSIC FROM: Various Count Basie albums; TV special (1974).
SELECTIONS: "Get It," "The Spirit Is Willing," "I Like It," "Still Swinging," "All of Me," "Corner Pocket," "Leroy Brown," "Splanky," "Big Stuff," "Shiny Stockings."

A TV special, *A Tribute to Count Basie,* from 1974—by which time the Basie band had long been settled into a butter-smooth mellowness that, to the untrained ear, sounds like bland middle-of-the-road schmaltz. But listen outward from the Count's own trademark abstemious piano, and you'll hear and feel the unique, swinging magic at the heart of one of the most important, influential, and enjoyable jazz orchestras ever. Eddie "Lockjaw" Davis on tenor sax and trombonist Al Grey are the featured soloists, and both are fine—except that an off-screen announcer intrudes on Davis's "Spirit Is Willing" solo (the announcer also spoils guitarist Freddy Green's "Corner Pocket"). Vocalist Fran Jeffries (on "I Like It," "Still Swinging," and "Leroy Brown") is gorgeous, and has a nice strong voice with interesting tinges of Billie Holiday on "I Like It." The best arrangements are a purring, occasionally exploding "All of Me," and Frank Foster's classic "Shiny Stockings."

□ TONI BASIL
WORD OF MOUTH

★★★

Pacific Arts, 1981, 30 minutes
DIRECTED BY: Toni Basil
MUSIC FROM: Word of Mouth (Chrysalis, 1981).
SELECTIONS: "Mickey," "Nobody," "Little Red Book," "Time After Time," "Be Stiff," "Space Girls," "You Gotta Problem."
Also available on Pacific Arts Stereo Laser videodisc.

Though *Word of Mouth* has been overtaken in sophistication of idea and execution by more recent home music videos, it still stands tall as one of the best pioneering efforts of the genre—one of the first all-conceptual video programs marketed to the home market concurrent with the same artist's audio-only album release. By the time Basil directed and choreographed *Word of Mouth*, all by herself, she already had a long and accomplished career in rock film and TV as dancer, choreographer, and actress, going all the way back to Elvis's *Viva Las Vegas!* and TV's *Shindig!*, on which she was assistant choreographer, up through her supporting roles in *Easy Rider* and *Five Easy Pieces*. She also discovered and worked with Los Angeles street-dance troupe the Lockers—even bringing them on *Saturday Night Live* a few times to show off their pre-breakdance pop-locking robotics.

It was undoubtedly this long-running involvement in the visual end of rock culture that inspired Basil to take such comparatively early advantage of the still largely untested home music video medium with *Word of Mouth*. Gratifyingly, she got an immediate hit out of it with "Mickey," her effervescent parlay of cheerleading and choreography set to an irresistibly bouncy tune; it became one of the first videos in America (or in the world, at least since Queen's "Bohemian Rhapsody" did it in the U.K. six years earlier) to send a record to the top of the charts without the artist touring to support it. With its overall strong sense of high-spirited fun and such adorable touches as heart-shaped inserts, "Mickey" remains an enduring, unforgettable rock video classic.

The rest of *Word of Mouth* fails to reach the high standards set by the opening "Mickey," sometimes becoming turgidly self-conscious (as in Basil's overdone, silent-movie–style shenanigans in "Nobody," which otherwise contains some neat visual puns) or so cute and light it threatens to float away ("Little Red Book," with its silly, cartoonish visualization). The music, which features some of her pals in Devo—who also supplied the songs "Be Stiff," "Space Girls," and "You Gotta Problem"—is accomplished, danceable synth-pop, but Basil really has little to say along with it. However, she *always* says it with style to spare, from her eye-popping garb to her resourceful choreography, which makes great use of colloquial gestures as well as traditional dance elements. The closing "Shopping A to Z" comes closest to "Mickey" as a video, with its consumer-critique conflation of *Supermarket Sweep* and sub–John Waters suburban perversity. Throughout, however, Toni Basil and *Word of Mouth* look and behave like no other home music video program ever, and there aren't many you can say *that* about.

☐ THE BEACH BOYS
AN AMERICAN BAND
★★★★½

Vestron, 1985, 103 minutes

PRODUCED BY: Malcolm Leo and Bonnie Peterson

DIRECTED BY: Malcolm Leo

MUSIC FROM: Various Beach Boys albums (Capitol, Brother/Reprise, Caribou, 1962–81).

SELECTIONS: "Surf's Up," "Surfin' U.S.A.," "Be True to Your School," "Surfin'," "Surfer Girl," "Fun, Fun, Fun," "I Get Around," "409," "Little Honda," "California Girls," "Help Me, Rhonda," "In My Room," "Student Demonstration Time," "Dance, Dance, Dance," "Please Let Me Wonder," "Wouldn't It Be Nice," "That's Not Me," "Sloop John B," "God Only Knows," "Good Vibrations," "Heroes and Villains," "Fire," "Do It Again," "I Can Hear Music," "Break Away," "Barbara Ann."

Considering writer/director/producer Malcolm Leo's previous *This Is Elvis* and the apparent amount of control the Beach Boys had over the project, we may never know if Leo really intended this documentary to play as subversively as it often does. A lot of people think (rightly, it must be said) that most of the narrative scenes by the various Beach Boys are stilted and lame—except, of course, for Brian Wilson's, in which he lies in his bed with the covers up to his chin, a beached whale, casually and candidly telling us how he had a nervous breakdown, got into LSD, and so on. Thing is, this is a great documentary, whether the Beach Boys know it or not, precisely because it shows the Beach Boys for what they really are—*very weird people.* That intriguing subtext aside, there's oodles of great footage (and, of course, great music), from very early music videos to film and TV variety show clips to career-spanning concert footage. Highlights include a hysterical, classically smarmy skit with Jack Benny and Bob Hope during "California Girls"; a classically hip bit with *Saturday Night Live*'s Dan Aykroyd and John Belushi as Beach Police forcibly dragging bedridden

Brian out to the sea to surf ("Come on Brian," chides Aykroyd, "Let's go surfin' now . . ."; Belushi chimes in, "Everybody's learnin' how . . ."; together, they conclude, "Come on a safari with us!"); and some genuinely tripped-out '60s footage set to *Smiley Smile*'s "Fire."

☐ **VARIOUS ARTISTS**
BEAT STREET
★★★

Vestron, 1985, 106 minutes
PRODUCED BY: David V. Picker and Harry Belafonte
DIRECTED BY: Stan Lathan
MUSIC FROM: Beat Street motion picture soundtrack LPs, Volumes One and Two (Atlantic, 1984).
SELECTIONS: Jazzy Jay: "Son of Beat Street"; Juicy: "Give Me All," "Beat Street Strut"; Tina B: "Nothin's Gonna Come Easy"; the Treacherous Three: "Santa's Rap"; Jenny Burton: "It's Alright by Me"; Jenny Burton and Patrick Jude: "Strangers in a Strange World (Love Theme from *Beat Street*)"; Rockers Revenge: "Battle Cry"; Ralph Rolle: "Wappin' (Bubblehead)"; LaLa: "Into the Night"; Grandmaster Melle Mel and the Furious Five: "Beat Street Breakdown"; the System: "Baptize the Beat"; Afrika Bambaataa and the Soul Sonic Force + Shango: "Frantic Situation"; Sharon Green, Lisa Counts, and Debbie D.: "Us Girls"; Cindy Mizelle: "This Could Be the Night"; Arthur Baker: "Breaker's Revenge"; Ruben Blades: "Tu Carino/ Carmen's Theme."

Unexpectedly dark, surprisingly realistic Hollywood rap-sploitation flick, not-so-metaphorically pitting bourgeois ethnic Rae Dawn Chong against genuine street-level rap/breakdance/graffiti artists and, in its most upbeat aspect, having them all united at the end to "put on a show *right here*" as movie-musical tradition demands. While the confused and confusing climax (with rap luminaries like Grandmaster Melle Mel and Afrika Bambaataa joining Chong's legit orchestra and dancers *and* a Harlem Gospel Choir at the Roxy, Manhattan's near-legendary home of rap) somewhat obscures it, *Beat Street*'s rather daring motif is to validate truth-to-cultural-roots and condemm the sell-out; though not a total success, it deserves credit for ambition (most of which is probably due to the original screenplay of Steven Hager, a New York journalist who was the first intrepid white man to cover the rap scene). The best musical moments are Bambaataa's "Frantic Situation," Melle Mel's "Beat Street Breakdown," the sassy "Us Girls," and the Treacherous Three's brilliant exercise in gallows humor and Christmas spirit, "Santa's Rap."

☐ **VARIOUS ARTISTS**
BEATLEMANIA, THE MOVIE
★/★★★

USA/IVE, 1982, 95 minutes
PRODUCED BY: Edie and Ely Landau with Steven Leber and David Krebs
DIRECTED BY: Joseph Manduke
MUSIC FROM: Beatlemania, The Movie (American Cinema, 1981).
SELECTIONS: "I Want to Hold Your Hand," "She Loves You," "Please Please Me," "Help!," "Day Tripper," "If I Fell," "Can't Buy Me Love," "Yesterday," "Eleanor Rigby," "We Can Work It Out," "Nowhere Man," "A Day in the Life," "Strawberry Fields Forever," "Penny Lane," "Magical Mystery Tour," "Lucy in the Sky with Diamonds," "Michelle," "Get Back," "The Fool on the Hill," "Lady Madonna," "Got to Get You into My Life," "Come Together," "With a Little Help from My Friends," "All You Need Is Love," "Revolution," "Helter Skelter," "Hey Jude," "The Long and Winding Road," "Let It Be," "The End."
Also available on USA Stereo Laser videodisc.

This is the 1981 film of the long-running Broadway show—"Not the

Beatles, but an incredible simulation!" (so why's the bassist right-handed?) Four look-alikes for John, Paul, George, and Ringo play a comprehensive (and predictable) sampling of the Fab Four's repertoire, accompanied throughout by "remember-those-crazy-'60s" film montages intercut with the performances (often using split screens). The clones do a good job of re-creating the look and sound (Tom Teely, who plays George, would go on to release a critically praised solo album in 1985), but the very idea of it, along with the meatgrinder trivialization of the '60s (*major* exception: a stupendous fashion montage for "Michelle"), makes this a fairly nauseating program (which is why it gets one star). Besides, why would anyone want this at all, since the real Beatles have several videos on the market? Because as the Broadway show's long-running success proved, you can fool lots of people all of the time. And, in the program's defense, many songs here are not available in any kind of footage being performed by the Beatles themselves, and they're all great songs. People who'd be inclined to go in for this sort of thing will find it well-produced and enjoyable (which is why it gets three stars).

□ THE BEATLES

LET IT BE

★★★★★

Magnetic, originally released 1970, 81 minutes

PRODUCED BY: Neil Aspinall

DIRECTED BY: Michael Lindsay-Hogg

MUSIC FROM: Let It Be motion picture soundtrack (Apple, 1970) and various other Beatles albums.

SELECTIONS: "Don't Let Me Down," "Maxwell's Silver Hammer," "I've Got a Feeling," "Oh, Darling," "One After 909," "Across the Universe," "I Dig a Pony," "I Me Mine," "For You Blue," "Besame Mucho," "You Really Got a Hold on Me," "Rip It Up," "Kansas City," "Lawdy Miss Clawdy," "Two of Us," "Let It Be," "The Long and Winding Road," "Get Back," "Dig It," "Maggie Mae."

Let It Be is generally considered to be the documentary of the Beatles' breakup, although it is neither a true documentary (since the Beatles controlled its content) nor really about their imminent breakup. That said, there's no question that seeing this film and knowing what's going to happen to these four guys can be a sad experience. In the years since the film's original release we've learned much about the Beatles, and this information (of which there seems to be an endless supply) allows us to view this film without the naïve preconception of the group as four bright and happy lads from Liverpool that made it such a downer for earlier audiences. For example, we know now that Paul, George, and Ringo did not necessarily hate Yoko Ono (an annoying presence here if you do believe that she alone broke up the band); that John and Yoko were doing heroin at this time; that things hadn't been really good among the four for some time; that Paul McCartney (whose reputation as a controlling, selfish goody two-shoes was crystallized the day this was released) admits he made some mistakes then, because he didn't know any other way to handle the band.

To see *Let It Be* without villains is to watch and witness what was truly wonderful about the band. Since they stopped touring so early on, there are few good films of them performing live. Those that do exist are marred by the formality of television clips or the noisy hysteria of live shows. You can't watch this without being touched by the obvious musical and personal rapport and sense of community they shared. Even in a scene where George takes offense at Paul's high-handed bossiness, the tension magically vanishes the minute they all start playing. When George shows Ringo a better way to structure the drummer's first version of "Octopus's Garden," we see an expression of friendship and care that you'd be hard-pressed to envision among the Rolling Stones, for example. And, most strikingly, when John and Paul make eye contact or smile after a stunning vocal harmony, or when they latch into the perfect groove during rehearsal, the intensity of their friendship, their working relationship—their love for each other—is clear. There's no question that there could not have been room in the Beatles for anyone outside the group, and, equally, that none of the four could ever lead.

The film ends with three finished songs performed live in the studio—"Two of Us," "Let It Be," and "The Long and Winding Road"—and the famous rooftop scene, when the group plays live for the public from the roof of the Apple executive offices in London. Cameras catch the looks of amazement, confusion, and surprise on the faces of the passersby, along with the rare complaint about the noise, and then show people scurrying up to the closest rooftops or standing mesmerized in the street. This set—"Get Back," "Don't Let Me Down," "I've Got a Feeling," "One after 909," "I Dig a Pony," and a reprise of "Get Back"—could be watched a hundred times. Despite all the bickering and the tension of the earlier studio sets, the rooftop scene proves to the world that despite all the other things the Beatles did—the modest stuff, like change the face of rock 'n' roll, for instance—they were a truly great band, probably the greatest. Twenty years hence, after all the tell-all scandal books have gone out of print or disintegrated and the group's lawsuits are settled, this is how your kids will know what the Beatles meant to you.—P.R.

□ THE BEATLES
MAGICAL MYSTERY TOUR
★★½

Media, 1982, 60 minutes
PRODUCED BY: Dennis O'Dell
DIRECTED BY: The Beatles
MUSIC FROM: Magical Mystery Tour (Capitol, 1967)
SELECTIONS: "Magical Mystery Tour," "The Fool on the Hill," "Flying," "Blue Jay Way," "Your Mother Should Know," "I Am the Walrus," "Hello Goodbye."

This confused and confusing, self-consciously surreal psychedelic artifact was never theatrically released in the United States after getting panned following its television debut in the United Kingdom. Even Queen Elizabeth publicly criticized it. For those who know and love the soundtrack LP, it could be either fascinating or disappointing to see the album's enclosed book-of-the-film come to, er, life. Some of the sequences—"Your Mother Should Know," especially—work on their own, and most do retain inevitable value as protean stabs at conceptual music video. But the awesome musical soundtrack itself is easily the best thing about this self-indulgent effort.

□ THE BEATLES
THE COMPLEAT BEATLES
★★★★★

MGM/UA, 1982, 119 minutes
PRODUCED BY: Stephanie Bennett and Patrick Montgomery
DIRECTED BY: Patrick Montgomery
MUSIC FROM: Various albums by the Beatles and others.
SELECTIONS: Bill Haley and the Comets: "See You Later Alligator," "Rock Around the Clock"; Chuck Berry: "Rock & Roll Music"; Lonnie Donegan: "Jack of

Diamonds," "Rock Island Line"; Gerry Marsden: "Jambalaya," "Living Doll"; Eddie Dixon: "Be-Bop-A-Lula," "Raunchy," "20 Flight Rock"; Frankie Avalon: "Venus"; Cliff Richard: "Living Doll"; Tony Sheridan: "I Like Love," "My Bonnie"; various (teenagers, etc.): "We Love You Beatles," "When the Saints Go Marching In," "She'll Be Comin' Round the Mountain," "Jingle Bells," "Rock Night Club Theme"; the Beatles: "Rock & Roll Music" (live and studio versions), "All My Loving," "Mr. Moonlight," "A Taste of Honey," "Kansas City," "Some Other Guy," "Hippy Hippy Shake," "Long Tall Sally," "Please Please Me," "I Saw Her Standing There," "She Loves You," "Twist and Shout," "It Won't Be Long," "I Want to Hold Your Hand," "From Me to You," "A Hard Day's Night," "I'm Happy Just to Dance with You," "I'm a Loser," "Things We Said Today," "Ticket to Ride," "Help!," "You're Gonna Lose That Girl," "Yesterday," "Nowhere Man," "If I Needed Someone," "She's a Woman," "Taxman," "Tomorrow Never Knows, " "Strawberry Fields Forever," "Penny Lane," "A Day in the Life," "Being for the Benefit of Mr. Kite," "Sgt. Pepper's Lonely Hearts Club Band," "Lucy in the Sky with Diamonds," "All You Need Is Love," "Love You To," "Magical Mystery Tour," "Hello Goodbye," "Yellow Submarine," "Hey Jude," "Revolution," "Glass Onion," "Revolution 9," "Why Don't We Do It in the Road?" "Get Back," "I've Got a Feeling," "Because," "The End," "I'm So Tired," "Let It Be," "Blackbird."

Also available on MGM/UA Stereo Laser videodisc.

The Compleat Beatles, the first home video program by the genre's foremost rockumentarian, Patrick Montgomery (who's also produced and/or directed such fine programs as *Rock and Roll: The Early Years* and *British Rock: The First Wave*), is *it* if you're a Beatles fan—and, beyond a certain age, who among us is not? And how could those born too late to live through the phenomenon that was the Beatles miss such a good opportunity to learn all about it? In other words, *The Compleat Beatles* is a mandatory purchase for anyone who believes they take rock 'n' roll seriously. It's got just about everything anyone could ever want to see: the personal histories from birth of each member of the Fab Four; the sociocultural milieu into which they were born, and the backdrop against which they gradually, and then suddenly, exploded into stardom; and all the rest of the rock history they wrote so large, from the exuberant innocence of their early years to their later self-conscious artiness to the band's painful death. It's all presented in exhaustive detail, with oodles and oodles of eye-opening, jaw-dropping archival photos and film clips showing Beatles performances, recording sessions, and so on from all phases of their career, as well as Beatlemaniacs in action, now-campy newsreels on Beatlemania, and more. There are interviews— some pulled from the archives (such as those with the late Beatles manager Brian Epstein), most done for this tape (with everyone from the manager of the Star Club in Hamburg, Germany, where the Beatles arduously polished their act in the early '60s, to their producer George Martin, who makes the most of the hefty chunks of screen time he gets). But *The Compleat Beatles* does have one problem, and it's a fairly good-sized one: Malcolm McDowell's narration (written by David Silver), which is so stuffily sober and joylessly portentous it makes an exhaustive program begin to seem exhaust*ing*. It also effectively removes a crucial Beatles element from the informative mix—*fun*, something those mail order Beatles Video scrapbooks, crudely compiled as they are, *do* have. It's McDowell who makes *The Compleat Beatles* come across, with incredible irony, as something predicted and pre-parodied by *The Rutles*.

☐ **THE BEATLES**
READY STEADY GO! SPECIAL EDITION: BEATLES LIVE
★★★★½

Sony, 1985, 20 minutes
PRODUCED BY: Jack Good
DIRECTED BY: Rita Gillespie
MUSIC FROM: Meet the Beatles (Capitol, 1964); *The Beatles' Second Album* (Capitol, 1964); *Something New* (Capitol, 1964); *Early Beatles* (Capitol, 1965); *The Beatles Again* (Capitol, 1970).
SELECTIONS: "Twist and Shout," "Roll Over Beethoven," "I Wanna Be Your Man," "Long Tall Sally," "Love Me Do," "Please Please Me," "From Me to You," "She Loves You," "I Want to Hold Your Hand," "Can't Buy Me Love," "Shout."

The Fab Four, at the height of Beatlemania—as opening footage of an army of screaming young girls marching into the *RSG!* studio with "We Love You (fill in name of a Beatle)" placards shows—on Britain's most crucial pop-TV show. And they do indeed sound very live, at least at the start: John has to gasp for air as he reaches for those high screams on "Twist and Shout," and George blows the guitar intro to "Roll Over Beethoven." But halfway through they embark on a cut-and-paste medley (from "Love Me Do" through "I Want to Hold Your Hand") that's either barely rehearsed, or the product of someone backstage madly cutting back and forth between different 45s; it *could* be live, but . . . Anyway, it's still a precious pop moment, wonderfully preserved.

☐ **THE BEATLES**
A HARD DAY'S NIGHT
★★★★★

MPI, 1983, 90 minutes
PRODUCED BY: Walter Sherson
DIRECTED BY: Richard Lester
MUSIC FROM: A Hard Day's Night (United Artists, 1964).
SELECTIONS: "A Hard Day's Night," "I Should Have Known Better," "If I Fell," "I'm Happy Just to Dance with You," "And I Love Her," "Tell Me Why," "Can't Buy Me Love," "Anytime At All," "I'll Cry Instead," "Things We Said Today," "When I Get Home," "I'll Be Back," "She Loves You," "I Want to Hold Your Hand."

☐ **THE BEATLES**
HELP!
★★★½

MPI, 1986, 92 minutes
PRODUCED BY: Walter Sherson
DIRECTED BY: Richard Lester
MUSIC FROM: Help! (Capitol, 1965).
SELECTIONS: "Help!," "The Night Before," "You've Got to Hide Your Love Away," "Ticket to Ride," "I Need You," "You're Going to Lose That Girl," "Another Girl," plus incidental music by George Martin.

A Hard Day's Night was the first true rock film, and thus the first truly great rock film. Though it *is* an antic, capering, careering comedy, it's also a very *pointed* farce much of the time, inasmuch as it so forcibly appears to project, nay embody, the Beatles' point of view (after all, the Beatles do play themselves in it). In taking that revolutionary step, *A Hard Day's Night*—which, not so incidentally, also happened to be an awesome merging of brilliant talents—delivered the rock film from the days of old, eschewing crass exploitation completely in favor of a forever-fresh, natural maturity and self-possession, which produced an abundance of witty irreverence and semi-serious absurdity. Even though Beatlemania was a new phenomenon at the time the film was released—new enough that the movie only intensified it—the phenomenon had been around long enough for the Beatles to begin to show traces of a surprising but attractively hip, world-weary cynicism, which may have seemed so hip mainly because it so nicely balanced the sweetness of those incredible songs (sort of the way Lennon balanced McCartney). Mainly, the Beatles and

Richard Lester and everyone else involved with *A Hard Day's Night* were able to come up with a rock movie in which a band plays itself and makes no apologies; a rock movie which is hysterically funny, yet definitely functions as quote-unquote serious entertainment and even cinematic art—and it was a world-conquering *hit* at the same time! It's that immediate popularity and lasting appeal that complete the equation, making *A Hard Day's Night* not only a great and important rock film, but one of the best and most significant films of the '60s, or of recent times, period.

The plot is so simple it's barely there (which doesn't matter because the movie is so full of energy and attitude anyway): the Beatles are on their way to appear on a television variety show, but the whole thing is constantly complicated by hordes of hysterical Beatlemaniacs and Paul's feisty, troublemaking "grandfather," played with diabolical brilliance by Wilfred Brambell. Devilish old Granddad convinces Ringo he has every right to wander off as a lark just before the start of the show. Panic ensues, but in the nick of time Ringo's found and everything goes as planned. Miraculously, *A Hard Day's Night* is not one bit as clichéd as this plot summary might indicate, and aside from the aforementioned reasons there are many others worth noting: Lester's bold introduction of avant-garde and *nouvelle vague* techniques (like those jump-cut clowning-in-formation bits that accompany some of the songs) into such a mainstream enterprise; Alun Owen's witty script, which complements the Beatles themselves so well; Victor Spinetti as the TV show's frazzled director, like Brambell brilliant in a scene-stealing supporting role; the Beatles themselves, of course, and their songs; and just the way the movie cracks so wickedly wise about the music biz and just plain *everything*—like those meet-the-press sequences, which are unforgettable. This is a must-see, must-own item. A technical note: this is the 1981 theatrically rereleased version, which adds an opening photo-montage to the tune of "I'll Cry Instead" to the original.

Help! once again found Lester directing the Beatles as themselves in a zippy, modishly fun cinematic gambol—but the results, while still most enjoyable and of undeniable historical/influential import, just don't quite measure up to *A Hard Day's Night*. Sure, the Beatles and their songs are as great as ever in this shaggy-dog mix of comedy and intrigue, in which a crazy scientist (Spinetti again) and his bumbling henchman (Roy Kinnear, another delight) *and* a crazy Eastern religious cult (led by Leo McKern and Eleanor Bron) are all frantically chasing the Fab Four because of a magical ring that's innocently found its way onto Ringo's finger. But *Help!* suffers from a kind of sophomore jinx or something: the "Lesterisms," those madcap/experimental touches on which the Monkees were predicated and which predated *Laugh-In,* seem a bit overdone for their own sake—just enough that they seem . . . well, *forced.* A much bigger budget than its predecessor's also probably led Lester and/or his producer to shoot in gaudy Technicolor and OD on scenic globe-trotting locations (which combine to give the movie something of a Elvis-movie feeling). But it must be emphasized that these complaints are comparatively minor, and that *Help!* is still well worth seeing.

☐ THE BEATLES

BUDOKAN CONCERT

★★★★½

VAP Import, 44 minutes
PRODUCED BY: Apple Corps Ltd.

MUSIC FROM: Various albums by the Beatles.

SELECTIONS: "Rock and Roll Music," "She's a Woman," "If I Needed Someone," "Day Tripper," "Baby's in Black," "I Feel Fine," "Yesterday," "I Wanna Be Your Man," "Nowhere Man," "Paperback Writer," "I'm Down."

□ THE BEATLES
VIDEO SCRAPBOOK
★★★½

Encore Entertainment import, 120 minutes

PRODUCED BY: Encore Entertainment

MUSIC FROM: Various albums by the Beatles; various films, theatrical trailers, and uncredited newsreels and TV shows.

SELECTIONS: "Twist and Shout," "She Loves You," "I'm Down," "I Saw Her Standing There," "Rock and Roll Music," "Give Peace a Chance," "All My Loving," "Ticket to Ride," "Can't Buy Me Love."

Budokan is available only as a Japanese import at this writing, and with the current dollar-to-yen exchange rate, it could cost up to $200 or more to acquire. But for the serious Beatles fan, it's worth it. This is the Fab Four's legendary "black suits concert," shot *beautifully* in *living color* June 30, 1966, at Tokyo's Budokan concert hall—and the very clean audio recording is in hi-fi stereo, yet. On their last tour ever, the group looks and sounds very good and very live. Since Japanese audiences have always been far more restrained than their Western counterparts, the music is actually more audible than the crowd's screams most of the way through. Before the concert starts, there's about fifteen minutes of black-and-white documentation of their arrival at the airport, police escort to hotel, two press conferences, and so on. During one press conference, after noting that they've never seen so much security anywhere before, the Beatles are asked who their favorite, most respected, and influential composers are. McCartney replies, "I dunno . . . John Lennon." Lennon obligingly adds, "Paul McCartney." Capturing rock's best and most important band ever just before their evolution into the rarefied *Sgt. Pepper* period, this is by far the best single record available of the Beatles in live performance. (Available by mail order from Playings Hard to Get.)

Video Scrapbook is a rough-edged, low-budget compilation of miscellaneous footage of concerts, press conferences, behind-the-scenes stuff, and Beatlemaniacs in action. It makes an absolutely fascinating counterpart to *The Compleat Beatles,* because most of the elements it patches together so crudely are in themselves quite impressive.

It opens with the Beatles onstage at the Hollywood Bowl on August 23, 1964, delivering "Twist and Shout" and "She Loves You"; the recording is grainy, uneven, but good enough overall. Next comes a rather bizarre, extended interlude from some forgotten documentary film or TV show: it opens with the Beatles, wearing longer hair and light-colored Nehru jackets, playing "I'm Down" onstage at a very roughly shot concert, with John Lennon on organ; late in the song, a Lennon voiceover cuts in, talking about the LSD experience. The camera finally cuts to him, *circa* 1970 or so, in long hair, beard, and wire-rim specs, walking with Yoko over the grounds of Tittenhurst Park, talking to the camera about acid, the youth movement, the generation gap, etc.; we then see John and Yoko on the telephone to some Berkeley, California, students who are occupying their dean's office and dangerously close to a riot situation with the police—a fairly revelatory '60s moment, captured nicely. Then it's back to John and Yoko traipsing through the woods, as John says beatifically (while Yoko gazes at him just as beatifically), "The '60s was just, like, wakin' up in the morning . . . I can't wait to be around to see what happens next."

Later comes a press conference in Australia: asked what they expect to find there, John shoots back, "Australians, I suppose." Then there's *What's Happening—The Beatles in the USA,* a documentary of their first U.S. tour that includes some stunning time-capsule footage: the camera in the car with the Fab Four as their car is mobbed by fans outside their hotel; a family, including two paralyzed-with-delight teenage girls, watching the Beatles on *The Ed Sullivan Show* at home; Ringo dancing at a discotheque with a stunning, classic '60s beauty who teaches him the Swim and other dances; more you-are-there black-and-white concert footage; and on-the-road hotel scenes with the Fab Four relaxing and just hanging around, appearing quite unguarded and natural with the camera there.

And there's more, much much more, blowing you away with its raw nostalgic power: some rare 1962 footage from a Liverpool teen dance; a *Sgt. Pepper*–era TV-interview snippet with Paul; a too-brief snippet of a 1964 or '65 press conference in America, where a reporter shouts out "Sam Phillips says you guys are nothing more than four British Elvis Presleys" and the Fab Four reply by swiveling and sneering *à la* Elvis while shouting back "Not true, not true!"; Lennon's "Give Peace a Chance" filmlet, from the 1968 Montreal Bed-In; a making-of–*Yellow Submarine* documentary and trailer that, at this writing, are the only footage of that rock-animation classic on home video; some great *A Hard Day's Night* and *Help!* trailers; a TV interview with Ed Sullivan followed by Beatles clips from his show; newsreels from the time of Lennons' deportation hearings; a priceless movie trailer for a closed-circuit theatrical showing of a 1964 Beatles show (the excited voiceovers of two "teenagers" includes lines like "It's gonna be the swinginest, you dig, chick?" "I dig, Chuck.") a newsreel-style making-of *Hard Day's Night* mini-documentary; a *Magical Mystery Tour* trailer, one for *Let It Be,* and another for *How I Won the War, The Magic Christian,* and every other film a Beatle ever made or appeared in—even a television commercial for the Beatles-parody film *The Rutles.* And on and on and on it goes, leaping about in no particular chronological order. For the Beatles fan, it's well worth investigating, at any cost. (Available by mail order from Playings Hard to Get.)

☐ ADRIAN BELEW
ELECTRONIC GUITAR
★★★★

DCI, 1985, 60 minutes

PRODUCED BY: Rob Wallis and Paul Siegel

DIRECTED BY: Rob Wallis and Paul Siegel

MUSIC FROM: King Crimson: *Three of a Perfect Pair* (Warner Bros., 1983); Adrian Belew: *The Lone Rhino* (Warner Bros., 1982) and *Twang Bar King* (Warner Bros., 1984).

SELECTIONS: "Big Electric Cat," "Hot Sun," "Final Rhino," "Dig Me," "Rail Song."

The good-naturedly gonzo guitar whiz Adrian Belew has exhibited his sonic sorcery through the years with David Bowie (on *Lodger* and *Stage*), Talking Heads (*Remain in Light*), and King Crimson (*Discipline, Beat, Three of a Perfect Pair*) among others, as well as on his own solo records. He's famous for extracting all manner of bizarre space-age sounds and seemingly impossible animal noises (seagulls, rhinos, elephants) from his guitar, and here he shows you how he does it: with an army of effects pedals, a slide, a tremolo bar, and a lot of ingenuity and energy (i.e., shaking the upper cutaway horn on his Stratocaster for extra tremolo). For the young or advanced guitarist who's interested in making his guitar sound like anything *but* a guitar . . . but—considering Belew's articulate discussions of two-handed fretboard technique (e.g., Eddie Van Halen), alternative tunings, and fretless *guitar*—also for anyone seeking a creatively off-the-wall approach to electric guitar. (Available by mail order from DCI Music Video.)

□ LOUIS BELLSON
THE MUSICAL DRUMMER
★★★★

DCI, 1985, 60 minutes
PRODUCED BY: Rob Wallis and Paul Siegel
DIRECTED BY: Rob Wallis and Paul Siegel
MUSIC FROM: Demonstration exercises by Louis Bellson with quintet.

Bellson is an outstanding big-band swing drummer who's played with Duke Ellington's Orchestra among others, and who has had to spend too much undeserved time in Buddy Rich's shadow. Here, he performs seven pieces in a variety of styles—swing, shuffle, bossa nova, samba, rock, and so on—while dissecting and discussing his own parts in each piece in relation to those of the other players and the music itself. Bellson also articulates on brush technique and double-bass drumming (at which he's an acknowledged master), and plays two jaw-dropping solos. An accompanying sixty-four-page instruction booklet is also available. (Available by mail order from DCI Music Video.)

□ LOUIS BELLSON BIG BAND WITH BILLY COBHAM
COBHAM MEETS BELLSON
★★★

VIEW, 1986, 36 minutes
PRODUCED BY: Tazio Tami and Guido Vanetti
DIRECTED BY: Stanley Dorfman
MUSIC FROM: Various Louis Bellson Big Band albums.

□ LOUIS BELLSON AND HIS BIG BAND
LOUIS BELLSON AND HIS BIG BAND
★★★

VIEW, 1986, 55 minutes
PRODUCED BY: Tazio Tami and Guido Vanetti
DIRECTED BY: Stanley Dorfman
MUSIC FROM: Various albums by Louis Bellson and His Big Band.
SELECTIONS: "The Drum Squad," "Samantha," "Blues for Freddy," "Niles Ahead," "We've Come a Long Way Together," "Explosion."

Cobham Meets Bellson features two generations of great drummers, in a 1984 concert in Switzerland. Louis Bellson has kept time for big-band giants like Count Basie, Duke Ellington, Benny Goodman, and Tommy Dorsey, and would probably be a household name were he not eclipsed in the general public's eye by Buddy Rich. Cobham had a wide range of jazz, rock, and R&B credits before becoming famous with pioneering jazz-rock fusion ensemble the Mahavishnu Orchestra. Here, the results of their meeting are mixed, partly because the musical format—one long suite, consisting mainly of drum solos and duos occasionally punctuated by the Bellson Big Band's riffs, vamps, and shouting choruses—is predictable. (It also ensures that some of the band's best players, trumpeters Lew Soloff and Randy Brecker, tenor saxist Michael Brecker, and baritone saxist Howard Johnson, never get a chance to show *their* stuff.)

The first Cobham-Bellson duo comes after a few short, midtempo flagwaving bars by the band: Cobham is predictably rambunctious as he tries to outdo Bellson with muscle, speed, and flash, but it's all in vain. The ever-tasteful, graceful, and wily Bellson effortlessly maintains the upper hand, evincing far more musicality, as well as a touch that's better suited to this setting. The solos and trade-offs between the two drum kings are *so* protracted that anyone but a drum fanatic would probably tune out before the band even comes back in to cue the next series of solos and duos. That would be a shame, because the *second* just-drums section is fascinating and musically rewarding. It starts in silence so complete that all you can hear is the hiss of the tape. Then Cobham delicately pings a pair of finger cymbals; Bellson drums ever so softly on a tom-tom with his fingers; Cobham gently taps the rims of his tom-toms with his sticks to evoke a ghostly, rustling clatter. Eventually, it builds to a mighty clamor of bangs, clangs, gongs, thumps, and rattles, before subsiding and building again. It has the well-ordered, careful execution of a written arrangement, and one overhead shot of Bellson, with sheet music spread over his floor toms, indicates that's just what it may be. This section ends fittingly, with Cobham finishing off another quiet passage by moving his sticks at his drums without hitting them, miming thus more and more slowly, and finally slowing to a standstill in mid-drum-striking motion. A musical and theatrical triumph that makes the tape well worth seeing, for fans of great drummers *and* those who enjoy good, challenging music.

Louis Bellson and His Big Band, shot in the same straightforward manner at what appears to be the same unidentified Swiss venue, gives the band and its capable soloists much more of a chance to stretch out. The band handles both spryly dynamic untempo charts (like the opening "Drum Squad") and more relaxed, Basie-style velvet-glove blues (e.g., "Blues for Freddy") with equal alacrity, taking their appropriate cue from leader Bellson's immaculate musicianship. Bellson is featured soloist on "Drum Squad"; Herb Geller comes out of nowhere in the poised, balladic "Samantha" with a squiggly, high-energy, barely contained alto sax solo. Tenor saxist Michael Brecker, Johnson on tin whistle (!), Soloff, and trombonist Jiggs Whigham all shine during "Blues for Freddy"; Randy Brecker is featured to good advantage on the strolling vamp "Niles Ahead"; veteran swing trumpeter Benny Bailey struts some beautiful, butter-smooth stuff on the tender "We've Come a Long Way Together." The exuberant, ever-accelerating "Explosion" kicks off with Bellson's awesome solo demonstration of percussive prowess, then goes on to feature Geller and Brecker in a heated sax battle, booted along by Bellson's boiling beat and the rest of the band's agile, muscular riffs and fills, before Bellson solos again (using his double bass drums brilliantly). Then, while still beating in time on nothing but a drum-head, he gets up from his kit and walks over to a smaller kit for *more* killer soloing, *then* goes back to his *original* kit for some *four-stick soloing* (two in each hand), finally taking the dynamics down to a whisper-soft snare drum roll before building back up and cueing the full band in for a great finish. *Whew!* Good show!

□ PAT BENATAR
IN CONCERT

★★

RCA/Columbia, 1983, 73 minutes

PRODUCED BY: Rick Newman and Richard Fields

DIRECTED BY: Marty Callner

MUSIC FROM: Various Pat Benatar albums (Chrysalis, 1979–83).

SELECTIONS: "Anxiety (Get

Nervous)," "Fire and Ice," "You Better Run," "Little Too Late," "Fight It Out," "Looking For a Stranger," "I Want Out," "We Live for Love," "In the Heat of the Night," "Shadows of the Night," "Heartbreaker," "Hit Me with Your Best Shot," "Hell Is for Children," "Little Paradise," "Love Is a Battlefield."

□ PAT BENATAR
HIT VIDEOS

★ ½

RCA/Columbia, 1984, 27 minutes

PRODUCED BY: Rising Star Video Productions, Rick Newman, Richard Fields

DIRECTED BY: Mark Robinson, Juliano Waldman, Bob Giraldi

MUSIC FROM: Get Nervous (Chrysalis, 1982); *Tropico* (Chrysalis, 1984).

SELECTIONS: "Anxiety (Get Nervous)," "Lipstick Lies," "Shadows of the Night," "Love Is a Battlefield."

With her classically trained voice and hard-rocking AOR-formula clichés, Benatar has won herself legions of fans. Those admirers probably already adore these two programs, and the fact remains that they are recommendable *only* to Benatar fans.

In Concert was shot in competent, uninspired fashion at the New Haven, Connecticut, Veteran's Memorial Coliseum in 1983, and Pat and her band (featuring hubby Neil Geraldo on guitar) churn out the hits with bland sterility and anonymous competence. Except for drummer Myron Grombacher, that is. He probably couldn't even tune his snare drum head without grimacing dramatically, as if he were in the midst of soundly thrashing Buddy Rich in a drum-off. Grombacher's forcibly obnoxious, but at least he's the most vivid and memorable personality on display here.

Hit Videos is similarly undistinguished, for the most part, unless you happen to be a Benatar fan. Its sole saving grace is Mark Robinson's neurotic, slapstick fear-of-dentistry joke, "Anxiety." Robinson's "Shadows of the Night" is a muddled, ultimately laughable homage to WW II Rosie-the-Riveter proto-feminism; Juliano Waldman's "Lipstick Lies" is, as its title suggests, the usual turgid, blue-lit, sexist rock video nonsense, dated with a *Flashdance* veneer.

And then there's Bob Giraldi's mysteriously acclaimed "Love Is a Battlefield." Like all the clips Giraldi made after his auspicious rock-video debut with Michael Jackson's "Beat It," "Love Is a Battlefield" is bombastically overproduced, and oozing the sorts of retro-showbiz clichés that give away Giraldi's roots in those all-singing, all-dancing Dr Pepper TV commercials he made in the '70s. At the time of its release, it sported the modest innovation of spoken dialogue in a dramatic, pre-song prelude, with Pat sullenly running away from her suburban home and berating father. But "Love Is a Battlefield" handles that stated theme with such clouded superficiality it actually appears to glamorize the act of running away to a life of degeneracy in the big city. Its climactic dance number remains one of the most dumbfoundingly repellent scenes in the history of rock video: runaway Pat, who appears to have become a hooker or some such modern-day variant on the classic dance-hall floozie, gets public revenge against the clip's villain—a venal spic pimp, and make no mistake, he's a *spic* pimp, with a grotesquely caricatured, gold-toothed, "hey-meester-you-want-my-seester" leer that leaves me wondering why Giraldi was never publicly lambasted for such blatant racism—by leading a group of girls-of-the-night in a routine where they all shake their breasts menacingly in his face. Honest. It dissolves from this side-show to an insultingly pat (pardon the pun) coda, in which Pat is seen in the light of the triumphant morning after, traipsing off, exhausted but fulfilled, into the distance while patting the shoulders of the other gals with that "Way to go!" manner that ersatz football players or volleyball-playing beach bums have of doing in soft-drink commercials. The irresponsible obnoxiousness of "Love Is a Battlefield" is only amplified in the smugly arrogant making-of documentary on this clip included in *Hit Videos.* And anyone seeking to avoid this video vileness by seeking out *In Concert* should be warned that "Love Is a Battefield" is also tacked on to the end of that program.

Oh well, perhaps it was to atone for the "Love Is a Battlefield" video (not to mention kicking off her career by shoving her black-spandexed derrière at the camera on her debut album cover) that Pat sang "Stop using sex as a weapon" in her 1985 hit. We can only hope . . .

□ TONY BENNETT

TONY BENNETT SINGS

★★★★½

Sony, 1986, 48 minutes

PRODUCED BY: Nicholas Wry

DIRECTED BY: John Blanchard

MUSIC FROM: Various Tony Bennett albums; Canadian TV special (Allarcom Prod., 1981).

SELECTIONS: "Another Opening, Another Show," "There'll Be Some Changes Made," "This Can't Be Love," "My Funny Valentine," "Just in Time," Medley: "Who Can I Turn To"/"Rags to Riches," "Lullabye of Broadway," "Something," "O Sole Mio (Di Capua)," "Sing You Sinners," "Because of You," "There Will Never Be Another You," "I Left My Heart in San Francisco," "I Wanna Be Around," "Don't Get Around Much Anymore," "Sophisticated Lady," "Solitude," "It Don't Mean a Thing," "For Once in My Life."

Tony Bennett is such a well-established pop figure that it's easy for rock-generation listeners to take him for granted and dismiss him as a square. But as his fans know, that's *their* loss. In the pop world, Bennett is also well loved, and in jazz circles he's well regarded. And, as he proves in this 1981 Canadian TV special, in which Bennett sings to a live audience in a large hall (Jubilee Auditorium in Edmonton, Alberta) backed by the very capable ITV Concert Orchestra, Bennett really, honestly, and truly is a very good, very hip Sinatraesque singer. He's got a nice voice with a pleasingly grainy edge to it; his artful phrasing shows abundant interpretive taste and grace; and he can be swaggeringly confident, or tender and reverent, as the case demands, while never sacrificing his satisfying swing and unerring musicality. Meanwhile, John Blanchard's classy and unobtrusive direction complements Bennett's easy-going, intimate performing style (while directing the lion's share of episodes of the great Canadian comedy series *SCTV,* Blanchard proved he could direct virtually any kind of television, and here he adds another notch to his belt). Also noteworthy—indeed, rather crucial to this program's overall success—is the very hip and swinging work of the ITV big band: under Ralph Sharon's leadership, it's just about the most authentically jazzy and tasteful TV orchestra I've ever heard, at least in such ostensibly middle-of-the-road circumstances. Highlights of the show include "My Funny Valentine," riveting in its hushed urgency; a gorgeous, gloriously swinging arrangement of "Lullabye of Broadway"; a believe-it-or-not cool "O Sole Mio (Di Capua)"; and "Solitude" and "For Once in My Life," which are simply outstanding performances.

□ BERLIN

BERLIN VIDEO 45

★★

Sony, 1984, 21 minutes

DIRECTED BY: Evan English and Paul Goldman, Dominic Orlando, Jim Yukich, Marcelo Epstein

MUSIC FROM: Pleasure Victim (Geffen, 1983); *Love Life* (Geffen, 1984).
SELECTIONS: "No More Words," "The Metro," "Dancing in Berlin," "Sex (I'm a . . .)," "Now It's My Turn."

This trendy L.A. synth-pop enterprise, fronted by onetime soap opera actress Terri Nunn, raised a few eyebrows with the serviceably suggestive and danceable "Sex (I'm a . . .)," the video of which finds Nunn and keyboardist John Crawford (*both* of them overly made-up) writhing around in tantalizingly quick seminude boudoir shots. It's basically trash and not even very good trash. But "Sex" and "The Metro," both directed by Marcelo Epstein, at least have the saving grace of his sexily chic, high-production-value look. Evan English and Paul Goldman's "No More Words" looks fine, but its silly *Bonnie and Clyde* scenario falls flat, and neither the bombastic tune nor Nunn's acting help very much. The rest are typical performance-dominated clips, prettily shot by Jim Yukich. Yes, Berlin does present a lovely, costly package, but the artifice is obvious, and it's all too clear that beneath the wrapping lurks an empty box. Berlin is the kind of band people are thinking of when they sneer at so-called video bands. Still, "video bands" *do* have their fans, and at least Berlin *do* grace the package with those lush production values.

□ CHUCK BERRY (WITH TINA TURNER)
CHUCK BERRY FEATURING TINA TURNER
★★★

JEM/Passport, 1985, 60 minutes
DIRECTED BY: Scott Sternberg
MUSIC FROM: Various Chuck Berry albums.
SELECTIONS: "Roll Over Beethoven," "Hail Hail Rock and Roll," "Sweet Little Sixteen," "Nadine (Is It You?)," "Around and Around," "Birmingham," "Maria, Maria," "Johnny B. Goode," "Brown-Eyed Handsome Man," "Too Much Monkey Business," "Rock & Roll Music," "Musical Piece," "Reeling and Rocking."

The brown-eyed handsome man, one of America's greatest poets and an undeniable musical titan, is caught in very typical latter-day just-another-gig form—and he still manages to amaze just often enough. Here, he's before a hasn't-a-clue whitebread crowd at L.A.'s Roxy in 1982. The bland direction reinforces the immediate impression of defiantly offhanded readings of those Berry treasures, but look and listen again and you will find a few nice, metallic-bluesy chordal solos (in "Nadine" and "Around and Around" among others). Then again, Chuck gives *waaay* too much solo time to shlockmeister Richie Zito. Still, by the time a pre-comeback Tina Turner sashays out in straight platinum-blonde hair and dancing better than she does now, and Chuck's gorgeous daughter Ingrid joins Dad for a "Reeling and Rocking" that gets the whole crowd onstage dancing with glee, it's hard not to be won over. Look, Keith Richards probably owns this tape—so why not you?

□ VARIOUS ARTISTS
BEST OF THE BIG BANDS
★★

Video Yesteryear, 1980, 75 minutes
MUSIC FROM: Various Panoram Soundies and Snader Telescriptions short musical films (1939–56).
SELECTIONS: Artie Shaw and His Orchestra: "Symphony of Swing"; Benny Goodman Trio: two unidentified selections; Lionel Hampton Orchestra: two unidentified selections; Harry James and His Orchestra: "All Star Bond Rally"; Ray Eberle with Joe Stafford, Glenn Miller Orchestra: "Swing into Spring"; Dorsey Brothers Orchestra: two selections from the film *The Fabulous*

Dorseys; Dorsey Brothers Orchestra with Lynn Roberts, Tommy Mercer: "Opus 1"; Count Basie Orchestra: two selections circa 1950; Larry Clinton and His Orchestra: "Chant of the Jungle," "Deep Purple"; Billy Eckstine Orchestra: two selections circa 1946; Charlie Barnet Orchestra: two selections circa 1942, 1950; Les Brown and his Band of Renown: two selections circa 1951.

Ragtag collection of various big-band Panoram Soundies, short musical films which were primitive forerunners of today's music video clips. Best of an odd lot include: Artie Shaw, whose band has a young Buddy Rich on drums, and whose "Soundie" features some intriguing montage effects; the always dependable Lionel Hampton; Count Basie; a rare look at the Benny Goodman Trio (with Teddy Wilson on piano and Gene Krupa on drums); and Harry James, whose guests include a young Frank Sinatra and a cameo appearance by Bing Crosby. Sound and picture quality erratic.

☐ **VARIOUS ARTISTS (BURNING SPEAR, STEEL PULSE, ASWAD, EEK-A-MOUSE, ET AL.)**

BEST OF REGGAE SUNSPLASH VOLUME ONE

★★★½

Sony, 1985, 60 minutes
PRODUCED BY: Stuart Reid
DIRECTED BY: Annie Rowe
MUSIC FROM: Reggae Sunsplash Festival, 1982.

SELECTIONS: Chalice: "Road Block"; Steel Pulse: "Blues Dance Raid"; Eek-a-Mouse: "Assassinator"; Aswad: "African Children"; Burning Spear: "Slavery Days"; Mutabaruka: "White Man's Country"; Big Youth: "War inna Babylon"; Marcia Griffiths: "Steppin"; Lloyd Parkes and We the People: "What More Can I Do?"; Mighty Diamonds: "Pass the Kutchie"; Blue Riddim Band: "My Name Is Nancy Regan."

☐ **VARIOUS ARTISTS**

BEST OF REGGAE SUNSPLASH VOLUME TWO

★★½

Sony, 1983, 60 minutes
DIRECTED BY: Annie Rowe
MUSIC FROM: Reggae Sunsplash Festival, 1982.

SELECTIONS: Chalice: "This Is Reggae Music," "A Song," "Shanty Town," "I've Got to Go Back Home," "Good to Be There," "Army Life"; Byron Lee and the Dragonairs: "Gypsy Girl"; Big Youth: "Mind Blowing Decision"; Toots and the Maytals: "Sweet and Dandy," "Everyday Is a Holiday"; Home T. Four: "Cool Runnings"; Taj Mahal: "Mail Box Blues"; Eek-a-Mouse: "A Wah Do Dem"; Mutabaruka: "Hard Times Love"; Yellowman: "My Life Story," "Amen," "Nick Nack Paddy Wack," "Banana Boat Song"; Lloyd Parks: "Redemption Song"; Deniece Williams: "Free," "My God's Amazing"; Twinkle Brothers: "Since I Throw the Comb Away."

Though both of these tapes, shot at the 1982 edition of Jamaica's annual Montego Bay outdoor reggae-fest, are quite mundane as productions (obtrusive inserts of travelogue footage, etc.) and sometimes worse, they each have enough to make them worth checking out for reggae fans. Volume One, in fact, has a strong enough lineup to make it more or less a must-have for reggae fans. Burning Spear's mesmerizing classic "Slavery Days" is the highlight—pure Rasta godhead with a powerful sociopolitical message; close behind are the Mighty Diamonds' "Pass the Kutchie" (later covered in pop fashion by Britain's Musical Youth as "Pass the Dutchie"), militant reggae poet Mutabaruka, 6-foot-6-inch nasal-voiced "toaster" (reggae's version of a rapper) Eek-a-Mouse, and England's two best reggae bands, Steel Pulse and Aswad. Volume One closes intriguingly, with Blue Riddim Band—a mostly white assemblage from Chicago—

making their barbed political commentary.

Volume Two is more problematic. Half of the performances are questionable, to say the least, in terms of their inclusion, e.g., notoriously lame disco-calypso tourist's band Byron Lee and the Dragonairs, and, with all due respect, Taj Mahal and Deniece Williams. Chalice are thoroughly mediocre, until they deliver the surprisingly powerful "Army Life" at the close, marching in time as they mock the military. The rest of the selections are all good to great—but are frequently marred by extremely annoying, abrupt cutaways in mid-song to the next selection. Still, Eek-a-Mouse and Yellowman are two delightfully bawdy toasters, and Eek-a-Mouse even appears to engage in some sort of live sex act onstage with a girl from the audience at one point. Mutabaruka's as ferociously militant as he is Volume One; Big Youth is caught on a good day—one of reggae's most erratic veteran stage performers is coherent, upbeat, and entertaining here; and Toots of the Maytals works the adoring throng like a seasoned politician in "Everyday Is a Holiday."

□ BETTY BOOP, VARIOUS ARTISTS BETTY BOOP—SPECIAL COLLECTOR'S EDITION, VOLUME ONE

★★★★½

Republic, 1985, 90 minutes
PRODUCED BY: Max Fleischer
DIRECTED BY: Dave Fleischer
MUSIC FROM: Various albums by various artists; various Betty Boop cartoons of the thirties.

SELECTIONS: Louis Armstrong and His Orchestra: "I'll Be Glad When You're Dead, You Rascal You"; Cab Calloway and His Orchestra: "St. James Infirmary," "The Old Man of the Mountain"; Royal Samoans: "Bamboo Isle Medley"; Rubinoff and His Orchestra: "Morning, Noon and Night"; Don Redman and His Orchestra: "Chant of the Weed," "I Heard"; Don Redman Orchestra with Betty Boop: "How'm I Doin'?"; various other unidentified vocal and instrumental cartoon music by unidentified artists.

Aside from being immortally creative and amusing masterpieces from the golden age of 1930s animation, Betty Boop cartoons are also early instances of music videos, "videos" in which the endlessly inventive, ceaselessly metamorphosing animated action was carefully synched with jazz-pop hits of the day as well as with the surreally shifting orchestral mixes of light classical, jazz, and pop that became known as "cartoon music." The brilliant work of the Fleischer brothers towers over virtually all modern-day cartoons in more ways than one: the animation itself is so much more carefully detailed—from characters to backgrounds—and distinctively stylish than, say, Hanna-Barbera's bland, cut-rate shlock that it's actually a sort of blasphemy to even consider the latter in the same breath. Furthermore, Betty Boop cartoons were far more sassily adult—and at times even a bit racy in tone—than almost everything that followed them, and still serve as by far the best remedy for the sickly sweet cuteness of the Disney school. The ever-winking and pouting Betty's girlishly high-pitched, adenoidal voice could probably be accounted for as a counterbalance to the obvious provocative sexiness of her flapper's attire—an extremely short skirt and stockings with her left garter always exposed.

The drug culture of the '60s rediscovered Betty Boop cartoons as classic "head trips," figuring the Fleischers and their animators *had* to be on *something* to come up with such irreverently tripped-out updates of *Through the Looking Glass*. Well, I don't know if the Fleischers were "on" anything, aside from an incredible creative roll, but it's not hard to see why hippies were charmed. Still, it must be emphasized that the cartoons' virtues easily surpass such callow trendiness, and thankfully programs like this will help their appeal endure.

Special Collector's Edition Volume One focuses impressively on the legitimate jazz greats that contributed music to which the fantastical antics of Betty and her anthropomorphic cohorts could be choreographed. And actual films of these artists are intercut with the cartoons in a manner unobtrusive enough to keep the emphasis on the animation—but also, perhaps, to leave serious jazz fans a bit frustrated. In one cartoon Betty and her pal Bimbo the dog are chased by cannibalistic natives (whose renderings are one of the occasional instances of the racist stereotyping that was the sole unfortunate aspect of these marvels). One of the natives' head grows larger and suddenly becomes the head of the *real* Louis Armstrong—via primitive but well-executed matting effects—as he growls out "I'll Be Glad When You're Dead, You Rascal You." Aside from that, Armstrong, Cab Calloway, and Don Redman and their bands are seen only in brief live-action intros playing overtures for the cartoons in which their songs are featured. Perhaps most notable is the chance to see Redman, one of the most underrated figures in jazz history (with Fletcher Henderson's Orchestra between 1923 and 1925, Redman virtually invented big-band jazz arranging—before Duke Ellington even went public with his first band in 1926), leading his orchestra in the splendid "Chant of the Weed" for a too-brief minute, rocking back and forth in their seats as they play the swaying, adventurously scored arrangement before a "Betty Boop's Saloon" cartoon set. And Redman's endearing, nasal-voiced talk-singing in "I Heard" and "How'm I Doin'?" makes perhaps the best musical complement to Betty's caricatured vocals. Meanwhile, some long-forgotten guy named Rubinoff is seen briefly, conducting his light-classical orchestra to intro "Morning, Noon and Night." And Max Fleischer makes a live-action appearance in the opening "Betty Boop's Rise to Fame," explaining and then demonstrating with pen and paper what Betty Boop is all about.

Anyone who's ever seen and been delighted by the work of the Fleischer brothers knows how recommendable a tape like this is. And if you haven't ever seen a Betty Boop cartoon, you haven't really lived, so check out this program posthaste. (Available in stores, or by mail order from Blackhawk Films and Republic Pictures Home Video.)

☐ **VARIOUS ARTISTS**

THE BIG CHILL

★★★½

RCA/Columbia, 1983, 103 minutes
PRODUCED BY: Michael Shamberg
DIRECTED BY: Lawrence Kasdan
MUSIC FROM: The Big Chill motion picture soundtrack (Motown, 1983).

SELECTIONS: Marvin Gaye: "I Heard It Through the Grapevine"; the Rolling Stones: "You Can't Always Get What You Want"; the Exciters: "Tell Him"; Procol Harum: "A Whiter Shade of Pale"; Smokey Robinson and the Miracles: "Tracks of My Tears," "I Second That Emotion"; the Rascals: "Good Lovin' "; the Temptations: "Ain't Too Proud to Beg," "My Girl"; the Beach Boys: "Wouldn't It Be Nice"; the Band: "The Weight"; the Spencer Davis Group: "Gimme Some Loving"; Percy Sledge: "When a Man Loves a Woman"; Creedence Clearwater Revival: "Bad Moon Rising"; Aretha Franklin: "A Natural

Woman (You Make Me Feel Like)"; Three Dog Night: "Joy to the World."

Though *The Big Chill* 's rock-and-Motown hit soundtrack isn't always thoroughly integrated into the film, or even anything more than incidental, it's still a great collection of music and deserves mention here if only for that reason. The film follows eight friends who came of age together during the mid- to late '60s on the '80s weekend following their friend Alex's funeral. Alex's unexplained suicide forces each character to consider the meaning of it all and the very meaning of friendship, and so on . . .

Fortunately, *The Big Chill* was cleverly written, and brilliantly acted by a cast that includes Glenn Close, William Hurt, Jeff Goldblum, and Mary Kay Place. Here and there the music does work magic, particularly at the opening (juxtaposing the arrivals of the eight friends at the funeral service and two morticians' hands as they dress Alex with Marvin Gaye's paranoid "I Heard It Through the Grapevine") and in the later funeral scene, where the Stones' "You Can't Always Get What You Want" sets the tone—and perhaps the theme—for all that follows. After that, it's just a very good film and some great music.—P.R.

□ BIG COUNTRY
BIG COUNTRY LIVE
★★½

Media, 1984, 75 minutes
PRODUCED BY: Aubrey Powell
DIRECTED BY: Nigel Gordon
MUSIC FROM: The Crossing (Mercury, 1983); *Wonderland* (Mercury, 1984); *Steeltown* (Mercury, 1984).
SELECTIONS: "1000 Stars," "Angle Park," "Close Action," "Lost Patrol," "Wonderland," "The Storm," "Pipe Band Sequence," "Porrohman," "Chance," "Inwards," "Fields of Fire," "Harvest Home," "Tracks of My Tears," "In a Big Country," "Auld Lang Syne."

When they first appeared on the scene in 1983, Big Country represented an intriguing fusion of post–new wave honed urgency and arena-rock grandiosity. The laughable pretensions of the latter are signaled right at the start of this concert tape, which opens with rolling clouds and thunderclaps, crashing waves, smoldering and erupting volcanos, and waterfalls. Big Country does strive for an epic scope in fusing their native Scottish tradition with rock's electricity, and it seems a safe bet that what attracted fans to their first two hits, "In a Big Country" and "Fields of Fire," was not the import of their particular fusion but the power of their anthemic guitar heroics—so, ridiculous as it is, that opening *is* rather aesthetically appropriate. Big Country guitarists Stuart Adamson (who shouts the lead vocals) and Bruce Watson specialize in guitars-sounding-like-bagpipes (which, as any devout Brit-rock fan knows, were first laid on wax by Mike Oldfield in his 1972 classic *Tubular Bells*) keening bansheelike over marching-drum patterns—an evocative, distinctive sound in limited doses that, for all but devout fans, the band wears out through simple overuse. Still, "In a Big Country" and "Fields of Fire" do work in their bracingly bombastic way—though, just as rewarding, at least, are more conventional rockers such as the moody, vaguely Springsteenish "Chance" and "Inwards," which features particularly galvanic, churning guitar counterpoint between Adamson and Watson. The bulk of the others, however, will leave all but Big Country fans unmoved. And their stiff, wrongheaded bludgeoning of Smokey Robinson's classic "Tracks of My Tears" is a pathetically ill-advised move. The concert is competently shot overall, though both the lighting and sound leave something to be desired at times. On the plus side for fans, this concert (originally cablecast live by MTV) took place on New Year's Eve 1983–84 in Glasgow, Scotland, and the band members—who signify their roots in Scottish tradition via plaid shirts and an onstage interlude by a pipe-and-drum band in full tartan regalia—perform at peak intensity for an adoring hometown crowd.

☐ **PETER GABRIEL, VARIOUS ARTISTS**
BIRDY
★★

RCA/Columbia, 1985, 120 minutes
DIRECTED BY: Alan Parker
MUSIC FROM: Birdy motion picture soundtrack (Geffen, 1985).

Alan Parker's *Birdy* is the seemingly endless story of a weirded-out Viet vet who thought he was a bird even *before* Nam (you guessed it, he's the title character) and his fellow Viet vet and longtime pal's attempt to draw Birdy out of his catatonia. With Matthew Modine as Birdy and Nicholas Cage as his pal Al, *Birdy* is a sort of Brat Pack version of *One Flew Over the Cuckoo's Nest*—but if any of you cynics out there found the *original* trite, boy are you in for big fun here. *Birdy* is larded with all sorts of self-consciously profound pretension and symbolism, between the title character's birdlike psychic fragility and internal war wounds and down-to-earth Al's more physical scars (he wears Invisible Man bandages over most of his face when he comes to visit his shell-shocked friend). Meanwhile, the characters are unappealing jerks we couldn't care less about, and the actors can't overcome that. And with Cage's voiceovers cueing flashbacks throughout, *Birdy* begins to resemble a more classic laugher—that camp masterpiece of the '50s, *The Oscar.*

Until, that is, the very end—when *Birdy* seems to deflate itself with a self-mocking, jokey little twist that leaves one wondering if the whole *thing* has been a sendup all along. But rather than leading me to admire Parker's black wit, the ending makes me feel even more abused, since I had to sit through two interminably "intense," "soul-searching," "deeply philosophical" hours of claptrap to get to it.

Peter Gabriel's soundtrack is so tasteful and accomplished it's almost dignified—and thus almost completely out of place here. It's almost entirely instrumental (a teensy bit of wordless Gabriel vocal can be heard at one point), occasionally refers to earlier Gabriel songs (such as the gorgeous piano figure from "Family Snapshot," which appears here in a too-brief snippet), and ranges from ethereal and/or abstract synth-musings to stately piano processionals and throbbing Afro-rock episodes. Along with Gabriel's original soundtrack music, a few '50s rock songs are heard in snippets during some pre-Vietnam flashbacks; in the wittiest touch, a prom band plays "Rockin' Robin" while Birdy awkwardly makes his way around the dance floor with a date who has no *idea* he's more than a few bricks shy of a load.

☐ **THE BIRTHDAY PARTY**
PLEASURE HEADS MUST BURN
★★★

Ikon, 1984, 60 minutes
PRODUCED BY: Malcolm Whitehead
DIRECTED BY: Malcolm Whitehead
MUSIC FROM: Pleasure Heads Must Burn (Rough Trade U.K., 1983).
SELECTIONS: "Dead Joe," "A Dead Song," "Junkyard," "Release the Bats," "Pleasure Heads," "Big Jesus Trashcan," "Nick the Stripper," "Hamlet," "Pleasure Avalanche," "Six Inch Gold Blade," "Wild

World," "Six Strings," "Sonny's Burning," "She's Hit."

With their theatrical lead singer Nick Cave moaning and howling and shuddering and gesticulating dementedly out front, the now-defunct British post-punk rockers Birthday Party (named after the Harold Pinter play, which is your first clue to their doomy subject matter—as if titles such as "A Dead Song" and "Release the Bats" didn't make it obvious) conjure an abrasive, assaultive rhythmic din in the two performances (July 1982 and February 1983) caught in *Pleasure Heads Must Burn*. Cult followers of the Birthday Party and Cave's subsequent solo work will relish this program, despite the extremely amateurish production values—or perhaps, in part, because of them, since it *is* shot in an up-close and grittily unadorned manner and since the Birthday Party's barbed-wire drone hardly begs for a glossy treatment anyway. At any rate, *Pleasure Heads Must Burn* is raw and raucous enough that it's certainly not for everyone, though it never tries to be. It should be noted, however, that as rough and noisy as they can be, the band play with confidence and assurance—and they're capable enough to swing convincingly from frenetic hardcore punk ("Dead Joe") to a grinding, thudding drone ("Junkyard"), from danceable punk-funk ("Release the Bats") to compelling post-punk blues mutations with twangy, reptilian guitar work redolent of Captain Beefheart ("Nick the Stripper"). The two concerts are broken up midway through by a concept clip for "Nick the Stripper" in which Cave, wearing only a diaper and with "Hell" and then "Porca Dio" painted across his chest, takes part in some sort of bizarre, mysterious pagan rites that effectively evoke his and the band's macabre motifs. All in all, though Cave's loony, hortatory bellowing can grate, *The Birthday Party* is intense and accomplished enough on its own terms to be worth a look from those of you who, reading this, think maybe you *might* like something like this. (Available in stores or by mail order from Factory.)

☐ **DUKE ELLINGTON AND HIS ORCHESTRA, BESSIE SMITH**
BLACK AND TAN/ST. LOUIS BLUES
★★★★

Republic, 1985, 36 minutes
PRODUCED BY: Dick Currier
DIRECTED BY: Dudley Murphy
MUSIC FROM: Film shorts *Black and Tan* (RCA Photophone, 1930); and *St. Louis Blues* (RCA Photophone, 1929); various albums by Duke Ellington and His Orchestra, and Bessie Smith.
SELECTIONS: Black and Tan: "Black and Tan Fantasy," other songs not identified; *St. Louis Blues:* "St. Louis Blues."

Here we have two black-and-white "race movie" shorts from the first few years of the sound era, each featuring a towering giant of twentieth-century Afro-American culture, on one cassette. While this program's most obvious value is as nostalgia and as a rare opportunity to see *the* seminal blues singer, Bessie Smith, as well as Duke Ellington and His Orchestra in their vintage Cotton Club days—value increased by the excellent quality of the prints—the program is also, for those who care to investigate, fascinating in its pioneering, pre–music video attempts to wed story to song.

Black and Tan attempts, and partially achieves, tragic poignancy in illustrating the varied moods of Ellington's classic "Black and Tan Fantasy." It starts off with an amazing few minutes of Duke, with the great wah-wah mute trumpeter (and co-composer of "Black and Tan Fantasy")

Bubber Miley, composing the piece at the piano in his apartment. A bumbling pair of piano movers—whose racist stereotyped portrayals, typical of the era, stand in stark contrast to the dignified reserve with which Duke and his men comport themselves—enter, with the news that they've come to repossess the struggling Duke's piano. Betty Washington, a chorus girl in Duke's floor show at the local club, follows them in and helps convince them—with the aid of some hooch—to leave the piano there. It's then revealed that she's been very sick with some mysterious malady, thus setting the stage for the tragic scenario: after we cut to Duke and his band in a Cotton Club–styled joint, backing several male tap dancers on a mirrored dance floor with an unidentified instrumental, we see the chorus girl (in an outrageous, glittery Josephine Baker–style revealing get-up) leaning against a backstage wall, looking faint, rolling her eyes back and holding her hand to her forehead, silent-movie-style. A subjective shot achieved with a primitive prismatic lens reveals her point of view via insectlike compound-vision multi-images of the floor show; she's introduced, bucks up, and tries to do her bush-dance number anyway, getting halfway through it before dramatically collapsing on the mirrored floor. We then cut to the final scene: in a strident, yet effectively atmospheric setup, she's on her deathbed in her apartment and Duke and his band are gathered around her playing the funeral march coda to "Black and Tan Fantasy," the shadows of the band and their uplifted horns cast supernaturally large on her high-ceilinged walls. The last thing she sees before she dies is Duke's face, beaming at her through a gray haze. And then, abruptly, it's over.

St. Louis Blues is an intriguingly proto-feminist parable, in which Bessie finds her good-time-Charlie beau two-timing her. She pleads with him to be good, he slaps her to the floor, laughs, and leaves; sitting on the floor, she begins wailing "St. Louis Blues"; a cut in midlyric finds her continuing the song while leaning disconsolately against the bar in a smoke-filled speakeasy, the crowd of sharp-dressed patrons responding to her awesome, elemental calls. In a rather stinging finale, her beau enters the speakeasy, dances for the appreciative patrons, spies Bessie at the bar, and calls her name; they embrace and he steals a wad of bills from her stocking while they dance. He then throws her back against the bar and struts out, laughing in her face again; she leans back against the bar, rolls her eyes heavenward, and resumes singing "St. Louis Blues." The End. Jazz fans will note that, while they aren't indentified, her backing musicians include the great stride pianist James P. Johnson and members of Fletcher Henderson's unsung-hero of an orchestra (though none of them appear to be Coleman Hawkins or Benny Carter, both in Henderson's band at the time, and Johnson, with his back to the camera at the rear of the tiny bandstand, is barely visible). As for Bessie Smith, Pauline Kael put it best: "Here she is, the greatest of our jazz singers, all five foot nine inches and two hundred pounds of her . . . and when she lets out her huge, thick voice, full of gin and love and humor, she is one of the most beautiful images that ever filled the screen." (Available by mail order from Blackhawk Films or Republic Pictures Home Video.)

□ BLACK FLAG
TV PARTY

★★★½

Target, 1983, 60 minutes
PRODUCED BY: Joe Rees
DIRECTED BY: Joe Rees

MUSIC FROM: Various Black Flag albums (SST, 1979–83).
SELECTIONS: "What Happened to Henry," "TV Party," "Rise Above," "Thirsty and Miserable," "Kill Me," "American Waste," "Overkill," "Gimmie Gimmie Gimmie," "Damaged," "Revenge," "Jealous."

Black Flag, the preeminent Los Angeles hardcore punk band, is captured here in Target Video's classic rough-and-ready style performing live at Target's San Francisco studios between 1979 and 1983. The first four songs feature vocalist Henry Rollins in his skinhead period and are mostly set to Target's "Culturewar" footage—guerrilla montages of TV advertisements and violence, from the Kennedy assassination "Zapruder film" to incidents of urban terrorism and war. There's also a crudely effective "concept" clip for the classic "TV Party," in which the band literally illustrates the lyrics by doing nothing but sitting around a messy living room, watching the tube and downing cans of brew. And there's a brief, rather ineffectual snippet of Black Flag fans in Bologna, Italy, on the band's 1979 tour—they look like punk kids everywhere, which may be the most remarkable thing about them. The rest of the songs feature original lead singer Dez Cadena, who moved to rhythm guitar when Rollins joined the band. (Available in stores, or by mail order from Target Video or Independent World Video.)

☐ **VARIOUS ARTISTS**

BLACK JAZZ AND BLUES

★★★½

Video Yesteryear, 1985, 44 minutes
MUSIC FROM: The films *St. Louis Blues* with Bessie Smith, James P. Johnson, Fletcher Henderson Orchestra (1929); *Symphony in Black* with Duke Ellington and His Famous Orchestra, Billie Holiday (1935); *Caldonia* with Louis Jordan Tympany Five (1945).
SELECTIONS: Bessie Smith: "St. Louis Blues"; Duke Ellington Orchestra: "Negro Moods," "Harlem Rhythm," "A Hymn of Sorrow"; Billie Holiday with Duke Ellington Orchestra: "Lost Man Blues"; Louis Jordan and His Tympany Five: "Caldonia! (What Makes Your Big Head So Hard?)."

Three "race movies," made by and for blacks in the '20s, '30s, and '40s, each of great historical value and then some. Bessie Smith—the one and only Bessie Smith, Queen of the Blues and a seminal figure in American music—makes her only surviving film appearance in *St. Louis Blues,* belting out the title song in a gin mill after her man's left her. Also appearing are the magnificent stride pianist James P. Johnson and members of the Fletcher Henderson Orchestra, who frequently backed Bessie on record. *Symphony in Black* compacts a number of scenes dramatizing different movements of Ellington's title piece, and among them is young Billie Holiday's movie debut, singing "Lost Man Blues" in a nightclub setting. *Caldonia* features jump 'n' jive master Louis Jordan, a great and innovative talent whom history has thus far overlooked, perhaps because of surviving contrived racist-comical trifles like this. This one's among Video Yesteryear's better offerings in terms of its historical *and* musical value, and for the uniform high quality of the artists preserved here. (Available by mail order from Video Yesteryear.)

☐ BLACK SABBATH

LIVE! FEATURING OZZY OSBOURNE

★★★

Media, 1984, 60 minutes
PRODUCED BY: Martin Baker
DIRECTED BY: Brain Wiseman
MUSIC FROM: Various Black Sabbath

albums (Warner Bros., 1970–78).

SELECTIONS: "Symptom of the Universe," "War Pigs," "Snowblind," "Never Say Die," "Black Sabbath," "Dirty Women," "Rock 'n' Roll Doctor," "Electric Funeral," "Children of the Grave," "Paranoid."

Black Sabbath's doomy, simplistic power-chording, Gothic imagery, and inherent ugliness and ridiculousness made them one of the premier "heavy" bands of the '70s. Here's a no-nonsense concert tape from late in that decade, featuring the band's original (fans would say best) lineup, with notorious lead vocalist Ozzy Osbourne, who's since gone on to a successful solo career (recently, three of the four musicians seen here left the band). Captured here in a nicely straightforward five-camera shoot, with plenty of close-ups on all the players, as well as shots of the capacity British audience responding with almost frightening intensity, Sabbath are in classic sludgemongering form. As expected, Ozzy provides a classic stoopid moment with the line, "We're gonna finish off with a number called 'Children of the Grave'—so let's see you *boogie!*" If you're into this kind of thing, here 'tis.

□ ART BLAKEY
JAZZ AT THE SMITHSONIAN
★★★★

Sony, 1983, 58 minutes

PRODUCED BY: Clark and Delia Gravelle Santee

DIRECTED BY: Clark and Delia Gravelle Santee

MUSIC FROM: Various Art Blakey/Jazz Messengers LPs (various labels, 1981–83).

SELECTIONS: "Little Man," "My Ship," "New York," "Webb City."

□ ART BLAKEY AND THE JAZZ MESSENGERS
AT RONNIE SCOTT'S LONDON
★★★½

JEM/Passport, 1986, 57 minutes

PRODUCED BY: RSVP/Wadham Films

MUSIC FROM: Various Art Blakey/Jazz Messengers albums.

SELECTIONS: "On the Ginza," "I Want to Talk About You," "Two of a Kind," "Dr. Jekyll."

Not only is Art Blakey a past master at bebop drumming, he's also a deservedly revered talent scout, whose hard-bopping Jazz Messengers ensembles have produced an inordinate share of great jazz talent since the 1950s. The 1982 edition caught in *Jazz at the Smithsonian* is no exception: on trumpet is Wynton Marsalis, just before he went on to win a Grammy and much wider acclaim. Also in the front line for some straight-up, smokin' jazz is Wynton's brother Branford, a superb saxophonist who would go on to join Police-man Sting's solo band.

The *London* program captures the next edition of Blakey's band, and while saxophonist Donald Harrison and trumpeter Terrence Blanchard have yet to achieve the fame of the Marsalis brothers, neither is a slouch. In fact, they're both just about as good as their predecessors, once again proving that yea, verily, Blakey's talent-scouting abilities surpasseth all understanding.

Both programs are shot straightforwardly, with a minimum of fuss and flash; both include interview snippets in which Blakey relates anecdotes with an animated, affectionately crusty personality and a marvelously coarse voice; and both feature him lighting a furious percussive fire beneath the young guns out in front of him on the bandstand. The *Smithsonian* is rated a tad higher than the *London* program solely because of the presence of the Marsalis brothers, which gives the program a bit of extra "star quality." But, really, they're pretty much equal, and equally good.

☐ BLANCMANGE
VIDEO 45

★ ½

Sony, 1983, 16 minutes
DIRECTED BY: Clive Richardson
MUSIC FROM: Happy Families (Island, 1983); *Mange Tout* (Sire, 1984).
SELECTIONS: "Living on the Ceiling," "Waves," "Blind Vision."

Unless you're a fan of this British synth-rock duo or a big admirer of '80s "new music" Anglos in general, you can ignore this tape. Clive Richardson's videos are okay, using some special effects to put the band into zero-gravity video space here and there, but it's certainly nowhere near enough to redeem the unremarkable music.

☐ BLONDIE
EAT TO THE BEAT

★ ½

Warner Home Video, 1983, 42 minutes
PRODUCED BY: Paul Flattery
DIRECTED BY: David Mallet
MUSIC FROM: Eat to the Beat (Chrysalis, 1979).
SELECTIONS: "Eat to the Beat," "The Hardest Part," "Union City Blue," "Slow Motion," "Shayla," "Die Young, Stay Pretty," "Accidents Never Happen," "Atomic," "Living in the Real World," "Sound-a-Sleep," "Victor," "Dreaming."

Eat to the Beat is pretty forgettable as a video program, though it does have a rather interesting place in music-video history as perhaps the very first "video album" to match it's audio-only counterpart cut for cut—and one of the first big bombs of the new medium. It was highly touted before its release as the first big music-video disc, but due to various forms of legal and corporate red tape, its release kept getting delayed, past the point where anyone cared. Finally, it came out on video*cassette,* three years after it was supposed to, and never on disc after all. And it wasn't worth the wait. *Eat to the Beat* is a thoroughly mundane and moribund assemblage of simple performance clips with occasional primitive or clumsy conceptual touches added. The whole thing—from director David Mallet's incessantly jarring and neurotic camera moves to such gratuitous special effects as the solarization in "Atomic"—is an eyesore. And even worse, *Eat to the Beat* was a crashingly disappointing album, coming as a lukewarm carbon-copy followup to their best album ever, *Parallel Lines*; and not only is most of the music here mediocre, but the best of it, like "Dreaming," is also included on *Best of Blondie,* which is infinitely more recommendable than this unless you were a *major* Blondie fan and/or *Best of* leaves you with an insatiable thirst for more.

☐ BLONDIE
THE BEST OF BLONDIE

★★★ ½

Pacific Arts, 1981, 48 minutes
PRODUCED BY: Keefco, various others
DIRECTED BY: Keith "Keef" MacMillan, various others
MUSIC FROM: The Best of Blondie (Chrysalis, 1981).
SELECTIONS: "Call Me," "In the Flesh," "X Offender," "Denis," "Detroit 442," "(I'm Always Touched by Your) Presence, Dear," "Picture This," "Hangin' on the Telephone," "Heart of Glass," "Dreaming," "Union City Blue," "Atomic," "The Tide Is High," "Rapture," "Sunday Girl."

☐ BLONDIE
BLONDIE LIVE!

★ ½

MCA, 1984, 55 minutes
MUSIC FROM: Various Blondie albums (Private Stock, Chrysalis, 1978–84).
SELECTIONS: "Heart of Glass," "Call Me," "One Way or Another," "Hangin' on the Telephone," "Dreamin'," "Rapture," "The Tide Is High," "Dance Way," "War Child," "Island of Lost Souls," "Start Me Up."

Though none of the clips in the more or less chronological *Best of Blondie* compilation is a great music video in and of itself, almost all of them do an adequate, or better, job of capturing the gorgeous Deborah Harry in all her awkwardly endearing charm. The tape not only shows the progress—and eventual regress—of Blondie's music from its '60s-retreat roots to eclectic sophisto-pop. It also brings home, again and again, just what a fine pop-rock band Blondie could be. For anyone who experienced Blondie firsthand during the band's lifespan, here's marvelous nostalgia and more. For anyone who missed 'em and is curious, here you go.

Blondie Live! is *not* the way to remember them. Recorded on their final tour before dissolving, they were promoting their last and worst album, *The Hunter*—and they look and sound as if they knew the end was near. Not a pretty picture. Even harder to look at is Harry's main squeeze and the band's driving musical force, guitarist Chris Stein, who was suffering from a mysterious internal disorder that made him look literally like death warmed over. Thus young gun Eddie Martinez—soon to gain greater fame for his crunching guitar on Run-D.M.C.'s rap-metal fusion hit "Rock Box"—was brought along to flesh out the sound, as was a horn section. Ironically or not, Martinez is about the only person onstage who seems energized and eager (not to mention able) to please the audience. The show is also shot rather sloppily. All in all, depressing is the word for this one.

□ BLOTTO
METALHEAD

★★★½

Sony, 1983, 12 minutes
PRODUCED BY: Blotto
DIRECTED BY: Gary Glinski and Tom Gliserman with Blotto
MUSIC FROM: Combo Akimbo (Blotto, 1982).
SELECTIONS: "Metalhead," "I Quit," "I Wanna Be a Lifeguard."

Sort of a lighthearted version of Devo, Blotto hail from Albany, New York, and produce their own records and videos on shoestring budgets. "I Quit" (about office politics) and the self-explanatory fun 'n' sun "I Wanna Be a Lifeguard" are entertaining slapstick pieces. But "Metalhead" is something else altogether: it's nothing short of a mini-masterpiece. One of the first and finest parody video clips ever, this devastating takeoff on heavy metal mania finds band member Sergeant Blotto (there's also Bowtie Blotto, Cheese Blotto, Lee Harvey Blotto, and Broadway Blotto) undergoing a transformation from a regular kinda guy to a raving, drooling metalhead. Along the way, there are allusions to Señor Wences and Ozzy Osbourne's animal-munching stunts, drums played with baseball bats and guitars played with hatchets (no wonder guitars are known as "axes" in the trade, right?), a guest appearance by real-life heavy-metal guitar hero Buck Dharma of Blue Oyster Cult, and the now-famous shot of Sergeant Blotto with smoke coming out of his headphones, which MTV used to use for one of its in-house promo spots. "Metalhead" would make an ideal short subject before theatrical showings of the subsequent *This Is Spinal Tap.*

□ VARIOUS ARTISTS
BLOW-UP

★★★½

MGM/UA, 1982, 102 minutes
PRODUCED BY: Carlo Ponti
DIRECTED BY: Michelangelo Antonioni
MUSIC FROM: Blow-Up motion picture soundtrack (MGM, 1966).
SELECTIONS: The Yardbirds: "Stroll On"; jazz soundtrack by Herbie Hancock.

Director Michelangelo Antonioni's Mod-era classic is a cryptic and provocative study of morality, amorality, and the artist's role in society, which along the way to its enigmatic conclusion manages to provide a most memorable travelogue through Swinging London's rock underbelly. David Hemmings stars as a hip fashion photographer who inadvertently photographs (or, er, "shoots") a murder-in-progress in London's Hyde Park one afternoon. The strange, haunting, and ultimately perplexing aftermath of his discovery forms the core of the film. Antonioni stages some wonderful scenes capturing the Mod-rock era's polymorphous perversity and general decadence, such as the famous quick-cut sequence of Hemmings engaged in a fashion shoot/ seduction with the model Verushka. The most famous scene in the movie, and what makes it most memorable and recommendable as a rock musical title, features the Yardbirds with Jeff Beck *and* Jimmy Page, onstage in a London club playing "Stroll On" and ending it with Beck's imitation of Peter Townshend's legendary guitar-destruction bit. In comparison, Herbie Hancock's cool acoustic-jazz score might seem a bit out of place, but it still works and makes for good listening on its own as well.

Aside from being perhaps *the* definitive portrait of Mod-era London, *Blow-Up* is also a definitive example of '60s self-consciously hip avant-garde strangeness, especially in its unforgettable closing scene: Hemmings, still unable to solve the riddle of the murder in the backgrounds of his Hyde Park photos, is left pondering in Hyde Park while some mimes play tennis without a ball. Antonioni tried with less success to make the same metaphysical statements about hip young rock-era America in *Zabriskie Point*.

□ THE BLUES BROTHERS
THE BLUES BROTHERS
★

MCA, 1984 (originally released in 1980), 133 minutes

PRODUCED BY: Robert K. Weiss

DIRECTED BY: John Landis

MUSIC FROM: The Blues Brothers motion picture soundtrack (MCA, 1980).

SELECTIONS: The Blues Brothers: "Stand by Your Man," "Theme from *Rawhide,*" "Gimme Some Lovin' "; Elmore James: "Shake Your Moneymaker"; John Lee Hooker: "Boogie Chillun' "; Sam and Dave: "Soothe Me," "Soul Man"; Kitty Wells: "Your Cheatin' Heart"; Otis Redding: "Can't Turn You Loose"; Louis Jordan: "Let the Good Times Roll"; Aretha Franklin: "Think"; Cab Calloway: "Minnie the Moocher"; Ray Charles: "Shake Your Tailfeather"; James Brown: "The Old Landmark."

John Belushi and Dan Aykroyd's Blues Brothers may have been cute the first dozen times on *Saturday Night Live*, but anyone with half a brain could see that a routine whose biggest laughs come when the fat guy does a somersault while the skinny guy runs in place is pretty limited. Judging from the Blues Brothers' phenomenal success both as a movie and a soundtrack, however, Jake and Elwood possessed a certain something people just couldn't get enough of. Yeah, yeah, yeah, I know—their shtick was really a "tribute" to those great soul stars of yesteryear that by the late '70s seemed to have been all but forgotten. That may have washed for the records, but judging from the embarrassing, stupid cameos by Aretha Franklin (though some critics loved her here), James Brown, Cab Calloway, and Ray Charles, one wonders how their legacies are served if they are remembered like this. I hesitate to charge that these fine artists were exploited, based on the assumptions that they (a) were not kidnapped or drugged, and (b) that they received and cashed their checks. Ditto for the great backing musicians (including Stax soul guitar guru Steve Cropper and bassist Donald "Duck" Dunne), singer Chaka Khan, Steve Lawrence (the *only* funny thing here), and the other victims. Blues great John Lee Hooker makes a rare screen appearance, which due to the filmmaker's incompetence, is all too brief and has no impact.

As for the film, the very idea that anyone thought this was even vaguely funny provokes more laughs than the movie itself. The glaring lack of judgment about such basics as the writing, direction, acting, and pacing are so appalling you can't help but wonder how a movie like this got made. Any thought about what drove all those millions to go see it—and like it—is too frightening to even contemplate. The fact that this was the only one of Belushi's movies to score at the box office, with the exception of *Animal House*, also calls his "comic genius" tag into question. Giving Belushi and Aykroyd the benefit of the doubt as to their intentions, you can do your part to keep the soul legacy alive: skip this and go buy the Atlantic Rhythm & Blues seven-album series and some Stax hits compilations.—P.R.

☐ **VARIOUS ARTISTS**

BLUES LIKE SHOWERS OF RAIN

★★★★½

Rhapsody, 1985, 30 minutes

PRODUCED BY: John Jeremy

DIRECTED BY: John Jeremy

MUSIC FROM: Various albums by various artists; various field recordings in the southern United States, 1960.

SELECTIONS: Not identified; artists include: Blind Arvella Gray, Otis Spann, J. B. Lenoir, Little Brother Montgomery, Lonnie Johnson, Henry Townshend, Sunnyland Slim and Robert Jr. Lockwood, Lightnin' Hopkins, Sam Price, Speckled Red, and others.

Billed as "an introduction to the world of blues," *Blues Like Showers of Rain* is really more an elegiac exegesis of country blues than a mere documentary. It's composed of sepia-toned historical photos, field recordings, and narrative voiceovers by a variety of blues artists, most of them (Spann, Montgomery, Lenoir, Hopkins, Price, Sunnyland Slim, and Lockwood, for instance) highly regarded. Singer Blind Arvella Gray provides the main narration. Producer/director/editor John Jeremy collected all of this material during field trips through the South in 1960, and considering that there's no actual live-action film—only the photographs—Jeremy has done an astoundingly good job of making *Blues Like Showers of Rain* a singularly compelling piece of cinema. He ably exploits the panoramic setups of most of the photos with camera zooms, pull-backs, and slow pans; but mostly, merely by juxtaposing image with sound, be it spoken word or music, Jeremy creates a profoundly poetic musical-visual synergy that makes this movie informative, entertaining, and absorbing—and then some. *Blues Like Showers of Rain* is lyrical and moving enough to transcend the documentary category, and for anyone interested in the blues, or Afro-American music and/or American culture in general, it's highly recommended. Indeed, it's so good that I dare anyone who thinks they're *not* interested in the subject to see it and not be absorbed, moved, and enlightened. (Available by mail order from Rhapsody Films.)

☐ **VARIOUS ARTISTS**

BODY ROCK

★

HBO/Cannon EMI, 1984, approximately

90 minutes

PRODUCED BY: Jeffrey Schechtman
DIRECTED BY: Marcelo Epstein
MUSIC FROM: Body Rock soundtrack (EMI-America, 1984).
SELECTIONS: Lorenzo Lamas: "Fools like Me," "Smooth Talker"; Maria Vidal: "Body Rock"; David Lasley: "Teamwork"; Roberta Flack: "One Thing Leads to Another"; Laura Branigan: "Sharpshooter"; Baxter Robertson: "Vanishing Point"; Ralph MacDonald: "Let Your Body Rock (Don't Stop)," "Smooth Talker"; Dwight Twilley: "Why You Wanna Break My Heart"; Ashford and Simpson: "The Jungle," "Do You Know Who I Am," "The Closest to Love"; Martin Briley: "Deliver."

It's hard to really appreciate the negligible standards of a subgenre such as rapsploitation until you see something as bad as this. Here Lorenzo Lamas (who looks like a cross between Desi Arnaz and a starving Arnold Schwarzenegger) plays Chilly D, a graffiti artist who learns how to rap, then how to dance (but never how to dress), from his friends, his neighborhood crew, the Body Rock Group. Why they help him and why the smarmy manager/art dealer/ impresario Terrence even cares about Chilly is never clear, since Chilly D doesn't appear to be very good at anything. But of course, Chilly makes it and becomes the star attraction of a chrome-and-strobe disco, where he croons stuff such as, "I'm a cannibal . . . gonna make your body pay." The rich, decadent, art-scene dilettante women love Chilly; but so do the men, especially Donald, who's been secretly backing Chilly's career from day one. When Donald kisses Chilly on the dance floor, it's Chilly's turn to pay. Naturally, he refuses, returns to the old neighborhood, where all the friends he sold out forgive him, and he shows *them* in a finale of bad rap that must be seen to be believed.

This is the *Rocky* of rap, but it's offensive for reasons besides just being dumb. Its depiction of the art world as peopled by nymphomaniacs and homosexual pedophiles is not for kids. These reactionary caricatures are unnecessarily ugly. There are a couple of dance scenes that do work (particularly some footage of breakers shot from under a transparent floor), though it's hard to recommend even those, especially when it appears that in some cases the film was sped up. Tacky.—P.R.

□ MARC BOLAN AND T. REX
MARC BOLAN ON VIDEO
★★★★

JEM/Passport, 1985, 60 minutes
PRODUCED BY: "Marc On Video"
DIRECTED BY: Various
MUSIC FROM: Various T. Rex albums, including *T. Rextasy* (Warner Bros., 1985).
SELECTIONS: "20th Century Boy," "Crimson Moon," "Laser Love," "Jewel," "Children of the Revolution," "Jeepster," "London Boys," "Mad Donna," "Life's a Gas," "Metal Guru," "Buick MacKane," "Get It On," "The Groover," "Ride a White Swan," "To Know You Is to Love You," "Telegram Sam," "Dreamy Lady."

This compendium of British TV appearances and primitive video clips is of more than mere historical value. Bolan, who died in a tragic car accident (his girlfriend Gloria Jones, who was driving at the time, is seen here in an eerily ironic duet on "To Know You Is to Love You") in 1977, was an avatar of chic rock style, a beautiful boy with Botticelli face and curls who somehow joined the hippie and glitter eras, pioneering androgyny along the way. Musically, he was a uniquely gifted pop-rock figure, whose unlikely mix of rockabilly and hard-rock guitar, delightfully trashy horn and string charts, masterfully ephemeral pop hooks, and constant conga comment matched his stage manner of oddly seductive elfin sexuality. None of these is a "great video" per se, but nearly all of Bolan's greatest hits (except "Hot Love") are here in from-the-video-vaults form—a lovely legacy of recent pop history, waiting to be rediscovered by a generation that may know Bolan only through the Power Station's bludgeoning of "Get It On."

☐ CLAUDE BOLLING, OTHERS
CONCERTO FOR CLASSICAL GUITAR AND JAZZ PIANO
★★½

Pioneer, 1982, 50 minutes
PRODUCED BY: Simon Fields and Paul Flattery
DIRECTED BY: Bruce Gowers
MUSIC FROM: 1982 concert in Pasadena, California.
SELECTIONS: "Hispanic Dance," "Mexicaine," "Invention," "Serenade," "Rhapsodic," "Africaine," "Finale," "Have You Met Miss Jones," "High and Inside."
Also available on Pioneer Stereo Laser videodisc.

Straightforwardly shot concert at Pasadena's Ambassador Auditorium, with pianist Bolling presenting his pretty, romantic, neo–"Third Stream" fusion of jazz, pop, and classical, very much in the same vein as his earlier hit with classical flautist Jean-Pierre Rampal. Here, he's accompanied by classical guitarist Angel Romero, and a jazz rhythm section comprised of esteemed pianist George Shearing, drummer Shelly Manne, and bassist Brian Torff. Pleasant but unspectacular.

☐ VARIOUS ARTISTS
BORN TO SWING
★★★★

Rhapsody, 1985, 50 minutes
PRODUCED BY: John Jeremy
DIRECTED BY: John Jeremy
MUSIC FROM: Various albums by Count Basie's Orchestra and other artists; soundtrack of the film *Born to Swing* (Silver Screen, 1973).
SELECTIONS: Various unidentified performances by Count Basie's Orchestra and others.

Very much like producer/director John Jeremy's documentary on country blues, *Blues Like Showers of Rain* (also distributed by Rhapsody), this look at the survivors of Count Basie's greatest big band—the 1936–43 edition—balances a poignantly elegiac tone with the dignity and vitality of its subjects. The featured Basie alumni include drummer Jo Jones, trombonist Dicky Wells, trumpeter Buck Clayton, and saxophonists Earle Warren and Buddy Tate—all of them superb players, first seen in their heydays via some too-brief black-and-white clips of that fabulous Basie band defining the essence of big-band swing.

We then cut to 1973 in color, and the jazz greats are seen as survivors who make ends meet with day jobs hardly befitting their status as great American musicians from one of the best and most important ensembles in modern musical history. Wells toils as a messenger for a Wall Street brokerage house; Jones gives the occasional drum lesson; Warren tells of the oompah band he once had to play in at a German restaurant in order to earn enough money to eat. As if to enforce our sneaking suspicions that all is not well in the world when such things can come to pass, Jeremy intercuts shots of Gene Krupa, who is white, discussing how much influence black jazz drummers such as Baby Dodds, Cozy Cole, and Chick Webb had on him. Without slighting Krupa, Jeremy makes us realize the ultimate inequities caused by racism in our society; after all, neither Webb nor Cole nor Dodds ever gained as much fame—or as much money—as Krupa did.

However, Jeremy never belabors this

point, avoiding preachiness in favor of a subtle poignancy. All of this is forgotten for a time when the musicians are united for a recording session at which trumpeter Joe Newman, representing a somewhat later generation of Basie alumni, is also present. The music is indescribably warm and soulful, and it's only here that the burdens of day-to-day life are completely lifted from these dignified gents' shoulders. There is also some nice footage of these noble old men *off* the performing stand—teaching, hanging out and bantering in musical instrument stores, at home with their wives. Throughout, Jo Jones is the most riveting presence: in the vintage Basie clips, he executes stunning licks all over his kit—including some crossover sticking of floor-toms on either side of him that must be seen to be believed—with a mile-wide grin on his face. In the '70s footage, he is a forebodingly truculent yet magnetic figure with what seems like a perpetual glower on his handsome face—obviously too proud to give in to the sands of time that threaten to obscure forever his enormous contributions to American culture. Thanks to films like this, though, Jones and his cohorts need not worry so much about that happening. (Available by mail order from Rhapsody Films.)

□ DAVID BOWIE
LOVE YOU TILL TUESDAY
★★★½

Mail order U.K. import, 1969, 30 minutes
PRODUCED BY: Kenneth Pitt
DIRECTED BY: Malcolm J. Thomson
MUSIC FROM: The World of David Bowie (London/Deram, 1967); *Images: 1966–67* (London/Deram), 1973).
SELECTIONS: "Love You till Tuesday," "Sell Me a Coat" (with Hermione and Hutch), "When I'm Five," "Rubber Band," "The Mask," "Let Me Sleep Beside You," "Ching-a-Ling" (with Hermione and Hutch), "Space Oddity," "When I Live My Dream" (with Hermione and Hutch).

This import-only obscurity has to be some sort of music-video first: a half-hour compilation of video clips from 1969. Bowie was still heavily into the mime he'd begun studying two years before, and while he's a less savvy and outrageous performer here than he would soon become, his heavily mannered, chameleonic essence is definitely there. Director Malcolm Thomson provides surprisingly high (for the period, and considering Bowie's status at the time) production values; he even gets arty here and there and pulls it off. The songs are very slight and forgettable, for the most part ("Space Oddity" is a much cruder arrangement here than the later hit version). A few numbers feature Bowie with the moribund folk duo Hermione and Hutch. Definitely worth the high import price for Bowiephiles and those interested in music video history. (Available by mail order from Playings Hard to Get.)

□ DAVID BOWIE
CHINA GIRL VIDEO 45
★★★

Sony, 1983, 14 minutes
PRODUCED BY: Various
DIRECTED BY: David Mallet
MUSIC FROM: Let's Dance (EMI-America, 1983).
SELECTIONS: "Let's Dance," "China Girl," "Modern Love."

Three solid clips from Bowie's *Let's Dance* LP are compiled in Sony's *China Girl Video 45.* "Let's Dance" and "China Girl" are both colorfully produced and divertingly substantial, though only the former really comes even close to living up to Bowie's statements at the time of their release that they were both analyses of Old World/New World cultural imperialism versus the Third World. In "Let's Dance," a pair of young Australian aborigines acquire a pair of red shoes (directly referred to in Bowie's lyric, as in "Put on your red shoes and dance the blues") symbolic of Western civilization—and near the end of the clip, symbolically destroy them on a hilltop overlooking Sydney Harbor. In between there's a memorable homage to a scene in Luis Buñuel's surrealist classic *Un Chien Andalou,* as the aborogine boy is suddenly seen pulling a huge piece of industrial machinery down the middle of a busy Sydney street.

"China Girl" finds Bowie and a striking Asian model engaged in various metaphorical setups for master-servant, exploiter-exploited, and evenly romantic relationships; it's all a bit too fast-moving and obscure for its own good, but note that the version here is the *uncensored* "China Girl"—with a *From Here to Eternity* tribute near the finale in which Bowie and the China Girl make love on a beach. You can spot Bowie's nude bottom through the pounding surf. Finally, "Modern Love" is the glittering concert clip taken from the *Serious Moonlight Concert* program. But, lovely as it is, it's not really a "concert" clip. Sure, the footage is from the concert—but would you believe that for the clip's initial MTV release to promote the "Modern Love" single, Bowie and director David Mallet actually spent hours carefully synching the live footage to the original album track, then post-dubbed subtle audience noises to make it seem live? They did, probably because there was some sort of unavoidable glitch in the concert recording or something. At any rate, it's hard to believe anyone would go to such trouble, but it's still easy to enjoy "Modern Love" as one of the most beautifully shot concert clips of recent memory.

□ DAVID BOWIE
JAZZIN' FOR BLUE JEAN
★★★★★

Sony, 1984, 22 minutes
DIRECTED BY: Julien Temple
MUSIC FROM: Tonight (EMI, 1984).
SELECTIONS: "Blue Jean," "Don't Look Down."

More than anything else, *this* really made good on Bowie's *Let's Dance*–era about-face declaration that he was throwing away the masks and just being a regular guy like the rest of us from now on. Never has he felt closer, seemed more human—unless one wants to count his only other deliberately comic performance, in the vastly underrated and barely seen 1978 film *Just a Gigolo.* The intelligence and integrity of director Julien Temple are also largely responsible for bringing Bowie's slight but charming conceit about the absurdities of the star-fan relationship to such delightfully comic life.

Bowie leads two lives in this mini-movie: as the ludicrously affected rock star Screaming Lord Byron, Bowie mocks his own past outrages; as the pathetic nerd Vic, who desperately tries to impress a date with his feigned friendship with Byron (and who of course ends up losing the girl to the star), Bowie makes a fascinating, and amazingly successful, attempt to identify with Us Normals. The "Blue Jean" song segment itself works infinitely better in context here than as a separate video clip. And there's a perfect coda, with the camera pulling up and away as Bowie goes back out of character to argue with Temple about how the story's supposed to end—a witty comment on the making of a witty comment about rock stardom.

☐ **DAVID BOWIE**
SERIOUS MOONLIGHT
★★★★

Music Media, 1984, 90 minutes
PRODUCED BY: Anthony Eaton
DIRECTED BY: David Mallet
MUSIC FROM: Various David Bowie albums (RCA/EMI, 1972–83).
SELECTIONS: "Look Back in Anger," "Heroes," "What in the World," "Golden Years," "Fashion/Let's Dance," "Breaking Glass," "Life on Mars," "Sorrow," "Cat People," "China Girl," "Scary Monsters," "Rebel Rebel," "White Light/White Heat," "Station to Station," "Cracked Actor," "Ashes to Ashes," "Space Oddity," "Young Americans," "Fame."
Also available in Pioneer Stereo Laser videodisc.

This lavishly produced concert program captures the new, *sans*-persona Bowie, live in Vancouver during his heralded 1983 world tour. Beneath huge balloons of planet earth and a silvery crescent moon, Bowie slickly spans his career, and the results can't help but be impressive (especially with Chic drummer Tony Thompson kicking things smartly along). Director Mallet's use of special post-production effects (as well as bits of the concept clip for "Let's Dance") is more tasteful than usual for him. You can't go wrong here—unless you're one of those who find Bowie minus masks a bit, er, dull.

☐ **DAVID BOWIE**
RICOCHET
★★★

JEM/Passport, 1985, 60 minutes
PRODUCED BY: Rebecca Dobbs, Bhaskar Bhattacharyya, Gerry Troyna
DIRECTED BY: Gerry Troyna
MUSIC FROM: Various David Bowie albums (RCA, EMI, 1972–84).
SELECTIONS: "Station to Station," "Modern Love," "Ziggy Stardust," "Look Back in Anger," "Warszawa," "Heroes," "Ricochet," "Fame."

Intriguing, slightly off-the-wall counterpart to Bowie's *Serious Moonlight* concert video, as the camera here follows him *off*-stage on the Singapore/Bangkok/Hong Kong swing of the same 1983 world tour. (It is this part of the tour that is so lavishly documented in the 1984 coffee-table book *Serious Moonlight*.) We see Bowie doing all sorts of sight-seeing, from a lavish dinner on a well-appointed boat with some rich locals to more typical Third World slum tours, both by bright daylight and eerie neon-lit night. Given the milieu, and Bowie's jarring Old World presence in it, one can't help but feel echoes of *The Year of Living Dangerously*—especially when we see such bizarre, unexplained scenes as that of Bowie sitting crossed-legged before a similarly posed old man in Bangkok, who spits tea in Bowie's impassive face—and this is annoyingly exaggerated with gratuitous freeze-frames of men in suits and shades who happen to be standing around (bodyguards? secret agents? *worse???*). Overall, however, it's quite atmospheric and unusual, though Bowie fans should note that *Ricochet* is as much travelogue as Bowie video. He's in only about half of it, really (most of the concert music is heard, not seen), and even in *that* footage he remains very guarded most of the time.

☐ **DAVID BOWIE**
ZIGGY STARDUST AND THE SPIDERS FROM MARS
★★

RCA/Columbia, 1985, 91 minutes
PRODUCED BY: D. A. Pennebaker
DIRECTED BY: D. A. Pennebaker
MUSIC FROM: Pinups (RCA, 1973); *Aladdin Sane* (RCA, 1973); *The Rise and Fall of Ziggy Stardust and the Spiders from Mars* (RCA, 1972); *Hunky Dory* (RCA, 1971); *The Man Who Sold the World* (Mercury, 1970).
SELECTIONS: "Hang On to Yourself," "Ziggy Stardust," "Watch That Man," Medley: "Wild Eyed Boy from Freecloud"/ "All the Young Dudes"/"Oh You Pretty

Things," "Moonage Daydream," "Changes," "Space Oddity," "My Death," "Cracked Actor," "Time," "Width of a Circle," "Let's Spend the Night Together," "Suffragette City," "White Light/White Heat," "Rock & Roll Suicide."

Pioneering concert-rockumentarian D. A. Pennebaker caught Bowie toward the tail end of his glitter phase, on his supposed "Farewell Tour" of the U.K. But despite the obvious historical value of such a program, the camerawork is extremely erratic, the lighting is virtually nonexistent (causing much of the action to be lost in a murky blackness), and the sound is sludgy, the result of both a rather lame band and horrendous recording. Honestly, these technical difficulties make it pretty tough for anyone but the most ardently devoted Bowie fan to sit through this without getting frustrated.

□ DAVID BOWIE, OTHERS
CHRISTIANE F.
★★★½

Media, 1984, 130 minutes
PRODUCED BY: Bernd Eichinger and Hans Weth
DIRECTED BY: Ulrich Edel
MUSIC FROM: The film *Christiane F.* (New World Pix, 1981); *Christiane F.* original soundtrack LP (RCA Germany, 1981); David Bowie albums *Station to Station, "Heroes," Lodger, Stage, Low* (RCA, 1976–81).
SELECTIONS: "V2 Schneider," "TVC 15," "Heroes," "Look Back in Anger," "Stay," "Sense of Doubt," "Boys Keep Swinging," "Warszawa," "Station to Station."

Grim, depressing, English-dubbed 1981 German docudrama about the descent of a seemingly normal and sensible but terminally bored thirteen-year-old girl into heroin addiction and prostitution. The protagonist also happens to be a David Bowie freak, which occasions lots of his songs on the soundtrack, and even a brief live appearance where he performs "Station to Station" onstage. The chic anomie of Bowie's music from this period (especially the avant-pop experiments of the atmospheric *Low* and *"Heroes"*) makes a nice ironic comment on the action—which happens to be so commendably flat in its graphic candor that you might find the drama a bit leaden. You have to think about what you're seeing to realize the horror of it all, and thanks largely to Nadia Brunkhorst's remarkably credible performance as the title character, you do. Based on a true story, *Christiane F.* is honest and intense, and unflinching in its portrayal of the seamier side of drug addiction, and generally a thousand times more powerful than typical "teen problem" films.

□ BOBBY BRADFORD AND JOHN CARTER
THE NEW MUSIC
★★★

Rhapsody, 1985, 29 minutes
PRODUCED BY: Peter Bull and Alex Gibney
DIRECTED BY: Peter Bull and Alex Gibney
MUSIC FROM: The New Music motion picture soundtrack (1980).
SELECTIONS: "Circle," "And She Speaks."

Bradford and Carter, like their alto saxophonist contemporary the free-jazz giant Ornette Coleman, grew up in Texas, where they heard and played a lot of bebop and blues before making the leap of faith into the avant-garde. Cornetist Bradford and clarinetist Carter subsequently moved to Los Angeles, where they were among the first on the West Coast to eke out a living playing nothing but Colemanesque "new music." As this brief, unadorned portrait/documentary/performance film tells us, they've taken teaching jobs to help pay the rent, but resolutely refuse to compromise their music. The two duets they play are daunting, but ultimately very rewarding, examples of avant-garde jazz, demonstrating not only their individual instrumental talents—Carter, one of the most highly regarded clarinetists in jazz, period, can play "straight" *and* get spine-tinglingly strange extreme-overtone noises out of the licorice stick—but a highly refined compositional logic that would probably reveal itself to most listeners only gradually, through repeated listenings.

Unfortunately, *The New Music* is so relentlessly smug about how uncompromised its subjects are that it ends up preaching polemically to the already converted. I like a lot of avant-garde jazz a whole lot more than many people I know, yet even I can plainly see that Bradford and Carter's music is not the most readily accessible to the majority; but directors Bull and Gibney seem to feel that anyone who can't immediately see the value in this music is a philistine who's wasting his or her time watching the film. So, even as it's practically beating its breast with pride over the refusal of its subjects to sell out for wider acclaim, *The New Music* virtually ensures that it won't convert anyone. It wastes a golden opportunity, not to mention some fine (if a bit cerebral) music by two admirable musicians, in doing so, which docks it a half-star—as does the short shrift it gives to background on these two undeservedly obscure musicians at its opening, again implying that if you don't *already* know about them you don't deserve to be told. About the only thing that makes the film's self-conscious, self-destructive bias understandable is the rather cantankerous attitude Carter and especially Bradford have about their self-determined stance in a city where studio musicians rake in top dollars all around them. But *The New Music* does, after all, feature two admirable musicians playing their music, and the performance is shot with intimate, straightforward taste; fans of these two, or of avant-garde jazz in general, will certainly want to check it out. (Available by mail order from Rhapsody Films.)

□ LAURA BRANIGAN
LAURA BRANIGAN

★★

RCA/Columbia, 1985, 60 minutes

PRODUCED BY: Marty Callner, Molly Miles

DIRECTED BY: Marty Callner

MUSIC FROM: Various Laura Branigan albums.

SELECTIONS: "The Lucky One," "All Night with Me," "Satisfaction," "Ti Amo," "I Wish I Could Be Alone," "Solitaire," "How Am I Supposed to Live without You," "Self Control," "Gloria," "Don't Show Your Love."

Also available on Pioneer Stereo Laser videodisc.

Given her mediocre voice, bombastic and vapid music, thoroughly unspectacular looks and physical ungainliness, it's nothing less than a miracle that Laura Branigan has managed to become an international pop star. Yet she has. So it would be pointless for me to say that even her fans might find this unspectacularly shot concert program, from Caesar's Tahoe in 1984, a deadly dull embarrassment. After all, anyone who goes for Branigan's music will go for this as well.

□ VARIOUS ARTISTS
BREAKIN'

★★

MGM/UA, 1984, 87 minutes

PRODUCED BY: David Zito and Allen DeBevoise

DIRECTED BY: Joel Silbert

MUSIC FROM: Breakin' motion picture soundtrack (Polydor, 1984).

SELECTIONS: Kraftwerk: "Tour de France"; Al Jarreau: "Boogie Down"; Art of Noise: "Beat Box"; Bar-Kays: "Freakshow on the Dance Floor"; Hot Streak: "Body Work"; Carol Lynn Townes: "99½"; Chris Taylor and David Storrs: "Reckless"; Re-Flex: "Cut It"; 3V: "Heart of the Beat"; Firefox: "Street People"; Rufus with Chaka Khan: "Ain't Nobody"; Ollie and Jerry: "There's No Stoppin' Us," "Showdown."

☐ **VARIOUS ARTISTS**

BREAKIN' 2—ELECTRIC BOOGALOO

★★

MGM/UA, 1985, approximately 90 minutes

PRODUCED BY: Allen DeBevoise

DIRECTED BY: Allen DeBevoise

MUSIC FROM: Breakin' 2—Electric Boogaloo motion picture soundtrack (Polydor, 1985).

SELECTIONS: Ice-T: "Reckless"; Carol Lynn Townes: "Believe in the Beat"; Firefox: "Stylin' "; George Kranz: "Din Daa Daa"; Steve Donn: "Gotta Have the Money"; Midway: "Set It Out"; Ollie and Jerry: "Electric Boogaloo," "Physical Clash," "When I C. U."; Rags and Riches "Oye Mamacita"; Jeff Tyzik: "Jammin' in Manhattan"; Mark Scott: "I Don't Wanna Come Down"; Satisfaction: "Do Your Thang."

A Menachem Golan and Yoram Globus production, *Breakin'* may be the most likeable of the breakin' flicks, but that's not really saying much. It's a lot less pretentious than *Beat Street* (partly because *Breakin'* is set in sunny Venice, California, not exactly the hip-hop capital of the world) and a lot less offensive to the thinking viewer than *Body Rock*—and it does have some genuinely fine breaking, courtesy of costars Adolfo Quinones (Shabba-Doo) and Michael Chambers (Boogaloo Shrimp), whom you might recognize from Chaka Khan's video for "I Feel for You." But, as with countless other teen movies, this one also hinges on that idealistic, simpleminded adolescent premise—If only *we* ran things. Sure.

Here Ozone (Quinones) and Turbo (Chambers) team up with a rich white girl, Kelly (Lucinda Dickey), to prove that they can overcome their differences—social, racial, political, economic—because they love to dance. She's a classically trained dancer whose teacher loves her, resents them, and does all he can to see that they don't get their big break (pardon the pun). Of course, they do (don't they always in these silly movies?) and they all live happily ever after.

Until *Breakin' 2—Electric Boogaloo,* that is, when some mean politicians and developers try to raze the local community center. Kelly postpones a career-making trip to Paris to come back and help Ozone and Turbo stage the big show that saves the community center. (Yay!) There's little to recommend this one, since it mostly repeats the same themes, only in a less believable context. But dance fanatics might be interested just to see some good steps.

If, on the other hand, you're picking up either of these for the music, don't bother. There are few good tracks on either tape, and even the good ones all sound like they were written to make the definitive statement about dancing as a metaphor for life, a limited and much-worn theme.—P.R.

☐ **VARIOUS ARTISTS**

BREAKIN' METAL

★½

JEM/Passport, 1985, 70 minutes

MUSIC FROM: Various albums by various artists.

SELECTIONS: Hanoi Rocks: "Oriental Beat," "Back to Mystery City"; Thor: "Knock Them Down," "Deathmarch," "Let the Blood Run Red"; Rock Goddess: "Satisfied the Crucified," "Hold Me Down"; Black Sabbath: "Paranoid"; Wrathchild:

"Sweet Surrender," "Hot Rock Shock," "Kick Down the Walls"; Lords of the New Church: "Going Downtown," "Black Girl White Girl"; Sledgehammer: "Garabandal"; Thin Lizzy: "Massacre," "Don't Believe a Word"; DiAnno: "Road Rat."

A gaggle of mostly deservedly unknown heavy-metal sludgemongers, shot on the ultra-cheap at various U.K. rock clubs. Hanoi Rocks, a delightfully dumb new New York Dolls joke by way of England and Scandinavia, are the class of the lot; their two cuts are actually closer to the proto-punk raunch of, say, the Heartbreakers than to actual metal, which of course is all to the good. Sub-Schwarzenegger bodybuilder Thor is the worst—as a singer and frontman, he bends metal bars with his teeth pretty well. In between are such curiosities as Wrathchild (a hard-pop band in glitter disguise) and all-girl headbangers Rock Goddess. Thin Lizzy, Lords of the New Church, and Black Sabbath are the only really well-known bands here; except for Sabbath (whose classic "Paranoid" is taken from the band's *Live! Featuring Ozzy Osbourne* program) they are in mediocre form here. Overall, for confirmed metalheads only.

☐ **VARIOUS ARTISTS**

BREATHLESS

★★★½

Vestron, 1984, 100 minutes
PRODUCED BY: Martin Erlichman
DIRECTED BY: Jim McBride
SELECTIONS: Mink DeVille: "Bad Boy"; Fripp and Eno: "Wind on Water, Wind on Wind," "Final Sunset"; Jerry Lee Lewis: "Breathless," "High School Confidential"; Elvis Presley: "Suspicious Minds"; Link Wray and the Wraymen: "Jack the Ripper"; Dexy's Midnight Runners: "Celtic Soul Brothers"; Joe "King" Carrasco: "Caca de Vaca"; X: "Breathless"; the Pretenders: "Message of Love."

Though this film was based on it, you have to forget about Godard's *A Bout de Soufflé,* for this isn't any kind of remake of any French film but a truly American portrait of pop culture and a pop culture antihero. Richard Gere is Jesse, a two-bit hood and car thief who accidentally kills a California highway patrolman, and *Breathless* recounts the few days between the murder and Jesse's own end. Jesse is immature, wild, and childishly charming—not unlike his hero Jerry Lee Lewis. He comes to L.A. to see a French architecture student named Monica—brainlessly played by Valerie Kaprisky—whom he worships, even though—or maybe because—they had a casual fling in Las Vegas. What makes Jesse so engaging despite his self-centered arrogance is that he longs to feel passion about something, anything. He'd love to die for the kind of love Jerry Lee or the Pretenders sing about, and in the end, he probably does.

Breathless is one of those "rock video" movies full of burning sunsets, pastel city streets, hot candy-colored cars, and atmosphere—lots and lots of atmosphere. What qualifies this film for inclusion here is the fantastic use of the soundtrack, which is eclectic (and also features, in bits and pieces, King Sunny Adé and Sam Cooke) but never gratuitous. Each bar works in the film the way music works in your life at those moments when no one else is home, or you're driving alone in your car. At the film's opening, Jesse is in Vegas casing out cars to steal, with Mink DeVille's "Bad Boy" in the background. When Jesse tears across the desert sunset in his stolen Porsche, he's singing Jerry Lee's "Breathless" at the top of his lungs, pounding on the steering wheel, rocking. He invades Monica's apartment and her life, fueled by a fantasy of love and crushed by her "betrayal," though she barely knows him—so he sings "Suspicious Minds" in the shower, using the shower head as his mike. This is probably one of the best uses of any Elvis song in any movie to date. When he and Monica spend their last night together running through Los Angeles to escape the cops, it's to a pounding "Message of Love." He spends what we believe are his last few seconds of life in a passionate, aching tribute to Lewis. In addition, this is far and away Gere's most likable role, and definitely worth seeing.—P.R.

□ MARTIN BRILEY
DANGEROUS MOMENTS
★★½

Sony, 1986, 14 minutes
PRODUCED BY: Len Epand, Claude Borenzweig
DIRECTED BY: Chris Gabrin, Don Letts
MUSIC FROM: One Night with a Stranger (Polygram, 1983); *Dangerous Moments* (Polygram, 1985).
SELECTIONS: "Dangerous Moments," "The Salt in My Tears," "Put Your Hands on the Screen."

This "Video 45" clip compilation contains one rock-video classic, sandwiched between two well-meaning also-rans. The classic is "The Salt in My Tears," a bitter take on divorce settlements inspired by Briley's own then-recent divorce; Marie Elise Gretner, who was in the cast of *Octopussy,* turns in a brilliantly parodic performance as the avenging Queen Bitch ex, which along with Chris Gabrin's deftly comic direction keeps the song's vast potential for wounded-macho sexist claptrap from being unleashed. "Dangerous Moments" clumsily, cloyingly updates the old "let's-have-sex-now-'cos-they-could-drop-the-bomb-anytime" line, while Don Letts's "Put Your Hands on the Screen" is an unfortunately muddled satire of a deserving target—money-grubbing TV evangelists. Is one exceptional piece enough to recommend a three-clip package from a guy who makes competent formula hard-rock pop, and about whom the most charismatic thing is the possible bald spot he keeps hiding by *never, ever removing his beret?* Well, I guess you could do worse.

□ VARIOUS ARTISTS (STING, OTHERS)
BRIMSTONE AND TREACLE
★★½

MGM/UA, 1982, 85 minutes
PRODUCED BY: Kenith Trodd
DIRECTED BY: Richard Longcraine
MUSIC FROM: Brimstone and Treacle motion picture soundtrack LP (A&M, 1982).
SELECTIONS: Sting: "Only You," "Spread a Little Happiness"; the Police: "I Burn for You"; the Go-Go's: "We Got the Beat"; Squeeze: "Up the Junction."

Sordid, intriguing little British film that might have worked better as a shorter-form *Twilight Zone* episode. Sting is, however, *very* effective as a creepy interloper into a stiff-upper-lip British household, run by two extremely capable actors (Denholm Elliott and Joan Plowright), whose daughter (Susan Hamilton, later to star in *1984*) has been in a catatonic state (turns out she walked zombielike in front of a car after seeing Dad at the office getting it on with his secretary). Sting somehow manages to ingratiate himself into the household by acting as if he can cure the girl; eventually he tries raping her to bring her out of her stupor, and then all hell breaks loose. Longcraine—whose best work has been in TV commercials, like the one for British Airways where the island of Manhattan appears to be landing in London—has the mood down, but the story's just a bit too slight, and the all-round strong performances can't quite save it. The dark screenplay is by Dennis Potter, who also brought us the marvelous, undeservedly overlooked Steve Martin/ Bernadette Peters remake of *Pennies from Heaven.* The music is generally ineffectual in the movie, and is not worth the price of admission on its own; Sting's upbeat, '30s-style closing theme is a heavily ironic touch after the nastiness that's preceded it.

☐ **VARIOUS ARTISTS**

BRITISH ROCK: THE FIRST WAVE

★★★½

RCA/Columbia, 1985, 60 minutes
PRODUCED BY: Patrick Montgomery
DIRECTED BY: Patrick Montgomery and Pamela Page
MUSIC FROM: Various albums by various artists.
SELECTIONS: Bill Haley and His Comets: "Rock Around the Clock"; the Vernon Girls: "Rip It Up"; Lonnie Donegan: "Rock Island Line"; the Beatles: "She Loves You"; "Twist and Shout," "I Saw Her Standing There," "Can't Buy Me Love," "She's a Woman"; Gerry and the Pacemakers: "It's Gonna Be Alright," "Ferry Cross the Mersey"; Brian Poole and the Tremoloes: "Do You Love Me"; the Hollies: "Just One Look"; the Rolling Stones: "I Just Wanna Make Love to You," "I Wanna Be Your Man," "Round and Round"; the Animals: "House of the Rising Sun," "We Gotta Get Outta This Place"; the Kinks: "All Day and All of the Night"; Freddie and the Dreamers: "I'm Telling You Now"; Manfred Mann: "Doo Wah Diddy"; Herman's Hermits: "Mrs. Brown, You've Got a Lovely Daughter"; Spencer Davis Group: "I'm a Man"; the Who: "I Can't Explain," "My Generation"; the Yardbirds: "Heart Full of Soul"; Cream: "Tales of Brave Ulysses"; the Zombies: "She's Not There."

Yours truly is a contributor to the narration script of *British Rock: The First Wave.* That noted, read what I have to say, check the tape out, and then you decide if I'm being overly biased.

Patrick Montgomery's Archive Film Productions (*The Compleat Beatles, Rock and Roll: The Early Days*) always manages to unearth the kind of archival footage that makes your eyes pop and your jaw drop, and here we go again: from the montages of skiffle, beat clubs, and boho blues bars (not to mention the Vernon Girls destroying "Rip It Up") to the rarely if ever seen Beatles bits (from their Royal Command Performance and the last concert ever, in San Francisco in 1966, among others); from the Animals' snarling "We Gotta Get Outta This Place" and the Yardbirds' melancholically mod "Heart Full of Soul" to the various scenes of Beatlemania, Stonesmania, Herman-mania (as in the Hermits), and Monkeemania. In fact, the most memorable moment in the whole program is this comment, from a teenage girl circa 1964 or '65 who's asked by a TV reporter why she loves the Rolling Stones: " 'Cos Keith is beautiful . . . and, 'cos—no, wait—they're so ugly they're appealing." That's one of the most brilliantly insightful, pithy, and articulate critiques of rock, British or American, I've ever heard. And you'd best believe it makes me wince to admit that that young lady's comment does a much better job of telling the tale than that part of the program to which I contributed—the narration, which falls back on too many clichés (gee, don't recall if I wrote those . . .), is obviously not as focused as *The Compleat Beatles,* nor as possessed of a point of view as *Rock and Roll: The Early Days.* And Michael York's rather pompous and humorless reading of it sure doesn't help. Still, the facts, the why's and wherefore's, of this particular corner of rock history are there, in what is on the whole a nicely assembled package. And it's got some outrageously good footage.

☐ JAMES BROWN
LIVE IN CONCERT
★★½

Media, 1984, 48 minutes
PRODUCED BY: Wendell Wilks
DIRECTED BY: Barrie McLean
MUSIC FROM: 1979 Summer Festival at the Forum in Toronto, Canada; various James Brown albums.
SELECTIONS: "Band Intro/Boogie Wonderland," "Too Funky in Here," "Body Heat," "Try Me," "Georgia," "Please, Please, Please," "Jam 1980s," "Mutha's Nature," "Too Funky in Here (Reprise)."

One of modern music's all-time greats, the one seminal figure who deserves most of the credit for creating that sexily syncopated, urgent form of black dance music known as "funk," the Godfather of Soul was well into his fifties when this 1979 Toronto show was shot. And though he's well past his prime (see *That Was Rock* for JB's Godhead), Mr. Dynamite still goes through those splits, spins, shimmies, and knee-drops that inspired Michael Jackson, Prince, and so many others, and still breaks out the old classic cape routine for "Please, Please, Please." But the band's far from his best, the only certified JB classics in the repertoire are the gospel-soul ballad "Try Me" and the protean R&B "Please, Please, Please," and the show suffers from an overdose of Vegasitis and overworking serviceable latter-day funk fodder like "Body Heat," "Jam 1980s" and "Mutha's Nature." Furthermore, the crass TV-special production values—cutting from JB to the trio of female backup singers just as Soul Brother Number One is going into a knee-drop; cutting away from "Try Me" in mid-song with a "The Forum Presents James Brown" logo on-screen; etc.—don't help a bit. Still, this *is* The Hardest Working Man in Showbiz, and "Too Funky in Here" represents the best of his more recent work. If you care about the roots of modern dance music you'll check this out.

☐ JAMES BROWN
LIVE IN LONDON
★★★★

Sony, 1986, 56 minutes
PRODUCED BY: Martin Brierly
MUSIC FROM: Various James Brown albums.
SELECTIONS: "Give It Up or Turnit a Loose," "Too Funky in Here," "Get Up Offa That Thing," "Try Me," "Prisoner of Love," "Cold Sweat, Parts 1 and 2," "Papa's Got a Brand New Bag," Medley: "I Got You (I Feel Good)"/"Out of Sight," "It's a Man's, Man's, Man's World," "Please, Please, Please," "Sex Machine."

Fronting an eleven-piece band (whose members are identified by a credit roll at the end of the tape!) in 1985 at London's Hammersmith Odeon, JB delivers a surprisingly smoking set in *Live in London.* Hot enough, in fact, to overcome the mediocre production, which is indifferently competent at best and occasionally descends to ill-advised slo-mo and freeze-frame inserts during and between songs, and the occasional clumsy odd-angle shot from the wings through a maze of band members. The three-piece horn section features longtime on-again/off-again saxophonist Maceo Parker on alto, to whom the Godfather of Soul gives several solo spots; overall they're fiery and precise, albeit still lacking the full flavor of the classic '60s JB bands. James coasts in places, but that's mainly because he really puts out in other places, especially a nicely extended "Prisoner of Love," which kicks off an extremely solid string of classics that takes up the last half of the show. There are, of course, the jarring moments here and there—the music jumping abruptly from Maceo's slow-burning solo in "Prisoner of Love" into the fast, jagged funk groove of "Cold Sweat" with no warning, for instance—but that sort of non-sequitur whimsy has always been part of JB's eccentric charm. "Papa's Got a Brand New Bag" and "I Got You (I Feel Good)" are notable in that they're *not* throwaway versions ("Try Me," however, is—consisting of no more than its title, trilled *once* by JB)—rather, they're taken at a hard clip and sound reasonably authentic. The classic "Man's World" is the highlight: there's an unforgettable moment with James on his knees, pleading "Help me somebody" off-mike as the band vamps softly behind him; later he recites a roster of dead stars in tribute, from Elvis to "not one, not two, but three princes of peace—John Lennon, Bob Marley, and Marvin Gaye"—but he also mentions Roberto Clemente (nothing *wrong* with that, it's just another of those delightfully strange James Brown Moments). There's another memorable shot of JB dancing with a white girl in the audience during "Sex Machine." But those are only the peak moments. All in all, this tape really testifies, and is easily the best *full-length* James Brown performance available on the market at this writing (*That Was Rock* is more intense, but also shorter).

□ BILL BRUFORD
BRUFORD AND THE BEAT

★★★½

DCI, 1982, 40 minutes
PRODUCED BY: Kenny Klompus and Steve Apicella
DIRECTED BY: Kenny Klompus and Steve Apicella
MUSIC FROM: Discipline (Warner Bros., 1981).
SELECTIONS: "Discipline."

Not so much an instructional home video as a "percussion profile," which is what its producer appropriately calls it. As any of his fans know, Bill Bruford (a British progressive-rock vet who's played with Yes, Genesis, King Crimson, and U.K. among others) is an unusually intelligent drummer, something that's quite evident in his comments on his background, equipment, playing style, and general musical philosophies. Yes guitarist Steve Howe and King Crimson guitarist Robert Fripp also offer brief comments on working with Bruford, and the drummer himself deconstructs the ingenious polyrhythms of Crimson's 1981 masterwork *Discipline* (apt title) before playing the actual composition with the band. My only disappointment as a big Bruford fan, is that the tape focuses on the mammoth mutant electro-acoustic kit Bill used with the re-formed Crimson since 1981. As any of his fans know, his accomplishments before then on conventional acoustic kit drums were also awesome and would certainly bear closer examination. (Available by mail order from DCI Music Video.)

□ JIMMY BUFFETT
LIVE BY THE BAY

★★★

MCA, 1986, 87 minutes
PRODUCED BY: Tammara Wells
DIRECTED BY: Jack Cole
MUSIC FROM: Various Jimmy Buffett LPs (Dunhill, ABC, and MCA, 1970–85).
SELECTIONS: "Door Number 3," "Grapefruit—Juicy Fruit," "We Are the People," "Stars on the Water," "Coconut Telegraph," "Come Monday," "Rag Top Day," "Who's the Blonde Stranger?," "Volcano," "Changes in Latitudes, Changes in Attitudes," "One Particular Harbour," "If the Phone Doesn't Ring, It's Me," "Why Don't We Get Drunk," "Cheeseburger in Paradise," "Fins," "Last Mango in Paris," "A Pirate Looks at Forty," "Margaritaville."

Jimmy Buffett's obsessively tropical mellowness can get a bit precious at times, but Mr. Miami Nice sure does have his fans, and if you're one of 'em, you should definitely settle back and enjoy this. Buffett's on his home turf at Miami's Marine Stadium (a former boat-racing facility), and he and his Coral Reefer Band easily charm an audience that's both in the stands and on the water. The very smooth direction and production complete the pretty picture.

□ ERIC BURDON, OTHERS
COMEBACK
★½

MGM/UA, 1984, 105 minutes
PRODUCED BY: Jochen Von Vietinghoff and Rocco-Film Project
DIRECTED BY: Christel Buschmann
MUSIC FROM: The movie *Comeback* (1983).
SELECTIONS: "Do You Feel," "House of the Rising Sun," "Sweet Blood Call," "No More Elmore," "Crawling King Snake," "Hurts Me Too," "Take It Easy," "Bird on the Beach," "The Road," "Lights Out," "Streetwalker," "Devil's Daughter," "Where Is My Friend," "Kill My Body."

Turgid, pretentious rock drama, with ex-Animal lead singer Eric Burdon as disillusioned superstar Rocco, who chucks it all at the peak of high-living success to find himself—which he finally does in the slums of West Berlin. Along the way, he bellows through an uneven blues-rock score, and tries to somehow wade through the muck of a silly, sordid story. It's pretty rough going in this pointless downer. Points of interest: Rocco's daughter is played by Soleil Moon Frye, of TV's *Punky Brewster*; and bluesman Louisiana Red appears, in a small supporting role, as a down-and-out Berlin bluesman (!) who sings a few songs and agrees with Rocco that "life sucks." Indeed it does—ending as it does here in Rocco's murder (the result of earlier shady dealings), just as he's launched his (you guessed it) comeback. *Yawn.*

□ KATE BUSH
LIVE AT HAMMERSMITH ODEON
★★★

HBO/Cannon, 1979, 52 minutes
PRODUCED BY: John Weaver
DIRECTED BY: Keith "Keef" MacMillan
MUSIC FROM: The Kick Inside, Lionheart, On Stage (Capitol/EMI, 1978).
SELECTIONS: "Moving Strange Phenomena," "Them Heavy People," "Violin," "Hammer Horror," "Don't Push Your Foot on the Heartbreak," "Wow," "Feel It," "Kite," "James and the Cold Gun," "Oh England My Lionheart," "Wuthering Heights."

With her exotic beauty and flighty woman-child warble, Bush is a true original—obviously gifted, but wildly eccentric enough that she's certainly not for everybody. She's hugely popular in England and Europe, but has never been more than a cult heroine in America. This concert program is not likely to widen her Stateside audience much—even though she sings and dances up a storm in this 1979 London show, making charmingly inventive use of multiple stage sets and costumes (like the dancing violins in "Violin") as well as mime and other theatrics. Director Keith MacMillan adds more than his usual complement of felicitous post-production touches (mirror-image superimpositions, slo-mo, etc.). In her own way, Bush is as endearingly bizarre as, say, Cyndi Lauper—but where Lauper's rooted in crass garden-variety American-surrealist junk culture, Bush is rooted in Old World extravagances and arcana, and until she finds some more direct pop hooks on which to hang her wardrobe of audio-visual weirdness, she'll probably remain just a curiosity here.

□ SAM BUSH
BLUEGRASS MANDOLIN
★★★★

Homespun, 1985, 90 minutes

PRODUCED BY: Happy Traum
DIRECTED BY: Happy Traum
SELECTIONS: "Paddy on the Turnpike," "Grey Eagle," "Sugar Foot Rag," "Sapporo," and others.

Another instructional winner from Homespun, as Bush takes you slowly and carefully through an historical variety of mandolin styles, from classic Bill Monroe to the recent "newgrass" country/bluegrass/jazz fusion, demonstrating tremolo, cross-picking, rhythm chops, and other techniques along the way. Homespun's usual felicitous use of split-screen helps you follow Bush's intricate left-hand fretting technique with ease. (Available by mail order from Homespun Tapes.)

□ JAKI BYARD
ANYTHING FOR JAZZ
★★★

Rhapsody, 1984, 25 minutes
PRODUCED BY: Dan Algrant
DIRECTED BY: Dan Algrant
SELECTIONS: Portions of several unidentified pieces by Jaki Byard solo and by Byard's Apollo Stompers big band.

Since the late '50s, Byard has been gaining critical respect as an incredibly gifted, accomplished, and stylistically eclectic pianist. He's played with such well-known jazz names as Charles Mingus, yet Byard remains one of contemporary jazz's many well-kept secrets. Dan Algrant's low-budget portrait/documentary *Anything for Jazz* contains tantalizing, but in the end frustratingly brief, snatches of his music—some dazzling solo piano that mercurially refracts classical, boogie-woogie, blues, and free-form expressionism with devastating musical logic; his young big band, The Apollo Stompers, sails through some boldly scored, hard-swinging arrangements. And that's prophetic in a way, for when it's over, the film itself seems somehow frustratingly short—we've been shown and told just enough about this benignly skewed genius to be left wanting to know *more.*

Noted jazz bassist Ron Carter and the late great pianist Bill Evans are both seen for a few moments, talking about how underrated Byard is—but they never say *why,* they never articulate (or are allowed to) from their privileged points of view just what's so special about Byard and his music. Of course, Byard answers that question every time he plays, or leads his band, or is shown teaching his students—but again, there's not enough of that, especially not enough of the music. And how, one has to wonder, can this sadly overlooked and underpaid musician manage to keep an actual big band together in this day and age? The only apparent clue to Byard's gratifying pluck is his intensely close relationship with his family (there are not-at-all gratuitous sequences from Byard's home movies, and various family snapshots are set to songs Byard dedicates to family members). In this regard, *Anything for Jazz* serves better as a raw but very realistic portrait of Jaki Byard the man, as opposed to the musician. And as such, despite the grainy look and sometimes erratic sound of it, *Anything for Jazz* is a passable document on a marvelous subject.

The highlight is not a musical sequence, but a moment when Byard sits in his apartment discussing his undeserved obscurity with an off-camera interviewer, as he says, "I *never* call anyone for gigs—let 'em call *me,* that way I know they want me." Just then, as if on cue, his phone rings—and rings, and rings, and rings, as Byard keeps rapping to the camera, ignoring the phone. After seven or eight rings, just as we're beginning to wonder if he'll *ever* answer it, Byard abruptly snorts, "That's a gig," and leaps out of his easy chair to get the phone. After the laughter at this sequence has faded, it's this moment that remains haunting enough to leave one wondering about the bittersweet paradox of someone who feels compelled to be such a "character" in the name of self-determined dignity—and at the expense of such richly deserved wider acclaim. (Available by mail order from Rhapsody Films.)

☐ DAVID BYRNE, OTHERS
THE CATHERINE WHEEL

★★★½

HBO/Cannon, 1986, 73 minutes

DIRECTED BY: Twyla Tharp

MUSIC FROM: Songs from the Broadway production of *The Catherine Wheel* (Sire/Warner Bros., 1981).

SELECTIONS: "His Wife Refused," "Two Soldiers," "The Red House," "My Big Hands (Fall Through the Cracks)," "Big Business," "Eggs in a Briar Patch," "Poison," "Cloud Chamber," "What a Day That Was," "Big Blue Plymouth (Eyes Wide Open)," "Light Bath," and others not listed.

From where I sit, this well-produced concert document of acclaimed choreographer Twyla Tharp's dance/theater/music happening *The Catherine Wheel* is recommendable mainly for David Byrne's music. I've never been very much of a fan of The Dance, and Tharp's bizarro splayings, postures, and contortions leave me pretty cold. Certainly, at the very least, they lack the cockeyed, offhand charm of Byrne's own trademark penguin-on-acid moves. Still, if you're at all into this kind of thing and already think Twyla Tharp is pretty hot stuff, and if you don't already have this, you ought to check it out right away. Meanwhile, anyone who can relate to the excellence of Talking Heads' music ought to check this out as well, for Byrne's score contains some of the best music he's ever made, within or without Talking Heads: specifically, the itchy polyrhythmic funk of "Big Business" and the ecstatic rush of "Big Blue Plymouth (Eyes Wide Open)" and "What a Day That Was." Occasionally, as in "Eggs in a Briar Patch" or "Cloud Chamber," the music degenerates into forgettable, self-consciously "abstract" avant-garde musings; but overall, it's as singular, strong, and steadily intriguing as almost all of Byrne's and Talking Heads' other works. Heck, it's enough to render Tharp's choreography expendable—unless you're into that sort of thing. Note that the companion soundtrack *album* does *not* contain the full Byrne musical soundtrack (it *is,* however, on the soundtrack cassette).

C

☐ **C.T.I.**
ELEMENTAL 7
★★½

Factory/Doublevision, 1981, 60 minutes
PRODUCED BY: Chris Carter, Cosey Fanni Tutti, John Lacey
DIRECTED BY: Chris Carter, Cosey Fanni Tutti, John Lacey
MUSIC FROM: Elemental 7 (Fetish UK, 1980).
SELECTIONS: "Temple Bar," "Dancing Ghosts," "Meeting Mr. Evans," "Invisible Spectrum," "Sidereal," "Well Spring of Life," "The Final Calling."

☐ **C.T.I.**
EUROPEAN RENDEZVOUS
★★

Factory/Doublevision, 1984, 50 minutes
PRODUCED BY: Chris Carter, Cosey Fanni Tutti, John Lacey
DIRECTED BY: Chris Carter, Cosey Fanni Tutti, John Lacey
MUSIC FROM: European Rendezvous (Fetish U.K., 1983)
SELECTIONS: "Intro," "Mary," "Funky," "The Need," "Loop," "Sequencer," "Slow," "Thy Gift," "Voice Echo," "Goodbye Deutschland," "October Love Song."

C.T.I., featuring two former members of Britain's semi-legendary post-punk dadaists Throbbing Gristle, Chris Carter and Cosey Fanni Tutti, does a somewhat gentler version of Throbbing Gristle's noisome, willfully dull, and annoying antimusic. *Elemental 7* is an ambient, "environmental" video, with electronic pastels washing over treated, often abstract imagery to relaxing and yet slightly disturbing effect, somewhat like Eno's *Thursday Afternoon* but a bit better. *European Rendezvous* sets recordings from a 1983 European tour to the similarly abstract, effects-treated slide projections used for visual accompaniment on that tour. While in both cases the "music" consists of soft, electronic drones that make it easy to forget that anything's happening at all, *Elemental 7* matches sound and image to better effect than *European Rendezvous.* Mainly for British avant-rock fans, Throbbing Gristle cultists, or those adventurous souls seeking a far-afield alternative to Eno's and Windham Hill's varieties of video wallpaper. (Available in stores or by mail order from Factory.)

☐ **CABARET VOLTAIRE**
JOHNNY YESNO
★½

Factory/Doublevision, 1984, 55 minutes
PRODUCED BY: Peter Care
DIRECTED BY: Peter Care
MUSIC FROM: Johnny Yesno (Factory U.K., 1984).
SELECTIONS: "Johnny Version," "Invocation," "Loosen the Clamp," "Hallucination," "Yashar."

☐ **CABARET VOLTAIRE**
DOUBLEVISION PRESENTS CABARET VOLTAIRE
★½

Factory/Doublevision, 1984, 90 minutes
PRODUCED BY: Various
DIRECTED BY: Various
MUSIC FROM: Various Cabaret Voltaire albums and singles (Factory U.K., 1982–84).
SELECTIONS: "Diskono," "Obsession," "Trash Part One," "Badge of Evil," "Nag Nag Nag," "Eddie's Out," "Landslide," "Photophobia," "Trash Part Two," "Seconds Too Late," "Extract from Johnny Yesno," "Walls of Jericho," "This Is Entertainment," "Moscow."

Cabaret Voltaire, one of British post-punk label Factory's more adventurous experimental-electronic sound-collagist acts, create some striking and evocative aural jumbles of *musique concrete*. Some of them, such as "Diskono," "Nag Nag Nag," and "Eddie's Out," are actually danceable in a fractured way; others, such as "Trash" and "Photophobia," are just plain striking and evocative, though certainly not for the meek. However, the music is hardly strong enough overall to salvage the atrocious visuals of Doublevision Presents, which mainly consist of Factory's all-too-typical amateurishly arty nonsense. In short, almost unwatchable and not quite listenable enough to make this recommendable to anyone aside from diehard devotees to this sort of self-consciously bizarre stuff. Ninety minutes of this is much too much to take.

Johnny Yesno is described in Factory's catalogue as "Peter Care's acclaimed short film, a story of paranoia and insanity." Insanity, yes, but paranoia is too exciting a term to apply to such a boring "avant-garde" irrational indulgence. While there are flashes of recognizable people and objects, this is a nonlinear, nonrepresentational attempt at post-literal, post-punk impressionism. Sounds pretty lofty, but unfortunately *Johnny Yesno* goes wrong by going nowhere, offering nothing to replace the "mundane artifice" of linear, representational, literal cinema that it has stripped away. The music is more of the same rhythm/tape loop/noise mélange and just as hit-or-miss as in *Doublevision Presents* . . . Hard to believe this is the product of Peter Care, who would go on to direct such striking videos as Cabaret Voltaire's "Sensoria" and Public Image's "Rise." (Available in stores or by mail order from Factory.)

□ CABARET VOLTAIRE
GASOLINE IN YOUR EYE

★★

Sony, 1986, 82 minutes

PRODUCED BY: Peter Care, Richard H. Kirk, Stephen Mallinder

DIRECTED BY: Peter Care, Richard H. Kirk, Stephen Mallinder

MUSIC FROM: Various albums and singles by Cabaret Voltaire.

SELECTIONS: "Introduction," "Crackdown," "Diffusion," "Sleepwalking," "Slow Boat to Thassos," "Sensoria," "Automotivation," "Big Funk," "Kino," "Ghostalk," "Fadeout."

Gasoline in Your Eye is yet another unconscionably extended, self-consciously *outré* avant-garde Cabaret Voltaire program. Once again, the music divides fairly evenly between soft, ethereal synth *études* and poundingly percussive computer-disco *études* with treated vocals and tape effects in deliberate place of a dance track's usual hummable choruses. Once again, the accompanying visuals consist of all manner of shot and found footage, with lots of fast edits and quick repetitions and other vertiginous, seemingly random or at most purely rhythmic treatments, and each clip seems to go on forever. "Sleepwalking" seems to be some sort of distracting stab at atmospheric mystery/suspense; there's some female nudity in "Diffusion," as Cabaret Voltaire toy with what appears to be a black-and-white '50s stag film of a woman moving about a kitchen in the buff; and there are even brief moments in "Crackdown" when one poker-faced Cabaret Voltaire member lip-synchs his vocal (which basically consists of sneering/chanting the title). Only one of these clips really stands out from the rest: Peter Care's "Sensoria," which is distinguished by its dizzying trick photography whereby a camera is mounted on a sort of special crane that does 180-degree slo-mo catapults perpendicular to the ground while gyroscopically keeping the camera focused on a single point on the ground. It's a real visual gas, even if it does tend to leave one reaching for the motion-sickness pills.

☐ CAB CALLOWAY AND HIS ORCHESTRA

BIG BANDS AT DISNEYLAND

★★★½

Disney, 1984, 57 minutes
PRODUCED BY: Ron Miziker
DIRECTED BY: Jim Gates
MUSIC FROM: Various Cab Calloway albums.
SELECTIONS: "Get Happy," "Good Time Charlie's Got the Blues," "You're Nobody till Somebody Loves You," "Learnin' the Blues," "Take a Plunge," "Just One of Those Things," "The Girl from Ipanema," "Bewitched," "Tippin' In," "Stormy Weather," "Greasy Brown Paper Bag," "Don't Cry Out Loud," "How Does It Feel Right Now?," "It Ain't Necessarily So," "Minnie the Moocher," "Caldonia"/ "When the Saints Go Marchin' In," "Blues Chaser."

This was shot in 1984 for cable TV's Disney Channel, in Disneyland's Plaza Gardens, where summer big band concerts have been a tradition for many years. Like the other programs in this series, it's shot nicely and straightforwardly, with good strategic close-ups compensating for occasional clumsy cuts and too many shots of dancing couples; and it's hosted by Peter Marshall, the former Mr. *Hollywood Squares*, who provides a quick artist-bio rap over a photo-montage career-review midway through, along with a brief, superficial interview with the artist. (Here, it's with Calloway's daughter Chris, who sings with Dad's band; Marshall says this was Cab's idea.) Speaking of Hollywood Squares, each of these programs opens with a '30s radio announcer-style intro by Gary Owens, of *Laugh-In* fame.

You've gotta love silver-haired Cab Calloway. His voice cracks and wavers all *over* the place—yet he keeps smiling that enormous smile, lighting up that cheshire-cat face of his, apparently relishing the chance for further potential embarrassment, and thus transcending the ridiculous with sublime evergreen jive. In "Good Time Charlie's Got the Blues," he even mutilates an operatically-held l-o-n-g note, with gusto. But while the voice is erratic, Calloway's spirit is *so* willing, and his flesh still *so* able when it comes to those marvelous jive dances of his, you can't help thinking they just don't make entertainers like this anymore. Especially when Cab suddenly gets it all together and brings it on home with a poignant, forceful, dramatic reading of "Stormy Weather"—although he does blow it at the *very* end with another of those sustained notes.

If "Stormy Weather" is the highlight, another classic provides the low point—and oddly enough it's the tune most closely associated with Calloway, his signature song "Minnie the Moocher." Here, it's presented in a *disco* desecration, which isn't awful because it's disco but because it's tossed off so perfunctorily you'd think Cab and the band are embarrassed by it. But that's the only real bummer in an otherwise fun program: the never-identified band is a wee bit ragged around the edges here and there, but they always swing nicely (there's a nice round of horn solos on the instrumental "Greasy Brown Paper Bag," especially a talking wah-wah plunger-mute turn by a trombonist); Calloway's daughter Chris is an attractive and capable singer and entertainer, if a bit more "mannered" and less effortlessly ingratiating than her father. (She performs on "Just One of Those Things," "The Girl from Ipanema," "Bewitched," "Don't Cry Out Loud," and "How Does It Feel Now?".)

☐ CAMEO

THE VIDEO SINGLES

★★★½

Sony, 1984, 27 minutes
PRODUCED BY: Len Epand

DIRECTED BY: Various
MUSIC FROM: She's Strange (Polygram, 1984); *Alligator Woman* (Polygram, 1982); *Cameosis* (Polygram, 1980).
SELECTIONS: "She's Strange," "Talkin' Out the Side of Your Neck," "Be Yourself," "Flirt," "Alligator Woman," "We're Goin' Out Tonight," "Shake Your Pants."

Cameo's music is simultaneously ultrasyncopated and razor sharp, and always slinkily danceable. In their videos, they present a sense of stylish fun and a "NuWave" image (e.g., wraparound shades). The video chronology from 1980 to 1984 also gives an opportunity to gauge the production-value progress made over the years in black-music videos.

□ CANNED HEAT
BOOGIE ASSAULT
★ ½

Monterey/IVE, 1983, 60 minutes
PRODUCED BY: Rick Percell
DIRECTED BY: Michael Barnard and Dusty V. Moss
MUSIC FROM: Various Canned Heat albums.
SELECTIONS: "Boogie for the Bear," "A Sleepy Hollow Baby," "Stoned Bad Street Fighting Man," "Gimme That Money," "Hell's Just On Down the Line," "Bye-Bye Blues," "I Need a Hundred Dollars," "Hard Rider," "Let's Work Together," "You Lied."

Long after the deaths of onetime bandleaders Alan Wilson and Bob "the Bear" Hite, these tireless blues-boogie band Canned Heat was somehow still puffing along in the early '80s (only drummer Fito de la Parra was left from the '60s originals). How they lasted that long, and why they bothered to inflict this lame, low-budget series of "concept" videos and horrendously lip-synched performance clips on us is anyone's guess. *Boogie Assault* is crude in more ways than one: the production values and filmmaking savvy of the producers are virtually nil; the band members are unattractive, to say the least, as are the scads of Hell's Angels who play supporting roles; and the "concepts" here include such unsavory activities as train robberies, a cocaine deal (amazingly, somewhat anticipatory of *Miami Vice* with its fancy-yacht setting and a colorful macaw perched next to the dealer). Most nauseating of all is a sequence in which bassist Ernie Rodriguez is seen in bed with his old lady, apparently dreaming about a hideously photographed birthday party. Waking, rolling over in bed, and rolling a joint are all done in close-ups, highlighted with solarized slow-motion quick cut-ins (including one *really* gross extreme close-up of his tongue licking the rolling paper). Meanwhile, the band's undifferentiated slabs of blooze rock are nowhere near inspired enough to elevate the proceedings; in fact, the music generally sounds like a disconnected afterthought to the ugly visuals.

□ THE VILLAGE PEOPLE, OTHERS
CAN'T STOP THE MUSIC
★ ½

HBO/Cannon, 1980, 117 minutes
PRODUCED BY: Allan Carr, Jacques Morali, and Henri Belolo
DIRECTED BY: Nancy Walker
MUSIC FROM: Cruisin' (Casablanca, 1979); *Go West* (Casablanca, 1979); *Can't Stop the Music*, motion picture soundtrack (Casablanca, 1980).
SELECTIONS: The Village People: "Can't Stop the Music," "Liberation," "I Love You to Death," "Y.M.C.A.," "Magic Night," "Milkshake," "Samantha," "Sophistication"; the Ritchie Family: "Give Me a Break," "The Sound of the City."

This legendary bomb—one of the biggest eggs ever laid during the disco era—actually signaled the end of disco while it closed the '70s. In fact, *Can't*

Stop the Music is pretty darned bad, though perhaps not quite as horrible as everyone thought initially. Then again, it's hard not to consider this disco's *Plan Nine from Outer Space*. Consider: it was directed, in almost competent fashion, by Nancy Walker—you know, "Rosie" from the Bounty paper towel commercials; its surreal cast includes Valerie Perrine, Olympic hero Bruce Jenner, Steve Guttenberg (later of *Diner, Cocoon*, and other films of greater distinction), Paul Sand (a gifted comic actor who had appeared on *Mary Tyler Moore*), and such onetime leading ladies as Tammy Grimes, June Havoc, and Barbara Rush, whose inexplicable presence here gives the proceedings the feel of a Bob Hope TV special; and its excuse for a plot—how jes-folks like Perrine and Jenner help the Village People and their manager, Jackie Morrell (Guttenberg), get a contract from record exec Sand—is an even worse joke than the Village People's *real* story. In *that* one, producer/impressario Jacques Morali cooked up the six-stereotype ensemble as a cynical gay-subculture in-joke, and against all odds it became a brief but smashing success. *Can't Stop the Music* isn't a sick joke that works, though; it's a moronic joke that doesn't work. Morali's salsa-fied follow-up to the Village People, the Ritchie Family, perform a couple of numbers along the way in a video that only be recommended for its kitschy camp value.

□ BELINDA CARLISLE
BELINDA

★★

MCA, 1986, 60 minutes
PRODUCED BY: Tina Silvey
DIRECTED BY: Jonathan Dayton and Valerie Farris
MUSIC FROM: Belinda (IRS, 1986); *Beauty and the Beat* (IRS, 1981).

SELECTIONS: "I Need a Disguise," "I Never Wanted a Rich Man," "Gotta Get to You," "Shot in the Dark," "We Got the Beat," "Band of Gold," "Lust to Love," "From the Heart," "Head Over Heels," "Mad About You," "Since You've Gone," "I Feel the Magic."

This is a nicely put-together profile of former Go-Go's lead singer Belinda Carlisle on the occasion of her maiden solo LP, mixing, according to an MCA press release, "revealing glimpses of Belinda in rehearsals, photo sessions, interviews and finally performing before a standing-room-only crowd at the famous Roxy in Hollywood" (where, before a friendly home-turf crowd, she kicked off her first solo tour in the summer of 1986). Belinda had shed quite a few pounds by this time and was no longer the cherubic chubette fronting that adorable all-girl post-punk pop band. But while she looks a darn sight cuter, she still can't dance worth a damn, her voice is easily strained, and overall she comes across in performance as just another vacuous chickie-poo *chanteuse* fronting an anonymous, mostly guy band (though former Go-Go's guitarist Charlotte Caffey is along, too). Her solo songs are even less substantial than those of the Go-Go's, and, as if to underscore just how featherweight they are, there's loads of chatter from Belinda, Charlotte, and the boys in the band over lots of tunes.

Meanwhile, those "revealing glimpses" of Belinda show her to be a cool, distant careerist with nothing of any significance to say; at best, she's an exemplary Yuppette, and if you think that's something worth aspiring to, you may really enjoy checking out Belinda's act here. Belinda chats a little bit about her then-recent marriage to Morgan Mason, son of the late actor James Mason. Further proof of Belinda's ultimate soullessness is offered up in her vapid desecration of Freda Payne's soul classic "Band of Gold." It's the hideous low point in what is basically an innocuous, forgettable program.

All in all, *Belinda* is enough to make me miss the Go-Go's even more. If you are an avid fan of Belinda's music, then nothing I say will keep you from enjoying this mindless swill. Oh, and speaking of mindless, Duran Duran's Andy Taylor guests on guitar for the last few songs of the show, reprising his guest-solo spot on Belinda's first solo hit single, "Mad About You." Thankfully this is the *concert* version of the song, rather than the promotional video clip—which was a sickeningly adulatory valentine to Belinda herself and to her relationship with Mason.

□ KIM CARNES
KIM CARNES VIDEO 45
★★½

Sony, 1984, 15 minutes

PRODUCED BY: MGMM and Picture Music International

DIRECTED BY: Russell Mulcahy and Jim Yukich

MUSIC FROM: Mistaken Identity (EMI-America, 1981); *Voyeur* (EMI-America, 1984).

SELECTIONS: "Bette Davis Eyes," "Voyeur," "Draw of the Cards," "Invisible Hands."

Also available on Pioneer 8-inch Stereo Laser videodisc.

With the Grammy-winning smash hit "Bette Davis Eyes" in 1981, Carnes came out of nowhere (although she had actually been around for several years before this hit), which is more or less where here career has gone *since* "Bette Davis Eyes." That video is easily the centerpiece of a collection that is mainly recommendable only to her fans. "Bette Davis Eyes," though, is something of a seminal rock video classic, and one of the first great successes for Russell Mulcahy, one of the field's leading *auteurs*. Its use of a Fellini-esque rogue's gallery dancing in what appears to be some sort of surreal ballroom, and its insinuation of jaded, decadent Attitude as Carnes serenades her audience with the insistently catchy tale of a femme fatale, would prove highly influential on many subsequent clips (Mulcahy's included). The rest of the selections here, however, try for a similar sort of chic mystery and provocative atmosphere but fall flat; meanwhile, the sandpaper-throated Carnes just isn't given the material to come up with anything inspired.

□ CARPENTERS
YESTERDAY ONCE MORE
★★★

A&M, 1985, 55 minutes

DIRECTED BY: Fred Paskiewicz

MUSIC FROM: Various Carpenters albums, including *Yesterday Once More* (A&M, 1985).

SELECTIONS: "We've Only Just Begun," "Those Good Old Dreams," "Superstar," "Rainy Days and Mondays," "All You Get from Love Is a Love Song," "Top of the World," "Ticket to Ride," "Only Yesterday," "Calling Occupants of Interplanetary Craft," "Beechwood 4-5789," "Touch Me When We're Dancing," "Hurting Each Other," "There's a Kind of Hush," "(They Long to Be) Close to You."

Also available on Pioneer Stereo Laser videodisc.

Considering the Kleenex potential inherent in a Carpenters video clip compilation being released after Karen's death by complications of anorexia nervosa, *Yesterday Once More* is executed with a lot of tasteful restraint. It's just one straightforward, rather primitive performance video after another, with no connecting material to intrude on the teary-eyed mood of nostalgia and melancholy this program is sure to create in any Carpenters fan. Everyone else can either catalogue the changes in Karen's hair and wardrobe, or just ignore this altogether.

□ THE CARS
HEARTBEAT CITY
★★½

Warner Home Video, 1984, 48 minutes
PRODUCED BY: Charlex, others
DIRECTED BY: Charlex, others
MUSIC FROM: Hearbeat City (Elektra, 1984); *Shake It Up* (Elektra, 1981); *Panorama* (Elektra, 1980).
SELECTIONS: "Hello Again," "Magic," "Drive," "Panorama," "Heartbeat City," "Shake It Up," "Why Can't I Have You?," "You Might Think."

Extremely erratic clips compilation by the icy-cool Boston-based new wave pop-rockers. It's worth having just for Charlex's ingenious "You Might Think," an antic masterpiece that proves the spirit of Ernie Kovacs can not just survive but thrive on high-tech video effects (Charlex also did the similarly cool between-clips material). But beyond that, and "Panorama"—a neat, *film noir*–like espionage concept with a killer ending directed by Devo's Gerald Casale—the quality drops off sharply. Some folks argue the virtues of Tim Hutton's self-consciously arty "Drive" and Tim Pope's daylight surrealism in "Magic," but the rest are either indefensibly dull ("Why Can't I Have You?"), indefensibly sexist ("Shake It Up"), or in the case of Andy Warhol's nauseating "Hello Again," just plain indefensible.

□ THE CARS
LIVE 1984–1985
★★

Vestron, 1984, 58 minutes
PRODUCED BY: Fiona Fitzherbert, Susan McGonigle, Peggy Pierrepont
DIRECTED BY: Larry Jordan
MUSIC FROM: Various Cars albums.
SELECTIONS: "Hello Again," "It's Not the Night," "Touch and Go," "Good Times Roll," "Moving in Stereo," "Just What I Needed," "Cruiser," "Drive," "You Might Think," "Let's Go," "Heartbeat City," "You're All I've Got Tonight."

Some groups could overcome a diffidently shot, acutely artsy concert film like this with—how you say?—good music, engaging stage presence, and a show of energy. But not these guys. Between the constant cuts to the *Heartbeat City* scenes playing on the screens around the stage, the occasionally sloppy performance, and general don't-give-a-damn attitude the Cars express, you wonder why on earth you're even watching. Judging by this, the Cars don't seem to know or care why they're doing it. God forbid someone should make eye contact, deliver his lyrics instead of mumbling them, or even pretend he's in public, on a stage, in front of people who've paid to see them. It's one thing to pull a Miles Davis or a Jeff Beck *if* your songs are even mildly interesting to begin with and *if* you can play them well. But the Cars aren't and don't. Their one engaging quality was their tight, crisp, power-poppy sound. Here, the rhythm section's so flatulent and the singing so halfhearted that good tunes like "Good Times Roll" and "Let's Go" don't snap and pop but lurch and lumber. Now and then Ben Orr's vocals get so deep and low in the mix that it sounds like his bass is singing, and Ric Ocasek's languid artiste pose is almost laughable. The one thing the Cars are good at is being earnest and affected and kind of tortured-looking. If I didn't know better I would think their songs were actually saying something!—P.R.

□ BENNY CARTER
JAZZ AT THE SMITHSONIAN
★★★★

Sony, 1984, 57 minutes
PRODUCED BY: Clark and Delia Gravelle Santee
DIRECTED BY: Clark and Delia Gravelle Santee

MUSIC FROM: Various Benny Carter albums.

SELECTIONS: "Honeysuckle Rose," "Misty," "Take the 'A' Train," "Cottontail," "Autumn Leaves."

Carter, one of jazz's grand old gentlemen, goes all the way back to the late '20s in terms of his career, impact, and influence on the music. And since then, he's never faltered. Here, Carter leads a letter-perfect backing trio (pianist Kenny Barron, bassist George Duvivier, drummer Ronnie Bedford) and shares the spotlight with the fine, underrecognized jazz violinist Joe Kennedy, in a set of silken standards that amply illustrate Carter's own skillful blend of dignified grace and sultry insinuation. There are also brief interview segments, in which this jazz giant exhibits a touching modesty and shows more of that same dignity and grace.

□ JOHNNY CASH
LIVE IN LONDON
★★★½

Continental, 1984, 50 minutes

DIRECTED BY: Rick Gardner

MUSIC FROM: Various Johnny Cash albums.

SELECTIONS: "Ring of Fire," "Folsom Prison Blues," "Gotta Do My Time," "The Baron," "I Walk the Line," "Don't Take Your Guns to Town," "Big River," "Ghost Riders in the Sky," "Casey Jones," "Orange Blossom Special"; Johnny Cash with June Carter Cash: "If I Were a Carpenter," "San Antonio Rose," "The Flatfoot Dance," "Jackson"; Johnny Cash with Cyndi Cash: "Lay Me Down in Dixie"; Johnny Cash with June Carter Cash and Cyndi Cash: "Will the Circle Be Unbroken."

□ JOHNNY CASH
RIDIN' THE RAILS—THE GREAT AMERICAN TRAIN STORY
★★★

Sony, 1986, 53 minutes

PRODUCED BY: Webster–Rivkin Productions

DIRECTED BY: Nicholas Webster

MUSIC FROM: 1974 TV special; various Johnny Cash albums.

SELECTIONS: "The Night They Drove Old Dixie Down," "The Legend of John Henry's Hammer," "Casey Jones," "Wreck of the Old '97," "City of New Orleans," "Brother Can You Spare a Dime?," "Ridin' the Rails," "Ribbon of Steel," and others.

In *London,* Cash—backed at this 1981 show by his regular band, and with wife June and daughter Cyndi joining on some numbers—dispenses his country classics with as much easy assurance and understated charm as any fan should expect. In fact, the only real problem with this show is that sometimes it seems a little *too* easy and cozy—but then, what else should we expect when a certified country legend performs before a typically reverent British audience? Video clips are intercut with performances of "The Baron" (an illustrative pool-hall showdown), "Casey Jones" (literal-minded train footage), and "Will the Circle Be Unbroken" (an inexplicable few seconds of a dove flying into a guy's long hair, or something, in slo-mo). Otherwise, the direction is commendable, straight to the point yet warm and intimate, and ultimately unobtrusive except for those video clip inserts.

The award-winning 1974 TV special *Ridin' the Rails* is aptly called a "docu-musical" by its producers: Cash travels through time (as well as space, as in all over the country) to show us great moments in the rich history of America's mighty railroads, and sings plenty of train songs along the way to illustrate the equally rich folkore that grew up around the epochal phenomenon of locomotion. It's solid, educational entertainment, done with seriousness, integrity, and commendable charm thanks to Cash's easygoing personality and evident sincerity.

Standing in the foreground, behind him the reconstructed historical moment when the west-bound and east-bound cross-country railroads first met at Promontory Point, Cash seems genuinely thrilled to be "present" and at the making of railroad history. Cash also wrote a few tunes (like the title track) especially for the show.

□ CARLOS CAVAZO
THE CARLOS CAVAZO PACKAGE
★★★★

Star Licks, 1984, 50 minutes
PRODUCED BY: Mark Freed and Robert Decker
DIRECTED BY: Mark Freed and Robert Decker
MUSIC FROM: Quiet Riot: *Metal Health* (Pasha, 1983); *Condition Critical* (Pasha, 1984).
SELECTIONS: "Metal Health," "Cum On Feel the Noize," "Battleaxe," "Run for Cover," "Red Alert," "Mama Weer All Crazee Now," "(We Were) Born to Rock," and thirteen other solos, melodies, chords and other licks from various other Quiet Riot songs and various untitled Carlos Cavazo improvised solos.

Though he may not look like the kind of guy you'd bring home to mother, Cavazo—who plays hair-raising heavy-metal guitar with those leering headbangers, Quiet Riot—comes across nicely and articulately enough in this instructional video to make skeptics think twice about underestimating the musicality (and humanity) of metal musicians. Whatever you think of Cavazo's playing and Quiet Riot's music, he's generously instructive on a number of his own techniques and those that have become genre conventions—from staccato picking, major and minor arpeggios, bottlenecking, and pedal tone trills to exotic modes and scales, switch-flipping (between guitar pickups, that is, for quick changes in tone), pick squeals, two-handed pick-tapping, string-scraping, vibrato bar technique and phrasing, and much more. There's also a section in which Cavazo improvises some pretty outrageous solos, which are notated in the accompanying booklet along with all his other exercises. And, as in all the Star Licks Master Series tapes, Cavazo plays everything once at normal speed, and once more at a slower speed—but then, since this is video, you can also rewind and play his licks back whenever you like. (Available by mail order from Star Licks.)

□ VARIOUS ARTISTS
A CELEBRATION
★★½

Monterey/IVE, 1980, 68 minutes
MUSIC FROM: 1979 TV special.
SELECTIONS: Gary Busey: "Rock and Roll Music"; Tanya Tucker: "Crossfire," "Lay Back in the Arms of Someone You Love"; Kris Kristofferson: "The Truth Will Set You Free," "Me and Bobbie McGee"; Delaney and Bonnie: "Only You Know and I Know"; Duane Eddy: "Rebel-Rouser"; Rocky Burnette: "Tear It Up"; Billy Burnette: "I Believe What You Say"; Maureen McGovern: "Like a Thief in the Night"; Roger Miller: "You Don't Want My Love," "Dang Me"; Glen Campbell: "Rhinestone Cowboy," "Hey Little One," "Southern Nights"; All: "Will the Circle Be Unbroken."

Glen Campbell, who had a hit with the great rockabilly singer-songwriter Dorsey Burnette's "Hey Little One," organized this 1980 L.A. Forum memorial concert after Burnette's death in 1979. As the concert kicks off, someone booms over the PA, "This ain't no eulogy—this here's a celebration!" Yet the show is highly erratic, and not till it nears the home stretch does it come close to working up the right spirit for the occasion. All of the performances through the first half are so-so at best; some, like the shakily reunited Delaney and Bonnie, are worse. It turns a corner when Duane Eddy twangs out his classic "Rebel Rouser"; Rocky Burnette, son of Dorsey's rockabilly pioneer brother Johnny, handles his uncle's "Tear It Up" with appropriate abandon in one of the highlights, and his cousin Billy Burnette (Dorsey's son) does all right with one of the hits his dad wrote for Ricky Nelson, "I Believe What You Say." Then it hits bottom as Maureen McGovern—*Maureen McGovern?!?!*—does an incongruous number (in an earlier surrealistic moment, Wink Martindale introduces Tanya Tucker!) and Roger Miller and Glen Campbell both animate unspectacular musical sets with a showily sincere emotional bluster that, given the circumstances, is almost a kind of psychodrama.

□ HARRY CHAPIN
THE FINAL CONCERT

★★★½

CBS/Fox, 1984, 89 minutes
PRODUCED BY: Rick Melchior, Barry McLean
DIRECTED BY: Barry McLean
MUSIC FROM: Heads and Tales, Short Stories, Verities and Balderdash, Portrait Gallery, Legends of the Lost and Found (Elektra, 1972–79); *Sequel* (Boardwalk, 1980).
SELECTIONS: "Story of a Life," "Shooting Star," "Taxi," "Mr. Tanner," "W.O.L.D.," "Better Place to Be," "Cat's in the Cradle," "Flowers Are Red," "Dreams Go By" "Mail Order Annie," "30,000 Pounds of Bananas," "Sequel," "You Are the Only Song," "Circle."
Also Available on CBS/Fox Stereo Laser videodisc.

Long before anyone ever heard of Bob Geldof, Chapin selflessly dedicated himself to charity with hundreds of concerts per year for World Hunger Year, which he cofounded in 1975. If fact, he was killed in a July 1981 auto accident en route to yet another benefit. Yet if one is to judge the art, and not the artist, it must be admitted that his commendable charitable efforts overshadow his pop-folk music, which suffers from both pretentiousness and a case of the cutes. Still, by the same token, this concert before a wildly enthusiastic audience in Hamilton, Ontario (not quite Harry's last actual show, but close), fully displays his warm, generous spirit and genuine folk troubadour's touch. Harry's brother Steve plays piano in the band, and brother Tom guests on some numbers, lending an especially warm feel to his family affair.

□ RAY CHARLES
BALLAD IN BLUE (A.K.A. BLUES FOR LOVERS)

★★★½

USA/IVE, 1981, 88 minutes
PRODUCED BY: Alexander Salkind
DIRECTED BY: Paul Henreid
MUSIC FROM: Various Ray Charles albums; *Ballad in Blue* motion picture soundtrack (TCF, 1966).
SELECTIONS: "Let the Good Times Roll," "Careless Love," "Hit the Road Jack," "Lucky Old Sun," "Unchain My Heart," "Hallelujah, I Love Her So," "Don't Tell Me Your Troubles," "I've Got a Woman," "Busted," "Talkin' 'bout You," "Light Out of Darkness," "What'd I Say."

A bit of an odd duck, this 1966 British film. It was produced by Alexander Salkind (later of *Superman* movie series fame) and directed by veteran screen actor Paul Henreid, the man who made cinema history by simultaneously lighting cigarettes for himself and Bette Davis in *Now, Voyager. Ballad in Blue* is a curious mix of superb Ray Charles concert footage with a mawkish soap opera of a story that ultimately gets in the way of The Genius's performances. In the soap opera, Brother Ray plays himself, on tour in England and Europe. In London's bohemian Mayfair district, he befriends a little blind boy and teaches him how to deal with his blindness. Ray convinces the boy's overprotective mother to take the kid to Paris when Ray goes to tour there, for an operation that might cure her son. The mother's boyfriend, played by Thom Bell (soon to become a big-time record producer and architect of the Philadelphia sound), is also hired as arranger for Ray's orchestra, which helps everything along. Ray carries himself in the "dramatic" scenes with his usual uncanny balance of spiritual dignity and wily, earthy grittiness, so you might want to watch this once just to see what happens. But the story *is* completely predictable, and nobody could be blamed for scanning through it to catch the concert sequences—basically the best Ray Charles concert video around.

□ RAY CHARLES
AN EVENING WITH RAY CHARLES
★★★★★

MCA, 1983, 50 minutes
MUSIC FROM: Various Ray Charles albums; British TV concert special.
SELECTIONS: "Riding Thumb," "Busted," "Georgia on My Mind," "Oh, What a Beautiful Mornin'," "Some Enchanted Evening," "Hit the Road, Jack," "I Can't Stop Loving You," "Take These Chains from My Heart," "I Can See Clearly Now," "What'd I Say," "America the Beautiful."
Also available on MCA/OPA stereo laser videodisc.

One of the hippest guys, and one of the most beautiful voices of all time, backed by the ITV Orchestra in a special shot for British TV at the Jubilee Auditorium in Edmonton, Alberta, Canada. Brother Ray is, of course, a living definition of soul, whether performing R&B, rock, gospel, country, or singing the phone book. Here he is in trademark powder-blue tux, with the trademark Raelettes, delivering so-hip-they-hurt rapped intros to a nice selection of his seminal R&B classics and the country songs he went on to make his very own, as well as some standards that can only benefit from the one and only touch of the man so rightly called "The Genius." Ray Charles is his own reward—come and get it!

□ CHEECH AND CHONG
GET OUT OF MY ROOM
★★★

MCA, 1984, 53 minutes
PRODUCED BY: Gillian Gordon and others
DIRECTED BY: Cheech Marin and others
MUSIC FROM: Get Out of My Room (MCA, 1984).
SELECTIONS: "Get Out of My Room," "I'm Not Home Right Now," "Love Is Strange," "Born in East L.A."

This four-video-plus-filler tape follows Cheech and Chong through the travails of making their first videos. It starts out cute enough, discussing the merits of the rock business and video ("If a song sucks, it will sell millions," "It doesn't have to make sense—it's a video") and contains the occasional funny line, such as Chong's explanation of the hows and whys of headbands: "You have to regulate the blood flow . . . you want to be somewhere between stupid and dumb." (Has Sammy Hagar seen this?) And "Born in East L.A.," a takeoff on Springsteen's "Born in the U.S.A." is as good as anything Weird Al Yankovic's done and achieves some genuine poignancy to boot. There are lots of scantily clad women, pot jokes, and double entendres for Cheech and Chong fans, and though it's not consistently hilarious (except for Cheech's Viking heavy metal character, Ian Rotten, star of "Get Out of My Room"), it's at least as funny as most of the current comedy movies of its time (not saying much, perhaps, but you get the point). Also included are some Cheech and Chong fans, whose diversity and comments show just how much a part of the mainstream culture these guys have become.—P.R.

□ CLIFTON CHENIER
HOT PEPPER
★★★★½

Flower Films, 1980, 54 minutes
PRODUCED BY: Les Blank with Maureen Gosling
DIRECTED BY: Les Blank with Maureen Gosling
MUSIC FROM: Various Clifton Chenier albums; *Hot Pepper* motion picture soundtrack (Flower Films, 1973).
SELECTIONS: "Zydeco Two-Step," "Big Mamou," "Hot Rod," "Baby, Please Don't Go," "Johnny Can't Dance," "I'm Coming Home," "Louisiana Blues," "Don't You Lie to Me," "I'm a Hog for You," "Zydeco Est Pas Sale."

The casual, homespun charms of folkloric traditions—from sage advice and native wisdom to rascally, cantankerous jive—that ethnic-subculture documentarian Les Blank loves so much are in abundance in this film, which is about the king of Louisiana zydeco music, accordionist Clifton Chenier. As Chenier plays it, zydeco is a rollicking, seamlessly organic mix of rockin' blues with Cajun-French accordion and lyrics. If you don't find yourself dancing to it, better check your pulse. In addition to showing Chenier and his band—which also features his brother Cleveland doing amazing polyrhythmic-percussive things with beer-can pop-tops scraped on a tin washboard—in action at sweaty dance halls, *Hot Pepper* follows Chenier along the streets and into the homes of his people. The "undisputed King of zydeco" talks with his dauntingly feisty 100-year-old grandmother; and in some of the most stunning photography in any Blank documentary, Chenier strolls his surrealistic homeland, where swampy bayous thick with tangled mangroves run smack dab into flat, dry farmland. Though Chenier never actually verbalizes the inspiration for his vibrant, joyous music, he doesn't have to: subtly, without condescending romanticism, Blank *shows* us his inspiration, in Chenier's family, friends, and surroundings. Another ace documentary from Blank. (Available by mail order from Flower Films.)

□ VARIOUS ARTISTS
CHESS MOVES
★★

RCA/Columbia, 1986, 26 minutes
PRODUCED BY: Nick Maingay
DIRECTED BY: David G. Hillier
MUSIC FROM: *Chess* original soundtrack (RCA, 1985).
SELECTIONS: Murray Head: "One Night in Bangkok," "Pity the Child"; Murray Head and Elaine Paige: "Nobody's Side"; Bjorn Skifs: "From Square One"; Elaine Paige and Barbara Dickson: "I Know Him So Well."

Fans of *Evita, Jesus Christ Superstar,* and Abba may want to check out this program. It's a sort of video teaser for *Chess,* a musical play based on the lives and loves of American and Soviet chess champs meeting for a world championship, with songs by Abba's Benny Andersson and Bjorn Ulvaeus along with Tim Rice, erstwhile partner of Andrew Lloyd-Webber. Between the five clips, Rice appears on-screen to explain each song's place in the play, and to impart various other bits of info—for instance, after the opening "One Night in Bangkok" (at this writing, the only hit the soundtrack had produced in over a year of release), he tells us that, as with *Jesus Christ Superstar* and *Evita,* the soundtrack album was released long before the musical was mounted to determine whether or not it would be a hit.

At this writing, *Chess* still had yet to open on Broadway—and, after sitting through *Chess Moves,* I pray it never will. Murray Head's "Bangkok," with its funky arrangement and fo-de-o-do megaphone-style rap, is an atmospherically fun piece of dance-pop fluff, but the rest is thoroughly turgid, bombastic MOR pop with the occasional rock or funk touches. Most egregious are the Pat Benatar/Bonnie Tyler–styled "Nobody's Side," which is just plain awkward songwriting, and "I Know Him So Well," which, with its two women both wanting and weeping for the same man, dramatizes soap-opera sexism on the part of the composers that the ultrapompous sweep of the music can't disguise. Meanwhile, the videos make tiresome overuse of chessboard motifs amidst all-too-typically inflated rock video productions, which are full of blue light beams piercing dry ice fog, big sets with lotsa extras, and all the other clichéd trimmings.

With alarming regularity, music and music video as lame, square, corpulent, flatulent, and just plain dull as this still manages to become a smashing success. It you're not the kind of person who buys this jive, steer clear.

□ CHICAGO BEARS SHUFFLIN' CREW
SUPER BOWL SHUFFLE
★★

MPI, 1985, approximately 30 minutes
PRODUCED BY: Richard E. Meyer, William D. Neal, James Hurley III, and Barbara Superter
DIRECTED BY: Dave Thompson
MUSIC FROM: "The Super Bowl Shuffle" (Red Label, 1985).

This was a cute idea for a good cause (Chicago's hungry) that you probably saw as much as you wanted to just before the Bears won the 1986 Super Bowl. The point of making this extended tape was to show the Bears in action rehearsing for the big shoot and just bein' guys. What you get is a lot of director Dave Thompson, depicted here in the overly long "making of" portion as if he's the De Mille of sports rap video, too much laughter over comments you can't hear clearly enough to know if they're funny, and jocks being jocks—lookin', actin', and talkin' real goofy and bored. Say what you will about male rock stars and crotch-intensive rock videos, at least those don't exhibit that compulsive self-touching that athletic cups seem to inspire. Couldn't that have been edited out, along with the other twenty-plus minutes of "sports history"?

As for the "music" end of this video: Since there isn't much, there isn't much to say. "Super Bowl Shuffle" may be the most gratifyingly funky and un-rah-rah sports-video tune to date, but as singers and dancers, the Bears make fine football players.—P.R.

□ VARIOUS ARTISTS
CHICAGO BLUES
★★★★½

Rhapsody, 1986, 50 minutes
PRODUCED BY: Harley Cokliss
DIRECTED BY: Harley Cokliss
MUSIC FROM: The film *Chicago Blues* (1972).
SELECTIONS: Johnie Lewis: "Poor Boy in a Strange City," unidentified gospel blues song; Willie Dixon: "Mississippi Field Holler"; Floyd Jones: "Stockyard Blues"; Liberty Union Church congregation: unidentified gospel hymn; portions of various songs by Muddy Waters, Buddy Guy and Junior Wells, and J. B. Hutto and the Hawks.

As its straightforward title indicates, *Chicago Blues* is a film as no-nonsense, direct, and immediate as its subject. British filmmaker Harley Cokliss went to the source of Chicago blues, the

South Side ghetto of the Windy City, to make this unjustly overlooked documentary, which is part gritty performance film, part starkly compelling ghetto travelogue. With only some shots of "Black Power" graffiti dating it, and against a backdrop of harrowingly poor tenement slums (occasionally seen reflected in skyscraper windows, the film's only cloying touch, though still a pretty powerful one), the film commendably captures both sides of the Chicago blues continuum. On the one hand are the country blues from the Mississippi Delta that came up north with migrant farmworkers after the Depression: Johnie Lewis, who came to Chicago in 1943, offers a rural blues song that poignantly captures the sheer exhilaration and terror of being a "Poor Boy in a Strange City," Chicago blues giant Willie Dixon offers up a Mississippi field holler to illustrate some seminal roots of the modern electric blues, and Floyd Jones plays another country blues in his living room.

Then there are the modern, urban Chicago blues that transformed the Delta original via electricity and the harsher, more urgent pace and post-industrial alienation of city life: here, we see such genuine hard-core Chicago blues greats as Muddy Waters, Buddy Guy and Junior Wells, and J. B. Hutto, all caught in intimate club gigs for virtually all-black inner-city audiences, an especially intriguing fact given that the film was made during the tail-end of the hippie subculture's fascination with "getting back to your roots" in general, and blues in particular. In fact, this may be why the movie's narration (shared by the musicians, comedian/activist Dick Gregory, a black Chicago politician, and others) is so stridently defensive in claiming the music for its originators and their people.

Meanwhile, Cokliss also illustrates the connection between the blues and gospel in Johnie Lewis's blues-tinged gospel song and in a hymn sung with joyful disregard for staying in key by a South Side church congregation. And his camera never flinches while prowling the poverty-stricken streets where these blues greats live, work, and play. A perfect urban counterpart to John Jeremy's superb country-blues-oriented *Blues Like Showers of Rain, Chicago Blues* is perhaps most remarkable not only in its appropriately raw intimacy but also in the way it never condescends to its subjects or audience. (Available by mail order from Rhapsody Films.)

☐ **VARIOUS ARTISTS**
CHULAS FRONTERAS
★★★★½

Brazos Films, 1980, 58 minutes

PRODUCED BY: Les Blank and Chris Strachwitz

DIRECTED BY: Les Blank

MUSIC FROM: Chulas Fronteras motion picture soundtrack (Arhoolie, 1976).

SELECTIONS: Ramiro Cavazos with Conjunto Tamalipas: "Cancion Mixteca"; Los Pinquinos del Norte: "Mi Texana," "Mexico Americano," "Corrido de Cesar Chavez"; Rumel Fuentes with Los Pinguinos del Norte: "Chicano"; Narciso Martinez: "Muchachos Alegres," "Luzita"; Lydia Mendoza and Family: "Panchita"; Lydia Mendoza: "Mal Hombre," "Pero Hay Que Triste"; Piporo: "Chulas Fronteras"; Dueto Reynosa: "Rinches de Texas"; Daniel Ramierez: "Corrido de Texas"; Flaco Jiminez: "La Nueva Zenaida," "Un Mojado Sin Licensia"; David Jiminez: "La Piedrera"; Santiago Jiminez: "Cotula"; Los Alegres de Teran: "Prenda del Alma," "Volver, Volver."

This award-winning look at the *Norteno* ("Northern," as in Northern Mexico, though most of it is actually set in South Texas) music of the Tex-Mex border—the exuberantly swinging and stomping, and/or soaringly romantic, Latinized-polka fusion that forms the folkloric roots of such classic rock sounds as those of Doug Sahm's Sir Douglas Quintet ("She's About a Mover," "Mendocino") and ? and the Mysterians ("96 Tears"), not to mention the new-wave *Norteno* of Joe "King" Carrasco—is one of the best documentaries from Les Blank. Blank, who's always been as much a folkloric galloping gourmet as musical documentarian, naturally examines local cuisine and other customs, but the delightful vitality and elegant romanticism of the music—which is dominated by accordions, acoustic guitars, and trilling tenor vocals as well as a jumping two-step rhythm—leaves the strongest impression. The best-known performer here is accordionist Flaco Jiminez, who has recorded and toured with Doug Sahm. But they're all marvelous, and so is *Chulas Fronteras.* (Available by mail order from Flower Films.)

□ HARVEY CITRON
BASIC GUITAR SET-UP AND REPAIR
★★★★

Homespun, 1984, 90 minutes
PRODUCED BY: Happy Traum
DIRECTED BY: Happy Traum

If you play electric guitar or bass, you really ought to own this tape, in which noted guitar authority Citron—a veteran player who used to market his own highly respected brand of axe—shows you all you need to know to take care of your instrument yourself: adjusting neck action, fixing fret-buzz, correcting intonation, raising or lowering the height of the nut or bridge-saddles, balancing pickups, cleaning volume and tone pots, and so on. It should be made clear that Citron doesn't really teach you *everything* (it just seems that way, he's so good). There *are* some conceivable things that could happen to a guitar or bass that you simply *cannot* fix yourself. But for the usual minor sorts of repairs and maintenance, Citron's got it covered, and with the simplest and most common tools and no prior knowledge whatsoever, you'll have it covered too, and save a lot of costly fix-it trips in the bargain. Citron's instructions are clear, slow enough not to intimidate yet never condescending, and the camerawork is as functionally excellent as in all Homespun Tapes. (Available by mail order from Homespun Tapes.)

□ ERIC CLAPTON
LIVE 85
★★★½

Vestron, 1986, 56 minutes
DIRECTED BY: Jim Yukich
MUSIC FROM: Various Eric Clapton albums.
SELECTIONS: "Tulsa Time," "Motherless Children," "I Shot the Sheriff," "Blues Power," "Tangled in Love," "Lay Down Sally," "Badge," "Let It Rain," "Cocaine," "Forever Man," "Layla."

The great veteran British rock guitarist, captured live in 1985 in Hartford, Connecticut, is in fine form: the band features onetime Booker T and the MGs bassist Donald "Duck" Dunn and stalwart U.K. session keyboardist Chris Stainton, and they blend taste and drive while delivering a mainly upbeat repertoire that contains such Clapton nuggets as "Blues Power," "Badge," "Let It Rain," and "Layla." Clapton, who had previously survived long and arduous personal battles with heroin addiction to attain his current reborn success, has the quiet dignity of the survivor, and it's all captured quite lovingly by Jim Yukich's tasteful direction.

□ THE CLASH
RUDE BOY
★★★★★

CBS/Fox, 1983, 123 minutes
PRODUCED BY: Jack Hazan and David Mingay

DIRECTED BY: Jack Hazan and David Mingay

MUSIC FROM: Rude Boy motion picture soundtrack (Buzzy Enterprises/ Atlantic Rel., 1980); *The Clash* (Epic, 1979); *Give 'Em Enough Rope* (Epic, 1978); *Black Market Clash* (EP) (Epic, 1980).

SELECTIONS: "Police and Thieves," "Career Opportunities," "Garageland," "London's Burning," "White Riot," "(White Man) in Hammersmith Palais," "I'm So Bored with the U.S.A.," "Janie Jones," "The Prisoner," "Tommy Gun," "All the Young Punks (New Boots and Contracts)," "Stay Free," "Complete Control," "Safe European Home," "What's My Name," "Let the Good Times Roll," "Rudie Can't Fail," "I Fought the Law."

□ THE CLASH

THIS IS VIDEO CLASH

★★½

CBS/Fox, 1986, 31 minutes

MUSIC FROM: Give 'Em Enough Rope (Epic, 1978); *London Calling* (Epic, 1979); *Black Market Clash* (EP) (Epic, 1980); *Sandinista!* (Epic, 1980); *Combat Rock* (Epic, 1982).

SELECTIONS: "Tommy Gun," "London Calling," "Bank Robber," "Train in Vain (Stand by Me)," "The Call-Up," "This Is Radio Clash," "Rock the Casbah," "Should I Stay or Should I Go."

Though critically underrated, and barely even a commercial cult item in America, *Rude Boy* remains one of the most fascinating and significant rock films ever made. As a punk-era meditation on the ultimate inability of rock music to transform momentary catharsis and protest into lasting transcendence and change, it makes a marvelously downcast counterpart to the Sex Pistols' burlesque cackle of hype and abnegation, *The Great Rock 'n' Roll Swindle.*

With the unromanticized dreariness of racially and politically tense London and the terminal humdrum of life on the road as backdrops, *Rude Boy* pits the Clash, one of Britain's best and most politically acute punk-rock bands, against co-screenwriter and co-star Ray Gange as the apparent "Rude Boy" of the title, a thick-headed bloke-off-da-street who fancies himself a Clash fan and, through a sheer stroke of luck, escapes his dead-end job in a sleazy adult book store to become a Clash roadie for a few weeks. The Clash and Gange should be complementary but are ultimately very much opposed. Gange looks a bit like a punk rocker, frequents punk clubs, and quietly sings Clash songs to himself as he walks home alone through London's darkened, empty streets. But unlike the Clash, Gange is suspicious of left-wing politics, and in fact while on the road with them reveals himself as a knee-jerk reactionary, provoking a series of violently pranksterish episodes with the band, who quickly get their fill of him. In "Garageland," Clash vocalist Joe Strummer sings, "The truth is only known by guttersnipes." While not exactly a guttersnipe, Gange is a total loser who makes a bleeding-heart-liberal mockery of that lyric.

This is *Rude Boy*'s central irony and dramatic crux—and, most importantly, its critique of rock culture: that is, that the band's relationship with Gange is exactly the opposite of what it should be. Gange is just the kind of guy the Clash mean to enlighten with their storm-the-barricades rhetoric, yet though he gets as close to them as anyone could hope, he remains pitifully benighted. And while the bountiful and generally outstanding concert footage of the Clash shows audience members seeming to be more positively involved in the band's music and message, *Rude Boy* doggedly focuses on this depressing motif of socio-cultural frustration. That apparently stacked deck is probably only partially why the band disavowed *Rude Boy*. The other reason must be that, for the most part, they are portrayed as being jerks almost on a par with Gange (though at least the Clash excel at *something*—their music). Guitarist Mick Jones seems a mere guitar-hero *poseur.* When he callously shouts Gange off the stage when the poor guy's only trying to untangle some guitar cords, Jones's meanness makes Gange's ineptitude seem all the more lovable by comparison. Bassist Paul Simonon comes off as an adorable thug most concerned with being the band's sex symbol. And drummer Topper Headon acts like a vicious little hoodlum who should be let out of confinement only to play drums (which he does brilliantly). Only singer/ guitarist Strummer, he of the wonderfully "toofless" delivery, emerges as a warm, sensitive human being who lives the band's message offstage. But in ironic reality, Strummer's real surname is Mellor, and he's the son of a bourgeois British politician—and thus, he probably *cares* about being a genuine working-class hero more than the rest of the band.

Rude Boy's only fault is that it deals awkwardly and incoherently with the *reason* for the unbridgeable chasm between Gange's lumpen tunnel vision and the Clash's high-minded ideology: the British class system and its profound reinforcement of racial and economic stratification. *Rude Boy* never really makes this explicit, and deals with it only in a botched subplot of police surveillance of black youths. That's a pretty glaring fault, but the rest of *Rude Boy* is good enough to make it a relatively small fault, too. What stays with you is not that gaffe, but moments like *Rude Boy*'s magnificently melancholy and subtly damning closing scene: Gange—having embarrassed himself into being unceremoniously kicked off the Clash tour—once again traipses alone through the London streets, softly singing the Clash's "Stay Free." That's all the Clash mean to him: not revolutionary rock 'n' roll, but just another song to be hummed. Of course, subsequent rock history has proven that, however polemical, *Rude Boy*'s analysis was all too painfully accurate.

This Is Video Clash unceremoniously strings together the band's seven video clips, and doesn't even bother to list production credits for them. No-nonsense delivery is one thing, but this verges on shoddy packaging. Still, if Clash fans and only Clash fans are likely to buy this, then they at least would probably be aware that most if not all Clash videos were directed by Don Letts (at this writing a member of Mick Jones's Big Audio Dynamite). The clips are a pretty erratic lot, though they do at least accompany what are basically the Clash's best-known songs. Both live-concert clips, "Train in Vain" and "Should I Stay or Should I Go?" (the latter filmed at New York's Shea Stadium), suffer from erratic camera work and muddy sound. "Tommy Gun" is a studio-shot performance clip focusing on Strummer's decayed teeth. The idiotic semi-concept clip for "Bankrobber" unfortunately makes the most literal use of the lyrics, which take rock 'n' roll's outlaw romanticism *way* too far by intercutting bandana-wearing bankrobbers with studio performance (the robbers take their loot to a Clash concert so they can buy tickets—surprise, surprise). "London Calling," with the band stomping out their angry anthem on a London bridge in the rain, is atmospherically effective as much because of as despite its comparative crudity.

The best clips are "The Call-Up" and the familiar "Rock the Casbah," which exhibit the seemingly opposed yet ultimately similar sides of the band's personality. The former illustrates the song's modestly majestic, subtly elegaic hymn to draft resistance with both concept (Her Majesty's draft notices arrive through front-door mail-slots; military police chase young men down fire escapes and through alleyways) and performance (the band in combat fatigues and bandit garb, playing in a studio remodeled as a bunker, complete with overhead artillery netting) footage in black and white. "Rock the Casbah" is a slapstick burlesque of U.S.–Middle Eastern political relations, taking off from the avant-funk song's nominal Iranian premise to show everything from a Hasidic rabbi and an Arab emir partying together by a hotel pool, to the Clash, again in their combat fatigues, lip-synching with a vengeance in front of a desert oil rig.

Overall, however, *This Is Video Clash* is mainly for diehard Clash fans, while *Rude Boy* provides food for thought for anyone who's ever cogitated on whether or not rock 'n' roll music really can and does effect positive social change.

□ JIMMY CLIFF
BONGO MAN

★★½

Media, 1985, 89 minutes
PRODUCED BY: Stefan Paul
DIRECTED BY: Stefan Paul
MUSIC FROM: Jimmy Cliff (Trojan JA, 1970); *The Harder They Come* (Mango, 1972); *Follow My Mind* (Warner Bros., 1975); *Give Thanx* (Warner Bros., 1978); *I Am the Living* (MCA, 1980).
SELECTIONS: "Bongo Man," "It's a Hard Road to Travel," "Stand Up and Fight Back," "Viet Nam," "She Is a Woman," "The Harder They Come," "That's My Philosophy," "Wanted Man," "Fundamental Reggae," "I Am the Living," "No Woman, No Cry," "Going Back West," "Let's Turn the Tables."

Bongo Man is an odd little documentary-cum-tribute to reggae singer/songwriter/star Jimmy Cliff, attempting to portray him as a man of his people during a time when Jamaica was fraught with internecine political battles and riots. It features some strong concert footage of Cliff performing both in Jamaica for the local embattled Rastafarians and in Soweto, South Africa, for the embattled people there. There are also shots of Cliff in the recording studio and some lovely moments with Cliff as hill-roaming, hand-drumming mystic, chanting the title tune amidst the breathtaking vistas of Jamaica's mountainous outback (the title song, from Cliff's sadly overlooked *Give Thanx* LP, shows the obvious influence of undeservedly obscure Rasta Afro-hymnal tribal sect, Ras Michael and the Sons of Negus).

We also see Cliff helping Rastas build a community cultural center in the forested hills—while Jamaican patois voiceovers, with the speakers never identified, say things like "Jimmy's a mon of de people, mon, dat's why we love him," and "Here dere'll be a festival of music and arts for de *people*—and no bloody *tourists,* mon." None but the German film crew shooting them building the thing, that is. Especially if one keeps in mind that Cliff is a Muslim and not a Rasta, and has taken some heat for that both within and without Jamaica's tight-knit reggae community, it doesn't take too long before *Bongo Man* starts coming off as pat and forced. Which is no slight to Cliff: he remains a very gifted songwriter (no less than Bob Dylan once said Cliff's "Viet Nam" was the greatest protest song ever written) with a magnificent voice. But even playing in Soweto he's hardly another Bob Marley, which is how *Bongo Man* halfheartedly tries to paint him.

Still, for Cliff fans, *Bongo Man* is a must, and it could prove both entertaining and somewhat enlightening to those with a more casual interest in his music. Ironically, though, *Bongo Man* makes the mistake of including a scene of Jamaicans in a movie theater vociferously enjoying Cliff's wonderful movie vehicle *The Harder They Come*—which, crude as it was, remains a far, far better film than *Bongo Man*.

□ CLIMAX BLUES BAND
LIVE FROM LONDON
★★½

RCA/Columbia, 1986, 60 minutes
PRODUCED BY: Philip Goodhand-Tait
DIRECTED BY: Don Coutts, Heather Staines, Debbie Sanders
MUSIC FROM: Various Climax Blues Band albums.
SELECTIONS: "Black Jack and Me," "Friends in High Places," "Movie Queen," "Chasing Change," "Country Hat," "Sign of the Times," "Couldn't Get It Right," "What You Feel," "Gotta Have More Love," "Going to New York."

As their name reveals, Climax Blues Band began in the late '60s as a hard-working but undistinguished British blues-revival unit. By the mid-'70s they'd matured into a hardworking but undistinguished AOR pop-rock outfit, reaching the U.S. Top 40 every now and then with creditable efforts such as 1973's "Rich Man" and their biggest hit, 1977's "Couldn't Get It Right" (included here). While their sound bears a reasonably distinctive trademark—the unison lead vocals of founders Colin Cooper and guitarist Peter Haycock, and Cooper's sax playing—onstage they are rather devoid of personality. That's not necessarily a bad thing, though: in a way, it's refreshing to see an AOR factory putting its head down and sweating through a set rather than indulging in the flashy posturing endemic to much of the genre. Of course, this could also be explained by the fact that here they're shot at London's Marquee Club, hardly the sort of arena where most AOR rock bands strut their portentous stuff.

For all their sweatily attractive qualities, Climax Blues Band still lack the spark, style, and standout songs to enthrall any but their devotees. Still, for those who like their blues-based rock straight-up and unfussy, this adequately photographed program could be something of a minor revelation.

□ GEORGE CLINTON AND PARLIAMENT-FUNKADELIC
THE MOTHERSHIP CONNECTION LIVE FROM HOUSTON
★★★

Sony, 1986, 30 minutes
PRODUCED BY: Alan Douglas, George Clinton, and Archie Ivey; Coco Conn; Peter Lippman
DIRECTED BY: Archie Ivey, Peter Conn, Wayne Isham
MUSIC FROM: The Mothership Connection Live from the Summit, Houston, Texas soundtrack album (Capitol, 1986).
SELECTIONS: "Let's Take It to the Stage," "Do That Stuff," "Mothership Connection," "Doctor Funkenstein," "Get off Your Ass and Jam," "Night of the Thumpasorus People," "Atomic Dog," "Double Oh-Oh/Bullet Proof."

This program consists of twenty minutes of early-'80s concert footage from the Summit Arena in Houston, Texas (exact dates of the concert recording aren't given, but announcements from the stage that Sly Stone and Bootsy Collins are present or will be present place it around 1981–83), of George Clinton's post-hippie funk-rock traveling circus, Parliament-Funkadelic, and two Clinton video clips. The concert footage isn't very well shot—in fact, with barely adequate lighting and apparently only two cameras having a hard time keeping up with the barely controlled anarchy onstage, it's pretty much an el cheapo production. But then, while Clinton may deserve better, so is the show itself in a way: the high point of the concert is the descent and arrival of the "Mothership" onstage. It's a tacky tinfoil prop, from which Clinton emerges wearing his "Dr. Funkenstein" mask. That low-budget, homemade aspect is part of P-Funk's charm, as well as one of the things—like natural funkiness and cosmic consciousness—Clinton has in common with Sun Ra, one of his acknowledged idols and influences (along with James Brown, Sly Stone, and Jimi Hendrix).

There's nothing cut-rate about the music, however. Clinton's a maximalist at heart, always has been: he has always liked to mass dozens of musicians (multiple guitarists, keyboardists, percussionists and drummers, horn players, and backup singers) onstage as he does here; and he has long been issuing loads of records under a bewildering variety of group names and on many different labels, in an ostensible effort to infiltrate the public consciousness wherever possible. As a businessman, Clinton's proven a bit too Dionysian for his own good, letting his Apollonian guard down and overextending himself without appreciably expanding his audience. That may account somewhat for the relative tackiness of the stage production here. But to return to the subject of the music, even though there are a *lot* of players on-stage, the P-Funk band sounds as tight as a drum, and man do they cut the funk. Especially on "Do That Stuff," "Get off Your Ass and Jam," and "Night of the Thumpasorus People," they ride herd on some killer funk grooves so demonically danceable that if you aren't moved to move to them, you'd better check your pulse.

It's that ability to shake booties so convincingly that's always grounded Clinton's high-flown gonzo philosophies, which mingle earthy ribaldry with space-age utopianism in an effort to liberate whoever'll listen from the sterility of corporate-political repression. To cite Clinton's best-known aphorisms by way of illustration: "Free your mind and your ass will follow"; and, more to the point here, "Funk is its own reward." Unfortunately, this program dangles a really tasty reward before our eyes and ears, and then denies it—Clinton's grooves are *meant* to go on for a while, so you can get lost in them. But here there are too few of them, and they're all cut short after just a few tantalizing minutes. It's *very* frustrating.

That hunger *will* be abated somewhat by the two video clips that follow the concert portion. Peter Conn's "Atomic Dog" is an award-winning blend of computer animation and special effects, with a high-tech set that looks like a Donkey Kong video game brought to three-dimensional life; within the erector-set maze, humans in mutant-animal costumes and masks and animated dog-people chase each other and cavort, while Clinton sits off in a corner cackling at the foibles of mutant mankind. Wayne Isham's "Double Oh-Oh/Bullet Proof" is just as good if not better as a video, more or less literally illustrating Clinton's urgent, seriocomic fusion of atom-spy intrigue, romantic/political fatalism, and antinuke protest—mainly via animation that, as in "Atomic Dog," smacks heavily of the cartoonish illustrations on so many P-Funk albums. Both "Atomic Dog" and "Double Oh-Oh/Bullet Proof" are also superdanceable pieces of music, and they're both thankfully allowed to run their entire courses here. Which only makes it even more frustrating that the live stuff—so valuable for its sheer rarity alone—had to be so chopped up. All we're left with is a good, worth-a-look program that could have been a fantastic must-have.

☐ **SISSY SPACEK**
COAL MINER'S DAUGHTER
★★★★

MCA, 1980, 124 minutes
PRODUCED BY: Bernard Schwartz
DIRECTED BY: Michael Apted
MUSIC FROM: Various albums by Loretta Lynn, other country artists.
SELECTIONS: "I'm a Honky Tonk Girl," "You Ain't Woman Enough to Take My Man," "You're Lookin' at Country," "Don't Come Home Drinkin' (with Lovin' on Your Mind)," "Coal Miner's Daughter," "We've Come a Long Way," "One's on the Way," and others.

One of the best music bios of recent years follows Lynn from her backwoods beginnings, through good times and bad, to her ascendancy to First Lady of Country status. Superbly directed and acted all the way around (Sissy Spacek won an Oscar, deservedly; Levon Helm shines as Loretta's dad), with Spacek—who started as a singer before turning to acting—singing uncannily like Loretta herself. Beverly D'Angelo's very fine turn as Patsy Cline provides fascinating contrast to Jessica Lange's portrayal of Cline in 1985's *Sweet Dreams*.

☐ **JOE COCKER (WITH VARIOUS OTHERS)**
MAD DOGS AND ENGLISHMEN
★★½

RCA/Columbia, 1985, 118 minutes
PRODUCED BY: Pierre Adidge, Harry Marks, and Robert Abel
DIRECTED BY: Pierre Adidge
MUSIC FROM: Mad Dogs and Englishmen motion picture soundtrack (A&M, 1971).
SELECTIONS: "Delta Lady," "Feelin' Alright," "Darlin' Be Home Soon," "She Came in through the Bathroom Window," "Change in Louise," "Let It Be," "The Letter," "Lawdy Miss Clawdy," "Bird on the Wire," "Honky Tonk Women," "Space Captain," "Something," "With a Little Help from My Friends," "Please Give Peace a Chance," "Mad Dogs and Englishmen Theme."

With its relentless split screens—even triple-split screens!—you can tell *Mad Dogs and Englishmen* was made in the wake of *Woodstock*. Thankfully, this 1971 documentary substitutes the boozy, down-to-earth on-the-road *bonhomie* of Cocker's Leon Russell–led rock 'n' soul traveling circus for *Woodstock*'s insufferably holier-than-thou hippie utopianism. That doesn't necessarily make *Mad Dogs* that much better a film than *Woodstock;* it simply makes its momentary lapses easier to take. *Mad Dogs* indulges in plenty of the usual dull rockumentary footage: backstage, rehearsals, on the tour plane, on the tour bus, the old ladies, their kids, their pets, the groupies, the rounds of radio interviews . . . all of which yields exactly two modestly memorable moments. One is hilarious, as a pair of very young hotel clerks face the entire bedraggled entourage late one night at the check-in desk; one is thought-provoking, as a Texas groupie calling herself "the Butter Queen" (I don't wanna *know* how she earned that moniker) muses, "At one show I saw twelve-year-old *girls* trying to get backstage—I mean, that was a bit much." Tour manager Smitty Jones, meanwhile, proves himself a genuine character throughout, getting people to get things done mainly through sterling pronunciation and a classy accent.

The music is as boisterously swinging as some of us remember from way back when, however, with that all-star band (including Carl Radle on bass, Jims Gordon and Keltner on drums, Bobby Keys on sax, and Rita Coolidge among the backup singers) cooking under Leon Russell's svengali-like guidance in that inimitable tight-but-loose fashion. The concert photography is erratic, and the reduction of images necessitated by the split screens hardly helps. There *are* plenty of great shots of a young Cocker lost in his spastically soulful thing onstage; offstage, he seems like a genuinely sweet bloke who, in quieter moments, probably wondered what the hell all the big fuss was about. There are few indications of what a grind the Mad Dogs and Englishmen tour would end up being; it left Cocker broke and drained, and it took him some time to fully recover.

□ PHIL COLLINS
PHIL COLLINS VIDEO 45

★★★

Sony, 1983, 17 minutes
PRODUCED BY: Rooster Productions
DIRECTED BY: Stuart Orme
MUSIC FROM: Face Value (Duke, 1982).
SELECTIONS: "In the Air Tonight," "I Missed Again," "Thru' These Walls," "You Can't Hurry Love."

□ PHIL COLLINS
LIVE AT PERKINS PALACE

★★★★

HBO/Cannon, 1984, 60 minutes
PRODUCED BY: DIR Broadcasting, Inc.
DIRECTED BY: Ken Ehrlich
MUSIC FROM: Face Value (Duke, 1982); *Hello, I Must Be Going!* (Duke, 1983).
SELECTIONS: "I Don't Care Anymore," "I Cannot Believe It's True," "Thru' These Walls," "I Missed Again," "Behind the Lines," "The Roof Is Leaking," "The West Side," "In the Air Tonight," "You Can't Hurry Love," "It Don't Matter to Me," "People Get Ready."

□ PHIL COLLINS
NO JACKET REQUIRED

★★★

Atlantic, 1985, 28 minutes
DIRECTED BY: Jim Yukich
MUSIC FROM: No Jacket Required (Atco, 1985).
SELECTIONS: "Sussudio," "One More Night," "Who Said I Would," "Don't Lose My Number," "Take Me Home."

Long before Genesis drummer/vocalist Phil Collins moved out on his own for a successful part-time solo career, fans of the veteran British progressive-rock band knew what everyone else would find out later: Collins is not only a capable singer and an outstanding drummer, but also an engagingly good-humored personality whose impish charm translates as well on video as it does onstage. Interestingly, the success of his funk-inflected melodic pop has influenced Genesis, resulting in the streamlined sound that has since revived them.

The promo clips collected on *Video 45* and *No Jacket Required* are, for the most part, straightforward performance pieces; what concepts there are usually serve as convenient platforms for Collins to display his comic gifts, as in *Video 45* 's "I Missed Again" (where Phil lip-synchs all the instruments without any instruments—that is, he plays "air guitar," "air drums," "air trombone," etc.) or *No Jacket Required* 's "Don't Lose My Number" (in which the video's scenario consists of Phil enduring the derivative, clichéd scenarios proposed by a succession of hack directors for his next video). Overall, there's a marked improvement in production values from *Video 45* to *No Jacket Required* (the reason being that the former was shot before Collins's solo career became a runaway success). Probably the best video of all is *No Jacket Required* 's "Take Me Home," which was obviously shot at just about every stop on Phil's 1984–85 world tour: brief shots of Collins singing a line in strategic locales in, say, London and Sydney and Tokyo and New York and Paris and all sorts of other places, are edited with a deliberate, lapping-wave tempo that perfectly synchs in with the techno-tribal groove of the stately, hymnal tune. It's one of the freshest and easiest to watch meditations on homesickness rock video's ever likely to produce, and it's got a cute comic tag to boot.

Live at Perkins Palace is a nicely shot record of Collins in Pasadena, California, during his 1983 U.S. tour. Leading a crack band (which includes drummer Chester Thompson, who's also been a regular on Genesis tours since 1977, as well as the Phoenix Horns Collins hired from one of his favorite bands, Earth, Wind and Fire) through a representative selection of material from his first two solo albums, Collins gets an even better platform than in his videos to demonstrate his talent and charisma. The capacity throng certainly approves, as will Collins fans viewing at home. In fact, since the concert stage is the perfect setting for Collins and since *Live* does such a nice job of catching Collins in his element, *it* is the most highly recommended.

☐ **VARIOUS ARTISTS**

COMEDY VIDEOS

★★

Vestron, 1985, 60 minutes
PRODUCED BY: Various
DIRECTED BY: Various
MUSIC FROM: Various albums by various artists.

SELECTIONS: Mel Brooks: "Hitler Rap"; Julie Brown: "The Homecoming Queen's Got a Gun"; the Shmenges (John Candy and Eugene Levy): "The Last Polka"; Ruth Buzzi: "Where's the Beef?": Garry Trudeau, Elizabeth Swados, unidentified Ronald Reagan impersonator: "Rapmaster Ronnie"; Durocs: "It Hurts to Be in Love"; Al Franken and Tom Davis: "Under My Thumb"; Jimmy Picker: "Sundae in New York"; Fat Boys: "Jailhouse Rap"; Bob and Ray with Jane Curtin, Laraine Newman, and Gilda Radner: "Do Ya Think I'm Sexy?"; Martin Mull: "This One Takes the Cake"; the Rutles: "Tragical History Tour (Piggy in the Middle)"; the Blues Brothers (Dan Aykroyd and John Belushi): "Hey Bartender."

Comedy Videos, as with comedy records especially but comedy films on cassette as well, falls victim to that old bugaboo—the comedy's got to be exceptionally good to make you want to see it over and over again. There are only five out of thirteen clips that hold up here: "Rapmaster Ronnie," a dense, deft, well-observed attack on Reagan (with an impersonator smoothly rapping as he obliviously tours an urban slum) by *Doonesbury* cartoonist Garry Trudeau and award-nominated off-Broadway and TV composer Elizabeth Swados; the Durocs' really, REALLY *gross* but also affectionately comical and well-executed "It Hurts to Be in Love" (the tune itself, a stomping three-chord roots-rocker, is also pretty fine); Franken and Davis's "Under My Thumb," which rates an historical place in modern comedy annals as the first time this duo's ever done anything remotely funny—in fact, Franken does an excellent, serious imitation of Mick Jagger, and Davis on guitar (looking more like Ron Wood or Mick Taylor than Keith Richards) contributes to a rather good Stones impression by the *Saturday Night Live* band; Jimmy Picker's "Sundae in New York," a clever and inventive if cloying short featuring a clay-animated New York Mayor Ed Koch singing "New York, New York" while touring the Big Apple (encountering claymation cameos by Frank Sinatra, David Letterman, Rodney Dangerfield, and many others); and the Rutles' dead-on, pre–*Spinal Tap* Beatles parody "Piggy in the Middle," a sharp aural and visual trashing of "I Am the Walrus" from *Magical Mystery Tour* (here called *Tragical History Tour*). The rest vary from the absolute nadir of trend-hopping swill (Ruth Buzzi's execrably dumb "Where's the Beef?") to the only so-so (Julie Brown's "The Homecoming Queen's Got a Gun") and too much of it isn't even very funny the first time around.

☐ **VARIOUS ARTISTS (GEORGE HARRISON, ERIC CLAPTON, BOB DYLAN, OTHERS)**
CONCERT FOR BANGLADESH
★★½

HBO/Cannon, 1981 (originally released 1972), 99 minutes

PRODUCED BY: George Harrison and Allen Klein

DIRECTED BY: Saul Swimmer

MUSIC FROM: The Concert for Bangla Desh (Apple, 1971).

SELECTIONS: George Harrison: "Wah Wah," "My Sweet Lord," "Beware of Darkness," "While My Guitar Gently Weeps," "Awaiting on You All," "Something," "Bangla Desh"; Bob Dylan: "A Hard Rain's A-gonna Fall," "It Takes a Lot to Laugh, It Takes a Train to Cry," "Just Like a Woman," "Blowin' in the Wind"; Billy Preston: "That's the Way God Planned It"; Ringo Starr: "It Don't Come Easy"; Leon Russell: Medley: "Jumpin' Jack Flash"/"Youngblood"; Ravi Shankar: "Bangla Dhun"; George Harrison and Pete Ham: "Here Comes the Sun."

This tape is of historical importance, since Harrison's August 1971 Madison Square Garden concert for the people of Bangladesh was the biggest of the early famine-relief rock shows. The proceeds from the concert, soundtrack, and film eventually raised more than $10 million for UNICEF—though most of it was tied up in an Apple audit for nine years, thus also making it one of the more grossly mishandled fundraisers of its type. As for the music, it's an all-star band, featuring Eric Clapton, Billy Preston, Leon Russell, Ringo Starr, Jim Keltner, Jesse Ed Davis, Badfinger, and others, and clearly an exciting show for the Garden audience. Trouble is, so little of that comes across on film. The sound, despite being produced for the film by Phil Spector and Harrison, is muddy, and the camerawork, which tries too hard to be unobtrusive, is so boring it's distracting. It seems that no allowances for the filming were made in either the stage setup or the lighting.

An exciting show might have overcome these technical obstacles, but this one just couldn't. The music's good, but these guys aren't *doing* anything. Clapton, then in the throes of his addiction, oozes a bemused sleepiness and Leon Russell turns in a rousing "Jumpin' Jack Flash"/ "Youngblood" with a blankness of expression that makes you start scanning the screen for his ventriloquist. Harrison's pained looks are also a considerable minus, especially if you were never a fan of his more spiritual stuff. The show's real highlights, Billy Preston's gospel rave-up on "That's the Way God Planned It" and Dylan's set, as unremarkable as it is, make this worth watching. Also watch for Ringo's wonderfully flubbed "It Don't Come Easy." If you really must have the music, stick with the soundtrack LP, and unless you're a Beatles or benefit completist, skip this one.—P.R.

☐ **EDDIE CONDON SEXTET**
GOODYEAR JAZZ CONCERT WITH EDDIE CONDON
★★★½

Video Yesteryear, 1980, 27 minutes

MUSIC FROM: 1961 TV concert special.

SELECTIONS: "Blue and Brokenhearted," "Stealin' Apples," others.

Of greater historical value than Video Yesteryear's other Goodyear Jazz Concerts, perhaps, if only because trad-jazz banjo/guitarist Condon was one cat who rarely if ever got before a camera of any kind, and aside from being a great player and a major force in the trad-jazz movement, Condon was also a hell of a laconically funny character. (To wit the remark attributed to him in the early '50s, when he was standing in the Manhattan jazz club named after him and a waiter dropped a tray of drinks; "Please," Condon winced, "no bebop!") Here, Condon's band includes such stalwarts of the form as Peanuts Hucko on clarinet (who is featured on "Stealin' Apples") and cornetist Wild Bill Davison (featured on "Blue and Brokenhearted").

□ **VARIOUS ARTISTS**

COOL CATS: 25 YEARS OF ROCK 'N' ROLL STYLE

★★

MGM/UA, 1984, 77 minutes

PRODUCED BY: Stephanie Bennett

DIRECTED BY: Terry Dixon

MUSIC FROM: Various albums by various artists.

SELECTIONS: Elvis Presley: "Ready Teddy"; Billy Fury: "Don't Knock upon My Door"; Dickie Pride: "Slippin' and Slidin' "; Cliff Richard: "Turn Me Loose"; David Bowie: "Fashion," "Boys Keep Swinging"; Judas Priest: "Victim of Changes"; the Stray Cats: "Runaway Boys," "Stray Cat Strut; Blondie: "The Hardest Part"; Kiss: "I Love It Loud "; Bill Haley: "Rip It Up," "Rock Around the Clock"; Jerry Lee Lewis: "Whole Lot of Shakin' Goin' On"; Chuck Berry: "Maybellene"; Gene Vincent: "Be-Bop-a-Lula"; Bobby Fuller Four: "Let Her Dance"; Jimi Hendrix: "Wild Thing"; Tina Turner: "Shake"; Buddy Holly: "That'll Be the Day"; Little Richard: "Tutti-Frutti"; Eddie Cochran: "Somethin' Else"; Everly Brothers: "Wake Up Little Susie," "Be-Bop-a-Lula"; the Who: "My Generation," "Substitute," "Pictures of Lily," "Anyway, Anyhow, Anywhere," "Baba O' Riley," "My Generation (Quadrophenia)"; the Rolling Stones: "Not Fade Away"; the Beatles: "She Loves You"; the Jefferson Airplane: "Aquarius," "Somebody to Love," "White Rabbit"; Matthews Southern Comfort: "Woodstock"; Janis Joplin: "Ball and Chain"; the Beach Boys: "Good Vibrations"; Elton John: "Pinball Wizard"; Blondie: "Heart of Glass"; Rod Stewart: "Maggie May"; Gary Glitter: "Rock and Roll, Part 2"; the Sex Pistols: "Pretty Vacant," "Anarchy in the UK"; Joan Jett: "Bad Reputation"; the Jam: "Going Underground"; the Kinks: "Predictable"; Culture Club: "Church of the Poison Mind"; Style Council: "Money Go Round"; Twisted Sister: "You Can't Stop Rock 'n' Roll."

Also available on MGM/UA Stereo Laser videodisc.

"Rock 'n' roll is a lot more than the music," says Stray Cat Brian Setzer during *Cool Cats,* "it's style, it's lookin' cool." Well put: clothes, makeup, hairdos, stage moves, and dancing have always been every bit as crucial to rock and pop as the music itself, and their importance has only grown along with the intensification of media scrutiny over the years. The rock-video explosion and the existence of this program are but the most recent proof. Yes, the history of rock style and fashion deserves a video document. Unfortunately, despite some good qualities and despite being based on a very ambitious British coffee-table book of the same title, *Cool Cats* isn't it.

Yes, there are lots of great archival snippets of all sorts of performers from many phases of rock history, but they all seem to go by too quickly, rendering the program more a tease than anything else. The same holds true for a too-brief glimpse of fab-gear Carnaby Street during the height of London's swinging '60s. Perhaps the best segment is a priceless interlude with a middle-aged British Teddy Boy proudly displaying his three sideburned, pompadoured pubescent sons. And many of the rock stars interviewed—Setzer, Jefferson Airplane/Starship's Grace Slick, the Who's Pete Townshend, Roger Daltrey, and John Entwistle—are refreshingly candid. But on the other hand, entire eras and subcultures—not to mention most of the female gender's contributions—are ignored outright, or at best given extremely short shrift. But for Jimi Hendrix and Tina Turner (who are both, of course, given only brief screen time), black musical style is completely absent.

Unlike the book it's based on, *Cool Cats* doesn't try to articulate the ways rock style has always cannibalized its own past, something which is evident only in *some* of the era-to-era cuts. Terence Dixon's direction is virtually *non*-direction, leaping about disjointedly all over the place and utterly mangling any sense of historical overview. It all becomes a blurred steeplechase of images, sadly suitable for the no-attention-span generation but sure to frustrate anyone else trying to cogitate on a worthy subject. There's also *way* too much of the Who talking—but then, one of the executive producers of this program is Who manager Bill Curbishley. Oh well, that kind of sleazy biz is another well-entrenched aspect of rock style, in a way. At one point in *Cool Cats,* Grace Slick chuckles, "None of this is *serious*—it's a silly business." That's not true, of course. But the problem with *Cool Cats* is, it leaves you ready to believe it.

□ STEWART COPELAND
THE RHYTHMATIST

★★

A&M, 1985, 58 minutes
PRODUCED BY: J. P. Dutilleux
DIRECTED BY: J. P. Dutilleux
MUSIC FROM: The *Rhythmatist* soundtrack album (A&M, 1985).
SELECTIONS: "Koteja," "Liberte," "Kemba," and others.

Long before its release, Police drummer Copeland hyped this program as a probing documentary into the relationships between rhythm and life-style in African tribal society; press releases touted "Rhythmatism" as "the study of patterns that weave the fabric of life"; producer/director J. P. Dutilleux is a genuine, respected documentarian noted for his field work in the Amazon. So what did we get? A slack collection of seemingly random footage of Copeland as Great White Hunter, moving freely among slightly suspicious tribes of East and West Africa; just *happening* to meet up with a lovely blonde who of course would be delighted to share his journey; and generally making a fool of himself while blithely missing the point of everything he sees. And there's a lot more footage of Copeland's ridiculous exercises in culture-crossing—setting up his drum kit in a cage and bashing away while some lions attack the cage; banging on a gigantic rock while postulating weighty theorems about its alleged mystical powers—than of the natives themselves and their own musical culture. An insulting, indulgent, wasted opportunity? Maybe. But Copeland *couldn't* be this insensitive, could he? Perhaps it's meant as a sendup of the music theorist's intellectualization of White Man's Burden—a self-parody? If so, it ain't the *Spinal Tap* of its genre, but it does provide a bit of junk food for thought. Overall, though, it's not even worth that much mental effort.

□ CHICK COREA
CHICK COREA VIDEO LP

★★★½

Sony, 1983, 60 minutes
PRODUCED BY: Michael M. Galer
DIRECTED BY: Gary Legon
MUSIC FROM: Echoes of an Era (Elektra Musician, 1981); *The Griffith Park Collection* (Elektra Musician, 1982).
SELECTIONS: "L's Bop," "Why Wait," "500 Miles High," "Guernica."

The accomplished jazz and jazz-fusion pianist Chick Corea is de facto leader of an estimable modern-jazz ensemble in this nicely shot concert tape. He's joined by his former Return to Forever rhythm section of bassist Stanley Clarke and drummer Lenny White—and the very fine bebop tenor saxophonist Joe Henderson—to play the thoughtfully swinging acoustic jazz arrangements this ensemble recorded on the *Echoes of an Era* and *Griffith Park Collection* albums (with R&B singer Chaka Khan on the former; she's replaced by MOR jazz *chanteuse* Nancy Wilson fronting the same ensemble in Sony's companion tape *A Very Special Concert,* released under Wilson's name but merely the second half of this same concert). For Corea, Clarke, and White, who rose to fame playing electric fusion music with Return to Forever, this gig represents a return to the neoclassic bop and post-bop milieu in which they started, a milieu Henderson never really left. They synch together very nicely as a band, delivering tight ensemble work and heated, exploratory solos on all four pieces. "L's Bop" is a darting, up-tempo opener; the pensive "Why Wait" and the more ebullient "500 Miles High" are nice mid-tempo numbers; and the closing "Guernica" is more a moody tone poem than anything else. A solid dose of straight-up jazz, presented with low-key tastefulness. While Henderson's playing is exceptional, if there's a real star here it's White, whose ambidextrous drumming style is intriguing to watch and who delivers some refreshingly humorous between-songs banter.

□ CHICK COREA AND GARY BURTON

LIVE IN TOKYO

★★★★

Pacific Arts, 1985, 60 minutes

PRODUCED BY: Chick Corea and Gary Burton with Ted Kurland Associates

DIRECTED BY: Yatsusune Kikuchi

MUSIC FROM: Crystal Silence (ECM, 1972); *Duet* (ECM, 1981).

SELECTIONS: "Mirror, Mirror," "Bud Powell," "Children's Songs," "Señor Mouse," "Song to Gayle," "La Fiesta."

Also available on Pioneer Stereo Laser Videodisc.

Jazz-fusion pianist Corea and jazz vibist Burton first engaged in their delicate, glowing duets on the aptly titled *Crystal Silence* album in 1972. Ten years later they renewed their musical acquaintance with the Grammy-winning *Duet* LP and the tour caught here at Tokyo's Yubin Chokin Hall. "Mirror, Mirror" sets the tone for their incandescent *pas de deux*, the music coiling and uncoiling with supple grace and a mercurial range of instantly shifting moods and spontaneous arrangements between two masters seemingly connected by telepathy. Corea's "Bud Powell," dedicated to the bebop piano giant, is appropriately sprightly and boppish and, at times, fractured and unpredictable (reminding us that Powell suffered from terrible mental illness). Corea's classic "Señor Mouse" (originally recorded as "Captain Señor Mouse" by his fusion band Return to Forever) moves from a skittish opening to the lovely, lilting theme over a strong Latin groove, then alternates pleasingly between that theme and interludes of pointillistic, cross-hatched counterpoint, now stormy, now reflective, now edgily assertive. "Song to Gayle" is an extended, complex, suitelike piece, impressive in its range and scope of mood and arrangement; it leads imperceptibly to the rollicking conclusion of "La Fiesta." Throughout, Corea and Burton not only evince individual mastery of their instruments, but surprise the viewer with the sheer variety of what would seem to be sonically limited tone poems. The only failure in the whole program is "Children's Songs," a series of seven brief sketches that never really grow beyond being mere exercises. Overall, however, this is a most rewarding musical dialogue, and the simple, straight-ahead production is all a fan needs to enjoy it.

☐ ELVIS COSTELLO AND THE ATTRACTIONS
THE BEST OF ELVIS COSTELLO
★★★½

CBS/Fox, 1985, 67 minutes
PRODUCED BY: Jake Riviera
DIRECTED BY: Various
MUSIC FROM: My Aim Is True (CBS, 1977); *This Year's Model* (CBS, 1978); *Armed Forces* (CBS, 1979); *Taking Liberties* (CBS, 1980); *Get Happy!!* (CBS, 1980); *Trust* (CBS, 1981); *Almost Blue* (CBS, 1981); *Imperial Bedroom* (CBS, 1982); *Punch the Clock* (CBS, 1983); *Goodbye, Cruel World* (CBS, 1984).
SELECTIONS: "Green Shirt," "Pump It Up," "Oliver's Army," "I Wanna Be Loved," "High Fidelity," "Clubland," "(What's So Funny About) Peace, Love, and Understanding," "New Lace Sleeves," "I Can't Stand Up (for Falling Down)," "Radio Radio," "New Amsterdam," "The Only Flame in Town," "(I Don't Want to Go to) Chelsea," "Possession," "Sweet Dreams," "Let Them All Talk," "Accidents Will Happen," "You Little Fool," "Love for Tender," "Good Year for the Roses," "Every Day I Write the Book," "Watching the Detectives."

If you really like Elvis, the new wave's Last Angry Man, you'll really like this comprehensive compilation of video clips. Some of them have rarely, if ever, been shown in the U.S.: Paul Henry's "Green Shirt" captures the young Elvis in all his youthful, twitchily intense glory; the Rich Kids' claustrophobic close-up "I Wanna Be Loved" is a fascinating comment on the song with one of Elvis's most interesting and unusual on-camera performances; Barney Bubbles's "Clubland" is a vicious, Brecht-Weillian illustration of the song; Rocky Morton and Annabelle Jankel's "Accidents Will Happen" is a brilliant synergism of fractured computer animation; Irving Rappaport's "Watching the Detectives" is a silly montage of gumshoe-flick clips. Most of the rest boil down to early, intense straight performance clips (Jon Roseman's "Pump It Up," "Radio Radio," and "Chelsea") or, as in Chuck Statler's *Get Happy!!* series, clips so deliberately low-budget and casual they offer the intrigue of seeing Elvis undercutting his image with farce. The music, of course, is uniformly brilliant, slackening only with the few misguided country covers and the slick, silly duet with Daryl Hall, "The Only Flame in Town."

☐ VARIOUS ARTISTS
COUNTRY COMES ALIVE
★★½

RCA/Columbia, 1986, 30 minutes
PRODUCED BY: Various
DIRECTED BY: Various
MUSIC FROM: Various albums by various artists
SELECTIONS: Kenny Rogers: "Morning Desire"; Ronnie Milsap: "Lost in the '50s Tonight (In the Still of the Night)"; Alabama: "There's No Way"; Earl Thomas Conley: "Crowd Around the Corner"; Waylon Jennings: "America"; the Judds: "Love Is Alive"; Juice Newton: "I Can't Wait All Night."

Countrypolitan Comes in a Convenient Package would have been a better title for this star-studded compilation of MOR-country hits circa 1985–86. Ronnie Milsap and Earl Thomas Conley both ply the nostalgia theme so popular among country-pop artists; the Judds and Alabama offer straight-up performance clips; Juice Newton lip-synchs while riding a horse along a beach; Kenny Rogers croons his way through a gauzily romantic clip that's like a Harlequin Romance version of sexual ecstasy; and Waylon Jennings turns in a rather disappointing "America" over travelogue footage of purple mountains' majesty, fruited plains, amber waves of grain, etc. A decent K-tel–style sampler for those so inclined, thanks much more to the music than to the rather pedestrian visuals.

☐ **VARIOUS ARTISTS**
COUNTRYMAN
★½

Media, 1983, 103 minutes
PRODUCED BY: Chris Blackwell
DIRECTED BY: Dickie Jobson
MUSIC FROM: Various albums by various artists; *Countryman* motion picture soundtrack (Island/Mango, 1982).
SELECTIONS: Wally Badarou: "Theme from *Countryman*" (three versions), "Guidance," "Obeah Man Dub"; Bob Marley and the Wailers: "Natural Mystic," "Rastaman Chant," "Rat Race," "Jah Live," "Three O'Clock Road Block," "Small Axe," "Time Will Tell," "Pass It On"; Rico: "Ramble"; Steel Pulse: "Sound System"; Aswad: "Mosman Skank"; Dennis Brown: "Sitting & Watching"; Toots and the Maytals: "Bam Bam"; Fabulous Five: "Ooh! Aah!"; Jah Lion: "Wisdom"; Human Cargo: "Carry Us Beyond"; Lee Perry: "Dreadlocks in Moonlight."

Countryman was the third reggae movie to feature a solid soundtrack compiled by Island Records chief Chris Blackwell. But, as the maiden production of Blackwell's Island Alive film company, *Countryman* was a deserved box-office bomb, and the other two reggae films Blackwell had been involved with—*The Harder They Come* and *Rockers*—were better films with better soundtracks. *Countryman*'s lame excuse for a plot involves two swingin' young Americans (Hiram Keller and Tina St. Clair) plane-wrecked in Jamaica's wilderness, Jamaican government evildoing, and mystical rescue machinations by the charismatic title character, an aboriginal Rasta fisherman who plays himself as a mightily clichéd noble savage. The plot is so dull and devoid of forward motion that the film can only serve as a first-the-good-news, then-the-bad-news Jamaican travelogue. The good news is that the country is gorgeous and the natives are sweet and will ply you with ganja and fresh lobster and fruit if you happen to get stuck in the wilderness; the bad news is that the police may be bumblers but they're also relentlessly nasty, so you'd better be lucky enough to hook up with an angelic natural-born savior like Countryman. It's sort of a would-be Rasta *E.T.*: an alien (to us) Rasta mystic has to help the alien (to him) rich Americans and make sure they get back safely to the girl's daddy's ship. But while Countryman himself does have a refreshingly natural presence, the American guy and girl are so *blah* there's no way we can care about what happens to them. Countryman himself and his humanist, in-harmony-with-nature ethos are the best things about this movie, though some extremely silly kung fu mysticism and other varieties of esoteric mumbo jumbo get in the way of even that. There is a lot of good reggae music on the soundtrack, from the gems by such stalwarts as Bob Marley and the Wailers, Toots and the Maytals, and Lee Perry to the original and highly atmospheric Afro-Caribe background grooves by Wally Badarou.

☐ **THE CRAMPS, OTHERS**
A FREE CONCERT AT THE NAPA STATE HOSPITAL
★★★½

Target, 1984, 60 minutes
PRODUCED BY: Joe Rees
DIRECTED BY: Joe Rees
MUSIC FROM: Gravest Hits EP (Illegal, 1979); *Songs the Lord Taught Us* (Illegal/IRS, 1980)

SELECTIONS: The Cramps: "Mystery Plane," "The Way I Walk," "What's Behind the Mask?" "Human Fly," "Domino," "She Doesn't Love Me," "Garbage Man," "TV Set"; Crucifix: "Prejudice"; Flipper: "Low Rider"; Black Flag: "TV Party"; Mark Pauline and Survival Research Laboratories: "A Scenic Harvest"; Toxic Reasons: "Destroyer"; MDC (Millions of Dead Cops): "John Wayne Was a Nazi"; Throbbing Gristle: "Excerpt from Kezar Stadium Show"; Crime: unidentified song outside San Quentin State Prison; Z'ev: untitled percussion performances.

On June 13, 1978, New York City punk-era neorockabilly band the Cramps played a free concert for patients at the California State Mental Hospital in Napa, California. The first half of this tape is a crude but fascinating document of that show, shot in black and white with a single early Sony half-inch Portapak and recorded with a single microphone. What's intriguing about it is not just the very idea of a band performing in a mental institution but also that the Cramps—with their grindingly primitive punkabilly sound and the stage antics of lead singer Lux Interior, which include stuffing the microphone into his mouth and generally acting quite mad—are generally regarded as borderline psychotics by all but their fans. So here we have a band that *acts* crazy playing for an audience that has been legally declared as more-or-less crazy. The reality of it doesn't totally live up to the expectations engendered by the very idea of it, but it's surely a unique experience to see Napa patients dancing—in some cases contentedly in one place, in others more wildly and peripatetically—and wandering about while the Cramps blast out their lurching, primeval ooze of thumping 4/4 sludge-beat, barbed-wire guitar twang, and trash-culture allusions to pulp-comic grotesquerie. One female patient in particular, a big-boned brunette, keeps leaping onto the low stage, often with a punky-looking blonde who seems to be her companion, to dance with Interior, scream with him into the mike, and at times grab the mike to scream incoherently all by herself. Some might recoil in distaste at the lunatics-taking-over-the-asylum setup of this event, but from watching it, it appears that the Cramps showed the patients a pretty good time. Unfortunately, there's no further documented proof that this show was anything more than a self-consciously crazy notion that probably worked out better than anyone expected, and there's no follow-up in terms of personal reactions from the patients other than what we see them do during the show itself. Still, just having a record of this show on tape makes this arguably *the* most unusual program in this entire book.

The second half of this tape consists of a bunch of Target Video trailers for other programs, featuring an array of hardcore punk bands—Black Flag's "TV Party" clip is the highlight, and the biggest disappointment is the band Crime playing a terrible punk song outside the walls of San Quentin State Prison—and culminating in excerpts from post-industrial performance artist/percussionist Z'ev's *Six Examples* Target Video cassette. (Available in stores, or by mail order from Target Video or Independent World Video.)

□ CREAM
THE FAREWELL CONCERT OF CREAM
★★★

Video Yesteryear, 1980, 84 minutes
PRODUCED BY: Robert Stigwood
DIRECTED BY: Tony Palmer
MUSIC FROM: Live Cream, Vol. 1 (Atco, 1970); *Live Cream, Vol. 2* (Atco, 1972); *Best of Cream Live* (Polydor, 1975); and other Cream albums.
SELECTIONS: "Spoonful," "Crossroads," "Politician," "I'm So Glad,"

"White Room," "Tales of Brave Ulysses," "Badge," "Sunshine of Your Love."

Just what it says, with the protean rock supergroup—arguably the first to make instrumental virtuosity an issue of debate among rock fans, thus opening the door for the progressive rock to come, prefigured by their opening act at this London swan song, none other than Yes in their first big gig (not included in the film)—stretching out into their improvisatory acid-blues rock, being interviewed briefly, and so on. The sounds are real groovy, man, and there's plenty of historical significance here, but to dig it you have to be patient enough to wade through an excess of period psychedelic camera tricks—pulsating focus, light-show overlays, abrupt cuts to close-ups of paisley shawls, ad nauseam. Still, it makes a heck of a psychedelic curio, at the very least.

□ CROSBY, STILLS AND NASH
DAYLIGHT AGAIN

★★½

MCA, 1983, 108 minutes
PRODUCED BY: Neal Marshall
DIRECTED BY: Tom Trbovich
MUSIC FROM: Various Crosby, Stills and Nash, Buffalo Springfield, Crosby, Stills, Nash, and Young, and Crosby and Nash albums (Atlantic, ABC, 1969–84).
SELECTIONS: "Turn Your Back on Love," "Chicago," "Just a Song Before I Go," "Wooden Ships," "Dark Star," "Barrel of Pain," "Wind on the Water," "You Don't Have to Cry," "Blackbird," "Wasted on the Way," "Delta," "Treetop Flyer," "Magical Child," "Suite: Judy Blue Eyes," "Cathedral," "Southern Cross," "Long Time Gone," "For What It's Worth" "Love the One You're With," "Teach Your Children," "Daylight Again."
Also available on MCA Stereo Laser videodisc.

I never cared much for these guys, though they did have their individual (Stills's "Suite: Judy Blue Eyes," "Love the One You're With," and "For What It's Worth") and collective moments. And I always thought that the longer they kept at it, the weaker they became. But the rapt audience at their 1982 show at L.A.'s Universal Amphitheater obviously felt differently, and if you do, too, you'll appreciate this tastefully shot concert documentary. It is morbidly fascinating that, as the '60s fade further and further into nostalgic memory, CSN here look and sound rather . . . resigned, as if delivering a requiem in three-part harmony.

□ THE CRUSADERS
CRUSADERS LIVE: MIDNIGHT TRIANGLE

★★½

MCA, 1984, 52 minutes
PRODUCED BY: Reiko Posner and Makoto Hasegawa
DIRECTED BY: Reiko Posner and Makoto Hasegawa
MUSIC FROM: Various Crusaders albums (Chisa, Blue Thumb, MCA, 1971–85).
SELECTIONS: "Sunshine in Your Eyes," "Soul Shadows," "Scratch," "Melodies of Love," "Someday We'll All Be Free," "African Spirit," "Snowflake," "Keep That Same Old Feeling."

Solid, unspectacular concert shoot of the veteran top-selling jazz/funk fusion band (some of whose members, like keyboardist Joe Sample and saxophonist Wilton Felder, have also found solo success), caught in a club setting, doing their usual smooth-and-slick, ultraprofessional job of straddling the line between a relaxed groove and a torpid trance.

□ CULTURE CLUB
A KISS ACROSS THE OCEAN

★★★½

CBS/Fox, 1984, 56 minutes
PRODUCED BY: Keefco
DIRECTED BY: Keith "Keef" MacMillan

MUSIC FROM: Kissing to Be Clever (Epic, 1982); *Colour by Numbers* (Epic, 1984).

SELECTIONS: "I'll Tumble 4 Ya," "Mister Man," "It's a Miracle," "Karma Chameleon," "Black Money," "Love Twist," "Do You Really Want to Hurt Me," "Miss Me Blind," "Church of the Poison Mind," "Victims," "Time," "White Boy."

While watching this 1984 London concert by the phenomenal British teen-pop band, what hits home most of all isn't Boy George's outrageous pan-cultural androgyny so much as the overall excellence of the band and its music. At their best, which covers most of this tape, Culture Club may not have much to say but they say it wonderfully. George himself is really a bonus: a genuinely nice guy (somehow calling him *good*-humored seems like damning him with faint praise) with a genuinely original act that has a strong impact on a large number of people. What also strikes you, of course, is the intensity of the teen-idol mania surrounding Culture Club, most evident here in the steady high-frequency banshee wail the audience sustains through the entire course of the concert. As '80s British teen-mania pop phenomena go, far better this than Duran Duran.

□ THE CURE

STARING AT THE SEA—THE IMAGES

★★★½

Elektra, 1986, 82 minutes

PRODUCED BY: Tim Pope and Robert Smith

DIRECTED BY: Tim Pope, Piers Bedford, David Hillier, Bob Rickerd, Mike Mansfield, Chris Gabrin

MUSIC FROM: Standing on a Beach (Elektra, 1986); *Boys Don't Cry* (PVC, 1979); *. . . Happily Ever After* (A&M, 1981).

SELECTIONS: "Killing an Arab," "10:15 Saturday Night," "Boys Don't Cry," "Jumping Someone Else's Train," "A Forest," "Play for Today," "Primary," "Other Voices," "Charlotte Sometimes," "The Hanging Garden," "Let's Go to Bed," "The Walk," "The Lovecats," "The Caterpillar," "In Between Days," "Close to Me," "A Night Like This."

Since their emergence in 1979, the Cure have proven to be one of Britain's most consistently unique and accomplished post-punk rock bands. As one can see and hear in this chronological clips compilation (well, not *quite* chronological: the songs are arranged that way, but some of the earlier tunes have clips shot in 1986 for this tape), based on the band's 1986 best-of LP, their music has grown from the taut, tingly minimalism of existential ditties such as "10:15 Saturday Night" through darkly enveloping drones such as "A Forest" to funkier, more fleshed-out, pop-savvy yet still distinctively jittery tunes such as "Let's Go to Bed" and "Close to Me." Throughout their career, however, the Cure have remained constant in their probing originality, intensity of focus, lean-and-hungry sound, and palpably wired psychological edge.

The music is more than pithy and listenable enough to virtually hold up this program by itself (especially considering the comprehensiveness of the selections), and while the videos are an uneven lot, there's enough good stuff here to make this a pretty strong program. (When the visuals *do* falter, there's always the music.) Most of the better videos were directed by Tim Pope, whose other well-known efforts include Men Without Hats' "Safety Dance," Bow Wow Wow's "Do You Wanna Hold Me," and Neil Young's "Wonderin'. " One of his best efforts here, the opening "Killing an Arab," works because of its restraint: the song is taken right out of the pages of Camus's novel *The Stranger*, thus perfectly setting the tone for the program's existential edge; the video is simply a series of stark black-and-white shots of a weathered old man aimlessly wandering around a wintry beachfront village—apparently living with the guilt, or deeply disturbing lack of guilt, caused by the murder he'd committed long before. Pope's "Boys Don't Cry" is also powerfully simple and quietly stunning, merely by having a surrogate band of young boys strum and lip-synch along to the plaintive pop ditty (probably the sweetest Cure song ever) while the real Cure cast their giant shadows behind the boys on an opaque screen (at the start, a title flashes on the screen reading "The Cure?")—the clip's magic is all in the poetic way Pope sets up his camera to catch the play of shadow-Cure off kiddie-Cure. Pope's "Let's Go to Bed" features self-deprecatingly comic shenanigans taking place in a domestic-Caligari set, while his "Close to Me" may be the best single clip here—it's a hilarious claustrophobia joke in which the whole four-man band is stuck inside a wardrobe closet (just ponder the implications of *that* vis-à-vis a British band in the '80s) perched precariously on the edge of a cliff. However, Pope's "The Lovecats" and "The Walk," while arguably complementary to the nervous auras of their songs, are also aggressively grotesque to the point of unwatchability. There's nothing retchingly gross, mind you, it's just that they wallow in unattractiveness beyond the point of redemption. Most of the rest are simply performance videos by other directors; Piers Bedford's "10:15 Saturday Night" is the best, while Mike Mansfield's moronic Surrealism 101 exercise for "Charlotte Sometimes" and Chris Gabrin's self-consciously bizarre *and* tritely literal-minded "The Hanging Garden" are the low points.

Throughout, however, there's a visual constant as riveting as the musical constant: Cure guitarist, vocalist, composer, and driving force Robert Smith—a frail, intellectual, at times vaguely androgynous and always slightly bizarre-looking little chap who remains magnetically charismatic as much because of as despite his obvious peculiarities and physical limitations. In clips like "A Forest," he has an appealingly self-conscious way of un-mugging for the camera, as if to deliberately parody the deadpan angst suggested by his music. Yet he also steals the show when he appears to be sincerely mugging it up the way he thinks rock stars are supposed to, as in "The Caterpillar." Smith somehow manages to project both casual sincerity and drolly ironic detachment, and is personally responsible for making these videos, all in all, as delightful to look at as the songs are to hear. Thanks largely to Smith and his singular presence, this is a Cure that really works—and one well worth taking.

D

☐ VARIOUS ARTISTS (THE SEX PISTOLS, OTHERS)
D.O.A.—A RIGHT OF PASSAGE
★★★★★

HarmonyVision/Vestron, 1981, 90 minutes
PRODUCED BY: Lech Kowalski
DIRECTED BY: Lech Kowalski
MUSIC FROM: Various albums by various artists.
SELECTIONS: The Sex Pistols: "Anarchy in the U.K.," "God Save the Queen," "Pretty Vacant," "Liar," "EMI," "Holiday in the Sun," "New York," "I Wanna Be Me"; Iggy Pop: "Nightclubbing," "Lust for Life"; X-Ray Spex: "Oh Bondage, Up Yours"; the Rich Kids: "Pretty Vacant"; Generation X: "Kiss Me Deadly"; the Clash: "Police and Thieves"; Sham 69: "Borstal Breakout," "Rip Off"; the Dead Boys: "I Wanna Be a Dead Boy"; Augustus Pablo: "A.P. Special."

Superb, outrageously powerful documentary on British punk rock band the Sex Pistols' first, last, and only U.S. tour—seven shows in 1978 that probably did more to break up the band than anything else. By juxtaposing gritty concert footage from a variety of cities (Atlanta and San Francisco stand out) with equally candid footage of Pistols-inspired bands from England (the Clash, Generation X, X-Ray Spex, Rich Kids, Sham 69), and America (Dead Boys), and obviously off-the-cuff interviews with punk fans and bemused regular folks on the streets, producer/director Kowalski makes it painfully obvious why British punk in its most virulent form hadn't a prayer of catching on in the United States, where the only popular minority music was disco. The movie's poster (which doubles as the cassette cover)—a dazed punkette lying wide-eyed on a street as a Rolls-Royce approaches her neck, a big safety pin through one tire—is a perfect metaphor for the inevitable self-destructiveness inherent in punk's uprising, and for the unvarnished way the film covers its demise. Particularly poignant are the scenes of pathetic would-be Brit-punks Terry and the Idiots trying and failing to make a go of punk's anyone-can-play ethos; somewhere beyond poignant and pathetic are the discomfiting scenes of Sid Vicious and his girlfriend, Nancy Spungen, who would both be dead before the film was released, alternately arguing and nodding out. *D.O.A.* makes a great, sobering counterpart to the equally recommended *Great Rock 'n' Roll Swindle.*

☐ VARIOUS ARTISTS
D-TV: GOLDEN OLDIES
★★★

Disney, 1984, 45 minutes
PRODUCED BY: Chuck Braverman
DIRECTED BY: Various
MUSIC FROM: Various albums by various artists.
SELECTIONS: The Supremes: "Baby Love"; Spike Jones: "Blue Danube," "Holiday for Strings"; Louis Prima and Keely Smith: "That Old Black Magic"; Marvin Gaye: "Can I Get a Witness"; Tennessee Ernie Ford: "Sixteen Tons"; Burl Ives: "Lavender Blue"; Smokey Robinson and the Miracles: "You Really Got a Hold On Me," "Mickey's Monkey"; Lena Horne: "Stormy Weather"; the Cadets: "Stranded in the Jungle"; Barrett Strong: "Money"; and others.

☐ VARIOUS ARTISTS
D-TV: POP AND ROCK
★★★

Disney, 1984, 45 minutes
PRODUCED BY: Chuck Braverman
DIRECTED BY: Various
MUSIC FROM: Various albums by various artists.
SELECTIONS: Martha and the

Vandellas: "Dancing in the Street"; Little Richard: "Tutti-Frutti," "Long Tall Sally"; Elvis Presley: "Stuck on You," "Hound Dog"; Stevie Wonder: "Uptight," "I Was Made to Love Her"; Johnny Burnette: "Dreamin' "; the Four Tops: "Reach Out (I'll Be There)"; Tommy Roe: "Dizzy"; the Diamonds: "Little Darlin' "; Danny and the Juniors: "At the Hop"; and others.

☐ **VARIOUS ARTISTS**
D-TV: ROCK, RHYTHM & BLUES
★★★

Disney, 1984, 45 minutes
PRODUCED BY: Chuck Braverman
DIRECTED BY: Various
MUSIC FROM: Various albums by various artists.
SELECTIONS: Hall and Oates: "Kiss on My List," "Private Eyes"; the Jackson Five: "Dancing Machine"; the Supremes: "Stop! In the Name of Love"; the Doobie Brothers: "It Keeps You Running"; Stevie Wonder: "Signed, Sealed, Delivered"; Marvin Gaye and Tammi Terrell: "Ain't No Mountain High Enough"; Jimmy Cliff: "Wonderful World, Beautiful People"; Gladys Knight and the Pips: "Friendship Train"; Burning Sensation: "Belly of the Whale"; Richard Thompson: "Two Left Feet"; and others.

☐ **VARIOUS ARTISTS**
D-TV: LOVE SONGS
★★½

Disney, 1985, 45 minutes
PRODUCED BY: Chuck Braverman
MUSIC FROM: Various albums by various artists.
SELECTIONS: Juice Newton: "Love's Been a Little Bit Hard on Me"; the Temptations: "Just My Imagination," "Ain't Too Proud to Beg"; Elvis Presley: "All Shook Up"; the Marvelettes: "Don't Mess with Bill," "Too Many Fish in the Sea"; Stevie Wonder: "My Cherie Amour"; Gene Chandler: "Duke of Earl"; the Drifters: "Some Kind of Wonderful"; Mary Wells: "Two Lovers"; Dee Clark: "Raindrops"; Otis Redding: "Try a Little Tenderness"; Yes: "Owner of a Lonely Heart"; Sister Sledge: "We Are Family."

Interesting approach to children's music video programming from The Mouse House. The tunes were obviously chosen to go with available vintage Disney cartoon footage, rather than the other way around, and in *Rock, Rhythm & Blues* especially that created some insurmountable problems in terms of synching appropriate visuals and sound. But, overall, what tunes! Someone at Disney had the exceptional and gratifying good taste to program most of these tapes with unbelievably listenable soundtracks. *Pop and Rock*, and *Rock, Rhythm & Blues* particularly are immaculately hip compendia of *Big Chill*–style, feel-good baby boomer epiphanies from the car radio of our collective memory.

Someone else at Disney—supervising producer Chuck Braverman, perhaps—had the smarts and sass to coolly mock MTV's station break promos (there are also on-screen song and artist IDs). For the kids these tapes are ostensibly aimed at, here's an entertaining and morally upright music video alternative to MTV-style sex and violence. Still, adults looking over the kids' shoulders at these won't help but notice that, even when the cartoons do synch cleverly with the music, Disney's trademark cuteness (*Love Songs* could kill a diabetic at ten paces) and painfully literal-minded visualizations trivialize completely any resonance the music may still have. Maybe Disney's crew just doesn't realize how hip little kids really are these days. But then, what does it say for the rest of the people making music videos when Disney has two of the greatest-sounding various-artists clip collections around?

☐ **THE CHARLIE DANIELS BAND**
THE SARATOGA CONCERT
★★★½

CBS/Fox, 1982, 75 minutes

PRODUCED BY: Richard Namm
DIRECTED BY: Richard Namm
MUSIC FROM: Various Charlie Daniels Band albums; 1981 HBO cable-TV special.
SELECTIONS: "In America," "Ain't No Ramblers Anymore," "Lonesome Boy from Dixie," "Legend of the Wooley Swamp," "Reflections," "The Lady in Red," "Sweet Home Alabama," "Carolina," "Makes You Want to Go Home," "The Devil Went Down to Georgia," "The South's Gonna Do It Again," "Orange Blossom Special," "Amazing Grace," "Will the Circle Be Unbroken."
Also available on CBS/Fox Stereo Laser videodisc.

Though this HBO cable-TV special was shot in upstate New York, the Saratoga Performing Arts Center is an amphitheater carved right out of the picturesque Ichabod Crane territory, and thus a perfect setting for Daniels's own rural, mythopoetic Americana ("The Devil Went Down to Georgia," "Legend of the Wooley Swamp"—which is intercut with a concept video telling its crime-caper narrative). As for Daniels's rebel-rousing anthems ("The South's Gonna Do It Again," Lynyrd Skynyrd's "Sweet Home Alabama") and classic Southern-styled rockaboogie ("Reflections" is a tribute to Duane Allman, Skynyrd's late Ronnie Van Zandt, Elvis—all them Southern rock pioneers), well, they might *seem* out of place in New York State, but you'd never know it from the wildly appreciative, stars-and-bars waving throng, It's all shot competently enough to be perfect for the Daniels fan, and a perfect introduction for the curious.

☐ **VARIOUS ARTISTS**
DANSPAK
★

Sony, 1983, 20 minutes
PRODUCED BY: Merrill Aldighieri and Joe Tripician
DIRECTED BY: Merrill Aldighieri and Joe Tripician
MUSIC FROM: Various albums by various artists.
SELECTIONS: Man Parrish: "Hip Hop BeBop (Don't Stop)": Shox Lumania: "Falling," "Pointy Headgear"; Richard Bone: "Alien Girl"; Living: "Boat Talk."

☐ **VARIOUS ARTISTS**
DANSPAK II
★ ½

Sony, 1984, 30 minutes
PRODUCED BY: Merrill Aldighieri and Joe Tripician
DIRECTED BY: Merrill Aldighieri and Joe Tripician
MUSIC FROM: Various albums by various artists.
SELECTIONS: Jim Carroll Band: "Sweet Jane"; Lenny Kaye Connection: "I've Got a Right"; Strange Party: "Imitators"; Michael Musto and the Must: "Jimmie, Gimme Your Love"; Go Ohgami: "Kids on the Street"; Jason Harvey : "Easy Street."

Both tapes are attempts at "alternative" music video clips that fall quite flat for the most part. Aldighieri and Tripician are video artists from New York's underground avant-garde scene, and the performers are from the same self-consciously "artistic" netherworld. The use of super-fast time-lapse imagery through most of *Danspak* is "interesting" at first, but eventually commits the unpardonable sin of becoming every bit as dull and pretentious as mainstream music video's most vapid clichés. And the unspectacular music doesn't help.

Danspak II is mostly more of the same. New York City gossip columnist Michael Musto (with *Rolling Stone* editor Brant Mewborn among his backup singers) stands out by default with an acceptable Motown homage accompanied by a clumsily cute video. But the best clip in the bunch (actually the only decent one) is Jim Carroll's "Sweet Jane," with a nicely done board-game motif and a guest appearance by the song's composer, Lou Reed—who, like Carroll, is a New York City poet who also happens to make rock 'n' roll (though Lou does it infinitely better than Carroll does).

☐ VARIOUS ARTISTS
DANSPAK 3: FUTURE POP
★★★

Sony, 1986, 28 minutes
PRODUCED BY: Merrill Aldighieri and Joe Tripician
DIRECTED BY: Merrill Aldighieri and Joe Tripician
MUSIC FROM: Various albums by various artists.
SELECTIONS: Carl Anderson: "Buttercup"; Jason Harvey: "In Hollywood"; Prince Charles: "Skintight Tina"; the Ordinaires: "Grace," "Industry"; Go Ohgami: "Sleeping the Town."

Danspak 3 is by far the most successful of the series, with Aldighieri and Tripician finally getting it together and really living up to all the video-art hype. In fact, Jason Harvey's "In Hollywood," a sequel to his *Danspak II* clip, is the only real dud: its cartoonish sendup of a tinseltown *soirée* quickly devolves into a dumb deca-dance. Carl Anderson's "Buttercup," a nice little soul-pop song written by Stevie Wonder, adds time-lapse footage with clothes and drawers that's rhythmically incisive and witty to a sweetly romantic scenario that's right in the black-pop tradition. Prince Charles's "Skintight Tina" is taut, sexy, faster-than-usual dance-funk music, with an engagingly sexy, fun video illustrating the singer's double life as singer and record-plant assembly-line worker. The Ordinaires, from Manhattan's Lower East Side, play a fractured, angular-yet-refined chamber-style fusion of classical, jazz, and rock; "Grace" is a bit overly arty, with its oddly shot performance footage and time-lapse dadaisms, but "Industry" is very good, using digital screen-division and other high-tech tricks to deconstruct Manhattan into a geometric, psychedelic abstract (and, along with "Skintight Tina," contains the tape's wittiest moments). Japanese singer Go Ohgami's "Sleeping the Town" is a strange, schmaltzy country-pop tune sung mostly in operatic Japanese (go figure), but the video is a beautifully shot, affectingly atmospheric, dreamily sleazoid urban dance of desire. *Danspak 3* isn't a must-have by any stretch, but compared to its predecessors, it's a masterpiece.

☐ RAY DAVIES
RETURN TO WATERLOO
★★★½

RCA/Columbia, 1986, 60 minutes
PRODUCED BY: Dennis Woolf
DIRECTED BY: Ray Davies
MUSIC FROM: The film *Return to Waterloo* (Waterloo Films/New Line Cinema 1985); *Return to Waterloo* motion picture soundtrack (Arista, 1985).
SELECTIONS: "Return to Waterloo," "The Ladder of Success," "Going Solo," "Have You Seen This Face?," "Sold Me Out," "Please Come Home," "The Empire Is Dying," "Not Far Away."

Return to Waterloo had a brief theatrical run in the United States several months prior to its home-video release. When it first appeared, its title no doubt made Kinks fans think of one of Ray Davies's greatest songs, the Kinks' 1967 classic "Waterloo Sunset," one of the most heartbreakingly tender and romantic hymns of melancholy resignation in rock. In fact, *Return to Waterloo* has only the most tangential connection to that song: if anything, it's an overwhelmingly downcast riposte from an older, wiser, and obviously much sadder Davies to the perhaps naïvely hopeful younger Davies who could croon "Waterloo Sunset."

Waterloo is fiction, but it's told

realistically. Written and directed by Davies—who appears only very briefly at the beginning and end as a street-singer in the Waterloo train station—it's basically a day in the life of a British rail commuter (well played by Ken Colley) whose teenage daughter has run away from home, and who may or may not be a most-wanted rapist (as newspaper headlines show us). Somewhat courageously, Davies goes beyond this Hitchcockian motif to leave the commuter's guilt or innocence completely open to question. Ultimately, then, the plot becomes a platform from which Davies relaunches his traditional themes: encroaching modernity and its attendant alienation and anomie vs. the quaint comforts of familiar tradition; the twilight of the British Empire; his addiction to the bittersweet taste of nostalgia; and so on.

Davies does a fairly solid job of accomplishing all this, by relying on the most tried-and-true of movie-musical conventions: rather than resorting to promo-clip–style quick-cut montages set to assembly-line pop, he has characters break right out into song in the midst of the action, the lyrics manifesting their inner thoughts and feelings as well as the story's subtexts. The songs—all but three of which are sung by cast members, with musical backing by Davies and all the rest of the Kinks except his brother Dave (Ray sings the other three, including the title track, himself)—advance or comment on the action, or both, but are never marketing-ploy afterthoughts. Musically and lyrically, they have the classic earmarks of the Kinks' music-hall–rock meld and subjective social comment—but some are also marred by the long-winded preachiness of the Kinks' uneven *Preservation* rock operas.

But when it works, it works brilliantly. Most effective are a pair of scenes involving Colley with some sullenly arrogant young punks in his railway car. In the first, Colley's eyeing them warily across the aisle, when suddenly their boom-box erupts with the nasty self-righteous vitriol of "Sold Me Out." Later, upper-class-twit businessmen and veterans of the wars in "Eenja" fire back with the desperately plaintive choruses of "The Empire Is Dying," and the punks respond with the sneering "Not Far Away"; as Davies has the punks and the old farts trading choruses back at each other with ever-increasing intensity, the sequence gets about as powerful as a traditionally structured rock musical ever could. On the other hand, "Going Solo," about a runaway daughter as seen through her parents' rather self-righteous and less-than-understanding eyes, comes off as an inferior gloss on the Beatles' classic "She's Leaving Home."

Overall, though, *Return to Waterloo* is quite remarkable in its artistic discipline, considering it's Davies's first go at near-feature-length filmmaking. Then again, considering Davies's track record as one of rock's most accomplished thespians (going all the way back to the Kinks' "Dead End Street" video in 1965), not to mention his pioneering behind-the-camera efforts at musical-visual synergy with his late-'60s soundtracks for the British TV-movie *Arthur* and the theatrical film *Percy,* it shouldn't surprise that he's turned in such an accomplished directorial debut. However, it should also be pointed out that for many, *Return to Waterloo* may prove to be *too* artistically disciplined: it's a *relentlessly* bleak and downbeat movie, adamantly refusing to crack a smile or let its audience off easy. But Davies wasn't just being doggedly faithful to his suspicious-of-progress muse by so convincingly portraying both personal and communal quiet desperation in

Return to Waterloo. He was also being painfully true to his subject: at the time this was made, at least, England was hardly swinging—unless one meant by the end of a rope.

□ MILES DAVIS QUINTET WITH THE GIL EVANS ORCHESTRA THE SOUND OF MILES DAVIS

★★★★★

Tokei Japan/Instant Replay (videodisc) and Playings Hard to Get, 1986, 27 minutes

DIRECTED BY: Jack Smight

MUSIC FROM: Miles Ahead (Columbia, 1957); *Kind of Blue* (Columbia, 1958); 1959 episode of the TV show *Robert Herridge Theater.*

SELECTIONS: "So What," "The Duke," "Blues for Pablo," "New Rhumba."

Also available on Tokei/Instant Replay Laser videodisc.

Taken from an episode of an obscure 1959 TV show, *The Sound of Miles Davis* captures one of jazz's all-time masters at the peak of his form and does so with an incredibly apt and unobtrusive estheticism that makes this a magnificent time capsule of '50s cool-jazz hipsterism *and* a transcendent, timeless artifact. Jack Smight, an accomplished director of early live television, shoots the performance in "behind the scenes" fashion in a stark television studio—the cameras, dolly tracks, lighting rigs, and other studio hardware are clearly visible (perhaps in deference to the perceived unvarnished artistic "truth" of jazz?)—swathed in a powerfully atmospheric chiaroscuro that looks so ravishing in black and white it's enough to make you glad color TV hadn't been invented yet.

And what a performance Smight captured. The program opens with the Miles Davis Quintet, easily one of the most influential jazz units of all time, playing the post-bop classic "So What" from the landmark album *Kind of Blue*. I'm not aware of any other footage of this group on video; but even more incredibly, this particular edition of the Quintet happens to include the late great John Coltrane on tenor sax—not to mention Wynton Kelly on piano, Paul Chambers on bass, and Jimmy Cobb on drums. Jazz fans need know no more, but for those who've never had the pleasure of hearing this music, it's tautly balanced, elegantly poised, soft yet penetrating, gorgeous but not prettified . . . it's immaculate. Following the superb, too-brief "So What," Davis and his trumpet join the Gil Evans Orchestra for three pieces from their then-current *Miles Ahead* LP. Here, the music turns sumptuous and heavenly, with Davis sighing and stretching in languid lyricism over Evans's lush, viscously flowing charts. Throughout, Smight's understated *mise en scène* (yes, it looks good enough to hold up to that term, even if this *is* TV) never gets in the way of the music, just subtly complements it.

Jazz music doesn't come any better than this. Neither does jazz video. It figures this is a Japanese release available here only as a mail order import. (Cassette available by mail order from Playings Hard to Get; videodisc available by mail order from Instant Replay.)

□ VARIOUS ARTISTS THE DECLINE . . . OF WESTERN CIVILIZATION

★★★★

Media, 1982, 105 minutes

PRODUCED BY: Gordon Brown and Jeff Prettyman

DIRECTED BY: Penelope Spheeris

MUSIC FROM: Various albums and singles by various artists; *The Decline . . . of Western Civilization* soundtrack (Slash, 1980).

SELECTIONS: Black Flag: "White Minority," "Depression," "Revenge";

Germs: "Manimal"; Catholic Discipline: "Underground Babylon"; X: "Beyond and Back," "Johnny Hit and Run Pauline," "We're Desperate"; Fear: "Beef Bologna," "Let's Have a War," "I Love Livin' in the City"; and others, including Circle Jerks, Alice Bag Band.

Fine, unflinching documentary of L.A.'s late-'70s punk rock scene, with Penelope Spheeris capturing not only the bands in action, but at home (X are friendly and nice; Darby Crash of the Germs, who later died of a heroin overdose, sits in a mumbling stupor in the kitchen, waking occasionally to fondle his pet tarantula). Spheeris also gets up close and personal with "regular" punk kids who follow the bands, such as Eugene, the terminally dumb skinhead punker whom she poetically shoots next to a dangling, naked lightbulb. One of the highlights is Fear, the gay-baiting San Francisco punk rockers, one of whose members was Lee Ving, who went on to star in movies like *Flashdance* and *Get Crazy;* their black-humored stage presence is hilarious. Overall, the impression one gets of the L.A. punk scene is, as the film's title indicates, that of a pathetic, dying culture, many times removed from meaning and reality, consuming itself in a perverse outburst of petulant entropy. However, bands like X and Black Flag manage to rise above their roots in this nowhere scene and make something more of them—something called grrreat rock 'n' roll.

☐ STEVE DEFURIA
SECRETS OF ANALOG AND DIGITAL SYNTHESIS

★★★★

DCI, 1985, 120 minutes
PRODUCED BY: SynthArts
DIRECTED BY: Joe Scacciaferro

DeFuria has programmed synthesizers for Frank Zappa, Stevie Wonder, and Lee Ritenour among others, and in this in-depth tape he seems well qualified indeed to explain the dizzyingly complex ins and outs of getting the sounds you want out of those daunting, high-tech machines. DeFuria covers both the older analog synths (e.g., Mini-Moogs and ARP Odysseys) *and* the newer digital synths (e.g., Yamaha DX7, Korg Poly800, Sequential Circuits Prophet). In simple, no-nonsense style, DeFuria shows you special techniques for both studio and stage performance with synthesizers, delves into the various nuances of different manufacturers' synths, and devotes special attention to programming Yamaha's DX7, which is probably *the* most popular newfangled digital synth in the world (at least, as of this writing; the way *this* area of high-tech goes, things get obsolete every other week). (Available by mail order from DCI Music Video.)

☐ VARIOUS ARTISTS
DÉJÀ VIEW

★★½

Karl-Lorimar, 1986, 50 minutes
PRODUCED BY: Joel Gallen
DIRECTED BY: Various
MUSIC FROM: Various albums by various artists.
SELECTIONS: The Rascals: "Good Lovin' "; the Zombies: "She's Not There"; Don McLean: "American Pie"; the Box Tops: "The Letter"; the Temptations: "I Can't Get Next to You"; Lesley Gore: "It's My Party"; the Beach Boys: "Don't Worry Baby"; Procol Harum: "A Whiter Shade of Pale"; the Hollies: "Bus Stop"; Sly and the Family Stone: "Everyday People"; John Sebastian, Ronnie Spector, Felix Cavaliere, Roger McGuinn, Richard Manuel: "You and Me Go Way Back."

Déjà View combines post-MTV video clips with fondly remembered '60s—and in the case of "American Pie," '70s—hits (with the exception of "You and

Me Go Way Back," which was recorded and shot in 1985 for this program). Some were shot by veteran video directors such as Stuart Orme ("American Pie"), David Hogan ("A Whiter Shade of Pale"), and Dominic Sena ("Bus Stop"); some by movie-makers like Tommy (*Halloween III*) Wallace ("Don't Worry Baby"), Jeremy (*The Journey of Natty Gann*) Kagen ("Everyday People"), and *Grease 2* director/choreographer Patricia Birch ("It's My Party"); and the rest by other notables (actor Bob Balaban directed "She's Not There"). Almost without exception, these newly minted clips are technically impeccable, with lavish production values. Most of them feature the original artists, or one or more members of the original groups, in cameo or featured roles, and many have name guest starts (Michael Pare of *Eddie and the Cruisers* and *Streets of Fire* in "The Letter"; Hollywood character actor Harry Dean Stanton in "A Whiter Shade of Pale"; Bronson Pinchot of *Beverly Hills Cop* and TV's *Perfect Strangers* in "I Can't Get Next to You"; Terri Garr in "She's Not There"; most of the cast of TV's *St. Elsewhere* in "Good Lovin' ").

Yet, as good-looking as most of these clips are, they're also pretty boring and useless—either pointlessly literal-minded, or self-consciously "bizarre" and "surreal" in that overdressed, cinema-chic way that's typical of too many rock videos, especially the kind that are so often accused of robbing people of their imaginations. Most of the people who would even care to see *Déjà View*—those who grew up when these songs were first hits—must have all manner of real-life experiences associated with these sounds. Do they really need to have those memories trampled by strained slapstick, cloyingly cute "comedy," and silly sub–*Twilight Zone* scenarios? *Déjà View:* an interesting idea, perhaps, but now you know why nobody ever thought of it before.

☐ VARIOUS ARTISTS
DEL MERO CORAZÓN (LOVE SONGS OF THE SOUTHWEST)
★★★★½

Brazos Films, 1980, 28 minutes

PRODUCED BY: Chris Strachwitz

DIRECTED BY: Les Blank

MUSIC FROM: Del Mero Corazon motion picture soundtrack (Arhoolie, 1976); *Love Songs of the Southwest* (Arhoolie, 1976).

SELECTIONS: Ricardo Mejia and Ruben Valdez: "Seis Pies Abajo"; Los Madrugafores: "La Zenaida"; Andres Berlanga: "Las Quejas de Zenaida"; Conjunto Tamalipas: "Camioncito Pasajero," "Al Pie de la Tumba," "El Troquero"; Leo Garza and His Conjunto: "En Cada Vida un Momento"; Chavela Ortiz: "Quiero Que Sepas"; Chavela Ortiz and Brown Express: "Besos Y Copas"; Little Joe and La Familia: "Las Nubes."

A lovely, lyrical little counterpart to Les Blank's award-winning *Chulas Fronteras, Del Mero Corazón* looks at the romantic side of this rich Chicano subculture through the folkloric love songs of the region. They, and those who perform them, are full of passion and humor, pain and nobility. Time and again—while also tracing how these songs pass through the community, and down through generations, always changing but retaining their aching essence—Blank dares you to think these artists and their music are corny. But their unpretentious sincerity blows away any such skepticism, easily living up to the title's English translation. Subtly, we are led to realize that as unpretentious as they are, these songs are also a medium for the poetry of daily life—the daily life of a vibrant culture that's worth getting to know for a too-short twenty-eight minutes. (Available by mail order from Flower Films.)

□ DEPECHE MODE
SOME GREAT VIDEOS
★★½

Warner Reprise, 1986, 51 minutes
DIRECTED BY: Clive Richardson and Peter Care
MUSIC FROM: Various Depeche Mode albums (Sire/Warner Bros., 1981–86).
SELECTIONS: "Just Can't Get Enough," "Everything Counts," "Love in Itself," "People Are People," "Master and Servant," "Blasphemous Rumours," "Somebody," "Shake the Disease," "It's Called a Heart," "Photographic," "A Question of Lust."

Some Great Videos has quite a title to live up to—and it doesn't. Clive Richardson, who did such a nice job on *Live in Hamburg,* directed all but two of the clips in this compilation (one of them, "Photographic," is from *Live in Hamburg*), and almost all of his videos have the exact same style: band performance superimposed over sundry other footage (traveling road footage in "Everything Counts," the band in a cavern in "Love in Itself," found war footage in "People Are People," and so on). It works better at some times than others, and overall it's, well, okay. But by no means can these videos be called great. Same goes for Peter Care's two clips: "Shake the Disease" is straight performance with weird camera angles and movements; "It's Called a Heart" finds the band carrying bizarre neotribal masks as they stalk through a cornfield (stalk? cornfield? is this a visual pun or something?). None of the clips are that *bad,* either, mind you. The Depeche Mode fan will certainly enjoy it, and it's not a bad sampler for non-fans—the opening "Just Can't Get Enough" and the closing "A Question of Lust," the two most overtly romantic songs here from this wordy but accomplished and rather charming band, are the musical standouts, with "People Are People" and "Blasphemous Rumours" close behind, and the rest not trailing by much. Once again, Depeche Mode prove themselves one of Britain's better synth-pop bands.

□ DEPECHE MODE
THE WORLD WE LIVE IN AND LIVE IN HAMBURG
★★★★

Warner Reprise, 1986, 57 minutes
PRODUCED BY: Melissa Stokes
DIRECTED BY: Clive Richardson
MUSIC FROM: Speak and Spell (Sire, 1981); *A Broken Frame* (Sire, 1982); *Construction Time Again* (Sire, 1983); *Some Great Reward* (Sire, 1984); *People Are People* (Sire, 1984).
SELECTIONS: "Something to Do." "If You Want," "People Are People," "Somebody," "Lie to Me," "Blasphemous Rumours," "Told You So," "Master and Servant," "Everything Counts," "Just Can't Get Enough."

One of Britain's first and best new wave synth-pop/electro-dance bands, Depeche Mode (translated literally from French, their name means "hurry fashion") make music that's at once direct, minimal, melodic, and danceable on one hand, and sophisticated, experimental, and darkly ironic on the other. There's also a form of black humor in the music, when singer David Gahan flatly delivers lyrics like "People are people so why should it be / You and I would get along so awfully?" or "I don't want to start any blasphemous rumours / But I think that God's got a sick sense of humor / And when I die I expect to find him laughing." (Okay, so they're a little wordy, but what do you expect from a bunch of British technoids?) The point is, there's some depth and invention to be discovered here. And in shooting Depeche Mode live in

Hamburg, Germany, in 1985, director Clive Richardson has done a smashing job of capturing the natural theater of their stage act. They don't just stand numbly at keyboards, but also clang hammers against anvils and strike hanging sheets of corrugated metal to form pointillistic rhythm vamps (especially well done in "Blasphemous Rumours"). Using simple, architectonic close-ups, starkly powerful lighting, sharply composed superimpositions, and an editing rhythm as sophisticated as the band's arrangements, Richardson not only elegantly documents Depeche Mode's ritualistic, self-absorbed intensity in performance, but draws viewers—both fans *and* the casually curious—into it as well. The program ends on an upbeat note with the marvelous pure pop love song "Just Can't Get Enough," one of the catchiest ditties of British electro-pop.

□ DER PLAN
EVOLUTION

★★★½

Import, 1984, 40 minutes

MUSIC FROM: Geri Reig (Atatak Germany, 1982); *Normalette Surprise* (Atatak Germany, 1983); *Evolution* (Atatak Germany, 1984).

SELECTIONS: "Gummitwist," "Ich Bin Ein Computer," "Alte Pizza."

Adventurous fans of avant-garde postmodern electronic new-wave rock with a playfully sardonic edge might want to check out this import concert tape of Germany's answer to the Residents, caught live in Japan. Der Plan is a Dusseldorf-based trio whose music can range from nursery-rhyme tuneful simplicity to daunting atonal noise—but it's always organized in an almost theatrical way that ends up making it slyly insinuating after a few listenings. Indeed, theatricality is a key with Der Plan, for like the Residents, they are as creative visually as aurally, with stunning costumes and stage sets that honorably update Germany's proud Bauhaus heritage. Though you might have to know the German language to fathom the lyrics of "Ich Bin Ein Computer (I Am a Computer)", you don't need a translator to know that Der Plan are chiding stereotypical Germans, in this case via Kraftwerk. But then, that's to be expected of a band whose first recordings (made before they knew how to play instruments; they taped ambient noise, edited and looped it, and made it sound like music!) included the charming "Da Vorne Steht ne Ampel" ("Over There Stands a Traffic Light"), which was all about the seemingly inbred German habit of *always* obeying traffic lights—stopping for a red even at 4 A.M. when there's not another car in sight. For those who dare, this tape is a chance well worth taking. (Available by mail order from Playings Hard to Get.)

□ RICK DERRINGER
ROCK SPECTACULAR

★★

Sony, 1983, 58 minutes

PRODUCED BY: Jake Hooker and Jeanne Suggs

DIRECTED BY: Tom Lupo and George Harrison

MUSIC FROM: Various albums by various artists.

SELECTIONS: Rick Derringer: "Easy Action," "Rock 'n' Roll Hoochie Koo," "Party at the Hotel"; Karla DeVito: "Is this a Cool World or What?," "Just Like You"; Southside Johnny: "Honey Hush," "Five Long Years"; Carmine Appice: "Have You Heard"; Tim Bogert: "Lady"; Ted Nugent: "Cat Scratch Fever," "Oh, Carol"; Ensemble: "Hang On Sloopy."

Also available on Pioneer Stereo Laser videodisc.

Onetime leader of the McCoys (whose "Hang on Sloopy" closes the program) later with Edgar Winter in the mid-

’70s, a record producer (bringing us gems like *The Wrestling Album*) and, as of 1986, a member of Cyndi Lauper’s band, Derringer is a competent enough rock guitarist and producer. He seems like a pretty nice guy, but hosting this 1982 show with an assortment of special guests at the Ritz in New York City, Derringer fails to show enough in the way of talent or inspiration to make this an exciting or interesting program. Ditto his guests, though Ted Nugent is in his usual lunatic form, and thus more diverting than anyone else. Derringer’s shortcomings as a guitarist are brought out during the two numbers with drummer Carmine Appice and bassist Tim Bogert, where they try to re-create something like the sound of the power trio Bogert and Appice had with Jeff Beck. Elsewhere, Karla DeVito enters twirling a parasol, as if she had just walked over from Broadway, where she had been appearing at the time in *The Pirates of Penzance. Yawn.*

□ RICK DERRINGER
SECRETS
★★★

DCI, 1985, 40 minutes
PRODUCED BY: Jake Hooker and Mark Sayous
DIRECTED BY: Mark Sayous
MUSIC FROM: All American Boy (Blue Sky, 1973).
SELECTIONS: “Rock & Roll Hoochie Koo,” “I Play Guitar.”

Veteran rock guitarist Derringer’s career goes back to the mid-’60s, when his band the McCoys topped the charts with the immortal “Hang On Sloopy,” to the ’80s, when he played on and produced *The Wrestling Album.* Here, he’s in an intimate setting, and is slickly shot as he gives tips and pointers on soloing, guitar scales, exercises to build endurance, and “chops” (sort of the musician’s jargon for learned, as opposed to natural, ability), and performs a couple of his better-known tunes with his band. Derringer comes across as a nice guy, and there’s something here to be learned by beginning and intermediate guitarists. (Available by mail order from DCI Music Video.)

□ DEVO
THE MEN WHO MAKE THE MUSIC
★★★★★

Warner Home Video, 1979, 55 minutes
PRODUCED BY: Devo, Inc.
DIRECTED BY: Chuck Statler and Gerald V. Casale
MUSIC FROM: Q: Are We Not Men? A: We Are Devo! (Warner Bros., 1978); *Duty Now for the Future* (Warner Bros., 1979).
SELECTIONS: “Jocko Homo,” “Secret Agent Man,” “Satisfaction,” “The Day My Baby Gave Me a Surprize,” “Come Back Jonee,” “Devo Corporate Anthem,” “Uncontrollable Urge,” “Wiggly World,” “Praying Hands,” “Smart Patrol/Mr. DNA,” “Red Eye.”

□ DEVO
WE’RE ALL DEVO
★★★★★

Sony, 1983, 60 minutes
PRODUCED BY: Chuck Statler
DIRECTED BY: Gerald V. Casale
MUSIC FROM: Q: Are We Not Men? A: We Are Devo!, Duty Now for the Future, Freedom of Choice, New Traditionalists, Oh, No It’s Devo (Warner Bros., 1978–82); *Dr. Detroit* (1982); *Human Highway* (NR).
SELECTIONS: “Satisfaction,” “The Day My Baby Gave Me a Surprize,” “Worried Man,” “Whip It,” “Girl U Want,” “Freedom of Choice,” “Beautiful World,” “Through Being Cool,” “Love Without Anger,” “Peek-a-Boo,” “That’s Good,” “Theme from *Dr. Detroit,*” “Jocko Homo.”
Also available on Pioneer Stereo Laser videodisc

Two outstanding clips-compilations-and-more from rock video’s original masters. The pioneering Spud Boys made the first such home rock-video program with *The Men Who Make the Music,* which neatly ties together their earliest clips, concert footage of the yellow-suited show that set the rock world on its eye and ear in the late '70s, de-evolutionary propaganda, and vicious rock-biz satire featuring extra players like New York actor Michael Swartz, brilliant as venal record exec Rod Rooter, and Robert Mothersbaugh, Sr. (father of Devo's Mark and Bob Mothersbaugh), as General Boy, Devo's benignly senile, vaguely paramilitary corporate figurehead.

We're All Devo finds Laraine Newman (Mark Mothersbaugh's girlfriend at the time) and Timothy Leary (!) joining Swartz in the connective scenes, and has a more comprehensive collection of Devo's masterful, technically and conceptually advanced, blackly seriocomic video clips. But *The Men Who Make the Music* has all that concert footage, and its between-clips scenes are funnier. Then again, *We're All Devo* has such rarities as "Worried Man," from Neil Young's never-released antinuke musical *Human Highway*. Since only a minimum of material is duplicated between the two programs, let's call it a toss-up and say that both are, in their own ways, remarkably funny, thought-provoking, entertaining, and highly recommended.

□ DEXY'S MIDNIGHT RUNNERS
THE BRIDGE

★★★½

RCA/Columbia, 1983, 52 minutes
DIRECTED BY: Steve Barron
MUSIC FROM: Too-Rye-Ay (Polydor, 1982).
SELECTIONS: "Old," "All in All," "Let's Make This Precious," "Respect," "Jackie Wilson Said," "Until I Believe in My Soul," "Kevin Rowland's Band," "Come On Eileen," "Celtic Soul Brothers."

This is not the original, 1980 Stax/Volt tribute-band version of Dexy's Midnight Runners; this is the 1982 reincarnation of the British band live in London, with only leader Kevin Rowland remaining—now dressed in *Hee Haw* wardrobe rejects, mixing the fatback horns of old with country-rockabilly and Irish traditional jigs and reels (with fiddles, concertinas, banjoes). It's an unlikely but rather bewitching sound, especially on the hit single "Come On Eileen." As the scruffy leader of this scruffy band, Rowland is an oddly intense, possessed presence, trying mightily to get as deep Into the Mystic as the Irish soul brother he's obviously emulating, Van Morrison (who originally recorded "Jackie Wilson Said," and whose "Until I Believe in My Soul" is the model for Dexy's version). Sometimes he strains way too hard, but just as often—e.g., "Let's Make This Precious"—he improvises some fairly riveting theatrical moments. And Steve Barron captures it all with gorgeous camerawork.

□ DENNIS DeYOUNG
THREE PIECE SUITE

★★★½

A&M, 1986, 20 minutes
PRODUCED BY: Paul Flattery and Tammara Wells
DIRECTED BY: Jack Cole
MUSIC FROM: Desert Moon (A&M, 1985); *Back to the World* (A&M, 1986).
SELECTIONS: "Desert Moon," "Don't Wait for Heroes," "Call Me."

Erstwhile Styx vocalist DeYoung applies only a modicum of his original band's neo-art-rock pomposity to his solo albums, and the result is a more listenable, intimate, and romantic form of modestly majestic pop rock. It meshes well with the directorial style of Jack Cole, who with clips like these three has become the Frank Capra of music video—a master of short-form sentimentality, with the narrative and character-development skills to craft genuine mini-movies that (for most people at least) are ultimately as moving as they are corny. Going back to Philip Bailey's "I Know" in 1982, Cole was one of the first rock video *auteurs* to make use of dialogue a constant in his clips. He uses it well, too, although in doing so Cole sometimes relegates the songs he's visualizing to distant background soundtracks for his own concepts. Here, DeYoung's music, pleasant as it may be, is far too bland and insubstantial to resist being overshadowed by Cole's strikingly effective deployment of rich production values and heartstring-tugging emotionalism.

That said, "Desert Moon" remains an affectingly bittersweet exercise in small-town, you-can't-go-home-again nostalgia; "Don't Wait for Heroes" uses a rock talent contest scenario to transform music-biz hopes and dreams into a go-for-it celebration; and "Call Me" is closest to most music videos in dropping dialogue completely, and focusing on DeYoung's performance of the song, with a band in a nondescript little bar while it pours outside. It's almost effortlessly effective at creating a Hopperesque (as in Edward) mood of melancholy and loneliness against its rain-spattered urban backdrop, and that mood does a lot to enhance what is really a very slight, Billy Joel–ish song.

All three clips are beautifully produced, and since they're all the work of the same director, they work together quite well. Recommended most highly to DeYoung fans, of course; but even if you don't care for the music, you've got to admire the care and quality of the videos.

□ NEIL DIAMOND

LOVE AT THE GREEK

★★★½

Vestron, 1977, 52 minutes

PRODUCED BY: Gary Smith and Dwight Hemion

DIRECTED BY: Dwight Hemion

MUSIC FROM: Various Neil Diamond albums including *Love at the Greek* (Columbia, 1977).

SELECTIONS: "Cherry, Cherry," "Sweet Caroline," "Play Me," "Beautiful Noise," "Street Life," "Lady Oh," "If You Know What I Mean," "Song Sung Blue," "Cracklin' Rosie," "Holly Holy," "I Am . . . I Said," "Brother Love's Traveling Salvation Show."

Also available on Vestron Stereo Laser videodisc.

Sure, it's schmaltzy—especially when Neil drags Henry Winkler out of the audience and, prancing in delight the whole while, forces him to sing "Song Sung Blue" as the Fonz would've. But Dwight Hemion's direction of this 1976 TV special is not only highly competent but also surprisingly tasteful. And you'd have to be crazy not to admit that Neil Diamond has written a hell of a lot of amazingly good songs, and that most of them are here. Cynics are advised to sit through this before dismissing Diamond out of hand; in the battle between Neil's camp-showbiz style and the timeless substance of his songs, the quality of those tunes wins. What helps a lot is that while Neil himself may deliver them with all the shlocky Vegas intensity he can muster, Robbie Robertson of the Band is supervising the sound (note that Neil was one of the Band's guests in *The Last Waltz*?).

□ MANU DIBANGO

KING MAKOSSA

★★★½

VIEW, 1985, 55 minutes

PRODUCED BY: Lagoon Productions

DIRECTED BY: Phillippe Antoine

MUSIC FROM: Various Manu Dibango albums including *Soul Makossa* (Atlantic, 1972).

SELECTIONS: "Soul Makossa,"

"Marabout," "Bokilo Boogie," "Ma Marie," "Manu's Rhythm," "Waka Juju," "Mangabolo."

Most people probably know Cameroonian Dibango as a saxophonist, from his 1972 hit "Soul Makossa," one of the first relatively uncut pieces of African pop music to become a hit in the United States. So it may be a surprise to see Dibango open this December 1981 Brussels, Belgium, concert with a great *marimba* solo that leads into "Soul Makossa," before he picks up his tenor sax. From there, Dibango and his eight-piece ensemble cruise through supple grooves that meld traditional and modern African music with influences from jazz and jazz-funk fusion. Some of Dibango's more fusion-oriented material gets a little tepid here and there, but generally there's enough piquancy and polyrhythms to keep things at least mildly interesting. Aside from the opener, the high point is "Bokilo Boogie," which despite its title is basically the distinctive ring of Afro-pop's juju and Congo guitars over an effervescent, bouncing rhythm that's half Afro-pop highlife and half calypso. By the same token, "Waka Juju" isn't really juju at all; it's more like Afro-Latin "Cubop," with a staccato melody line slightly reminiscent of the spidery runs in King Sunny Adé's juju music. Director Antoine does a pretty classy job most of the way through, though his inserts of super-slo-mo shots of the various musicians and singers onstage can annoy. The Hi-Fi Stereo sound itself is lovely, but the *original* sound recording on the program has the band sounding frustratingly thin and distant at times, as if it were a remote recording, instead of one taken directly from the sound board. All that really means is that you'll have to boost the volume a little more than usual to really hear and feel it.

☐ **VARIOUS ARTISTS**

DICK CLARK'S BEST OF *BANDSTAND,* VOLUME ONE

★★★★

Vestron/Dick Clark Video, 1986, 60 minutes

PRODUCED BY: Paul Brownstein

MUSIC FROM: Various albums by various artists; various late '50s and early '60s episodes of the ABC-TV show *American Bandstand*.

SELECTIONS: Bill Haley and His Comets: "Rock Around the Clock"; Buddy Holly and the Crickets: "Peggy Sue"; Sam Cooke: "You Send Me"; Jerry Lee Lewis: "Great Balls of Fire"; the Silhouettes: "Get a Job"; the Big Bopper: "Chantilly Lace"; Fabian: "Turn Me Loose"; Dion and the Belmonts: "A Teenager in Love"; the Fleetwoods: "Come Softly to Me"; Paul Anka: "Lonely Boy"; Mark Dinning: "Teen Angel"; the Everly Brothers: "Cathy's Clown"; Edd "Kookie" Byrnes and Connie Stevens: "Kookie, Kookie (Lend Me Your Comb)"; Chubby Checker: "The Twist."

At this writing *American Bandstand* (about which I may be biased, having cowritten a book on its history with Dick Clark), which debuted on ABC-TV in August 1957, was the longest-running network show. Dick Clark must have been doing something right, and much of that something from the show's late '50s/early '60s heyday—the performers and their music—is here. In fact, longtime *Bandstand* fans, or those who recall it fondly from their youth, may be disappointed that this program focuses almost exclusively on performances to the exclusion of such other hallmarks of this modern American institution as Rate-a-Record and the dance contests. There are, however, quite a few delightful snippets of Dick Clark in the stands chatting with various gum-snapping girls in sweaters, A-line skirts, bobby sox, and saddle shoes.

Best of Bandstand, Volume One opens with some wonderful behind-the-scenes black-and-white footage of technicians setting up *Bandstand*'s original stage set (including the podium Clark has since donated to the Smithsonian Institute) at Philadelphia's WFIL-TV studios. The bleachers are rolled out, the kids start filtering into the auditorium, and it's all so real and genuinely nostalgic the viewer is instantly riveted. But it's soon interrupted by a period WFIL station ID, and then a voiceover from Clark brings us back to the present before telling us that since 99 percent of *Bandstand*'s "performances" were lip-synchs, so are most of these (excepting Jerry Lee Lewis and Buddy Holly) and that the original recordings have been remastered to better suit the capacities of hi-fi VCRs; and that, in fact, not all the performances are from *Bandstand* itself. Some are taken from Clark's Saturday-night show that ran a few seasons in the early '60s, and was really just a prime-time extension of *Bandstand* in a more formal setting. And while all of the performances are kinescopes—where a movie camera records a TV show as it's playing on a TV screen—the visual quality throughout is excellent.

So are many of the "performances" themselves, lip-synched or not. The standouts, of course, are the two genuine live takes, by Jerry Lee Lewis and Buddy Holly and the Crickets. Performing "Great Balls of Fire," Jerry Lee is *extremely* live, like a loose power line dangerously whipping around in a gale—he's in classic, abandoned form. And the teenybopper-bobby soxer crowd screams right back at him, while primitive pyrotechnic explosions at the back of the stage burn out the camera every time Jerry Lee yelps out the chorus.

The Buddy Holly sequence is by far the most amazing thing here—and, ironically, it's not even from a Dick Clark show. As Clark notes in his intro, *Bandstand* 's only Holly footage was lost somewhere along the line. Instead, we have a December 1957 appearance on, of all things, *The Arthur Murray Party,* a sedate showcase for the venerable ballroom-dance instructor and his students. Murray's wife Catherine gives Holly and band a bizarre intro: she starts off sweetly sincere about being tolerant of those crazy kids and their rock 'n' roll music, but as she says, "So here they are, Buddy Holly and the Crickets!" she starts breaking up into hysterical laughter—at what, that name? Her own pro–rock 'n' roll speech? No matter, for the camera dollies over to Holly and the two Crickets in bowties and tuxedoes, urgently and earnestly kicking off "Peggy Sue" in the middle of a huge ballroom, while in the background, gowned debutantes and their beaus stand stiffly against the back wall. Look closely and you'll notice a deb or two bouncing in time.

Other highlights include Sam Cooke, a real treat because there's so little extant footage of this legendary performer, and because here—even though he's lip-synching—we can see *why* he's a legend. He oozes confident sex appeal and looks wonderful. In a completely different vein, Edd "Kookie" Byrnes and Connie Stevens provide a camp classic with their brilliantly stilted lip-synch to the novelty hit "Kookie, Kookie (Lend Me Your Comb)"—where the *real* attraction is Ms. Stevens's nose—her real, *original* nose, not the pertly upturned version most of us know. Meanwhile, the Everly Brothers and Paul Anka both look *so young!* And it's fascinating to see that at so tender an age, Anka already had his showbiz act down pat.

The other selections all make for enjoyable nostalgia, at least; even

Fabian's turn is worth watching if only for the frenzied audience's primo demonstration of the original teen-idol phenomenon in action. But the presence of the likes of Fabian, the Big Bopper and Mark Dinning only points up my one complaint, which is the comparative lack of seminal black rock 'n' roll performers. Chuck Berry and Ike and Tina Turner, among others, appeared on *Bandstand* in the late '50s, and hopefully they and others will be featured in future volumes. That one complaint aside, this is a classily produced program that retains the straightforward lack of pretension that's always been one of *Bandstand* 's most appealing traits.

☐ **VARIOUS ARTISTS**

DINER

★★★★★

MGM/UA, 1984, 110 minutes

PRODUCED BY: Jerry Weintraub

DIRECTED BY: Barry Levinson

MUSIC FROM: Various albums by various artists; *Diner* motion picture soundtrack (Elektra, 1982).

SELECTIONS: Jerry Lee Lewis: "Whole Lotta Shakin' Goin' On"; Dion and the Belmonts: "A Teenager in Love," "I Wonder Why"; the Heartbeats: "A Thousand Miles Away"; Eddie Cochran: "Something Else"; Carl Perkins: "Honey, Don't"; the Fleetwoods: "Mr. Blue"; Lowell Fulson: "Reconsider Baby"; Clarence "Frogman" Henry: "Ain't Got No Home"; the Del-Vikings: "Come Go with Me"; Bobby Darin: "Beyond the Sea," "Dream Lover"; Percy Faith and His 1001 Strings: "Theme from *A Summer Place*"; Jane Morgan: "Fascination"; Dick Haymes: "Where or When"; Tommy Edwards: "It's All in the Game"; Fats Domino: "Whole Lotta Loving"; Jimmy Reed: "Take Out Some Insurance"; Elvis Presley: "Don't Be Cruel"; Howlin' Wolf: "Smokestack Lightning"; Chuck Berry: "Run Rudolph Run," "Merry Christmas Baby"; Jack Scott: "Goodbye Baby."

Diner is similar to *American Graffiti* in more ways than one: yes, it's an intelligent, empathetic examination of a group of teenagers in one city (Baltimore in this case); yes, while the '50s are turning into the '60s, the kids featured are also on the cusp of adulthood; yes, it features an outstanding golden-oldies musical soundtrack; and yes, it sports some astoundingly good ensemble acting. But also like *American Graffiti, Diner* is one magnificent must-see of a movie, a funny, sad, deeply considered, and affectionate work of art that's marvelous to see the first time, and bears up incredibly well to repeated viewings. There is one major difference between the two in terms of their status as *music* movies: *American Graffiti* uses its music much more actively, to comment on and further its plot; in *Diner,* it's essentially an atmospheric backdrop most of the time—though as such it's as perfectly observed as every other aspect of the film. So *Diner* gets the full five stars mainly because it's such a damned good film. The ensemble actors—Steve Guttenberg, Mickey Rourke, Kevin Bacon, Daniel Stern, Timothy Daly, and Paul Reiser—are all magnificent. In the sole featured-female role (as Stern's wife), the tragically underutilized Ellen Barkin is also superb.

There are, however, some musical moments that bear pointing out. For one thing, the soundtrack thankfully rescues some unjustly obscure gems of '50s R&B, like Lowell Fulson's "Reconsider Baby," Jimmy Reed's "Take Out Some Insurance," and most wonderfully of all, Clarence "Frogman" Henry's delightfully skewed "Ain't Got No Home," in which Henry sings like both a frog and a girl (while Stern, blasting the tune on his car radio, sings right along). And then there's that unforgettable scene of Stern screaming at his uncomprehending wife Barkin because she's messed up his record collection—not only something any music aficionado can instantly relate to, but also enough in its way to redress much of the balance in terms of music-appreciation between this and *American Graffiti.*

If you've never seen it, do so at once. If you have, then you already know that to see it again on video would be just like a visit from an old friend. It's *that good.*

☐ DIO
A SPECIAL FROM THE SPECTRUM
★★★

Warner Music Video, 1985, 51 minutes
PRODUCED BY: Steve Sabol for NFL Films
DIRECTED BY: Phil Tuckett
MUSIC FROM: Holy Diver (Warner Bros., 1983); *The Last in Line* (Warner Bros., 1984).
SELECTIONS: "Stand Up and Shout," "Don't Talk to Strangers," "Mystery," "Egypt," "Heaven and Hell," "The Last in Line," "Rainbow in the Dark," "The Mob Rules," "We Rock."

Sure, you get loud, hard music and a "singer" who's really a screamer, and the requisite lasers, pyrotechnics, and an enormous Egyptian stage set. But this document of a 1984 show at the Philadelphia Spectrum just may be the thing to raise the eyebrows of those who fear, hate, or sneer at heavy metal. Former Rainbow and Black Sabbath vocalist Ronnie James Dio comes on like the genre's Mr. Nice Guy, with gracious between-songs patter and more smiles than snarls. Accordingly, the most exceptional song here, "Mystery," is really a nice pop song in heavy-metal clothing. Much of the rest is almost punk in its rampaging pace. The only lows are indulgent drum and guitar solos that seem straight out of *Spinal Tap.* And this is one arena-rock show produced by NFL Films—they *know* how to shoot the kind of mammoth macho spectacle that makes milder souls wince.

☐ DIRE STRAITS
MAKING MOVIES
★★★★

Warner Home Video, 1980/84, 22 minutes
PRODUCED BY: Mervyn Lloyd
DIRECTED BY: Lester Bookbinder
MUSIC FROM: Making Movies (Warner Bros., 1980).
SELECTIONS: "Romeo and Juliet," "Tunnel of Love," "Skateaway."

☐ DIRE STRAITS
ALCHEMY: DIRE STRAITS LIVE
★★½

Media, 1984, 95 minutes
DIRECTED BY: Peter Sinclair
MUSIC FROM: Dire Straits (Warner Bros., 1978); *Communique* (Warner Bros., 1979); *Making Movies* (Warner Bros., 1980); *Love Over Gold* (Warner Bros., 1982); *Twisting by the Pool* (Warner Bros., 1983); *Dire Straits Live—Alchemy* (Warner Bros., 1984).
SELECTIONS: "Once upon a Time in the West," "Expresso Love," "Romeo and Juliet," "Private Investigations," "Sultans of Swing," "Two Young Lovers," "Tunnel of Love," "Telegraph Road," "Solid Rock," "Going Home (Theme from *Local Hero*)."

When people first said that *Miami Vice* was inspired by music videos, the three clips of *Making Movies* were the kind of music videos they meant: sumptuously art-directed, lit, and photographed, each shot a carefully composed image. It's art and graphic beauty for their own sake, and development of plot and character be damned. Within the limitations of the four-minute music video clip, that's a sensible approach—especially if you're as gifted a director as Lester Bookbinder. He butters his bread making British and European TV commercials, and here he carries the graphic acuity, textural lushness, and comparatively mature tone and content of Continental ads to music video with great aplomb. His visualizations of Dire Straits' vaguely jazzy/bluesy/folkish pop-rock are both literal and obvious (a blithe-spirited roller-skating waif for "Skateaway," various tunnel motifs for "Tunnel of Love," etc.)—yet at the same time, so imaginative, striking, and beautifully executed that each clip occupies a pleasantly hazy middle ground between the music and the imagery, preserving the integrity of both. You don't have to think about anything, just sit back and enjoy an audio-visual feast. Even if you don't care for Dire Straits' music, the visuals are good enough to try anyway.

Alchemy, the video counterpart to their double live 1984 LP of the same title, suffers from a lack of pretty imagery to divert you from the visual dullness of Dire Straits live. But if you're a fan of the band, you don't care about pretty imagery—you *want* to be able to see Mark Knopfler's fingers making his guitar sing with those distinctive, sweet-toned, bluesy licks. And you won't want or need any other distractions from the band's tasteful refinements of J. J. Cale's mellow-to-laconic-to-catatonic country-blues-funk. In short, a must for fans; others may find the perfunctory visual nature of the performance a bit tedious.

□ DIRE STRAITS

BROTHERS IN ARMS—THE VIDEO SINGLES

★★★½

Warner Reprise, 1986, 20 minutes

PRODUCED BY: Siobhan Barron, Anne Marie Mackay, Simon Fields

DIRECTED BY: Steve Barron, Pete Cornish, Steven Johnson, and Bill Mather

MUSIC FROM: Brothers in Arms (Warner Bros., 1985).

SELECTIONS: "Money for Nothing," "So Far Away," "Walk of Life," "Brothers in Arms."

If it weren't for "Walk of Life," a completely asinine and annoying mélange of Dire Straits stage performance footage with totally irrelevant shots of athletes and fans at sporting events (hard to believe this was directed by Stephen Johnson, who proved he knows better with such brilliant clips as Talking Heads' "Road to Nowhere" and Peter Gabriel's "Sledgehammer"), this would be an excellent compilation of video clips. And since "Walk of Life," with its jolly sea-chantey feel and chirping Farfisa-like synthesizer hook, is such a pleasantly ingratiating tune—as well as the fact that most people don't mind and/or are used to (courtesy NFL Films) slo-mo sports set to music, and because the clip does show a great deal of Mark Knopfler in action—Dire Straits fans probably already *do* consider this a very nice little program.

At any rate, "So Far Away" combines pretty performance shots with striking, weird-camera-angle aerial shots of metropolitan cityscapes to forge an appropriately evocative complement to the lovely tune's air of long-distance longing. It's a good video; the other two are *great* videos. In "Brothers in Arms," first-time music video director Bill Mather (who had previously worked on BBC programs and commercials) uses highly atmospheric charcoal animations of wartime scenes and a raging ocean to illustrate the song's unknown-soldier's-eulogy lyrics—*and* he expertly metamorphoses these scenes into Dire Straits performance footage that's treated so it has the same grainy, gray, charcoal-rubbing look. It's one of the most strikingly original clips of the '80s, as is "Money for Nothing," which is not only an eye-catching example of state of the art computer animation, but also a fascinating multitextual, self-reflective exercise in music video autoanalysis (not to mention a killer funky-metal riff). Knopfler claims he actually overheard the lyrics—apparently the anti-MTV rantings of a mid-American member of the booboisie—being spouted by a man in an appliance store as he disapprovingly watched MTV on a bank of television sets; the video has a computer-animated appliance-store delivery man and his young helper lip-synching, while MTV's logo and a series of quick mock-MTV music videos play on the bank of TV sets in the background (one of the fake clips, featuring a leggy bimbo in lingerie, is identified as being by the "Ian Pearson Band"—Ian Pearson being the man who created the clip's distinctive computer graphics). All in all, this is one of the stronger short-form clips compilations out there.

□ THE DIRT BAND
THE DIRT BAND TONITE

★★★

HBO/Cannon, 1982, 58 minutes
DIRECTED BY: Derek Burbidge
MUSIC FROM: Various albums by the Dirt Bank, a.k.a. Nitty Gritty Dirt Band, (Liberty/UA, 1967–82).
SELECTIONS: "Too Close for Comfort," "Fire in the Sky," "An American Dream," "Harmony," "Fish Song," "Randy Lynn Rag," "Rocky Top," "Make a Little Magic," "Some of Shelly's Blues," "Mr. Bojangles," "Badlands," "Bayou Jubilee"/"Sally Was a Goodun," "Battle of New Orleans," "Jealousy," "Will the Circle Be Unbroken."
Also available on Pioneer Stereo Laser videodisc.

Formerly known as the Nitty Gritty Dirt Band, these veteran country/folk/bluegrass fusioneers had only recently had their first hit in a long time—with the Jimmy Buffet–style whimsy of "An American Dream" in 1979—when this concert was shot at the Denver Rainbow Music Hall in 1981. So the eclectic, folksy Americana of their Nitty Gritty days is leavened with a little good-time country-rock. But they still trade off on all manner of acoustic stringed instruments and demonstrate great prowess on all of them. Fans will love this, though depending on how much they like watching these accomplished instrumentalists plying their trades, they may wonder why director Derek Burbidge keeps splicing in silent-movie and Max Fleischer cartoon footage (I *love* Max Fleischer cartoons, but *here?*). It's all well-performed and well-shot, and worthwhile for fans.

□ THOMAS DOLBY
LIVE WIRELESS

★★★½

HBO/Cannon, 1983, 58 minutes
DIRECTED BY: Thomas Dolby
MUSIC FROM: The Golden Age of Wireless (Capital, 1982); *She Blinded Me with Science* EP (EMI, 1983).
SELECTIONS: "Europa and the Pirate Twins," "Windpower," "One of Our Submarines," "Radio Silence," "New Toy," "Urban Tribal," "Flying North," "Jungle Line," "Puppet Theater," "Samson and Delilah," "She Blinded Me with Science," "Airwaves."
Also available on Pioneer Stereo Laser videodisc.

Don't let his spectacles and bookworm demeanor fool you; Dolby may be a techno-rock whiz kid, but he invests the form with more wit, emotional depth, and thoughtful humanity than most. Here, he provides a cute triple-allusive Chinese box motif within which to present a concert video: in black-and-white, we see Dolby as a projectionist, showing the color film of Dolby's concert; the film itself has Dolby—who despite his exceptional qualities is *not* the world's most exciting stage performer—backed onstage by a bank of monitors playing footage (some from his video clips) that provides a running commentary on his stage act. "Europa," "Radio Silence," and "One of Our Submarines" exemplify Dolby's peculiarly affecting nostalgic/melancholic musings on the Empire and technology; new wave warbler Lene Lovich livens things up by coming out to do "New Toy," a hit Dolby wrote for her; and there is the clever slapstick video clip for "She Blinded Me with Science."

□ THOMAS DOLBY
THOMAS DOLBY VIDEO 45
★★★★

Sony, 1984, 16 minutes

PRODUCED BY: Limelight Film and Video

DIRECTED BY: Thomas Dolby, Danny Kleinman

MUSIC FROM: The Flat Earth (Capitol, 1984); *The Golden Age of Wireless* (Capitol, 1982).

SELECTIONS: "She Blinded Me with Science," "Hyperactive!" "Europa and the Pirate Twins," "Radio Silence."

Also available on Pioneer 8-inch Stereo Laser videodisc.

Thomas Dolby's wire-rimmed spectacles and generally bookish demeanor may make him *look* like a sterile techno-nerd, but that impression is disspelled upon close inspection of his music and his video, which both display an uncommon degree of humor and humanity. Of course, his *is* pretty clever and techno-oriented, too. And, after Devo, Dolby was one of the first rock performers to direct his own video and do it well.

"She Blinded Me with Science," Dolby's first hit, is a deft musical mix of pummeling funk-rock rhythm, staccato electronics, and a lovely neo-classical violin bridge, with Dolby assuming a variety of vocal guises; its serio-comic equation of lust with science is an example of what makes Dolby different. The video is silent-movie-style slapstick comedy (one of the first and only clips to make the comment that most conceptual music videos are, in essence, silent movies that accompany songs) set in what one imagines is a typically stately loony bin in the English countryside. An actual eccentric British scientist, Dr. Magnus Pike (who has a *Mr. Wizard*–type show on British TV), plays the caricatured twit analyst to perfection.

"Hyperactive," this program's highlight, makes dazzlingly inventive and comic use of high-tech video effects, blooming at a time-lapse pace with the music, another successful marriage of high-tech and funk racing at a supersonic pace to match the title. Dolby again uses the psychiatrist's couch—only this time, both he and the shrink wear boxes over their heads which flash various digitally inserted images on each side (reminiscent of the visual puns used by the offbeat Swiss mime troupe Mummenschanz), and at one point Dolby transforms himself into his own ventriloquist's dummy.

"Europa and the Pirate Twins" and "Radio Silence" are nicely done performance clips capturing Dolby's multimedia concert presentation; both highlight his cerebral, atmospheric side, which frequently conjures a peculiarly affecting sort of metaphysical melancholy—a nostalgia for quaint, long-forgotten dreams of futures that would never be. All in all, an exceptional little program by an exceptional artist who seems to have the goods to go from "little" to "major," given a break or two.

□ FATS DOMINO
FATS DOMINO LIVE!
★★★

MCA, 1986, 19 minutes

PRODUCED BY: T. V. Grasso, Jeff Kranzdorf
DIRECTED BY: T. V. Grasso
MUSIC FROM: Various Fats Domino albums
SELECTIONS: "My Girl Josephine," "Blue Monday," "Blueberry Hill," "Ain't That a Shame," "I'm in Love Again," "I'm Ready," "I Want to Walk You Home."

Recorded in the summer of 1985 at L.A.'s Universal Amphitheater—at the same time and venue, and by the same crew, as MCA's *Ricky Nelson In Concert,* and with the same straightforward, unadorned production values—this video seems rather perfunctory, clocking in at just nineteen minutes. But in that time Fats, with his rolling New Orleans piano strides and his molasses voice and his big smile—not to mention his solid band, featuring those booting tenor and baritone saxophones—is guaranteed to put a smile on your face. And while I'm sure there must have been many better Fats Domino performances before and maybe even after this one, I have no reason to believe he was holding back here for any reason; and besides, there are no other Fats Domino concert programs to my knowledge at this writing. Yes, you may want to think twice about spending approximately a dollar a minute for a fine but less-than-earthshaking (and ultimately disappointing in its shortness) Fats Domino program. But if Fats is your man, by all means check it out.

☐ **VARIOUS ARTISTS**
DON'T WATCH THAT, WATCH THIS! VOLUME 1
★★★

Sony, 1986, 48 minutes
MUSIC FROM: Various albums by various artists.
SELECTIONS: Tears for Fears: "Mothers' Talk"; Shakatak: "Down on the Street"; Lloyd Cole and the Commotions: "Perfect Skin"; Zerra 1: "Ten Thousand Voices"; Fiat Lux: "Blue Emotion"; Big Country: "Wonderland"; Feelabeelia: "Feel It"; Marilyn: "Cry and Be Free"; the Mighty Wah: "Come Back"; Frank Chickens: "We Are Ninja"; Dire Straits: "Love Over Gold"; Swan's Way: "Soul Train"; Boomtown Rats: "You Drag Me Down."

☐ **VARIOUS ARTISTS**
DON'T WATCH THAT, WATCH THIS! VOLUME 2
★★½

Sony, 1986, 47 minutes
MUSIC FROM: Various albums by various artists.
SELECTIONS: Tears for Fears: "Shout"; the Kane Gang: "Respect Yourself"; Lloyd Cole and the Commotions: "Rattlesnakes"; Big Country: "Just a Shadow"; Jodie Watley: "Where the Boys Are"; Flying Lizards: "Dizzy Miss Lizzie"; Two People: "Rescue Me"; Bananarama: "Hotline to Heaven"; Boomtown Rats: "A Hold of Me"; Junior: "Do You Really (Want My Love)"; Sharpe and Numan: "Change Your Mind"; Band Aid: "Do They Know It's Christmas?"

These two video-clip compilations feature all-British various-artists lineups, with each volume dominated by comparatively little-known mid-'80s bands. Individually, the songs and videos in both volumes fall somewhere between being pleasant and uncompelling, competent but not too distinguished, not bad but not great. But taken collectively, they're not bad, really, and do make convenient alternative pop samplers for Anglophiles.

Volume 1 rates a slight edge over *Volume 2.* Highlights of the former include: Lloyd Cole and the Commotions' "Perfect Skin," a nice jangly '60s pop-rock tune with an intriguing video in which superimposed lyrics zoom around the prettily shot, lip-synching band; Fiat Lux's "Blue Emotion," refined post-punk protest rock with the band in hardhats at a factory and parading with proletarians through London streets, to eventually take over a fat cat's mansion; Feelabeelia's "Feel It," with colorful, graphically acute new-wave visuals and animation delightfully visualizing the sprightly soul-pop tune; the Mighty Wah with "Come Back," a slightly eccentric, hard-driving pop-rocker that's the best song in the program, visualized in bizarre, antivideo (I *think*), on-the-street fashion; and Frank Chickens, a self-conscious but still effectively strange pair of Japanese women, whose deadpan, cracked-rap "We Are Ninja" is enlivened by a video with a few feminist stings (mostly directed at traditional Japanese paternalism). Elsewhere, Dire Straits perform "Love over Gold" in concert (intercut, for some reason, with slow-motion footage of trapeze artists in flight); Boy George's less flamboyantly androgynous pal Marilyn (a guy, of course) sings a mediocre gospel-pop song in a manner much like his more famous pal's; and the pre–Band Aid/Live Aid Bob Geldof and the Boomtown Rats lip-synch "You Drag Me Down" while working in a coal mine.

Volume 2's highlights are fewer: former Shalamar member Jodie Watley's "Where the Boys Are" (*not* the Connie Francis oldie) is only a so-so synth-funk pop song with a so-so performance-oriented video, but Watley's gorgeous, sexy, and dynamic in it; the Boomtown Rats offer a stronger song and a more straightforward performance clip for "A Hold of Me"; Band Aid's "Do They Know It's Christmas?," the first rock charity video of the '80s; and, best of all, the Flying Lizards use trick photography to do their typical deadpan-dada thing to "Dizzy Miss Lizzie" (surely you remember their similar deconstructions of "Money" and "Summertime Blues"). Meanwhile, the Kane Gang offer a limp cover of the Staple Singers' classic "Respect Yourself"; Bananarama deliver cute, light-as-a-feather record-biz satire in "Hotline to Heaven"; Sharpe and Numan (as in Gary Numan—remember *him*?) indulge in dumb, self-conscious weirdness; and Junior leads his soccer game to victory for little apparent reason to illustrate his decent funk-pop song.

□ THE DOORS
A TRIBUTE TO JIM MORRISON
★★★

Warner Home Video, 1981, 60 minutes

MUSIC FROM: Various Doors albums (Elektra, 1967–71).

SELECTIONS: "5 to 1," "Back Door Man," "The End," "Moonlight Drive," "People Are Strange," "Light My Fire," "Touch Me," "Changeling," "Unknown Soldier," "Celebration of the Lizard" (excerpt), "Crawlin' King Snake," "When the Music's Over."

□ THE DOORS
DANCE ON FIRE
★★★★★

MCA, 1985, 65 minutes

PRODUCED BY: George Paige

DIRECTED BY: Ray Manzarek, various others

MUSIC FROM: Various Doors albums (Elektra, 1967–71).

SELECTIONS: "Break On Through," "People Are Strange," "Light My Fire," "Wild Child," "L.A. Woman," "Unknown Soldier," "Roadhouse Blues," "WASP (Texas Radio and the Big Beat)," "Love Me Two Times," "Touch Me," "Horse Latitudes," "Moonlight Drive," "The End," "Crystal Ship," "Riders on the Storm."

Also available on Pioneer Stereo Laser videodisc.

This is a tough choice for real diehard Doors fans: some of the same material (e.g., "Light My Fire" performed on *The Ed Sullivan Show,* with a cheesy backdrop of—what else?—doors; and "Touch Me" on *The Smothers Brothers*

Show, and what's that black eye doing on Robbie Krieger?) overlaps between the two programs, yet each has vintage concert footage that the other doesn't. *Tribute to Jim Morrison* has "Changeling," "Unknown Soldier," "Crawlin' King Snake," "When the Music's Over," "5 to 1," "Back Door Man," and a bit of "Celebration of the Lizard" in grainy concert takes. *Dance On Fire* has mostly better-produced stage shots of "Roadhouse Blues," "WASP (Texas Radio and the Big Beat)," "Love Me Two Times," and "The End." *Tribute,* a bit too obviously based on the Danny Sugerman–Jerry Hopkins Morrison bio *No One Here Gets Out Alive,* has interviews with the Doors and their producer, Paul Rothchild. Yet what insight these interviews shed on the tragic rock poet's life and death runs neck-and-neck with a queasiness brought on by the ghoulish way people like Ray Manzarek have of wearing bare the carpet in Morrison's corner of the Rock Myth Hall of Fame.

In this regard, *Dance On Fire* rates the edge, because nothing—no interviews that restate the obvious, no portentious voiceover narration, none of Manzarek's "Oh, Morrison, maaaan . . . " maunderings—gets in the way of a marvelous collection of archival footage that *really* serves as a fitting tribute to Jim. There he is, in classic mesmerized/mesmerizing poet/shaman form: in ahead-of-their-time promotional video clips for "Break On Through" and "Moonlight Drive"; in the long-censored "Unknown Soldier" clip, where Jimbo is tied to a stake, shot, and drools out blood in slo-mo; and during the anarchic concert footage of "Roadhouse Blues," where we get a different side of Morrison—his bemused, mocking shrug as cops drag him offstage. There are also two newly produced video clips for two Doors classics: "Wild Child" (which is strangely missing its technical credits) makes fine, apposite use of old footage of Indian rituals and newfangled special effects; the Manzarek-directed "L.A. Woman," though, is a dumb slasher scenario starring John Doe of the L.A. punk rock band X (whom Manzarek produces), and is the sole drawback in all of *Dance On Fire.*

Finally, in regard to *Dance On Fire*'s moodier, lower-key approach, all its clips are linked with atmospheric mini-segments featuring Morrison reading his poetry over dreamy abstract-effect shots. Maniacal Doors fans will want both, but those whose interest is somewhat less ardent are advised to try *Dance On Fire.*

□ THE DREAM ACADEMY
THE DREAM ACADEMY
★★½

Warner Reprise, 1986, 16 minutes

PRODUCED BY: Leslie Libman and Larry Williams; Peter Kagen and Paula Greif

DIRECTED BY: Leslie Libman and Larry Williams; Peter Kagen and Paula Greif

MUSIC FROM: The Dream Academy (Warner Reprise, 1985).

SELECTIONS: "Life in a Northern Town," "This World," "The Love Parade," "Please Please Please Let Me Get What I Want."

The Dream Academy emerged from Britain in 1985 and achieved minor success with a pleasant enough neo-'60s sort of folk-pop: light, airy, tuneful, though quite derivative—not just of '60s British hippie-folk from Donovan to early Marc Bolan, but also, in the cases of "This World" and "The Love Parade," extremely redolent of the distinctive neofolk sound of the '80s Scottish band Aztec Camera. The music may be nice enough, but the videos themselves are a very mixed bag. "This

World" and "The Love Parade" are both by Peter Kagen and Paula Greif, a duo with a singularly annoying, meaninglessly arty style that arbitrarily slaps together moodily lit performance shots with gratuitous, quick-cut grainy Super 8 footage (incredibly, all of their clips look exactly alike, whether for the Dream Academy or Scritti Politti or Steve Winwood—how do they keep getting work?). "Life in a Northern Town" is the most distinctive song here, with a lovely African choral chant added to the delicate '60s-folk mix, though its video by Leslie Libman and Larry Williams resembles Kagen and Greif's work (yet to the former's credit, they intercut *their* moodily lit performance footage with gray travelog shots of the overcast northern British countryside). However, their "Please Please Please Let Me Get What I Want" is the best music video here, complementing the simple, plaintive ballad with a stately performance clip, with the camera constantly sweeping slowly around the band (two guys and a girl) in 360-degree pans as they lip-synch inside a large room in a mansion. All in all, mainly for Dream Academy fans.

☐ **VARIOUS ARTISTS**

DRY WOOD

★★★★½

Flower Films, 1980, 37 minutes

PRODUCED BY: Les Blank with Maureen Gosling

DIRECTED BY: Les Blank with Maureen Gosling

MUSIC FROM: Dry Wood motion picture soundtrack (Flower Films, 1973).

SELECTIONS: Bois Sec Ardoin: "Mardi Gras Song," "Untitled," "Home Sweet Home"; Bud Ardoin and Canray Fontenot: "Lachez-Les"; Canray Fontenot: "Untitled Instrumentals 1 and 2," "Jole Blon."

Yet another small wonder from rural-Americana archivist and folkoric gourmet Les Blank, who here documents the cuisine and music of the Cajun Creoles of the Louisiana bayou. Blank focuses on two families, the Ardoins and the Fontenots. We see them prepare gumbos, barbecues, and other feasts; a hog-butchering party (in which Blank follows the beast from slaughter to sausage); country Mardi Gras; a "Men's only" supper, and work in the rice fields. Through it all Blank gets up close and personal in his distinctively unobtrusive way, as "Bois Sec" ("Dry Wood") Ardoin, his son Bud, and Canray Fontenot make their music, a less-refined version of the "zydeco" made famous by Clifton Chenier, it's an insistently jumping, wildly energetic, rough-hewn mix of blues, washboard/jug-band stomps, field hollers, and romantically folkloric Acadian accordian music. We also get to see a church congregation sing a lovely version of "Kumbaya." The music is rollicking good fun, as are the people—though Blank *never* oversentimentalizes them as noble-savage caricatures. And in the cooking and barbecuing sequences, you can practically taste the food. *Dry Wood* is sure to make you hungry, even as it satisfies some of your other senses.

☐ DURAN DURAN

DURAN DURAN (Short Version)

★★★½

Sony, 1983, 11 minutes

PRODUCED BY: Chryssie Smith and MGMM

DIRECTED BY: Godley and Creme, and Russell Mulcahy

MUSIC FROM: Rio (Capitol/EMI, 1982); *Duran Duran* (Capitol/EMI, 1981).

SELECTIONS: "Girls on Film," "Hungry like the Wolf."

☐ DURAN DURAN
DURAN DURAN (Long Version)
★★½

HBO/Cannon, 1983, 60 minutes
PRODUCED BY: MGMM
DIRECTED BY: Russell Mulcahy, Godley and Creme, Ian Emes
MUSIC FROM: Duran Duran (Capitol/EMI, 1981): *Rio* (Capitol/EMI, 1982).
SELECTIONS: "Planet Earth"; "Lonely in Your Nightmare," "Careless Memories," "My Own Way," "Rio," "Hungry like the Wolf," "Night Boat," "Girls on Film," "Save a Prayer," "The Chauffeur," "Is There Something I Should Know?".
Also available on Pioneer Stereo Laser videodisc.

☐ DURAN DURAN
DANCING ON THE VALENTINE
★★

Sony, 1984, 15 minutes
PRODUCED BY: MGMM/Duran Duran
DIRECTED BY: Russell Mulcahy, Simon Milne, Brian Grant
MUSIC FROM: Seven and the Ragged Tiger (Capitol/EMI, 1983); *Arena* (Capitol/EMI, 1984).
SELECTIONS: "The Reflex," "Union of the Snake," "New Moon on Monday."

☐ DURAN DURAN
SING BLUE SILVER
★★½

HBO/Cannon, 1984, 85 minutes
PRODUCED BY: Paul Berrow, Michael Berrow, and Duran Duran
DIRECTED BY: Michael Collins and Russell Mulcahy
MUSIC FROM: Duran Duran (Capitol/EMI, 1981); *Rio* (Capitol/EMI, 1982); *Seven and the Ragged Tiger* (Capitol/EMI, 1983); *Arena* (Capitol/EMI, 1984).
SELECTIONS: "Is There Something I Should Know?," "Planet Earth," "Is Anybody Out There?," "Wild Boys," "Union of the Snake," "Girls on Film," "New Religion," "Eyes of a Stranger," "Save a Prayer," "The Reflex," "Hungry like the Wolf," "Careless Memories," others.

No matter what you think of Duran Duran's music (personally, I think their "music" is so unmusical and coldly contrived it would be avant-garde were it not so devoid of humor, personality, substance, or musical spark—but then, millions would argue the opposite, so there you go . . .), the marriage of their shallowly chic soundcraft with video *auteur* Russell Mulcahy's trademark avalanches of derivative, chic images was made in rock video heaven. Mulcahy, in working with these pretty boys, takes the rock-video director's promotional imperative to transcendent heights: he keeps such feverish torrents of provocative, sexy, beautifully shot images on-screen you can't even *think* about the music.

But too much of a good thing is still just *too much*, and watching *Duran Duran* the long version is like eating a dozen pieces of cheesecake. Thus, the short version of *Duran Duran* is recommended to all but the band's most ardent fans, because Mulcahy's "Hungry like the Wolf" and Godley and Creme's "Girls on Film" are two rock-video classics that are more than enough on their own: the former is a dizzying *Raiders of the Lost Ark* tribute (there's also an homage to *Apocalypse Now*, when Simon Le Bon is seen rising in slo-mo out of a river amidst a torrential downpour), the latter a paradigm of rock-video sexism that's half ladies' mud-wrestling, half fashion show, and all soft-core porn, with the band intriguingly kept in the distant background throughout.

Dancing on the Valentine has two unbelievably dumb, cliché-ridden clips (Simon Milne's grossly overdone "Union of the Snake," and Brian Grant's offensively specious stab at "revolutionary politics," "New Moon on Monday"), and one fantastic one: Mulcahy's "The Reflex," a monumental, exalted concert video with vertiginous *North by Northwest* photography, and a dazzlingly apt special-effects sequence in which an animated tidal wave washes out over the audience from the lip of the stage. Once again, Mulcahy goes above and beyond the promotional call of duty, and accomplishes the impossible: he actually makes a Duran Duran concert look *exciting*.

No such luck with *Sing Blue Silver*, the handsomely produced but ultimately run-of-the-mill documentary on Duran Duran's 1984 U.S. tour. All the usual trimmings are here: the band on- and offstage, rehearsing and performing, talking and being interviewed, sight-seeing and hanging out and passing time and cutting up and so on; management and crew people in action; and the fans, those teenybopper girls, horde after horde of them, all giddy and trembling and screaming with insane affection/lust/worship for their idols. In fact, what distinguishes *Sing Blue Silver*, aside from its lush production values, is the fact that those fans are on camera nearly as much as the band. Too bad they aren't on *more* than the band—because the fans are a *lot* more interesting than Duran Duran.

□ DURUTTI COLUMN
DOMO ARIGATO
★★★½

Factory/Ikon, 1985, 50 minutes
PRODUCED BY: Anthony Wilson
DIRECTED BY: Anthony Wilson
MUSIC FROM: Domo Arigato (Factory, 1985).
SELECTIONS: "Sketch for Summer," "Sketch for Dawn," "Little Mercy," "Mercy Dance," "The Room," "e . . . e . . . ," "Blind Elevator Girl," "Belgian Friends," "The Missing Boy."
Available only on Factory compact disc.

While this 1985 concert tape from Japan suffers from Factory's usual no-budget—and not much more visual aptitude—look, musically it's one of the wayward, self-consciously arty British post-punk label's strongest offerings. Durutti Column, led by guitarist/composer/arranger Vini Reilly, play a soothing trance-rock that mates the pleasing sonorities of Mike Oldfield's *Tubular Bells*–era progressive-pop minimalism with the layered repetitive-drone techniques of Philip Glass/Steve Reich modern-classical minimalism. That Reilly achieves this, and distinctively flavors his steady-state ambience with Oriental pentatonic scales and strains of pastoral folk and fluid jazz, is remarkable considering the two guitars/bass/drums lineup. Visually, there's not much to watch, but aurally this makes an intriguing alternative to Windham Hill's watercolor-whimsy school of musical hypnosis. (Available in stores or by mail order from Factory.)

□ BOB DYLAN, OTHERS
DON'T LOOK BACK
★★★★★

Paramount, 1986, 95 minutes
PRODUCED BY: Albert Grossman and Don Court
DIRECTED BY: D. A. Pennebaker
MUSIC FROM: Various Bob Dylan albums (Columbia, 1962–65); *Don't Look Back* motion picture soundtrack (Leacock-Pennebaker, 1967).
SELECTIONS: Bob Dylan: "Subterranean Homesick Blues," "All I Really Wanna Do," "Only a Pawn in Their Game," "The Times They Are A-Changin'," "The Lonesome Death of Hattie Carroll," "Lost Highway," "I'm So Lonesome I Could Cry," "Don't Think Twice, It's All Right," "It's All Over Now, Baby Blue," "Bob Dylan's 115th Dream," "It's Alright, Ma (I'm Only Bleeding)," "Gates of Eden"; Joan Baez: "Sally Go Round the Roses," "Turn,

Turn Again"; Alan Price: "Little Things That You Do"; Donovan: "To Sing for You."

Originally released in 1967, *Don't Look Back* was the first rock documentary by D. A. Pennebaker. Some twenty years later, it remains every bit as riveting as it must have been back then. Pennebaker and a skeleton crew went along for the ride when Bob Dylan toured England in 1965—at the peak of his folk-boom superstardom and just before he "went electric." In classic rough-hewn, hand-held, up-close fashion, Pennebaker's camera caught a succession of privileged moments—some funny, some sad, some surreally silly, most just plain scintillating—that occurred between the humdrum of life-on-the-road and the hysteria surrounding the tour. While it was Dylan's songs that ostensibly made him such a sensation, they aren't the real subject of *Don't Look Back* by a long shot: most of them are presented in quick snippets from various concerts, and virtually the only one heard in its entirety is the opening "Subterranean Homesick Blues"—a self-contained, non-sequitur prelude of sorts and a pioneering music video in which Dylan stands in an alley holding up cue cards bearing one word from each line of the frantically spoken-sung song (could Dylan have already worked out a sardonic commentary on lip-synching, even then?) while beatnik poet Allen Ginsberg does who knows what in the background.

No, the real subjects of *Don't Look Back* are Dylan himself and his sycophantic entourage, including loutish manager Albert Grossman (compare the scene here where Grossman berates an innocently inquiring member of a hotel staff to a comparable scene in *The Song Remains the Same* featuring Led Zeppelin's notorious manager Peter Grant, and *you* decide who seems more vile). Also included are Joan Baez (who seems to croon folk songs incessantly, leaving one praying that John Belushi's Bluto would come crashing into the frame from *Animal House* to bash an acoustic guitar over her head), professional nobody Bob Neuwirth, and the assorted British fans, press people, and others who gawk at Dylan in awe, dismay, or bemused perplexity. Thus, by extension, *Don't Look Back* is really all about the performer-audience relationship, the artist's own art-life gap, and the artist's place in society. Dylan himself is constantly pressed for revelations on just these issues by the press *and* the fans and various hangers-on, and his sometimes frivolous, sometimes antagonistic, almost always cryptic replies form the film's most memorable leitmotif. Something more than merely memorable is the film's closing press-interview sequence, in which Dylan methodically castigates and devastates a poor pitiful *Time* magazine reporter who's just trying to do his job.

Other highlights include: a brief insert of a *very* young Dylan performing "Only a Pawn in Their Game" on a Southern farm for black sharecroppers; teenage British girls outside Dylan's hotel, sighing and cooing "Oooh, pinch me, pinch me!" when their idol glances out a window at them; Dylan meeting an unnamed British rock band who tell him they play electric rock versions of his songs—"You'd prob'ly hate 'em," they say modestly, but Dylan wrinkles his brow, says, "Hmmm . . ." and moments later is seen gazing in fascination at electric guitars in a music store window; the twittish wife of some British politico lavishing praise on Dylan, then rendering the singer speechless by inviting him and his entourage to stay at her palatial home next time they come through; Dylan laboriously typing lyrics in his hotel room while Baez sings in one corner and Marianne Faithful sits quietly in another; a very young and very nervous Donovan (who's something of a running joke in the movie, as Dylan keeps reacting to the Donovan headlines he keeps seeing in the British pop press) performing for Dylan—who, surprisingly, gives the kid a break, says he likes his song, and plays "It's All Over Now, Baby Blue" for him in return; and a squirmingly pathetic backstage encounter between Dylan and a hapless nerd of a British fan who brazenly invades Dylan's privacy, naïvely hoping for an instant hands-across-the-water humanistic bond—and who's so bent on bonding with Dylan that the latter's not-so-subtle ways of telling the kid to go to hell fall on deaf ears.

Throughout, Dylan is a fascinating presence: sometimes soft-spoken and pleasant, sometimes impassively enigmatic, but mostly arrogant as all get-out—a cocksure young man who seems to know fully and exactly why he's such a big deal and who sure as hell isn't telling what he knows. And, unlike everyone else in the film, he's *never* nervous or awkward with the camera around—though he's as acutely aware of the camera's presence as everyone else is. Meanwhile, the only member of his entourage who comes across as likable is Animals keyboardist Alan Price, and the only other person Dylan expresses any respect, admiration and/or affection for is bearded old folkie Derrol Adams, who toddles along with Donovan to Dylan's hotel room.

With *Don't Look Back*, Pennebaker has done a hard-nosed, no-nonsense job of capturing a fascinating and significant moment in rock history. His ultimate triumph may be that the film is so pithy and piercingly *human*, it should continue to resonate forever.

□ BOB DYLAN WITH TOM PETTY AND THE HEARTBREAKERS
HARD TO HANDLE
★★★★

CBS/Fox, 1986, 60 minutes

DIRECTED BY: Gillian Armstrong

MUSIC FROM: Knocked Out Loaded (Columbia, 1986); *Pat Garrett and Billy the Kid* (Columbia, 1973); *Blonde on Blonde* (Columbia, 1966); *Highway 61 Revisited* (Columbia, 1965); *Empire Burlesque* (Columbia, 1985); *Nashville Skyline* (Columbia, 1969).

SELECTIONS: "In the Garden," "Just like a Woman," "Like a Rolling Stone," "It's Alright Ma (I'm Only Bleeding)," "Girl from the North Country," "Lenny Bruce," "When the Night Comes Falling from the Sky," "Ballad of a Thin Man," "I'll Remember You," "Knockin' on Heaven's Door."

Hard to Handle is a superior concert video all the way: Dylan's in good, energetic form and doesn't appear to be parodying himself as he delivers a strong selection of vintage and contemporary tunes; Petty and the Heartbreakers, augmented by four gospel-soul backup singers, may not be the Band but provide solid, up-to-snuff accompaniment; and Australian filmmaker Gillian (*My Brilliant Career, Starstruck*) Armstrong has shot it all beautifully, with gracefully gliding camera moves and classy angles and lighting and 35-mm film stock (or so it looks—if it's 16-mm, she's even better than I thought) that, speaking of the Band, reminds me of *The Last Waltz.* Dylan and Petty sound good enough together that it's hard to believe this was shot at one of their first shows, in Australia in the spring of 1986—a few months before they brought their "True Confessions" summer tour to the U.S. Dylan performs "It's Alright Ma (I'm Only Bleeding)" and "Girl from the North Country" in solo acoustic versions.

E

□ SHEILA E. (WITH SPECIAL GUESTS PRINCE AND THE REVOLUTION)
LIVE ROMANCE 1600
★★★½

Warner Reprise, 1986, 55 minutes
PRODUCED BY: Limelight
DIRECTED BY: Danny Kleinman
MUSIC FROM: The Glamorous Life (Warner Bros., 1984); *Romance 1600* (Paisley Park, 1985); *Krush Groove* motion picture soundtrack (Warner Bros., 1985).
SELECTIONS: "Sister Fate," "Erotic City," "Toy Box," "S-Car-Go," "Holly Rock," "Merci for the Speed of a Mad Clown in Summer," "The Glamorous Life," "A Love Bizarre."

Sheila E. (for Escovedo) has recorded with her father, Latin percussionist Pete Escovedo, and played with the likes of Marvin Gaye and Lionel Richie. But it took Prince's patronage to make her a star in her own right with the 1984 album *The Glamorous Life*, which was a nicely Latin-flavored variant on Prince's classic Minneapolis Sound, a danceable rock-funk fusion featuring heavy use of synthesizer "brass" parts. In concert—as here, in a triumphant homecoming show at San Francisco's Warfield Theater in the spring of 1986—the Prince-clone effect can get to be a bit much, with Sheila E. and most of her band dressed in Princely Edwardian lace and ruffles, their hair swept around stylishly, *à la* Prince and his band in the *Purple Rain* period, and dancing-in-unison choreography that smacks very much of Prince's distinctive revival of Motown-era routines. Also, Sheila E.'s playfully childish teasing of the audience as a prelude to "Toy Box"—taunting in a little-girl voice that she has bubblegum and the crowd doesn't, putting on pajamas over her glittery stage costume, and engaging in naughty double entendres about toy boxes and playing doctor with saxophonist Eddie Minnefield—starts off nauseating and gets even worse as she drags it out way too long.

But those are the only downsides to what is basically a beautifully shot and produced, slickly entertaining show that Sheila's many fans should love. Highlights include: "S-Car-Go," a Latin-percussion jam with Sheila and her brother and bandmate Juan on congas and father Pete on timbales (it's Pete who gets the sharpest polyrhythmelodics going); "Merci for the Speed of a Mad Clown in Summer," which despite its ludicrous title boasts a fairly awesome drum kit solo by Sheila E., in which she applies Latin-percussion techniques to the traps—with more than enough power and alacrity to make a believer out of anyone; her biggest hit, "The Glamorous Life," featuring a timbale solo by Ms. E. in which the houselights are dimmed so she can show off her glow-in-the-dark sticks; and the show-closing "A Love Bizarre," a song Prince wrote with Sheila for her *Romance 1600* album and on which he performed (it's also in the rap movie *Krush Groove*, as is "Holly Rock"). Here, Prince and the Revolution take over the stylishly set stage for the tune, with Sheila E. joining *them* in an extended, neo–James Brown jam that turns up the heat and shows how it's *really* done, in one of the first performances by the band's expanded twelve-piece lineup. Prince, wearing a classy camel hair coat over a midriff-baring lavender two-piece outfit, flashes some outrageous dance moves and is obviously having himself a ball. The highlight of this highlight comes when Prince leads his three male backup singers (including Jerome Benton,

Morris Day's former sidekick in the Time) and then the rest of those onstage in "The Wooden Leg," a vicious parody of former Prince protégé Morris Day—who abruptly left the Prince camp just as the film *Purple Rain* was making him a star—and his dance-craze hit "Oak Tree." It's Prince and "A Love Bizarre" that take a good but essentially rather slight program up another half star.

□ EARTH, WIND AND FIRE
IN CONCERT
★★★

Vestron, 1984, 58 minutes
PRODUCED BY: Michael Schultz, Gloria Schultz, Maurice White
DIRECTED BY: Michael Schultz
MUSIC FROM: Various Earth, Wind and Fire LPs (Warner Bros., Columbia, 1970–84).
SELECTIONS: "Let Your Feelings Show," "In the Stone," "Fantasy," "Sing a Song," "Reasons," "Remember the Children," "Where Have All the Flowers Gone," "Shining Star," "Keep Your Head to the Sky," "Gratitude," "That's the Way of the World," "I've Had Enough," "Jupiter," "Let's Groove."
Also available on Pioneer Stereo Laser videodisc.

Maurice White's sophisticated, Latin-jazz pop-funk enterprise plays most of its biggest hits before an Oakland, California, audience in 1982. With their space-age glitter costumes, laser-light show, and dabbling in Egyptian mythology, EWF reveal as much of an influence from veteran psychedelic jazz giant Sun Ra as George Clinton's Parliafunkadelicment Thang—except, as one can see here, where Clinton does it in a wilder, looser, nastier, polymorphously perverse manner, White takes it in a much more Vegasy, slick direction, while still laying down some solid grooves. Schultz's direction is unspectacular, but with such an overdone spectacle to capture, that's okay.

□ SHEENA EASTON
LIVE AT THE PALACE, HOLLYWOOD
★★½

HBO/Cannon, 1982, 60 minutes
PRODUCED BY: David G. Hillier
DIRECTED BY: David G. Hillier
MUSIC FROM: Sheena Easton (EMI, 1981); *You Could Have Been with Me* (EMI, 1981); *Madness, Money and Music* (EMI, 1982).
SELECTIONS: "Prisoner," "Help Is on Its Way," "I Wouldn't Beg for Water," "Are You Man Enough," "Fooled Around and Fell in Love," "When He Shines," "Modern Girl," "Madness, Money and Music," "In the Winter," "Weekend in Paris," "Morning Train (9 to 5)," "You Could Have Been with Me," "Raised on Robbery," "Wind beneath My Wings," "For Your Eyes Only."
Also available on Pioneer Stereo Laser videodisc.

□ SHEENA EASTON
SHEENA EASTON VIDEO EP
★★½

Sony, 1983, 15 minutes
DIRECTED BY: Steve Barron, David G. Hillier
MUSIC FROM: Sheena Easton (EMI, 1981); *Telefone* (EMI, 1983).
SELECTIONS: "Telefone (Long Distance Love Affair)," "Machinery," "Ice Out in the Rain," "Morning Train (9 to 5)."
Also available on pioneer 8-inch Stereo Laser videodisc.

Sheena Easton is a wee little Scottish cutie who has a nice enough voice and who has a shown an adaptability to pop trends—specifically in the grooming of her punkier image in 1985 with the hits "Strut" and "Sugar Walls" (the latter a controversial Prince-penned ode to sexual excitation)—that suggests a parallel with Olivia Newton-John. Unfortunately, both of these videos were made *before* Sheena's image change, during her MOR phase. *Live* finds her extremely awkward on her first U.S. tour, delivering a stifferoo of a Vegas-style set while obviously wondering if she should try, er, rocking out a bit here and there, and just as obviously unable to do so convincingly.

The Sony *Video EP* catches her at the very beginning of her image transformation, with three slickly produced concept videos shot by Steve Barron (who's done hundreds of memorable clips, from Michael Jackson's "Billie Jean" and the Human League's "Don't You Want Me?" to a-ha's "Take On Me" and Z.Z. Top's "Rough Boy"), and "Morning Train" from the nicely shot *Live* just as a reminder of where she was coming from. As regards those three slick clips—"Telefone," "Machinery," and "Ice Out in the Rain"—suffice to say Sheena, whose acting skills seem severely limited, has not inspired Barron to anything resembling his best work. The monster-movie slapstick antics of "Telefone" might amuse some. But overall, both programs are strictly for fans.

□ SHEENA EASTON
VIDEO 45
★★

Sony, 1984, 14 minutes
PRODUCED BY: Various
DIRECTED BY: Various
MUSIC FROM: Various Sheena Easton albums (EMI-America).
SELECTIONS: "Telefone (Long Distance Love Affair)," "Machinery," "Ice Out in the Rain," "Morning Train."

Easton's *Video 45* is strictly for her fans only. "Telefone (Long Distance Love Affair)," a stupid and insipid monster-movie takeoff, is probably the most familiar clip due to its MTV exposure. "Morning Train," her first big hit, is present in a straightforward concert clip and should be the most familiar tune. It's also the best, which should give you discerning listeners a good idea of just how mediocre this music really is overall. The other songs and clips are totally unremarkable: in "Machinery," the wee bonnie lassie makes a lame women's-lib statement of sorts, playing a secretary rebelling against the automation in her office; "Ice Out in the Rain" is a turgid lost-love ballad, accompanied by one of those moodily lit performance clips that zooms in on Sheena's ever-so-expressive kisser and looks more like some sort of high-toned perfume ad than anything else. Unless you just can't get enough of the look and sound of Sheena, steer clear.

□ DUKE ELLINGTON AND HIS ORCHESTRA
THE DUKE ELLINGTON STORY
★★★½

Video Yesteryear, 1980, 86 minutes
MUSIC FROM: "Goodyear Jazz Concert" with Duke Ellington and His Orchestra (TV special, 1962); *Black and Tan* (two-reel film, 1930); *Duke at the Cote d'Azur* (1966).
SELECTIONS: "Take the 'A' Train," "Black and Tan Fantasy," and others.

Three Duke films on one cassette. The opening "Goodyear Jazz Concert," a TV special from 1962, finds that year's well-oiled orchestra—including Harry Carney, Johnny Hodges, Russell Procope, Jimmy Hamilton and Paul Gonsalves on reeds, Ray Nance, Cat Anderson, Shorty Baker and Lawrence Brown on brass, and Aaron Bell and Sam Woodyard in the rhythm section—cruising through "Take an 'A' Train" and five other selections. The closing *Duke at the Cote d'Azur* is a French performance filmlet of Duke with a bass-drums rhythm section giving a rare trio concert at a French art museum in Antibes, France (site of annual jazz festivals). They bracket *Black and Tan*, a fascinating look back at the Harlem of 1930, with Duke involved in various contrived tragicomic situations while trying to compose and present the title work. A rare look at Duke comparatively early in the prime of his "Cotton Club" period.

☐ EMERSON, LAKE AND PALMER
PICTURES AT AN EXHIBITION
★★★

Magnum, 1986, 95 minutes
PRODUCED BY: Lindsay Clennel
DIRECTED BY: Nicholas Ferguson
MUSIC FROM: Emerson, Lake and Palmer (Cotillion, 1970); *Pictures at an Exhibition* (Cotillion, 1971).
SELECTIONS: "Pictures at an Exhibition," "The Barbarian," "Take a Pebble," "Knife Edge," "Nutrocker."

Though it was released in 1972, this concert documentary was shot on videotape. And while the concert shots themselves are fairly straightforward, ELP's extravagant stage show (with Carl Palmer's enormous drum kit, and Keith Emerson's enormous array of organs and synthesizers, which he at times kicks and throws around in a sub-Hendrix anarchic furor) is treated with an excess of silly psychedelic visual effects that ELP fans will probably find a tiresome, distracting eyesore. Emerson's pneumatic, calisthenically bombastic transcription of Moussorgsky's series of classical suites, "Pictures at an Exhibition," provides the program's centerpiece, but fans get the bonus of three other tracks from the band's best-selling debut album (the lovely ballad "Take a Pebble" is bracketed by the charging, frenetic progressive-rock pieces "The Barbarian" and "Knife Edge") and their fast, fun update of the 1962 hit "Nutrocker." Like ELP's music, this video is strictly for their fans only.

☐ BRIAN ENO
THURSDAY AFTERNOON
★½

Sony, 1986, 82 minutes
PRODUCED BY: Brian Eno
DIRECTED BY: Brian Eno
SELECTIONS: "Seven video paintings of Christine Alicino filmed in San Francisco in April 1984; treated and assembled at Sony in Tokyo."

Self-professed nonmusician Eno has made some marvelous mutant-pop records (from *Here Come the Warm Jets* through *Before and After Science*). He's also been known to mouth off about the general vapid insipidity of music videos. *He* should talk after *this*! *Thursday Afternoon* exists in a turgid netherworld, somewhere between pretentious ambient video art and tiresome soft-core porn. The modestly attractive Christine Alicino (could she be related to the artist, as in Christine Alice Eno?) lounges about semi- or totally nude, in a chair, on a couch, in the bath . . . Eno plays back her soporific, languid non-movements at *ultra*-slow speed, and treats it all with very subtle special effects (colorizations, image-trails, etc.). It gets to be like watching paint dry after a while, and if you're in the proper spaced-out state of mind, that could be fun. Eno's whisper-soft pastel music tinkles along in appropriately s-l-o-w, quiescent fashion. But get this: Eno has a note on the back cover of the cassette telling us, "This is a vertical format video; please turn your television set up on its right side." Sure Brian, whatever you say.

☐ JOHN ENTWISTLE
BASS GUITAR MASTER CLASS
★★★★

Hot Licks, 1985, 60 minutes
PRODUCED BY: Arlen Roth
DIRECTED BY: Mark Kaplan
MUSIC FROM: Instructional demonstrations by John Entwistle and

musical exchanges between Entwistle and Arlen Roth

The Who's brilliant bassist—who innovated the "lead bass" style along with Paul McCartney and Chris Squire of Yes—demonstrates a vast variety of his (mostly) idiosyncratic and more traditional techniques: fingering, plectrum-playing, octave technique, chords, solos, hammer-ons and pull-offs (Entwistle is the original Eddie Van Halen of the bass, really treating it as a bass *guitar*) as well as phrasing, walking bass lines, harmonics, string-bending, and more.

The first half of this instructional tape finds Entwistle talking and playing alone before the close-up camera; he's a bit uncomfortable and withdrawn, but his trademark droll deadpan and sheer awesome skill as a player get him through. Things pick up in the second half when he's drawn out for jamming and dissection-through-discussion by guitarist Arlen Roth, who's obviously an old hand at such encounters and gets a smooth musical and verbal dialogue going. Along the way, Entwistle reveals that his treble-toned melodic style was influenced not by bassists but guitarists, Duane Eddy in particular. On-screen musical notation of what's being played and good camerawork showing what both right and left hands are doing—often with split-screens—add immeasurably to the instructive value. And, of course, you can replay the hardest parts over and over as often as you need to. (Available by mail order from Hot Licks.)

☐ **VARIOUS ARTISTS**

EUBIE!

★★★½

Warner Home Video, 1984, 85 minutes

DIRECTED BY: Julianne Boyd

MUSIC FROM: Eubie! original cast soundtrack album (Warner Bros., 1979); cable TV special (HBO, 1981).

SELECTIONS: "I'm Just Wild About Harry," "In Honeysuckle Time," "Shuffle Along," "Memories of You," others.

Gregory and Maurice Hines reprise their roles from the original cast for the cable-television version of this award-winning Broadway musical salute to the timeless songs of Eubie Blake, the seemingly ageless ragtime-jazz pianist/composer/entertainer who died shortly after his 100th birthday in February 1983. The entire cast is as capable as the songs are enduringly tuneful—which is to say, plenty—and all told, this is a most enjoyable all-singing, all-dancing remembrance of a long-gone era in American culture, complete with a full complement of sets and costumes approximating the period, and an ebullient spirit that does justice to the memory of the indomitable Eubie Blake himself.

☐ EURYTHMICS

★★★½

SWEET DREAMS (THE VIDEO ALBUM)

RCA/Columbia, 1983, 64 minutes

PRODUCED BY: Kate Burbidge, Maurice Bacon, and Jon Roseman

DIRECTED BY: Derek Burbidge

MUSIC FROM: Sweet Dreams (Are Made of This) (RCA, 1982); *Touch* (RCA, 1984).

SELECTIONS: "This Is the House," "Never Gonna Cry Again," "Take Me to Your Heart," "I've Got an Angel," "Satellite of Love," "Love Is a Stranger," "Who's that Girl?" "This City Never Sleeps," "Jennifer," "Sweet Dreams (Are Made of This) (Live)," "I Could Give You," "Somebody Told Me," "Wrap It Up," "Tous Les Garçons et Les Filles," "Sweet Dreams" (video clip).

Also available on Pioneer Stereo Laser videodisc.

Eurythmics, the British post–new-wave pop duo that took the music world by storm in 1982 with their debut single, the mysteriously moody and chamber-like "Sweet Dreams," are tailor-made for the music video age—what with mannish girl Annie Lennox's strikingly androgynous looks and piercing blue eyes, and partner Dave Stewart's quietly bizarre, moussed-mop-topped presence. Onstage, they are eye-catchingly entertaining, surprisingly lively, and always accomplished; in their videos, they display a gift for provocative, enigmatic if self-consciously "surreal" imagery ("Sweet Dreams," "Love Is a Stranger"), as well as an ability to exploit the obvious in surprising ways (e.g., Lennox's multiple disguises and the multiple spot-the-guest-star cameos in "Who's that Girl?"). *Sweet Dreams* includes both concept clips ("Sweet Dreams," "Love Is a Stranger," "Who's that Girl," and "This City Never Sleeps") and concert footage shot at London club Heaven.

The Eurythmics may surprise some people with their onstage energy—those who know them only through their coolly stylized videos, that is. Those same folks may be equally surprised to see that Dave Stewart—the guy who sits there at computer consoles in the "Sweet Dreams" video, punching out those string-quartet synths—is a heck of a guitar player as well as a synth-whiz. There's also some nice pixilated-animation sequences (produced by Bura & Hardwick Animation). All in all, a solid value for fans; and those who don't consider themselves fans may find more to enjoy here than they think.

☐ BILL EVANS
BILL EVANS ON THE CREATIVE PROCESS

★★★½

Rhapsody, 1984, 20 minutes

DIRECTED BY: Louis Cavrell

MUSIC FROM: Unidentified television show (1966).

SELECTIONS: "Star Eyes," several other unidentified compositions and improvisations by Bill Evans.

The late, great jazz pianist Bill Evans was an unusually reticent personality, which is largely why this particular video is so very fascinating. This extremely curious artifact is an excerpt from a mid-'60s TV show in which Evans plays show-and-tell at the piano with his older brother Harry, a music teacher. It starts out with Steve Allen, with classic all-kidding-aside-folks pomposity, telling us what a great and important player Evans is. The rest of it is simply the two Evans brothers in a room, at a piano, and then chatting while seated on a pair of folding chairs on a podium. With their haircuts and clothes and the whole look of the thing, it's not only a classic time capsule of the deadly dull nerdball gray-flannel-suit Eisenhower era, but also—given when it was made—all the proof any latter-day hippies ought to need that the spirit of the repressive '50s really did live on a lot longer into the souped-up '60s than anyone may have dreamed.

With Evans showing step-by-step how he approaches jazz construction, augmenting chords, improvising melodically on standard songs, and the like, the show starts off as an almost campy antiquated instructional film-strip—like the ones you used to have to sit through in grade school. But right before your eyes and almost before you know it, it turns into an admirably (though probably unintentionally) telling portrait of Bill Evans—a nice guy and a brilliant musician who was way too shy to blow his own horn the way Allen does for him in his intro. And who never really gets to dip too deeply into his own bag of musical tricks, because he's so shy he lets brother Harry act just like an older brother—prodding Bill at the piano, telling him with theatrical patience and more than a little condescension what he wants Bill, the wayward artiste of the family, to show the folks at home. Harry also generally stifles the articulate impulses of his shy, tremulously tentative brother with that same officious *I'm*-the-*real*-teacher-here attitude—and that's the major tragedy of *Bill Evans on the Creative Process,* for while Evans gets to *show* the way he transmogrifies a song such as "Star Eyes" from the basic and easily recognizeable melody to radically altered post-improvised/augmented form, he never really gets to *explain how and why* he's treated the song the way he has and arrived at his remarkable remake/remodel job. After a while, the viewer wants to reach right into the screen and forcibly shut Harry up so that his obviously far more gifted brother can just do his thing. Bill does get to play a bit, in his inimitable delicate and thoughtful manner, but only enough to leave the viewer starving for a whole lot more. It ends with an interesting but inconclusive chat between the two brothers about the relative merits of an institutionalized education in jazz.

Despite its problems and too-short duration, *Bill Evans on the Creative Process* is definitely one of the most unusual jazz videos out there, and it provides just about the only known film or video documentation extant of a jazz great who's no longer with us. (Available by mail order from Rhapsody Films.)

□ GIL EVANS ORCHESTRA

GIL EVANS AND HIS ORCHESTRA

★★★★

V.I.E.W., 1986, 57 minutes

PRODUCED BY: Tazio Tami and Guido Vanetti

DIRECTED BY: Stanley Dorfman

MUSIC FROM: Various albums by Gil Evans and His Orchestras

SELECTIONS: "Hotel Me," "Friday the 13th," "Copenhagen Sights," "Stone Free," "Waltz/Variation on the Misery," "Orange Was the Color of Her Dress," "The Honey Man," "Gone," "Eleven."

Veteran post-bop big-band leader, arranger, and pianist Evans, who's most famous for his heavenly collaborations with Miles Davis (e.g., *Sketches of Spain, Porgy and Bess*), here leads a solid twenty-piece band in a very nicely shot 1983 Swiss concert. Evans's inimitable musical stamp is all over this tape, in the velvety yet vivid voicings and the relaxed, meditative, amorphous ebb and flow—this music is free-floating and sometimes free-form, but it's always pleasingly consonant. Most of the pieces proceed at a slow, rising-and-falling pace, gradually evolving from random collectively improvised ruminations to lush, swinging swells of more traditional orchestral glory. The band includes such highly regarded players as Howard Johnson (baritone sax, tuba), Randy Brecker (trumpet), Michael Brecker (tenor sax), Lew Soloff (trumpet), and Billy Cobham (drums), and they do a remarkable job of bringing Evans's evanescent muse to life—especially considering that the gaunt, gray, frail-looking (some might even say almost cadaverous) Evans doesn't "conduct" them at all—he just sits at his piano, occasionally bouncing to the beat of the airy Latin vamps that gently prod the music along, almost always with his eyes closed, lost in the music, sometimes smiling or just plain beaming. Well he should: it sounds beautiful. The highlights include Charles Mingus's majestic and funky "Orange Was the Color of Her Dress" and Gershwin's "Gone," rendered as a hushed, gossamer tone poem of unutterable beauty and tenderness. Some may be taken aback, however, by the liberties Evans takes as an arranger:

his version of Thelonious Monk's "Friday the 13th," for instance, starts with a long, grippingly rhythmic baritone sax solo by Johnson, leading to five minutes or so of quiescent collective improvisation—and when the distinctively blowsy Monkian theme finally saunters in, played by the full band, the piece suddenly ends. Jimi Hendrix's "Stone Free" is turned into an absolutely unrecognizable (and rather anonymous, if pleasant), vaguely Latinish vamp that sets up a French horn solo by John Clark. Weird. But it still sounds beautiful. And thanks to the apt, tasteful direction—which follows the featured players through the arrangements with great accuracy and features lots of nice close-ups—it looks great, too.

□ KENNY EVERETT

THE BEST OF THE KENNY EVERETT VIDEO SHOW

★★½

Thorn–EMI, 1982, 104 minutes
PRODUCED BY: David Mallet
DIRECTED BY: David Mallet
MUSIC FROM: Various albums by various artists.

SELECTIONS: Elvis Costello: "Oliver's Army"; David Essex: "Imperial Wizard," "Twenty Flights Up"; Dave Edmunds, Nick Lowe, and Rockpile: "Trouble Boys"; Thin Lizzy: "Waiting for an Alibi"; the Pretenders: "Stop Your Sobbing"; Roxy Music: "Trash"; David Bowie: "Boys Keep Swinging"; the Moody Blues: "Nights in White Satin"; Rachel Sweet: "I Go to Pieces"; the Darts: "Get It While You Can"; Cliff Richard: "Green Light"; Squeeze: "Cool for Cats."

Kenny Everett was a rock video pioneer: the first video jock, so far as can be ascertained. His mid-to-late-'70s British TV show was directed by another rock video pioneer, *Shindig!* vet David Mallet—whose manic style and daring, advanced use of video effects were right at home in this daft, tarted-up, slap-happy milieu (and whose studio-shoots of guest bands are, in fact, primitive vid-clips). Everett's pretty manic himself, but most of his relentless shtick is really just a slightly hipper version of Benny Hill, an impression the too-frequent appearance of the Hot Gossip Dancers reinforces (Arlene Phillips's soft-core striptease "choreography" was another pioneering rock-video aspect of the show). Most likeable is Sid Snot, Everett's arrogant-punk character. But incredibly, the best line I ever saw Snot deliver while the show was syndicated on late-night American TV is missing here: "I came from a broken 'ome, y'know . . . I broke it." Maybe you've got to be British to get the "humor," but it all goes beyond wearying with the constant smug laughter of Everett's off-camera crew. What's best about Everett as a pre-MTV VJ is his outrageous irreverence toward rock stars: he slaps Rod Stewart on the head with a rubber club, ties Cliff Richard up and dangles him from the ceiling, pies David Essex. In the tape's best sequence, David Bowie sings "Boys Keep Swinging" on the same set as the famous video clip—but here he's loose, smiling, and there are no drag-costume gambits. It fades out with a dissolve to Bowie, sawing along on violin on a London rooftop. Everett appears as a repressed-pervert type (wearing a banker's suit in front; bra, panties, and garters in back) who goads Bowie into chasing him across the rooftops. But on the whole, this program is of mainly historical, not hysterical, interest.

□ THE EVERLY BROTHERS

THE EVERLY BROTHERS' ROCK 'N' ROLL ODYSSEY

★★★★½

MGM/UA, 1984, 73 minutes
PRODUCED BY: Stephanie Bennett
DIRECTED BY: Richard Deligter

MUSIC FROM: Various albums by the Everly Brothers and others.

SELECTIONS: The Everly Brothers: Medley: "Bye Bye Love / All I Have to Do Is Dream / Wake Up Little Susie / Cathy's Clown / Bowling Green / Let It Be Me," "Kentucky," "Don't Let Our Love Die," "Long Time Gone," "Bye Bye Love," "Devoted to You," "Wake Up Little Susie," "All I Have to Do Is Dream," "Walk Right Back," "Lucille," "Rattlesnakin' Daddy" (with Tennessee Ernie Ford), "Bird Dog," "(Til) I Kissed You," "Cathy's Clown," "When Will I Be Loved," "Crying in the Rain," "Don't Blame Me," "Bowling Green," "The Last Thing on My Mind," "So Sad (to Watch Good Love Go Bad)," "Patiently," "Amazing Grace," "Temptation," "Let It Be Me"; Ike Everly: "Ike Everly Lick 1 and 2"; Mose Ragur: "Mose Ragur Lick"; the Mills Brothers: "Paper Doll"; Lefty Frizzell: "Mom and Dad's Waltz"; Hank Williams: "Hey Good Lookin' "; Bo Diddley: "Hey Bo Diddley"; the Beatles: "She Loves You."

The Everly Brothers' Rock 'n' Roll Odyssey is a superb recounting of their saga—from child stardom with their dad, Ike Everly, and the Everly Family on radio, through teen idol–hood, to the fallow "has-been" years, through their bitter breakup, and up to their long-overdue reconciliation and reunion in 1983—with Don and Phil talking us through it all together. This personal touch is especially valuable to this program because, as Phil says here in footage from the press conference announcing their reunion, "You can't sing together without having a personal reconciliation."

The spine-tingling distinctiveness of the Everly Brothers' music was the result not only of perfect vocal harmony but of a deep personal bond as well. However, some things are apparently just *too* personal, and the program's biggest lapse is allowing the Everlys to gloss over their decline and dissolution, a ten-year period of separation riddled with drugs, divorces, and other ugliness. An understandable omission in a way, certainly; but still, part of what makes their odyssey so remarkable is that such a close pair could endure such a rupture in their relationship and then resume it. That reunion loses some of its impact and significance when we aren't shown what had to be overcome to let it happen in the first place. *Odyssey* also indulges in a bit of rock history revisionism that amounts to another forgivable mistake—implying that the British Invasion ended the duo's pop reign (even as the Beatles are quoted acknowledging the Everlys' influence on the Fab Four's harmonies and music in general) when such was not historically the case. (The British Invasion started in early 1964. The Everlys had their last big hit in the spring of 1962, "That's Old Fashioned"; they had no hits at all in 1963 and only a couple of very minor ones in '64.)

Otherwise, *Odyssey* is excellent, packed with the usual hefty dose of wonderful archival footage and photos found in Delilah Films rockumentaries (such as *The Compleat Beatles* and *Girl Groups*): the Everlys on an *Ed Sullivan Show* when they were fresh out of Marine Corps boot camp and sporting crew cuts and dress uniforms; family patriarch Ike Everly pickin' and singin' and jokin' with the boys on their '60s summer-replacement series; and, in the course of illustrating the Everlys' influences, a fabulous bit of footage of Hank Williams in action, as well as a revelatory '40s Panoram Soundie short by the Mills Brothers for "Paper Doll" that proves definitively that "conceptual" rock video clips are really nothing new (in this one, a Mills Brother cuts a picture of a pretty dancing girl out of a newspaper, places her on the patio at the outdoor party at which the Brothers are hanging out—

and through a neat "special effect" she comes alive and dances while the Mills Brothers watch). There are also interviews with Linda Ronstadt (who confesses, adorably, to having had a major crush on one of the Everlys in her youth), Chet Atkins (illuminating an often-overlooked but very crucial element in the Everlys' move to Nashville, something the Everlys themselves make very clear in their obvious respect and affection for Atkins), and Felice and Boudleaux Bryant, the husband-and-wife songwriting team that composed most of the Everlys' timeless hits (Felice has a wonderful quote to the effect that the Everly Brothers "sounded like . . . first love").

Toward the end, things get intriguingly complex, as the omission of details on the great separation comes back to haunt us when the Everly Brothers go home to Kentucky for a family reunion and even a visit to their father's grave. There's a deeply affecting sense of fulfillment, of finally coming full circle—yet it's not as satisfying as it should be. That's the only really bad news about *The Everly Brothers' Rock 'n' Roll Odyssey*: you don't quite get *everything* here, but you sure do get everything *else*. And since it leads right up to the triumphant Royal Albert Hall comeback show recorded in *Reunion Concert*—even rolling the credits over "Let It Be Me" from that concert—the two programs complement each other perfectly and are recommended as a pair.

☐ THE EVERLY BROTHERS

THE EVERLY BROTHERS REUNION CONCERT

★★★★

MGM/UA, 1984, 60 minutes

PRODUCED BY: Stephanie Bennett and Alan Yentob

DIRECTED BY: Rick Gardner

MUSIC FROM: The Everly Brothers Reunion Concert (Passport, 1984).

SELECTIONS: "Claudette," "Walk Right Back," "Cryin' in the Rain," "Cathy's Clown," "Love Is Strange," "When Will I Be Loved," "Bird Dog," "Be-Bop-a-Lula," "Barbara Allen," "A Long Time Gone," "Step Up and Go," "Bye Bye Love," "Wake Up Little Susie," "Devoted to You," "Love Hurts," "(Til) I Kissed You," "All I Have to Do Is Dream," "Lucille," "Let It Be Me."

Following a phenomenal string of late-'50s and early-'60s rock classics, Don and Phil Everly became an oldies act. They broke up in public in 1973 when Phil smashed his guitar onstage in the middle of a show and walked off. Ten years later, they reunited at London's Royal Albert Hall, and those spine-tingling high-lonesome harmony vocals sounded as inimitably beautiful as ever. Backed by a crack band led by British session guitarist Albert Lee (who also took part in John Fogerty's 1985 comeback performance), the Everlys were simply magnificent. A generous sampling of the best of their work is lovingly performed, taking them back to their roots and amply displaying how influential the Everlys were on British rock royalty like the Beatles and Dave Edmunds. Meanwhile, Don Everly's lead vocals sound stronger than ever, and Lee's band backs the brothers with all the joy and precision the Everlys themselves bring to their singing.

There's a bit of the usual documentary interview stuff around the edges, which is nice, but director Rick Gardner commendably focuses on the show itself, and shoots it with a minimum of fuss and a maximum of respectful competence. He neatly captures the show's emotional highlight when, in the closing "Let It Be Me," both Everlys cry as they sing more to each other than to the audience. It feels more like a movie than a documentary.

□ THE EVERLY BROTHERS

ALBUM FLASH

★★★

Sony, 1986, 26 minutes
PRODUCED BY: Stephanie Bennett
DIRECTED BY: Richard Deligter
MUSIC FROM: EB '84 (Mercury, 1985).
SELECTIONS: "You Make It Seem So Easy," "The Story of Me," "Following the Sun," "On the Wings of a Nightingale."

Album Flash is the Cinemax pay-cable channel's forum for what are basically record label video press kits. This one is about the Everly Brothers' classy first post-reunion concert album, *EB '84,* produced by British roots-rocker Dave Edmunds and featuring songs by such Everlys-influenced British pop-rock stars as Paul McCartney and Jeff Lynne of ELO, and it's fairly good, such as it is. The camera follows Don and Phil Everly to recording studios in London and Nashville as they make their first record together in ten years; the Everlys and Edmunds discuss the album and each song presented here, and Edmunds talks about how bowled over he is to be producing his idols. Don Everly has a nice line about why Edmunds—who has been recording fine rock 'n' roll music in the vintage mode of the Everlys, Chuck Berry, Buddy Holly et al. for years—was chosen to produce: "Well, because of his interest . . . I felt, you know, he'd done his homework." *That's* an understatement.

Too bad the video producer's weren't as skilled at their job as Edmunds was at his. "The Story of Me," which sure sounds like a Jeff Lynne song, gets a dull, mushily romantic concept-video presentation, while McCartney's lovely "On the Wings of a Nightingale" suffers from moronic footage of the Everlys restoring a classic '50s car that's totally wrong for the song's mood. Don's "Following the Sun" and the beautiful "You Make It Seem So Easy" fare better with straightforward montages of the Everlys performing them in the studio.

F

☐ VARIOUS ARTISTS
A FACTORY VIDEO
★½

Factory/Ikon, 1983, 60 minutes
PRODUCED BY: Malcolm Whitehead, Anthony Wilson
DIRECTED BY: Malcolm Whitehead, Anthony Wilson
MUSIC FROM: Various albums by various artists (Factory, 1980–83)
SELECTIONS: Section 25: "New Horizon"; New Order: "Ceremony," "In a Lonely Place"; A Certain Ratio: "Forced Laugh"; Orchestral Manoeuvres in the Dark: "Electricity"; Cabaret Voltaire: "No Escape"; the Names: "Nightshift"; Durutti Column: "The Missing Boy"; Kevin Hewick: "Ophelia's Dreaming Song"; Crispy Ambulance: "The Presence"; Stockholm Monsters: "Soft Babies."

☐ VARIOUS ARTISTS
A FACTORY OUTING
★½

Factory/Ikon, 1984, 60 minutes
PRODUCED BY: Malcolm Whitehead
DIRECTED BY: Malcolm Whitehead
MUSIC FROM: Various albums and singles by various artists (Factory, 1983–84).
SELECTIONS: New Order: "Your Silent Face"; James: "Stutter"; Stockholm Monsters: "Life's Two Faces"; 52nd Street: "The Rapp"; A Certain Ratio: "Showcase," "Back to the Start"; Swamp Children: "You've Got Me Beat"; Durutti Column: "The Beggar"; the Wake: "Uniform"; Section 25: "Warhead"; Quando Quango: "Go Exciting."

Musically speaking, these are both erratic but overall conveniently eclectic samplers of the British label Factory's stable. They cover a wide aural range, spanning New Order's melancholy big-beat trance-rock, A Certain Ratio's abstract, cerebral jazz-funk fusion, and Durutti Column's meditatively minimal, quietly hypnotic guitar mosaics. Those three constitute the highlights shared between the two tapes. The others are: on *A Factory Video,* Orchestral Manoeuvres in the Dark's "Electricity," as irresistibly perfect a piece of percolating electro-pop as we're ever likely to hear, and, on *A Factory Outing,* James's delicately fractured folk-pop and Quando Quango's exuberant electro-Latin dance funk. The rest, however, consists of various sorts of crude, noisy, self-consciously experimental avant-rock that's definitely an acquired taste.

Unfortunately, the visuals on both tapes are so uniformly mediocre-to-awful that only the most forgiving diehard fans of this sort of thing will be able to put up with them. Worse, the murky, amateurish, and indulgent visuals guarantee that no potential converts will acquire *this* taste. *Video* consists of promo clips, either dourly depressive, performance-oriented lip-synchs or lamely cryptic concepts that go nowhere s-l-o-w-l-y. *Outing* is all poorly lit and clumsily shot live performances at Factory's Manchester club, the Hacienda. Both tapes seem to have been shot by first-year film students who'd never touched a camera before. *Video* and *Outing* get their one and a half stars each solely on their uneven musical merits. (Available in stores or by mail order from Factory.)

☐ FALCO
ROCK ME FALCO
★★★½

A&M, 1986, 18 minutes
MUSIC FROM: Einzelhaft (A&M, 1982); *Falco 3* (A&M, 1985).
SELECTIONS: "Der Kommissar," "Rock Me Amadeus," "Vienna Calling," "Jeanny."

Austrian disc jockey Falco burst onto the international music scene in 1982 with "Der Kommissar," a slick, sassy, and altogether smashing amalgam of rock, rap, and funk. While its central rhythm certainly owes a heck of a lot to Rick James's classic "Super Freak," Falco's playful German-English rapping and his cohort Robert Ponger's craftily rockish music just as surely invest it with its own distinctive personality. So distinctive, in fact, that after an initial radio and TV battle, Falco beat out an all-English copy of "Der Kommissar" by British band After the Fire. The three-year lapse that followed made some people think Falco was a one-shot novelty, but the equally off-the-wall and seductive 1985 smash "Rock Me Amadeus" finally disproved that notion.

In his videos, Falco presents an irreverent, incessantly mugging persona that you either love or hate. "Der Kommissar" finds him preening and posing like a mock-Brando in *The Wild One,* and running in place occasionally while superimposed over footage of police cars driving toward the camera—he's fleeing the authorities while giving them lip in the chorus. Ultimately, it's both a celebration and a lampoon of rock-rebel iconography. And as much because of as despite its low-budget look, it's infinitely cooler and easier to take than the sickeningly self-conscious cinema-chic of After the Fire's clip.

"Rock Me Amadeus" is also entertaining in a cockeyed way, with Falco portraying Mozart as a punk-rock star in old Vienna, although after a while it begins to look too much like a Ken (*Tommy, Lisztomania*) Russell or Derek (*Jubilee*) Jarman version of *Amadeus.* "Vienna Calling" is yet another super-catchy and danceable tune, but here the video—choreographed frivolity with telephones—just gets silly and dull.

"Jeanny," however, is brilliant enough as a video to make you completely forget that the leaden hard-rock ballad is by far the weakest song in the collection. With its CinemaScope borders at the top and bottom of the screen, its artful *trompe l'oeil* dissolves, and its frequent shots of moodily lit, lavishly rainswept deserted city streets, it has all the trappings of another shoot-the-works, over-the-top Russell (Duran Duran's "Hungry Like the Wolf," the Motels' "Only the Lonely," Billy Joel's "Pressure" to name but a few) Mulcahy mini-movie classic. That impression is strongly reinforced about halfway through, when the girl Falco's been following and crooning to throughout the clip is suddenly seen straitjacketed and cowering in the shiny tiled corner of an insane asylum room—a direct allusion to Mulcahy's 1979 classic "Making Plans for Nigel" for XTC.

Yet, after the halfway point, "Jeanny" suddenly turns into a savage indictment of Mulcahy's—and too much other rock video's—oppressive cinema-chic-anery, dolly-bird sexism, and ever-spewing new-wave-photography clichés: In a twist finale, Falco is revealed in the straitjacket, and the girl appears and disappears around him, alternately taunting and ignoring him. One image—loony Falco in long shot, framed between the lovely, sexily stockinged legs of a lady standing right in front of the camera—really brings home the point: If you actually swallow all that sexist claptrap rock videos keep puking out, you're either already crazy or about to become so.

A video like "Jeanny" ought to be enough on its own to make this program a mandatory purchase with a four-star rating. So why only three-and-a-half? Because there are no credits at all, which shows a lack of respect for the producers of the clips, Falco, music video as a genre, and the home music video consumer. Research revealed that "Jeanny," along with "Rock Me

Amadeus" and "Vienna Calling," were directed by Falco's Austrian friends Hannes Rossacher and Rudi Dolezal, so kudos to them, and condolences for not getting credited.

□ THE FALL

PERVERTED BY LANGUAGE BIS

★★★

Factory/Ikon, 1983, 53 minutes

MUSIC FROM: Perverted by Language (Rough Trade, 1983); *Hex Enduction Hour* (Kamera UK, 1982); *Kicker Conspiracy* EP (Rough Trade, 1981); various other Fall singles.

SELECTIONS: "Wings," "Totally Wired," "Kicker Conspiracy," "Hexen Definitive/Strife Knot," "Eat Y'Self Fitter," "The Confidence of Glaspance," "Tempo House," "The Man Whose Head Expanded," "Smile," "Drago," "Hip Priest," "Container Drivers."

Combining the stripped-down abrasion of punk, mutated country overtones, driving folkish rhythms, and leader Mark E. Smith's eccentrically enunciated blank-verse sing-speech, the Fall have proven one of the most remarkably resilient and distinctive—and least compromising—survivors of 1977's British punk uprising. Here, they're captured in concert and in some deliberately anticommercial promo clips; in both cases the footage is crude but acceptable. The classic "Totally Wired" is the best live cut; "Kicker Conspiracy," a deadpan satire of the British obsession with soccer, the best promo clip. The Fall are not for everyone, but then, they don't try to be. For those who dare, a taste worth acquiring.

□ TAL FARLOW

TALMAGE FARLOW

★★★½

Rhapsody, 1984, 58 minutes

PRODUCED BY: Lorenzo de Stefano

DIRECTED BY: Lorenzo de Stefano

MUSIC FROM: Various Tal Farlow albums; the film *Talmage Farlow* (Prod. A-Propos, 1981).

SELECTIONS: Several unidentified songs performed by Tal Farlow with Tommy Flanagan and Red Mitchell.

Tal Farlow bent a lot of ears way, way back when he first arrived on the New York jazz scene in the early 1950s—a shy, unassuming kid with a guitar who turned out to possess both a startlingly unique and adventurous sense of harmonic invention and the gloriously accomplished technique to pull it off. Quickly, this meek young unknown came to be regarded as a masterful jazz guitarist—and, just as suddenly, in 1958, he vanished from the scene. Farlow has continued to shun the spotlight since then, which has stamped him with a legend-in-his-own-lifetime aura that's the product of his estimable talent and—as this film makes clear—his admirable resolve to be his own man.

This intimate portrait/documentary visits Farlow—a tall, rangy North Carolina native with a weathered frontiersman's face—in his Sea Bright, New Jersey, home, where he's returned to his first profession, sign painting. He tells us he enjoys painting signs as much as playing guitar. George Benson—one of the best and best-known jazz guitarists in the world—comments aptly that "when you think about Tal Farlow, the first thing that comes to mind is this incredibly wild sense of harmony that's associated with the name. And then if you know the man in person, or have ever had the occasion to meet him, you can see how humble and meek he is. It just doesn't quite match up." As we see Farlow painting signs and leisurely fishing and then see him pull out a guitar and casually play a few mind-bendingly brilliant licks, Benson's comments really hit home. Lenny Breau, another fine, overlooked jazz guitarist, offers glowing comments on Farlow's musicianship, and bemused respect for Farlow's Thoreauvian status. Farlow, who is a man of resolutely few words throughout, says in a politely impatient tone of voice, "Just because I stopped playing in New York, doesn't mean I stopped playing." He also says, by way of explaining why he abruptly left New York as stardom seemed at hand, "I don't want to be a star in music, I just want to be a participant."

Unfortunately, Farlow is so truculent, and de Stefano so understandably respectful that *Talmage Farlow* never delves into exactly what it was about impending celebrity that so turned off Farlow. Knowing what we know *now* about the exigencies of the jazzman's life and the vicissitudes of celebrity in general, and considering that Farlow was a country boy coming to the bright lights of the big city in the early '50s—long before relentless media scrutiny and Hollywood myth-making had educated us to the perils of stardom—it's hard not to want to know a lot more about it. But far more unfortunate is the unduly contrived subtext that's really the only thing marring *Talmage Farlow*: the forced notion that the film itself was made at just the right time, because an upcoming "triumphant return" gig at New York's Public Theater would signal a comeback from Farlow's long self-imposed exile. Subsequent history has proved that idea wrong, but the problem here is that, as Gary Giddins wrote in the *Village Voice,* "we're never quite sure if the movie is documenting Farlow's return, or if Farlow is returning so that a movie can be made." The modest hype the movie connects to the Public Theater concert—even including clichéd shots of newspaper headlines trumpeting Farlow's long-awaited return—places so much importance on Farlow's appearance in the media capital that it virtually insults the guitarist by ignoring and/or denying all he's been saying about how much more important music is to him than media attention.

The concert itself, in which Farlow performs with two other highly accomplished jazzmen, pianist Tommy Flanagan and bassist Red Mitchell, is delightful. But even better are their rehearsals at Flanagan's apartment, where we get a very intimate look at the way musicians playing only for each other can hook into a very pure form of spontaneous inspiration, an ineffably magical muse that somehow smacks of a higher form of jazz than we're used to hearing, even when we think we're hearing great jazz. This is such marvelous musical footage, and we owe de Stefano so much for having captured it, that it makes up for his lapses elsewhere. As does the fact that, overall, de Stefano does allow Farlow to portray himself as more of a genuine human being than a living legend. Recommended as much as a general interest, offbeat character study as for jazz and guitar afficionados. (Available by mail order from Rhapsody Films.)

□ ART FARMER
JAZZ AT THE SMITHSONIAN
★★★★

Sony, 1984, 58 minutes
PRODUCED BY: Clark and Delia Gravelle Santee
DIRECTED BY: Clark and Delia Gravelle Santee
MUSIC FROM: Various Art Farmer LPs.
SELECTIONS: "You Know I Care," "Red Cross," "Cherokee Sketches," "Recorda Me," "Blue Monk," "Firm Roots."

Expatriate jazz fluegelhorn master Farmer, who now resides in Vienna, is personable, warm, and humble in both his offstage comments and his onstage playing of tasteful, slow- and medium-tempo, straight-up arrangements (add tenderly lyrical for his playing). His abundantly evident mastery of the mellow, round-toned horn (here fronting an able rhythm section propelled by the outstanding drummer Billy Hart) ought to be more than enough to banish the memory of Chuck Macaroni from the mind of anyone with ears.

□ FAT BOYS
FAT BOYS ON VIDEO
★★½

MCA, 1986, 30 minutes
PRODUCED BY: Kris P., Julie Pantelich
DIRECTED BY: Zbigniew Rybczinski, Simeon Soffer
MUSIC FROM: Fat Boys (Sutra, 1986); *The Fat Boys Are Back!* (Sutra, 1985).
SELECTIONS: "Sex Machine," "Jailhouse Rap," "Stick 'Em," "Can You Feel It," "Hard Core Reggae," "Fat Boys."

The "heavyweight champions of rap," the "Three Stooges of rap"—whatever you call them, the Fat Boys are one of rap music's biggest, heaviest acts simply because they made a rap act out of being big and heavy. Darren "The Human Beat Box" Robinson was, along with the less-publicized Doug E. Fresh, the first popularly acclaimed "human beat box"—that is, one who mimics the sounds of rap rhythm machines and even turntable "scratch" effects with his mouth. His partners, Mark "Prince Markie D" Morales and Damon "Kool Rock Ski" Wimbley, rap along with relish over heaping portions of solid rhythms—which helps explain why this novelty act caught on. And when it comes to putting their money where their mouths are, the Fat Boys can be just plain big fun. Every one of these videos tries to put them into some sort of setup conducive to self-deprecating fat jokes. "Jailhouse Rap" is probably the best, with the boys almost regretting their pizzeria gluttony. After a while, however, the joke tends to wear a bit, er, thin.

□ FELA ANIKULAPO KUTI AND AFRIKA 70
FELA IN CONCERT
★★★★★

VIEW, 1986, 57 minutes
PRODUCED BY: Lagoon Productions
DIRECTED BY: David Niles
MUSIC FROM: Army Arrangement (Celluloid, 1985); *Original Sufferhead* (Celluloid, 1985).
SELECTIONS: "Untitled Instrumental," "Army Arrangement," "Original Sufferhead," "Power Show."

The dissident Nigerian singer/songwriter/instrumentalist/bandleader Fela Anikulapo Kuti is both a popular superstar and a constant pain in the necks of corrupt governments in his homeland, where despotic regimes have had him jailed and physically beaten dozens of times since he launched his career in the late '60s. In September 1984, on the eve of his first major American tour, Fela was arrested for the umpteenth time at the airport in Lagos, Nigeria's capitol, on a trumped-up currency smuggling charge. His cause went international when, thanks in part to the efforts of Amnesty International, he was finally freed after a year and a half, just a month before the June 1985 Amnesty International "Conspiracy of Hope" all-star rock tour. Fela, looking a bit frail, out of place, and overwhelmed but still as defiant and unbowed as ever, appeared briefly at the concluding Amnesty show. Unfortunately, he only got to play a bit of piano with salsa star Ruben Blades and a little percussion with the Neville Brothers. The United States still had yet to taste the full power and glory of Fela's "Afro-beat" music, as played by his Afro-jazz-funk-rock orchestra, Afrika 70.

As of this writing, Fela still had not brought his full band to America. But no matter: *Fela in Concert* is an indispensable record of the sound, fury, and spectacle that is Fela in performance—recommended whether you've seen him in person or not. Shot in Paris in June 1981, *Fela in Concert* does a very serviceable job of capturing a show that's a treat for the eyes and ears, though there are occasional minor technical problems with short-term drop-outs of volume and color. In Fela's typical, hypnotically extended Afro-beat numbers, like those here, Afrika 70 (which can number anywhere from fifteen to twenty or more members) lays down a thick, sinuous, polyrhythmic carpet, intertwining chattering hand-percussion, syncopated James Brown–style scratchy rhythm guitar, and stolid bass and electric piano vamps. Meanwhile a horn section, anchored by the bull-roaring baritone sax of longtime Fela sideman Lekan Animashaun, alternately barks, brays, bleats, and blasts out the most distinctively ferocious brass charts I have ever heard. Fifteen of Fela's more than twenty wives join their leader in call-and-response vocalizing, and perform suggestive bush dances in their very scanty and colorful tribal costumes and intricate face-paint. Above it all, Fela dances seductively and stalks the stage like a caged tiger as he talk-sings angrily outspoken lyrics in a mixture of Nigerian and pidgin English, often in a gleefully mocking tone punctuated by snorts of derisive laughter at the various government officials who hassle him but can't hope to eclipse his popularity with the Nigerian people. He also plays probing, staccato organ solos and full-bodied, authoritative tenor sax solos.

Fela's Afro-beat adds up to a riveting, thrilling fusion of African tribal music with Western funk and jazz—and it's as significant as it is exciting, because it's a fusion from an African's point of view, drawing on elements like funk and jazz which, though they sprouted in the West, are rooted in Africa. Furthermore, if rock 'n' roll can be defined as danceable electric protest music, then Fela must be the world's last genuine rock 'n' roll rebel: his music is certainly danceable and electric enough, and he doth protest so much in his music that his own government would rather risk global embarrassment by jailing him than let him tour abroad. Considering all that—as well as the rarity of his visits to America—the hour here, great as it is, hardly seems like enough.

□ THE FIRM

FIVE FROM THE FIRM

★★½

Atlantic, 1986, 26 minutes

PRODUCED BY: Aubrey Powell

DIRECTED BY: Peter Christopherson

MUSIC FROM: The Firm (Atlantic, 1985); *Mean Business* (Atlantic, 1986).

SELECTIONS: "Radioactive," "Satisfaction Guaranteed," "All the King's Horses," "Tear Down the Walls," "Live in Peace."

Jimmy Page's first band after Led Zeppelin, formed with former Bad Company vocalist Paul Rodgers, may have fallen victim to the inevitable hype surrounding it and everyone's long-brewing expectations. But hype is not all that made the Firm a flop with critics (of course) *and* fans, who failed to make it the runaway hit many expected. To be blunt, the Firm's material was less than inspired at best, and at worst flat-out boring rehash of '70s hard-rock clichés. Page's *outré,* Captain Beefheart–styled guitar licks enliven "Radioactive," which is accompanied by a decent-enough but unspectacular performance video.

"Satisfaction Guaranteed" is a tasteful but hardly exceptional slow blues-rock groove; its concept video is set in what appears to be a bayou bar (Page's hero, the veteran guitar whiz and inventor Les Paul, cameos as the bartender), and effectively conveys an atmosphere of ultra-humid, sub–Tennessee Williams torpor, with the fulfillment promised in the song's title coming at the end, as a lovely young lady shining with sweat steps outside the bar and it starts raining. The other three clips are all from the Firm's *Mean Business* album, and were composed by Rodgers alone, while the earlier two were co-written with Page. Their accompanying videos, full of globe-trotting political imagery and apocalyptic motifs, are ostensibly meant to form some kind of antinuke trilogy or something. But while their production values are lovely, and director Peter Christopherson has done a solid job overall, the songs are simply too weak to support such heavy inferences. For fans only.

□ THE FIXX
LIVE IN THE USA

★★½

MCA, 1985, 58 minutes
PRODUCED BY: Suni Castrilli
DIRECTED BY: John Annunziato
MUSIC FROM: Shuttered Room (MCA, 1982); *Phantoms* (MCA, 1984); *Reach the Beach* (MCA, 1983).
SELECTIONS: "Priviledge," "Questions," "Less Cities, More Moving People," "Are We Ourselves?," "In Suspense," "Wish," "Saved by Zero," "Lost in Battle Overseas," "Deeper and Deeper," "Red Skies at Night," "One Thing Leads to Another."

Straightforward concert documentary on the arty, cerebral British "new-music" band on their 1984 U.S. tour. While they often sound tepid and pretentious to this listener, they do have their fans, as this tape demonstrates with its requisite audience shots; and even I have to admit that on the hits "Red Skies at Night" and "One Thing Leads to Another," the Fixx do flash some decent hooks (even if they still show no personality). Fans of the band will enjoy this, no matter what.

□ VARIOUS ARTISTS
FLASHDANCE

★★½

Paramount, 1983, 95 minutes
PRODUCED BY: Don Simpson and Jerry Bruckheimer
DIRECTED BY: Adrian Lyne
MUSIC FROM: Flashdance motion picture soundtrack (Casablanca, 1983).
SELECTIONS: Irene Cara: "Flashdance (What a Feeling)"; Laura Branigan: "Gloria," "Imagination"; Michael Sembello: "Maniac"; Kim Carnes: "I'll Be Here Where the Heart Is"; Joan Jett: "I Love Rock 'n' Roll"; Jimmy Castor Bunch: "It's Just Begun"; Donna Summer: "Romeo"; Karen Kamon: "Manhunt"; Cycle V: "Seduce Me Tonight."
Also available on Pioneer Stereo Laser videodisc.

Adrian Lynne's box-office monster of 1983 is essentially a pathetically trite, corny Cinderella story dressed up in the hippest latter-day colors of its time—that is, it supersedes such quaint old matters as narrative consistency and credible characters with music-video techniques like LOUD music edited forcefully to the pounding beat, quick-cut montages that dazzle the viewer with fleeting glimpses of sexy stuff and/or athletic action, and lighting and camera angles that are infinitely more carefully considered than the script. The featured actors, Jennifer Beals and Michael Nouri, are both wooden beyond belief—especially Beals, whose thespian arsenal consists solely of a blankly satiated or a blankly horny vapid space-cadet gaze. The premise that Beals is a Pittsburgh welder by day who "flash dances" at night—a sort of new-wave striptease executed onstage in a steel-workers' watering hole that just happens to have a fancily designed and lit stage—is so laughable it's to die. But that didn't matter: *Flashdance* was a latter-day triumph of style over content, and though it was not, contrary to popular belief, the first feature film to function as an extended music video (*Pink Floyd The Wall*, for one, predated it), it was certainly one of the first truly potent and successful examples of that new genre. For that and that alone, *Flashdance* has some historical significance. It's also interesting for the way it mirrored '80s attitudes: Nouri sums up its ostensible point when he tells Beals, "You lose your dreams, you die," but *Flashdance* is all about following that dream as a way of looking out for Number One. Its post–Me Generation solipsism, along with its high-tech music-video gloss, made it a thoroughly modern movie for its time, despite the hoariness of so much of its conception and execution.

Otherwise, the soundtrack is highly erratic: Irene Cara's "Flashdance (What a Feeling)" and Michael Sembello's "Maniac" were both major hits, with the former epitomizing the sappily romantic *Rocky*-style corn at the heart of the film, and the latter a serviceable computer-disco pounder. The rest is overinflated bilge, typified by Laura Branigan's heinous "Gloria" and "Imagination," or uninspired background stuff by Giorgio Moroder, who produced the soundtrack along with Keith Forsey (composer of "Flashdance" and produce for Billy Idol). As far as the other performances in the movie are concerned, there's only one real actor here, and he's Lee Ving, the singer from San Francisco punk band Fear who is very fine as the sleazoid operator of an old-fashioned striptease club that competes with Beals's flashdance joint.

Oh yeah, one more thing: we can also thank *Flashdance* for prompting Hollywood to produce a ceaseless stream of crappy teen-oriented-movies-with-rock-soundtracks.

□ BELA FLECK
BANJO PICKING STYLES
★★★★

Homespun, 1985, 60 minutes
PRODUCED BY: Happy Traum
DIRECTED BY: Happy Traum
SELECTIONS: "Texas Bar-B-Que," "Brilliancy," "Natural Bridge Suite," "John Henry," "Wind That Shakes the Barley," and others.

Another "newgrass" jazz/country/bluegrass star (like fellow Homespun teachers Mark O'Connor and Tony Rice), Fleck takes the viewer through a variety of banjo styles that don't begin and end with bluegrass—just as his "newgrass" background would indicate. Still, in covering single-string picking, harmonics, blues improvisation, Keith tuners, and more, Fleck is articulate enough to be relevant to beginners, intermediate players, or those who think they're hot stuff on banjo already. They may find they still have some things to learn from this tape. (Available by mail order from Homespun Tapes.)

□ FLEETWOOD MAC
IN CONCERT: MIRAGE TOUR 82
★★½

RCA/Columbia, 1983, 78 minutes
PRODUCED BY: Marty Callner
DIRECTED BY: Marty Callner
MUSIC FROM: Fleetwood Mac (Warner Bros., 1975); *Rumours* (Warner Bros., 1977); *Tusk* (Warner Bros., 1979); *Fleetwood Mac Live* (Warner Bros., 1980); *Mirage* (Warner Bros., 1982).
SELECTIONS: "The Chain," "Gypsy," "Love In Store," "Not That Funny," "You Make Loving Fun," "I'm So Afraid," "Blue

Letter," "Rhiannon," "Tusk," "Eyes of the World," "Go Your Own Way," "Sisters of the Moon," "Songbird."

Also available on Pioneer Stereo Laser videodisc.

The half-Californian/half-British popmeisters are caught here at the L.A. Forum in 1982—at the tail end of a *long* tour in support of their *Mirage* LP. Understandably—but unfortunately for the viewer—they appear more than a bit fatigued, and while most of the songs are of course excellent, their performances here will prove disappointing to all but the most devout Mac fan. Even ardent admirers might be put off by the undue preponderance of Lindsay Buckingham tunes, and by Stevie Nicks's apparent exhaustion, which takes the obvious form of her constantly leaving the stage (her larynx is so far gone that Buckingham has to finish the last verse of "Sisters of the Moon" for her). A band this good deserves a better concert memento; Marty Callner's non-direction is straightforward but about as inspired and inspiring as the band's own half-hearted performance.

□ FLOCK OF SEAGULLS
FLOCK OF SEAGULLS VIDEO 45
★

Sony, 1983, 13 minutes

PRODUCED BY: Tony Van Den-End, Rupert Style

DIRECTED BY: Tony Van Den-End, Mike Brady

MUSIC FROM: Flock of Seagulls (Arista, 1982); *Nightmares* (Arista, 1983).

SELECTIONS: "Wishing (If I Had a Photograph of You)," "Nightmares," "I Ran."

As post–new wave British exponents of techno-bubblegum pop, Flock of Seagulls are much less pretty but, overall, much more likable than, say, Duran Duran. But their *videos—ugh!* This is the worst sort of "Surrealist Sci-Fi 101" claptrap, ranging from the merely dumb and dull to the wretchedly unwatchable. There *is* one really swell tune here, the gorgeous, plaintive "Wishing," but the tape omits the band's other best song, the similarly rapturous though slightly harder "Space Age Love Song." Stick to the audio records.

□ THE FOOLS
WORLD DANCE PARTY
★★★

JEM/Passport, 1986, 30 minutes

DIRECTED BY: Bob Tingle

MUSIC FROM: World Dance Party (JEM/PVC, 1985).

SELECTIONS: "Life Sucks, Then You Die," "Doo Wah Diddy," "She Makes Me Feel Big," "World Dance Party."

The Fools, who first burst onto the music scene from their native Boston in the late '70s with "Psycho Chicken," a sendup of Talking Heads' "Psycho Killer," are always ready to live up (or down, as the case may be), to their name with some irreverent kidding around. That's about all they do during these four video clips with connective material (in the latter, the band are seen as senile residents of the "Old Rockers Home"). "Life Sucks . . ." is country-punk gallows humor, with a cute video making clever use of chroma-key and toy sets; "Doo Wah Diddy" uses slapstick to take a horny teen stud from the elated pickup of the original song through the dreariness of domesticated drudgery; "She Makes Me Feel Big" is a laconic jazz-jive number, here set in a self-mocking recording-studio video; and "World Dance Party" is the Fools' answer to a world war, complete with life-size sex-dolls amidst the war room revelry. Lightly enjoyable fun—and anything you can say to put the Fools down, they've already done in their video, so *there*.

☐ **VARIOUS ARTISTS**
FOOTLOOSE
★★½

Paramount, 1984, 107 minutes
PRODUCED BY: Lewis J. Rachmil and Craig Zadar
DIRECTED BY: Herbert Ross
MUSIC FROM: Footloose motion picture soundtrack (Columbia, 1984).
SELECTIONS: Kenny Loggins: "Footloose," "I'm Free (Heaven Helps the Man)"; Mike Reno and Ann Wilson: "Almost Paradise"; Shalamar: "Dancing in the Sheets"; Sammy Hagar: "The Girl Gets Around"; John Cougar Mellencamp: "Hurts So Good"; Foreigner: "Waiting for a Girl Like You"; Quiet Riot: "Metal Health"; Bonnie Tyler: "Holding Out for a Hero"; Deniece Williams: "Let's Hear It for the Boy."

Though at first *Footloose* looks like just another teen movie, it actually raises some pretty big issues, such as censorship, community standards, and the role of the church in government. But the way these themes are presented makes you wonder if they didn't just show up in the film by accident. Ren (Kevin Bacon) and his mother move to a small, churchgoing town full of repressed teens. The source of the kids' unhappiness is the town ban on dancing and fun in general, and its leader is the local preacher (John Lithgow). His daughter, Ariel (Lori Singer), is—no surprise—the wildest kid in town, partially because, we suppose, it was her brother's death in a car accident after a night out that inspired her father's crusade for morality. Ren loves to dance, and with his cohort Willard (played by Christopher Penn, and easily the most likable character in the bunch), he convinces the town to let him hold a dance (by quoting from the Bible, no less). All goes well, Ariel's dad returns to the real world, the end.

It's a movie with a message, as they say, and that's a lot more than can be said for many films of this ilk. The factors rating its inclusion here—the music and the dancing, if you could call it that—are actually the film's weakest points. It's not that the music is bad, only that it's often used so poorly that it fails to make the statement—that music and dance are life-affirming forces—you think it intends. Also, there's a pretty nasty scene with Ariel's old boyfriend beating her viciously, which is *not* for little kids. Still, not a total loss.—P.R.

☐ **VARIOUS ARTISTS (OINGO BOINGO, OTHERS)**
FORBIDDEN ZONE
★★★

Media, 1984, 75 minutes
PRODUCED BY: Richard Elfman
DIRECTED BY: Danny Elfman
MUSIC FROM: Various albums by Oingo Boingo and other artists; original motion picture soundtrack for *Forbidden Zone* (Hercules Films, 1980).
SELECTIONS: Oingo Boingo: "Witch's Egg," "Minnie the Moocher," "Yiddishe Charlston," "Grand Finale"; Cab Calloway and His Orchestra: "Some of These Days"; Josephine Baker: "La Petite Tonkinoise"; Miguelito Valdez: "Bim Bam Boom"; Marie-Pascale Elfman: "Pleure"; Felix Figueroa and His Orchestra with the Boulevard Stompers: "Pico and Sepulveda."

Warning: this is a very strange, very *gross* movie, and it's NOT for everybody. It's for people who *like* very strange and *gross* movies. You have been warned.

Forbidden Zone is a black & white hyper-self-conscious, garbage-surrealist homage to the midnight-cult-movie genre and all its attendant phenomena: from *Rocky Horror* to John Waters gross-out epics, from Three Stooges slapshtick to Fleischer Brothers Betty Boop cartoons (i.e., the animation of John Muto), from the post-dubbed *Putney Swope/Jive* lunacy of Robert

Downey to *Eraserhead*'s dreamlike *mise en scène.* Herve Villechaize (yes, *that* Herve Villechaize) plays the king of the sixth dimension—the "Forbidden Zone," located behind a mysterious door in the basement of the humbly nutso Hercules family's home, reached through an intestinal steeplechase that literally shits people out, and oozing with hideously degraded denizens. In a trash project like this, Villechaize actually comes across as likable and talented. Susan Tyrell, a veteran of such epics, camps it up as Herve's queen and sings the best original soundtrack song ("Witch's Egg") to '50s-style rock by Oingo Boingo (some members of whom play bit parts, billed under the band's original name, "The Mystic Knights of the Oingo Boingo"). Marie-Pascale Elfman (sister of producer/director Richard Elfman and Oingo Boingo's Danny Elfman—this was a real family affair) is delightful as the French spitfire heroine.

But what really steals the show—aside from the wigged-out imagination and ingenuity of the set design—are the invigoratingly loony musical set-pieces, most of which (and the best of which) have nothing to do with Oingo Boingo, but rather are black-comic lip-synchs to big-band swing and Latin bossa-nova ready-mades from the '20s and '30s. Perhaps the best of them all stars those two British kamikaze performance artists, the Kipper Kids (one of whom, Martin von Hasselberg, married Bette Midler a few years after *Forbidden Zone* was released), as robotic boxers who grunt and punch themselves in the face in perfect time to the '30s samba "Bim Bam Boom"—while a fat, dumpy-looking kid in a sort of Mickey Mouse Club hat stands impassively before them, with *someone else's mouth* superimposed over his own to lip-synch the Spanish lyrics. It makes for three of the more galvanically absurd minutes of movie viewing I can recall, but you'd have to see it to even begin to believe it.

Indeed, *Forbidden Zone* works best—certainly as a "music video" program, at least—if you forget about following the plot and just go with the scrofulously zany flow of those outrageous '30s/'80s production numbers. Writer Roy Trakin once aptly described those sequences as "sort of like Devo remaking the Herbert Ross–Steve Martin remake of *Pennies from Heaven.*" If you can relate to *that,* then *Forbidden Zone* just might be for you.

□ FRANKIE GOES TO HOLLYWOOD

FROM A WASTELAND TO AN ARTIFICIAL PARADISE

★★½

RCA/Columbia, 1985, 28 minutes
PRODUCED BY: Various
DIRECTED BY: Bernard Rose, David Mallet, Godley and Creme
MUSIC FROM: Welcome to the Pleasuredome (Island, 1984).
SELECTIONS: "Relax" (version one), "Two Tribes," "Welcome to the Pleasuredome," "Relax" (version two).

Despicable as this "band" of arrogantly inept English poofters flaunting their venality as a marketing ploy may be, there *are* some things to recommend this clips compilation. Mainly, there's Godley and Creme's brilliant "Two Tribes" video clip, a diabolical mix of media agit-prop and global politics as figurehead mud-wrestling. This is the "long" version of this controversial, provocative masterpiece, with "scratch" edits of Richard Nixon and the like. There's also the first of the several controversial versions of the "Relax" video—the one censored by the BBC and MTV, complete with implied golden showers in a Fellini-esque gay bar and all that. Then there's the unendurable boondoggle of "Welcome to the Pleasuredome." And the last version of "Relax," one of the more hilariously ironic moments in rock video history, as the band plays live onstage and is attacked by an ecstatic audience of teenage *girls*.

□ JAY JAY FRENCH
HEAVY METAL PRIMER
★★★★

Hot Licks, 1986, 60 minutes
PRODUCED BY: Arlen Roth
DIRECTED BY: Mark Kaplan
MUSIC FROM: Various demonstrations and performances by Jay Jay French and Arlen Roth.
SELECTIONS: Power warm-ups, power chords, string bending, chromatic runs, metal licks, whammy bar technique, blues roots and influences, discussion/jam with Arlen Roth.

For serious heavy-metal guitarists who haven't yet reached the national-stardom stage and for beginning guitarists who like heavy metal, Twisted Sister's guitarist Jay Jay French offers a solid *Heavy Metal Primer.* Drawing on his considerable fourteen years of rock experience with Twisted Sister, French details a very helpful array of basic techniques and tricks of the trade, along the way demonstrating to any doubters out there that heavy-metal guitarists are nice people (and good teachers) too. French's emphasis on heavy metal's long-forgotten and/or overlooked roots in blues is especially gratifying, and his discussion and jam with guitarist Arlen Roth (the man who runs Hot Licks) sheds further light on the not-always-as-simple-as-it-looks-or-sounds heavy-metal guitar style. And as with all Hot Licks instructional tapes, fine camerawork, split-screens for right- and left-hand work, and on-screen notation of licks being played all add to the program's instructional value. (Available by mail order from Hot Licks.)

G

□ STEVE GADD
UP CLOSE
★★★★

DCI, 1983, 60 minutes
PRODUCED BY: Rob Wallis and Paul Siegel
DIRECTED BY: Rob Wallis and Paul Siegel
MUSIC FROM: Paul Simon's *One Trick Pony* (Warner Bros., 1980); various Steve Gadd jam sessions and demonstrations.
SELECTIONS: "Mozambique," "Late in the Evening," other untitled demonstrations and jams.

□ STEVE GADD
IN SESSION
★★★★

DCI, 1985, 90 minutes
PRODUCED BY: Rob Wallis and Paul Siegel
DIRECTED BY: Rob Wallis and Paul Siegel
MUSIC FROM: Jam sessions with two trios.

Gadd is one of the most tasteful, accomplished, and widely recorded drummers of the past decade or so; his most famous work is probably on Steely Dan's *Aja,* but you've also heard him on innumerable other funk, pop, R&B, and fusion tracks by a multitude of artists, as well as on hundreds of TV and radio commercial jingles. In *Up Close*, Gadd discusses and demonstrates his own marching-band roots; his approach to the trap set; drum rudiments and chart-reading; maintaining strict tempo; practice routines; bass drum technique; how to play just like the incredible jazz and fusion drummer Tony Williams; how to play sambas and other Latin patterns on a drum kit; and, most incredibly of all, the four-stick technique Gadd employed for that great "Mozambique"-derived Afro-Latin polyrhythm he played on Paul Simon's hit "Late in the Evening." *In Session* opens with an awesome Gadd jam with a drum machine, then has Gadd discussing and playing funk, reggae, bebop, R&B, slow blues, and a variety of Latin grooves with two different trios—one composed of bassist Will Lee (of the *Late Night with David Letterman* band and quite a few sessions himself) and noted session pianist Richard Tee (who's made his own DCI instructional cassette); the other, for Latin and bebop, with superb jazz bassist Eddie Gomez and underrated, New York–based pianist Jorge Dalto.

In Session, which comes with its own accompanying instructional booklet, contains a wealth of teaching by simply showing Gadd playing his relentlessly impeccable licks in loose improvisatory jams, and fleshing them out with illustrative voiceover comments. Overall, both tapes are invaluable for any drummer. (Available by mail order from DCI Music Video.)

□ DIAMANDA GALAS
THE LITANIES OF SATAN
★★★½

Target, 1986, 30 minutes
PRODUCED BY: Joe Rees
DIRECTED BY: Joe Rees
MUSIC FROM: The Litanies of Satan (Rough Trade, 1982)
SELECTIONS: "The Litanies of Satan."

As much performance artist as vocalist, Diamanda Galas is known as "the diva of electro-acoustic music," a sobriquet that in no way prepares the unsuspecting for the maniacal madness and visceral virtuosity of "The Litanies of Satan," the thirty-minute piece for voice, two stereo microphones, live tape-loops, and electronic modifications that she performs here (in a July 1985 show at the I-Beam Club in San

Francisco). "The Litanies of Satan," according to a title that appears on-screen just before the piece begins, is from the poem by Charles Baudelaire and "devotes itself to the emeraldine perversity of the life struggle in hell." *That* prepares the unsuspecting better than Galas's title. So does this critique, from the London magazine *Time Out*: "Whore, saint, demon, lover, madwoman or angel, there is no other voice in rock, jazz, or the avant-garde with her violence, consuming passion and pure elemental force."

Punkishly attired in a black leather corset, the exotically attractive, raven-tressed Galas clutches two microphones to her mouth and proceeds to deliver a blithering torrent of anguished sighs, screams, moans, chants, glottal gurgling sounds, and speaking-in-tongues gibberish; through electronic modifications (like echo, reverb, and distortion) and live tape-loops, her vocal emissions are layered and transmogrified into a dense, hellishly swarming and buzzing mass of atavistic sound and noise that makes it hard to believe it could have come out of just one human being's mouth. Wildly original and intense, this is absolutely, positively NOT for everyone. But as the *New York Times* noted, Galas is "undeniably virtuosic" at what she does, and, for those who dare, *The Litanies of Satan* makes for one hell (sorry, couldn't resist) of a trip. Target Video's low-budget production—in which what looks like a single-camera up-close performance shoot is treated with occasional slow-motion and solarization effects—could be technically cleaner but does the trick well enough. To those with adventurous tastes who are still a bit faint of heart—or who have someone *else* in their home who's faint of heart—I would strenuously recommend NOT playing this tape after dark. (Available in stores, or by mail order from Target Video or Independent World Video.)

□ GAP BAND

VIDEO TRAIN

★★½

Sony, 1986, 23 minutes

PRODUCED BY: Len Epand and Claude Borenzweig

DIRECTED BY: Don Letts, Nick Saxton, Jim Sotos, Lawrence Bridges

MUSIC FROM: Gap Band III (Polygram, 1981); *Gap Band IV* (Polygram, 1982); *Gap Band V—Jammin'* (Polygram, 1983).

SELECTIONS: "Party Train," "Early in the Morning," "You Dropped a Bomb on Me," "Burn Rubber (Why You Wanna Hurt Me)," "Jam the Motha."

The Gap Band—brothers Charlie, Robert, and Ronnie Wilson of Tulsa, Oklahoma—make some mean state-of-the-art funk music, and some of the best of it ("Early in the Morning," "You Dropped a Bomb on Me," "Jam the Motha") is here. The videos themselves, however, are another story. Unless you really get off on the sight of the Wilson brothers doing their unison steps, you'll be bored by "Early in the Morning," "You Dropped a Bomb on Me," and "Burn Rubber." "Party Train" does an okay but unexceptional job of communicating the life-affirming power of funk with its good-times atmosphere. But Lawrence Bridges's "Jam the Motha" is by far the best of this mediocre lot: the band perform live on a huge video-billboard, while below them L.A. goes through another sunny day in faster-than-the-speed-of-light time-lapse photography. Oh well, if nothing else, the soundtrack makes for a nice little half hour of dancing.

□ J. GEILS BAND

VIDEO 45

★★½

Sony, 1982, 13 minutes

PRODUCED BY: Various
DIRECTED BY: Paul Justman, Chuck Statler
MUSIC FROM: Freeze-Frame (EMI-America, 1981; *Love Stinks* (EMI-America, 1980).
SELECTIONS: "Angel in Blue," "Centerfold," "Freeze-Frame," "Love Stinks."

An extremely erratic clips compilation by the Boston-based veteran blues-rockers, who by the time this was released had evolved (or devolved, depending on your perspective) into a competent but unspectacular, corporate party-rock bank. "Centerfold," the best song and best-known video here, is a rousing musical arrangement with an irresistible singalong chorus and a video (directed by keyboardist Seth Justman's brother Paul) that sets singer Peter Wolf in a fantasy classroom full of lovely young ladies cavorting around him in cheerleader outfits and sexy lingerie. It takes off literally from the song's lyrics but also adds some imaginative and nicely executed dreamy touches, and its inherent sexism stays just this side of offensiveness. "Freeze-Frame" is an unwatchable eyesore by Justman, mixing silent-movie clips and cheap-looking solarization and superimposition effects with shots of the band having a paint-spattering melee. This is one of those clips in which a band is basically saying, "We haven't got a damned clue what to do with our video budget, but hey—we *do* have a video budget . . ." "Love Stinks," shot by video pioneer and onetime Devo associate Chuck Statler, is similarly uninspired, but it does have its moments of blankly downcast off-the-wall humor. Justman's "Angel in Blue" is the sleeper here: a rarely shown clip that's a surprisingly thoughtful and heartfelt consideration of a starlet's Marilyn Monroe–style rise-and-fall saga. This program is most worth checking out for this clip.

□ GENESIS
THREE SIDES LIVE
★★★½

HBO/Cannon, 1982, 90 minutes
DIRECTED BY: Stuart Orme
MUSIC FROM: Three Sides Live (Atlantic, 1982).
SELECTIONS: "Behind the Lines," "Duchess," "Misunderstanding," "Dodo," "Abacab," "No Reply At All," "Who Dunnit," "In the Suite Cage"/"Cinema Show"/"Slippermen," "Afterglow," "Me & Sarah Jane," "Man on the Corner," "Turn It On Again."

□ GENESIS
LIVE: THE MAMA TOUR
★★★½

Atlantic, 1986, 102 minutes
PRODUCED BY: Cynthia Biedermann
DIRECTED BY: Jim Yukich
MUSIC FROM: Genesis (Atlantic, 1983); *Abacab* (Atlantic, 1981); *Wind and Wuthering* (Atlantic, 1977); *The Lamb Lies down on Broadway* (Atlantic, 1975); *Selling England by the Pound* (Atlantic, 1974).
SELECTIONS: "Abacab," "That's All," "Mama," "Illegal Alien," "Home by the Sea," "Second Home by the Sea," "Keep It Dark," "It's Gonna Get Better," Medley: "In the Cage"/"Cinema Show"/ "Afterglow"/"Turn It On Again."

By 1982, when Genesis were caught in concert at the Nassau Coliseum on Long Island, New York, for *Three Sides Live,* the veteran British progressive-rock band had been through a lot of changes. Original vocalist Peter Gabriel and guitarist Steve Hackett had departed, and drummer/vocalist Phil Collins had recently undertaken a successful solo career in which he displayed his affection for R&B and funk. In fact, Genesis's 1982 tour proved to be their most successful U.S. jaunt since Gabriel's last tour with them in 1975, because the band had been dramatically influenced by Collins and was now playing what amounted to R&B- and funk-inflected rock with an art-rock veneer. And as this tape shows, audiences responded. With regular touring members Daryl Steurmer on guitar and bass, and drummer Chester Thompson joining Collins, bassist/guitarist Mike Rutherford, and keyboardist Tony Banks, Genesis are in good musical form, though Collins provides the sole point of visual interest with his energetic, good-humored, down-to-earth stage presence. There is a pretty impressive light show if you go in for that sort of thing (with dry-ice fog as well!), and the concert is shot nicely by Stuart Orme. There are also some snippets of on-the-road footage, and brief interviews in which Collins's vitality appears even more desperately important to the band's success—what with Banks and Rutherford droning on drily like a pair of upper-class-twit professors in a *Monty Python* sketch.

Live: The Mama Tour is more slickly directed, which is appropriate because it finds the band, in England in 1984 to promote the *Genesis* album, slicker and more cagily pop-oriented than ever. The spotlight's focused on Collins's irreverent-emcee bit, and he's honed his comic presence to a fine, seemingly spontaneous edge. Tunes like "That's All," "Mama," and "Illegal Alien," from *Genesis,* were all hit singles, and it's easy to see why: they're catchy pieces of pure pop in a McCartneyesque vein. As in *Three Sides Live,* the poppier latter-day material is emphasized over the earlier, lengthier progressive-rock exercises, which are given short shrift with another medley. Big fans of the band will probably want both programs.

☐ **VARIOUS ARTISTS**

GET CRAZY

★★★

Embassy, 1983, 98 minutes

PRODUCED BY: Hunt Lowry
DIRECTED BY: Allan Arkush
MUSIC FROM: The film *Get Crazy* (D&P Prod., 1983); various albums by various artists.

SELECTIONS: Doris Troy: "Just One Look"; Adrian Belew: "Big Electric Cat"; the Surfaris: "Wipe Out"; Johnny Otis: "Harlem Nocturne"; Flo & Eddie: "Walking in the Clouds"; Mikey Dread: "Headline News"; Marshall Crenshaw: "It's Only a Movie (But, But)"; T. Rex: "Metal Guru"; the Ramones: "Chop Suey"; Sparks: "Get Crazy"; Bill Henderson: "The Sky Is Crying," "The Blues Had a Baby and They Named It Rock and Roll," "Hoochie Coochie Man"; Lee Ving and Fear: "Hoochie Coochie Man"; Malcolm McDowell: "Hoochie Coochie Man," "Hot Shot"; Black Uhuru: "Carbine"; Howard Kaylan: "Auld Lang Syne"; Lori Eastside and Nada: "You Can't Make Me," "I'm Not Gonna Take It"; Lou Reed: "Little Sister."

Get Crazy isn't the greatest rock parody, but it *is* an enjoyable lightweight rock comedy. If it has a problem, it's director Allan Arkush, a Roger Corman protégé whose touch is something less than subtle. Just about everything and everyone in *Get Crazy* is a "thinly veiled" takeoff on something or someone: the plot concerns a real cool old rock palace that's a thinly veiled Fillmore West (to which the film is fondly dedicated), which a nasty record exec/promoter (Ed Begley, Jr.) wants to shut down for his own nefarious reasons; Daniel Stern of *Diner* and *Blue Thunder* fame is the stage manager of the cool old rock palace, the Saturn Theater—he's the one who organizes the Saturn's annual New Year's Eve blow-out, and to save the Saturn from the evil exec this year's bash has to be *really* big, and so *Get Crazy* cheerily falls into movie-musical clichéville.

Among the stars Stern rounds up: Malcolm McDowell as Reggie Wanker, a dissolute British rocker who's a thinly veiled Mick Jagger/Rod Stewart figure; Lou Reed as Auden, a thinly veiled Dylan-type rock poet who's so zoned-out on his own genius his songs consist of his conversation—and his conversation consists of repeating back whatever anyone says to him; and New York post-punk rock-aerobics queen (yes, such a person does exist) Lori Eastside as a maniacal punk-rock queen. Thing is, they're all pretty funny, especially McDowell and Reed. Also cute: the bit at the New Year's Show when "Hoochie Coochie Man" is performed first in traditional blues fashion by Bill Henderson, then in overwrought heavy-rock fashion by McDowell, and finally in furious punk fashion by Lee Ving, who was so good in *Flashdance* and is allowed to chew up a bit too much scenery (literally) as rabid punk-rocker Piggy; and the recurring riff of a magical drug dealer who keeps appearing *Star Wars*–style out of nowhere, accompanied by glowing special effects and the pounding drums and loopy guitar wail of Adrian Belew's "Big Electric Cat" (a particularly canny use of rock music, that). Yes, *Get Crazy* is hit-or-miss, but if you've never seen it and you happen to be in the mood, it's worth checking out.

□ BARRY GIBB
NOW VOYAGER
★★

MCA, 1984, 79 minutes
PRODUCED BY: Aubrey Powell
DIRECTED BY: Storm Thorgeson
MUSIC FROM: Now Voyager (MCA, 1984).
SELECTIONS: "Shine, Shine," "Fine Line," "I Am Your Driver," "Temptation," "Lesson in Love," "Shatterproof," "Stay Alone," "One Night," "Hunter."

Conceptually linked series of MTV-style videos, in which the Bee Gee, playing off the title, is transported to various "exotic" and "mysterious" places. Director Storm Thorgeson (who got his start with Hipgnosis, the album-cover people) has a nice way with highly produced, lavishly odd images; but while it's pleasurable in a superficially sensory way, there's nothing deep enough here visually or musically to merit much attention. Unless you're a major Gibb fan, that is.

□ DIZZY GILLESPIE ORCHESTRA, OTHERS
JIVIN' IN BEBOP
★★★½

Video Yesteryear, 1982, 59 minutes
MUSIC FROM: The film *Jivin' in Bebop* (1947).

Straight performance film of young Diz, before his trumpet began bending upward, with his adventurous "Cubop" big band, which included the nucleus of the Modern Jazz Quartet in vibraphonist Milt Jackson and pianist John Lewis. They play compositions by Diz, Charlie Parker, and others. Dizzy does his own unique brand of scat-singing, and guest vocalists Helen Humes and Kenny Hagood are along as well. As on many Video Yesteryear releases, reproduction quality is a bit grainy, but worth it for jazz-history buffs seeking out this sort of gold. (Available by mail order from Video Yesteryear.)

□ DIZZY GILLESPIE, OTHERS
JAZZ IN AMERICA
★★★★½

Embassy, 1983, 90 minutes
PRODUCED BY: Gary Keys
DIRECTED BY: Stanley Dorfman
MUSIC FROM: Various Dizzy Gillespie albums.
SELECTIONS: "Manteca," "Night in Tunisia," "Groovin' High," "Poppa Joe,"

"Hot House," "Lover Man (Oh, Where Can You Be)," "Tin Tin Deo," "Salt Peanuts."

□ DIZZY GILLESPIE, OTHERS
DIZZY GILLESPIE'S DREAM BAND/JAZZ IN AMERICA

★★★½

Sony, 1983, 16 minutes
PRODUCED BY: Gary Keys
DIRECTED BY: Stanley Dorfman
MUSIC FROM: Various Dizzy Gillespie albums; the video program *Dizzy Gillespie: Jazz in America* (Embassy, 1983).
SELECTIONS: "Groovin' High," "Hot House."

Both of these programs are taken from the same 1981 concert at New York's Lincoln Center, during which the great bebop trumpeter led an all-star big band in recreating some of the gems of the late-'40s/early-'50s "Cubop" era, an era when Diz was leading the way in fusing bebop with Latin music. The band includes Max Roach and Grady Tate on drums, Candido on congas, Gerry Mulligan and Pepper Adams on baritone sax, John Lewis and Sir Roland Hanna on piano, Milt Jackson on vibes, Paquito d'Rivera on alto sax, Jon Hendricks on vocals, and many others—suffice to say it's a hell of a band, and just about everyone in it gets plenty of chances to stretch out and dig in to these hard-swinging, neoclassic arrangements (which, by the way, are by the very respected Chico O'Farrill). The music is sublime throughout, Diz is in his usual good humor and generous spirits as host/leader, and it's all shot very classily and competently, with loads of nice strategic close-ups and the wonderful added touch (too rare in such videos) of on-screen identification of the soloists. Both Embassy's long version and Sony's two-song excerpt are recommendable, but the Embassy has to get the nod—because you don't just have to be a jazz fan to want more, rather than less, of *this.*

□ DIZZY GILLESPIE
IN REDONDO BEACH/JAZZ IN AMERICA

★★★½

Embassy, 1986, 60 minutes
PRODUCED BY: Gary Keys
DIRECTED BY: Stanley Dorfman
MUSIC FROM: Various Dizzy Gillespie albums.
SELECTIONS: "Be-Bop," "Kush," "Birk's Works," "Brother 'K,' " "Woody'n You," "Jazz America."

Diz fronts a unique septet, featuring an acoustic bassist *and* an electric bassist, in *Redondo Beach,* which is the first Jazz in America program I can recall that's marred by far too many intrusive audience-reaction shots. That drawback and the serviceable if unimaginative direction aside, it's pretty primo stuff musically, as Diz and band—which also features alto saxophonist Paquito d'Rivera, pianist Valerie Capers, and trombonist Tom McIntosh—deliver a highly authoritative and satisfying set of Latin-inflected modern bebop. Sure, they really smoke, as the ol' jazzbo's term has it, especially on the supercharged opener, "Bebop." But that's not why you'll occasionally notice what looks like smoke emitting from Dizzy's upturned trumpet bell as he solos—this show was recorded on a chilly night in Redondo Beach. Anyway, d'Rivera and Capers are close behind Diz in the soloing sweepstakes here, and Diz is his usual irrepressible self in his between-songs patter. At the start of the show, he tells the audience, "I'd like to introduce the members of the band right now" and proceeds to introduce them—to each other.

□ DAVID GILMOUR
DAVID GILMOUR

★★½

CBS/Fox, 1984, 101 minutes
DIRECTED BY: Michael Hurll, Norman Stone

MUSIC FROM: Pink Floyd: *The Wall* (Columbia, 1982); *David Gilmour* (Columbia, 1982); *About Face* (Columbia, 1984).
SELECTIONS: "Until We Sleep," "All Lovers Are Deranged" (two versions), "There's No Way Out of Here," "Short and Sweet," "Run like Hell," "Out of the Blue," "Blue Light" (two versions), "Murder," "Comfortably Numb," *After the Floyd*.

Though Pink Floyd is a critically underrated band, guitarist David Gilmour solo is strictly for fans only. Yes, he's a uniquely bluesy rock guitarist and all, but his uncanny resemblance to rock critic Dave Marsh (who probably *hates* hearing this likeness mentioned) is more remarkable than anything he has to say musically or lyrically. Still, his and Floyd's fans will certainly appreciate this nicely produced program, which contains concept clips for "Blue Light" and "All Lovers Are Deranged," a nine-song concert, and *After the Floyd*, a thirty-minute special on Gilmour's solo career featuring interviews with Gilmour and Pete Townshend of the Who.

□ VARIOUS ARTISTS
GIRL GROUPS: THE STORY OF A SOUND
★★★★½

MGM/UA, 1983, 65 minutes
PRODUCED BY: Stephanie Bennett and Steve Alpert
DIRECTED BY: Steve Alpert
MUSIC FROM: Various albums by various artists.
SELECTIONS: The Angels: "My Boyfriend's Back"; Frankie Lymon: "Why Do Fools Fall in Love?"; the Chantels: "Maybe"; the Shirelles: "Will You Love Me Tomorrow?"; the Drifters: "On Broadway"; Dee Dee Sharp: "Mashed Potato Time"; Little Eva: "The Loco-Motion"; the Dixie Cups: "Chapel of Love," "You Should Have Seen the Way He Looked at Me"; the Exciters: "Tell Him"; Martha and the Vandellas: "Dancing in the Street"; Mary Wells: "My Guy"; the Marvelettes: "Please Mr. Postman"; the Shangri-Las: "Leader of the Pack," "Remember (Walkin' in the Sand)," "Give Him a Great Big Kiss"; the Ronettes: "Shout," "Be My Baby"; Darlene Love: "He's a Rebel"; the Blossoms: "Needle in a Haystack"; the Supremes: "Come See About Me," "Baby Love," "Stop! In the Name of Love," "Back in My Arms Again," "Someday We'll Be Together."

This superb documentary, based on Alan Betrock's book of the same title, recounts the history, roots, and influence of one of baby-boomer-pop music's best-loved and best-remembered sounds. Through interviews with such performers as Ronnie Spector of the Ronettes, Mary Wilson of the Supremes, and Darlene Love, and behind-the-scenes *auteurs* like songwriters Ellie Greenwich, Jerry Leiber, and Mike Stoller, *Girl Groups* paints a telling and complete portrait not only of the girl-group sound, but also of its historical milieu and both its timely and timeless significance. There are also some fascinating, comparatively prehistoric music video snippets—the most surreal being the Exciters' "Tell Him," which is set in, of all places, the Bronx Zoo.

□ PHILIP GLASS
KOYAANISQATSI
★★★★★

Pacific Arts, 1984, 87 minutes
PRODUCED BY: Godfrey Reggio
DIRECTED BY: Godfrey Reggio
MUSIC FROM: Koyaanisqatsi soundtrack album (Island/Antilles, 1983).
Also available on Pacific Arts/MCA Stereo Laser videodisc.

Godfrey Reggio, working under the auspices of the Institute for Regional Education and with Francis Ford Coppola (who gets "presented by" billing), took seven years to make this movie. And while at times it may feel like it's taking seven years to watch

Koyaanisqatsi, all in all it's one *hell* of a trip, and surely one of the ultimate examples of a feature film that's really an extended music video. It's a nonnarrative, faster-than-the-speed-of-light travelogue, with no dialogue and only the Earth and mankind as characters.

Koyaanisqatsi counterpoints gorgeous, unspoiled natural vistas with nervously energetic time-lapse shots of urban centers and industry at work. The title is a Hopi Indian word meaning "life out of balance," and the movie's message seems to be that humanity is an ugly blight on the face of this beautiful planet. In a way, that's a hard point to argue with, but this breathtakingly photographed (by Ron Fricke) film proposes no solutions either—and its point could have been made in at least a third less running time. Those time-lapse light trails of city traffic have their trippy beauty all right, but the ostensibly critical time-lapse shots of Grand Central Station commuters and a weiner-factory assembly line are too obvious and heavy-handed. Perhaps the fact that Reggio is an ex-monk explains this relentlessly misanthropic one-sidedness. Whatever, Reggio's ultimately wearing bias pushes the "educational film" angle suggested by the IRE's involvement deep into the realm of the didactic—a bit too deep for what is basically an abstract, sensory feast.

And yet, *Koyaanisqatsi* really *is* a sensory feast—an awesome and epic one that grabs you and stays with you enough to be undersold by an adjective like "powerful." The untitled, nonlyrical score, by New York–based modern-classical minimalist composer/keyboardist Philip Glass, is very much a part of the experience. Glass's typical mantrically repeated, intricately overlaid layers of tintinnabulating organ ripples and wordless choral vocals are fleshed out to appropriately monumental proportions with full choir and some orchestral passages. Glass makes full and vibrantly visceral use of the palette at his disposal, moving with grace and assurance from an ethereal whisper to a spine-tingling scream. Glass is every bit as responsible as Reggio and Fricke's visuals for effecting *Koyaanisqatsi*'s most riveting synergistic epiphanies.

☐ **VARIOUS ARTISTS**

GO, JOHNNY, GO!

★★★

Media, 1985, 75 minutes
PRODUCED BY: Alan Freed
DIRECTED BY: Paul Landres
MUSIC FROM: The film, originally released in 1959.
SELECTIONS: Jimmy Clanton: "My Love Is Strong," "It Takes a Long Time," "Ship on a Stormy Sea," "Angel Face"; Chuck Berry: "Johnny B. Goode," "Little Queenie," "Memphis"; Sandy Stewart: "Playmates," "Heavenly Father"; Ritchie Valens: "Ooh My Head"; Jackie Wilson: "You'd Better Know It"; Eddie Cochran: "Teenage Heaven"; the Cadillacs: "Jay Walker," "Please Mr. Johnson"; the Flamingoes: "Jump, Children"; Jo-Ann Campbell: "Mama, Can I Go Out"; Harvey Fuqua: "Don't Be Afraid to Love Me."

Better than most '50s jukebox musicals because the "plot" (hero Jimmy Clanton competes in an Alan Freed talent show, and that's about it) is *so* thin it barely gets in the way of the cavalcade of performances it occasions. And a pretty good cavalcade it is, too: Chuck Berry, Ritchie Valens, Jackie Wilson, and Eddie Cochran all stand out, and Clanton is grittier-voiced and easier to take than most '50s teen idols were (which may explain why he never went as far as most '50s teen idols).

☐ **THE GO-GO'S**

TOTALLY GO-GO'S

★★★

HBO/Cannon, 1982, 77 minutes

MUSIC FROM: Beauty and the Beat (IRS/A&M, 1981); *Vacation* (IRS/A&M, 1982).

SELECTIONS: "Vacation," "You Can't Walk in Your Sleep (If You Can't Sleep)," "Skidmarks on My Heart," "How Much More," "Fading Fast," "Tonite," "London Boys," "Cool Jerk," "We Got the Beat," "Surfing and Spying," "Automatic," "The Way You Dance," "Beatnik Beach," "Lust to Love," "Can't Stop the World," "This Town," "Our Lips Are Sealed," "Let's Have a Party," "Remember (Walkin' in the Sand)."

□ THE GO-GO'S

PRIME TIME

★★★½

RCA/Columbia, 1985, 25 minutes

MUSIC FROM: Talk Show (IRS, 1984); *Vacation* (IRS, 1982); *Beauty and the Beat* (IRS, 1981).

SELECTIONS: "Our Lips Are Sealed," "We Got the Beat," "Vacation," "Get Up and Go," "Head over Heels," "Turn to You," "Yes or No."

The Los Angeles all-girl pop rockers gave the concert recorded in *Totally Go-Go's* at an L.A. high school in December 1981, as a triumphant homecoming show following a world tour, and with their debut album *Beauty and the Beat* in the Top Ten. Not only does the crowd go crazy, but the Go-Go's are obviously pretty worked up themselves. While this adds to the overall excitement level, it also makes their performance ragged in spots, much more so than in the later *Wild at the Greek.* But the Go-Go's just happily churn out a generous portion of serviceably fun '60s-style rock. They also talk about themselves and their band in some brief interview snippets, where they don't have very much to say but come off as sweet and genuine anyway.

Prime Time is a solid compilation of video clips that proves that you don't have to be an analytically inclined media maven to enjoy the Go-Go's. Unlike, say, Bananarama, the Go-Go's may project an air-headedly kicky image, but they were a talented and resourceful '60s-inspired pop-rock band, whose sheer energy, smarts, and personality carry the day—and that's despite the erratic quality of the clips themselves. "Our Lips Are Sealed," "We Got the Beat," and "Yes or No" are thoroughly dispensible blends of bubbleheaded shenanigans and gawky, lackluster stage performance (the first two pulled from *Totally Go-Go's*). "Vacation," with its inane Cypress Gardens water-skiing fantasy, epitomizes the sweet escapism for which some loved and others derided the Go-Go's. Much better are two perfectly fine clips that, for some reason, never got much exposure: "Get Up and Go" (directed by Douglas Martin) features delightful, rollicking clay-animation; and "Turn to You" (directed by Mary Lambert) is a clever gender-bending prom party, with the Go-Go's cast as both bouffanted party dolls *and* in male drag as the prom band. Finally, there's the tape's masterpiece, the one clip that really makes the cassette worth owning: "Head over Heels." It's one of their hardest-hitting and musically best-arranged tunes, and director Douglas Martin enhances it magnificently with a beautifully lit, studio-mounted performance, razor-sharp on-and-around-the-beat edits, rhythmic multi-split-screens, and abrupt cut-ins (not to mention his neat use of slo-mo when the band drops out for Kathy Valentine's bass break three-quarters of the way through). The video is as dynamic and delightful as the song, and as the charismatic, camerawise Go-Go's were at their best. It can be watched over and over, and you can still enjoy it while growing to appreciate the subtle sophistication of its perfect execution.

You would have to have a heart of stone to resist it.

☐ THE GO-GO'S
WILD AT THE GREEK
★★★

RCA/Columbia, 1985, 52 minutes
PRODUCED BY: Simon Fields
DIRECTED BY: Chris Gabrin
MUSIC FROM: Beauty and the Beat (IRS, 1981); *Vacation* (IRS, 1982); *Talk Show* (IRS, 1984).
SELECTIONS: "Head over Heels," "Our Lips Are Sealed," "Forget That Day," "We Got the Beat," "Turn to You," "Tonight," "You Thought," "Yes or No," "I'm with You," "This Town," "Can't Stop the World," "Vacation," "I'm the Only One."

Pleasantly straightforward shoot of the L.A.-based all-girl, post-punk, pop-rock band playing to a hometown crowd in 1984 outdoors at the Greek Theater. While the now-defunct Go-Go's look more mild than wild, and sound a lot more ragged outside the studio, watching them here it's undeniable that they were more than a mere gaggle of cute, bubbly bubbleheads who could actually play. The Go-Go's crafted some very fine examples of '60s-based rock, most of the best of which ("We Got the Beat," "Our Lips Are Sealed," "Head over Heels," "Vacation," "Yes or No," "Turn to You") are here. No matter how some people out there may or may not feel about them, the Go-Go's look and sound just fine, now that their absence and this video can make the heart grow fonder.

☐ GOLDEN EARRING
GOLDEN EARRING VIDEO EP
★★★★

Sony, 1984, 30 minutes
DIRECTED BY: Dick Maas, Paul DeNoojier
MUSIC FROM: Cut (Polydor, 1982).
SELECTIONS: "Twilight Zone," "Something Heavy Going Down," "N.E.W.S.," "Clear Night Moonlight," "When the Lady Smiles."

One of the very best clips compilations of relatively short length without added connective material. Which should come as no surprise to those familiar with Dick Maas's immortal "Twilight Zone" video—a mini-movie filled with wit, sexy style, high production values, and one of the better surrealist homages in the nascent genre's history (in this case, to Buñuel's *Discreet Charm of the Bourgeoisie,* when the paranoid protagonist opens the red curtains in a drawing room to find himself onstage before a theater audience). The rest of the clips maintain that level of accomplishment. Paul DeNoojier's "Something Heavy Going Down" and "N.E.W.S." make delightful use of assorted visual puns, masks, special effects, and various self-referential gambits, all accentuated with deadpan comic flair. Maas proves he's got panache to burn with "Clear Night Moonlight," a *Bonnie and Clyde* gloss with a legitimately shocking and powerful conclusion, and the Freudy-cat-and-mouse psychodrama of "When the Lady Smiles," which is for *mature* audiences only. As for the music . . . well, it backs the visuals very nicely, and the more you dig those classy visuals, the more you're likely to appreciate Golden Earring's craftily competent, if ultimately rather unspectacular pop rock.

☐ GOLDEN EARRING
LIVE FROM THE TWILIGHT ZONE
★★★

RCA/Columbia, 1984, 60 minutes
PRODUCED BY: Robert Swaab, Laurens Geels
DIRECTED BY: Dick Maas
MUSIC FROM: Something Heavy Going Down (Live from the Twilight Zone) (Polygram, 1984).
SELECTIONS: "Mission Impossible,"

"When the Lady Smiles," "Long Blond Animal," "The Devil Made Me Do It," "Radar Love," "Twilight Zone."

Also available on Pioneer Stereo Laser videodisc.

Live from the Twilight Zone is exactly what its title implies: a concert (shot at the Groenoordhallen in Leiden, Holland, in June 1984) that's based on the "Twilight Zone" video, complete with two leather-clad dancing girls. The program opens with Maas's conceptual intro, a follow-up to the "Twilight Zone" clip in which the spy character is hit by a car, brought to a hospital, and given face-altering plastic surgery. It's done with as much toney, chic style as "Twilight Zone," but once the concert starts, Maas's resources limited. Golden Earring is a slickly competent band, and here it's obvious that they have their adoring homeland fans. But onstage and on their own they're not exciting enough, nor is their material distinguished enough, to appeal to any but the already converted—despite the fact that Maas shoots the concert with his usual panache.

☐ **VARIOUS ARTISTS**

GOODTIME ROCK 'N' ROLL, VOLUME ONE

★★

MCA, 1986, 27 minutes

PRODUCED BY: Arthur Forrest

DIRECTED BY: Arthur Forrest

MUSIC FROM: Various albums by various artists.

SELECTIONS: Fabian: "Old Time Rock 'n' Roll"; the Diamonds: "Little Darlin' "; Bo Diddley: "Bo Diddley"; Little Anthony: "Tears on My Pillow"; the Crystals: "He's a Rebel"; Lou Christie: "Lightnin' Strikes"; Lesley Gore: "It's My Party"; the Coasters: "Yakety Yak"; Chubby Checker: "Let's Twist Again," "The Twist."

This cavalcade of '50s and '60s nostalgia acts was shot in competent, unspectacular fashion at an unspecified Louisiana venue on the banks of the Mississippi River in August 1985. Judging by the slightly tawdry feel of the whole affair, the venue was probably a theme park or something. Fabian, who I've heard sound passable on many occasions, sings hideously here to open proceedings. The Diamonds' pudgy, middle-aged lead singer's voice cracks on the falsetto parts of "Little Darlin'." Bo Diddley turns in a more-or-less okay performance that's sabotaged by a drummer who can't—or at least won't—even play a Bo Diddley beat! "The Crystals" sound great but look way too young to be anything near the genuine article. Little Anthony sounds okay, and after a shaky start Lou Christie, paunch and double chin and all, actually manages to get his middle-aged voice to scrape the sky for "Lightnin' Strikes." Lesley Gore may be the biggest embarrassment of all: she looks and sounds totally foolish trying to sing "It's My Party" in her deep, womanly voice. By the time the Coasters (who seem pretty authentic) and Chubby Checker cruise through their bits . . . well, let's just say that if you're a pretty big afficionado of these sorts of things, or are really hard up for some rock nostalgia, this *could* be for you.

☐ **VARIOUS ARTISTS**

GOSPEL

★★★★½

Monterey/IVE, 1983, 92 minutes

PRODUCED BY: David Leivick and Fred Ritzenberg

DIRECTED BY: David Leivick and Fred Ritzenberg

MUSIC FROM: The 1982 film; various albums by various artists.

SELECTIONS: The Mighty Clouds of Joy: "Mighty High," "Walk Around Heaven," "I Came to Jesus"; the Clark Sisters: "Name It and Claim It," "Is My

Living in Vain," "Hallelujah"; Walter Hawkins and the Hawkins Family: "Goin' to a Place," "He Brought Me," "Until I Found the Lord," "Right On"; Shirley Caesar: "He's Got It All in Control," "No Charge," "(This Joy) The World Didn't Give It to Me"; the Reverend James Cleveland: "Waiting on You," "I Don't Feel Noways Tired," "Can't Nobody Do Me like Jesus," "I Have a Determination."

Excellent concert documentary of some of gospel's biggest names performing *very* live in Oakland, California's Paramount Theater. The spirit *and* sass, the preaching *and* the showbiz sweat 'n' savvy, of such mountain-movers as the Clark Sisters or the Hawkins Family (which includes Edwin of "Oh Happy Day" fame) is pretty hard to resist whatever your faith or lack thereof. Especially awesome are Shirley Caesar and the Reverend James Cleveland. But all of them make it plain just how far a newcomer like Amy Grant will have to go to get even *close* to the real power of gospel music.

☐ **VARIOUS ARTISTS**
THE GOSPEL AT COLONUS
★★★★

Warner-Reprise, 1986, 90 minutes
PRODUCED BY: David Horn and Yvonne Smith
DIRECTED BY: Kirk Browning
MUSIC FROM: The Gospel at Colonus original cast recording (Warner Bros., 1985).
SELECTIONS: "Live Where You Can," "Stop Do Not Go On," "How Shall I See You Through My Tears," "A Voice Foretold (Prayer)," "Never Drive You Away (Jubilee)," "Numberless Are the World's Wonders," "Lift Me Up (Like a Dove)," "Sunlight of No Light," "Eternal Sleep," "Lift Him Up," "Now Let the Weeping Cease (Hymn)."

The Gospel at Colonus is based on the Greek tragedy *Oedipus at Colonus,* here transformed into a striking and poignant series of gospel revelations. The elemental gravity and joy of gospel music mesh surprisingly (or not so surprisingly) well with the source matter's timeless motifs of human suffering and redemption. At least part of the success of this fusion is due to the music and lyrics, by Bob Telson and Lee Breuer, and the performances by, among others, the Institutional Radio Choir, the J. D. Steele Singers of Minneapolis, and especially the semilegendary Clarence Fountain and the Five Blind Boys of Alabama. For those who may be put off by the idea of a classical Greek tragedy at first, this could at least serve as an unusual and relatively easy way of getting into some good stuff. Those more familiar with Greek tragedy may never look at it the same way again after *The Gospel at Colonus*. It should also be pointed out that fans of *Cats* and *Jesus Christ Superstar* may be left a bit cold by this production's comparative starkness and avoidance of grandstanding musical-theater clichés. But to me, that only makes *The Gospel at Colonus* infinitely better theater than either *Cats* or *Jesus Christ Superstar*.

☐ **AMY GRANT**
AGE TO AGE
★★★

A&M, 1985, 90 minutes
PRODUCED BY: Kitty Moon and Marc Ball
DIRECTED BY: Marc Ball
MUSIC FROM: Various Amy Grant albums, including *Age to Age* (A&M, 1983).
SELECTIONS: "Shaddai," "Father's Eyes," "Fat Baby," "Sing Your Praise to the Lord," and others.

☐ **AMY GRANT**
FIND A WAY
★★★

A&M, 1985, 30 minutes
PRODUCED BY: Various
DIRECTED BY: Various

MUSIC FROM: Unguarded (A&M, 1985).
SELECTIONS: "Find a Way," "Wise Up," "Angels," "Don't Run Away," "It's Not a Song."

Grant is sort of a cross between Madonna and Elmer Gantry, a Bible-thumping pop-rock-gospel *chanteuse* who knows what it takes to get as many people as possible turned on to her heavenly message: a heavenly body which she's not afraid to flaunt in the service of the Lord. *Find a Way,* the slickly produced compilation of promo clips from *Unguarded,* the LP that crossed Grant over to mainstream popularity, contains a most telling scene in the midst of the *Fame*-styled concept video for "Don't Run Away." Just as we start thinking it's Amy's song and message that are inspiring the stagehands and rehearsing dancers and actors to put on a really good show and all that, we get a quick-cut series of close-ups of those stagehands and actors and musicians all widening their eyes, smiling appreciatively, and pointing and staring at something off-camera. Then it cuts to a slow-motion close-up—which tellingly focuses on Amy's torso and cuts off her head—of Amy seductively doffing her overcoat to reveal a low-cut zebra-striped blouse and skin-tight red leather pants. I've heard of "erecting a pulpit," but this is a bit much.

So, Grant is a sort of whitebread answer to Prince, who also likes to trade on the provocative paradoxes of liberated sexuality and God-squad religious conviction. Whether you find that neat or nauseating depends on your own tastes and degree of liberation. But this sort of unlikely *frisson* probably explains her recent runaway popularity. Certainly her performance, as captured in the nicely shot *Age to Age* concert video (shot in 1983, before she crossed all the way over), doesn't. She's as bland as she is cute, and she's very cute. Her black gospel backup singers easily out-sing her, and she's nowhere near entertainer enough to disguise how hard she's working, nor to divert attention from the calculation in her whole act. Her fans will eat up both of these, for sure, but the curious are advised to avoid the unendurable-at-ninety-minutes *Age to Age*.

□ THE GRATEFUL DEAD
DEAD AHEAD
★★½

Warner Home Video, 1982, 90 minutes
PRODUCED BY: Richard Loren
DIRECTED BY: Len Dell'Amico
MUSIC FROM: Various Grateful Dead albums (Warner Bros., Arista, 1967–82).
SELECTIONS: "Uncle John's Band," "To Lay Me Down," "On the Road Again," "Ripple," "Don't Ease Me In," "Lost Sailor," "Saint of Circumstance," "Franklin's Tower," "Rhythm Devils," "Fire on the Mountain," "Not Fade Away," "Good Lovin.' "
Also available on Pioneer Stereo Laser videodisc.

□ THE GRATEFUL DEAD
THE GRATEFUL DEAD MOVIE
★★

Monterey/IVE, 1979, 131 minutes
PRODUCED BY: Ron Rakow, Edward Washington
DIRECTED BY: Jerry Garcia, Leon Gast
MUSIC FROM: 1977 film; various Grateful Dead albums.
SELECTIONS: Opening medley: "U.S. Blues"/"Beat It on Down the Line"/"The Wheel"/"He's Gone," "Another Saturday Night," "Going Down the Road Feeling Bad," "Truckin'," "Eyes of The World," "Sugar Magnolia," Intermission medley: "St. Stephen"/"Ripple"/"Golden Road to Unlimited Devotion," "Playing in the Band," "Casey Jones," "Morning Dew," "Stella Blue," "Johnny B. Goode," "Maybe It Was the Roses," others.

Dead Ahead is a competently shot, straightforward documentary of the Dead at New York City's Radio City

Music Hall on Halloween night, 1980. After being introduced by Al Franken and Tom Davis, one of the unfunniest comedy teams ever, the Dead launch into an acoustic set of the first four tunes in the program. The rest of the set is played with electric instruments—though whether or not you think the music itself is really "electric" depends on whether you're a Dead Head or not. If you're not, well . . . "Uncle John's Band" and "Ripple" are nice little tunes, and their version of Buddy Holly's "Not Fade Away" has its loping, spaced-out charm, but "Rhythm Devils" is an excruciatingly extended drum/percussion duet between Mickey Hart and Bill Kreutzmann, and overall the admittedly distinguished musicianship of guitarist Jerry Garcia and bassist Phil Lesh can't keep the heav-*ee* air of aging-hippie somnolence from dragging your eyelids down . . . down . . . down . . .

The Grateful Dead Movie documents a series of shows at San Francisco's Winterland Theater in 1974. It opens with a bang: Gary Gutierez's extended, animated, psychedelic, interstellar-pinball fantasy on Grateful Dead album covers and their associated visuals. But from that high it's straight downhill to for-Dead-Heads-only territory. Lesh is by far the most commanding musical presence, and steps out beautifully on "Eyes of the World." But the sound recording and camerawork are mediocre and worse. And the Dead are just that: dead on their feet, so laid-back they're out cold—as enervatingly dull as all the excess footage of band members and roadies backstage, with assorted Hell's Angels, latter-day hippies, and earth mother groupies milling about.

☐ **VARIOUS ARTISTS**
GREASE
★★★

Paramount, 1978, 110 minutes

PRODUCED BY: Robert Stigwood
DIRECTED BY: Randal Kleiser
MUSIC FROM: Grease motion picture soundtrack (RSO, 1978).
SELECTIONS: Sha-Na-Na: "Rock 'n' Roll Is Here to Stay," "Tears on My Pillow," "Hound Dog," "Born to Hand Jive," "Blue Moon"; Frankie Avalon: "Beauty School Drop-Out"; Olivia Newton-John and John Travolta: "You're the One that I Want"; Olivia Newton-John: "Hopelessly Devoted to You"; John Travolta: "Greased Lightnin'."

☐ **VARIOUS ARTISTS**
GREASE 2
★

Paramount, 1982, 115 minutes
PRODUCED BY: Robert Stigwood and Alan Carr
DIRECTED BY: Patricia Birch and Johnny Leghood
MUSIC FROM: Grease 2 motion picture soundtrack (RSO, 1982).
SELECTIONS: The Four Tops: "Back to School Again."

Coming at the height of '50s nostalgia, *Grease* was a huge hit. The original Broadway play, lauded for its cleverness, ran for years and audiences loved it—though judging from this film, you'd be hard-pressed to say why. John and Newton-John make a cute enough couple, and the dumb intrigues of American teenagers circa 1960 or so obviously have some appeal. Still: real afficionados of the period should see *American Grafitti* and leave this for the kids. Ditto for the "starless" sequel.—P.R.

☐ **VARIOUS ARTISTS**
GREENPEACE NON-TOXIC VIDEO HITS
★★★½

Vestron, 1986, 60 minutes
MUSIC FROM: Various albums by various artists, *Greenpeace Non-Toxic Hits* (A&M, 1985).

SELECTIONS: Peter Gabriel: "Shock the Monkey"; Tears for Fears: "Mad World"; Queen: "Is This the World That We Created"; Talk Talk: "It's My Life"; Thomas Dolby: "Dissidents"; Heaven 17: "Crushed by the Wheels of Industry"; Kaja: "Turn Your Back on Me"; Mai Tai: "Our Love Is History"; Madness: "On the Wings of a Dove"; Roger Taylor: "Strange Frontier"; Depeche Mode: "Blasphemous Rumours"; Hazel O'Connor and Chris Thompson: "Push and Shove"; Snowy White: "Bird of Paradise"; George Harrison: "Save the World"; Kelly Groucutt and the children of Blanford Mere Primary School: "We Love Animals."

Through the first half of this rather complicated bureaucratic benefit video for the British-based, international antinuke/pro-environment Greenpeace group (the video itself doesn't benefit Greenpeace, but the videos are of songs from which the artists donate royalties to Greenpeace), I kept thinking, could this be the first genuine, politically acute, thematic anti-establishment various-artists clips compilation? It sure seemed that way. The general theme of madness and destruction, accompanied by the implicit challenge to the viewer to feel and/or do something about it is stated in nicely oblique fashion by the opener: Brian Grant's brilliant, psychodramatic *Altered States* gloss for Peter Gabriel's "Shock the Monkey," in which a businessman wrestles with his subconscious demons and surrenders with honor. While both the pretentiously poker-faced Tears for Fears and the hideous-as-usual Queen are vapidly blatant about reinforcing the theme, they do have their fans, and the point is there. Tim Pope's fascinating integration of wildlife footage into Talk Talk's "It's My Life" alludes to Greenpeace's pro-environment causes with the same sort of subtle, sideways-attack approach as the opening clip. Thomas Dolby's "Dissidents," with its saga of Eastern European underground freedom fighters, focuses the program's latent critique of government policies, and stumbles only once (though badly, with an idiotically stereotypical subtitle in which one of the freedom fighters sadly recalls the night the authorities took his mother away: "We were eating a simple meal of barleycorn and water when they came . . . "). And Heaven 17's delightfully Devo-ish "Crushed by the Wheels of Industry" echoes "Shock the Monkey" and amplifies and sharpens the theme with cartoonish wit.

Then—suddenly, horribly—the video hits become very . . . toxic, if you will. What are Kaja's bland "new music," Mai Tai's innocuous girl-group dance pop, and the turgid irrelevancies of Hazel O'Connor and Chris Thompson and Queen drummer Roger Taylor doing here? Obviously there are only so many music videos around that commit to political issues while maintaining some degree of pop appeal, and the compilers of this program just plumb ran out (as if they'd never seen, say, the Rolling Stones' "Undercover," the Raybeats' "Jack the Ripper," Devo's "Beautiful World" . . .). So they grasp at these musically and visually unappetizing straws, cutting in animals-vs.-humans footage to cloyingly play off Kaja's song title; Taylor's unlistenable bilge has a video that juxtaposes a *Rebel Without a Cause*–style game of "chicken" with nuclear apocalypse. Madness's contribution fits in name only, at least, but their heavy Cockney singing obscures whatever lyrical message might be there, and the video itself is more of their usual horsing around. Depeche Mode's "Blasphemous Rumours," an ace clip taken from their excellent *Live in Hamburg,* relates to the overall theme only in the most tenuous way. Onetime Pink Floyd tour guitarist Snowy White plays pretty notes while his song puts you to sleep;

George Harrison's contribution is wretched hippies-revisited hokum; and the post-credits "We Love Animals" anthem by ex-ELO Kelly Groucutt and all them kids is—how do the British say it?—twee.

So, a good idea runs aground. And yet, it *is* a good idea, and at times a *thrillingly* good idea. It's related to a great cause, and any such concerted consciousness-raising in music video is welcome. This program may be only half-successful, but it gets a better-than-good rating because . . . well, it's like those old Peace Corps ads: a glass is filled halfway with water—is it half-empty or half-full? This program is half-full.

□ JOHNNY GRIFFIN

THE JAZZ LIFE: JOHNNY GRIFFIN

★★★½

Sony, 1985, 50 minutes

PRODUCED BY: Ben Sidran

DIRECTED BY: Parker Y. Bird

SELECTIONS: "Blues for Gonzie," "A Monk's Dream," "When We Were One," "56."

The great bebop tenor saxophonist caught live in a 1981 set at New York's Village Vanguard, backed by a splendid rhythm section (Ronnie Matthews, piano; Ray Drummond, bass; Kenny Washington, drums) who stay with him every step of the way, through smoking bop, tender ballads, and a lovely tip o' the pork-pie to Thelonious Monk. The no-frills, straight-ahead production mirrors the music's no-nonsense quality. Griffin, a longtime expatriate, reveals warmth and wit in his between-numbers patter.

□ GTR

THE MAKING OF GTR

★½

RCA/Columbia, 1986, 30 minutes

PRODUCED BY: Paul Flattery

DIRECTED BY: Jim Yukich

MUSIC FROM: GTR (Arista, 1986).

SELECTIONS: "When the Heart Rules the Mind," fragments of various others.

Only the most dogged progressive-rock die-hards could conceivably care about this program, which documents in tiresome and flatulently fatuous fashion the formation of GTR, a corporate-AOR rock enterprise led by former Yes and Asia guitarist Steve Howe and onetime Genesis guitarist Steve Hackett. From the "initial meetings" of Howe and Hackett, through their recruitment of bassist Phil Spalding (from Mike Oldfield's backing band), drummer Jonathan Mover (from progressive-rock revivalists Marillion), and vocalist Max Bacon (from hunger, basically), to in-studio work with producer and former Buggles/Yes keyboardist Geoff Downes, not a single moment rings with a shred of spontaneity or human interest. The same can easily be said for their music, which loads lamely baroque ornamentation onto a tired, corpulent formula. The video for one such monstrosity, "When the Heart Rules the Mind," is included in its entirety, while band members are seen working out snippets of various others from GTR's self-titled debut LP. Come to think of it, even a lot of die-hard progressive-rock freaks are liable to be put off, or put to sleep, by the way GTR falls flat on its collective face between the two stools of vintage symphonic rock and crassly commercialized AOR pomp.

□ THE GUESS WHO

TOGETHER AGAIN

★★½

Media, 1984, 118 minutes

PRODUCED BY: David Wolinsky, Bill Ballard, Dusty Cohl, Michael Cole, Anthony Eaton

DIRECTED BY: Michael Watt

MUSIC FROM: Various Guess Who albums, including *Best of the Guess Who Volumes 1* and *2* (RCA, 1972, 1973); *Best of Bachman–Turner Overdrive* (Mercury, 1976).

SELECTIONS: "Shakin' All Over," "Prairie Tune," "This Mornin'/46201," "Hang On to Your Life," "You Ain't Seen Nothin' Yet," "Undun," "No Sugar Tonight," "New Mother Nature," "Clap for the Wolfman," "Laughing," "Hand Me Down World," "American Woman," "Albert Flasher," "Rain Dance," "Taking Care of Business," "No Time," "These Eyes."

Some ten years after Canada's first massively successful pop-rock band bitterly disbanded, they reunited for a tour in 1983. Here we have their Toronto performance, shot in bland, typical-TV fashion, the band mixing hits with solo material from the post–Guess Who careers of singer Burton Cummings and guitarist Randy Bachman, as well as new songs composed for the tour by the reunited group. In the late '60s and early '70s, the Guess Who had a superlative string of quality hit singles, matched in its time only by Creedence Clearwater Revival for consistency in bringing hard-hitting excellence to the Top 40. Those classics—"These Eyes," "Laughing," "Undun," "No Sugar Tonight," "American Woman," and others—still sound great, as do Bachman's BTO classics "You Ain't Seen Nothin' Yet" and "Taking Care of Business." But the newer material is undistinguished, and many of the high points are offset by the interviews with the band, which usually degenerate from the usual we-love-each-other blandishments to outright self-serving pretentiousness. Unless you're a real diehard fan, you'd probably be better off sticking with the *Best of* album.

H

☐ BOBBY HACKETT SEXTET
GOODYEAR JAZZ CONCERT WITH BOBBY HACKETT

★★★

Video Yesteryear, 1980, 24 minutes
MUSIC FROM: TV concert special, 1961.
SELECTIONS: "Goodyear Blues," "Swing that Music," others.

Hackett, an estimable mainstream-jazz trumpeter, here leads a fine sextet through its straight-swinging paces for a 1961 TV special. The band includes Urbie Green on trombone, Bob Wilber on clarinet, and Dave McKenna on piano—a fine group, and McKenna has rarely played outside of his usual forceful barrelhouse solo gigs.

☐ VARIOUS ARTISTS
HAIR

★

MGM/UA, 1979, 121 minutes
PRODUCED BY: Lester Persky, Michael Butler
DIRECTED BY: Milos Forman
BASED ON the play by Jerome Ragni and James Rado; music by Galt MacDermot
MUSIC FROM: Hair motion picture soundtrack (RCA, 1979).
SELECTIONS: "Aquarius," "Sodomy," "Donna/Hashish," "Colored Spade," "Manchester, England," "Abie Baby/Four Score," "I'm Black/Ain't Got No," "Air," "Party Music-1930s," "My Conviction," "I Got Life," "Frank Mills," "Hair," "Initials," "Electric Blues/Old-Fashioned Melody," "Hare Krishna," "Where Do I Go," "Black Boys-White Boys," "Walking in Space," "Easy to Be Hard," "3-5-0-0," "Good Morning Starshine," "What a Piece of Work Is Man," "Somebody to Hold," "Don't Put It Down," "The Flesh Failures/Let the Sunshine In."

When *Hair* first played Off-Broadway in 1967, it was revolutionary, addressing such themes as interracial love, the draft, drugs, and hippies. The timeliness that was its virtue then is its biggest flaw in this 1979 film. Here the separate skits and numbers are joined together in the tale of a young straight, Claude (John Savage), and his adventures with a group of hippies (which includes Treat Williams, onetime Chicago lead guitarist Don Dacus, and Annie Golden of the Shirts) and a straight, rich girl (Beverly D'Angelo). The plot is too silly to recount, and Twyla Tharp's ballyhooed choreography is off-puttingly stunning and tricky. As for the music, you've heard whatever was worth hearing a thousand times before, though Melba Moore and Nell Carter contribute a couple of good performances. While you have to assume that part of the film's purpose was to salvage the reputation of the much-maligned subspecies *Homo hippieus*, it fails miserably. These guys, especially Treat Williams's Berger, are real jerks—selfish, nasty, deceitful, and inconsiderate in their idiotic naïveté. The ending (which turns on the same kind of ironic twist of fate as another of Forman's films, *One Flew over the Cuckoo's Nest*) could have served as a real "message," since it features the big Central Park gathering of untold thousands of used-to-be hippies in a staged peace rally. The problem is the film that precedes it. Instead of feeling part of the Age of Aquarius, you may find yourself changing your mind about former Chicago mayor Richard Daley.—P.R.

☐ HALL AND OATES
THE DARYL HALL AND JOHN OATES VIDEO COLLECTION: 7 BIG ONES

★★½

RCA/Columbia, 1984, 30 minutes
PRODUCED BY: BLTV, Neo-Plastics,

Jay Dubin, and Beth Broday

DIRECTED BY: Mick Haggerty and C. D. Taylor, Jay Dubin, and Tim Pope

MUSIC FROM: Private Eyes (RCA, 1981); *H2O* (RCA, 1982); *Rock'n Soul Part 7* (RCA, 1983).

SELECTIONS: "Say It Isn't So," "Family Man," "Maneater," "Private Eyes," "Adult Education," "I Can't Go for That (No Can Do)," "One on One."

At the peak of their form as the most successful duo in pop-music history, Hall and Oates released a pair of programs that amounted to two different greatest-hits packages. *7 Big Ones* compiles MTV-era video clips for a quick dose of nouveau blue-eyed soul for the short-attention-span generation. *Rock'n Soul Live*, shot on the 1983 *H_2O* tour at the Montreal Forum, offers a much lengthier, unspectacularly shot, career-spanning, in-concert best-of. In both cases, the music is indubitably remarkable: a relentlessly catchy, easy to listen—and usually dance—to blend of black and white pop roots and influences, which may be most remarkable in the extent to which its appeal crosses over pop's usual color barriers. However—despite Hall's matinee idol looks, the fact that both he and Oates are sharp dressers, and the pretty production values sported by most of their video clips—Hall and Oates are not the world's most visually exciting act. And unless you're *really* a fan of theirs, you'll have to admit that fact after sitting through either *7 Big Ones* or *Rock'n Soul Live*.

□ HALL AND OATES
ROCK'N SOUL LIVE
★★★

RCA/Columbia, 1984, 90 minutes

PRODUCED BY: Danny O'Donovan

DIRECTED BY: Marty Callner

MUSIC FROM: Various Hall and Oates albums (RCA, 1972–83).

SELECTIONS: "Family Man," "Diddy Doo Wop (I Heard the Voices)," "Italian Girls," "Kiss on My List," "She's Gone," "Art of Heartbreak," "One on One," "You've Lost That Loving Feeling," "I Can't Go for That (No Can Do)," "Sara Smile," "Wait for Me," "Maneater," "Private Eyes," "Open All Night," "You Make My Dreams," "Room to Breathe."

Also available on Pioneer Stereo Laser videodisc.

Supporting their 1983 *H_2O* LP at this Montreal Forum gig, Hall and Oates were just arriving at the peak of their latter-day golden period of seamlessly melded black-and-white pop hits, and most of them up to that point are here—as well as older favorites like "She's Gone" and "Sara Smile." Daryl Hall's a good-looking guy with a great voice, and he and John Oates both display sharp sartorial sense with their impeccable '50s tweeds and sharkskins, and they and their backing band do a highly competent job of rendering all the material. But H & O are still far from the world's most exciting live act. However, their fans shouldn't give a darn about that, and this straightforwardly shot concert video should satisfy them well.

□ DARYL HALL AND JOHN OATES
LIVE AT THE APOLLO WITH DAVID RUFFIN AND EDDIE KENDRICKS
★★★½

RCA/Columbia, 1985, 30 minutes

PRODUCED BY: Al Smith

DIRECTED BY: Jeb Brien, John Jopson, and John Oates

MUSIC FROM: Daryl Hall and John Oates Live at the Apollo with Special Guests Eddie Kendricks and David Ruffin (RCA, 1985).

SELECTIONS: "You Make My Dreams," "Get Ready," "Ain't Too Proud to Beg," "The Way You Do the Things You Do," "My Girl," "Every Time You Go Away," "When Something's Wrong with My Baby."

In May 1985, as a way of thanking their longtime supporters in the black-music community, and of generating benefit dollars for the United Negro College Fund, Hall and Oates played Harlem's legendary Apollo Theater with special guests, and original Temptations, singers David Ruffin and Eddie Kendricks. It's obviously a dream come true for blue-eyed soul stars Hall and Oates, and Ruffin's manly growl and Kendricks's skyscraping falsetto are both in fine fettle. And the white boys get that classic unison choreography down . . . well, not too badly. The only problem is that at only a half hour it is somehow disappointing: it looks and feels and sounds like an exciting, momentous occasion, and then it's over before you know it. Still, what's there *is* very nice.

□ HALL AND OATES
THE LIBERTY CONCERT
★★½

RCA/Columbia, 1986, 60 minutes
PRODUCED BY: Paul Flattery
DIRECTED BY: Jim Yukich
MUSIC FROM: Various Hall and Oates albums (RCA).
SELECTIONS: "Dance on Your Knees/Out of Touch," "Family Man," "Rich Girl," "Say It Isn't So," "You've Lost That Lovin' Feelin'," "Method of Modern Love," "Maneater," "Adult Education," "You Make My Dreams," "Hot Fun in the Summertime."

On July 4, 1985, pop music's most successful duo ever played a concert at Jersey City, N.J.'s Liberty Park—which in reality is probably closer than any spot in Manhattan to the Lady herself— to benefit the Statue of Liberty restoration project. On paper it probably seemed like a great idea to preserve this show on video: Daryl and John and their super-slick band playing most of the blue-eyed soul-funk classics that their '80s-generation fans know by heart, while the sun set over a suitably impressive panoramic vista, with the show culminating in a fireworks display and the lighting of the Liberty torch as a grand finale. But what may make H&O an exciting concert duo to their fans doesn't translate too well to video, unless you're a rabid admirer of theirs—for instance, Hall's seemingly endless call-and-response protraction of "Method of Modern Love" with his live audience might have been fun if you were there, but becomes a real drag while you watch at home. Meanwhile, the fireworks—which go off during H&O's decent but unspectacular encore of Sly Stone's classic "Hot Fun in the Summertime"—and torch-lighting are shot from such a great distance over the duo's shoulders that you end up wondering (a) whether Liberty Park really *is* that close to Liberty Island, and (b) if, given the enormous and kinda neat Liberty Torch model onstage, this isn't some sort of subliminal way of elevating Daryl and John above the cause and the icon for which they were ostensibly playing. Again, as in the dully competent *Rock'n Soul Live*, and the fun but somehow not-wholly-satisfying *Live at the Apollo*, H & O live are a bit of a letdown.

□ CHICO HAMILTON
THE JAZZ LIFE
★½

Sony, 1985, 53 minutes
PRODUCED BY: Ben Sidran
DIRECTED BY: Parker Y. Bird
MUSIC FROM: Various Chico Hamilton albums.
SELECTIONS: "The Theme" (performed twice), "Encore," "Sweet Dreams Too Soon," "The Baron," "Space for Stacy," "First Light," "Clinton Avenue," "Erika."

Veteran jazz drummer Hamilton is seen here in concert at Manhattan jazz landmark the Village Vanguard, sedating the audience with a two-guitar brand of easy-listening "jazz" that's so mellowed-out it wouldn't sound out of place in a dentist's office. Frustratingly, when a female singer tries to join in, she's so far off-mike we can only guess how good or bad she might be. About the most interesting thing about this tape is Hamilton's drum kit itself—he keeps his ride cymbal slung *real* low, so he has to lean down into the beat. How ironic that the music's somnambulistic groove is so very far from a beat that one would have to lean into.

□ LIONEL HAMPTON AND HIS ORCHESTRA

LIVE HAMP!

★★★½

Sony, 1983, 24 minutes
PRODUCED BY: Wesley Ruggles, Jr., and Gary Reber
DIRECTED BY: William Cosel
MUSIC FROM: Various Lionel Hampton albums.
SELECTIONS: "Air Mail Special," "Smooth Sailing," "Hamp's Boogie Woogie."

Master vibraphonist Hampton has always led one of the swingingest big bands in jazz, and the one captured in this 1982 show at Paul Anka's Jubilation! club in Las Vegas is no exception. Straightforward photography captures leader and band, roaring through the flagwaving "Air Mail Special" and "Hamp's Boogie Woogie," which bracket the slower "Smooth Sailing," a showcase for the superb Texas tenor sax of Arnett Cobb. All in all, a solid little sender.

□ LIONEL HAMPTON AND HIS BIG BAND

BIG BANDS AT DISNEYLAND

★★★★

Disney, 1984, 57 minutes
PRODUCED BY: Ron Miziker
DIRECTED BY: Jim Gates
MUSIC FROM: Various Lionel Hampton albums.
SELECTIONS: "Vibramatic," "Sweet Georgia Brown," "Air Mail Special," "P.S. I Love You," "Milestone," "Skylark," "Hamp's Boogie Woogie," "Glad Hamp," "Flyin' Home," "When the Saints Go Marchin' In."

This is the best Lionel Hampton program currently available, despite the sometimes clumsy direction (offset by a lot of nice camera angles), the annoying overabundance of shots of couples dancing on Disneyland's fantasy bandstands, and the disconcerting and unctuous presences of announcer Gary *(Laugh-In)* Owens and host Peter *(Hollywood Squares)* Marshall. That's because there's enough good stuff, hefty sustained doses of it, to offset the bad stuff—and the good stuff is just straight-up Hamp, an ageless wonder, playing the hell out of the vibes and leading yet another fine-tuned, hard-swinging jazz orchestra (sadly unidentified in the credits) through a solid repertoire of mostly stomping flagwavers.

This unit kicks ass like no other contemporary jazz big band this side of Sun Ra's Arkestra. Like Ra, with his reverently by-the-book yet irreverently punk-paced takes on vintage Duke Ellington and Fletcher Henderson stompers, Hamp understands two secrets of *serious* big-band swing that too many other bandleaders seem to have either forgotten or never learned: the kind of kick-out-the-jams energy that turns a jazz orchestra into a huge acoustic rock 'n' roll band and the vibrant, gutbucket full-band voicing achieved by balancing the shrill, strident screech of the brass with a throaty, earthy roar from the saxophones. Maybe Ra and Hamp are unique in this regard because they're just about the only bandleaders left who actually lived and played through the era when big-band swing was *the* popular dance music defining the cutting edge of, as they used to call it, "ultramodern rhythm."

Highlights include Hamp's vibes on the only ballads here, "P.S. I Love You" and "Skylark." In both, he wafts delicate tone-clusters that float like fireflies on smoke-ring phrasing; just as you start thinking what a nice, surprising change of pace this is from Hamp's usual ecstatic effervescences of many fast hard-swinging notes, he starts winding up into his usual ecstatic, effervescent style. Other musical pinnacles include "Milestone," a sharp arrangement of a challenging, beboppish line, and "Glad Hamp," with Hamp at the drums executing a wonderful exchange of four- and eight-bar solos with his drummer (he also plays some of his trademark two-fingered piano). There's also a brief interview between Marshall and Hamp, in which the only revealing moment comes when Hamp smiles and says he likes to play drums "when I'm feeling savage" and a photomontage history of Hamp narrated by Marshall—both ladle on the blandishments at the expense of any real substance, but so what? You don't expect hard-hitting interviews or in-depth history in a program like this, and you don't need them, either. Hamp and his music are enough. He's a natural, national resource.

□ HERBIE HANCOCK AND THE ROCKIT BAND

HERBIE HANCOCK AND THE ROCKIT BAND

★★★

CBS/Fox, 1984, 73 minutes

DIRECTED BY: Ken O'Neill

MUSIC FROM: Future Shock (Columbia, 1983) and other Herbie Hancock albums.

SELECTIONS: "Rockit," "Autodrive," "Hard Rock," "Future Shock," "You've Got Stars in Your Eyes," "Chameleon," and others.

Also available on CBS/Fox Stereo Laser videodisc.

With his Grammy-winning instrumental smash "Rockit," Hancock proved he's one jazz fusionist who can apply the taste, smarts, and daring of "pure" jazz to the pop arena, with an adventurous, immaculately hip, and danceable form of electronic funk-fusion that prominently features the rap turntable "scratching" of Grandmixer D. ST. (*sic*). Aurally, this is one of the best examples yet of the improvements in VCR sound made by VHS and Beta HiFi (laser videodiscs have always sounded better than any cassettes, and now hifi tapes have merely evened the score), with the dramatic difference in brightness, fullness, presence, dynamic range, and signal-to-noise ratio especially evident in the percussive instruments, which not only sound better but actually can be *felt.* And given the extremely percussive nature of Hancock's music here, that's an extra bonus.

"Rockit" dominates not only the feel of the music, but the stage show as well: the stage is full of breakdancers (more appropriate here than in most music video programs), and the robots created by British artist Jim Whiting, which were immortalized in Godley and Creme's "Rockit" video clip (which is included here along with Godley and Creme's similarly inventive "Autodrive" clip). Director Ken O'Neill keeps the visuals serviceably straightforward for the most part. My one complaint is with his constant jarring quick-cuts to extreme close-ups of the robots as they go through their perverse, fractured Rube Goldberg motions. After a while, all the cuts from band members to robots make man and machine look interchangeable. Was this intentional?

□ HANOI ROCKS
ALL THOSE WASTED YEARS
★★★

Sony, 1985, 55 minutes
DIRECTED BY: Mark Over
MUSIC FROM: All Those Wasted Years (Dutch Import, 1983).
SELECTIONS: "Pipeline," "Oriental Beat," "Back to Mystery City," "Motorvatin'," "Until I Get You," "Mental Beat," "Beer and a Cigarette," "Don't You Ever Leave Me," "Tragedy," "Malibu Beach Nightmare," "Taxi Driver," "I Feel Alright," "Train Kept A-Rollin'," "Under My Wheels," "Blitzkreig Bop."

Hanoi Rocks was a cool little neo-glam-rock band who came to the United States from Finland via Britain in the mid-'80s, but broke up before they ever had a chance to make any impact here. Sadly, the friendship they'd begun developing with Mötley Crüe, which could conceivably have allowed Hanoi Rocks to make an impact in America, led to their demise when their drummer Nicholas "Razzle" Dingley was killed in an auto accident in 1985, while a passenger in a car driven by Crüe's vocalist Vince Neil. A real tragedy: Hanoi Rocks wanted to be the New York Dolls, but they were born too late—an inherent ridiculousness that, in this straightforward live video from London's Marquee Club in 1983, somehow makes them only more appealing as they shamble and pose all over the stage in their mascara. At any rate, their brand of rock 'n' roll is definitely in the Dolls/Heartbreakers mold of post-Stones twin-guitar raunchola, which is a great mold to be in, and Hanoi Rocks can play. The show itself is shot decently enough, but one wonders why they bothered to interview the band if they were only going to use micro-second snippets between songs. Unless, that is, Hanoi Rocks were in the same hilariously besotted state they appeared to be in when vocalist Mike Munroe (who sports a wonderfully ridiculous fake-British accent) and guitarist Nasty Suicide were interviewed once by MTV VJ Mark Goodman. But then, as this concert video shows, that's Hanoi Rocks—engagingly cool rock 'n' roll trash, even in spite of themselves when need be. Further proof can be found by noting that the show ends with four carefully chosen covers: the Stooges' "I Feel Alright," "Train Kept A Rollin' " (the blues standard made famous by the Yardbirds and then Aerosmith), Alice Cooper's "Under My Wheels," and the Ramones' "Blitzkreig Bop." If you agree that that's pretty cool, then you'll also be glad this tape exists. It's not awesome or anything, but at least it does a nice job preserving a band that died before its time, that coulda and shoulda been contenders.

□ VARIOUS ARTISTS
HARDCORE MUSIC, VOLUME ONE
★★★½

Target, 1984, 60 minutes
PRODUCED BY: Joe Rees
DIRECTED BY: Joe Rees
MUSIC FROM: Various albums and singles by various artists.
SELECTIONS: Toxic Reasons: "Riot Squad," "Destroyer," "Drunk and Disorderly"; Black Flag: "Rise Above," "American Waste"; Code of Honor: "Stolen Faith," "Fight or Die," "Code of Honor"; Flipper: "Love Canal," "Turn-a-way," "Nothing"; D.O.A.: "Get Outta My Life," "New Age"; MDC (Millions of Dead Cops): "My Family," "Stupid Shit," "John Wayne Was a Nazi"; Lewd: "Flight"; Sex Pistols: "EMI".

Hardcore music is the hardest, fastest, most abrasively thrashing school of punk rock: tempos are so blurringly fast that melody and lyrical coherence inevitably get whipped to shreds in the tornadoes of cathartic noise. If hardcore is your thing, then this tape is for you. In fact, aside from this and the other *Hardcore Music* volumes assembled by Target Video of San Francisco (which is mainly Joe Rees), there's precious little hardcore music on home video, which is hardly a surprise given hardcore's willful fringe-cult status. Joe Rees's production values are not high, of course, but they are definitely good enough, and the rawness of his footage is a perfect esthetic match for hardcore's chaotic live shows, in which audience members frequently leap onstage only to dive right back into the "slam dancing" throng. Here, with a selection of Southern California and Bay Area bands, the high points include: Black Flag, one of hardcore's most popular and influential groups (with lead singer Henry Rollins in his skinhead phase); Flipper, just about the only *slow* hardcore band; D.O.A., the tightest and most listenable band here; and the seminal British punk rockers the Sex Pistols, at their San Francisco swan-song show. Rees mixes the live footage with polemically antiestablishment montages of boob-tube imagery, which can be predictable (scenes from Duke movies for MDC's "John Wayne Was a Nazi"), witty (Flipper's "Love Canal" introduced with a snippet from the old *Flipper* TV show), or just plain antiestablishment. (Available in stores or via mail order from Independent World Video or Target Video.)

☐ **VARIOUS ARTISTS (JIMMY CLIFF, OTHERS)**

THE HARDER THEY COME

★★★★½

HBO/Cannon, 1982, 93 minutes
PRODUCED BY: Perry Henzell
DIRECTED BY: Perry Henzell
MUSIC FROM: The Harder They Come motion picture soundtrack (Capitol/Mango, 1972).

SELECTIONS: Jimmy Cliff: "The Harder They Come," "You Can Get It If You Really Want," "Many Rivers to Cross," "Sitting in Limbo"; Scotty: "Draw Your Brakes"; the Melodians: "Rivers of Babylon"; the Maytals: "Sweet and Dandy," "Pressure Drop"; the Slickers: "Johnny Too Bad"; Desmond Dekker: "Shanty Town."

The first reggae feature film, *The Harder They Come* introduced reggae to the world outside of Jamaica, made an international star of Jimmy Cliff, and almost instantly became one of the first and hardiest midnight-movie cult hits. Its technical crudity may be off-putting to some at first, but as the story develops it's hard not to be drawn in anyway, at which point the crudity becomes bracing—not to mention aesthetically appropriate in many ways, since the film meshes folkish roots and rockish urgency to become something of a manifesto of Jamaican cultural determinism. The tragic-ballad of a plot, which is based on a modern-day Jamaican folktale, follows Jimmy Cliff as Ivan, an aspiring musician and singer from Jamaica's craggy inland who comes to the comparatively cosmopolitan capitol of Kingston to seek his fame and fortune. He does find them, but along the way to stardom he runs afoul of both crass capitalism and political corruption, two enemies he tries to fight through both his music—which he steadfastly fights to keep free of commercial adulteration—and his fame. In a genuinely gripping, edge-of-your-seat climax, he's ambushed by the police and shot down in cold blood at the peak of his folk-hero notoriety.

Because of its unrepentant grittiness, many viewers will have to watch *The Harder They Come* very closely to be able to follow it. But it's well worth the effort, for it's one of the first populist films to convincingly posit "the pop star as cultural guerrilla," as David Ehrenstein and Bill Reed succinctly put it in *Rock on Film*. Considering when it was made, its unflinching focus on the corruption and perversion that colonialism and capitalism have wreaked on Jamaica's native culture and society, as well as its bold identification of the recording star as political martyr, make *The Harder They Come* a truly remarkable film. It also remains one of the best introductions to the reggae milieu available, especially through its musical soundtrack, which cannot be overpraised. The angelic-voiced Cliff is at his singing and songwriting peak with the title track, the similar but more upbeat "You Can Get It If You Really Want," and the strikingly melancholy "Sitting in Limbo" and "Many Rivers to Cross" (which is much more gospel-pop than reggae). The rest of the songs by various other artists are as uniformly excellent, from the Melodians' exquisite "Rivers of Babylon" to Toots and the Maytals' driving "Pressure Drop," with two particular highlights being Desmond Dekker's "Shanty Town" and the Slickers' "Johnny Too Bad," both immortal classics of pre-reggae modern Jamaican pop. Indeed, it's *such* a magnificent soundtrack that I urge everyone to get the record album so the tunes can be enjoyed on their own.

Meanwhile, Cliff is effortlessly charismatic and extraordinarily effective in his screen acting debut, and producer/director Perry Henzell (what the heck ever happened to him after this movie, anyway?) not only keeps the story moving along smartly, he also uses all the music with dramatic felicity *and* never loses sight of his militant political subtexts. Latter-day reggae converts may also note that the martyrdom climax eerily foreshadows Bob Marley's untimely passing in a way—but don't ponder that *too* much, because it's probably just coincidence in the end.

□ BARRY HARRIS
PASSING IT ON

★★★½

Rhapsody, 1986, 23 minutes

PRODUCED BY: David Chan and Kenneth Freundlich

DIRECTED BY: David Chan and Kenneth Freundlich

MUSIC FROM: Various Barry Harris albums; the soundtrack of the film *Passing It On* (Rhapsody, 1985).

SELECTIONS: Several unidentified songs performed by Barry Harris with Pepper Adams, Clifford Jordan, Red Rodney, and others.

This is a slight but affectionate and modestly rewarding portrait of the estimable bebop pianist Barry Harris, a Detroit native who has resided in New York since the late '50s. The title of this day-in-the-life documentary refers to the amply illustrated fact that Harris is a teacher as well as a musician—we see him talking and demonstrating for his students and jamming with such bebop stalwarts as baritone saxist Pepper Adams, tenor saxist Clifford Jordan, and trumpeter Red Rodney—but, more than anything else, he's a perpetual student with an open heart and an open mind who ultimately sees little difference between his three roles. Indeed, in under a half hour, *Passing It On* does a remarkable job of showing just how similar these roles can be, as well as endearing Harris to the viewer for this philosophical fountain of youth. We also get shots of Harris reminiscing about the jazz greats he's played with in the past—from Lester Young to Charlie Parker, whom Harris describes as "the most gracious man I ever met." Viewing *Passing It On*, one has difficulty imagining anyone passing anything less of a judgment on the diminutive, professorial Harris himself. About all this charming little film lacks is more of Harris's music, not to mention more of the man himself. That said, however, what's there is fine. (Available by mail order from Rhapsody Films.)

☐ **VARIOUS ARTISTS**

HEAR-N-AID—THE SESSIONS

★★★

Sony, 1986, 30 minutes
PRODUCED BY: Marie Cantin and Wendy Charles
DIRECTED BY: Wendy Charles
MUSIC FROM: Stars (Polygram, 1986).
SELECTIONS: "Stars."

For the heavy-metal fan, this documentary on the making of the famine-relief benefit single "Stars" offers a unique, competently executed, up-close look at the making of an all-star record. And profits from the video go to famine relief, too. Hear-N-Aid, the name for this all-star heavy metal assemblage, numbers forty musicians, including: vocalists Eric Bloom (Blue Oyster Cult), Kevin Dubrow (Quiet Riot), Don Dokken (Dokken), Ronnie James Dio (Dio), Rob Halford (Judas Priest), Blackie Lawless (W.A.S.P.), Vince Neil (Mötley Crüe), and Geoff Tate (Queensryche); guitarists Ted Nugent, Vivian Campbell (Dio), Carlos Cavazo (Quiet Riot), Brad Gillis (Night Ranger), George Lynch (Dokken), Yngwie Malmsteen (Rising Force), Mick Mars (Mötley Crüe), Dave Murray (Iron Maiden), Eddie Ojeda (Twisted Sister), Donald "Buck Dharma" Roeser (Blue Oyster Cult), and Neal Schon (Journey); bassists Jimmy Bain (Dio) and Rudy Sarzo (Quiet Riot); and drummers Carmine Appice (King Kobra), Vinnie Appice (Dio), and Frankie Banali (Quiet Riot). In a wonderfully cool move, Michael McKean and Harry Shearer were also included, in their roles as David St. Hubbins and Derek Smalls of the metal-parody group Spinal Tap. As Ronnie James Dio explains at one point, the whole idea of Hear-N-Aid was inspired by Live Aid and USA for Africa and originally conceived and composed (the song "Stars") by Dio's Campbell and Bain.

"Stars" is a decent enough heavy-metal song in the genre's poppier, more melodic vein, although it's still full of heavy metal's usual breast-beating, aural hallmarks—such as shrilly shrieking singers and soundalike, fleet-fingered calisthenic guitar solos, not to mention the portentously phrased lyrics, which could have come from a *Classics Illustrated* comic-book version of some medieval legend. But hey, it's for a good cause, right? The construction of the song in the studio is illustrated in four sections—"basic tracks," "lead vocalists," "guitarists," and "the choir" of massed backing vocals—leading to the presentation of "Stars, the record" in straightforward performance-video form. But while the production itself is commendably tight and restrained, the program is still padded with a lot of dull, redundant chatter from many of the participating musicians about what a great cause it is, what a nice project it is, how much fun it is to all be together in this, etc. Only occasionally does anyone say anything interesting; say, Dio or Halford commenting that it was about time "this kind of music" got into the rock-charity act, or Neil describing he and his fellow metal heroes as regular guys (in some cases family men) underneath it all. But by far the best crack is from, naturally, Spinal Tap's St. Hubbins, referring to the incredibly fleet-fingered, but even more incredibly egotistical, Scandinavian guitar hero Yngwie Malmsteen: "I like how he puts 'Yngwie *J.* Malmsteen' on his records, so you don't confuse him with all the other Yngwie Malmsteens out there."

All in all, while this *is* a good idea

and a great cause, *Hear-N-Aid—The Sessions* is definitely meant more for the heavy-metal fan than anyone else. However, if "anyone else" were to get *one* heavy metal cassette, this wouldn't be a bad choice, considering the cause, the all-star nature of the venture, and the comparative accessibility of the song "Stars." Of course, there's the extra point for coolness for the inclusion of two members from Spinal Tap, the mythical metal band to end all metal bands.

□ HEART
VIDEO 45

★½

Sony, 1986, 18 minutes
DIRECTED BY: Jeff Stein
MUSIC FROM: Heart (Capitol, 1986).
SELECTIONS: "Never," "These Dreams," "What About Love," "Nothin' at All."

Heart's career was just about to finally peter out when they came back from the depths with the bombastic, slickly produced *Heart*, one of the biggest sellers of 1986. But unless you're a huge fan of the band, you'll have to either crack up laughing or leave the room clutching your stomach when this video is played. Heart ingeniously waited until two full years after *Purple Rain* to adopt Prince's Edwardian-fop look; lead singer Ann Wilson can't be shown in anything other than extreme closeup or extreme longshot, and rarely if ever do we see below her shoulders—if we do she's inevitably shrouded in darkness to camouflage her "mature" figure; Ann's sister, guitarist Nancy, resorts to inane sub–Mötley Crüe guitar-hero posturing, a pathetic and obnoxious substitute for her former great looks. And the clips themselves are either crashingly dull performance pieces or stilted and stultifying conceptual jobs. The problems of the latter are epitomized by "These Dreams," with its unbelievably moronic succession of asinine music-video clichés that are, one supposes, designed to make four-year-olds go, "Oh wow!" For instance, those slo-mo shots of Ann and Nancy and the others falling into pools of water—and *then* rising back up out of the pools as the film is run backward, WOW!!! How very, very artistic. Meanwhile, only one song is actually listenable: "Nothin' At All," which sports taut verses and an irresistible, killer chorus. All in all, however, Heart's *Video 45* is indisputable evidence that some bands just haven't got a clue of how ridiculous their videos make them look.

□ VARIOUS ARTISTS
HEARTLAND REGGAE

★★★★½

Continental, 1984, 90 minutes
PRODUCED BY: John W. Mitchell
DIRECTED BY: J. P. Lewis
MUSIC FROM: Various albums by various artists and the film (1980).
SELECTIONS: Jacob Miller and Inner Circle: "Tired Fe Lick Week in a Bush," "Peace Treaty," "I'm a Natty," "Run for Cover," "Jah Dread"; Bob Marley and the Wailers: "Trenchtown Rock," "War," "Jammin'," "Natty Dread," "Jah Live"; Peter Tosh: "Legalize It," "400 Years," "African," "Get Up, Stand Up"; Althea and Donna: "Uptown Top Ranking"; Judy Mowatt and Light of Love: "Black Woman"; Dennis Brown: "Whip Them Jah"; U-Roy: "Natty Don't Fear," "Soul Rebel"; Junior Tucker: "Enjoy Yourself."

This is a documentary of a unique moment in recent pop-music history: the One Love Peace Concert in Kingston, Jamaica, on April 22, 1978. The concert was hastily organized by the government to prevent calamitous riots from destroying Jamaica, as thousands had already recently died in internecine wars between the factions of Prime Minister Michael Manley and opposition leader Edward Seaga. Bob

Marley truly rose to the occasion, as the musician chosen by the battling politicians to soothe the people of Jamaica. This is easily the best Marley ever captured on film or video, the *real* Lion of Judah at the peak of his powers and *deep* into it, infinitely more intense than later shows shot closer to his 1981 death. *Heartland Reggae* includes the famous scene of Marley himself bringing Manley and Seaga out onstage to shake hands and make friends again—an incredible moment, especially as Marley does it during the climactic "Jammin'," which is surely appropriate.

Elsewhere, the late Jacob Miller is exuberantly militant, Peter Tosh is dourly militant, Dennis Brown is beautifully, plaintively militant, and "toaster" (reggae's answer to rappers) U-Roy is in classic ribald, tongue-twisting court-jester form. The only real drawbacks are an overly militant Rasta voiceover that pops up from time to time, and the sometimes shaky camerawork. But for reggae fans, this is genuine manna, and you're not likely to get a more intimate and street-level look at reggae music and its element.

□ VARIOUS ARTISTS (WILLIE NELSON, JERRY GARCIA, BO DIDDLEY, JOHNNY PAYCHECK)
HELL'S ANGELS FOREVER
★

Media, 1984, 93 minutes

PRODUCED BY: Richard Chase, Sandy Alexander, Leon Gast

DIRECTED BY: Richard Chase, Kevin Keating, and Leon Gast

MUSIC FROM: The movie *Hell's Angels Forever* (1983); various albums by various artists.

SELECTIONS: Willie Nelson: "I Can Get Off on You," "Angel Flying Too Close to the Ground"; Bo Diddley: "Do Your Thing," "Nasty Man"; Jerry Garcia: "That's All Right," "It Takes a Lot to Laugh, It Takes a Train to Cry"; Mission Mountain Wood Band: "Take a Whiff on Me"; Bobby Van Dyke: "Gimme a Harley"; Johnny Paycheck: "Too Bent to Boogie," "Angel of the Highway," "Ride On, Sonny"; Elephant's Memory: "Pirates Ball," "Angels Forever."

A documentary that tries to portray the Hell's Angels as the last true Americans, an unjustly beset-upon fraternity of honorable outlaws. Well, to be perfectly, cynically ironic about it, one could easily argue that compared to a dangerously two-faced, white-collar criminal like, say, Richard Nixon, the Angels really *are* commendably up-front and sincere. But you'd really have to be predisposed to like the Angels to enjoy this sloppily made, seemingly endless movie; otherwise, you'll not only be ultimately bored silly, but every now and then you'll be put off by the sordid antics of these sexist, violence-prone bikers. The occasional musical interludes with Willie Nelson, the Grateful Dead, Bo Diddley, and others are chaotically shot, poorly recorded sound-wise, and not nearly inspired enough as music to make much difference either way.

□ JIMI HENDRIX
RAINBOW BRIDGE
★½

IUD, 1971, 108 minutes

PRODUCED BY: Michael Jeffrey and Barry De Pendergrast

DIRECTED BY: Chuck Wein

MUSIC FROM: Rainbow Bridge (Reprise, 1971).

SELECTIONS: "Dolly Dagger," "Ezy Ryder," "Hey Baby (New Rising Sun)," "Foxey Lady," "Voodoo Chile (Slight Return)," "Earth Blues," "Pali Gap," "Purple Haze," "Star Spangled Banner," "Hear My Train a-Comin'," "Look Over Yonder."

By the time Jimi Hendrix began filming *Rainbow Bridge* in the summer of 1970, he was so deeply involved with a legion of music business hustlers that he had almost given up on the hope of ever controlling his own career again.

According to Hendrix biographer Jerry Hopkins, Hendrix never wanted to make this film and was so adamant about not participating that the producer—Hendrix's manager—Michael Jeffrey had him drugged, kidnapped, and sent to Hawaii against his will. The movie was to document Hendrix performing with Mitch Mitchell and Billy Cox at the Rainbow Bridge Occult Center on the slopes of Maui's Haleakala Crater before an audience of local hippies. Hendrix took drugs all day, the audience drank LSD-spiked punch, the producers shot forty hours of film and spent a cool million bucks, and this is what you get: about an hour of totally incomprehensible psychedelic footage starring actress Pat Hartley, lots of groovy if antiquated effects, and, at the end, a substandard Hendrix performance.

Hendrix was of course one of rock's most charismatic figures, and like Jim Morrison, he could make even a bad show at least interesting. There are solid versions of "Voodoo Chile (Slight Return)," "Dolly Dagger," and "Purple Haze," along with some interesting background music, and for guitar maniacs, a rare look at Hendrix playing in daylight. Sadly, though, *Rainbow Bridge* stands as a classic example of the self-indulgence that was the '60s' undoing and the unconscionable greed and disrespect of Hendrix's great talent that may have been his end—only weeks later, Hendrix was dead. Also note that because of the poor quality of the music in the film, the alleged "soundtrack" album features alternate takes of these songs.—P.R.

□ JIMI HENDRIX
JIMI PLAYS BERKELEY
★★★

Vestron/HarmonyVision, 1982, 45 minutes
PRODUCED BY: Michael Jeffrey
DIRECTED BY: Peter Pilafian
MUSIC FROM: Various Jimi Hendrix albums (Reprise, 1967–71).
SELECTIONS: "Johnny B. Goode," "Hear My Train a-Comin'," "Star Spangled Banner," "Purple Haze," "I Don't Live Today," "Little Wing," "Lover Man," "Machine Gun," "Voodoo Chile (Slight Return)."

□ JIMI HENDRIX
THE JIMI HENDRIX CONCERTS VIDEOGRAM
★★½

Vestron/HarmonyVision, 1983, 38 minutes
PRODUCED BY: Stuart S. Shapiro
DIRECTED BY: Dara Birnbaum, W.T.V., John Sanborn and Kit Fitzgerald, Dan Reeves, Stephen Beck, Shalom Gorewitz, Woody Wilson
MUSIC FROM: The Jimi Hendrix Concerts Album (Warner Bros., 1982).
SELECTIONS: "Fire," "Little Wing," "Wild Thing," "Hey Joe," "Voodoo Chile (Slight Return)," "Hear My Train a-Comin'," "Bleeding Heart," "Star Spangled Banner."

□ JIMI HENDRIX
JIMI HENDRIX
★★★★★

Warner Home Video, 1984, 103 minutes
PRODUCED BY: Joe Boyd, John Head, and Gary Weis
DIRECTED BY: Gary Weis
MUSIC FROM: Soundtrack Recordings from the film, Jimi Hendrix (Warner-Reprise, 1973).
SELECTIONS: "Rock Me," "In from the Storm," "Wild Thing," "Johnny B. Goode," "Hey Joe," "Purple Haze," "Like a Rolling Stone," "Star Spangled Banner," "Machine Gun," "Hear My Train a-Comin'," "Red House."

The 1971 movie *Jimi Plays . . .* documents Hendrix's 1970 Memorial Day show in Berkeley, California, with Billy Cox on bass and Mitch Mitchell on drums. As the only Hendrix movie or video containing a more-or-less complete single concert, it's recommended. Hendrix is in vintage form, and it's shot nicely enough, though there is a bit of psychedelic-era overreliance on a few odd camera angles. But it's also fascinating for its ten minutes or so of extra-musical footage: student demonstrations; an argument on the street between an establishment adult-bookstore owner and some hippies protesting the movie *Woodstock* "because they're charging us three dollars and fifty cents to see a movie that we made—us, the people, man." As time marches on, such sequences begin to seem less like nostalgic trifles and more and more like actual social history.

Jimi Hendrix is an excellent all-round 1973 rockumentary, featuring a comprehensive selection of performance clips from London's Marquee Club in 1967, and the Monterey Pop, Woodstock, and Isle of Wight festivals. There's also Jimi on *The Dick Cavett Show,* and reminiscences by Pete Townshend, Eric Clapton, Little Richard (in one of whose mid-'60s backing bands a young Jimi once played), Lou Reed, Jimi's father, and various girlfriends, other musicians, groupies, and friends. Being the kind of performer he was, Hendrix makes a perfect case for music video: why just own the soundtrack LP when you can *see* him, too?

Concerts Videogram, however, sort of undoes the case for music video, though it is an intriguing and offbeat idea, originally developed by USA cable network's adventurous *Night Flight.* The idea was to have a bunch of avant-garde video artists from New York's downtown scene make experimental visual correlatives to whatever Hendrix song they chose from *The Concerts Album.* While none of it looks like typical music video, much of it is at least as boring as music video can be, and even the best of it is self-consciously arty, usually to a distracting degree. Dara Birnbaum's pointless cut-ups of sullen suburban kids for "Fire" and WTV's infantile warmed-over psychedelia for "Little Wing" are the worst; among the best, and most ambitious, are Dan Reeves's "Hey Joe," Shalom Gorewitz's "Hear My Train a-Comin' " and "Star Spangled Banner" (which all treat topical social-comment footage with dizzying high-tech video effects), and John Sanborn and Kit Fitzgerald's "Wild Thing" (a quick-cut burlesque on sex roles, with Manhattan nightclub maven Clark Render seducing himself in drag). But the most easily enjoyable video is Stephen Beck's op-art effects fest for "Voodoo Chile (Slight Return)"—an unpretentious celebration of pure psychedelia as its own reward.

□ JIMI HENDRIX
JOHNNY B. GOODE
★★

Sony, 1986, 26 minutes
PRODUCED BY: Alan Douglas and various others
DIRECTED BY: Various
MUSIC FROM: Various albums by the Jimi Hendrix Experience.
SELECTIONS: "Are You Experienced?," "Johnny B. Goode," "All Along the Watchtower," Medley: "Hey Joe"/"Foxey Lady"/"Purple Haze"/"Crosstown Traffic"/ "Fire," "Star Spangled Banner," "Voodoo Chile."

Johnny B. Goode is an uneven compilation of various Hendrix clips: the title cut is from *Jimi Plays Berkeley*; "Are You Experienced?" and the medley beginning with "Hey Joe" are '80s concept videos set to album tracks; and "All Along the Watchtower," "Star Spangled Banner," and "Voodoo Chile" are concert clips from the Atlanta Pop Festival. Wayne Isham's opening clip for "Are You Experienced?" is excellent, a pixilated fantasia with a stunning and rather prophetic opening image—dozens of reels of master tapes coming alive and crawling from their cans inside the Hendrix vaults, threading themselves into machines in time to the tune's tape-reverse opening. The Atlanta concert footage is fine—and rarely seen. Those are the tape's good points.

But the rest is bad. Most regrettable is the way the concert footage of "Voodoo Chile" is intercut with some really rancid contemporary rock video choreography (even including overhead shots of circular formations, *à la* the June Taylor Dancers!)—this is tackiness beyond comprehension, and some of the strongest fuel yet for those who accuse producer Alan Douglas of improperly plundering the Hendrix vaults. In a further lack of discretion on Douglas's part, "Star Spangled Banner" fades out early to make way for the desecration of "Voodoo Chile." Meanwhile, the tastelessness continues apace with a cheap cut-and-paste medley, set to a simply bizarre video accompaniment: a bearded guy with a beret traipses through a city slum, looks up to see Jimi materialize in concert singing "Hey Joe," and is inspired by this epiphany to start splatter-painting a quickie Hendrix portrait on an alley wall. There *is* some good footage here for the Hendrix completist, but the extremely questionable parts of *Johnny B. Goode* are unsettling enough to keep it from getting a higher rating.

□ WOODY HERMAN AND THE YOUNG THUNDERING HERD

BIG BANDS AT DISNEYLAND

★★★½

Disney, 1984, 57 minutes

PRODUCED BY: Ron Miziker

DIRECTED BY: Jim Gates

MUSIC FROM: Various Woody Herman albums.

SELECTIONS: "Blue Flame," "Things Ain't What They Used to Be," "The Four Brothers," "Early Autumn," "Woodchopper's Ball," "Misty," "Peanut Vendor," "Perdido," "Pavanne," "Sonny Boy," "John Brown," "Country Cousins," "Caldonia," "Blue Flame (reprise)."

Bandleader/reedman Herman was in his forty-eighth year at the helm of his Thundering Herd jazz orchestra when this 1984 Disneyland concert was shot (originally for Disney Channel cable specials). And while he does look a bit weathered, and his whiny tone on clarinet and alto sax is more shrill and nasal than ever, it's a tribute to one of the all-time best-loved bandleaders that he still leads a pretty mean band. He's still got the unique "Four Brothers" sax section of three tenors and a baritone; tenors Dave Rickenberg, Gerry Penter, and Frank Taglieri, and baritone Mike Brignola (who has definitely inherited the talents of his father, baritone saxist Nick Brignola) do a superb job in both their solo and section work of responding to the calls of the eight brass. Throughout, the arrangements are solid and swinging, with the band cruising confidently from a plush purr to precise yet lusty flagwaving.

Musical highlights include the cooking "Things Ain't What They Used to Be" and "Four Brothers"; a stately, richly textured "Early Autumn," with Herman taking an alternately tender and bitter alto sax solo; and, best of all, a stupendous "Pavanne" that gracefully parades a captivating series of exotic interludes—Herman opens it with a bit of sinuous low-register clarinet rhapsodizing that's in vivid contrast to his usual sound, and then piquant flutes weave hypnotically beneath evocative solos by Brian Wagstaff on piccolo trumpet, Taglieri on bassoon (breathtaking), and Brignola on bass clarinet.

Unfortunately, from that lofty peak,

the program coasts downhill to a rather disappointingly lightweight conclusion: on "Sonny Boy," Woody "sings," once again proving that reed instruments are really just extensions of the human voice (if you get my drift); "John Brown" and "Country Cousins" are really one long, blah attempt at swinging "Battle Hymn of the Republic" (why bother?); "Caldonia" is more of a joke than anything else, not an especially hilarious one as done here, and really less than a band this good deserves, though the capable and energetic Young Thundering Herd do try to make the best of it. Sadly, the smolderingly atmospheric "Blue Flame" clips that frame the program are really just brief, soft backup for host Peter Marshall's hellos and good-byes. The direction is straightforward, with some great camera angles and close-ups more than making up for the shots of middle-aged couples dancing.

☐ **JERRY LEE LEWIS**
HIGH SCHOOL CONFIDENTIAL
★★★½

Blackhawk, 1985, 85 minutes
PRODUCED BY: Albert Zugsmith
DIRECTED BY: Jack Arnold
MUSIC FROM: The film *High School Confidential* (MGM, 1958).
SELECTIONS: "High School Confidential."

In the trash-movie watermark *High School Confidential*, you don't have to wait very long for the memorable musical highlight: the film opens with Jerry Lee Lewis and his combo on the back of a flat-bed truck, riding around a schoolyard as The Killer pumps out the torrid title tune. The rest of it is the hilariously sensationalized story of copper Russ Tamblyn going undercover to smash a drug ring in a high school where delinquency is studied far more assiduously than the three R's. In the most surreal touch, the busting-out-all-over Mamie Van Doren (whose curves are so sharp she could almost be a Picasso cubist canvas come to life) slinks around as Tamblyn's *aunt*—even though half the time she acts as if she's a member of the high school drug ring and she's forever making none-too-subtle sexual advances to Tamblyn. Yes, it's inordinately silly, classic cool-cat camp—and yet, as hyperbolic and literally unrealistic as it was, *High School Confidential* was attacked at the time of its release for *promoting* drug abuse through sensationalism, even as its producers claimed it was an attack on the problem. Furthermore, it was only the first snowball in an avalanche of similarly overstated, off-the-mark teen-exploitation flicks; as '80s detritus such as, say, *Class of '84* or *Dangerously Close* illustrate, the same old formula is still being churned out nearly thirty years later.

So *High School Confidential*, as the pacesetter for this particular genre, has its historical significance, however dubious. Still, it also has that opening with Jerry Lee, one of the more unforgettably cool images in the history of rock cinema. And it's got some classic dialogue, such as: Mom to kid—"How did school go today?"; kid, sullenly—"It went." (Available by mail order from Blackhawk Films.)

☐ **THE HOOTERS**
NERVOUS NIGHT
★★½

CBS/Fox, 1986, 42 minutes
PRODUCED BY: Karen Bellone
DIRECTED BY: John Jopson
MUSIC FROM: *Nervous Night* (CBS, 1985).
SELECTIONS: "And We Danced," "Hanging on a Heartbeat," "Don't Take My Car Out Tonight," "Where Do the Children Go," "All You Zombies," "Blood from a

Stone," "Time After Time," "Nervous Night," "Day by Day."

The Hooters broke onto the pop music scene in 1985 with an endearing and rather refined, if insubstantial, sound most significant for its effective integration of reggae rhythms, dub-reggae effects, mandolin folk melodies, and the haunting sound of the humble melodica (or "hooter" as they call it). Here, a triumphant homecoming concert before their rabid Philadelphia fans is bracketed by conceptual videos for "And We Danced" and "Day by Day." Keyboardist Rob Hyman performs "Time After Time," the hit he wrote with and for Cyndi Lauper, a reminder that the Hooters' first break was backing Lauper on her debut LP, *She's So Unusual.* Despite the ephemeral charms of the music, and the good looks, high energy, and talent of head Hooters Hyman and guitarist Eric Bazilian, explosive rock 'n' roll stage charisma is not their forté. Nor is their personal charisma very spectacular: the "up close and personal" interview segments are regrettable.

□ LIGHTNIN' HOPKINS (WITH OTHERS) THE BLUES ACCORDIN' TO LIGHTNIN' HOPKINS

★★★★½

Flower Films, 1980, 31 minutes

PRODUCED BY: Les Blank with Skip Gerson

DIRECTED BY: Les Blank with Skip Gerson

MUSIC FROM: Various Lightnin' Hopkins albums and *The Blues Accordin' to Lightnin' Hopkins* motion picture soundtrack (Flower Films, 1967).

SELECTIONS: Lightnin' Hopkins: "Untitled Instrumental Improvisation," "I'm Walkin'," "Good Mornin' Little Schoolgirl," "Meet Me in the Bottom," "Might Have to Tell You in the Morning," "How Long Has It Been," "Untitled Instrumental Improvisation," "Bring It Home to You," "Woman Named Mary"; Billy Bizor with Lightnin' Hopkins: "Untitled Rodeo Music"; Mance Lipscomb: "Cried All Night"; Billy Bizor: "Hurt Me So Bad."

Hopkins was a seminal Texas—as distinguished from Mississippi Delta—bluesman, adept at both acoustic and electric guitar, and influence (conscious or not) on many blues and rock guitarists. A careful listen to some of his more adventurous licks here will reveal a diabolical, rough-hewn, high-energy invention redolent of, yes, Jimi Hendrix—who, documentarian Les Blank subtly makes you realize, was most likely one of the many influenced by Hopkins. But that's far from all Blank shows us, as he shoots the blues giant at home in Centerville, Texas. Hopkins was a remarkable character: impish enough to seem dangerously arrogant at times, but always wily and tenacious; as he talks about and plays his marvelous country blues, he reveals a poker-faced, near-existential sense of black (no pun intended) humor that marks him as something of a musical cowboy, if you will. At one point, Hopkins ponders his inspiration and influences, then just starts casually plucking out some hauntingly beautiful deep-blues guitar, letting the music do the talking. Blank then cuts to a rowdy outdoor barbecue, where Hopkins's guitar boogie sets some little kids to frenzied dancing—an unforgettable image that says even more. There's also footage of Hopkins hanging out at a black rodeo, and there a brief musical contributions from harmonica player Billy Bizor and Texan songster Mance Lipscomb (subject of another great Blank documentary, *A Well-Spent Life*) during some other get-togethers. All in all, a beautiful little portrait of a departed master and the rapidly disappearing culture he represented. (Available by mail order from Flower Films.)

☐ VARIOUS ARTISTS
HOT ROCK VIDEOS, VOLUME ONE
★★

RCA/Columbia, 1984, 28 minutes
PRODUCED BY: Various
DIRECTED BY: Various
MUSIC FROM: Various albums by various artists.
SELECTIONS: Eurythmics: "Sweet Dreams (Are Made of This)"; the Kinks: "Come Dancing"; Alan Parsons Project: "Don't Answer Me"; Jefferson Starship: "No Way Out"; Rick Springfield: "I've Done Everything for You"; Lou Reed: "I Love You Suzanne"; Icicle Works: "Whisper to a Scream (Birds Fly)."

☐ VARIOUS ARTISTS
HOT ROCK VIDEOS, VOLUME TWO
★½

RCA/Columbia, 1985, 26 minutes
PRODUCED BY: Various
DIRECTED BY: Various
MUSIC FROM: Various albums by various artists.
SELECTIONS: Thompson Twins: "Hold Me Now"; Meat Loaf: "Modern Girl"; Jefferson Starship: "Layin' It on the Line"; Lou Reed: "My Red Joystick"; Rodney Dangerfield: "Rappin' Rodney"; Elvis Presley: "Blue Suede Shoes."

There's a reason why they are making fewer and fewer various-artist hit-video collections as time goes by: it's because they usually don't work. Here are two examples of why they don't work: nothing, either visually or musically, really ties anything together, and the inevitable can't-please-everybody phenomenon here tends to cancel out rather than multiply any possible audience. Volume One has two really good clips to recommend it: Eurythmics' classically nonsensical surrealism-dabbling in "Sweet Dreams" (love those contented cows), and Julien Temple's poignant "Come Dancing," a felicitous visualization of a classic melancholy exercise in bittersweet nostalgia by the Kinks' Ray Davies, who also turns in a heck of an acting job. The Alan Parsons Project's animated "Don't Answer Me" was acclaimed upon its release for some reason, even though the animation is crude and awfully cute. Starship, Rick Springfield, and Icicle Works are basically unwatchable unless you're a fan of theirs, and Lou Reed's "I Love You Suzanne" is a great tune indifferently visualized, with the added perversity of a blatant double for Lou breakdancing. Volume Two is even slimmer on the recommendables: Starship's "Layin' It on the Line," with its "vote Mick and Slick" takeoff on politics, and "Rappin' Rodney," with the world's greatest standup comedian in rock-video fantasyland. That's about it. Oh, also noteworthy, but for the wrong reasons: Martin Kahan's "Blue Suede Shoes" is a desecration of the King's memory.

☐ **WHITNEY HOUSTON**
THE #1 VIDEO HITS
★★★

RCA/Columbia, 1986, 18 minutes
DIRECTED BY: Brian Grant
MUSIC FROM: Whitney Houston (Arista, 1985).
SELECTIONS: "You Give Good Love," "Saving All My Love for You," "How Will I Know," "The Greatest Love of All."

Whitney Houston has the face, body, grace, and poise of the fashion model she used to be—*and* she's got those powerful, gospel-soaked pipes as well. When someone looks and sounds that good, what's not to love? Not much—so no wonder she rocketed to massive popularity with her debut album, which featured the four tunes videoized here. However, the more you look at these clips, the more you begin to notice what's not to like—or rather, what's not to see. That is, *personality* and/or *soul*, something real and raw behind that blinding ultrabright smile.

It's all given away, really, right at the top, with Whitney's first video, "You Give Good Love." It's a performance clip in which she tries self-consciously, and fails to seem funky. She fares infinitely better in "Saving All My Love for You," a well-crafted middle-of-the-road love ballad which she performs with suitable dignity and power—while her finishing-school dignity and poise carry her far above the clichéd "other woman" scenario of the clip. "How Will I Know" is a bouncy dance-pop number, with Houston strutting that fashion-runway walk of hers through a funhouse-maze set the color of psychedelic vomit, while inane choreography keeps getting in the way all around her. It's basically a tolerable video until the mistake is made of inserting a shot of Aretha Franklin, from her "Freeway of Love" video, for the line "I'm asking you 'cos you know about these things." All it does is make you realize just how unfunky Whitney is, with her fixed smile, robotic mince, and mechanically strident whoops and shouts. The crushing irony of it all is that this was probably a sincere attempt to show off what are in fact genuine connections to legitimate soul roots—Whitney's mom, Cissy Houston, a vastly underrecognized gospel-soul singer herself, used to sing with the Sweet Inspirations, who backed Aretha on some early recordings.

Speaking of Cissy, she appears in the program's final video, "The Greatest Love of All"—and her role in this tribute-to-stage-mothers-everywhere actually goes miles toward helping the video salvage the impossibly elephantine song, which lumbers about in so many melodramatic directions it ends up spent and splayed on the floor, huffing and puffing and stinking of hollow sentiment. Not only that, it reminds one of Gordon Lightfoot's classic "If You Could Read My Mind"—the part that goes "I don't know where we went wrong, but the feeling's gone . . ." in the section that starts, "I decided long ago never to walk in anyone's shadow . . ." And once again a queasy wrong note is struck, as Whitney croons, "I believe the children are our future . . ." and all that other pious rot *while doing her mascara in her makeup mirror!* And then, of course, there's the crowning moment of absurdity: Whitney singing that line "If I fail, if I succeed . . ." "If I *fail* "?!? *Her*, fail? *Hah!* Not when she look and sounds *this* good to those who made her debut album a million-seller. And since so many of those fans really *don't* think she has any faults, and since this program shows her first public flowering off to nice advantage, it gets three stars despite the unsettling aspects that reveal themselves to hardened cynics such as yours truly.

□ FREDDIE HUBBARD
STUDIOLIVE

★★

Sony, 1981, 59 minutes
PRODUCED BY: Allyn Ferguson
DIRECTED BY: Ric Trader
MUSIC FROM: Hubbard's Cupboard (Prestige, 1981).
SELECTIONS: "Hubbard's Cupboard," "Two Moods for Freddie," "Birdland," "Ride like the Wind," "Brigitte," "Condition Alpha," "This Is It."

Hubbard, a superb jazz trumpeter, is documented as he makes a record with a collection of top-notch L.A. studio cats. One session's with horns, one with strings. The horn session is by far the better of the two: the music's livelier, and Hubbard is challenged by fine players such as reedman Bud Shank and trombone virtuoso Bill Watrous.

The string session consists of the kind of smoothed-out, easy-listening fusion (as in not *really* jazz) that critic Peter Occhiogrosso once so aptly termed "fuzak" (as in fusion Muzak). Anyone who's ever been in on a recording session can tell you that there are long moments of boredom and waiting between the moments of excitement—and more boring than exciting moments are captured here. Still, Hubbard's fans will enjoy a chance to see him work (and coast) close-up in straightforward documentary fashion.

☐ VARIOUS ARTISTS
HULLABALOO
★★★★

Video Yesteryear, 1981, 47 minutes
PRODUCED BY: Gary Smith
DIRECTED BY: Bill Davis
MUSIC FROM: Two episodes of 1965 TV show.
SELECTIONS: David McCallum: "Agent Double-O Soul"; the Animals: "We Gotta Get Out of This Place," "Club A Go-Go"; Beau Brummels: "Don't Talk to Strangers"; Brenda Lee: "Rusty Bell"; Michael Landon: "I Like It like That," "You Were on My Mind"; the Byrds: "The Times They Are a-Changin' "; Paul Revere and the Raiders: "Steppin' Out"; Jackie DeShannon: "A Lifetime of Loneliness"; Chad and Jill: "No, My Love, No."

Two episodes of the Mod-era go-going TV-pop showcase—and ah, what fab, campy nostalgia for baby boomers.

The September 27, 1965, show was hosted by David McCallum in his *Man from U.N.C.L.E.* spy character of Illya Kuryakin (his deadpan singing is pretty funny). The running jokes about his show include a ticking Animals album cover he holds up while introducing the band; he tosses it away, it explodes, and we cut to the band—performing amid smoking ruins! Michael Landon provides comic relief in the October 4, 1965, episode, by *insisting* on singing. Also, the Byrds do Dylan, and Paul Revere and the Raiders deliver their second hit, the superb "Steppin' Out."

☐ THE HUMANS
HAPPY HOUR WITH THE HUMANS
★★½

Pacific Arts, 1984, 40 minutes
PRODUCED BY: Sterling Storm, L. B. Johnson, and Stephen Greenberg
DIRECTED BY: Sterling Storm, L. B. Johnson, and Stephen Greenberg
MUSIC FROM: Happy Hour (IRS, 1981).
SELECTIONS: "Waiting at the Station," "Don't Be Afraid of the Dark," "Invisible Man," "Buena Serte," "Lightning," "Human Eyes," "Farewell Kiss."

This is a mildly intriguing and, considering that it was made in 1982, rather ambitious program. But its good qualities are somewhat undone by the fact that the Humans make mediocre, anonymous post-new-wave rock music, and the fact that much of the imagery and motifs seen here have since been beaten into the ground. *Happy Hour* ties together seven video clips by the Humans with various *Twilight Zone*–style vignettes that introduce or echo the themes of the songs: romance, ego loss, guerrilla warfare, bourgeois liberal guilt, covert political action, cosmic sexual mysticism, nuclear dread, and general unarticulated teen anomie. Interestingly, *Happy Hour* often behaves more like a "real" musical than a mere collection of clips: certain motifs and their accompanying songs actually *recur,* rather than just parading past one by one. But *Happy Hour* has its artistic and technical ups and downs. The directorial trio—which includes one band member, lead singer Sterling Storm—shows potential with some striking lyrical/poetic images. But just as often they let those poetic/lyrical impulses run away with themselves, leading *Happy Hour* smack dab into film-school clichés, something that always looks even worse when the production budget's this low. Furthermore, despite its overall ambition and cohesion, *Happy Hour* disappoints by petering out on a note of inconclusive solipsism that echoes too much other music video. The music's far too undistinguished to make anyone really care very much about weighing this program's good points against its bad.

□ ENGELBERT HUMPERDINCK
THE ENGELBERT HUMPERDINCK SPECTACULAR
★★★

Vestron, 1986, 59 minutes
PRODUCED BY: Des Good
DIRECTED BY: Bob Marsland
MUSIC FROM: Various Engelbert Humperdinck albums (Parrot/Epic, 1967–86).
SELECTIONS: "A Lovely Way to Spend an Evening," "I'm So Excited," "Hello," "After the Lovin'," "Mona Lisa," "Those Lazy Hazy Crazy Days of Summer," "Ramblin' Rose," "Too Young to Go Steady," "When I Fall in Love," "I Just Called to Say I Love You," "I'll Walk Alone," "Help Me Make It through the Night," "Follow My Heartbeat," "Release Me," "This Moment in Time"/"Les Bicyclettes de Belsize"/"Am I That Easy to Forget"/"Quando? (When?)"/"A Man without Love"/"There Goes My Everything"/"Spanish Eyes"/"The Last Waltz'/ "Release Me," "If We Only Had Love"/"I Won't Care."

Born Arnold Dorsey in India, Humperdinck is a mellow hunk of a middle-of-the-road crooner—sort of halfway between Tom Jones and Perry Como—with many fans. They'll probably enjoy this well-shot document of an aptly titled, lavish 1985 show at London's Royal Albert Hall—complete with multitiered stage set, the London Philharmonic Orchestra, and four dancing girls—even though ol' 'dinck seems to have put on a pound or two. But non-fans looking on (don't ask why, for argument's sake) will note that as far as his qualities as an entertainer (he mostly sings but essays a few dance steps, too) go, the line "I'll sing you to sleep . . ." from his big 1976 hit "After the Lovin' " just about says it all: chiseled visage aside, he's a pretty stiff and limited performer. And one and all will have to laugh at Arnie Dorsey's earnestly spoken intro to "If We Only Had Love," part of which goes "If we only had love . . . we could all use our own names . . ." Not to mention when he pauses during the long medley near the end of the program, after having sung a fast, mostly Spanish "Spanish Eyes," and asks—an eyebrow cocked in rhetorical sassiness—"How was *that,* Julio?" To his credit, though, he does take some interesting liberties with a few Nat "King" Cole tunes, and succeeds surprisingly well with a breezy "Mona Lisa" to flamenco guitar accompaniment.

□ ALBERTA HUNTER
JAZZ AT THE SMITHSONIAN
★★★★

Sony, 1985, 58 minutes
PRODUCED BY: Clark and Delia Gravelle Santee
DIRECTED BY: Clark and Delia Gravelle Santee
MUSIC FROM: Various Alberta Hunter albums.
SELECTIONS: "My Castle's Rocking," "Downhearted Blues," "Handyman," "When You're Smiling," "Nobody Knows You When You're Down and Out," "Without Rhythm," "Without a Song," "Darktown Strutter's Ball," "Rough and Ready Man," "Time Waits for No One," "Blackman," "You Can't Tell the Difference After Dark," "Remember My Name."

Back in the 1920s, Alberta Hunter was one of the leading blues belters. After branching out into more mainstream pop singing, she eventually retired from performing to become a nurse. She launched a comeback in the mid-1970s that soon made her the toast of New York City nightlife. Here, it's easy to see why. Sure, she and her 1982 concert audience overindulge each other a bit, but Hunter's character, dignity, and vitality—not to mention her mastery as a vocalist—are very evident throughout, and overall the presentation (as in all Sony's Jazz at the Smithsonian tapes) is respectful and straightforward. A few of Hunter's colorful reminiscences with off-camera host (and veteran Voice of America DJ) Willis Conover break up an intimate hour onstage with a most remarkable lady.

I

☐ VARIOUS ARTISTS
IN HEAVEN THERE IS NO BEER?
★★★★½

Flower Films, 1984, 51 minutes
PRODUCED BY: Les Blank
DIRECTED BY: Les Blank
MUSIC FROM: Various albums by various artists; *In Heaven There Is No Beer?* motion picture soundtrack (Flower Films, 1984).

SELECTIONS: Dick Pillar Orchestra: "No Beer in Heaven," "Polish Power"; Mrozinski Brothers Aleatoric Ensemble: "Polka Shoes," "Beer Barrel Polka," "Don't Let the Stars Get in Your Eyes"; Happy Louie: "Jak Sie Masz," "Polish Blood," "Springtime Oberek"; Eddie Blazonczyk and the Versatones: "Sweet Mary Lou," "Pretty Mary Ann," "Na Lewo," "Potato Chips Polka"; "Joe Pat" Paterek: "Hail Mary," "Melody of Love"; Jimmy Sturr Orchestra: "Rock of Ages Medley," "How Swiftly Time Flies"; Marion Lush: "Hot Peppers Polka"; Marv Herzog Bavarian Band: "Im Leben"; Stefan Skrabar I Jego Chlopska Orchestra: "Wianek Majowy"; Makow Orchestra: "Frolicking with the Girls"; the Nu-Trels: "Ukranian Polka"; the Versa-J's: "Polish Hoedown"; Walt Solek: "Julida," "Who Stole the Kishka?"; Brave Combo: "Julida"; Johnny Prytko's Good Time Orchestra: "Die Bougie Die"; Frankie Yankovic: "Duluth Polka"; Li'l Wally: "At My Wedding"; Glahe Musette Orchestra: "Beer Barrel Polka"; Renata and Girls, Girls, Girls: "I'd Like To"; the Musicales: "Beer in Heaven."

Les Blank's high-spirited documentary on America's surprisingly vast polka subculture is dizzying in its frantic scope. From New London, Connecticut's, annual Polkabration festival to International Polka Association conventions, and with all manner of stops in between, many of them in the Midwestern "polka belt," Blank's camera captures polka dance, food, clothing, social rituals, and music with the hither-and-thither voraciousness of a beggar at a smorgasboard. The range of music alone is remarkable: from polka megastars like Grammy-winner Frankie Yankovic and the exuberantly virtuosic Eddie Blazonczyk, to such endearing novelties as Walt Solek's "Who Stole the Kishka? " and Renata and Girls, Girls, Girls' "I'd Like To" (polka, that is; and with a name like theirs, you've gotta love 'em); from Solek's straight-up and traditional version of the *Norteno*-related (see Blank's *Chulas Fronteras*) "Julida," to a version of the same song by Texas-based *punk-rock polka band* Brave Combo. There's even a polka mass.

In Heaven There Is No Beer? bursts with the energy, warmth, and friendly spirit of polka and the people who love it, and amidst all the kielbasa, beer, and accordions, there's also a bounty of funny moments and genuinely good music (for those of you who can't take polka seriously). Blank's films are often distinguished by his unique ability to observe so unobtrusively he's able to be present at those moments when a partygoer's head begins to throb (and/or stomach begins to churn) from a bit too *much* excess—and, boy, do those polkaholics like to go cheerfully overboard. In such moments, one can almost begin to read the question mark Blank has appended onto the polka song title that names the film as his way of nudging the viewer and poking fun at his potbellied, polyestered subjects. But that's strictly a value judgment in the eyes of each beholder, and no matter what, *In Heaven There Is No Beer?* is more than rich enough to be entertaining and informative.

☐ VARIOUS ARTISTS
IN OUR HANDS
★★½

Continental, 1984, 90 minutes

PRODUCED BY: Robert Richter and Stan Warnow
DIRECTED BY: Barbara Kopple, Tom Cohen, Don Lenzer, Robert Leacock, and others
MUSIC FROM: 1982 film; various albums by various artists.
SELECTIONS: Carly Simon: "Turn of the Tide"; Holly Near: "Singing for Our Lives"; Rita Marley: "That's the Jury," "My Kind of World"; Peter, Paul and Mary: "Where Have All the Flowers Gone?"; James Taylor: "You've Got a Friend"; John Hall: "Children's Cry"; House of the Lord Choir: "We Cry Disarmament"; Are and Be Ensemble: "If There Is No Struggle"; Pete Seeger: "It's the Bomb That Has to Die," "If I Had a Hammer."

Part antinuke agit-prop, *à la Atomic Cafe* (with scores of filmmakers compiling and/or contributing all sorts of footage, such as Japanese A-bomb survivors discussing their plights, and so on); part document of the June 12, 1982, antinuke rally in New York City's Central Park, which was attended by about a million people (the largest such rally in U.S. history). *In Our Hands* is pretty powerful as antinuke advocacy documentary; but while the events of June 12, 1982, are interesting and inspiring to antinuke partisans, and celebs from Orson Welles and Meryl Streep to Drs. Helen Caldicott and Benjamin Spock take part in the rally, and there is the sheer presence of *all those people* with the urgency and weight of their message, the music is unfortunately the weakest part of the whole thing. Pete Seeger's always great, and having Bob Marley's widow Rita Marley and feminist folksinger Holly Near along is interesting, but old folkies like Peter, Paul and Mary and perpetual wimps like James Taylor and John Hall (not to mention Carly Simon, who's heard on the soundtrack but didn't play at the rally) are simply boring, boring, boring. Too bad.

□ INXS
THE SWING AND OTHER STORIES
★★½

Atlantic, 1985, 57 minutes
PRODUCED BY: Richard Lowenstein and Tim Issacson
DIRECTED BY: Richard Lowenstein and Tim Issacson
MUSIC FROM: *Shabooh Shoobah* (Atco, 1982); *The Swing* (Atco, 1984); *Dekadance* (Atco, 1983).
SELECTIONS: "The One Thing," "Don't Change," "The Spy of Love," "To Look at You," "Original Sin," "I Send a Message," "Love Is (What I Say)," "Melting in the Sun," "Burn for You," "Dancing on the Jetty," "All the Voices."

This annoyingly produced mix of interviews, video clips, and onstage footage (from Australia and Japan) does a disservice to the fine Australian funk-rock band. On their first two American albums, INXS have come up with more than their share of fine songs: "The One Thing," "Don't Change," "Original Sin," "To Look at You," and "Burn for You" are the ones included here. But just about every song is interrupted by insubstantial and ultimately intrusive interview snippets with the band answering dumb questions like "what's your favorite food?" This is especially stupid when the banal banter ruptures the soaring power of "Don't Change" and the seductively atmospheric "To Look at You" and "Original Sin"; the same thing also ruins the ultrasensual, *Tom Jones* banquet-scene takeoff of the video clip for "The One Thing." Lowenstein does cut in some playful animation effects that comment humorously on the interviews (e.g., when a band member says his biggest influence is "Leon Trotsky," an animated question mark appears and floats around his head), but it's not nearly enough. A shame: INXS deserves better than such disrespectful treatment. Still, fans of the band may enjoy it.

☐ TONY IOMMI

THE TONY IOMMI PACKAGE

★★★

Star Licks, 1984, 60 minutes
PRODUCED BY: Mark Freed and Robert Decker
DIRECTED BY: Mark Freed and Robert Decker
MUSIC FROM: Various Black Sabbath albums (Warner Bros., 1970–80).
SELECTIONS: "Neon Knights," "N.I.B.," "Heaven & Hell," "Paranoid," "Iron Man," "Black Sabbath," "Master of Reality," and others.

For aspiring metalhead guitarists, here's another solid entry in the Star Licks series of instructional home videos, featuring Black Sabbath's veteran left-handed axeman. He covers the usual territory of heavy-metal guitar-instruction programs—from the basics all the way to sophisticated, flashy techniques like hammer-ons and pull-offs and all that—and gives it his own personal spin, which in a word is *heavy*. As an on-camera presence, Iommi is very much in the splendidly well-off British rock star mold, though he's also gratifyingly less distant and effete than one might expect. He also comes off a lot less, er, foreboding than he looks.

☐ DONNIE IRIS AND THE CRUISERS

BLOSSOM

★★

Sony, 1982, 46 minutes
PRODUCED BY: Mike Belkin
DIRECTED BY: Chuck Statler
MUSIC FROM: Back on the Streets (MCA, 1980); *King Cool* (MCA, 1981).
SELECTIONS: "Agnes," "That's the Way Love Ought to Be," "King Cool," "Sweet Merilee," "I Can't Hear You," "Broken Promises," "Love Is like a Rock," "Ah! Leah! "

Iris, a bespectacled rocker from Pittsburgh who slightly resembles a rangy Buddy Holly, had a number-one hit in 1970 as leader of the Jaggerz with "The Rapper." He then disappeared for nearly ten years before reappearing as leader of the Cruisers (and this was a few years before that dreadful movie *Eddie and the Cruisers*), who made two albums of crafty, eclectic, comparatively down-to-earth AOR pop-rock that showcased Iris's command of a wide range of vocal styles. They slid back into obscurity, and looking through this collection of low-budget, primitive, mainly performance-oriented clips shot by Chuck Statler (who did much better pioneering work with Devo, who were no doubt much more creatively stimulating to work with), it gradually becomes apparent why. For all their well-meaning capability, Iris and the Cruisers are ultimately rather feckless and unspectacular. Then again, plenty of feckless, unspectacular bands go pretty far in AOR pop rock, so one guesses that Iris just never had the right management or something. Too bad: "Love Is like a Rock" and "Ah! Leah!, " the best tracks here, showcasing talent that could conceivably have developed into something genuinely interesting.

☐ IRON MAIDEN

BEHIND THE IRON CURTAIN

★★½

Sony, 1985, 38 minutes
PRODUCED BY: Rod Smallwood and Andy Taylor
DIRECTED BY: Jim Yukich, Kenny Feuerman, Tony Halton
MUSIC FROM: Power Slave (Capitol, 1984); *The Number of the Beast* (Capitol, 1982).
SELECTIONS: "Aces High," "Hallowed Be Thy Name," "2 Minutes to Midnight," "Run to the Hills."

☐ IRON MAIDEN

VIDEO PIECES

★★½

Sony, 1984, 18 minutes

PRODUCED BY: Picture Music International
DIRECTED BY: David Mallet and Jim Yukich
MUSIC FROM: The Number of the Beast (Capitol, 1982); *Piece of Mind* (Capitol, 1983).
SELECTIONS: "Run to the Hills," "The Number of the Beast," "Flight of Icarus," "The Trooper."
Also available on Pioneer 8-inch Stereo Laser videodisc.

Not your typical rock band tour documentary, *Behind the Iron Curtain* captures this British heavy metal band touring Poland, Czechoslovakia, Hungary, and Yugoslavia in 1984. The band serves up its brand of speedy, screeching hard rock in such no-nonsense fashion that lead singer Bruce Dickinson is affectionately known to his fans as "the Air Raid Siren." There are some intriguing bits of behind-the-scenes footage: one Polish man says in broken English that they have maybe a concert a month there if they're lucky—and this inability to take rock for granted may be the reason that Iron Maiden's Iron Curtain fans seem even more rabidly appreciative than their British and American counterparts. At another point a Polish kid has a friendly argument with Dickinson, who keeps trying to explain why the kid can't play *real* heavy metal on a synthesizer. Overall, however, there's not enough of such footage to make sociologists happy, and by the same token, there may be too much travelogue to keep Iron Maiden fans from seeing it as an unnecessary distraction. Certainly, whoever had the idea to intercut WWII newsreel footage of the Battle of Britain into "Aces High," and battle scenes from Eisenstein's classic *Alexander Nevsky* into "Hallowed Be Thy Name," never should have had the idea in the first place. Fans, who usually just want to see their heroes in action, will probably be annoyed at the intrusions; anyone else would have to find the use of such imagery in this context more than a bit pretentious. And the inclusion of promo clips for "Aces High" and "2 Minutes to Midnight" instead of on-the-road live versions, could be seen as a bit of a rip-off.

Video Pieces, a collection of video clips, show how rock video directors can screw up things by not leaving well enough alone. David Mallet's three clips—"Run to the Hills," "The Number of the Beast," and "The Trooper,"—feature nice performance footage that any fan would probably drool over, yet each also severely undercuts the anthemic intensity of its song with dumbly literal and witless cut-ins of silent Western footage ("Run to the Hills," which is an Indian warrior's view of fighting off the White Man), horror-movie footage ("The Number of the Beast"), and silent-movie battle footage ("The Trooper"). By default, Jim Yukich's "Flight of Icarus" is the best clip because, despite its dumbly literal solarized mystical symbolism, it's at least more appropriate to the band's sincerely serious pulp-comic motifs.

□ IRON MAIDEN
LIVE AFTER DEATH
★★★

Sony, 1986, 90 minutes
PRODUCED BY: Tammara Wells
DIRECTED BY: Jim Yukich
MUSIC FROM: Iron Maiden (Capitol, 1980); *The Number of the Beast* (Capitol, 1982); *Piece of Mind* (Capitol, 1983); *Powerslave* (Capitol, 1984).
SELECTIONS: "Intro: Churchill Speech," "Aces High," "2 Minutes to Midnight," "The Trooper," "Revelations," "Flight of Icarus," "Rime of the Ancient Mariner," "Powerslave," "The Number of the Beast," "Hallowed Be Thy Name,"

"Iron Maiden," "Run to the Hills," "Running Free," "Sanctuary."

Live After Death is probably the ultimate concert video for the Iron Maiden fan, who gets ninety full minutes of the band caught at California's Long Beach Arena in March 1985 during its "World Slavery Tour." Iron Maiden perform on a massive stage adorned (if you can call it that) with huge Egyptian sphinxes on either side and a gigantic mummy in the middle that shoots pyrotechnic sparks from its eyes. If that seems like mammoth-scale dumbness to you, well, sure it is—but don't try telling that to the thousands of kids in the crowd loving every ear-splitting minute of it. Meanwhile, director Jim Yukich captures the show with all the state-of-the-art high-tech razzle-dazzle shot-on-film camerawork anyone could ever ask for.

☐ VARIOUS ARTISTS
ISLAND REGGAE GREATS
★★★½

RCA/Columbia, 1985, 28 minutes
MUSIC FROM: Various albums by various artists.
SELECTIONS: Burning Spear: "Jah Is My Driver"; Third World: "Now That We've Found Love"; Black Uhuru: "Solidarity"; Aswad: "Cashing for the Breeze"; Bob Marley: "War"/"No More Trouble"; Linton Kwesi Johnson: "The Great Insurrection"; Toots and the Maytals: "Reggae Got Soul."

This solid compilation of reggae video clips, mainly of concert performances spans the deeply entrancing, hard-core reggae bedrock of Burning Spear; the militant modern reggae of Black Uhuru; the smooth, sweet pop-reggae of Third World; and the ebulliently soulful, classic reggae of Toots and the Maytals. Also included is the late great reggae messiah, Bob Marley, in good if not peak form. And there are two especially valuable inclusions from the British reggae scene—Aswad, who are as good, though not as commercially adept, a British reggae band as the better-known Steel Pulse; and non-Rasta reggae poet-rapper Linton Kwesi Johnson, whose intelligently incendiary lyrics provide a scaldingly articulate record of British racism. Johnson's presence and his revolutionary fervor (not to mention the superb reggae music provided him by Dennis Bovell's Dub Band) make his clip the most exceptional entry in a powerful and commendably eclectic collection.

J

☐ JERMAINE JACKSON
DYNAMITE VIDEOS
★★

RCA/Columbia, 1985, 25 minutes
PRODUCED BY: Antony Payne, Jon Roseman
DIRECTED BY: Bob Giraldi, James Ewart
MUSIC FROM: Various Jermaine Jackson albums.
SELECTIONS: "Dynamite," "When the Rain Begins to Fall," "Sweetest Sweetest," "Do What You Do," "The Making of 'Do What You Do.' "

"Do What You Do" is a nice little pop-soul ballad; otherwise, there's no reason to go near this unless you're a MAJOR Jermaine Jackson fan. Bob Giraldi directed all the clips except "Sweetest Sweetest" (a smoochy soul ballad, shot by director James Ewart for British producer Jon Roseman, in which Jermaine's in a hotel giving room service—with a smile), proving again that he really should stay away from music videos. The guy makes brilliant TV commercials, like those Miller Lite sports-celeb ads and the tennis-motif "Thank you, Paine-Webber" spots. But when he makes music videos he loses all sense of artistic discipline; he stops making sense and starts getting bombastic and slick, which is just what he does here. "Dynamite" is a lavishly lame jailbreak scenario with the requisite Giraldi "let's-stop-dead-in-our-tracks-here-for-one-of-my-classic-Dr-Pepper-commercial-big-dance-numbers." "When the Rain Begins to Fall" is a duet between Jermaine and, of all people, Pia Zadora—so it does have its own slightly redeeming built-in camp-comedy factor. "Do What You Do" is another of Giraldi's muddled attempts at "mini-movie" scope and depth, here with a suspense plot featuring Jermaine as a gangster and the high-fashion model Iman as a femme fatale. The documentary on the making of this clip is an extended advertisement on behalf of Jermaine and Giraldi, where everyone struts around acting very impressed with the urgency and timeless significance of their endeavors. Still, as I said, if you like Jermaine you'll like this, and he *is* a trouper as he runs through the high-production-value paces.

☐ JOE JACKSON
THE BIG WORLD SESSIONS
★★★

A&M, 1986, 30 minutes
PRODUCED BY: Joe Jackson and David Kershenbaum
DIRECTED BY: Bob Lampel
MUSIC FROM: Big World (A&M, 1986).
SELECTIONS: "Right and Wrong," "(It's a) Big World," "Home Town," "Soul Kiss," "The Jet Set," "Man in the Street."

Jackson made rather a big deal out of the way he recorded his *Big World* album: he made it "live," onstage before an audience at New York City's Roundabout Theater in January 1986. In this handsomely shot video, you'll occasionally notice Jackson reading lyrics off a music stand, as well as see the engineers at work in a mobile studio right outside the theater. There's even a false start on "Soul Kiss." Jackson fronts a very capable bass-guitar-drums trio, also accompanied by four backing vocalists. The music is a tuneful, tasteful melange of pop, light rock, and funk, with tinges of Latin and classic soul. It may not be overly inspired or distinctive, but it's inevitably accomplished and enjoyable. Plus, Jackson's truly live recording is unique, especially in an era when few other artists would attempt such a feat. However, unless you're a Jackson fan, he reverts to annoying form too much of the time here: a sneering whine about how disappointing the rest of the world is, which indicates a guy with one heck of a superiority complex. What makes it so annoying is that (a) Jackson's always undoing such pleasant music with that self-righteousness, and (b) his attitude gets in the way of his obvious talent. This Jacksonian phenomenon really starts to manifest itself with "Soul Kiss" and remains prominent for the rest of the program. It's like a friend of mine, who is *not* a Joe Jackson fan, once said: "Here's my Joe Jackson impression: 'I *hate* rock 'n' roll . . . Rock 'n' roll is *dead* . . . I *am* rock 'n' roll."

And it's too bad, because some nice music gets ruined along the way: especially noteworthy are the Arabic-flavored "(It's a) Big World" and "Man in the Street," and the vintage surf-rock sound of "The Jet Set"; guitarist Vinnie Zummo shines on the latter two. Musically, the only really down moment is "Home Town," a flyweight sub-Springsteenism. An interesting sidelight: not *one* audience shot.

I must repeat, the fine music is ruined only if you're *not* already enamored of Jackson's style. If you are, chances are you'll really like this classy little program.

□ MICHAEL JACKSON
MAKING MICHAEL JACKSON'S "THRILLER"
★★★

Vestron, 1983, 60 minutes

DIRECTED BY: Jerry Kramer, John Landis, Bob Giraldi, Robert Abel

MUSIC FROM: Thriller (Epic, 1982); the Jacksons: *Triumph:* (Epic, 1981).

SELECTIONS: "Thriller," "Beat It," "Billie Jean," "Can You Feel It."

Also available on Vestron Stereo Laser videodisc.

Michael Jackson's John Landis–directed "Thriller" video was the crowning moment of 1983's Michaelmania: the longest (a six-minute song worked up into a fourteen-minute short subject), most expensive (a one-and-a-quarter-million-dollar budget), most ballyhooed rock video ever. It's also one of the most ponderous productions in rock video's short history. The only interesting thing about it is that at the peak of his popularity, Michael Jackson (as Landis excitedly explains) had this burning desire to portray himself to his millions of admirers as a monster. That's a highly intriguing fact, but *Making . . .* offers no insight into it. Documentarian Jerry Kramer has done a good job directing his portion of this program, yet that still doesn't keep it from deteriorating to the usual on-set smugness; let's face it, if "Thriller" is the ultimate rock video vanity production, *Making Michael Jackson's "Thriller"* is a vanity production about a vanity production.

Still, there is a lot of good, watchable stuff: transformational-makeup artist Rick Baker showing how he does his thing; Jackson rehearsing his "Beat It"–like dance routines with choreographer Michael Peters; snippets of Jackson 5 home movies; the J5 on *The Ed Sullivan Show;* Michael's electrifying "Billie Jean" from the "Motown 25" TV special (available in complete form on *Motown 25: Yesterday, Today, Forever*); and Michael's "Beat It" clip (directed by Bob Giraldi) and the Jacksons' awe-inspiring computer-animated "Can You Feel It" video (directed by Robert Abel)—both of which easily surpass "Thriller" for sheer synergistic excitement. And, of course, there are all those glimpses of Michael, being his own incomparably bizarre self. Not to mention the latent time-capsule value of this program: years from now we can look back and chuckle at what all the fuss may have been about, right?

☐ THE JACKSONS

LIVE AT THE RAINBOW

★★★½

Import, 1978, 58 minutes

MUSIC FROM: The Jackson 5's Greatest Hits (Motown, 1972); *Dancing Machine* (Motown, 1973); *Anthology* (Motown, 1977); *Goin' Places* (Epic, 1977); *Destiny* (Epic, 1978).

SELECTIONS: "Dancing Machine," "Things I Do for You," "Ben," "Keep on Dancing," "ABC," "The Love You Save," "Enjoy Yourself," "Destiny," "Goin' Places."

This competently shot 1978 concert at London's Rainbow catches the slick soul family act after they had out grown their Jackson 5 package—and long before the repugnant indulgences of 1984's *Victory* tour. While this is only a portion of their show on the *Destiny* tour—omitting such classics as their first hit, "I Want You Back," and their then-current hit, "Shake Your Body (Down to the Ground)"—what's here is a sequinned-suited, group-choreographed, disco-era soul spectacular. Michael Jackson was every bit as remarkable and riveting a stage performer then as he would be later—and hey, it's *before* his nose job, too. This is *much* more recommendable than a costly—and illegal—bootleg of the *Victory* tour show. However, be warned that since this *is* an import tape, it will cost more than a domestic tape and could take up to twelve weeks to arrive from across the ocean. (Available by mail order from Playings Hard to Get.)

☐ MICK JAGGER

RUNNING OUT OF LUCK

★★★

CBS/Fox, 1986, 88 minutes

PRODUCED BY: Mick Jagger, Nitrate Films

DIRECTED BY: Julien Temple

MUSIC FROM: Mick Jagger: *She's the Boss* (Columbia, 1985); the Rolling Stones: *Get Yer Ya-Ya's Out* (London, 1970); *Sticky Fingers* (Rolling Stones, 1971).

SELECTIONS: Mick Jagger: "Running Out of Luck," "Half a Loaf," "Turn the Girl Loose," "Hard Woman," "Secrets," "She's the Boss," "Lucky in Love," "Just Another Night," "Lonely at the Top"; Rolling Stones: "Jumpin' Jack Flash," "Brown Sugar."

This musical/adventure/comedy feature-length music video was originally shot just before the 1985 release of Mick Jagger's solo debut *She's the Boss*. For reasons that have never really been made very clear, its release was held up for over a year. *Running Out of Luck* is interesting and entertaining enough that, had it come out along with its companion audio album, it could have made a pretty big splash; being released a year later, as a seeming afterthought, its chances are lessened considerably—especially considering its retail price of $79.95, which seems designed to make it a rental rather than sales item. As a rental, though, *Running Out of Luck* is certainly worth a look.

The main thing to keep in mind is that *Running Out of Luck* was shot in and around Rio de Janeiro by Julien Temple, one of rock video's leading *auteurs*. In his best work, Temple inevitably likes to cast rock stars in multiple, usually less-than-flattering roles: David Bowie as both a loony-tune rock star and a pathetic nerd in *Jazzin' for Blue Jean*; Ray Davies of the Kinks as both himself and as a sleazy old lounge lizard type in "Come Dancing"; Jagger as a mummified museum exhibit and Rolling Stones bassist Bill Wyman as a museum security guard in the Stones' *Video Rewind*; Jagger as himself, a Central American revolutionary, *and* a shady, deal-making journalist in the Stones clip "Undercover"; and so on. Temple's often gone on record as saying he despises the usual role music videos play, that of merely glorifying a rock star. With his deliberately provocative casting moves Temple not only deglamorizes rock stars, but often accomplishes a sort of surprising, back-handed image-enhancement—making the stars seem more human, normal, and accessible by taking them down a peg, which is just what he does with Jagger.

Jagger plays himself, in Rio to make a suitably lavish music video, accompanied by his famous-model girlfriend, Jerry Hall, and a nutso music video *auteur*, well played by the movies' Mr. Gonzo himself, Dennis Hopper. You'd probably have to be a music-video insider of sorts to know that Temple is poking fun at big-bucks-adman-turned-pretentious-music-video-*auteur* Bob Giraldi when he has Hopper bring the on-set activity to a screeching halt at one point by shouting, "There's only *one* star on my sets—and that's ME!" From the beginning, Jagger and Hall are at odds, and they each flirt with extras on the set to piss the other one off. Jagger ends up getting pretty drunk and walking off with a trio of lovelies—he's too soused to notice that the three are actually guys in drag. They proceed to mug Jagger and, after pummeling him, leave him for dead.

Jagger ends up alone, lost in the wilderness outside Rio. Looking incredibly haggard, he mistakenly wanders into a banana plantation run by a whip-cracking, middle-aged woman (Zeni Pereira) who not only works Jagger like a slave, but makes him her sex-slave as well. In some strongly Buñuelian scenes, Temple intercuts scenes of Jagger being forced to satisfy her in her darkened bedroom with bright-daylight shots of Jagger, equally repelled, fending off tarantulas as he hacks down bananas. Eventually, of course, Jagger meets up with a pretty, friendly jungle girl (Rae Dawn Chong) who helps him escape and leads him back to civilization—where, instead of trying to prove who he is to a world that believes him dead, Jagger ends up more-or-less starting all over again, rehearsing in a nondescript London loft with a young band while Fleet Street wags snoop around trying to flesh out rumors that Jagger may be alive and back at work.

Along the way, the songs from *She's the Boss* are worked into the narrative with rather literal-minded but credible facility (it should be noted that "Hard Woman" is *not* the beautifully computer-animated clip that accompanied the song on MTV; rather, here the song backs a fairly intense soft-core love scene between Jagger and Chong). And Temple sets up one priceless, very memorable sequence in which Jagger tries in vain to convince the middle-aged man and woman running a little bodega in the Brazilian outback that he's a world-famous rock 'n' roll star: "I'm Mick Jagger," he says to their uncomprehending faces, "you know . . . Micky Jagiero?"; he scans the pile of record albums in one corner of the shop, and behind about twenty-five Julio Iglesias albums finds a copy of the Stones' *Through the Past Darkly*, throwing it on their turntable to sing and prance along with "Jumpin' Jack Flash" and "Brown Sugar" while the man and woman stare in blank nonrecognition, and a little boy has a ball mocking Jagger's legendary moves.

Overall, Jagger is very good, seemingly quite comfortable with all that Temple wants him to do—in fact, perhaps *too* comfortable. In fact, aside from leaving a few of the plot's loose ends untied at its conclusion, if *Running Out of Luck* has a fault it's that it all seems just a tad pat, in a way—as if it's all too cozily planned to make us believe Jagger's taking all of Temple's fictitious abuse so we'll end up liking him more. Maybe Temple needs to find another way to effect his purposefully deglamorizing motifs, or maybe there was some sort of problem with this particular production.

☐ THE JAM

VIDEO SNAP!

★★★½

Media, 1984, 47 minutes

PRODUCED BY: John Benedict, Peter Olliff

DIRECTED BY: Various

MUSIC FROM: In the City (Polydor, 1977); *This Is the Modern World* (Polydor, 1977); *All Mod Cons* (Polydor, 1978); *Setting Sons* (Polydor, 1979); *Sound Affects* (Polydor, 1980); *The Gift* (Polydor, 1982); *Snap!* (Polygram, 1984).

SELECTIONS: "In the City," "Art School," "News of the World," "Strange Town," "Butterfly Collector," "When You're Young," "Going Underground," "Start!," "Town Called Malice," "Precious," "Funeral Pyre," "The Bitterest Pill," "Absolute Beginners," "That's Entertainment."

☐ THE JAM

TRANS-GLOBAL UNITY EXPRESS

★★★★

Sony, 1985, 29 minutes

PRODUCED BY: Peter Henton

DIRECTED BY: Gordian P. Troeller

MUSIC FROM: Various Jam albums (Polydor, 1977–82).

SELECTIONS: "Town Called Malice," "Carnation," "Precious," "Ghosts," "Move On Up," "Private Hell," "Pretty Green," "Trans-Global Express," "The Gift."

The chronological clips compilation *Video Snap!* is as straight-ahead and no-nonsense as the now-defunct British Mod-influenced punk band was; mainly straight-performance clips ("Butterfly Collector" is an actual live concert clip) perfectly document the Jam's relentless energy and leader Paul Weller's dour assessment of contemporary Britain, and in the main the production values are surprisingly high. *Video Snap!* could make those who never much cared for the Jam realize what they missed, and taken with the fiery concert tape *Trans-Global Unity Express,* it represents the band's legacy well indeed in the home video market.

The latter tape opens with Paul Weller's dad, the Jam's manager, introducing the boys. Away they go with the charging, Motownish "Town Called Malice," and for twenty-nine fairly riveting minutes, their energy level remains at an unremitting, vein-popping pitch. Much of the music follows the soul-inflected lead of the first track, and there's even a cover of Curtis Mayfield's "Move On Up," which somewhat presages Weller's later move to the Style Council's sophisto-soul dabbling. The Jam build up a serious head of steam toward the climax with "Private Hell" and "Pretty Green." Throughout, the commendably straightforward camerawork catches the band's all-out, clenched-fist intensity very well.

☐ AL JARREAU

AL JARREAU IN LONDON

★★

Warner Music Video, 1985, 54 minutes

PRODUCED BY: Jacqui Byford

DIRECTED BY: David Mallet

MUSIC FROM: Various Al Jarreau albums (Warner/Reprise, 1975–85).

SELECTIONS: "Raging Waters," "Trouble in Paradise," "We're in This Love Together," "Let's Pretend," "Our Love," "Take Five," "High Crime," "Boogie Down," "Roof Garden."

Also available on Pioneer Stereo Laser videodisc.

A classic case of mismatching between director and artist. David Mallet—David Bowie's longtime video clip maker—is a true child of the post-modern, no-attention-span generation; he can never hold the same shot for longer than, say, five seconds. And while Jarreau's formidable vocal instrument does make athletic leaps all over the place, Mallet's hyperactive style is completely at odds with the mellow, intimate groove that runs through Jarreau's silken jazz-funk fusion. In the end, the poor pairing would seem to drive away both possible audiences for the program: Jarreau's fans will probably be annoyed with all the flashy camera angles and ceaseless quick-cuts; and somehow, I don't think Mallet's contributions will win Jarreau new converts from the rock crowd.

□ TOMMY JARRELL
SPROUT WINGS AND FLY
★★★★★

Flower Films, 1983, 30 minutes
PRODUCED BY: Alice Gerrard and Cece Conway
DIRECTED BY: Les Blank
SELECTIONS: Tommy Jarrell: "Drunken Hiccups," "John Brown's Dream," "When Sorrows Encompass Me Around," "Cluck Old Hen," "Cripple Creek," "Back Step Cindy," "Breakin' Up Christmas," "Molly, Put the Kettle On," "Fortune"; Tommy Jarrell with Blanton Owen and Paul Sutphin: "John Hardy"; B. F. Jarrell: "When Sorrows Encompass Me Around"; Julie Jarrell: "Come Take a Trip"; Melvin Slaydon: untitled instrumental; church congregation: "When Sorrows Encompass Me Around."

Though all of Les Blank's humbly revelatory little documentaries are delightful, *Sprout Wings and Fly* just may be the very best of them all. Nominally, it's a portrait of "old-timey music" (a form of bluegrass-folk mainly peculiar to the southern Appalachians), fiddler Tommy Jarrell, and his home in the breathtaking Blue Ridge Mountains of North Carolina. Jarrell is one marvelously spry old cat, sage and lovable but never presented as a folksy cliché. He's positively demonic on his fiddle, easily negotiating the lightning-quick double-stops and tricky fingerings of old-timey music; he further belies his aged appearance when he opens his mouth to sing a ballad and out comes a strong, deep, limber voice. The folks who live in Jarrell's mountain community form a colorful and intriguing supporting cast; and the scenery is gorgeous.

But beyond that, *Sprout Wings and Fly* has a poignancy and profundity that are so plainspoken, simple, and obvious one could hardly be faulted for missing it at first. It's a meditation on culture (as in music, dance, food, art) as a manifestation of man's will to live and create in harmony with nature—and to do so with joy, while always knowing that death is inevitable. Sound heavy? It is, if you think about it. Yet Blank *never, ever* makes it seem gooey and sentimental, nor does the film ever cluck its tongue or shake its head at the way such bedrock folkways are disappearing in the face of encroaching modernity the way so many message-films do. As always, Blank leaves things just the way his camera found them: far from perfect, but in many ways a lot closer to perfection than the industrial world beyond Jarrell's mountains, and always unpretentiously genuine. *Sprout Wings and Fly* is the very embodiment of such oft-abused terms as "life-affirming" and "celebratory." (Available by mail order from Flower Films.)

□ KEITH JARRETT
LAST SOLO
★★★½

Sony, 1986, 92 minutes
PRODUCED BY: Masafumi Yamamoto
DIRECTED BY: Kaname Kawachi
MUSIC FROM: Last Solo (ECM/Warner Bros., 1984).
SELECTIONS: "Tokyo '84 #1," "Tokyo

'84 #2," "Over the Rainbow," "Tokyo '84 Encore."

Keith Jarrett is not for everyone—but then, he doesn't try to be. Notice that there are only four selections in this program, which runs over ninety minutes. Jarrett's a very gifted jazz pianist who likes to spin out long and winding solo improvisations that shift through an often dazzling and inevitably dizzying panoply of moods—almost all of which Jarrett physically mirrors with his lost-in-the-mystic facial expressions, grunts and moans, and expressive bodily gestures and postures. If you're not going along with his musical flow, you'll more than likely find Jarrett an exasperatingly pretentious presence. If you *do* stay with him musically, you may find him refreshingly extroverted—or you may *still* think he's annoyingly self-important with all of his grimaces of exertion. At any rate, since this beautifully directed and recorded concert program provides such a hefty and intense dose of Jarrett doing his solo thing, it's recommended mainly for initiates who are prepared to accept the challenge of following Jarrett as he chases his muse.

☐ **VARIOUS ARTISTS**
JAZZ IN EXILE
★★★½

Rhapsody, 1985, 58 minutes
PRODUCED BY: Chuck France
DIRECTED BY: Chuck France
MUSIC FROM: Various albums by various artists; the film *Jazz in Exile* (Francerelli Films, 1982).
SELECTIONS: Dexter Gordon Quartet: "Gingerbread Boy"; Johnny Griffin Quartet: "Soft and Furry"; Woody Shaw Quintet: "Why"; Art Farmer Quartet: "In a Sentimental Mood"; Richard Davis Trio: "All Blues"; Randy Weston: "Hi-Fly"; Dexter Gordon/Johnny Griffin Quintet: "Red Top"; Phil Woods Quartet: "Last Night When We Were Young"; Richard Davis: "Summertime"; unidentified musical excerpts by the Art Ensemble of Chicago, Gato Barbieri, Carla Bley, Gary Burton, Betty Carter, Slide Hampton, Freddie Hubbard, and Mal Waldron.

Producer/director Chuck France, who also made the award-winning documentary *The War at Home*, here trains his no-frills camera on expatriate American jazz musicians residing in Europe. They not only state both the familiar and unfamiliar pluses and minuses of life abroad, but also contemplate their places in the scheme of things and play some fine music (which is unfortunately presented mainly in snippets rather than complete pieces). Dexter Gordon, Phil Woods, bassist Richard Davis's bowed solo rendition of "Summertime," and the too-few moments of the Art Ensemble of Chicago's surreal theatrics are the musical highlights. The conversations range from the righteously irate to the drolly resigned. Carla Bley, in a typically irreverent yet serious moment, notes that the food, wine, cars, and cigarettes in America are inferior to those in Europe—so why should America deserve better music and musicians? Hitting home the hardest, perhaps, is alto saxophonist Phil Woods, who flatly notes that the great onetime Ellington tenor saxophonist Ben Webster died in Amsterdam simply because he couldn't get any work in the U.S.

The unfamiliar minuses of the jazz life in Europe—where these musicians are inevitably more appreciated, and in many cases even coddled, by foreign audiences—mainly have to do with the simple inescapable human fact that these players are far from home and miss their roots. This fascinating flip side of the grass-is-always-greener motif manifests itself most obviously in the stated as well as the apparent-but-unspoken desires of most of these musicians to make triumphant homecomings.

However, *Jazz in Exile* does have one fault: it omits those expatriate musicians (the most famous of whom is probably the great swing-to-bop tenor saxophonist Don Byas) who have become successful and happy over there and have no apparent desire to ever return to the land that ignored them. It comes closest to documenting that attitude only in the tentative ambivalence expressed by soprano sax master Steve Lacy. As a result, *Jazz in Exile* has a certain underlying one-sidedness that could be seen by some as rather smug. But then, that's an occupational hazard for the independent producer/director documenting comparatively obscure musicians on a low budget—there's a natural, implicit tendency toward aggrandizing advocacy of the subject, a phenomenon only Les Blank has managed to consistently overcome with his unvarnished down-to-earth folksiness. Still, *Jazz in Exile* has more than enough substance, musical and otherwise, to make it recommendable to the jazz fan as well as to anyone interested in a different sort of angle on the complex, subtle relationships between America and the rest of the world. (Available by mail order from Rhapsody Films.)

☐ **VARIOUS ARTISTS**

JAZZBALL

★★½

Spotlite, 1985, 60 minutes

PRODUCED BY: Leslie Roush and Justin Herman

DIRECTED BY: Leslie Roush, Fred Waller, Aubrey Scotto, Jerry Hopper, Alvin Ganzer, Herbert Moulton

MUSIC FROM: Various albums by various artists; *Jazzball* compilation of Panoram Soundie musical short films (NTA Pictures, 1958).

SELECTIONS: Cab Calloway and His Orchestra: "Smoky Joe"; Rudy Vallee and His Connecticut Yankees: "You'll Do It Someday, So Why Not Now?"; Duke Ellington and His Orchestra: "Rockin' in Rhythm," "Stormy Weather," "Bundle of Blues" (tap dance medley with dancers Bessie Dudley and Florence Hill); Mills Brothers: "I Ain't Got Nobody"; Red Nichols and His Modern Mountaineers: "When I Meet My Baby in New Orleans"; Ina Ray Hutton and Her All-Girl Orchestra: "Truckin' "; Louis Armstrong and His Orchestra: "Shine"; Russ Morgan and His Orchestra: "Wabash Blues"; Louis Prima and His Orchestra: "Chinatown, My Chinatown"; Bob Crosby and His Bobcats: "How'd You Like To?," "Dixieland Parade"; Betty Hutton with the Vincent Lopez Orchestra: "Dipsey Doodle"; Isham Jones and His Orchestra: "Liszt's Second Hungarian Rhapsody"; Henry Busse and His Orchestra: "Hot Lips"; Bob Chester and His Orchestra: "Boogie Woogie Blues"; Hal Kemp and His Orchestra: "Swamp Fire"; Jimmy Dorsey and His Orchestra: "Yo Ho Ho"; Johnny "Scat" Davis: "Praise the Lord and Pass the Ammunition"; Gene Krupa and His Orchestra: "Jungle Madness"; Peggy Lee with the Dave Barber Orchestra: "It's a Good Day"; Lawrence Welk and His Orchestra: "Ain't She Sweet?"; Artie Shaw and His Orchestra featuring Buddy Rich: unidentified song; Will Mastin Trio featuring Sammy Davis, Jr.: "Boogie Woogie Piggy."

Jazzball is a late-'50s compilation of "Panoram Soundies": short musical films, usually of the straightforward performance type but sometimes enhanced with primitive "conceptual" gambits, that were made by jazz and pop artists for theatrical and film-jukebox use in the late '30s, '40s, and early '50s—and thus, pioneering instances of what is now known as music video. But while the idea of such a tape is a most intriguing one, and though *Jazzball* does have its moments, it's a disappointment for a couple of major reasons: one, the majority of the clips are rather unremarkable, static performance setups, and more damagingly, the newsreel-style narration (written by Charles Leonard, spoken by Art Gilmore) not only intrudes all over the music, but is riddled with historical inaccuracies and hyperbole (according to the voiceover, Duke Ellington invented jam sessions, Red Nichols was the only cornetist in all of jazz to compare with Bix Biederbecke, and Lawrence Welk really did play swing music at one time).

Still, this is at the very least reasonably good nostalgia viewing for those who care to revisit or rediscover the big-band era (though the selection suffers from an overload of such boring whitebreads as Russ Morgan, Louis Prima, Bing's little brother Bob Crosby, Henry Busse, and Bob Chester, not to mention Welk). And there are some notable moments. Perhaps most remarkable is the Duke Ellington medley clip: "Stormy Weather" cuts in midperformance to a succession of shots of rain falling on various locales, all connected by wipes that bleed liquidly down the screen (Gilmore's voiceover drops a groaner of a pun about "syrupy special effects"); and "Bundle of Blues" features not only musical-note-shaped wipes and dissolves, but also some *very* pre-MTV quick, on-the-beat cutting between various sections of the big band and dancers Bessie Dudley and Florence Hill. Rudy Vallee's clip features him playing clarinet and alto sax more than he croons. The Mills Brothers' "I Ain't Got Nobody" (yes, the one David Lee Roth covered) is a classic example of the follow-the-bouncing-ball lyric-subtitle bit. Isham Jones's orchestra shows why it was one of the best white bands of its era, with a swinging classical gas of a rearrangement of a Liszt piece. Ina Ray Hutton dances, sings, and then tap-dances marvelously while conducting her all-girl big band; at this writing, Bette Midler was planning to produce and star in a movie bio about Hutton, and from her sassy vivacity here it's easy to see why. Louis Armstrong performs "Shine" in what the narration calls "a jazz parody of paradise"—a tacky otherworldly set with jungle costumes and an inexplicable abundance of soapsuds all over the place, bizarre enough to distract you from what may be the hottest music on the whole tape. But then, as Louis's trumpet solo heats up to the boiling point, the image of his head and horn spins faster and faster through a cheaply effective, primitive special effect. Hal Kemp, who this writer at least expected to be just another forgettable bandleader, delivers a surprisingly swinging arrangement in a starkly lit performance clip that makes beautiful use of shadows and chiaroscuro (directed by Leslie Roush, this is easily the best-looking clip here).

Vying with Louis Armstrong and Duke Ellington for musical high point is the clip of Gene Krupa's band, which features one of the greatest trumpeters in jazz history, Roy Eldridge (a crucial figure in the transition from swing to bebop), swinging high and hard; there's also a great percussion interlude in which every band member pounds out a steady tattoo on his own little tom-tom while Krupa embroiders throbbing polyrhythms around the beat. For those post–baby boomers who've only seen the older Peggy Lee, the sight and sound of her when she was a very young, attractive, and hard-swinging vocalist will be an absolute revelation. As will the sight of Buddy Rich looking like a *kid* with Artie Shaw's orchestra. Sammy Davis, Jr., in a clip from the film *Sweet and Low* with the Will Mastin Trio of singer/dancers (the narration screws up again, calling this Sammy's film debut, when we've all seen that clip of him stealing a similar scene as a little kid, haven't we?) won't surprise anybody—he's his same old inimitable self. But some eyebrows may be raised when he and one of his partners throw some proto-breakdance moves into their tap routine.

If all that makes it seem that *Jazzball* is actually more high spots than low, well, all I can say is, that's ultimately in the eye of the beholder—but I'll add that there are enough low points to make *Jazzball* seem a lot longer than its sixty minutes. (Available by mail order from Republic Pictures Home Video or Blackhawk Films.)

□ EDDIE JEFFERSON (WITH RICHIE COLE)
LIVE FROM THE JAZZ SHOWCASE

★★★

University of Illinois at Chicago, 1982, 50 minutes

PRODUCED BY: Susan Markle

DIRECTED BY: William Mahin

MUSIC FROM: Various Eddie Jefferson albums.

SELECTIONS: "Jeaninne," "Night in Tunisia," "Trane's Blues," "I Cover the Waterfront," "So What?," "I Got the Blues," "When You're Smiling," "My Baby Has Gone Away," "Body and Soul," "How High the Moon," "Benny's from Heaven," "Moody's Mood for Love," "Summertime," "Freedom Jazz Dance."

This is the only known video record of the late great bebop scat singer, captured in an intimate club date at the University of Illinois on May 6, 1979—just two days before his mysterious shooting death in Detroit. Jefferson gets fine support from Charlie Parker–inspired alto saxophonist Richie Cole.

Jefferson was a unique character: cramming his rapid-fire scats with all sorts of tributes and references to great jazzmen; echoing his rough-edged, intense vocals with awkwardly enthusiastic, endearing sorts of dances. He starts out coarse enough to unsettle any Mel Torme fan, but gets warmed up soon enough and is in fine form by the fitting closer, "Moody's Mood for Love," his best-known tune (and dig the Sly Stone reference he throws in here!).

(Available by mail order from the University of Illinois at Chicago.)

□ JEFFERSON STARSHIP
JEFFERSON STARSHIP

★★

RCA/Columbia, 1983, 65 minutes

PRODUCED BY: Nelvana and Ease Media

DIRECTED BY: Stanley Dorfman

MUSIC FROM: Jefferson Starship Gold (RCA, 1979); *Freedom at Point Zero* (RCA, 1979); *Modern Times* (RCA, 1980); *Winds of Change* (RCA, 1982); *The Worst of the Jefferson Airplane* (RCA, 1970).

SELECTIONS: "Winds of Change," "Ride the Tiger," "Stranger," "Black Widow," "Find Your Way Back," "Somebody to Love," "Be My Lady," "Girl with the Hungry Eyes," "Out of Control," "White Rabbit," "Jane," "Stairway to Cleveland."

Also available on Pioneer Stereo Laser videodisc.

The Jefferson Starship were the Jefferson Airplane, one of the more politically radical San Francisco psychedelic rock bands, before they saw the light in 1974: Airplane became Starship, politics went out the door, and fuzzy-headed sub–*Star Wars* space-age motifs came in the window, tailor-made for the heavy-metal/AOR-rock generation. To put it bluntly, they sold out. That's the audience watching them in this 1983 concert, shot at the Queen Elizabeth Theater in Vancouver, Canada, and you can bet none of 'em are old enough to remember the Airplane's "Somebody to Love" and "White Rabbit" firsthand. You can be sure from their cheers that it matters not a whit to them that Airplane founder Paul Kantner (who was soon to leave the band) and longtime outrageous co-lead vocalist Grace Slick have little to do onstage, what with the music being given over to Mickey Thomas's voice and Craig Chaquico's feckless guitar flash. And you can rest assured that none but such converted fans of the Starship's corporate rock could manage to sit still through this indifferently shot concert program, which is sporadically interrupted by a dumb space-age DJ named "Shortwave Mike."

☐ LEROY JENKINS
SOLO VIOLIN
★★★★

Rhapsody, 1984, 29 minutes
PRODUCED BY: Leroy Jenkins
DIRECTED BY: Leroy Jenkins
MUSIC FROM: The film *Solo Violin*, (1984).
SELECTIONS: Seven untitled solo violin compositions, four of them played twice.

In this remarkable tape, the diminutive bespectacled avant-garde jazz violinist Leroy Jenkins simply stands before a camera trained on his hands, face, and violin, plays a series of eleven brief (two to five minutes each) solos, and stares coolly into the camera for about a half minute after each one. Jenkins's music is as uncompromising and forthright as his elegantly concise direction of the visuals—from frenetic crazy quilts of fractured melodic fragments to seemingly atonal free-form sawing that qualifies more as theoretical exercise than actual traditional composition, this is rigorously dry, unconventional, inaccessible stuff (only three pieces, the fifth and the last two, come close to traditional melodicism).

Jenkins—who's led a number of respected avant-jazz units since the early '70s, from the acoustic trio the Revolutionary Ensemble to his '80s electric quintet Sting—is not just messing around, however. His calm self-possession is one indicator that *he* knows what he's doing, even if you don't. Furthermore, he ingeniously sequences the solos so that he plays four of them twice, back to back each time—thus making the tape almost instructive in allowing the viewer/listener to study the two versions of each piece, comparing to find out where composition ends and improvisation begins. This "noise" really does get more musical with repeated listening. There's an innate dignity to the take-it-or-leave-it, unabashed and unadorned manner in which Jenkins presents his extremely uncompromising music that makes a particularly instructive comparison to another Rhapsody Films title, *The New Music*—which is so self-consciously proud of how uncompromising its subjects, avant-garde jazz cornetist Bobby Bradford and clarinetist John Carter, are, that it's a turnoff. And Jenkins pulls all this off without saying or showing a word throughout. He's not for everyone, but he sure doesn't try to be, either. (Available by mail order from Rhapsody Films.)

☐ VARIOUS ARTISTS
JESUS CHRIST SUPERSTAR
★★

MCA, 1984, 105 minutes
PRODUCED BY: Norman Jewison and Robert Stigwood
DIRECTED BY: Norman Jewison
BOOK AND LYRICS BY: Tim Rice
MUSIC BY: Andrew Lloyd Webber
MUSIC FROM: Jesus Christ Superstar motion picture soundtrack (MCA, 1973).
SELECTIONS: include Yvonne Elliman: "Everything's All Right," I Don't Know How to Love Him"; ensemble: "Superstar."

Jesus Christ Superstar, which in earlier incarnations was a London hit and a Broadway smash, spawned hit LPs from the Broadway show and this movie's soundtrack. In many ways, it is one of the very few real rock operas, with fewer than a dozen spoken lines, and an interesting example of what rock can do. The question of how well *Superstar* does it, though, is another issue.

For those who may have missed it, *JCS* is the story of Jesus's last seven days on earth. As the title suggests, this is a view of Jesus Christ as a superstar in the current sense, a product of the "media," which then was word-of-mouth. But it's also told in an attempt to "strip away the myth from the man." It's a tall order, and as this proves, one nearly impossible to fill, though the film does try. Coming to it with a head full of Cecil B. DeMille cinemagraphic images and Sunday-school-book watercolors, *JCS*'s visual starkness is at first stunning and disconcerting. There's little grandeur here, and the barren desert sets seem to diminish the characters, including (unintentionally?) Jesus.

In emphasizing the politics behind Jesus' (Ted Neely) fate and his effect on those around him, particularly Mary Magdalene (Yvonne Elliman) and Judas Iscariot (powerfully portrayed by Carl Anderson), the movie presents Jesus as a political threat and charismatic figure but never makes clear exactly why. And there's the catch. We know why—now. But to make that part of the movie work, we need to bring along much of the so-called myth, and that's probably a good thing, too. This Jesus, besides being short of stature and temper, hardly seems the type to single-handedly change the world. He asks a lot of questions, is shocked to learn that he's going to die for his followers, whom he alternately seems to tolerate and openly despise, and can be pretty sarcastic. As he says to God at one point, "I didn't start it."

What do work are many of the songs, which combine the ages-old story with contemporary music and language. Dismissing Jesus's importance early on, Caiaphas asserts that he's "just a craze," only to be told by one of his advisers that Jesus is in fact "at the top of the poll," and "bigger than John was when John did his baptism thing." "I Don't Know How to Love Him," a big hit single back then, is a beautiful song, and the title theme is as grand as the very idea. The rest, however, seems paralyzed in the heavy-guitar clichés and cast-of-thousands background vocals.

In addition, some of the devices just don't work. Setting the Last Supper as the last picnic and turning the apostles into something like the Yale Glee Club, or making Herod (Joshua Mostel) a fat, spoiled, depraved hippie who in a sarcastic ragtime tune prods Jesus to prove himself is either brave or disgusting, depending on your point of view. Then again, showing heaven as an all-white Las Vegas set or Pilate as enraged by the slightest suggestion that Jesus could be right isn't totally inconsistent. Presenting the movie as a play on film, with the hippie troupe taking a bus to the desert, then shown packing up at the end, is, however, a mistake. I suppose showing us—as if we didn't know—that Ted Neely really isn't Jesus goes hand in hand with the myth-stripping.

The only truly great thing about this film is Carl Anderson as Judas Iscariot. His portrayal rings the truest of all, for his role is the clearest. His Judas is a full character with burning doubts, conflicts, passions, questions—surprisingly unlike this Jesus. His acting is histrionic at points, but his voice is so fine and soulful that you feel his anguish. At both the beginning and the end, it is Judas who presents *Jesus Christ Superstar*'s main themes and its writers' real views, though even these don't always satisfy.

The idea of myth outstripping, distorting, perverting, even dictating reality will probably always be relevant. But nearly two thousand years after the fact, you can't help but wonder what the point of this at times fascinating exercise was. When this play was first conceived, only rock stars were called superstars, and hippies drew parallels between their own lives in 1960s America and the early Christians'. With its repeated allusions to communications and media, it might make you wonder how history might have been changed if Christ had had a video on MTV, and that's just the simpleminded sort of argument mass communications freshmen—and this movie—would love. What the film can't show us is how, despite the lack of "communications," Jesus Christ became what he is today to billions of people. If Christ had indeed been the way he's portrayed here and if we follow this metaphor to the logical end, he'd be an obscure folkie whose work could be found only in the local cutout bins.—P.R.

□ JETHRO TULL
SLIPSTREAM
★★★

Pacific Arts, 1984, 60 minutes
DIRECTED BY: David Mallet
MUSIC FROM: Aqualung (Chrysalis, 1971); *Thick as a Brick* (Chrysalis, 1972); *Too Old to Rock 'n' Roll* (Chrysalis, 1976); *Songs from the Wood* (Chrysalis, 1977); *Heavy Horses* (Chrysalis, 1978).
SELECTIONS: "Black Sunday," "Dun Ringill," "Flying Dale Flyer," "Songs from the Wood," "Heavy Horses," "Sweet Dreams," "Too Old to Rock 'n' Roll, Too Young to Die," "Skating Away on the Thin Ice of a New Day," "Aqualung," "Locomotive Breath."

I used to be a Jethro Tull fan, but mad flautist Ian Anderson and company lost me with the unbearably precious indulgences of 1973's *A Passion Play.* Those diehard fans who stuck with the veteran British progressive rockers, however, should enjoy this eye-catching program, a comparatively early and adventurous example of long-form home music video. *Slipstream* combines a live concert shot in 1981 at London's Hammersmith Odeon with rock video *auteur* (and regular David Bowie video collaborator) David Mallet's garish, self-consciously arty conceptual inserts. The former finds an edition of Tull featuring onetime Roxy Music and U.K. keyboardist/violinist Eddie Jobson tackling much of Anderson's post–*Passion Play* work, a convoluted and roccoco synthesis of Olde English folk whimsy with tortuously complex classical rock; the latter finds an analog to "Aqualung," Anderson's scrofulous guttersnipe character, going on a variety of bizarre, sci-fi–style adventures which cue various Tull tunes. Interestingly, the live sound from the London show is used over both concert and concept clips. Like I said, latter-day Tull fans ought to love it; former fans like me, or those who are just curious, will probably want to avoid this—but may also note that the last half of *Slipstream,* starting with "Too Old . . . ," is at least an improvement on the first.

□ BILLY JOEL
LIVE FROM LONG ISLAND
★★★

CBS/Fox, 1983, 80 minutes
PRODUCED BY: Jon Small
DIRECTED BY: Jay Dubin
MUSIC FROM: Piano Man (Columbia, 1973); *Streetlife Serenade* (Columbia, 1974); *Turnstiles* (Columbia, 1976); *The Stranger* (Columbia, 1977); *52nd Street* (Columbia, 1978); *Glass Houses* (Columbia, 1980); *Songs in the Attic* (Columbia, 1981); *The Nylon Curtain* (Columbia, 1982); *An Innocent Man*

(Columbia, 1983), *Greatest Hits, Volume I & II* (Columbia, 1985).

SELECTIONS: include "Allentown," "My Life," "Angry Young Man," "Sometimes a Fantasy," "Piano Man," "The Stranger," "Scandinavian Skies," "You May Be Right," "Movin' Out (Anthony's Song)," "Pressure," "Big Shot," "Italian Restaurant," "Just the Way You Are," "It's Still Rock 'n Roll to Me," "Only the Good Die Young."

Also available in CBS/Fox Stereo Laser videodisc.

The one thing you can say about this tape is that it accurately captures Billy Joel's live act. *Live from Long Island* (taped on Joel's home turf at the cavernous Nassau Coliseum) features some fine performances but gets bogged down in Joel's small gestures and lack of movement, his annoying tendency to focus his attention on his band rather than the audience, and the show's poor pacing. Joel's earnest approach is fine for a small club, but it's evident here that after a while even the audience tires of picking out the star, sequestered behind the baby grand at stage left. (Jerry Lee Lewis, Little Richard, and Elton John know how to solve this problem.) As for the music itself, it's all the greatest hits—with "Angry Young Man," "Pressure," and "Just the Way You Are" the standouts—done up nicely by a good tight band and sung by Joel, who is nothing if not sincere. Even though this tape does not contain any of his popular videos, it is interesting to note on seeing them here just how much the clips for "Allentown" and "Pressure" enhanced those songs. This tape contains some obscenity.—P.R.

☐ BILLY JOEL

THE VIDEO ALBUM, VOLUME ONE

★★★½

CBS/Fox, 1986, 48 minutes
PRODUCED BY: Various
DIRECTED BY: Various
MUSIC FROM: Piano Man (Columbia, 1973); *Street Life Serenade* (Columbia, 1974); *The Stranger* (Columbia, 1977); *52nd Street* (Columbia, 1978); *Glass Houses* (Columbia, 1980); *The Nylon Curtain* (Columbia, 1982); *An Innocent Man* (Columbia, 1983); *The Bridge* (Columbia, 1986).

SELECTIONS: "Piano Man," "Pressure," "Tell Her About It," "Keeping the Faith," "All for Leyna," "Honesty," "Sometimes a Fantasy," "While the Night Is Still Young," "Stiletto/My Life," "A Matter of Trust."

☐ BILLY JOEL

THE VIDEO ALBUM, VOLUME TWO

★★★

CBS/Fox, 1986, 50 minutes
PRODUCED BY: Various
DIRECTED BY: Various
MUSIC FROM: Various Billy Joel albums (Columbia, 1973–86).

SELECTIONS: "Baby Grand," "Root Beer Rag," "You May Be Right," "Allentown," "Uptown Girl," "The Longest Time," "It's Still Rock 'n' Roll to Me," "Big Shot," "You're Only Human (Second Wind)," "Los Angelenos," "Everybody Loves You Now."

More a career retrospective than a greatest-hits package, *The Video Album, Volume One* includes a surprising number of forgotten early clips, almost all of them of the primitive, straight-performance variety with Joel looking eye-openingly young: "All for Leyna," "Honesty," and "My Life." The latter is preceded by the purely musical prelude "Stiletto," which consists of a few moments of rather ludicrous footage of Billy and his band strutting a city street like a gang of young toughs; but as their descent into a subway dissolves into the older-looking Billy and band entering a studio to lip-synch "My Life," the inherent ridiculousness of the prologue seems to be acknowledged. That's only one of several cute touches: there's a brief cartoon of Billy's piano swallowing him that serves as a thematically appropriate intro for "Pressure," Russell Mulcahy's to-the-hilt phantasmagoria of paranoia and special effects that remains one of the best videos here and one of the best videos *ever*; and a surprise twist ending for "Sometimes a Fantasy," which somewhat raises the quality of a silly, stilted early concept clip in which a burglar forces Joel to make a crank call to a pretty blonde who answers the phone while lying in her bed, wearing a nightgown. "While the Night Is Still Young" is a nicely produced mini-movie, more-or-less literally illustrating the song's hackneyed theme of making the most of one's youth. "Piano Man," newly produced for this program, is another more-or-less literal interpretation of Joel's classic, with BJ at the ivories in a moody, mainly black-and-white barroom scenario. "A Matter of Trust" is a performance video notable mainly because Joel wears an electric guitar in it and stands up at the microphone, instead of sitting at his piano as usual; otherwise, it functions like one of those obnoxious sun-and-surf soft drink commercials that are full of annoyingly good-looking people having an annoyingly exuberant time—it manages to make Manhattan's funky St. Mark's Place, where it was shot, look like somewhere in L.A., which is some feat. "Keeping the Faith" and "Tell Her About It" are both highly produced high-visibility clips with which most people are already familiar; to this observer, Jay Dubin's warmly romantic, comedy-tinged "Tell Her About It," which opens with Will Jordan's Ed Sullivan impression and closes with the real Rodney Dangerfield, is right up there with "Pressure" as the class of the lot. Joel fans will appreciate the whole package, however.

At this writing, *The Video Album, Volume Two* wasn't scheduled for release for a few more months—so I haven't had a chance to see its newest clips, "Los Angelenos," "Big Shot," "Everybody Loves You Now," "Root Beer Rag," and "Baby Grand," the latter an eagerly anticipated duet between Joel and Ray Charles. Of its remaining clips, many of which will be familiar from exposure on MTV and other music-video showcases, Russell Mulcahy's "Allentown" is probably the best—it's not only typical of Mulcahy's high-production-value epic sprawl, but also contains some uncommonly emotional and humanistic moments for a Mulcahy clip. Also notable is "You're Only Human (Second Wind)," a cute homage to Frank Capra's *It's a Wonderful Life* that was seriously addressed to the problem of teen-suicide.

□ ELTON JOHN
LIVE IN CENTRAL PARK, NEW YORK

★★

Media, 1980, 59 minutes

PRODUCED BY: Danny O'Donovan and Mike Mansfield

DIRECTED BY: Mike Mansfield

MUSIC FROM: Various Elton John albums; cable-TV special (HBO, 1981).

SELECTIONS: "Saturday Night's All Right for Fighting," "Little Jeannie," "Bennie and the Jets," "Imagine," "Someone Saved My Life Tonight," "Goodbye Yellow Brick Road," "Philadelphia Freedom," "Sorry Seems to Be the Hardest Word," "Your Song," "Bite Your Lip."

Also available on Pioneer Stereo Laser videodisc.

□ ELTON JOHN
TO RUSSIA . . . WITH ELTON

★★★½

CBS/Fox, 1982, 75 minutes

PRODUCED BY: Allan McKeown and Ian La Frenais

DIRECTED BY: Dick Clement and Ian La Frenais
MUSIC FROM: Various Elton John albums; the film *To Russia . . . With Elton* (1979).
SELECTIONS: "Pinball Wizard," "Saturday Night's All Right for Fighting," "Back in the USSR," "Get Back," "Your Song," "Daniel," "The Man Who Wants to See You Smile," "Part Time Love," "Bennie and the Jets," "Sixty Years On," "Candle in the Wind," "Better Off Dead," "Rocket Man," and others.

□ ELTON JOHN
VISIONS (Long Version)
★★½

Embassy, 1982, 45 minutes
PRODUCED BY: Al Schoneberger
DIRECTED BY: Russell Mulcahy
MUSIC FROM: The Fox (Geffen, 1981).
SELECTIONS: "Breaking Down Barriers," "Nobody Wins," "Fascist Faces," "Carla/Etude," "Chloe," "The Hunter and the Haunted," "Heart in the Right Place," "Just like Belgium," "Fanfare," "The Fox," "Elton's Song."
Also available on Pioneer Stereo Laser videodisc.

□ ELTON JOHN
VISIONS (Short Version)
★★★½

Sony, 1983, 13 minutes
PRODUCED BY: Al Schoneberger
DIRECTED BY: Russell Mulcahy
MUSIC FROM: The Fox (Geffen, 1981).
SELECTIONS: "Breaking Down Barriers," "Elton's Song," "Just like Belgium."

□ ELTON JOHN
NIGHT AND DAY: THE NIGHT TIME CONCERT
★★★★

Vestron, 1985, 53 minutes
PRODUCED BY: John Reid and Mike Mansfield
DIRECTED BY: Mike Mansfield
MUSIC FROM: Various Elton John albums.
SELECTIONS: "Sorry Seems to Be the Hardest Word," "Blue Eyes/I Guess That's Why They Call It the Blues," "Your Song," "Saturday Night's All Right for Fighting," "Goodbye Yellow Brick Road," "Too Low for Zero," "Kiss the Bride," "I'm Still Standing," "Crocodile Rock," Medley: "Whole Lot of "Shakin' Goin' On"/"I Saw Her Standing There"/"Twist and Shout."

□ ELTON JOHN
THE BREAKING HEARTS TOUR
★★★★

Vestron, 1986, 55 minutes
PRODUCED BY: John Reid and Mike Mansfield
DIRECTED BY: Mike Mansfield
MUSIC FROM: Various Elton John albums.
SELECTIONS: "Rocket Man," "Daniel," "Restless," "Candle in the Wind," "The Bitch Is Back," "Don't Let the Sun Go Down on Me," "Sad Songs (Say So Much)," "Bennie and the Jets."

To Russia . . . is of historical interest and significance, both in terms of Elton's career and rock in general. It documents his 1979 tour of the Soviet Union: the first by a Western pop-rock star, and a whopper of a career-boosting publicity stunt, coming as it did after rock's onetime paragon of flamboyant outrage had adopted a more subdued later-'70s approach, released several indifferently received albums, and temporarily retired from the road in 1977. While we could do without Dudley Moore's precious narration, this mix of travelogue footage with on- and offstage business can't help but fascinate. Even though Elton was in the midst of his slump toward the '80s, and was no longer quite the camp spectacle that had made him one of the biggest superstars of the '70s, the Soviet authorities wouldn't let him bring a full band on tour. Only percussionist Ray Cooper is there to accompany Elton's piano and vocals, so there isn't much to tone down—but that's just what the Russkies keep nervously admonishing

Captain Fantastic to do. Considering that, and the fact that the selections in these Moscow and Leningrad shows hardly constitute an EJ best-of, the interaction between Elton and the uptight Soviets is almost better than the concert itself, except for the sight of those Russian audiences: staring blankly, glaring imperiously, or knitting their brows in bemused incomprehension at Elton's onstage antics. You've got to wonder why they even bothered letting him into the U.S.S.R. in the first place.

Central Park finds Elton's career in deeper decline as the '80s begin. With this August 1980 free concert, Elton was reduced to another publicity move—though, in keeping with his characteristic taste for the overdone, at least it's a pretty *grand* one—and it seems to show, as he remains comparatively subdued and detached through most of the set. There is an interesting moment in "Someone Saved My Life Tonight": a woman from the audience somehow manages to jump onstage, and as security's about to toss her off, Elton intercedes and sits her back down at the piano bench next to him for the rest of the song (he may have regretted that move later, for the woman carries on like a complete fool the whole time with her nervous giggles and "Hi Mom" arm-waving). For the closing "Your Song" and "Bite Your Lip," Elton reverts to ridiculous form by trading his piano-key-bedecked bellboy's suit for a seriously ludicrous Donald Duck outfit. The matter-of-fact direction seems to acknowledge as well as reflect the low ebb being captured.

The two versions of the *Visions* video clip album compare and contrast in much the same manner as Duran Duran's pair of eponymous programs, and the involvement of rock video *auteur* Russell Mulcahy has everything to do with that. Mulcahy's feverishly febrile, gusher-of-flashy-imagery *mise en scène* has singlehandedly created most of rock video's visual clichés (glass shattering or water splashing in hard-lit or strobe-lit slo-mo; backlit, diaphanous windblown curtains and women's gowns; etc.), and over the long haul of Embassy's *Visions* it becomes quite wearing. Sony's abridged version, however, takes the three best clips from the longer program, for a much more manageable and digestible audio-visual experience. "Breaking Down Barriers" finds Elton performing with fair exuberance amidst an ancient/futuristic fantasy set and stunning *Star Wars*–style special effects; "Elton's Song" and "Just like Belgium" take intriguingly opposite approaches to treating the theme of homosexuality: the former with a sensitive (for Mulcahy, anyway) story of a young British schoolboy's crush on an upperclassman, *à la Brideshead Revisited*; the latter with Elton stomping out the tune in a rowdy gay bar.

The Night Time Concert and *The Breaking Hearts Tour* make up the class of this lot, and should prove most satisfying overall to both diehard and casual Elton fans. The pair (with *Hearts* to have been originally titled, *The Day Time Concert*), together document Elton's complete summer '84 farewell-to-the-stage (again) concerts for his British fans, at Wembley Stadium—a fitting sight for, as Elton explains in a rather stiff studio intro, it's home to his beloved soccer when it's not a rock venue. Call it set and setting or whatever, but Elton rises to the occasion with tight, spirited performances spanning his hit-laden career. Meanwhile, the audience is so rapturously adoring that it actually intensifies the whole experience. Mike Mansfield's direction is elegantly simple and eminently tasteful, making effectively judicious use of the visual spice of special effects and video clip inserts—and making an instructive contrast to Mansfield's uninspired work on *Central Park.*

☐ LOUIS JOHNSON

THE LOUIS JOHNSON PACKAGE

★★★★

Star Licks, 1984, 60 minutes

PRODUCED BY: Mark Freed and Robert Decker

DIRECTED BY: Mark Freed and Robert Decker

MUSIC FROM: Various albums by the Brothers Johnson (A&M, 1976–84).

SELECTIONS: "Tokyo," "Street Wave," "Stomp," "Strawberry Letter #23," "Get the Funk out Ma Face," "Q," and others.

Johnson, who with guitarist sibling George forms the popular soul-funk duo the Brothers Johnson, is known as "Thunder Thumbs" because he's done such an incredible job of perfecting that ultrafunky "thumb-thwack" bass-playing technique that produces a bright, popping twang and has been the dance-music standard since Larry Graham, among others, pioneered it in the early '70s. Here, he demonstrates that technique, as well as many others, while running through a bunch of Brothers Johnson hits and some other tunes, practice patterns, and riffs. He comes across as a nice, articulate guy in the process, as well as an extremely gifted bassist.

☐ ELVIN JONES

DIFFERENT DRUMMER

★★★★½

Rhapsody, 1984, 30 minutes

PRODUCED BY: Edward Gray

DIRECTED BY: Edward Gray

MUSIC FROM: The film *Different Drummer* (1979).

SELECTIONS: "Three Card Molly."

Elvin Jones began revolutionizing modern conceptions of rhythm and the drummer's place in an ensemble in the early '60s with John Coltrane's legendary quartet (which also included pianist McCoy Tyner and bassist Jimmy Garrison). Jones's rampaging, multidirectional rhythmelodics seemed at first a chaotic, atavistic explosion, but upon closer inspection revealed a singularly daunting level of rhythmic and melodic sophistication, not to mention a genuinely frightening coordination of mental and physical acuity. A different drummer indeed—try imagining the careening force-of-nature sprawl of Keith Moon's playing with the Who, only harnessed to a more considered and refined musical sensibility, and you start to get the idea.

Edward Gray's *Different Drummer* is a superb short film that demystifies this jazz giant as both performer and personality. From Jones's club appearances, most of his fans know him as a rather forebodingly charismatic onstage presence, an irrepressible character who likes to smoke cigarettes in the midst of his furious polyrhythmic solos, emit animalistic growls and moans, and make gruff, no-holds-barred cracks and exclamations from behind his kit to spur on the other players in his bands. He forcefully projects a sort of noble-savage candor that marks him in stark contrast to the jazzman's usual air of dignified, low-key diffidence. But *Different Drummer* also shows us a side of Elvin Jones most of us have never seen and may never have suspected even existed in the first place—a sensitive, soft-spoken side that, ultimately, only makes sense given the innate musicality of his playing. We go back home to Flint, Michigan, with Jones and see him in church (his father was a deacon), with his family (including brothers Hank, a pianist, and Thad, a trumpeter, both highly respected jazzmen in their own rights) and with friends at picnics and in a

Detroit jazz club. Jones effortlessly comes across as both irascible—as his fans have always perceived him being in performances—and profoundly loving.

Inevitably, the personal and professional aspects of Jones's life begin to intersect, as he discusses his years playing with both Coltrane and the great bebop pianist Bud Powell, a musical genius who went insane. As we see a too-brief clip of the Coltrane quartet performing, Jones's voiceover succinctly states the obvious—"We didn't have to talk too much, it was telepathy." More riveting are Jones's comments on the tragic figure of Bud Powell, of whose sets at the legendary Birdland club in New York City Jones recalls, "The club atmosphere was always like a cathedral. Nobody talked, nobody drank. I'd very often find myself wiping tears out of my eyes." Not only is this an especially eloquent testimonial to Powell's legendary prowess, but it's also among the film's most affecting demonstrations of that side of Elvin Jones so few fans know.

All of these sequences are bracketed by an ingeniously simple and effective device—having Jones personally dissect the composition and performance of his piece "Three Card Molly." This starts off with Jones articulating his unique concept of the drum set as a painter's palette, with various drums and cymbals offering primary pigments and secondary shadings for his expressionistic/impressionistic musical canvas. Finally, Jones performs the piece with his quartet—which features guitarist Ryo Kawasaki, saxophonist Pat LaBarbera, and bassist David Williams—and, in the process, provides a handy demonstration of how to construct a drum solo, which we can appreciate better for what we've already learned about Jones's composition and his own approach to playing it.

Within the severe limitations of the short-form, low-budget documentary, producer/director Gray has done a truly marvelous job of painting an intimate, informative portrait of a remarkable musician and man—and, in the process, he's come up with an unprepossessingly revelatory guide to modern-jazz composition and improvisation that makes a perfect intro for those who've always been suspicious of, or intimidated by, the music. (Available by mail order from Rhapsody Films.)

□ GRACE JONES
A STATE OF GRACE
★★★★½

RCA/Columbia, 1986, 50 minutes
PRODUCED BY: Eddie Babbage
DIRECTED BY: Jean-Paul Goude
MUSIC FROM: Portfolio (Island, 1977); *Fame* (Island, 1978); *Muse* (Island, 1979); *Warm Leatherette* (Island, 1980); *Nightclubbing* (Island, 1981); *Living My Life* (Island, 1982); *The Best of Grace Jones* (Island, 1985).
SELECTIONS: "Warm Leatherette," "Walking in the Rain," "Feel Up," "La Vie en Rose," "Demolition Man," "Pull Up to the Bumper," "Private Life," "My Jamaican Guy," "Living My Life," "Slave to the Rhythm."

Sure, Grace is not much of a singer, but she makes one hell of a walking style statement. Besides, her flat monotone is swathed in slinky, state-of-the-art funk-disco-reggae from a band paced by the stellar reggae rhythm team of Sly Dunbar and Robbie Shakespeare (British superproducer Trevor Horn and some Washington, D.C., "go-go" funk players are heard on "Slave to the Rhythm"). Add that to Jean-Paul Goude's sensationally sensual visuals and acute graphic sense—every single shot appears to be carefully composed, and executed with high-fashion *élan*—and you have a sumptuously cool synaesthetic treat. By the way, this program is a reissue of *One Man Show*, the conceptualized concert video once distributed by Vestron, with the 1985 "Slave to the Rhythm" clip added; that clip itself is an intriguingly flawed little gem. It cuts together all sorts of gaudy Goude imagery, from *One Man Show* and (as in the case of those stunning shots of Grace's gape-mouthed head disgorging a car onto a desert) various racy European TV commercials. But it cuts it all together at a rapid pace that's more divorced from, than at odds with, the song's laid-back, supple groove.

□ HOWARD JONES
LIKE TO GET TO KNOW YOU WELL
★★½

Warner Home Video, 1985, 59 minutes
DIRECTED BY: Brian Simmons, Danny Kleinman, Chris Gabrin, Manatees in Motion
MUSIC FROM: Howard Jones (Elektra, 1984).
SELECTIONS: "Hunt the Self," "What Is Love," "Pearl in the Shell," "Hide and Seek," "Equality," "Like to Get to Know You," "Conditioning," "Bounce Right Back," "New Song."

Jones presents a pleasantly scruffy, elfin synth-whiz image and plays pleasantly chirpy synth-pop that's basically unexceptional and disposable, despite Jones's claims of philosophical significance. This tape mixes late-1983 concert footage of material from his early-1984 debut album (Jones is almost a one-man-band onstage, accompanied only by a stand-up drummer and a mime who acts out the think-positive philosophy of the lyrics), and razzle-dazzle MTV video clips for "What Is Love," "Hide and Seek," and "New Song." Fans should find this entertaining.

□ HOWARD JONES
LAST WORLD DREAM
★★★½

Elektra, 1986, 58 minutes
PRODUCED BY: Curt Marvis
DIRECTED BY: Wayne Isham
MUSIC FROM: Dream into Action (Elektra, 1985); *Human's Lib* (Elektra, 1984).
SELECTIONS: "Pearl in the Shell," "You Know I Love You, Don't You," "Like to Get to Know You Well," "No One Is to Blame," "Life in One Day," "Look Mama," "Will You Still Be There," "Always Asking Questions," "Hide and Seek," "Dream into Action," "What Is Love?," "New Song," "Things Can Only Get Better."

As seen in *Last World Dream,* Jones is more engaging in concert, where he makes nifty use of high-tech—his headset mike allows him to dance around between several synthesizers, as well as all over the stage, while singing; his drummer plays standing up, inside a cagelike array of electronic drum pads. This program is a beautifully directed and produced document of the final show on Jones's 1985–86 world tour at the National Exhibition Centre in Birmingham, England (thus explaining the program's title), and Jones's disarmingly friendly interaction with a rabidly appreciative home-turf crowd is as much a factor as the slick production values (which include some split-screens and a page-turning tour-book continuity device) in giving *Last World Dream* some appeal to Jones fan and others.

There's a very brief black-and-white interview snippet with HoJo at the beginning, bits of concept-clip footage are cut into the renditions of "Like to Get to Know You Well" and "Life in One Day" (the latter clip by Godley and Creme), and footage of Jones performing "Hide and Seek" at Live Aid in London is mixed with the

Birmingham performance. Jones gets particularly intense crowd participation (clapping and singing) in "No One Is to Blame" (which, along with "Things Can Only Get Better," demonstrates Jones's ever-increasing mastery of the irresistible pop single); features mask-wearing mime Jed Hoile in some numbers; gets a neat guitar sound out of the synth slung over his shoulder as he strikes guitar-hero poses in "Always Asking Questions"; and pulls a guy and girl out of the crowd in "New Song" to play along on synth (they can do it, through the magic of sequencers, by hitting one key). The music is relentlessly sprightly, hook-filled, and danceable throughout. You'd have to *really* hate this guy to find this program anything less than tolerable.

□ SPIKE JONES

SPIKE JONES AND HIS MUSICAL DEPRECIATION REVUE

★★★

Video Yesteryear, 1985, 28 minutes
MUSIC FROM: 1954 network TV show.
SELECTIONS: "Mule Train," "Wild Bill Hiccup," and others not listed.

Jones was probably pop music's first satirical dadaist, keeping time with a starter's pistol, substituting the sound of breaking windows or screeching trains for cymbal crashes in well-known pieces, and so on. Here, in an episode of Jones's 1954 prime-time network TV series, the following takes place: someone calling himself Sir Frederick Gas claims to be a bird imitator—then spreads his arms and tries to "fly" around the stage; a midget, a fat lady, and a seven-foot giant do a square dance together; an Indian brave wearing a shirt labeled "Cleveland" (get it, baseball fans?) sings "Mule Train" in Chinese; the lovely Nilssen Twins introduce the show by speaking in perfect unison; and so on. Vaude-video madness and mayhem *way* before *Laugh-In*.

□ LOUIS JORDAN

REET, PETITE AND GONE

★★★

Video Yesteryear, 1980, 67 minutes
MUSIC FROM: The film *Reet, Petite and Gone* (1947).
SELECTIONS: "Let the Good Times Roll," "That Chick's Too Young to Fry," "Reet, Petite and Gone," and others.

Jordan, an often-unsung hero of the pre-rock days with his fun-loving jazz-blues-pop fusion known as "jumpin' jive," became a huge star in 1946 with his million-seller "Choo Choo Ch-Boogie." A year later he played two roles in this farcical all-black "race musical," which thankfully features a lot of his music with his regular backing band, the Tympany Five. So, if you're so inclined, make like a shovel and dig it.

□ STANLEY JORDAN

MAGIC TOUCH

★★★

Sony, 1986, 19 minutes
PRODUCED BY: Picture Music International
DIRECTED BY: John Jopson and Dick Fontaine
MUSIC FROM: Magic Touch (Blue Note, 1985); *One Night with Blue Note, Vol. 1* (Blue Note, 1985).
SELECTIONS: "When You Wish upon a Star," "Touch of Blue," "Jumpin' Jack," "The Lady in My Life."

Jordan's a jazz guitarist, but Eddie Van Halen fans will notice a familiar technique at work while watching this video: Jordan taps the strings on the fretboard with both hands, rather than using fingers or pick to pluck the strings with one hand while fretting with the other; it's something Van

Halen does to add fast multinote filigrees to his solos, but Jordan plays *everything* that way. As an onscreen crawl quote from Jordan claims at the start of the tape, that way he gets an orchestral freedom on the guitar previously possible only on keyboard instruments. Electricity—which amplifies a string's vibrations enough so that they can be clearly heard even when the string is only lightly vibrated by tapping it against the fretboard—is what makes Jordan's "Magic Touch" technique possible. Fortunately, as he shows in the three nicely shot performance clips (two of which, "When You Wish . . ." and "Jumpin' Jack," are taken from the outstanding *One Night with Blue Note, Vol. 1*), Jordan's not just a whiz-bang technician, but also a *musician,* harnessing his neat ideas to a delicate, exploratory muse that often produces dazzling little pointillistic guitar symphonettes. He can swing, too, as "Jumpin' Jack" convincingly demonstrates.

"The Lady in My Life," which closes the program, is a concept video directed by Dick Fontaine that casts Jordan as a street musician who fantasizes falling in love with a pretty girl who watches him play, while he's also being shadowed by an exotic mystery lady in sunglasses. It's probably trying to make some sort of connection between corporeal women and the spiritual muse as the ladies in a guitar player's life. It's okay, I guess, but nothing special, and in no way does it enhance the music—although Jordan's guitar musings sound all right as a soundtrack for the *video.* All of which leaves me wondering about priorities and such.

□ JOURNEY
FRONTIERS AND BEYOND
★★★

Music Media, 1984, 98 minutes
PRODUCED BY: Steve Sabol
DIRECTED BY: Phil Tuckett
MUSIC FROM: Frontiers (Columbia, 1973); *In the Beginning* (Columbia, 1979); *Departure* (Columbia, 1980); *Captured* (Columbia, 1981); *Escape* (Columbia, 1981).
SELECTIONS: "Chain Reaction," "Wheel in the Sky," "Still They Ride," "Open Arms," "Stone in Love," "Escape," "Separate Ways (Worlds Apart)," "After the Fall," "Keep on Runnin'."

Journey, masters of melodramatically romantic AOR pomp rock, are caught taking their act on the road during their 1983 world tour. Considering Journey's status as kings of arena rock, this mix of concert and interview footage was fittingly shot by NFL Films, who specialize in unsubtle, large-scale, all-American sporting events. It's also an appropriate, and funny, touch to have John Facenda, the gloriously grave voice of *NFL Highlights* lo these many years, narrate the whole thing—although at times one does wonder if the band truly realizes just how funny Facenda's portentous recounting of the logistics of big-time touring can get, or if they even intended it to be funny in the first place. At any rate, Journey do their thing well, have just about as little to say in their interviews as in their music, are adored by their fans, and it's all put together well enough by the pigskin producers that any Journey fan'll love it.

□ JOY DIVISION
HERE ARE THE YOUNG MEN
★½

Factory/Ikon, 1984, 60 minutes
PRODUCED BY: Richard Boone and Bob Jones
DIRECTED BY: Richard Boone and Bob Jones
MUSIC FROM: Unknown Pleasures (Factory U.K., 1980); *Closer* (Factory U.K., 1980); *Still* (Factory UK, 1981); *Power, Corruption and Lies* (Factory/Rough Trade, 1983).
SELECTIONS: "Dead Souls," "Love Will Tear Us Apart," "Shadowplay," "Day

of the Lords," "Digital," "Colony," "New Dawn Fades," "Auto-suggestion," "Transmission," "The Sound of Music," "She's Lost Control," "Walked in Line," "I Remember Nothing," "Love Will Tear Us Apart" (conceptual clip).

Joy Division was a powerful and critically admired British post-punk rock band that set the doom-struck visions of lead singer Ian Curtis to a thick, dark, Velvet Underground–styled thudding drone out of which a poignantly yearning melodic line occasionally arose. Call it *sturm und strum,* if you will—and note that Curtis bore out his gloomy lyrics by hanging himself in 1980 while the band was becoming a hit on America's semi-underground new wave club scene.

Here Are the Young Men is virtually the sole visual record of the band in action—which is unfortunate, for it consists of "salvaged" Super 8 and VHS footage that's so dark, grainy, sloppily shot, half-unfocused, and chaotically edited that it's absolutely unwatchable. The sound isn't much better. The only redeeming part of the whole program is the concept clip for their most pop-oriented song, the soaring "Love Will Tear Us Apart," which is tacked on to the end of all that blurry, muddy-sounding concert material: it's a haunting performance clip shot in a spacious loft, enhanced with vertiginous tracking shots of doors flying open in series, shots that somehow mesh with the music's driving pace and plangent harmonies to ineffably touching effect. Still, it's not enough to elevate this program's rating; it gets its star and a half solely for that closing clip and its historical value. (Available in stores or by mail order from Factory.)

☐ **VARIOUS ARTISTS (ADAM ANT, TOYAH WILCOX, OTHERS)**
JUBILEE
★

Media, 1984, 103 minutes

PRODUCED BY: Howard Malin and James Whaley

DIRECTED BY: Derek Jarman

MUSIC FROM: Jubilee soundtrack album (Polydor, 1978).

SELECTIONS: Chelsea: "Right to Work"; Siouxsie and the Banshees: "Love in a Void"; Suzi Pinns: "Rule Britannia," "Jerusalem"; Adam Ant: "Plastic Surgery"; "Deutscher Girls"; Wayne County: "Paranoia Paradise"; Toyah Wilcox: "Wargasm in Pornotopia"; background and title music by Brian Eno..

Onetime Ken Russell set designer Derek Jarman's 1978 film was a deliberately perverse anticelebration of that year's Queen's Jubilee: in the film, Queen Elizabeth I (played by the fine young British actress Jenny Runacre, who doubles as a present-day punkette) is zapped into the future by her court mystic, only to find a Britannia ruled by soporific/anarchic/decadent punks running amok through the ruins of the Empire. Not a bad idea, but done with a pretentiousness and turgidity that render *Jubilee* almost unwatchable. It's mainly of historical interest to punk rock fans: Adam Ant looks *very* young and gawky in his small role; the Slits, England's first all-girl punk band, have an even smaller part; and Brit-punk scenemaker Little Nell has a featured role, which she handles with sexy, proto-Madonna aplomb.

☐ **JUDAS PRIEST**
FUEL FOR LIFE
★★½

CBS/Fox, 1986, 39 minutes

MUSIC FROM: British Steel (Columbia, 1980); *Point of Entry* (Columbia, 1981); *Screaming for Vengeance* (Columbia, 1982); *Defenders of the Faith* (Columbia, 1984); *Turbo* (Columbia, 1986).

SELECTIONS: "Living after Midnight," "Breaking the Law," "Don't Go," "Heading Out to the Highway," "Hot Rockin'," "You've Got Another Thing Coming," "Freewheel Burnin'," "Love Bites," "Locked In," "Turbo Lover."

□ JUDAS PRIEST
LIVE
★★★

Media, 1984, 83 minutes
PRODUCED BY: Judas Priest and Nocturne, Inc.
DIRECTED BY: Mick Anger
MUSIC FROM: Hell Bent for Leather (Columbia, 1979); *British Steel* (Columbia, 1980); *Point of Entry* (Columbia, 1981); *Screaming for Vengeance* (Columbia, 1982).
SELECTIONS: "The Hellion"/"Electric Eye," "Riding on the Wind," "Heading Out to the Highway," "Metal Gods," "Bloodstone," "Breaking the Law," "Sinner," "Desert Plains," "Ripper," "Devil's Child," "Screaming for Vengeance," "You've Got Another Thing Coming," "Victim of Changes," "Living after Midnight," "Hell Bent for Leather."

Fuel for Life, a collection of promo clips by the veteran British heavy-metal band, was released hot on the heels of CBS/Fox's *This Is Video Clash*—and continued that program's shoddy policy of completely omitting production and direction credits. Not one of these clips is remotely close to being a work of art, but if they can try to make money from them, can't they at least credit the people responsible for making them in the first place?

At any rate, *Fuel for Life* breaks down almost evenly between typically dumb/overblown/clichéd concept and/or performance videos, and clips that stand out from the run of the mill to some degree. The latter include: "Breaking the Law," a surprisingly good bank-robbing scenario to match the song's surprisingly punky lyrics, about what Britain's ravaged economy does to its young; "Hot Rockin' " starts out with the band working out at an exercise machine (?!) and taking a sauna, then moves to onstage performance with pyrotechnic effects—the highlight comes when vocalist Rob Halford dips his microphone into the flames and keeps lip-synching into it; the classic "You've Got Another Thing Coming" finds the band defiantly blasting away in a noise-pollution testing zone—at the very opening, which is usually cut off on MTV, the camera pans right by a sign that tells us so—and eventually blowing apart a bowler-hatted noise-pollution authority figure with the might of their music; and "Freewheel Burnin' " has a British schoolboy playing a laser-blasting Judas Priest video game that eventually beats him into submission. But from the eyes-rolled-back expression on his face as he slumps down in his seat, the kid loves it. These last two were directed by Julien Temple.

But, unless you're a Judas Priest fan, the lousy videos here outnumber the good ones. "Living after Midnight" is a mundane performance clip notable solely for its use of kids in the audience playing along on cardboard guitars (predating the use of the same device in 1982 by Australian band Heaven for "In the Beginning"). "Don't Go" is moribund studio-mounted performance, intercut with silly/self-consciously surreal/sexist concept stuff to highlight the paranoia indicated by the song's title. "Locked In" (directed by Wayne Isham) tries for *Romancing the Stone*–style comic-adventure here and there, with the band rescuing Halford from a desert torture chamber run by man-eating Amazons; it's hard to laugh, though, when such rampantly rapacious misogyny is being shoved down your throat.

The rest are basically not worth commenting on—except for "Love Bites," which may be both the best *and* worst video in the whole bunch. With the band onstage lip-synching bombastically beneath an enormous metal insect skull ("the Metallion") looming over their stage set, it's Spinal

Tap come to hysterically real life.

Thankfully, *Judas Priest Live* was shot on an earlier tour, before the Tap-alike stage set arrived. But that's not the only good thing about it, if you're a Judas Priest fan: it's a totally straightforward, no-nonsense concert video, with multiple cameras at good strategic angles showing Halford and duo lead guitarists Glenn Tipton and K. K. Downing gritting their teeth and getting into some serious, heads-down boogieing, writhing (and assuming other postures suggesting maximum energy expenditure) in their black-leather-and-silver-studs uniforms. Halford rides a huge Harley on stage for the encores. Judas Priest are certainly good at what they do, with a disciplined relentlessness to their attack that's sort of the musical equivalent of a scorched-earth policy. Their audience here responds with gusto, as will any of their fans; it's shot in such a direct, unfussy way the odds are less than 50-50 it will convert any nonbelievers.

☐ **VARIOUS ARTISTS**

JUKEBOX SATURDAY NIGHT

★★½

Video Yesteryear, 1980, 85 minutes
MUSIC FROM: Various Panoram Soundies and other short musical films, 1941–62.

SELECTIONS: No titles listed, but performers include: Fats Waller, Louis Armstrong, the Ink Spots, Cab Calloway, the Mills Brothers, Benny Goodman, Count Basie Orchestra, Lionel Hampton Orchestra, Dinah Washington, Nat "King" Cole Trio, Charlie Barnet Orchestra, Peggy Lee, Diahann Carroll with Sammy Davis, Jr., Mel Torme, Bobby Darin with Diana Ross and the Supremes.

Something you should know about Video Yesteryear: their catalogue lists only a certain amount of information for each tape (in this case, performers but no song titles) and they don't provide anyone with cassettes for review. So, not having seen this, I can only guess at what the interesting lineup of artists plays. I do know that Bobby Darin and Diana Ross and the Supremes fit in the midst of all that '40s swing and '50s supper-club stuff with a segment from their TV special salute to Rodgers and Hart. Video Yesteryear's catalogue says sound and picture quality on this collection of protean music videos is erratic, so take that as a warning. But for those interested in nuggets of pop-culture history, this may well be worth a look. (Available by mail order from Video Yesteryear.)

K

□ KAJAGOOGOO
KAJAGOOGOO VIDEO 45
★½

Sony, 1984, 11 minutes
PRODUCED BY: Eric Fellner
DIRECTED BY: Simon Milne
MUSIC FROM: *White Feathers* (EMI-America, 1983).
SELECTIONS: "Too Shy," "Ooh to Be Ah," "Hang On Now."

Kajagoogoo is one of those groups people are referring to when they deride the concept of "video bands": conveniently pretty, trendily attired and coiffed, lip-synching to bouncy, vacuously modern pop. In this case, we have a British teen-idol band of the post–Duran Duran school. "Too Shy," their lone hit before cockatoo-haired vocalist Limahl departed, is a decidedly minor piece of romantic fluff, but at least its video is tastefully done. In it, a pretty waitress in the club where the band is playing thinks she's time-traveling and it's really a WWII canteen full of soldiers on leave . . . anyway, this *Twilight Zone* motif is handled with elegant restraint by director Simon Milne, who also integrates it deftly into Kajagoogoo's performance, making this a very efficient promo clip indeed. Actually, fans of this sort of thing could do worse. The other two clips, however, share only the high production values with "Too Shy"—the music, scenarios, and performances are all much less inspired.

□ KANSAS
BEST OF KANSAS LIVE
★★½

Sony, 1982, 87 minutes
PRODUCED BY: Jim Duncan
DIRECTED BY: Phil Olesman
MUSIC FROM: Various Kansas albums (Kirshner, 1974–82).
SELECTIONS: "Paradox," "Windows," "Right Away," "Sparks of the Tempest," "Diamonds and Pearls," "Mysteries and Mayhem," "No One Together," "Hold On," "Dust in the Wind," "Chasing Shadows," "Crossfire," "Face It," "Play the Game Tonight," "Carry On Wayward Son," "Portrait (He Knew)," "Down the Road."

Kansas was celebrating its tenth anniversary as a flagship of bombastic, corporate AOR formula rock—heavily influenced by the more pompous and portentously philosophical strains of majestic British classical rock—in this 1982 concert at the Omaha, Nebraska, Civic Auditorium, which was originally shot for showing on MTV. So, for Kansas fans this concert tape is especially noteworthy. They'll love it. But the unspectacular direction and the overwrought, lumpen existentialism of such AOR standbys as "Dust in the Wind" and "Carry On Wayward Son" will leave nonfans resolutely unmoved.

□ KATRINA AND THE WAVES
WALKING ON SUNSHINE
★

Sony, 1985, 30 minutes
PRODUCED BY: Lynn Rose
DIRECTED BY: Chris Tookey
MUSIC FROM: *Katrina and the Waves* (Capitol, 1985).
SELECTIONS: "Walking on Sunshine," "Red Wine and Whisky," "Do You Want Crying," "Que Te Quiero."

By the time Katrina and the Waves burst on the scene in 1985, this half-American, half-British rock band had been kicking around on small-time British and Canadian labels for several years. At any rate, their major-label debut was one of the strongest albums of straightforward, unpretentious, unself-consciously rootsy rock 'n' roll of that year, and all of the songs here are good musically. But the accompanying videos are all either dull or dumb or both, which can be attributed to both unimaginative direction and the total lack of personality on the part of Katrina and the Waves. She's a good singer, and chief songwriter Kimberly Rew (a guy) plays great guitar and composes neat tunes, but collectively this is one band that hasn't got anything to say in the video medium. They don't belong there. Stick with the album and forget about this.

□ KID CREOLE AND THE COCONUTS

LIVE—THE LEISURE TOUR

★★★½

Embassy, 1986, 60 minutes
PRODUCED BY: Philip Goodhand-Tait
DIRECTED BY: Peter Orton
MUSIC FROM: Off the Coast of Me (Ze/Island, 1980); *Fresh Fruit in Foreign Places* (Ze/Sire, 1981); *Wise Guy* (Ze/Sire, 1982); *Tropical Gangsters* (Ze/Sire, 1982); *Doppelganger* (Ze/Sire, 1983).
SELECTIONS: "Don't Take My Coconuts," "Male Curiosity," "Table Manners," "Mr. Softie," "Annie, I'm Not Your Daddy," "Laughing," "Mona," "Lifeboat Party," "Endicott," "Indiscreet," "Caroline Was a Dropout."

August Darnell, formerly of the underappreciated Dr. Buzzard's Original Savannah Band, first began parading the Kid Creole show in the late '70s: part all-singing/all-dancing Broadway spectacular, part neo–Cotton Club nightclub revue, part funky dance party, with Darnell as Kid Creole singing double-entendre battle-of-the-sexes lyrics witty enough to call to mind a sort of streetwise Cole Porter, fronting a band that slickly covers big-band swing, Latin and Caribbean grooves, soul, rock, funk, and pop while dancing in unison. There are also, of course, the Coconuts, Darnell's chorus line of three pretty blondes in scanty attire who sing and dance and strut their hearts out. It's a hell of a show—full of style, smarts, and sass, engaging melodies and irresistible rhythms and clever lyrics, savvy staging and dynamic dancing. And as this tape amply demonstrates, the Kid and crew cut the funk a lot harder live than they do on record. Even those who already like Darnell's stuff from the records may be surprised at just how intensely he and the band are pumping on "Endicott."

Thing is, there aren't nearly as many Kid Creole fans in America as Darnell, with his manifestly vast talents, deserves. Maybe he's a little too old-fashioned show-biz for people or something, but Darnell's always been relegated to the undeserved status of critic's-fave cult hero here. As if to bear that out, *The Leisure Tour* was shot before an adoring throng—in Paris, at a club called Le Zenith. It's sad, really. It's just as sad that the production quality of this concert video doesn't measure up to the high standard of the show. The lighting, photography, and sound are all a bit off at times. But the typical rock concert video techniques—odd-angle close-ups to the max, too many shots from the wings and behind the stage, jarring edits—that are put to uninspired use here actually backfire, because Darnell has so much going on he's got people all the way across the stage on *two levels.* The overuse of close-ups deprives us of a true sense of the show. Besides, there's more than enough happening with Darnell's wardrobe, stage sets, and choreography—he doesn't *need* the extra added visual goosing. Worse yet, director Orton suffers from another typical rock-video affliction: he spends so much time on the Coconuts' anatomies the camera almost gets comically fixated after a while. As a consequence of all this, by the way, Darnell's antic sidekick Coati Mundi—actually "Sugar Coated" Andy

Hernandez, the vibraphonist who also used to be in Dr. Buzzard's Original Savannah Band—is rarely seen through the entire show.

Still, not even the annoying direction can ultimately stay in the way of what's on display for long. The Kid Creole show is captured at least well enough that one can still see that it's a heck of a show, and for that, I guess, we should be thankful, and better yet, *The Leisure Tour* seems to have been caught on a particularly hot night: not only "Endicott" (about a goody-goody next-door neighbor who's too good to be tolerated by the more merely mortal Kid), but also "Annie, I'm Not Your Daddy," "Male Curiosity," "Mr. Softie" (about male impotence), and "Table Manners" all ride their panethnic dance grooves with uncommon vigor. Renting this tape should be a lot cheaper than buying a concert ticket, and chances are if you dig this you'll pay to see Kid Creole live when he comes to town anyway.

□ B. B. KING
LIVE AT NICK'S

★★★★

Sony, 1985, 60 minutes
PRODUCED BY: Steve Moss
DIRECTED BY: Miles Kidder
MUSIC FROM: Various B. B. King albums.
SELECTIONS: "Every Day (I Have the Blues)," "Nightlife," "Better Not Look Down," "Never Make a Move Too Soon," "Sell My Monkey," "Love Me Tender," "Inflation Blues," "The Thrill Is Gone," "There Must Be a Better World Somewhere."

B. B. King is a figure of towering accomplishment, importance, and influence in the contemporary blues genre, and this 1983 show at the Nick's Uptown club in Dallas does a good job of showing why. In this relatively intimate setting, King's refined, sophisticated urban blues are infused with a funky urgency. His soulfully sincere vocals are as elegant and scintillating as the signature commentary of his immaculately finger-vibratoed licks on his guitar named Lucille. Of course "The Thrill Is Gone" and "There Must Be a Better World Somewhere" (title cut of his Grammy-winning 1981 album) are among the highlights, but so is a modestly intense version of "Love Me Tender" in which King's passionately resigned saloon singing sounds, believe it or not, like Sinatra's. Scattered throughout are brief interview bits, including one nice, colorful tale about how Lucille got her name. King is such an institution that it's increasingly amazing how hard he keeps working, as here, to please the crowds. Yes, his style is so . . . seemingly *archetypal* that it's predictable and all, but King delivers it with such sweaty integrity that it stays fresh. Kidder's direction of the concert footage is perfectly straightforward and tasteful, and the same holds for the unobtrusive way the interview snippets are edited in between songs. All in all, recommended to both fans and neophytes.

□ CAROLE KING
ONE TO ONE

★★★★

MGM/UA, 1983, 60 minutes
PRODUCED BY: Michael Brovsky
DIRECTED BY: Scott Garen
MUSIC FROM: Various Carole King albums, including *Tapestry* (Ode, 1971); *Rhymes and Reasons* (Ode, 1972); *Fantasy* (Ode, 1973); *Her Greatest Hits* (Ode, 1978).
SELECTIONS: "Jazzman," "Tapestry," "The Loco-Motion," "Lookin' Out for Number One," "Take Good Care of My Baby," "It Might As Well Rain Until September," "Smackwater Jack," "Hey Girl," "One Fine Day," "Chains," "Up on the Roof," "I Feel the Earth Move," "So Far Away," "It's a War," "One to One," "A

Natural Woman," "You've Got a Friend."
Also available in Pioneer Stereo Laser videodisc.

Handsomely produced documentary on the life and music of the brilliantly accomplished singer/songwriter. At home and onstage, she talks about her early Brill Building days and her later solo success, playing songs from both eras. Just about all the hits you'd want to hear are covered, and in her interviews, King seems relaxed and candid (what the heck, she *is* at home). A must for her fans, and I bet many of those who take her mainstream status for granted will be surprised at how much they like it, too.

□ KING CRIMSON
THREE OF A PERFECT PAIR—LIVE IN JAPAN
★★★½

JEM/Passport, 1985, 82 minutes
PRODUCED BY: Hirotishi Hario
DIRECTED BY: Ryuji Sasaki
MUSIC FROM: Discipline (Warner Bros., 1981); *Beat* (Warner Bros., 1982); *Three of a Perfect Pair* (Warner Bros., 1983); *Larks' Tongues in Aspic* (Atco, 1973).
SELECTIONS: "Three of a Perfect Pair," "No Warning," "Larks' Tongues in Aspic, Part III," "Thela Hun Ginjeet," "Frame by Frame," "Matte Kudasai," "Industry," "Dig Me," "Indiscipline," "Satori in Tangier," "Man with an Open Heart," "Sleepless," "Larks' Tongues in Aspic, Part II," "Elephant Talk," "Heartbeat."

□ KING CRIMSON
THE NOISE—FREJUS 82
★★★

JEM/Passport, 1985, 55 minutes
PRODUCED BY: Robin Nash
MUSIC FROM: Discipline (Warner Bros., 1981); *Beat* (Warner Bros., 1982); *Larks' Tongues in Aspic* (Atco, 1973).
SELECTIONS: "Waiting Man," "Matte Kudasai," "Sheltering Sky," "Neal and Jack and Me," "Indiscipline," "Heartbeat," "Larks' Tongues in Aspic, Part II."

The last of many versions of the venerable British art-rock band plays a sophisticated, unusual fusion of ethnic trance music, modern-classical minimalism, and rock. The music is bracingly inventive and energetic, if at times a bit dry, and definitely not for easy listening; the musicians—founder/guitarist Robert Fripp and fellow art-rock vet Bill Bruford on drums, both Brits, and Yanks Tony Levin (bass) and Adrian Belew (guitar, vocals)—are obviously highly accomplished. Bruford is a joy to watch, as he casually plays remarkably complex yet flowing polyrhythms on his mammoth, electronic fortress of a kit. It's intriguing to note the contrast between Fripp's ascetic, intense yet contained demeanor and Belew's wound-up, exuberant extroversion (with his gaunt frame and whiny, mannered vocals, Belew suggests David Byrne of Talking Heads, with whom Belew once played). But, overall, King Crimson's stimulation is more aural than visual. That said, fans won't care anyway, and will probably want both. Others are advised to check out *Three of a Perfect Pair* first: it's shot better than the murkier *The Noise* (though perhaps you'd prefer that atmospheric stuff); it's longer, covers a wider range of material, and includes brief interviews; and the band seems in slightly better form.

□ VARIOUS ARTISTS
KING OF JAZZ
★★★

MCA, 1983, 93 minutes
PRODUCED BY: Carl Laemmle, Jr.
DIRECTED BY: John Murray Anderson
MUSIC FROM: The film *King of Jazz* (Universal, 1930).
SELECTIONS: Not listed but include: Paul Whiteman Orchestra: "My Lord Delivered Daniel," "Linger Awhile," "Rhapsody in Blue"; Whiteman Orchestra

with various singers and dancers: "The Bridal Veil," "A Bench in the Park," "My Ragamuffin Romeo," "I Like to Do Things for You," "Melting Pot"; the Rhythm Boys with the Whiteman Orchestra: "Mississippi Mud," "The Bluebird and the Blackbird," "Happy Shoes"; Joe Venuti: "Oh How I'd Like to Own a Fish Store"; Willie Hall: "Pop Goes the Weasel," "Stars and Stripes Forever"; John Boles with Whiteman Orchestra: "Song of the Dawn"; John Boles, Jeanette Loff, and Whiteman Orchestra: "Monterey."

For Jazz Age nostalgists and those interested in '20s pop culture and the history of movie musicals in general, *King of Jazz* is quite a curio. For starters, it was the first Technicolor movie musical ever made; interestingly, the color here is nowhere near as gaudy as the '40s and '50s Technicolor we're more accustomed to, but rather casts everything in pale amber, rose, and turquoise shades that render the visuals rather otherworldly and ethereal. It's an appropriate touch in a way, because what's on display in this singing/dancing/comedy variety cavalcade is, by now, very much of another world. *King of Jazz* is overflowing with real-life Betty Boop flappers cooing in nasal voices, and operatically warbling male vocalists in swallowtail coats and slicked-down hair; and there are a half-dozen or so mammoth chorus-line-style production numbers that predate the surreal excesses of Busby Berkeley. There are also numerous fascinatingly primitive stabs at what are by now *de rigueur* special effects—for instance, there are lots of attempts at superimposition and lingering dissolve edits where we can see double images for several flickering frames before the intended effect finally clicks in with jarring abruptness.

King of Jazz was ostensibly a tribute to the subject of its title, bandleader Paul Whiteman—who has the dubious distinction of probably being the first whitebread cultural bwana in modern mass-culture history. The aptly named Whiteman became hugely popular by co-opting '20s black jazz, smoothing out its rough edges, and tailoring it for acceptance by the squarehead white bourgeoisie. Another key to his success, which *King of Jazz* implicitly and amply demonstrates, is his bigger-is-better philosophy, evidenced by the size of his orchestra—so what if all those string players and added banjoists and horn players and whatever made it all sound cumbersome, the sheer size of it all would knock 'em dead anyway—and the extravagance of the production numbers. Indeed, the comparative crudeness of the execution actually makes it easier to see the ways *King of Jazz* crystallized an industrial-strength crassness and condescension that have continued to dominate Hollywood and much mass culture in general.

King of Jazz takes the form of a flip through "Paul Whiteman's Scrapbook," a gigantic book whose pages are turned to introduce each musical production number, as well as the dumb, vulgar comedy skits that punctuate the musical interludes. The opening "My Lord Delivered Daniel" is an animated episode by Walter Lantz (yes, the guy who brought us Woody Woodpecker) telling how Paul Whiteman became King of Jazz (apparently by taking a gun into the jungle and capturing animals—as apt a metaphor as any for the essential repugnance of Whiteman's cultural imperialism, I guess). Then Whiteman himself appears: a big fat guy with about three chins and a pointy little moustache he keeps tweaking, which is just one of the ways in which he constantly mugs with obnoxious unctuousness. He opens a little satchel and in one of those primitive special effects, his band troops out of it onto a mini-bandstand. From there we have the succession of musical and comedy numbers, which are a mixed bag to say the least.

The musical centerpiece is certainly the Whiteman Orchestra's rendition of Gershwin's magnificent "Rhapsody in Blue": they play it while perched atop a mammoth blue piano, following a prelude in which a black dancer in ceremonial feathered headdress dances atop a giant tribal drum. This is as close as we're ever likely to get to seeing and hearing what this classic piece of music sounded like when the Whiteman orchestra premiered it, at their historic February 1924 concert at New York's Aeolian Hall. And for once, with music of true quality and lasting appeal to play, the Whiteman band doesn't sound so awfully ofay. Yet incredibly, this performance is stuck in the *middle* of the movie; it's bizarre to see it followed by more dumb comic blackouts and the like.

Also worth noting: a very young Bing Crosby can be spotted as one of the Rhythm Boys in the three numbers where this vocal trio is featured; violinist Joe Venuti, one of the genuinely good jazz musicians who got lost in the Whiteman band's sugary sauce, is wasted with a surrealistically silly talk-singing feature, "Oh How I'd Like to Own a Fish Store" ("I'm a fisherman," he ends it, apparently by way of explanation, "aren't we all?" Uh, yeah, sure Joe); another fiddler, one Willie Hall, parades a rather stupendous vaudeville act, using hair-trigger timing to slip all manner of comical juggling and mime tricks between his violin licks, and *then* plays a convincing "Stars and Stripes Forever" on a *bicycle pump*; and the production numbers for "Happy Shoes," "I Like to Do Things for You," and "Melting Pot" are all rather stunning in their sheer size and extravagance.

□ THE KINKS
ONE FOR THE ROAD
★★★½

Vestron, 1980, 60 minutes

MUSIC FROM: One for the Road (Arista, 1980); various other Kinks albums.

SELECTIONS: "Opening," "All Day and All of the Night," "Lola," "Low Budget," "Superman," "Attitude," "Celluloid Heroes," "Hardway," "Where Have All the Good Times Gone," "You Really Got Me," "Pressure," "Catch Me Now I'm Falling," "Victoria."

By the time this was shot, the Kinks had finally come through their protracted (roughly from 1969's *Arthur* through 1975's *Schoolboys in Disgrace*), exasperating/endearing/self-destructive/artistically fertile drunken-shambles period, and resuscitated a failing career by cleaning up and slicking up their act. Thus, much of their boozy rock 'n' roll cachet was virtually all gone; the more crassly commercial the Kinks got, the less interesting and compelling they became. It's especially poignant for one like me, who remembers seeing their original Edwardian-fop/proto–heavy-metal attack on TV (talk about poignant—bits of that period from an old *Shindig!* are intercut here with the live "Where Have All the Good Times Gone," a painfully literal but still effective choice) and that drunken-shambles period from live shows. However, leader/genius Ray Davies and crew *do* look remarkably, gratifyingly healthy here after all that has gone before, they sound okay, and the songs constitute a pretty good sampling of Davies classics. Then again, the cringe-worthy "Jumpin' Jack Flash" rip-off "Catch Me Now I'm Falling" makes a poignant statement of its own. At this writing, and to my knowledge, there *is* no other live Kinks on video; so as much as I may want to nitpick, *One for the Road* will have to do.

☐ THE KINKS
COME DANCING WITH THE KINKS
★★★

RCA/Columbia, 1986, 35 minutes
PRODUCED BY: Ray Davies, Chris Pye, others
DIRECTED BY: Julien Temple, Ken O'Neill
MUSIC FROM: One for the Road (Arista, 1980); *Give the People What They Want* (Arista, 1981); *State of Confusion* (Arista, 1983); *Word of Mouth* (Arista, 1984).
SELECTIONS: "Come Dancing," "Predictable," "Lola," "State of Confusion," "Don't Forget to Dance," "You Really Got Me," "Do It Again," "Celluloid Heroes."

Come Dancing is an uneven but ultimately delightful compilation of conceptual and performance clips, most of them aptly demonstrating bandleader Ray Davies's stunning thespian abilities. It opens with a killer one-two punch—the concept clips "Come Dancing" and "Predictable," two of the best ever made, both demonstrating not only Davies's acting (as a rakish hood with a heart of gold in "Come Dancing," and in a succession of comic guises in "Predictable") but also the unique talents of rock video *auteur* Julien Temple, who directed both of them. His gift for narrative momentum is especially evident in "Come Dancing," while both show his flair for the historical motif—"Come Dancing" through tender nostalgia prompted by an old dance hall being torn down (a theme that's a Ray Davies classic and one example of why he and Temple make a perfect match); "Predictable" with a sarcastic parade-through-rock-icon-history (complete with subtitles, and Davies going from dowdy housewife drag to '50s greaser, to '60s mod, to hippie, to '70s punk).

The rest of the program, which includes live concert clips of "Lola," "You Really Got Me," and "Celluloid Heroes," has a hard time living up to such an auspicious opening: Temple's "Don't Forget to Dance" is a disappointingly lethargic sequel to "Come Dancing"; his "State of Confusion" lives down to its title only too well, with inane fast-motion sequences; and the live clips are competently shot, but no more, and should leave all but the greenest of Kinks kollektors cursing the fact that rock video wasn't around to tape concerts back in the late '60s and early '70s, when the Kinks were a wild 'n' woolly, drunkenly unpredictable, always entertaining in-concert spectacle. Only Temple's "Do It Again," a strong song with a video in which Davies takes a sardonic, funhouse look at his band's history, comes anywhere near the high standards set by "Come Dancing" and "Predictable." However, for those two alone, this is a worthy purchase for any serious rock video collector.

☐ KISS
ANIMALIZE LIVE UNCENSORED
★★★

RCA/Columbia, 1985, 90 minutes
PRODUCED BY: John Weaver
DIRECTED BY: Keith "Keef" MacMillan
MUSIC FROM: Various Kiss albums (Casablanca, Polygram, 1974–85).
SELECTIONS: "Detroit Rock City," "Cold Gin," "Creatures of the Night," "Fits Like a Glove," "Heaven's on Fire," "Thrills in the Night," "Under the Gun," "War Machine," "Young and Wasted," "I Love It Loud," "I Still Love You," "Love Gun," "Lick It Up," "Black Diamond," "Rock and Roll All Night."
Also available on Pioneer Stereo Laser videodisc.

Sure, they're obnoxious. But Kiss *were* just about the first heavy metal act to explicitly seal the connection between thud-rock's macho strut and its now-ubiquitous cartoon parody-of-evil image-mongering. And beneath all the silly bluster, they *do* have a few actually decent rifferama exercises ("Love Gun," "Black Diamond," "Rock and Roll All Night"). If you're a Kiss fan, you'll just love this straightforwardly shot concert extravaganza—though you may wish Kiss had been captured in their original mid-'70s prime. Otherwise, of course, you'd have absolutely nothing to do with trash like this.

□ THE KNACK
LIVE AT CARNEGIE HALL
★★

Pioneer Artists, 1982, 50 minutes
PRODUCED BY: Robby Kenner
DIRECTED BY: Ethan Russell
MUSIC FROM: Get the Knack (Capitol, 1979); *. . . But the Little Girls Understand* (Capitol, 1980); *Round Trip* (Capitol, 1982).
SELECTIONS: "Rave Up," "Let Me Out," "Your Number or Your Name," "Oh Tara," "The Hard Way," "It's You," "Heartbeat," "End of the Game," "Hold On Tight and Don't Let Go," "Good Girls Don't," "Frustrated," "C'mon Everybody," "She's So Selfish," "My Sharona," "Not Fade Away," "A Hard Day's Night."
Available only on Pioneer Stereo Laser videodisc.

Derided by rock critics as record-company hype, adored by millions for a brief moment in time (the late '70s, remember?), the Knack have now been *so* forgotten that this concert shoot is available *only* on videodisc, a sure sign of lack of public interest if ever there was one. It's easy to see why critics blasted them: the Knack were very sexist in their lyrics, appeared to have no qualms with their deliberately contrived Beatles references—here they even have the gall to cover "A Hard Day's Night" as a show-closer—and leader Doug Feiger projected an air of singular vileness. It's harder to understand why they became so popular, however briefly: their songs are competent but undistinguished, and this kind of updated-'60s power pop never really caught on big. One wonders who's going to be interested in this piece, aside from the Feiger family; but if you are interested, here's the Knack shot straightforwardly, onstage just as they were on the brink of sliding back into obscurity. Next!

□ GLADYS KNIGHT AND THE PIPS AND RAY CHARLES
GLADYS KNIGHT AND THE PIPS AND RAY CHARLES
★★★

Vestron, 1979/1984, 78 minutes
PRODUCED BY: Neal Marshall, Susan Solomon, Mary Callner
DIRECTED BY: Marty Callner
MUSIC FROM: Various albums by Knight and the Pips and Charles; 1979 HBO concert special.
SELECTIONS: Introduction "Friendship Train"/"Georgia on My Mind"; Gladys Knight and the Pips: "How Can You Say (That Ain't Love)," "Every Beat of My Heart," "So Sad the Song," "On and On," "Best Thing That Ever Happened to Me," "Midnight Train to Georgia," "I've Got to Use My Imagination," "I Heard It Through the Grapevine"; Gladys Knight: "Evergreen," "The Way We Were"; Ray Charles with the Raelettes: "I Can See Clearly Now," "America the Beautiful"; Ray Charles with Gladys Knight: "Georgia on My Mind," "Neither One of Us," "Hit the Road, Jack."

For fans of these two giants of black popular music—or for anyone interested in digging two of the most soulful singers in history—this 1979 concert at L.A.'s Greek Theater should satisfy, though between the middle-of-the-road appearance of the audience and the good-natured stage manners of both Knight and Charles, it's at least as much innocuous entertainment as genuine get-down. But then, with Knight and Charles around you know it's gotta be at least somewhat soulful. It's all shot in fine but unspectacular fashion; director Marty Callner's only mistake is in using too many cutaways to audience members singing along or standing there dumbly while others around them applaud wildly.

□ KOOL AND THE GANG
TONIGHT!
★★★½

RCA/Columbia, 1985, 84 minutes
PRODUCED BY: Jon Small
DIRECTED BY: Jay Dubin
MUSIC FROM: Various Kool and the Gang albums, including *Tonight!* (Polygram, 1985).
SELECTIONS: "Celebration," "Ladies Night," "Hollywood Swinging," "Tonight," "You Can Do It," "Trilogy: Too Hot/No Show/Jones vs. Jones," "In the Heart," "Take My Heart," "Summer Madness," "Joanna," "Get Down on It," "Let's Go Dancin' (Ooh La La La)."

Kool and the Gang took about a decade to do it, but by the time this New Orleans concert was shot in 1984, they had become a state-of-the-art pop-dance hit machine, with classics like "Celebration," "Ladies Night," and "Joanna." They do nod to their roots in harder, blacker party-funk-disco here with "Hollywood Swinging," but mostly, they stick with the smoother, homogenized danceable pop that got them a vast, multiracial audience. There's plenty of slick Motown-style choreography in Kool and the Gang's stage show, and you'll hear the ladies in the house scream with delight whenever lead singer James "J.T." Taylor executes his smooth moves (trumpeter/vocalist Michael Ray flashes some pretty hip steps as well). Jay Dubin's direction is every bit as clean, classy, and accomplished as Kool and the Gang themselves.

□ VARIOUS ARTISTS
KOOL STREET VIDEOS
★★

Continental, 1984, 60 minutes
PRODUCED BY: Lyn Henderson
DIRECTED BY: Dennis De Vallance and various others
MUSIC FROM: Various albums by various artists.
SELECTIONS: Earth, Wind and Fire: "Let's Groove"; Kool and the Gang: "Let's Go Dancin' (Ooh, La, La)," "High De High," "Get Down on It"; Lakeside: "Turn the Music Up"; Stephanie Mills: "Pilot Error"; Shalamar: "Dead Giveaway," "A Night to Remember"; Midnight Star: "Freak-a-Zoid," "Can't Give You Up"; Ray Parker: "The Other Woman"; the Whispers: "In the Raw"; Rick James: "69 Times," "Throwdown."

An uneven collection of black videos, this tape ranges from the ridiculous (anything by Lakeside) to the sublime (Rick James) and includes some good tunes, such as Stephanie Mills's "Pilot Error" and Ray Parker's "The Other Woman." It suffers badly from uneven sound from clip to clip, poster- and solarization sickness, and a general look of cheapness. Although there was really no morally acceptable defense for MTV's pre-*Thriller* reluctance to air black clips, if this is a good representation of the pickings it's safe to say that from a strictly entertainment point of view, you didn't miss much.
—P.R.

□ KENNY KOSEK
LEARNING BLUEGRASS FIDDLE
★★★★

Homespun, 1984, 90 minutes
PRODUCED BY: Happy Traum
DIRECTED BY: Happy Traum
SELECTIONS: "Sally Goodin," "St. Anne's Reel," "The Orange Blossom Special," and others.

Oriented much more toward the beginning fiddler than Mark O'Connor's *Contest Fiddling* Homespun cassette, Kosek's tape starts you off from step one, showing you how to hold the instrument, proper use of the bow, riffs, double-stops, solos, and more. Kosek's a personable, good-humored teacher, which ought to make learning even more fun. (Available by mail order from Homespun Tapes.)

□ KROKUS
THE VIDEO BLITZ
★★½

RCA/Columbia, 1984, 60 minutes
PRODUCED BY: Marty Callner
DIRECTED BY: Marty Callner
MUSIC FROM: Various Krokus albums.
SELECTIONS: "Opening/Animation," "Long Stick Goes Boom," "Heatstrokes," "Our Love (uncensored version)," "Screaming in the Night," "Stayed Awake all Night," "Ready to Rock," "Ballroom Blitz," "Midnite Maniac," "Eat the Rich," "Headhunter."

Also available on Pioneer Stereo Laser videodisc.

Producer/director Marty Callner really, really tries to do right by the Swiss heavy metal band: he shoots their 1984 New York City concert with nicely placed multiple cameras, uses all sorts of fancy, eye-catching strobe edits and other effects, and cuts in comparably well-produced (if rather silly and subtly sexist in the heavy metal video tradition) concept videos for "Our Love" and "Ballroom Blitz." But the fact remains that, even with a great song title like "Long Stick Goes Boom," Krokus are grindingly dull. For fans only.

□ VARIOUS ARTISTS
KRUSH GROOVE
★★★

Warner Home Video, 1986, 95 minutes
PRODUCED BY: Michael Schultz and Doug McHenry; co-produced by Russell Simmons
DIRECTED BY: Michael Schultz
MUSIC FROM: *Krush Groove* motion picture soundtrack (Warner Bros., 1985); Sheila E.: *Romance 1600* (Paisley Park, 1985); Fat Boys: *Fat Boys* (Sutra, 1984); *Fat Boys Are Back* (Sutra, 1985).
SELECTIONS: Run-D.M.C.: "King of Rock," "It's Like That," "Can You Rock It like This," "You're Blind"; Fat Boys: "Don't You Dog Me," "Pump It Up—Let's Get Funky," "All You Can Eat," "Fat Boys"; Sheila E.: "A Love Bizarre," "Holly Rock"; UTFO: "Pick Up the Pace"; Kurtis Blow: "If I Ruled the World"; Deborah Harry: "Feel the Spin"; LL Cool J: "I Can't Live without My Radio"; Nayobe: "Please Don't Go"; New Edition: "My Secret (Didja Get It Yet)"; Beastie Boys: "She's on It"; Chad: "I Want You to Be My Girl"; Force M.D.'s: "Tender Love"; Gap Band: "Love Triangle"; Autumn: "Kold Krush"; Fat Boys, Run-D.M.C., Sheila E., and Kurtis Blow: "Krush Groovin' "; Chaka Khan: "Can't Stop the Street (Krush Groove)."

Despite its hackneyed story (basically just a shallowly updated cavalcade of hoary jukebox-musical clichés), *Krush Groove* succeeds as fun, energetically entertaining rapsploitation—thanks almost totally to its "fresh," in every sense of the word, young cast. All except one play themselves, which may account for their refreshing performances. That one exception, however, happens to be *Krush Groove*'s central character, "Russell Wright"—who is based on Russell Simmons, the young enterpreneur whose rags-to-riches rise via his Rush Productions/Profile Records artists including Run-D.M.C., Kurtis Blow, and the Fat Boys inspired *Krush Groove.* Simmons's Hollywood factotum is portrayed by the earnest, handsome Blair Underwood, who despite his obvious talent and charisma can't help but come off like an out-of-place pretty boy, surrounded as he is by so much street-level *verismo.*

The story's so half-baked and hand-me-down it's barely worth recounting, but here goes: audacious ghetto visionary knows he can beat the odds and land a ticket out of his local dump on the talent of his pals and relations, but he has to compromise his ethics and deal with the local Mafia-type for cash, *and* suffer legitimized corporate corruption via a major label and its sleazoid exec. Along the way, there are bad times and good times, and naturally some romance (provided by Sheila E.). In the desperate fight for fame and fortune, money supercedes blood and brother (Joseph "Run" Simmons of Run-D.M.C., who is Russell Simmons's brother) turns against brother (Russell). Family and roots are betrayed for a taste of the good life—then returned to and rejuvenated for the inevitable, contrived happy ending.

Still, most of the performers manage to rise above such predictable claptrap. Shelia E., though not quite a genuine "street" type since being remade and remodeled by Prince, is disarmingly easy and natural on camera, with her own down-to-earth charm. Rick Rubin, in real life the suburban guerrilla who founded Profile's subsidiary Def Jam label out of his NYU dorm room (a real-life saga that's even more interesting than Russell Simmons's), makes the most of his scant screen time and comes off like a professional wrestler—a natural-born, crazily inspired ham who can turn on the scene-stealing juice anytime. And as for the Fat Boys, well, *Krush Groove* isn't just a piece of cake—it's the whole *bakery.*

Most impressive of all, though, is Joseph "Run" Simmons, who makes one of the acting debuts of the '80s: the way he breathes poignant life into a classic modern archetype of the swaggeringly macho yet very vulnerable young black urban male is nothing short of magnificent. Really. *Krush Groove* is worth seeing for him alone—though Sheila E., Rick Rubin, and a generally quite solid soundtrack of rap and related dance-funk and dance-pop don't hurt a bit, either. Just don't think too hard about the "plot."

L

□ PATTI LABELLE
LOOK TO THE RAINBOW
★★★½

I.V.E./USA, 1986, 67 minutes
PRODUCED BY: Glenn Ellis, Sr.
DIRECTED BY: Michael Bernhaut
MUSIC FROM: Various albums by Labelle and Patti LaBelle.
SELECTIONS: "The Spirit Lives," "I'm in Love Again," "Such a Joy," "Afraid of Who I Am," "The Best Is Yet to Come," "Tell Me How," "Shoot Him on Sight," "Lady Marmalade," "Lover Man (Oh, Where Can You Be)," "Wind Beneath My Wings," "Up Where We Belong," "You Are My Friend," "Over the Rainbow," "Look to the Rainbow."

By the time this 1985 concert was shot at the Schubert Theater in Patti LaBelle's hometown of Philadelphia, she had proved herself a genuine showbiz survivor, having outlasted the girl-group and disco eras with her group LaBelle (originally Patti LaBelle and the BlueBelles in the girl-group years) and forged a comeback several months before this concert by stealing the show from Diana Ross and all others with her rendition of "Over the Rainbow" at the *Motown Returns to the Apollo* show. She stole the show there with some soulfully showboating vocal gymnastics, so it's no wonder she applies that same gutsy, bombastic approach to virtually every song in this program—even the tenderly bittersweet Billie Holiday–associated ballad "Lover Man." Her muscular voice swoops all over the place in what amounts to an exhausting excess of pyrotechnic testifying; she veers from high-pitched baby-talking gurgles and squeals to throaty warbles to hair-raising shrieks, and while she never misses a note and always convinces us that her voice is one hell of an instrument, Patti ultimately wears us down with it. Still, it's hard to blame any entertainer for giving the people what they want, especially when Patti manifests her joyful excitation physically in a series of endearingly awkward and enthusiastic expressive dances—even jumping, falling to the floor, and writhing around in "Tell Me How." Following that song, she reappears in one of her bizarre hairdos and an equally unique-looking glittery gown and is joined by five young breakdancers for the LaBelle disco classic "Lady Marmalade" (you remember, "Voulez vous couchez avec moi ce soir?") in the single most gratuitous moment on the whole tape. A gospel choir joins her for "Up Where We Belong" and the rest, as the live audience gives the sweat-drenched Patti a long and loud standing ovation. If you're a fan of hers, or of this sort of histrionic vocalizing, so will you—especially considering the wealth of fine up-close camera angles used by director Michael Bernhaut, which at times almost make you feel like checking your TV screen for perspiration stains.

□ STEVE LACY
LIFT THE BANDSTAND
★★★★

Rhapsody, 1985, 50 minutes
PRODUCED BY: Peter L. Bull
DIRECTED BY: Peter L. Bull
MUSIC FROM: Various albums by Steve Lacy and His Sextet, Sidney Bechet, Thelonious Monk, John Coltrane, and the Gil Evans Orchestra; soundtrack to the film *Lift the Bandstand* (Jigsaw Productions, 1985).
SELECTIONS: Steve Lacy Sextet: "Prospectus," "Gay Paree Bop"; Sidney Bechet: "St. Louis Blues"; John Coltrane: "Afro Blue"; Thelonious Monk Quartet: "Criss Cross"; Gil Evans Orchestra: "Blues for Pablo"; Steve Lacy (solo): "Gay Paree Bop."

This is a very fine and thorough musical/personal portrait of Steve Lacy, a post-modern master of jazz soprano sax whose uncompromisingly tart, intelligently abstracted music has kept him from the wide audience his talent so richly deserves. As the first real soprano saxophonist in modern jazz, Lacy influenced John Coltrane as much as the late great Trane influenced him. Furthermore, Lacy turns out to be as articulate a subject as he is a significant one, and it's no wonder director Peter Bull lets him tell his own story: Lacy proves to be disarmingly candid, as when he calls the sound of the soprano sax comparable to "a high, shrill infant," and he himself will probably strike the most responsive chords with viewers who may come to this program unaware of Lacy's musical accomplishments.

Lacy's unusual range of influences is illustrated through a succession of great vintage film clips: Lacy began on soprano sax after hearing jazz's first master of the instrument, Sidney Bechet, whom we get to see in performance; after working with Dixieland masters such as Pee Wee Russell and Pops Foster, Lacy swung all the way over and out, working with the savagely inventive avant-garde jazz pianist Cecil Taylor, who according to Lacy "had me swimming furiously in the avant-garde ocean." There's a clip of Lacy's next mentor, Gil Evans (the clip of "Blues for Pablo" appears to be from the superb *The Sound of Miles Davis* videodisc program), and another of his biggest influences, Thelonious Monk, playing "Criss Cross" with his quartet. It was Monk, says Lacy, who showed him how to "lift the bandstand" with one's music and musicianship; after leaving Monk's ensemble in the early '60s to make a better living in Europe, Lacy remained sufficiently inspired to form a quintet that played nothing but Monk tunes, and his own music certainly reflects much of the distinctive angularity and deliberately awkward grace of Monk's music. Finally, there's a clip of John Coltrane on soprano sax, as Lacy's voiceover claims that Trane was inspired to play the small horn after hearing Lacy play it.

What emerges most strikingly in the footage of Lacy playing solo and with his Sextet, however, is not just the range of his influences, but how very much he's transcended them to become his own man. His soprano sax playing bears scant if any obvious similarity to the styles of Bechet and Coltrane, and while his compositions may be Monk-rooted, they are also a quantum leap beyond those roots. Most instructive is the comparison between Lacy's solo version of "Gay Paree Bop" and his sextet's take on it (at a 1983 show at New York's Public Theater): solo, he's an introvert, carefully considering each note; with the group, he's a soaring extrovert, flying high above the rhythm section's rolling-and-tumbling propulsion in tandem with the wordless vocals of cellist Irene Aebi. What connects in both settings is Lacy's near-Zen mastery of his instrument and his music, his effortless ability to achieve the master jazzman's precariously poised balance between control and abandon, learned technique and spontaneous wit, and the very human keening that is the soul of his laughing, sighing, crying, singing sound on soprano sax. While Peter Bull also did a commendable job of letting the music and musicians do the talking in his *The New Music* (about avant-garde jazz cornetist Bobby Bradford and clarinetist John Carter, also distributed by Rhapsody), *Lift the Bandstand* is more enjoyable—no doubt due to its subject and his music. (Available by mail order from Rhapsody Films.)

☐ CHERYL LADD
FASCINATED
★★

HBO/Cannon, 1982, 50 minutes
DIRECTED BY: John Goodhue
MUSIC FROM: Cheryl Ladd (Capitol, 1978); *Dance Fever* (Capitol, 1979); *Fascinated* (Capitol, 1982).
SELECTIONS: "Fascinated," "Think It Over," "Just like Old Times," "Lesson from the Leavin'," "Lady Gray," "Just Another Lover Tonight," "Sakura, Sakura," "The Rose Nobody Knows," "I Love How You Love Me," "It's Only Love," "Try a Smile," "Cold as Ice," "Victim of the Circumstance."

Ms. Ladd is an attractive woman and not completely without talent (just to give her the benefit of the doubt), and the plot device providing a theme for this series of concept videos—Cheryl as a professional photographer whose subjects inspire her musical fantasies—is more convenient and less contrived than most, and it's all decently produced and directed. That said, you'd have to be a really *big* fan of her work on TV's *Charlie's Angels* to even care that this program exists. I mean, she's just *not* a good singer, and the music is L.A.-studio soft rock of the most soporific and forgettable sort.

☐ VARIOUS ARTISTS
THE LAST OF THE BLUE DEVILS
★★★★★

Rhapsody, 1984, 91 minutes
PRODUCED BY: John Kelly, Bruce Ricker and Edward Beyer
DIRECTED BY: Bruce Ricker
MUSIC FROM: Various albums by various artists; soundtrack of the film *Last of the Blue Devils* (Rhapsody, 1979).
SELECTIONS: Bennie Moten Orchestra: "South," "Moten Swing"; Big Joe Turner and Jay McShann: "Piney Brown Blues"; Jay McShann: "Jay's Blues"; Jay McShann and His Big Band: Medley: "Jumpin' the Blues"/"Hootie Blues"/"After Hours," "One O'Clock Jump"; Big Joe Turner with the Jay McShann Big Band: "Roll 'Em Pete"; Big Joe Turner: "Shake, Rattle and Roll"; Count Basie and His Orchestra: "Moten Swing," "Jumpin' at the Woodside," "Night Train," "One O'Clock Jump"; Jesse Price: "Jesse's Blues"; Oklahoma City Blue Devils: "Squabblin' "; Paul Quinichette, Eddie Durham, and Charles McPherson: "Lester Leaps In"; Lester Young: unidentified tenor sax solo; Crook Goodwin: "Until the Real Thing Comes Along"; Charlie Parker: "Hot House"; Art Jackson: "Body and Soul"; Count Basie and Jo Jones: "Dickie's Dream"; Claude Williams: untitled violin solo; Buster Smith Quintet featuring Jo Jones and Budd Johnson: "Buster's Tune"; Jo Jones and Baby Lovett: untitled drum duet; Speedy Huggins: untitled tap dance.

Bruce Ricker's *Last of the Blue Devils* is a magnificent documentary on a fabled time and place in American musical history: Kansas City in the '20s, '30s, and '40s, when it was Manhattan-in-the-Midwest as much as Chicago ever was—an "open city" with a wild and woolly nightlife of booze, gambling, and prostitution, supported by the powerful political machine of Mayor "Boss" Tom Pendergast, who in effect took his city and said, "To hell with Prohibition—let's party!" Besides some high times, some very high-caliber music came out of it all by the likes of Count Basie, Big Joe Turner, Jay McShann, Jimmy Rushing, Lester Young, Charlie Parker, "Papa" Jo Jones (considered by most critics the first modern drummer), and more. Ricker covers this storybook scene by documenting a March 1974 reunion of Kansas City jazzmen who hang out and reminisce at the city's Mutual Musicians Foundation Hall. Basie, Turner, and McShann are there, as are, gratifyingly, some musicians who played crucial roles in the historical evolution of jazz but who never got their due because they chose to remain in Kansas City rather than migrate to media centers such as New York or Los Angeles—as did alto saxophonist Buster Smith (a major influence on Charlie Parker) and drummer Baby Lovett (whose friendly rivalry with Jo Jones certainly influenced the latter).

Ricker approaches his subjects with a perfect-for-video intimacy, probably cued by the warmth and camaraderie of the entire reunion scene: all of these grand old men are delightful characters as well as marvelous musicians. This aspect makes *The Last of the Blue Devils* (the title referring to the Oklahoma City Blue Devils big band of the late '20s, a legendary territorial band in which many of the key figures in Kansas City jazz got their starts) seem at times like an elongated version of one of Les Blank's distinctively down-to-earth and folksy shoestring documentaries. But Ricker also packs the film with informative conversations, performances, and archival stills and footage that trace the spread and influence of the K.C. approach throughout post–World War II jazz and other forms of popular music. *Blue Devils* follows the chronology of the Blue Devils band as its members moved into unsung-hero Benny Moten's orchestra and then, upon his untimely death in the mid-'30s, into Count Basie's band. Big Joe Turner says, "We were doing rock 'n' roll before anybody ever heard of it" and a subsequent mid-'40s clip of him belting out "Shake, Rattle and Roll" proves it. After Buster Smith and others discuss his influence on Charlie Parker, Smith plays some alto sax that's positively startling in its adventurous vivacity, coming from such a seemingly frail old gent; then we see a vintage black-and-white clip of Parker with Dizzy Gillespie playing "Hot House," Parker's bow tie fluttering in time to his straining neck muscles.

But as important as such specific revelations are, they're overshadowed here by a more generalized historical value: while musicians such as these may be well documented on recordings and in photographs in most cases, there's always been a terrible dearth of film capturing the wholeness and presence of these creators; in traversing the life/art gap and literally letting these musicians speak for themselves, *The Last of the Blue Devils* becomes a living oral/visual history of the faces and places that made the music a celebration of the personalities and emotional commitments of the players—their music, their homes, their time, and the timelessness of their art. As such, *Blue Devils* is also loaded with epiphanies, personal, musical, and both:

Big Joe Turner slowly, painfully ascends the stairs of the musicians' hall aided by a cane and another person, and then we see him in a chair before a piano, singing the blues with commanding authority and no perceptible effort; an archival clip of the Basie orchestra performing "Moten Swing," their original theme song, provides a perfect paradigm of the distinctively tasteful restraint and concision that was Basie's musical calling card—at the piano, the eternally laconic Basie hits the same stark, single note *three times* over the course of twelve bars of muted-brass riffing, and as it peals lonesomely over the leashed power of the band it makes for magnificent music as well as a pithy character study of a jazz giant. There's original Blue Devils drummer Ernie Williams, in the abandoned lot that was once the famous "12th Street and Vine," telling some little black kids, "Now don't use your head as a hatrack, and go to school and get yourself an education—that's Ernest Walter Williams talking, sixty-nine years old. Can you make it? I made it. Will you?" Later, in the midst of a tour of where all the hot clubs used to be, Williams tells us that when his wife once demanded he choose between her and the music, he chose the music. Jay McShann, a look of imperturbable good humor playing about his face as he casually tosses off ingenious barrelhouse symphonettes at the piano, governs the proceedings like some benevolent, bluesy oversoul. Cigar-chomping Milton Morris, who used to own the Reno Club in Kansas City, tells hilariously vivid anecdotes about the high life under Boss Pendergast, about the legendary all-night jam sessions in his former club, about Count Basie's renowned love for K.C. barbecued ribs. White-haired tap dancer Speedy Huggins executes whirlwind moves that would do James Brown proud, and, as he finishes to a roomful of applause and appreciative laughter from his friends, the camera captures his face being lit up by a barely restrained, humbly boyish joy. And then there's Papa Jo Jones and Baby Lovett: Jones, one of the most notoriously difficult personalities in jazz history, is in buoyant spirits as he duets with his mentor; but Lovett provides perhaps the most haunting presence in the whole movie—quiet, withdrawn, he barely utters a single word in the whole course of the film and seems touched by some sort of inexpressible sadness that wouldn't bear retelling.

There's a whole lot more in *The Last of the Blue Devils,* but telling you any more would only spoil what is ultimately a mandatory viewing experience. There are just two quibbles: its historical summation of Kansas City jazz somehow neglects two significant exponents, Andy Kirk and Marylou Williams; and the musicians, in their reminiscences and backslapping repartee with one another, often speak in rough-hewn dialects that are hard for outsiders to decipher. But it's worth the effort to catch the anecdotal pearls dropped by these weathered marvels of exuberant agelessness. And, for those rock-generation viewers who think this may be too quaint a topic for them to bother checking out, remember what Big Joe Turner said.

The Kansas City sound, with its rollicking swagger, was probably the most intensely rhythmic swing-era subgenre and presaged the coming of rock 'n' roll more than any other subgenre of the time; Count Basie's reiterative riff approach had a sizable influence on rock 'n' roll arranging techniques. Thus, the chapter of musical history that's brought to such affecting life in *The Last of the Blue Devils* may be more relevant to the here and now than you think. But essentially, this film's virtues are timeless, and, with both Basie and Turner now gone at this writing, need any more be said? (Available by mail order from Rhapsody Films.)

□ LED ZEPPELIN
THE SONG REMAINS THE SAME
★★★½

Warner Home Video, 1980, 136 minutes
PRODUCED BY: Peter Grant
DIRECTED BY: Peter Clifton and Joe Massot
MUSIC FROM: Led Zeppelin (Atlantic, 1969); *Led Zeppelin II* (Atlantic, 1969); *Led Zeppelin IV (Untitled)* (Atlantic, 1971); *Houses of the Holy* (Atlantic, 1973); *The Song Remains the Same* (Atlantic, 1976).
SELECTIONS: "Black Dog," "Rock 'n' Roll," "Since I've Been Loving You," "No Quarter," "The Song Remains the Same," "The Rain Song," "Dazed and Confused," "Stairway to Heaven," "Moby Dick," "Heartbreaker," "Whole Lotta Love."

Though derided by non-fans as a laborious, amateurish indulgence, *The Song Remains the Same* is more than just manifold manna for the Zep-head. It's also one of the most prophetic rock films of the mid-'70s. It consists mostly of a 1973 Led Zeppelin concert at New York's Madison Square Garden—nicely photographed, though the sound is muddy and erratic, and the band is in typical onstage form, which is less impressive than the way they sounded on record—along with the usual attendant behind-the-scenes tour-documentary stuff (limos from the airport to the gig, etc.), and some "fantasy sequences" intercut with the live footage (which is often psychedelicized with solarizations and double images).

Each band member gets his own fantasy: vocalist Robert Plant has a sword-wielding Arthurian bit for the title song; guitarist Jimmy Page metamorphoses from contemporary form to child to baby to wizened and bearded old wizard, climbing a mountaintop during Page's violin-bow/theremin extravaganza in the *long* version of "Dazed and Confused"; bassist/keyboardist John Paul Jones plays a masked marauder in the eighteenth-century British countryside wreaking havoc on horseback with a band of similarly masked vandals for "No Quarter"; and drummer John "Bonzo" Bonham, at first seen tinkering on his farm with his tractors, cars, and motorcycles, becomes a race-car driver in his fantasy, set to his spotlight-piece "Moby Dick." Even the band's notorious manager, Peter Grant, gets one to open the film—he's a '20s-style pinstripe-suited gangster leading his henchmen on a violent hit, machine-gunning a bunch of fantastical (one's faceless, another's a werewolf) tycoon/politico types in their mansion as they play a warlike board game. Grant's particular "fantasy," according to some reports, was discomfitingly close to his real-life management style. Yet, when we see Grant in a later scene backstage at the Garden, berating a security guy because someone's been caught selling unauthorized Led Zep T-shirts at the gig, he comes across merely as a harried, hardworking manager who's *exceedingly* intent on making sure his boys don't get ripped off.

At any rate, most of these fantasy sequences are pretty dumb and all that. But they are absolutely, positively anticipatory of conceptual rock videos, more so than anything in any other pre-MTV rock movie. As with contemporary music videos, these interludes either took off literally from a song's lyrics (as in Jones's "No Quarter" bit) or referred to a mystique previously elaborated in the band's album cover artwork (such as Page's wizard-on-the-mountain bit, illustrated in the gatefold drawing for the untitled fourth Led Zep LP—a.k.a. *Zoso*—the one with "Stairway to Heaven"). And they were designed not just to flesh out and enhance the filmgoer's experience, but mainly to elicit a big "Oh, *wow!*" from that viewer (e.g. Page's bit, climaxing with rainbow-rotoscoped multi-image trails following his sword as he waves it around atop the mountain, visually echoing his violin-bow moves in the song)—not unlike latter-day heavy metal videos.

While the bountiful concert stuff makes this a must-have for any Led Zeppelin fan, it's those fantasy sequences that lend *The Song Remains the Same* its historical significance and make it worth checking out for those who take a genuine interest in the roots of rock video.

□ ALBERT LEE
THE ALBERT LEE PACKAGE
★★★★

Star Licks, 1984, 40 minutes
PRODUCED BY: Mark Freed and Robert Decker
DIRECTED BY: Mark Freed and Robert Decker

MUSIC FROM: Various albums by Albert Lee and others.

SELECTIONS: "Country Boy," and nineteen other "licks" drawn from other songs and various riffs, solos, and other exercises.

Like all the other excellent instructional cassettes in the Star Licks Master Series, *The Albert Lee Package* offers a low-key, intimate lesson taught by an accomplished and respected contemporary guitarist who shows you a variety of licks and tricks, playing all the exercises, solos, fills, etc., twice, once at normal (usually blinding) speed and once at extra-slow (as in merely mortal) speed. And, like the others in the series, it comes with a booklet that carefully notates each exercise.

Lee is a superb British country-rock guitarist, who since the late '60s has played with Eric Clapton, Jerry Lee Lewis, Don Everly, Rosanne Cash, Ricky Scaggs, Emmylou Harris, and John Fogerty, among others. Here, he runs through twenty different exercises on about a half dozen different instruments, including two Fender Telecasters (one is a battered blond '53 autographed by everyone Lee has ever played with), a Gibson J-200 acoustic given to him by Don Everly, a Gibson Les Paul given to him by Eric Clapton, and a Gibson electric mandolin. The techniques he demonstrates include "slick chicken pickin' " (lightning-fast bluegrass-style runs full of complicated fingerings that will have you thanking God for the scan button so you can watch them over and over), double stops, scale-running, open tunings, pick-hand pulls, mixing picking and fingering, steel-guitar effects, and more. Lee does it all with a casual, sometimes self-deprecating friendliness that's in marked contrast to his stunning technical displays. (Available by mail order from Star Licks).

□ JOHN LENNON
INTERVIEW WITH A LEGEND
★★★★

Karl-Lorimar, 1981, 60 minutes

SELECTIONS: John Lennon interviewed by Tom Snyder, April 28, 1975, on NBC-TV's *The Tomorrow Show;* Jack Douglas, producer of Lennon's *Double Fantasy,* interviewed December 9, 1980.

Interview with a Legend affords a rare, unique look at Lennon in a nonmusical, interview setting. It's the December 9, 1980, edition of NBC-TV's *Tomorrow Show,* with Tom Snyder, which was actually a rebroadcast of Snyder's April 28, 1975, interview with Lennon on the show, plus interviews conducted that same day after John died, with rock journalist Lisa Robinson and record producer Jack Douglas, who worked on *Double Fantasy,* the last Lennon-Ono recording released in John's lifetime. The Lennon-Snyder interview is essentially a low-key, friendly chat, more wide-ranging than in-depth. Throughout, Lennon is a wee bit guarded and careful not to be too outrageous—this was, after all, during his deportation hearings, and his lawyer comes out for the second half, which is dominated by a discussion of John's case—yet always his candid, witty, irreverent, sincere, dignified self. As for Snyder, well, it's hard not to think of Dan Aykroyd savaging him on *Saturday Night Live.* There's one priceless moment when Snyder, during a discussion of Beatlemania, refers to "those silly haircuts"; without missing a beat, John retorts, "Which you have now!" Other topics include the Beatles ("We broke up out of boredom"; "I, and the others, I think, am most happy for Ringo's success"), his musical likes ("Disco's great, and that thing in Jamaica called reggae"), Yoko, the Toronto Bed-In, and stardom, which prompts the eternally ironic Lennon statement "It used to be I couldn't go anywhere without being hassled, but now we go anywhere we want." There's also a prescient dialogue about whether Lennon would do an antidrug campaign on TV; he'd rather not—"People can't be told, they have to learn for themselves."

In the later show Lisa Robinson talks about Lennon as happy househusband and Yoko's positive influence on him. Snyder, trying to keep things cool and calm the day after the tragedy, acts like his usual buffoonishly suave self, only a bit more restrained. He's even that way with Jack Douglas, who manages to reminisce about John in a quavering voice, while blinking back tears—serious lump-in-the-throat stuff.

□ JOHN LENNON
LIVE IN NEW YORK CITY
★★★★

Sony, 1986, 55 minutes

PRODUCED BY: John Lennon, Yoko Ono, and Gerard Meola

DIRECTED BY: Steve Gebhardt and Carol Dysinger

MUSIC FROM: Some Time in New York City (Apple/Capitol, 1972); *Plastic Ono Band* (Apple/Capitol, 1970); *Imagine* (Apple/Capitol, 1971); *Live Peace in Toronto, 1969* (Apple/Capitol, 1969); the Beatles: Abbey Road (Capitol, 1969).

SELECTIONS: "Power to the People," "New York City," "It's So Hard," "Woman Is the Nigger of the World," "Sisters O Sisters," "Well, Well, Well," "Instant Karma," "Mother," "Born in a Prison," "Come Together," "Imagine," "Cold Turkey," "Hound Dog," "Give Peace a Chance."

Also available on Pioneer Stereo Laser videodisc.

The August 30, 1972, benefit at Madison Square Garden for One to One (a charity for mentally handicapped children) was the only solo show Lennon ever performed after the Beatles stopped touring in 1966 (he also made a surprise guest appearance at Elton John's November 1974 Garden show). Having this as our only record of post–Fab Four John in action is something of a mixed blessing: he was much more into causes and effecting political change at this point in his career than he was into making music, and he obviously played this show (at the reported urging of TV journalist Geraldo Rivera) more as a grand gesture for a good cause than to make any musical statement. He and the Plastic Ono Elephant's Memory Band are obviously *very* underrehearsed, something John openly acknowledges throughout the show with his typically sharp, bittersweet wit. Thc band itself is simply awful, serving to remind us of just how bad so much post-psychedelic rock really sounded back then; the addition of star session drummer Jim Keltner doesn't help much, and Yoko Ono's alien-cat-in-heat vocals and random piano plonks graphically illustrate not only her legitimate claim to ahead-of-her-time avant-gardism, but also why so many people hated and ridiculed her for so long (they may turn off a whole new generation now that this program is out).

But this *is* John Lennon, after all, and the man and his music make this memento triumph against those odds. It's a good thing, considering the lame, ill-prepared band, that songs like "Imagine," "Instant Karma," and "Well, Well, Well" are as durable as they are. But even more powerful is the way this program captures Lennon the Character: that witty between-songs patter (e.g., his intro to "Mother": "Here's another song from one of those albums I made after I left the Rolling Stones"); his courageous spiritual generosity and crusader-for-change indomitability (vividly evident in women's-lib anthems like "Woman Is the Nigger of the World" and "Sisters O Sisters"); his equally courageous (given the tides of public reaction) and boundless affection for Yoko, poignantly captured in intimate close-ups of him smiling and blowing kisses at her from across the stage. And, considering when it was made, it's surprisingly well shot, with multiple cameras focusing on the onstage action felicitously, and keeping the obligatory audience shots to a gratifying minimum (in fact, the quality of the shooting makes it all the more frustrating that the 1972/1985 credits obscure who's responsible for what). Maybe Lennon deserves an even better memorial, but it's highly unlikely he'll ever get one.

□ JOHN LENNON (WITH YOKO ONO)
IMAGINE
★★½

Sony, 1986, 55 minutes

PRODUCED BY: John Lennon and Yoko Ono

DIRECTED BY: John Lennon and Yoko Ono

MUSIC FROM: Imagine (Apple, 1971); Yoko Ono: *Fly* (Apple, 1971).

SELECTIONS: "Imagine," "Crippled Inside," "Jealous Guy," "Don't Count the Waves," "It's So Hard," "Mrs. Lennon," "I Don't Want to Be a Soldier," "Power to the People," "Gimme Some Truth," "Oh My Love," "How Do You Sleep?," "How?," "Oh, Yoko!"

Like David Bowie's earlier *Love You Til Tuesday, Imagine* has great ahead-of-its-time historical value, being essentially one of the first album-promoting compilations of what are basically pioneering music video clips. In this case, *two* albums were being promoted by the original 81-minute feature film. The home video version, however, plays it sensibly safe by cutting a half hour of what must have been the rest of Yoko's *Fly* album, which is represented here by only two cuts. Her "Don't Count the Waves" is very avant-garde, very post-psychedelic and aleatoric, with Yoko's repetitive psycho-babbling counterpointing heavily echoed free-form percussion and electronic noises; "Mrs. Lennon" is basically Yoko trying to sing, and perhaps even more trying than the ostensibly much weirder "Waves." Lennon's *Imagine* songs, by vivid contrast, hold up magnificently for the most part, with elegantly powerful writing and starkly emotional performances. The title anthem, of course, is a highlight, but so are "How?" and "Oh, Yoko!" and especially the unutterably tender "Jealous Guy." "It's So Hard," "Gimme Some Truth," "Oh My Love," and "How Do You Sleep?" aren't too far behind.

It's a good thing the music's so strong, because visually, *Imagine* stakes a sadly legitimate claim to true pioneer status: that is, it may have been ahead of its time, but it also happens to be as indulgent and tiresome as the Beatles' *Magical Mystery Tour,* as well as many modern-day conceptual music videos. *Imagine* ups the artistic ante a bit from *Magical Mystery Tour.* Here, higher production values but also a much higher level of pretentious artiness rule. The songs are accompanied by an enervating stream of home movies (featuring John and Yoko alone together, and with such hip pals as Andy Warhol, Dick Cavett, George Harrison, and Phil Spector, mostly shot in and around what one assumes is their gorgeous, sprawling country estate, Tittenhurst) and self-consciously "bizarre" and "surreal" shenanigans, some of them actually documents of Yoko's "bagism" and other forms of her performance- and conceptual-art gambits. Lennon's grand wit is nowhere in evidence to relieve the self-serious air. Only the classy, predominant performance clip "Imagine" is watchable enough, and substantive enough in subtextual implication, to qualify as a good video. Its slow, dignified pace is indubitably a suitable visual complement to the music—but are its wintry-white colors and austere, near-elegaic mood at odds with the song's hopeful idealism, or do they illuminate subtle shades of fatalistic resignation in it?

The rest of *Imagine,* however, quickly devolves into the kind of aimless stuff-and-nonsense that could appeal only to diehard Lennon-Ono fans—who will probably be excited to note that *Imagine* turns out to have been the source for the similarly meandering escapades of Lennon's "Nobody Told Me" video; that there are no visual references to Paul McCartney, the alleged subject of "How Do You Sleep?," in that song's visual accompaniment; and to see John on the potty for a moment here, John and Yoko kissing and kissing and kissing there . . . But otherwise, title track aside, there's nothing in *Imagine* that does very much to enhance some already great music.

☐ JULIAN LENNON
STAND BY ME
★★½

MCA, 1986, 58 minutes
PRODUCED BY: Martin Lewis
DIRECTED BY: Martin Lewis
MUSIC FROM: Valotte (Atlantic, 1984).
SELECTIONS: "O.K. for You," "On the Phone," "Lonely," "Well I Don't Know," "Valotte," "Let Me Be," "Say You're Wrong Jesse," "Day Tripper," "Space," "Stand by Me," "Too Late for Goodbyes."

Thoroughly standard tour documentary on John Lennon's eldest son's first U.S. tour, with the usual, predictable mix of stage footage, interviews, backstage and offstage shenanigans, on-the-road blahs, crews at work (do we *really* have to keep seeing those interminable shots of crews unloading crates of gear?) . . . While Julian is remarkably confident onstage, he really *shouldn't* be compared to his late great dad (no matter how eerie the vocal and facial resemblance): John Lennon was an irascible rebel ("He could be nasty . . . and he could be nice," Julian says at one point, and that seems to say it well enough) possessed of genius; so far, Julian Lennon has proved to be a talented, but basically shallow and mild entertainer. He does act like a bratty kid sometimes, but hasn't evidenced a shred of his father's fabulous wit; most of his comments are quite bland and boring. In fact, the most interesting thing in the program is a shot of some people waiting in line for tickets to one of Julian's shows, being asked what they like about him. It made me sit up and smile when a black man stepped forward and said, "I liked his father, John Lennon, that's why I'm here."

☐ HUEY LEWIS AND THE NEWS
VIDEO HITS
★★★½

CBS/Fox, 1985, 46 minutes
PRODUCED BY: Various
DIRECTED BY: Various
MUSIC FROM: Huey Lewis and the News (Chrysalis, 1980); *Picture This* (Chrysalis, 1982); *Sports* (Chrysalis, 1983); *Back to the Future* motion picture soundtrack (MCA, 1985).
SELECTIONS: "National Anthem," "Heart of Rock & Roll," "Is It Me," "Some of My Lies Are True," "Don't Ever Tell Me That You Love Me," "Heart & Soul," "If This Is It," "Bad Is Bad," "Back in Time," "Power of Love," "I Want a New Drug," "Workin' for a Living," "Finally Found a Home."

☐ HUEY LEWIS AND THE NEWS
THE HEART OF ROCK & ROLL
★★★½

Warner Home Video, 1985, 53 minutes
PRODUCED BY: Tony Eaton

DIRECTED BY: Bruce Gowers
MUSIC FROM: Sports (Chrysalis, 1984); *Picture This* (Chrysalis, 1982); *Huey Lewis and the News* (Chrysalis, 1980).
SELECTIONS: Medley: "Star Spangled Banner / Ain't No Stoppin' Us Now," "The Heart of Rock & Roll," "Heart & Soul," "Walking on a Thin Line," "Workin' for a Living," "Buzz Buzz Buzz," "I Want a New Drug," "Trouble in Paradise," "If This Is It," "It's All Right," "Hope You Love Me Like You Say You Do."

In many ways, Huey Lewis and the News are a refreshing '80s pop phenomenon. At their best, they present a canny, pop-savvy update of classic, straight-from-the-roots rock 'n' roll, and in so doing, they studiously avoid bizarre fashion statements, gravity-defying haircuts, and other flavor-of-the-month trendiness. And as hits such as "Heart & Soul" (which, truth to tell, they didn't compose, but did rearrange successfully), "I Want a New Drug," and "Power of Love" proved, they have a knack for the proverbial killer hook. The downside, however, is that beyond their nice-guy veneer, one never finds anything deeper, more dangerous—more, shall we say, *rock 'n' roll*; after a while their resolute niceness makes them a little *too* easy to take, casting a not-so-flattering light on the slick, calculated blandness that's as crucial to their success as those manicured roots-rock references. But that's something that would matter only to those who care to think that much about the culture they consume. For the vast majority of average rock fans, Huey Lewis and the News are simply a consistently tuneful, gratifyingly unaffected pop enterprise with a good beat you can dance to.

Video Hits provides career-spanning evidence of the band's growth (or, depending on your perspective, slide) from earnestly scruffy pub-rockers (picking up where Huey's first band, Clover, left off; they had backed Elvis Costello on his debut album, *My Aim Is True*) to sleek corporate-rock hit-making machine. In early tunes, such as "Some of My Lies Are True" and "Workin' for a Living," Huey and the boys sport a lean-and-hungry sound driven by the delightfully cheesy retro sound of the Vox organ, not to mention a credible working-class attitude and a rather endearing, self-deprecating sense of humor. The videos are appropriately low-budget, direct performance clips. By the time of the *Sports* clips, the band's sound is fuller and more conservatively pop-oriented, and the videos are slicker—which tends to take away some of the credibility of their self-deprecating wit (e.g., "Bad Is Bad," "If This Is It"). It's nice that they try to keep that ingratiating wit happening amidst all the higher production values, but it only ends up seeming more and more strained as it mutates from the attitude/lyric–based earlier humor to the later variety, which is epitomized by the inanely choreographed shenanigans of "If This Is It." But maybe I just think too much about such things.

Having reached the multiplatinum plateau with *Sports,* the band triumphantly returned to its Bay Area home for the San Francisco's Kabuki Theater show, shot for *The Heart of Rock & Roll*. They play the hits and play 'em well, it's all competently if not spectacularly shot (but then, such a nice normal rock band hardly calls for spectacular production—competent is just about right), and the Kabuki crowd, of course, loves the homeboys to death. The only real wrench in the works, aside from the overlap of six tunes between this and *Video Hits,* is bassist Mario Cipollina. He spends virtually the entire show in a slouch-shouldered, slack-jawed tough-guy pose, a cigarette butt permanently plastered to his lower lip—projecting an attitude that's so pathetically unconvincing it wouldn't scare Emmanuel Lewis, fails utterly as parody (if in fact that's how it's intended), and either way gets *really* tired *really* fast.

☐ JERRY LEE LEWIS
THE KILLER PERFORMANCE
★★★

JEM/Passport, 1986, 50 minutes
DIRECTED BY: Anthony Wall
MUSIC FROM: Various Jerry Lee Lewis albums.
SELECTIONS: "Whole Lot of Shakin' Goin' On," "Down the Line," "Trouble in Mind," "I Don't Wanna Be Lonely Tonight," "The One Rose," "Mona Lisa," "Lucille," "Chantilly Lace," "Me and Bobby McGee," "I'll Make It Up to You," "Little Queenie," "You Win Again," "Great Balls of Fire," "(I Don't Want to) Hang Up My Rock 'n' Roll Shoes."

An indifferently shot 1984 London concert, in which a genuine rock 'n' roll genius more or less goes through the motions. The producers make the mistake of opening the program with a fantastic archival clip of Jerry Lee in the '50s, letting his hair down on a smoking "Whole Lot of Shakin' Goin' On." In fact, usually the best way to judge the intensity of a Jerry Lee performance is by how messy his hair is at the end. Here, nary a greased-back lock is out of place when he concludes the show. And yet, even though a latter-day concert couldn't hope to compare to that incendiary opening clip, even though the Killer is just going through the motions, this is an enjoyable program. Just remember to keep your expectations lowered. The set balances rockin' boogie-woogie and balladic country pretty evenly, and Jerry Lee's in relaxed, good-humored form, bantering so casually between numbers you eventually realize he's having his own private party up there and doesn't give a damn whether the crowd comes along with him or not. Of course, the reverent British audience goes along anyway. The revelatory stomping on Nat "King" Cole's classic "Mona Lisa" is an early highlight, but Jerry Lee doesn't really hit his classic full-tilt stride until "Little Queenie." Every so often throughout the show, there are moments when the Killer casually starts pumping that turbine-drive eight-to-the-bar rhythmic bedrock along, and those moments are thrilling. And overall, the chance to see a certified rock 'n' roll legend in action should not be passed up.

☐ MEL LEWIS JAZZ ORCHESTRA
JAZZ AT THE SMITHSONIAN
★★★

Sony, 1984, 55 minutes
PRODUCED BY: Clark and Delia Gravelle Santee
DIRECTED BY: Clark and Delia Gravelle Santee
MUSIC FROM: Various Mel Lewis Jazz Orchestra albums.
SELECTIONS: "One Finger Snap," "Dolphin Dance," "Make Me Smile," "Eye of the Hurricane."

Lewis is a fine, sensitive jazz drummer who for many years has led his Jazz Orchestra every Monday night at Manhattan's Village Vanguard jazz club; his lyrical, low-profile, ever-adaptable approach makes an intriguing contrast to the forceful flamboyance and furious flash of that other bandleading drummer, Buddy Rich. While Lewis's orchestra is not one of the best known in modern jazz annals, it has always been highly respected by knowledgeable insiders, and repeated viewings of this program will show why: they're quite good. And it's always intriguingly entertaining, not to mention instructive, to watch the subtle way Lewis guides his mostly-young charges through their charts with his drums more than anything else.

☐ MEL LEWIS JAZZ ORCHESTRA
MEL LEWIS AND HIS BIG BAND

★★★

VIEW, 1986, 38 minutes
PRODUCED BY: Avshalom Katz and Uzi Peled
DIRECTED BY: Dan Birron
MUSIC FROM: Various Mel Lewis Jazz Orchestra albums.
SELECTIONS: "I'm Getting Sentimental Over You," "Ding Dong Din," "I Get a Kick Out of You," "I Want to Be Happy," "Little Pixie."

Mel Lewis and His Big Band, a straightforward five-camera recording of a 1985 Jerusalem concert, is a bit erratic. That's mainly because of the two numbers featuring vocalist Lynn Roberts, who's competent but also, as David Letterman used to say about *Entertainment Tonight*'s Mary Hart, too damn perky—especially on "I Get a Kick *Out of* You" (not "I Get a Kick *Over* You" as the cassette-cover credits have it). The band's arrangements on "Kick" and "I Want to Be Happy" are okay, but nothing spectacular. On the three instrumentals, though, they shine, with Lewis again pushing his solid young charges with understated authority from his drum throne, and locking in beautifully with bassist Dennis Irwin and pianist Phil Markowitz (Lewis's big bands are notable for their guitarless rhythm sections) for some lovely cruise-control propulsion. The standouts are "Ding Dong Din," a dark, moody piece with a sophisticated arrangement, its Gershwinesque neoclassical overtones highlighted by Markowitz's solo; and "Little Pixie," with its fast, boppish tempo and darting, skirling sax-section phrases, arranged and played much in the marvelously crisp manner of Benny Carter's vintage '30s charts for himself and Fletcher Henderson. The five-man sax section excels at both the sectional work and their round-robin solos in this superb show-closer.

☐ LIBERACE
LIBERACE LIVE

★★★★

Vestron, 1985, 56 minutes
PRODUCED BY: Stewart Morris
MUSIC FROM: Various Liberace albums.
SELECTIONS: "Our Love," "Tonight We Love," "Chopsticks," "Blue Danube Waltz," "Spanish Eyes," "Mexican Hat Dance," Medley: "Memory"/"Send in the Clowns"/"New York, New York"/"As Long as He Needs Me"/"Chariots of Fire"/ "Boogie-Woogie"/"You Made Me Love You"/"Beer Barrel Polka," "I'll Be Seeing You."

☐ LIBERACE
LIBERACE IN LAS VEGAS

★★★½

Warner Home Video, 1981, 84 minutes
PRODUCED BY: Philip Bonnell
DIRECTED BY: Thomas V. Grasso
MUSIC FROM: Various Liberace albums.
SELECTIONS: "Our Love," " 'South of the Border' Medley," "Strauss Medley," "Mexican Medley" (with Ballet Folklorico of Mexico), "Mexican Fiesta" (with Ballet Folklorico of Mexico and Lorenzo Escovia)," "The Stripper," "The Old Fashioned Way," "It's Impossible," "As Time Goes By," "Chopsticks," "Send in the Clowns," "Boogie-Woogie," "Polish Polka Medley," "Spanish Eyes," "I'll Be Seeing You," Marco Valenti: "Tribute to Mario Lanza."

Midway through *Liberace Live,* a 1985 concert at London's Wembley Centre with the London Philharmonic Orchestra, Liberace pauses between numbers, smiles that devilish little-boy smile, and quotes Mae West: "Too much of a good thing . . . is just *won*derful!" That just about says it as far as Liberace goes, and if you're a fan, you'll probably love this program. It's directed in a straightforwardly functional manner that's perfect for the singularly ostentatious spectacle that was Liberace. Only occasionally does it descend to typical TV-special production values by fading to black after panning the applauding audience. Actually, though, Liberace's show itself is a bit understated, perhaps out of deference to the LPO: there's this itty bitty, rather tacky little electric candelabra, and the only thing in the way of a stage set is Liberace himself, and his six costume changes (three of them, before the encore, just to parade on and off in different jewel-encrusted, dramatically cowled hoods). Which is enough, and kind of refreshing in a way, come to think of it.

In fact, a large part of what makes this program so good is its intimacy, which makes it perfect for the TV medium. Indeed, it opens with Liberace, alone in his dressing room, introducing the show, seemingly right to the viewer. The camera follows Liberace as he shakes hands with the fans clustered at the lip of the stage during the finale—he sings "I'll Be Seeing You" while pressing the flesh with fans and chuckling, "Gee, I feel like the Pope." However, Liberace is most impressive not in his tinkly, facile piano playing (though there is a nice Spanish tinge to "New York, New York"), nor in his peacock finery, but in his close relationship with his audience. Plainly, they love him, and he loves them. And when he gets all coy and gushes things like, "You know, I enjoyed myself so much tonight that I almost feel guilty about taking the money . . . but I'll take it! Know why? Remember that bank I always laughed all the way to? Well—I bought it!," he really does come across as the most lovable "Mr. Showmanship" in Las Vegas. Liberace asks if there are any requests, and listens attentively to the crowd shouting them out for a full *three minutes* before playing most of them in an extended medley. The crowd sings along spontaneously on "You Made Me Love You," *with no prompting whatsoever.* If this is just a feigned act, well, it works anyway.

Though quite similar to the London show, the 1980 Las Vegas Hilton extravaganza captured (with a serviceable restraint similar to that of the London show) in *Liberace in Las Vegas* is also crucially different. Obviously, it's much more grandiose and less intimate than the London show, and the Liberace completist who gets both programs may find *Las Vegas* enhancing the refreshingly low-key quality of *Liberace Live.* Here, we have a Spanish-tinged spectacular against a dancing-waters backdrop, as Liberace (accompanied by the Jimmy Mullador Orchestra) is joined periodically by the Ballet Folklorico de Nacionale of Mexico, a Mariachi band, and lariat artist Lorenzo Escovia, all of whom are good, colorful tourist-attraction acts. Liberace also introduces singer Marco Valenti, who does a mediocre tribute to Mario Lanza that you may want to fast-forward. Appropriately, the program opens with a proto-*Dynasty* montage of Liberace in one his eye-poppingly lavish homes, toying with all manner of piano-motif items (his pool is ringed with a painted keyboard, and he's even served a piano-shaped cake in the kitchen), before getting into a Rolls-Royce with a license plate reading "88 KEYS." The montage fades as we see the Rolls driving Liberace onstage. At which point an Incredible Camp Moment occurs: Liberace introduces his chauffeur, Scott Thorson—the one who would later claim to be Liberace's ex-lover and try to sue Liberace (unsuccessfully) for palimony.

As in the London show, Liberace gushes those same entrance ("Hey look me over . . .") and exit ("Remember that bank . . .") lines, and the same

Mae West quote, with the same impossibly ingratiating warmth and sincere, self-satisfied delight. Aside from all the Mexicana, by way of Vegas flamboyance he also shows off a black diamond mink cape by strutting and swirling it in time to "The Stripper"; he then sighs and coos, "Oooh, I get so horny when I do that! . . . you too?" as the audience roars. For the finale, he flies on wires over the stage, crying, "Mary Poppins, eat your heart out!" The musical highlight is probably his interpolation of "I Pagliacci" into "Send in the Clowns."

Liberace also manages to overcome the showbiz trappings and build a sense of intimacy with *this* audience, not only through his adorably childlike banter, but also by striding out into the crowd, picking out Harriet from Minneapolis, and bringing her onstage for a few minutes fox-trotting to "The Old Fashioned Way." You can't help but love the guy. Even a skeptical nonfan would have to envy the good time Liberace and his audiences have with each other. And you rock fans who think Liberace was a square old fart should note that in many ways he was the first glitter-rock star—in the sense that he predated figures like Elton John, Boy George, and even Prince, among others.

□ MANCE LIPSCOMB
A WELL-SPENT LIFE
★★★★½

Flower Films, 1981, 44 minutes

PRODUCED BY: Les Blank with Skip Gerson

DIRECTED BY: Les Blank with Skip Gerson

MUSIC FROM: Mance Lipscomb, Texas Songster, Volumes 1–6 (Arhoolie, 1960–74); *Trouble In Mind* (Reprise, 1970).

SELECTIONS: Mance Lipscomb: "Captain, Captain," "Big Boss Man," "You Don't Love Me," "Take Me Back Babe," "Nighttime Is the Right Time," "Sugar Babe," "Rock Me All Night Long," "Keep On Truckin'," "Motherless Children," "St. James Infirmary"; church congregation: "I Shall Not Be Moved," "Old Time Religion."

Discovered during the early-'60s folk boom, Texas "songster" Lipscomb (who died in 1974, three years after Blank shot this portrait/tribute) was more than a bluesman, as a look at the songs in this film indicate: songsters didn't limit their repertoires to the blues, but also performed stomps, reels, shouts, breakdowns, and ballads at picnics, dances, and other social functions.

A link to the days of seminal Texas country blues giant Blind Lemon Jefferson, and a contemporary of that other Texas blues great Lightnin' Hopkins (Lipscomb appears in both of Blank's Hopkins films, *The Blues Accordin' to Lightnin' Hopkins* and *The Sun's Gonna Shine*), Lipscomb was a highly gifted guitar and violin player, who at one point in this film demonstrates the way bottleneck-slide guitar was *first* played—with a knife-edge.

But just as remarkable as the deep wellspring of his music is Lipscomb himself. Prior to his discovery, Lipscomb had spent almost his entire life (he was born in 1895, and spent all his years in Navasota, Texas) sharecropping on farms, surviving in a system not much better than the kind of slavery the Civil War was supposed to abolish. Yet when Blank's camera found Lipscomb, it found a man who those long, hard years had made unutterably sweet instead of bitter. "This world is made for everybody," he muses at one point, with no trace of rancor, "we got to share it. Ain't no lovin', ain't no gettin' along." Then, in one of the film's most charming and memorable moments, we see Lipscomb and his wife—whom he married in 1913—eating dinner at separate tables in other modest kitchen. Mrs. Lipscomb explains that one time, fifty years earlier, she had set the table for Mance and he hadn't come home that night; ever since, she always ate on her own. "Well," Lipscomb dryly comments, "she's the boss." You gotta love a guy like this—and a movie like this, for preserving his person and his music. (Available by mail order from Flower Films.)

☐ **VARIOUS ARTISTS(ANNE CARLISLE, OTHERS)**
LIQUID SKY
★★★

Media, 1983, 114 minutes
PRODUCED BY: Slava Tsukerman
DIRECTED BY: Slava Tsukerman
MUSIC FROM: The film *Liquid Sky* (1983).

David Denby, in *New York* magazine, called *Liquid Sky* "the funniest, craziest, dirtiest, most perversely beautiful science fiction film ever made." Well, it *is* funny, crazy, dirty, perverse, and at times, yes, perversely beautiful—especially when it comes to star Anne Carlisle, who is strikingly effective in both male and female lead roles. Set in Lower Manhattan's artsy/bohemian fringe, *Liquid Sky* is about intergalactic aliens and heroin addicts, and can't (or won't) decide which of the two is more strange (but then, who could, or would?). Despite the obvious debt to William Burroughs that such a premise suggests, *Liquid Sky* is more like what Fellini might make if he took a *lot* of LSD. Producer/director Tsukerman also did the music, and it's the perfect soundtrack for this colorful nightmare-circus: swarming electronic insectine noise that savagely mutates old-world marches and waltzes, it's amazingly reminiscent of the post-modern electro-chamber-rock of the Residents (yes, that's a compliment).

☐ **VARIOUS ARTISTS**
LISZTOMANIA
★

Warner Home Video, 1981, 105 minutes
PRODUCED BY: Roy Baird and David Puttnam
DIRECTED BY: Ken Russell
MUSIC FROM: *Lisztomania* original soundtrack album (A&M, 1975).
SELECTIONS: "You Tear Me Up" and others.

If you think about it, Ken Russell's idea of treating classical giants like Franz Liszt and Richard Wagner as rock stars (complete with groupies, screaming teen audiences, etc.) is rather interesting. Unfortunately, you *can't* think because Russell's usual vulgar excess is so relentless and aggressive in its ham-fisted attempts to be "outrageous." Who lead singer Roger Daltrey appears to be too flummoxed and wide-eyed at the proceedings to really "act"—and what healthy, handsome young rock star wouldn't be, when the film is question seems to have been made with one of *Playboy*'s "Sex in Cinema" issues in mind? Ringo Starr and former Yes keyboard wizard Rick Wakeman have cameo roles; Wakeman provides the flatulent classical-rock score, which brings off neither classical nor rock with any conviction, and which occasions some of Daltrey's worst bellowing ever.

☐ LITTLE RIVER BAND
LIVE EXPOSURE
★★★

HBO/Cannon, 1981, 75 minutes
DIRECTED BY: Derek Burbidge
MUSIC FROM: *Beginnings* (Capitol, 1978); *Sleeper Catcher* (Capitol, 1978); *First under the Wire* (Capitol, 1979); *Backstage Pass* (Capitol, 1980); *Time Exposure* (Capitol, 1981).
SELECTIONS: "It's a Long Way There," "Man on Your Mind," "Mistress of Mine," "Happy Anniversary," "Don't Let

the Needle Win," "Reminiscing," "Ballerina," "Cool Change," "The Night Owls," "Help Is on Its Way," "Lonesome Loser," "It's Not a Wonder," "Just Say That You Love Me."
Also available on Pioneer Stereo Laser videodisc.

Australia's Little River Band, or LRB as they've come to be known, started out as a slick country rock band but went even slicker in the mid-to-late '70s to catch the growing audience for soft-rock pablum. Here, they're caught in concert at the Summit in Houston, Texas, in 1981, before blond surfer-boy singer/guitarist Glenn Shorrock left the band. Live, they rock a bit harder than on record, but this is still some mighty bland stuff. While it's all shot quite nicely, it's for LRB fans only.

□ KENNY LOGGINS
ALIVE
★★★

CBS/Fox, 1981, 60 minutes
PRODUCED BY: Ken Ehrlich
DIRECTED BY: Don Mischer
MUSIC FROM: Various Kenny Loggins albums.
SELECTIONS: "On a Lonely Night," "I Believe in Love," "Love Has Come of Age," "Lucky Lady," "Angry Eyes," "I'm Alright," "House at Pooh Corner," "Danny's Song," "Fall in the Fire," "Celebrate Me Home," "Do It Tonight," "This Is It," "Roll Over Beethoven," "Keep the Fire."
Also available on Pioneer Stereo Laser videodisc.

Loggins, one of these avenging wimps from the L.A. pop-folk singer/songwriter school who's somehow managed to hang in there, is insufferably bland and terminally cute, but he's also exuberant as hell and rarin' to please (which may explain why he's been able to hang in there; that and the "new wave" look he adopted in the early '80s). Here, he's caught in not one but two different outdoor shows, both on the same day (one in the afternoon and one at night) in Santa Barbara, California. So of course the director indulges the rather pointless diversion of cutting right on the beat between daylight and nighttime versions of the same song. On his home turf, Loggins smiles through a set that's sure to please his followers, and leave everyone else cold, as they've been from the beginning.

□ LORDS OF THE NEW CHURCH
LIVE FROM LONDON
★★½

RCA/Columbia, 1984, 60 minutes
PRODUCED BY: Philip Goodhand-Tait
MUSIC FROM: Lords of the New Church (IRS, 1982); *Is Nothing Sacred?* (IRS, 1983); *Method to Our Madness* (IRS, 1984).
SELECTIONS: "New Church," "Eat Your Heart Out," "Livin' on Livin'," "Dance with Me," "Johnny Too Bad," "Russian Roulette," "Bad Timing," "Live for Today," "Open Your Eyes," "Black Girl, White Girl," "Partner in Crime," "Going Down Town," "You Really Got Me," "Li'l Boys Play with Dolls," "Holy War."

If you're a fan of the Lords, you'll probably enjoy this straightforwardly shot 1984 London concert. Otherwise, you're liable to be bored silly or grossed right out. The Lords are a thoroughly mediocre heavy-metal-influenced new-wave band with nothing beyond the usual live-fast/die-young rock 'n' roll bromides. While their membership includes guitarist Brian James, formerly of seminal Brit-punks the Damned—a good musician who's never really risen to the potential shown in his superb 1981 solo single "Ain't That a Shame"—they are dominated by grotesque lead singer Stiv Bators, formerly of the Cleveland-based Dead Boys. Bators is one of the most hideous frontmen in rock history, with an ugly snivel of a voice and the face of a rodent. For fans only.

☐ **VARIOUS ARTISTS (HOWARD ARMSTRONG, OTHERS)**
LOUIE BLUIE
★★★★★

Pacific Arts, 1986, 60 minutes
PRODUCED BY: Terry Zwigoff
DIRECTED BY: Terry Zwigoff
MUSIC FROM: Various albums by Howard "Louie Bluie"; Armstrong, and the folk trio Martin, Bogan and Armstrong; *Louie Bluie* motion picture soundtrack (Zwigoff Superior Pictures, 1985).
SELECTIONS: "State Street Rag," "That Will Never Happen No More," "Cotton Gin," "Listenin' for my Name," unidentified Tyrolean folk song, "My Four Reasons," "Vine Street Rag," "Diamond Dog Blues," "Wrap Your Troubles in Dreams."

In a way, *Louie Bluie* is the ultimate Les Blank documentary: a small, independent film made with loving care, about a fascinating, lovably down-to-earth, culturally significant subject that embodies and illustrates folkloric Americana. But Les Blank didn't make *Louie Bluie.*

What's most remarkable about Terry Zwigoff's 1985 film *Louie Bluie*—aside from the exceedingly gratifying fact that it exists in the first place—is its subject, Howard Armstrong: Tennessee fiddler and mandolinist; longtime leader of southern black string bands, playing a rollicking mélange of blues, folk, bluegrass, jazz, gospel, country, and pop tunes originally sprung from a classically American marriage of African and European roots; member of the trio Martin, Bogan and Armstrong, formed in the '50s and popular during the early- '60s folk boom; accomplished painter, poet, and *raconteur;* and a beautiful human being who is one *hell* of a character, sort of a down-home version of Castaneda's Don Juan Mateus—wily, witty, and wise, with a zest for life that almost makes you jealous of what a cool dude he is. As Armstrong says at the film's opening (right before bragging about his still-potent sexual prowess), "I'm not seventy-five years old—I'm seventy-five years *young.*" That he is, looking amazingly good for his age (he says his secret is "Curiosity—that's what keeps you young"), dashingly handsome, and physically vital enough (he's much more than "spry") to be half the figure he quotes. He exudes a forever-young vibrancy, a rogueish charisma, and a refreshingly irreverent and bawdy humor that ensure that he could never be sentimentalized as a cute cliché. An example, in reference to the irrelevance of institutionalized religion, and Jesus Christ in particlar: "Who in the fuck cares about somebody noddin' his damn head when some guy's gettin' ready to kick his ass? . . . Jesus was too meek and humble." Another, as Armstrong stands disdainfully beneath one of those typical abstract scrap-metal-sculpture monstrosities in a Chicago plaza: "Boy, I'd *hate* to wake up to see *that* in the mornin' . . . I'm a realist, see, if you're gonna paint, paint something real that people can *relate* to—*this* looks like it jumped right outta the twilight zone!" Perhaps the best example of Armstrong's spiritually and philosophically healthy hell-raising is his "whorehouse bible," *The ABC's of Pornography*—a lavishly calligraphed, illustrated, and collaged handmade book Armstrong keeps under lock and key, full of serio-comic and explicitly ribald fables about human sexuality. Here's hoping he lets someone publish it.

Howard Armstrong is the kind of guy you might chance to run into somewhere, sometime, if you were lucky enough; he'd leave you wishing somebody would document his life on film, so others could experience the life-affirming joy that *is* this man's very presence. *Louie Bluie* is exactly that movie, but it's even better—more significant, more enjoyable—because it also does such a great job of documenting the culture Armstrong embodies. The music is as buoyant and delightful as Armstrong himself, and it's presented in a marvelous variety of combinations and settings: Armstrong solo; with a sister-in-law who divorced Armstrong's brother long before, but for whom he still feels a sisterly affection (and whom he reduces to priceless, embarrassed laughter with a childhood anecdote about an off-color church recitation having to do with "woodpeckers"); rehearsing for a Chicago concert (which we also see in part) with such other genuine original musical masters as guitarist Ted Bogan (Armstrong's buddy, whom he describes as "such a ladies man we used to call him 'Mr. Black Gable' "), mandolinist Yank Rachell, banjoist Ikey Robinson, and mandolinist Tom Armstrong (whose possible relationship to Howard Armstrong is something I must have missed, if it is pointed out in the film); and in other footage shot in and around his native milieu of La Follette, Tennessee. Armstrong also reminisces about such long-gone cultural phenomena as medicine shows, and points out the different kinds of music his string bands played for their audiences (blues and country for black fish fries and picnics; pop tunes only for white banquets and outings). *Louie Bluie* does a superb job of fleshing out Armstrong's oral history, illuminating his fascinating contradictory world of black and white, past and present, country and city, familiar and exotic with phenomenal archival photos and, in the cases of early buck-and-wing proto-tap dancers and a jug band, some truly amazing film footage.

There's a whole lot more, but telling it would only spoil the experience of seeing it yourself. You can never get enough of a guy like Howard Armstrong, or of a movie that does such an engaging and rewarding job of portraying such a man and his world.

□ LOVERBOY
LOVERBOY LIVE
★★

Vestron, 1982, 59 minutes
PRODUCED BY: Joe K-Fisher
MUSIC FROM: Loverboy (Columbia, 1980); *Get Lucky* (Columbia, 1981).
SELECTIONS: "Turn Me Loose," "The Kid Is Hot Tonite," "Working for the Weekend," "Only the Lucky Ones," "When It's Over," others.

More hard pop than heavy metal, Loverboy manage to string together some decent riffs every now and then, and at their best ("Working for the Weekend," "Only the Lucky Ones") could even become a guilty pleasure for rock fans who ought to know better. But their all-too-typical corporate-rock rut and breast-beating macho strut don't come close to making this nicely shot but run-of-the-mill document of a 1982 show at the Pacific Coliseum in Canada (their home turf) a must-have for anyone but already converted fans.

□ STEVE LUKATHER
THE STEVE LUKATHER PACKAGE
★★★★

Star Licks, 1984, 35 minutes
PRODUCED BY: Mark Freed and Robert Decker
DIRECTED BY: Mark Freed and Robert Decker
MUSIC FROM: Various albums by Toto and others.
SELECTIONS: "Rosanna," "Carmen," "Hold the Line," "Lovers in the Night," "Mama," "Breakdown Dead Ahead," and fourteen other solos, melodies, and other

licks from various other songs and Steve Lukather solos.

Like all the other cassettes in the Star Licks Master Series, this one presents a top-rank contemporary guitarist showing and telling all about his equipment, techniques, and tricks of the trade in intimate, low-key fashion. All exercises are played through twice, once at normal speed and once again at slower speed, and all licks are notated in an accompanying booklet. Lukather is as nice and generous with the information as the other players in this series. But this guy plays with the highly successful corporate-rock band Toto, as well as in sessions for the likes of Michael Jackson, Lionel Richie, Elton John, Donna Summer, George Benson, Paul McCartney, Hall and Oates, Diana Ross, Michael McDonald, and many others. In short, Lukather's a top-drawer Hollywood hired hand, who's renowned and sought-after enough to have all sorts of exotic high-tech gear and custom-crafted state-of-the-art instruments at his disposal. While he's admirably forthcoming about just how important all that costly gear is to his studio-perfect sound, the fact remains that the beginning guitarist seeking instruction here could easily be intimidated by the mammoth cost of trying to get the Lukather sound.

The only other fault with the tape (and it's a fault that is really a matter of personal perspective and taste) is that it concentrates on soloing to the complete exclusion of anything on comps, fills, rhythm licks, etc. That said, Lukather is forthright and articulate on such techniques as speed-picking, position-shifting, traveling scales, false harmonics, and vibrato-bar phrasing (he's especially good here, as he shows those who just got a new high-tech locking vibrato bridge installed on their guitars what whammy-bar clichés to *avoid*). (Available by mail order from Star Licks.)

□ LORETTA LYNN
LORETTA

★★★

MCA, 1980, 61 minutes
PRODUCED BY: Allan Nadohl
DIRECTED BY: Gene Weed
MUSIC FROM: Various albums.
SELECTIONS: "You're Lookin' at Country," "Out of My Head and Back in Bed," "Pregnant Again," "One's on the Way," "The Pill," "In the Ghetto," "Naked in the Rain," "You Ain't Woman Enough," "Coal Miner's Daughter," "They Don't Make 'Em Like My Daddy," "I Wanna Be Free," "I Saw the Light."

Also available in MCA Stereo Laser videodisc.

Sure, this show was shot in very straightforward fashion at Harrah's Reno—but as the lady herself sings at the top of the show, when you look at her, you're lookin' at country. Miss Loretta's warmth and wit, charm and grace, and sheer talent can't help but come shining through, and should win over even staunch noncountry fans right quick. The selection of hits, of course, leans to the more commercial side, and there is a Vegasy sheen to much of the proceedings. But this program still has Loretta (who also provides a family slide show and a clip from her movie bio *Coal Miner's Daughter*), and that's a lot.

M

☐ PAUL McCARTNEY AND WINGS
ROCKSHOW
★★½

HBO/Cannon, 1981, 102 minutes
PRODUCED BY: MPL Communications
MUSIC FROM: Various albums by the Beatles, Paul McCartney, and Wings, including *Wings Over America* (Capitol, 1977).
SELECTIONS: "Rock Show," "Jet," "Spirits of Ancient Egypt," "Medicine Jar," "Venus and Mars," "Maybe I'm Amazed," "Band on the Run," "Live and Let Die," "Bluebird," "Falling," "Yesterday," "Let Me Roll It," "Magneto and Titanium Man," "Go Now," "Listen to What the Man Said," "Let 'Em In," "Silly Love Songs," "Beware My Love," "Letting Go," "Hi, Hi, Hi."
Also available on Pioneer Stereo Laser videodisc.

In this concert recorded at the Seattle King Dome during Wings' 1976 world tour, McCartney covers just about all of his career and plays most everything anyone could ever want to hear him play. But unless you're a big McCartney fan, you're still liable to get bored, mainly because it's shot in such a pedestrian, unimaginative manner. The visuals are also quite grainy and underlit much of the time. No wonder there's no credit for a director. Still, it *is* McCartney, and there *are* all those great songs—though whether you end up liking the live versions better than their recorded counterparts really depends on how big a McCartney fan you are.

☐ PAUL McCARTNEY
GIVE MY REGARDS TO BROAD STREET
★

CBS/Fox, 1984, 109 minutes
PRODUCED BY: Andros Epaminondas
DIRECTED BY: Peter Webb
SCREENPLAY BY: Paul McCartney
MUSIC FROM: Give My Regards to Broad Street (Columbia, 1984); and various Beatles, Paul McCartney, and Wings albums (thirteen of the sixteen album cuts).
SELECTIONS: "Good Day Sunshine," "Yesterday," "Here, There, and Everywhere," "Wanderlust," "Ballroom Dancing," "Silly Love Songs," "Not Such a Bad Boy," "So Bad," "No Values," "For No One," "Eleanor Rigby/Eleanor's Dream," "Band on the Run," "The Long and Winding Road," "No More Lonely Nights."
Also available on CBS/Fox Stereo Laser videodisc.

One of the biggest box-office bombs of 1984, Paul McCartney's *Give My Regards to Broad Street* reeks of the blandness and lack of imagination that's characterized McCartney's recordings for some time. The alleged plot is really a daydream in the life of a prosperous rock star (McCartney), wherein a trusted employee is believed to have disappeared with the master tapes to his next precious album. Due to some clandestine financial arrangements, the loss of the album could lead to McCartney losing his label to some nasty businessmen. Never one to react, McCartney carries on with his usual schedule—recording with Beatles producer George Martin and Ringo Starr; rehearsals with a band that includes Dave Edmunds, Chris Spedding, Starr, and wife Linda; a live solo radio performance; and rehearsals for a couple of big production numbers (from which we get the silly and overdone "Ballroom Dancing" and "Silly Love Songs"). Then in a dream inside the dream . . . Never mind. Of the several Beatles tunes recast here, only "Yesterday," performed in a comical blues style by a penniless busker McCartney, is noteworthy. Given all the real-life problems McCartney has had with the industry, you'd think he could have produced something that was at least somewhat satirical. The seemingly total lack of any kind of direction makes this movie drag, and just a few minutes into it, you may wish that *this* tape had been lost too.—P.R.

☐ ROB McCONNELL BOSS BRASS
LIVE!
★★½

Sony, 1983, 25 minutes
PRODUCED BY: Wesley Ruggles, Jr., and Gary Reber
DIRECTED BY: William Cosel
MUSIC FROM: Various Boss Brass LPs.
SELECTIONS: "Waltz I Blew for You," "My Man Bill," "Street of Dreams."

Canadian trombonist McConnell's popular big band plays live in 1981 at Howard Rumsey's famed Southern California club, Concerts by the Sea. Yet, while the visuals clearly show that we *are* in a crowded jazz club (with a bandstand as crowded as the seats in the audience are), you can't help but feel you're watching a prime-time private eye series or something—*that's* how brassily bombastic and one-dimensional McConnel's charts are. If you like this kind of stuff (i.e., if you think Stan Kenton was a real musical genius), you'll dig this too.

☐ AL McKAY
THE AL McKAY PACKAGE
★★★★

Star Licks, 1984, 40 minutes
PRODUCED BY: Mark Freed and Robert Decker
DIRECTED BY: Mark Freed and Robert Decker
MUSIC FROM: Various Earth, Wind and Fire albums.
SELECTIONS: "Power," "In the Stone," "I'll Write a Song for You," "Shining Star," "Getaway," plus ten other rhythm patterns, grooves, and other exercises, some taken from parts of other songs.

Another winner in the Star Licks Master Series of instructional home music videos, here with McKay, of the top funk-pop band Earth, Wind and Fire, demonstrating a variety of funk rhythm-guitar techniques. After some show-and-tell on his various guitars, amps, and effects pedals, McKay then carefully shows you how he constructs a series of parts, some from EWF tunes, others just all-purpose exercises that could easily be worked into any number of pre-existing or newly composed arrangements. McKay not only shows how to build a hot rhythm-guitar groove; with the help of Lionel Richie's bassist, King Henry Davis, taped drum patterns, and complete band tracks, he also shows how rhythm guitar parts fit into the complex, polyrhythmic latticework of EWF's typically sophisticated arrangements.

Like all Star Licks Master Series tapes, this one is intimate and low-key, with McKay playing all exercises twice, once at normal speed and again slower, and there's an accompanying booklet that notates each exercise. What sets this apart from most of the rest of the Star Licks tapes, though, is McKay himself: his bluff, down-to-earth, endearingly unpretentious attitude gives him more personality than most of the other players in the series, and combined with his well-rounded approach to instruction, makes this one potentially more appealing to the novice guitarist. (Available by mail order from Star Licks.)

☐ MALCOLM McLAREN
DUCK ROCK
★★★

RCA/Columbia, 1985, 45 minutes
MUSIC FROM: Duck Rock (Island, 1983); *D'ya Like Scratchin'* (Island, 1984).
SELECTIONS: "D'Ya Like Scratchin'," "Soweto," "Punk It Up," "Jive My Baby," "Buffalo Gals," "Obatala," "Song for

Chango," "Zulus on a Time Bomb," "Roly Poly," "Duck for the Oyster," "Hobo Scratch," "Legba," "Merengue," "Double Dutch."

Following his masterminding of the Sex Pistols and Bow Wow Wow in the late '70s and early '80s, British culture-huckster McLaren hatched a new scheme—an idiosyncratic vision of postmodern global pop, mingling elements as diverse as African, Caribbean, and Latin American pop and folk musics, South Bronx rapping and turntable-scratching, square-dance music. He combined the latter two for the delightful hit single "Buffalo Gals." Then he went globe-trotting to Kwazuland, Botswanaland, and Swaziland in Africa, as well as Cuba, Brazil, the Peruvian Andes, and the Appalachian Mountains of America, and, after treating much of what he recorded there with rap-and-scratch effects by the South Bronx's "World's Famous Supreme Team," as well as between-cuts radio-DJ phone-in patter by World's Famous, he came up with the *Duck Rock* album. It's an exercise in culture-plundering that offset its disquieting-to-disgusting imperialist implications (the locals get scant, if any, credit) with McLaren's usual good taste in what music to plunder. The irrepressible bounce of such Afro-pop juju/highlife-styled numbers as "Jive My Baby," "Double Dutch," and "Zulus on a Time Bomb" is especially hard to resist. The panculturalism of the music is accompanied by lively low-budget videos with the look and feel of on-the-fly field recordings—the camera jostling among dancing Zulus or South Bronx girls masterfully performing "double-dutch" jump rope that end up appearing as clumsy and chopped-up as they are surreally free-associative. McLaren himself, a diminutive guy wearing one or more ridiculously large hats (as the cover photo on the cassette sleeve shows, he sometimes stacks one atop another), tends to just interfere with the hand-held documentary footage, which is poetic justice in a way. But heck, ultimately it *is* his program. And the "guerrilla" feel to the field footage is almost a refreshing break from MTV overload, especially with its far-flung subject matter. The "Buffalo Gals" video clip, however, shows how it should be done—with just-slick-enough-for-MTV production values (the clip did in fact play on MTV for a while, long enough to start its own mini-fashion trend with the "Buffalo Gal" look of oversized, loosely layered "poor boy" clothes featuring enormous window-pane check patterns), and editing as rhythmic as the music and the mutant square dance in which the Buffalo Boys and Gals engage. It is perhaps telling that Joe Butt, who did such a nice job directing "Buffalo Gals," is credited nowhere on *Duck Rock*'s sleeve. On the other hand, it's merely appropriate that whoever shot the globe-trotting documentary footage isn't credited, either.

☐ **VARIOUS ARTISTS (ROGER DALTREY, ADAM FAITH, OTHERS)**
McVICAR
★★½

Vestron, 1984, 90 minutes
PRODUCED BY: Roy Baird, Bill Curbishley, and Roger Daltrey
DIRECTED BY: Tom Clegg
MUSIC FROM: McVicar original motion picture soundtrack (Polydor, 1980); *McVicar* (The Who Films, 1980).
SELECTIONS: "Free Me," "Just a Dream Away," "White City Lights," "Waiting for a Friend," "Without Your Love," "McVicar."

Effective jailbreak drama based on real-life story of famed British recidivist John McVicar, with strong performances all around, especially from Daltrey as the title character and onetime U.K. teen idol Adam Faith as his prison buddy. Only problem is it fails to provide any real insight into McVicar's tenacious rebelliousness, a frustration compounded by a closing title that tells us he went on to become a successful member of society. The Who, augmented by an orchestra, perform most of the score, with a so-so assortment of tunes written mainly by Russ Ballard, formerly of Argent.

□ CHRISTINE McVIE
THE VIDEO ALBUM
★★★

Vestron, 1984, 60 minutes
PRODUCED BY: Kate and Derek Burbidge
DIRECTED BY: Kate and Derek Burbidge, Alan Arkush
MUSIC FROM: Songbird (Warner Bros., 1984), and various albums by Christine McVie and Fleetwood Mac.
SELECTIONS: "Love Will Show Us How," "Keeping Secrets," "The Challenge," "Who's Dreaming this Dream?," "I'm the One," "So Excited," "Got a Hold on Me," "One in a Million," "You Make Loving Fun," "Don't Stop," "World Turning," "Songbird."

As a member of Fleetwood Mac since 1970, and as a sometime solo artist, Christine Perfect McVie has gained a sterling reputation with critics for her ability to write beautifully crafted, stylish, and mature pop-rock songs—a reputation that's deserved because it passes the ultimate acid test of mass popularity. Here, she's shot straightforwardly on her 1984 solo tour to promote the *Songbird* album, leading a band that includes rockabilly hopeful Billy Burnette (who had co-written a few tunes with Christine) on rhythm guitar and vocals, Muscle Shoals session vet George Hawkins on bass, and former Average White Band drummer (who joined Duran Duran in 1986) Steve Ferrone.

Talented McVie may be, but unless you're a rabid fan of hers, you may find her stage presence rather underwhelmingly sedate. That combined with her very adult music's lack of flash and the less-than-inspired direction make for something less than the world's most exciting rock concert. The crowd finally gets really excited when Mick Fleetwood sits in on drums for three Fleetwood Mac hits late in the set: "You Make Loving Fun," "Don't Stop," and "World Turning." The program opens with a concept video for "Love Will Show Us How," directed by Alan Arkush, the Roger Corman grad who also shot the rock comedy movie *Get Crazy.* "Love Will Show Us How" is a satire of the making of a big-budget rock video, with cult filmmaker Paul Bartel (*Eating Raoul*) guest-starring as the officious oaf of a video *auteur* who subjects McVie to all manner of production absurdities. Like *Get Crazy,* it's not the wittiest comedy ever created, but it has a basic good-naturedness to its slapstick that's quite winning. Midway through the program, we cut from the concert to a performance video for "Got a Hold on Me," which is shot in moodily lit black-and-white turning to color for the middle verse, then back to black-and-white. For McVie fans, or those in a general soft-rock mood, this just might be the ticket.

□ MADONNA
MADONNA
★★★

Warner Music Video, 1984, 17 minutes
PRODUCED BY: Various
DIRECTED BY: Various
MUSIC FROM: Madonna (Sire, 1983); *Like a Virgin* (Warner Bros., 1984).
SELECTIONS: "Burning Up," "Borderline," "Lucky Star," "Like a Virgin."

☐ MADONNA
THE VIRGIN TOUR LIVE
★★★

Warner Music Video, 1985, 50 minutes
PRODUCED BY: Simon Fields
DIRECTED BY: Danny Kleinman
MUSIC FROM: Like a Virgin (Warner Bros., 1984); the films *Vision Quest* (1985) and *Desperately Seeking Susan* (1985).
SELECTIONS: "Dress You Up," "Holiday," "Into the Groove," "Everybody," "Gambler," "Lucky Star," "Crazy for You," "Over and Over," "Like a Virgin," "Material Girl."

Say what you will about Madonna's discomfitingly unscrupulous, calculatedly sleazy persona, but the camera sure loves her as much as any Madonna-wanna-be. Yet paradoxically, the clips compilation *Madonna* is disappointing because it fails to include her one really good promo clip—Mary Lambert's farrago of ambiguous deceit, "Material Girl"—and the ones that are included here are pretty lame. Steve Barron's "Burning Up" sports luscious superannuated color cinematography by King Baggot (what a name!), but the sight of Madonna wriggling like a speared fish all over some L.A. street is queasily ridiculous. Lambert's "Borderline" is a muddled attempt at a vaguely feminist motif, with Madonna ticking off her macho boyfriend by landing a modeling job (yeah, I guess there's a bit of art-imitates-life *frisson* there, too). Arthur Pierson's "Lucky Star" finds Madonna and two other people, er, "dancing" on a barren studio set, and features what may be the most revoltingly calculated-to-appear-uncalculated wink at the camera of all time. Lambert's "Like a Virgin," with the zaftig bottle-blonde siren writhing in Venetian gondolas (come on, admit it—don't you keep wishing she'd bang her head into one of those bridges that keep passing overhead?) and chasing a guy in a lion mask, is so idiotic it borders on camp. With the exception of the pedestrian "Burning Up," the music at least is state-of-the-art '80s techno-funk-rock-pop—for which Madonna's songwriters and producers are at least as much to thank as she herself.

Virgin Tour Live captures America's favorite navel reserve at the triumphant Detroit homecoming stop on her 1985 U.S. tour. Again, the Reaganite siren's music percolates along, and she expends a considerable amount of energy onstage—while her two male dancers expend an *overbearing* amount of energy, their nonstop Vegas aerobics quickly veering into self-parody. Unfortunately, the stage show itself suffers from a major case of slick, shallow, mechanical Vegasitis—many observers accused Madonna of using backing tapes for the shows, and there are moments when she seems to be out of breath from dancing and/or pretty far off-mike, yet we can hear her voice loud and clear, *just like on record*—and though the camera does like her, Madonna displays virtually zero personality. Still, the hordes of screaming Madonna-wanna-be's lap it up, and if you're a fan, you might too. Director Danny Kleinman usually goes special-effects crazy when he makes video clips (like Thomas Dolby's "Hyperactive!" or Pat Benatar's "Sex as a Weapon"), but here his touch is commendably restrained and fluid. Every now and then his camera catches the ice-cold, gold-digging glint in Madonna's eyes as she aerobicizes through her paces.

☐ MAGNUM
LIVE!
★½

Embassy, 1986, 60 minutes
PRODUCED BY: Philip Goodhand-Tait
DIRECTED BY: Peter Orton

MUSIC FROM: Various Magnum albums.

SELECTIONS: "How Far Jerusalem," "Before First Light," "Story Teller's Night," "All England Eyes," "Les Mort Dansant," "Just Like an Arrow," "Lights Burned Out," "Endless Love," "Two Hearts," "Soldier of the Line," "Kingdom of Madness," "The Sacred Hour."

Magnum is a British heavy metal band that, as of this writing, is obscure in the U.S. Deservedly obscure. Magnum is a stupefyingly nondescript, pathetically bombastic example of a genre that at its worst is given to unforgivably stupefying, pathetic bombast anyway. Oh well, in a way it makes sense: Embassy, which released this upon an unsuspecting public, also released *This Is Spinal Tap.* Would that this show, shot in competent fashion at the Camden Palace in London in 1985, were meant as a joke as well. However, if you're an insatiable metalhead, you may want to check this out. Then again, if you're *that* insatiable a metalhead, I'd love to know what you're doing reading a *book.*

□ MIKE MAINIERI
THE JAZZ LIFE

★★★

Sony, 1982, 60 minutes
PRODUCED BY: Ben Sidran
DIRECTED BY: Parker Y. Bird
MUSIC FROM: 1982 concert at Seventh Avenue South club, NYC.

SELECTIONS: "Crossed Wires," "Flying Colors," "Sara's Touch," "Bamboo," "Song for Seth," "Bullet Train," "T-Bag."

Fusion-jazz vibist Mainieri, who's also produced albums for pop singer Carly Simon, is joined here by such top-rank fellow fusionists as Weather Report drummer Omar Hakim (more recently with Sting), pianist Warren Bernhardt (a member with Mainieri of Steps Ahead), reedman Bob Mintzer (who excels on electrified bass clarinet and sax), and the redoubtable bassist Eddie Gomez. Despite the synthlike sonorities of Mintzer's amplified horns and Hakim's clean-machine polyrhythms, Mainieri's music is closer to hearty, traditional acoustic bebop than trendily superficial electric fusion; in other words, it's pretty satisfying, tasteful stuff. The handsome, confident, effortless Hakim especially is a pleasure to watch as he digs into this demanding music. The camerawork on the whole band is given to too many odd angles, but it does get right up close.

□ MELISSA MANCHESTER
THE MUSIC OF MELISSA MANCHESTER

★★★

Warner Home Video, 1982, 60 minutes
PRODUCED BY: Michael Lippman
DIRECTED BY: Marty Callner
MUSIC FROM: Various albums by Melissa Manchester, including *Greatest Hits* (Arista, 1982).

SELECTIONS: "Help Is On the Way," "Midnight Blue," "O, Heaven (How You've Changed to Me)," "Whenever I Call You Friend," "Working Girl (for the)," "As Time Goes By," "It's All in the Sky Above," "Home to Myself," "This Lady's Not Home," "Peace in My Heart," "Good News," "We've Got Time," "Easy," "Talkin' to Myself," "Don't Cry Out Loud," "Boy Next Door," "Come in from the Rain."

Also available on Pioneer Stereo Laser videodisc.

After being discovered by Bette Midler and her then-arranger Barry Manilow, Melissa Manchester went on to gradually build a career as an MOR superstar singer-songwriter, with adult-contemporary classics like "Midnight Blue" (which, like many of the songs here, she co-wrote with Carole Bayer Sager; "Whenever I Call You Friend" was co-written with Kenny Loggins). Here, in an unidentified hall, Manchester sings at her piano before a large audience, accompanied by an orchestra. Unless you're a fan of hers, you won't find her an especially scintillating performer—though anyone would have to agree that she does have a refreshing, down-to-earth stage manner, sort of a normalized, milder-mannered cross between Midler and Streisand. Marty Callner's direction is competent but uninspired—or, depending on your perspective, tastefully restrained. Either way, this program is pretty much for Manchester fans only; but for them; it's a nicely done overview of the lady's work.

□ HENRY MANCINI (WITH ROBERT GOULET AND VIKKI CARR)
HENRY MANCINI AND FRIENDS

★★★

Sony, 1986, 49 minutes
PRODUCED BY: Nicholas Wry
DIRECTED BY: John Blanchard
MUSIC FROM: Various albums by Henry Mancini, Robert Goulet, and Vikki Carr; Canadian TV special (Allarcom Prod., 1980).
SELECTIONS: Henry Mancini and Orchestra: "Moon River," "Theme from *Charlie's Angels,*" "Inspector Clouseau Theme," "It's Easy to Say," "Bier Fest Polka," "Speedy Gonzales," "Moonlight Sonata Op. 27 No. 2 'Moonlight,' " "*Roots* Theme," "Oluwa (Many Rains Ago)," Vikki Carr with Mancini and Orchestra: "The Best Is Yet to Come," "A Song for You," "Granada"; Robert Goulet with Mancini and Orchestra: "Around the World," "Soliloquy."

The idea of Mancini conducting a big orchestra in a large hall (Jubilee Auditorium in Edmonton, Canada) before a large audience and doing "Theme from *Charlie's Angels*" is, depending on your taste, either ridiculous or—if you've got a highly developed sense of camp—ridiculously cool. Let's be as kind as possible and just say that Mancini's music is "light"—he's obviously accomplished at it, but nevertheless this stuff is so light it could almost blow away and often so cloying you wish it would. Mancini himself is a stiff presence, Vikki Carr is not to my taste, and Robert Goulet is someone I cannot take seriously as a singer. Still, it's all shot nicely enough, and if you happen to be a fan of this sort of thing you'll probably enjoy this.

□ MANHATTAN TRANSFER
VOCALESE

★★★

Atlantic, 1985, 28 minutes
PRODUCED BY: Martin Fischer
DIRECTED BY: Bud Schaetzle
MUSIC FROM: *Vocalese* (Atlantic, 1985).
SELECTIONS: "That's Killer Joe," "Blee Blop Blues," "Another Night in Tunisia," "To You," "Ray's Rockhouse."

Fans of the Grammy-winning jazz-pop vocal group should be delighted with their first home video, a very nicely produced collection of performance and concept videos from their *Vocalese* album. The concepts include a very cosmopolitan late-night big-city street-scene for the opening "That's Killer Joe," and an ingenuous tribute to *I Love Lucy* for "Blee Blop Blues." But whether in conceptual or performance videos, director Bud Schaetzle not only keeps the production values up there, but also matches Manhattan Transfer's sound and image with a tasteful "uptown" attitude, manifested in the lighting, camerawork, sets, costumes, and so on.

□ BARRY MANILOW
THE FIRST BARRY MANILOW SPECIAL

★★½

MGM/UA, 1977, 52 minutes
DIRECTED BY: Steve Binder
MUSIC FROM: 1977 ABC TV special; various Barry Manilow albums.

SELECTIONS: "It's a Miracle," "This One's for You," "Could It Be Magic," "Mandy," "Jump Shout Boogie," "Avenue C," "Jumpin' at the Woodside," "Cloudburst," "Bandstand Boogie," "New York City Rhythm," "Sandra," "Early Morning Strangers," "I Write the Songs."

Also available on MGM/UA Stereo Laser videodisc.

□ BARRY MANILOW
THE MAKING OF 2:00 AM PARADISE CAFE
★★½

RCA/Columbia, 1985, 55 minutes

PRODUCED BY: Les Joyce

DIRECTED BY: Don Clark

MUSIC FROM: 2:00 AM Paradise Cafe (Arista, 1984).

SELECTIONS: "Paradise Cafe," "When Love Is Gone," "What Am I Doing Here," "Blue," "When October Goes," "Say No More," "Big City Blues," "Night Song."

The First . . . is Mr. Shlock's Emmy-winning 1977 ABC TV special, with tasteful-as-usual (well, tasteful as can be expected, in this case) production from Steve Binder, who also shot such commendable TV-rock spectaculars as *The T.A.M.I. Show* and Elvis Presley's 1968 "Singer Presents" comeback special. Alan Thicke was one of the writers for the special, which shifts from the first few opening tunes to a soundstage salute to '40s big-band items (from "Jump Shout Boogie" through Barry's lyrics-added version of the *American Bandstand* theme "Bandstand Boogie"), with special guest Penny Marshall and Barry's girl-singer backup trio Lady Flash. Before another big-production medley-salute, this time to life in The Big City, Barry provides what may be the most intriguing section for his non-fans: a medley of commercial jingles he wrote for Kentucky Fried Chicken, McDonald's, State Farm Insurance, Stridex Medicated Pads, and Dr Pepper. In the ironic climax, Barry sings his "trademark" tune, "I Write the Songs"—which Bruce Johnston of the Beach Boys wrote.

In *The Making of . . .* , Barry is appropriately blown away that such jazz greats as baritone saxophonist Gerry Mulligan, guitarist Mundell Lowe, bassist George Duvivier, drummer Shelly Manne, and vocalists Sarah Vaughan (guesting on "Blue") and Mel Torme (on "Big City Blues") would somehow consent to appear on his "first jazz-inspired album." This documentary of its making is Barry's tribute to that tribute. While the music may indeed still be shlock, at least it's the best-sounding shlock he's ever performed. But his gushing narration is unbelievably obnoxious, and watching him alternate between eyelid-batting coyness and unconvincing displays of in-studio "intensity" is a truly sickening experience.

□ BOB MARLEY AND THE WAILERS
LIVE AT SANTA BARBARA COUNTY BOWL
★★★

HBO/Cannon, Pioneer Artists, 1981, 60 minutes

PRODUCED BY: Bill Phelps

DIRECTED BY: Don Gazzaniga

MUSIC FROM: Various albums by Bob Marley and the Wailers (Island, 1973–80).

SELECTIONS: "I Shot the Sheriff," "Jamming," "Exodus," "Stand Up For Your Rights," "Ambush in the Night," "Crazy Baldhead," "Stir It Up."

Also available on Pioneer Stereo Laser videodisc.

Marley was a legendary performer, but unfortunately *Live at Santa Barbara County Bowl* won't really show you why. It's directed nicely enough, has excellent picture and sound quality throughout, and catches the late, lamented Dylan *and* Beatles of reggae leading his finely tuned band through a solid set of good-to-classic reggae outdoors on a sunny California day. But, sadly, it happened to be shot not long before Marley's death from cancer in 1981. And looking at it as we must after his death, it's almost impossible not to think that Marley *looks* like he's near death: it's not that he appears physically ravaged, but rather that he's remarkably listless. Especially compared to his supercharged performance in *Heartland Reggae,* in which he more than embodies all those hyperbolic hosannas critics always used to ladle on about his onstage charisma. That, and not this, is what skeptics, and those believers lucky enough to have seen vintage Marley live in person, should check out first. That said, it should be emphasized that while *Live at Santa Barbara County Bowl* is *not* prime-period Marley, it *is* still a good program. You could always do worse than even middling Marley.

☐ BOB MARLEY AND THE WAILERS
LEGEND: THE BEST OF BOB MARLEY AND THE WAILERS
★★★

RCA/Columbia, 1985, 55 minutes
PRODUCED BY: Torquil Dearden and Don Letts
DIRECTED BY: Torquil Dearden and Don Letts, various others
MUSIC FROM: Various Bob Marley and the Wailers albums, including *Legend* (Island, 1984).
SELECTIONS: "Want More," "Is This Love," "Jammin'," "Could You Be Loved," "No Woman No Cry," "Stir It Up," "Get Up Stand Up," "Satisfy My Soul," "I Shot the Sheriff," "Buffalo Soldier," "Exodus," "Redemption Song," "One Love"/"People Get Ready."

Modestly produced but effective compilation of various Wailers footage—concert footage (from Keith MacMillan's 1978 documentary film of a London show), promotional videos early (the vintage "Stir It Up" finds Marley and band looking *very* young) and late ("Buffalo Soldier" was made *after* Marley's tragic death), and not too illuminating but at least comprehensible bits of Marley interview footage between songs. "One Love" (with cameos by Paul McCartney and Madness among others) and "Is This Love" are both intriguingly ambitious and charming early concept videos. Decent as this is for the Marley fan, if it's the definitive Marley video portrait then it's only by default.

☐ BOB MARLEY AND THE WAILERS
LIVE AT THE RAINBOW
★★★★½

RCA/Columbia, 1986, 40 minutes
PRODUCED BY: Scott Millaney
DIRECTED BY: Keith "Keef" MacMillan
MUSIC FROM: Various albums by Bob Marley and the Wailers (Island, 1973–77).
SELECTIONS: "Trenchtown Rock," "Them Belly Full (But We Hungry)," "I Shot the Sheriff," "Rebel Music (3 O'Clock Roadblock)," "Lively Up Yourself," "Crazy Baldhead," "War," "No More Trouble," "The Heathen," "No Woman, No Cry," "Jamming," "Get Up, Stand Up," "Exodus."

Live at the Rainbow has to be *the* best single program for the Marley fan, either casual or hard-core. Shot in 1977 at the famed London venue, it catches Marley and his band at or very near the very peak of their powers and is infinitely more urgent and gripping than the later *Live at Santa Barbara County Bowl.* Marley isn't *quite* as galvanically possessed as he is in *Heartland Reggae,* but he's close enough to that pinnacle of intensity here that *Rainbow* more than makes up for the fact that *Heartland Reggae,* for the Marley purist, contains so many other attractions or distractions. A solid edition of the Wailers is on display here, featuring lead guitarist Junior Marvin, and they do a beautiful job playing a top-notch selection of songs from Marley's awesome repertoire. Veteran rock video director Keef does an ace job of catching it all. In such a uniformly superb show, it's hard to pick highlights, but if forced, I'd go for "Crazy Baldhead" and the comparatively obscure "The Heathen." Yes, this *has* to be *the* Marley program to get first—though if you're turned on by this, you should then spring for *Heartland Reggae* as well.

□ DAVE MASON
IN CONCERT
★★★

Monterey/IVE, 1981, 60 minutes
PRODUCED BY: Neal Marshall
DIRECTED BY: Dave Levisohn
MUSIC FROM: Various Dave Mason albums.
SELECTIONS: "Just a Song," "Stand by Me," "Shining Deep As You," "Dust My Blues," "We Just Disagree," "Let It Go," "Feelin' Alright," "All Shook Up," "Maybe," "Every Woman," "The Words," "Bring It On Home," "All Along the Watchtower," "Take It to the Limit."
Also available on Pioneer Stereo Laser videodisc.

In this 1981 concert at Perkins Palace in Pasadena, California, Mason does a pleasantly competent and seemingly sincere job of running through the wimpiest soft-rock wet noodles from his post–Traffic solo career, as well as a wide variety of covers (some of them, like "Dust My Blues," are very ill-advised undertakings on his part). The whole show is acoustic, Mason accompanied only by another acoustic guitarist (and a violinist on "Sad and Deep As You"), and with only Mason's greatest, hardest-hitting composition ever, "Feelin' Alright," to stand up to such greeting-card sucrose as "Every Woman" and "We Just Disagree" . . . well, you've *got* to be a real fan of this sort of romantic twaddle to be able to sit through it. If you *are* a fan, though, you'll probably enjoy this; it's shot decently enough, and you'll probably find yourself thinking after a while that, with his crafty mush-headedness, Mason is a father of California popsters like, say, Kenny Loggins or even Jackson Browne. And with his full beard and Hawaiian shirt, he looks the part, too.

□ YUMI MATSUTOYA
TRAIN OF THOUGHT
★★★★

Sony, 1986, 58 minutes
PRODUCED BY: Aubrey Powell
DIRECTED BY: Storm Thorgeson
MUSIC FROM: Train of Thought (Toshiba-EMI, 1984).
SELECTIONS: "Pessimist," "Time Passing," "Heartbreak," "Hotel Without Time," "Dang Dang," "Like a Swallow," "Destiny," "Mysterious Experience."

Train of Thought may be the single strangest program in this whole book, which is one of the reasons it gets four stars. Yumi Matsutoya is a singer/actress who's apparently very popular in her native Japan, where this program was number 2 on the home-video charts in the summer of 1986 when it was released here. This is a highly produced compilation of concept and performance clips, placing each music video within a sophisticated, ambiguously open-ended mini-movie scenario that starts with Matsutoya boarding a train—yes, the train of thought—and leads to all manner of fantasy sequences to cue the music videos. *Train of Thought* was directed by Storm Thorgeson, the onetime chief of Hipgnosis, the album cover art firm that dominated the biz in the '70s, and whose music videos include Yes's "Owner of a Lonely

Heart." That gives you some idea of what kind of highly produced mini-movie stuff we're talking about here.

But what makes *Train of Thought* such a kick is the East-meets-West culture clash that results when a Japanese pop star is given the full feature-program music-video mini-movie treatment by a hot-shot MTV-style director. Most of the way through, the program is simply surreal, but in a disarmingly carefree, "so what?" sort of way. If you can handle Matsutoya's feather-light pop songs, almost all sung in Japanese, you might find yourself getting seduced in an off-the-wall way by this program.

The best thing of all about *Train of Thought* is the English translations of Matsutoya's lyrics ("poetically descriptive . . . filled with psychological insight," say the liner notes). Check this out: "I couldn't help wanting to see you/In spite of the pouring rain/I'm near your apartment/Your voice sounded so cool on the phone/And I know that your love is distant/So please tell me/You were happy with me, weren't you?/Only with you I had a fiery passion, I'm right?/Can we still be friends?/You're joking, that only happens in books!/I just wanted to see/How you could break our love to pieces . . ." This, sung cheerfully as she ambles down a rain-spattered city street while sexy, scantily clad female dancers writhe in the background. Like, wow!

I've got it—*Train of Thought* is the gaudily zany, casually surreal Scopitone filmlet of the '50s/'60s reborn. Cool!

□ BRIAN MAY
STAR LICKS MASTER SERIES
★★★★

Star Licks, 1984, 45 minutes
PRODUCED BY: Mark Freed and Robert Decker
DIRECTED BY: Mark Freed and Robert Decker
MUSIC FROM: Various Queen albums (Elektra, 1973–82); Brian May and Friends: *Star Fleet Project* (Capitol, 1983).
SELECTIONS: "Brighton Rock," "Bohemian Rhapsody," "Tie Your Mother Down," "Crazy Little Thing Called Love," "Dragon Attack," "Father to Son," "March of the Black Queen," "Somebody to Love," "Dead on Time," "Put Out the Fire," "Hard Life," "Star Fleet," "Keep Yourself Alive," "Love of My Life."

An instructional video, and then some, as Queen's guitarist—one of the most accomplished, respected, and distinctive in all of rock—takes you painstakingly through his highly personal equipment set-up, style, and technique, playing passages from a wide variety of Queen songs twice, first at regular (usually supersonically fast) and then slower (as in normal) speeds. Finally, Brian shows you his famous technique for simultaneous three-part guitar harmonies in a solo situation. Throughout, May seems just a bit uncomfortable on camera, yet at the same time a sweet, rather retiring type (you wouldn't expect him to be picking out those flaming licks on an arena stage next to Freddie Mercury!) who does his darnedest to give you as much of his experience and insight as he can. Even nonguitarists and non–Queen/May fans may find themselves fascinated. (Available by mail order from Star Licks.)

□ JOHN MAYALL, VARIOUS OTHERS
BLUES ALIVE
★★½

RCA/Columbia, 1984, 92 minutes
PRODUCED BY: Jonathan Stathakis, Pat Weatherford
DIRECTED BY: Len Dell'Amico
MUSIC FROM: Various albums by various artists.
SELECTIONS: John Mayall and the Bluesbreakers: "Hard Times Again," "My time after Awhile," "Dark Side of

Midnight"; Etta James with the Bluesbreakers: "Let It Roll," "You Got Me (Where You Want Me)," "Baby What Ya Want Me to Do"; Buddy Guy and Junior Wells: "Messin' with the Kid," "Don't Start Me Talkin' "; Sippie Wallace: "Shorty George Blues"; Albert King with the Bluesbreakers: "Born under a Bad Sign," "Stormy Monday"; Mayall, Bluesbreakers, et al.: "C.C. Rider Jam," "Room to Move."

Throughout the '60s, John Mayall was the patron saint of the British blues boom, giving such stars as Eric Clapton, Jack Bruce, onetime Rolling Stones guitarist Mick Taylor, and Fleetwood Mac's namesake rhythm section of bassist John McVie and drummer Mick Fleetwood their first big breaks. Some twenty years later, Mayall toured the United States in 1982 with a reunited edition of his Bluesbreakers band, here featuring McVie, Taylor, and drummer Colin Allen (who had played with Mayall and Dutch progressive rock band Focus). The concert captured here, from the Capitol Theater in Passaic, New Jersey, features such notable guest stars as veteran R&B belter Etta James, stalwart Chicago bluesmen Buddy Guy (guitar) and Junior Wells (vocals, harmonica), blues legend Sippie Wallace, and the great blues guitarist Albert King. But despite all the accomplished talent onstage, this program is erratic and disappointing enough that it should perhaps be retitled *Blues Embalmed.*

The problems rest squarely on the shoulders of Mayall and the Bluesbreakers, who appear shockingly listless, lethargic, lackadaisical, lame . . . any other term for "uninspired" will do just as well. Taylor, whose solos with the Stones were always so tasteful, is a major letdown; either he was sick this night, or his mind was elsewhere for some reason, or *something*—but it just wasn't happening for him. McVie and Allen make a leaden rhythm section, and Mayall himself—never known to have musical talent commensurate with his talent-scouting abilities—can't help very much. So it's up to the guest stars to transcend their surroundings, by providing even more spirited dignity than one might reasonably expect. This James, Wallace, and King manage to do (King blows Taylor off the stage effortlessly), but not Guy and Wells.

□ MAZE FEATURING FRANKIE BEVERLY

HAPPY FEELIN'S

★★★

Sony, 1984, 20 minutes

PRODUCED BY: Picture Music International

DIRECTED BY: Michael Collins and Philip Olesman

MUSIC FROM: We Are One (Capitol, 1984).

SELECTIONS: "We Are One," "Never Let You Down," "Southern Girl," "Happy Feelin's."

As Maze's producer, arranger, composer, and lead vocalist, Frankie Beverly is the driving force behind the band's uniquely tasteful and danceable blend of mellow funk and laid-back jazz. And while there's nothing visually exceptional in this collection of clips, there's nothing grossly stupid or offensive, either, and they all do a good enough job of capturing Beverly and Maze in action that both fans and the curious should find it a satisfying little item. In "We Are One," the universality of the lyrics is rather patly illustrated with cuts between the band performing in a studio and shots of diverse types of people on the streets of L.A. "Never Let You Down" is a *Casablanca*-inspired performance set-piece, the band crooning in tuxes while an elegant couple mime and dance in literal counterpoint to the romantic lyrics. "Southern Girl," the most upbeat tune here, and "Happy Feelin's" are both straightforward concert clips, shot before an enthusiastic audience.

☐ MEAT LOAF
LIVE AT WEMBLEY
★★

JEM/Passport, 1985, 60 minutes
PRODUCED BY: Ian Trotter
DIRECTED BY: Mike Mansfield
MUSIC FROM: Bat Out of Hell (Cleveland International, 1977); *Dead Ringer* (Cleveland International, 1981); *Midnight at the Lost and Found* (Cleveland International, 1983).
SELECTIONS: "Bat Out of Hell," "You Took the Words Right Out of My Mouth," "Deadringer for Love," "All Revved Up with No Place to Go," "Promised Land," "I'm Gonna Love Her for the Both of Us," "Two Out of Three Ain't Bad," "All Revved Up (Reprise)."

Offstage, say when he's an MTV guest VJ or something, Meat Loaf seems like a genuinely nice guy. But put him onstage with those hideously overdone Springsteen burlesques of producer Jim Steinman's, and he's just a pathetic pile of blubber and bluster; "All Revved Up with No Place to Go," indeed. For his fans, this serviceably shot London '84 show will do; the rest of us can at least take solace in the fact that this tape thankfully does *not* include Meat's notorious sexual opus "Paradise by the Dashboard Light," the gross-out duet which both Ellen Foley and Karla DeVito once took as a low road to later, greater success.

☐ MEAT LOAF
BAD ATTITUDE LIVE!
★★½

Vestron, 1986, 55 minutes
PRODUCED BY: Michael Appleton
DIRECTED BY: Tom Corcoran
MUSIC FROM: Bad Attitude (Cleveland Int'l, 1985); *Midnight at the Lost and Found* (Cleveland Int'l, 1983); *Dead Ringer* (Cleveland Int'l, 1981); *Bat out of Hell* (Cleveland Int'l, 1977).
SELECTIONS: "Bad Attitude," "Dead Ringer for Love," "Paradise by the Dashboard Light," "Piece of the Action," "All Revved Up with No Place to Go," "Modern Girl," "Bat out of Hell."

Bad Attitude Live!, adequately shot (though the lighting is quite erratic) in London (again—at least he still has a career *somewhere*) in 1985, is more of the same, with the gum-snapping Meat Loaf before a huge motorcycle stage set (harking back to his hit debut album *Bat out of Hell*) lamely interacting with a pair of female backup singers. The lowlight comes during "Paradise by the Dashboard Light," with Meat Loaf and one of the girls engaging in a dumb, dull seduction pantomime in which the girl strips down to black bra, tap pants, garters and stockings, leading to a strobe-lit "consummation." *Yawn.* For Meat Loaf fanatics only.

☐ JOHN COUGAR MELLENCAMP
AIN'T THAT AMERICA
★★★½

RCA/Columbia, 1985, 49 minutes
PRODUCED BY: Alan Hecht, Fred Seibert, Alan Goodman
DIRECTED BY: Alan Hecht, Fred Seibert, Alan Goodman, and others
MUSIC FROM: Uh-Huh (Polygram, 1984); *American Fool* (Polygram, 1982); *Nothin' Matters and What If It Did* (Riva, 1980); *John Cougar* (Riva, 1979); *A Biography* (Riva, 1978).
SELECTIONS: "Jack & Diane," "Hand to Hold On To," "Hurts So Good," "This Time," "Ain't Even Done with the Night," "I Need a Lover," "Miami," "Small Paradise," "Crumblin' Down," "Authority Song," "Pink Houses."
Also available on Pioneer Stereo Laser videodisc.

Solid video portrait of mid-America's answer to Springsteen, containing some interview material from pay-cable network Cinemax's 1984 *Album Flash* special on the *Uh-Huh* album. The program wins extra points for having the guts to show Mellencamp back when he was Johnny Cougar—an embarrassment of misguided poses foisted on the poor young hick by a onetime Bowie manager. Considering what a determinedly sincere and legitimately important rock artist Mellencamp has become, it really is a trip to see such crude early videos as "Miami" and "Small Paradise" and take note of Cougar's neo-Travolta *Saturday Night Fever* hairdo (!). And, even though the program for some reason avoids strict chronology, fans will still be fascinated to see the artist's slow but steady development of a more natural and appropriate rocker's image—and the increase in production values as his star began to rise—in such clips as "This Time," "I Need a Lover," and "Ain't Even Done with the Night." Between-clips interview bits with Mellencamp and other denizens of his Indiana hometown don't hurt in painting a picture of a deservedly proud and defiant Midwestern rock rebel who's lucky to have survived such early image gaffes. The program ends triumphantly with the superb trio of videos from *Uh-Huh*: Chris Gabrin's stupendously stylized starkness in "Crumblin' Down," Jay Dubin's fine metaphor for rock's handing-down of the rebellious tradition in "Authority Song," and Gabrin's nobly ambitious yet soberly clear-eyed meditation on patriotic ambivalence in "Pink Houses."

☐ **VARIOUS ARTISTS**
MELLOW MEMORIES
★★½

USA/IVE, 1984, 60 minutes
PRODUCED BY: Various (none credited)
DIRECTED BY: Various (none credited)
MUSIC FROM: Various albums by various artists.
SELECTIONS: Neil Diamond: "Cherry, Cherry"; John Denver: "Leavin' on a Jet Plane"; Helen Reddy: "I Don't Know How to Love Him"; the Association: "Never My Love"; Bobby Sherman: "Cry like a Baby"; Jerry Reed: "Amos Moses"; Tommy James and the Shondells: "Mony Mony"; the Supremes: "I Hear a Symphony"; Nitty Gritty Dirt Band: "Mr. Bojangles"; Wayne Newton: "Daddy Don't You Walk So Fast"; John Denver: "Country Road"; Shirley Bassey: "Diamonds Are Forever"; Billy Joe Royal: "Cherry Hill Park"; the Osmonds: "One Bad Apple"; Brian Hyland: "Gypsy Woman"; Loggins and Messina: "Nobody But You"; Harper's Bizarre: "The 59th Street Bridge Song (Feelin' Groovy)"; David Cassidy: "I Think I Love You"; Dionne Warwick: "Alfie"; Sonny and Cher: "Beautiful Story"; Mickey Newbury: "American Trilogy."

A curious assemblage of in-studio and on-location lip-synchs from various TV shows circa the late '60s and early '70s, completely oriented toward what was big on the AM radio dial in those years, but not necessarily always "mellow" memories—I mean, I wouldn't call Neil Diamond's "Cherry, Cherry" or Tommy James and the Shondells' "Mony Mony" mellow. But they more than make up for that with *two* John Denver numbers, and the Osmonds doing their hideous Jackson 5 Minstrel Show, and the unbearable Helen Reddy and Wayne Newton, and . . . Really, it's as much yuppie nostalgia as it is video Valium, and these are all parts of the roots of today's music videos, primitive and/or tacky as they may be. Some modestly revelatory moments: Harper's Bizarre's blond lead singer was none other than Warner Bros. Records executive Ted Templeman, the man who produced Van Halen's albums; Billy Joe Royal's "Cherry Hill Park," a bit of AM fodder that I remembered with a smile when it first came on—and then I began realizing just how sexy (and sexist, I guess) the lyrics really were; and it all ends strongly, with Mickey Newbury performing his composition medley "American Trilogy," which Elvis Presley made a hit.

☐ MEN AT WORK
LIVE IN SAN FRANCISCO OR WAS IT BERKELEY?

★★½

CBS/Fox, 1984, 58 minutes
PRODUCED BY: George Paige
DIRECTED BY: Bruce Gowers
MUSIC FROM: Men at Work (Columbia, 1982); *Cargo* (Columbia, 1984).
SELECTIONS: "Overkill," "Dr. Heckyll and Mr. Jive," "Underground," "The Longest Night," "Down Under," "Blue for You," "High Wire," "No Sign of Yesterday," "Who Can It Be Now?," "Helpless Automaton," "It's a Mistake," "Mr. Entertainer," "Be Good Johnny."

Led by that wall-eyed wallaby with the disconcertingly deadpan demeanor, Colin Hay, Men at Work crafted some pleasant if insubstantial pop hits before disintegrating in late 1985. Nobody ever said they were the world's hottest stage act, and nobody ever will after seeing this decently shot but nevertheless ultimately dull program, shot in Berkeley (though Hay keeps thinking it's San Francisco, something the audience keeps trying to correct—hence the title) in 1983. If Hay's strangeness isn't enough to put you off, keyboardist/reedman Greg Ham's relentlessly cloying attempts to live up to his name will. Bits of video clips for "Down Under," "High Wire," and "It's a Mistake" are cut into the concert footage to try to make things more exciting, but it's useless—or is it hopeless? For fans only.

☐ MENUDO
UNA AVENTURA LLAMADA MENUDO

★★

Embassy, 1983, 90 minutes
PRODUCED BY: Jorge Garcia and Orestes A. Truco
DIRECTED BY: Orestes A. Truco
MUSIC FROM: Una Aventura Llamada Menudo motion picture soundtrack (Sono Cinematografia Padosa, 1982).
SELECTIONS: "A Volar," "Lluvia," "Clara Dame un Beso," "Sube a Mi Moto," "Estrella Polar," "La Banda Toca Rock," "Quiero Rock."

Una Aventura Llamada Menudo ("An Adventure Called Menudo") gets two stars *only* because it will appeal to Menudo fans—those who speak Spanish, that is, since it's presented here in their native tongue, with no dubbing or subtitles. For those non-Latins who fail to see Menudo's charms, that's not the least of the problems with this program. The plot's even dumber and more banal and predictable than you might expect: the boys fly a balloon to their next concert, just for fun; balloon flight goes awry, boys land in field—next to mammoth home in which resides *really* cute blonde whom they happen upon, along with her *very* attractive but strangely stern aunt. Turns out the aunt's so stern, and seems to want to keep the boys locked up in her mansion, because she's a big secret admirer of theirs. They sing her a song and she's so grateful she flies them to their gig in a convenient helicopter.

But the production values take the whole thing past the point of mere dullness into a whole other realm of stupefaction that, Menudo converts aside, only a sexual pervert could love: *Aventura* is so laboriously ham-fisted and inept in its direction, so stupidly obvious in its use of not-even-that-gorgeous travelogue footage as maxi-filler, it's just about as dumbfoundingly awful and insulting as Menudo's featherweight Eurodiscopop (for a Yankee analogy, try listening to the "rock music" in a *Partridge Family* episode sometime); but worse, it dotes so peculiarly on the cuteness of the Menudo kids and the blonde girl and her smoldering-'neath-the-primness aunt that it almost begins to play like a child-porn epic minus the sex scenes. Now, you may think that's an insane idea, but the filmmaking skill on display here is exactly equal to that in your average porno loop. Which is disgusting enough in itself.

On the other hand, *Una Aventura Llamada Menudo* seems innocuous enough in and of itself and may prove entertaining to little kids—especially if they're Spanish, speak the language, or have an unnatural craving for Menudo. However, my entire take on this program is colored by the knowledge that Menudo is really a cynical extension of the logic of the teen-idol huckster/promoters who've been slinking around since the '50s. You know, the guys in Menudo get bounced out once they hit puberty and their voices deepen. The assembly-line commerciality of it all might seem inhuman at first, and in some ways it surely is, but we cynics know it's really all *too* human. Still, this is only one repulsive aspect of *Una Aventura Llamada Menudo;* furthermore, it's not even made well enough to be sat through and enjoyed as an ironic artifact of such exploitative leisure-capitalism. How awful is *Una Aventura Llamada Menudo?* That all depends on what you know.

□ MABEL MERCER
A SINGER'S SINGER
★★★★

VIEW, 1986, 42 minutes

MUSIC FROM: Various Mabel Mercer albums.

SELECTIONS: "That's for Me," "Blame It on My Youth," "My Love Is a Wanderer," "Get Well Soon," "If Love Were All," "Wait til You're Sixty-five," "Clouds," "Experiment," "Bein' Green," "More I Cannot Wish You," "Isn't He Adorable," "The Times of Your Life," "Trouble Comes," "Some Fine Day," "It Amazes Me," "Remind Me," "It's All Right with Me."

Mabel Mercer was as old as the century when she died in 1984, but she left behind a forever young and vibrant musical legacy of uniquely timeless and touching interpretive singing. No less than Frank Sinatra has always maintained that "Mabel Mercer taught me everything I know." Cole Porter, Ernest Hemingway, F. Scott Fitzgerald, and the Prince of Wales, among other, were steadfast admirers in the '30s when Mercer was the toast of Paris's cabarets. Later, when she gained the same regal stature in Manhattan's toney cafe society, Billie Holiday, Nat "King" Cole, Margaret Whiting, and many other notables attended her appearances. Mabel Mercer was one heck of a singer, and one heck of a lady.

Here, in an absolute must-own for any Mercer fan, she's caught live at Cleo's in Manhattan, a tiny bistro where this grand dame of supper-club singers seems perfectly at home. The intimate, well-considered, no-frills camerawork perfectly complements Mercer's own disarmingly personable, conversational style, which makes each note her own. Though this was recorded in the twilight of her years, she's imperially great. Hard-core Mercer fans may wish for a more vintage visual record of her, but it's unlikely they'll get one that's this well produced. By the way, for those rock-generation kids who think this sort of thing is square or something, "Clouds" is actually Joni Mitchell's "Both Sides Now." And a warning to those who are considering checking this program out, so they can impress house guests with what's on their video shelves: sample her records first. She was the epitome of her style of singing, yes, but it's a very mannered style which is not to everyone's taste (her arch English diction bothers some), and may easily seem impossibly precious and mannered to greenhorns on such turf. By the same token, though, her quietly dignified reading of "Bein' Green," by *Sesame Street* composer Joe Raposo, easily tops the version Van Morrison (no slouch as a vocalist himself) recorded in the mid-'70s.

☐ **VARIOUS ARTISTS**
METROPOLIS
★★★½

Vestron, 1985, 84 minutes
PRODUCED BY: Michele Cohen, Keith Forsey, Laurie Howard, George Naschke
DIRECTED BY: Fritz Lang
MUSIC FROM: Metropolis motion picture soundtrack (Columbia, 1985).
SELECTIONS: Cycle V: "Blood from a Stone"; Pat Benatar: "Here's My Heart"; Jon Anderson: "Cage of Freedom"; Billy Squier: "On Your Own"; Adam Ant: "What's Going On"; Bonnie Tyler: "Here She Comes"; Freddie Mercury: "Love Kills"; Loverboy: "Destruction."

Fritz Lang's towering, 1926 post-futurist vision of a post-modern, mechanized dystopia has a plot that's a bit too schematic and polemical, but that's more than offset by its awesome set design and stunning command of cinematic technique (e.g., dissolves, superimpositions). Really, it's impossible to watch this movie without going "Wow!" every few minutes. In this sense especially, *Metropolis* (like Luis Buñuel's 1928 *Un Chien Andalou*) is one of those certified classics that not only foreshadowed but has often been plundered for the imagery of music videos. German disco record producer Giorgio Moroder undertook the daunting task of assembling a "complete" *Metropolis,* filling in long-lost sequences with unearthed production stills, and adding snazzy color tints, other special visual effects (such as moving blue skies in some outdoor scenes), appropriate sound effects and decent, synth-and-sequencer soundtrack music. For all of that, he is to be commended. So why does this get only three-and-a-half stars? Because Moroder is also to be damned for degrading his and Lang's accomplishments with a blandly bombastic, trivializing rock score. Still, you could always supply better music on your own, and visually, this *is* the *Metropolis* to see. (Interestingly Moroder's use of color here foreshadowed Ted Turner's controversial Colorization process, whereby classic black & white films are "colored" through a computerized tinting process. Purists should note two points: Moroder's work here does enhance the film, and black & white prints are available.)

☐ **BETTE MIDLER**
DIVINE MADNESS
★★★

Warner Home Video, 1981, 87 minutes
PRODUCED BY: Michael Ritchie
DIRECTED BY: Michael Ritchie
MUSIC FROM: Various Bette Midler albums, including *Divine Madness* (Atlantic, 1980).
SELECTIONS: "Big Noise from Winnetka," "Paradise S," "My Mother's Eyes," "The Rose," "Fire Down Below," "Stay with Me," "Ebb Tide," "Hawaiian War Chant," "My Way," "Chapel of Love," "Boogie Woogie Bugle Boy," "E Street Shuffle," "Summer," "Leader of the Pack," "Rain," "Ready to Begin Again," "Do You Want to Dance?," "You Can't Always Get What You Want," "I Shall Be Released."

Beautifully shot documentary of Midler in concert in Pasadena, California, in 1979. She's in typical-to-classic form, alternately vulgar, brilliant, brilliantly vulgar, self-indulgent, and—when she tries to tackle rock 'n' roll like "Fire Down Below"—just plain bad. If you're a Midler fan, it's hard to believe you don't have this already. Otherwise, as good-looking as Michael Ritchie's lavish production is, it does tend to run on in spots and may make you grateful for the scan button.

□ BETTE MIDLER
THE BETTE MIDLER SHOW

★★★★

Embassy, 1982, 84 minutes

DIRECTED BY: Tom Trbovich

MUSIC FROM: Various Bette Midler albums; pay-cable TV special (HBO, 1976).

SELECTIONS: "Friends," "Oh My My," "I Sold My Heart to the Junkman," "Salt Peanuts," "In the Mood," "Flat Foot Floogie," "Come On-a My House," "Lullaby of Broadway," "Boogie Woogie Bugle Boy," "Fiesta in Rio," "Hello in There," "Hurry On Down," "Delta Dawn," "Long John Blues," "Up the Ladder to the Roof."

The Bette Midler Show, an HBO pay-cable special shot live in Cleveland in 1976, is the heftiest dose of vintage vulgar Bette available on home video (the earlier snippets in *Art or Bust* are even more vintage, but much shorter). She looks a lot younger, and a lot more zaftig, than in later and perhaps better-known films and videos—and she's a heck of a lot more vulgar, liberally sprinkling her tacky-cabaret act with all manner of filthy jokes, puns, and asides (and, in the case of items such as "Long John Blues," filthy songs). She's backed by her trio of female vocalists, the Harlettes, and they all go through a number of calculatedly campy set and costume changes. Bette sings "Fiesta in Rio" as her mock–lounge singer character Vicki Eydie, and "Hello in There" as her bag lady character. Director Tom Trbovich manages to keep up with Bette's energetic show in ultracompetent but never overdone fashion, making this program an interesting counterpart to *Art or Bust,* which some Midler fans feel smothers the star with much too much in the way of gratuitous extras. Overall, *The Bette Midler Show* is a delightful dose of good, dirty fun (especially the string of classic Sophie Tucker jokes)—which also has its deeper, more serious moments, such as an intense version of "Delta Dawn" in which Bette performs the marvelous service of forever banishing the memory of the hideous Helen Reddy.

□ BETTE MIDLER
ART OR BUST

★★★½

Vestron, 1985, 82 minutes

PRODUCED BY: Peter Kauff and Bob Meyerowitz

DIRECTED BY: Thomas Schlamme

MUSIC FROM: Original stage production produced by Jerry Blatt; various Bette Midler albums; cable-TV special (1984).

SELECTIONS: "Pink Cadillac," "Cadillac Walk," "Don't Look Down," "All I Need to Know," "We'll Run Away," "Sweet Marijuana," "Chattanooga Choo-Choo," "Say Hello," "Pretty Legs and Great Big Knockers," "Is It Love," "I Got My Eye on You," "Disco Memories Medley: "Proud Mary"/"We Are Family"/"I Will Survive," "In the Mood," "You're My Favorite Waste of Time," "Broken Bicycles," "Everyone's Gone to the Moon," "Here Comes the Flood," "Stay with Me," "The Rose."

Also available on Vestron Stereo Laser videodisc.

Taking right off with a flying leap from the highbrow/lowbrow pun of the title, *Art or Bust* never lets you forget its theme for a moment. There's the relentlessly effervescent presence of the Divine Miss M herself, the spot-the-20th-century-art-master references in the costumes and stage design (Picasso, de Chirico, and Miro are pretty prominent, among many others), and the heavy post-production that often turns Bette into a sort of live painting herself. In fact, it all gets so ceaselessly frenetic at times that you start wondering if someone thought Bette herself wasn't entertainment alone. If all that isn't enough, the vintage black-and-white footage of pre-stardom Bette getting her start at New York's Continental Baths, and the old color-TV footage of Bette being outrageous on a 1973 United Jewish Appeal telethon, make it quite clear that *Art or Bust* is no ordinary concert program. Both for Bette freaks and curious others, this one's highly recommended.

□ MIDNIGHT STAR
IN CONCERT
★★★

USA/IVE, 1984, 48 minutes
PRODUCED BY: Gary Delfiner
DIRECTED BY: Lou Tyrrell
MUSIC FROM: No Parking on the Dance Floor (Solar/Elektra, 1983).
SELECTIONS: "Electricity," "Playmates," "Slow Jam," "Wet My Whistle," "Night Rider," "No Parking on the Dance Floor," "Freak-a-zoid."

The nine-piece Cincinnati, Ohio, funk band who took the dance-music world by storm with their platinum debut album, *No Parking on the Dance Floor,* is caught onstage in L.A. before a most appreciative, and mostly black, audience. Midnight Star really jam on their razor-sharp, upbeat dance numbers, which overlay burbling, hip-hop-derived sequencer polyrhythms with staccato funk rhythmelodics and robotic, vocodered vocals: for instance, the opening "Electricity" and their two best numbers, the show-closing "No Parking on the Dance Floor" and "Freak-a-zoid." Their slow ballads, like "Playmates" and "Slow Jam," on the other hand, are rather pedestrian and for fans only. The concert is shot in competent, unspectacular, straightahead fashion; occasionally the cameras jostle distractingly as they get up close, and at times they linger mysteriously on band members who aren't singing or soloing. But overall, this should satisfy Midnight Star fans, and funky freakazoids everywhere will get down to those cooking hit singles.

□ KID PUNCH MILLER
'TIL THE BUTCHER CUTS HIM DOWN
★★★½

Rhapsody, 1986, 53 minutes
PRODUCED BY: Philip Spalding
DIRECTED BY: Philip Spalding
MUSIC FROM: The film *'Til the Butcher Cuts Him Down* (1971).
SELECTIONS: Portions of various songs by Kid Punch Miller with various other Dixieland jazz performers.

Ernest "Kid Punch" Miller was a great, seminal New Orleans jazz trumpeter. A few years older than Louis Armstrong, Miller played with Louis as well as such jazz greats as Jelly Roll Morton, Kid Ory, and Jack Carey—but somehow never struck gold and found the fame his talents deserved. William Russell, curator of Tulane University's jazz archives and narrator of *'Til the Butcher Cuts Him Down,* says in the film that it was Miller who first came up with the "fast fingering" that has become a standard part of every jazz trumpeter's vocabulary.

As its title indicates, *'Til the Butcher Cuts Him Down* does get mawkish and morbidly melodramatic at times, but since Miller died just as filming was completed, that's understandable. It's also quite forgivable, because this film is our only chance to see a marvelous, irascible character—and an embodiment of a lost age of classic twentieth-century Americana. While this dying old man appears very pained and fragile as he's helped up steps to his hospital bed, when he struggles onstage at the 1970

New Orleans Jazz and Heritage Festival, he comes alive and his trumpet sounds as lustily alive as it must've in the halcyon Jazz Age. We also see Miller performing at New Orleans's famous Preservation Hall (he led one of the very first editions of the Preservation Hall Dixieland Jazz Band); and in one great scene, Dizzy Gillespie is present at a Festival rehearsal, struck dumb by Miller's vitality and authority on his horn.

Miller also sings a few blues choruses during his show, in a surprisingly smooth, ingratiatingly droll manner—which carries over into his conversational reminiscences about his own life and career. He tells most of the stories from his hospital bed, which he festoons with old photos, posters, and other memorabilia that spark his recollections. His tales of the Jazz Age high life in New York and Chicago (which include a rueful admission that he was tossed out of Jelly Roll Morton's band for drinking too much) are as rich and colorful as anyone could hope. The only bum note is a needlessly long digression on jazz funerals. All in all, *'Til the Butcher Cuts Him Down* proves that Miller fully deserved such a tribute, and at the same time gives him one. (Available by mail order from Rhapsody Films.)

□ STEVE MILLER BAND
STEVE MILLER BAND LIVE
★ ½

HBO-Cannon, 1983, 50 minutes
MUSIC FROM: Steve Miller Band Live (Capitol, 1983).
SELECTIONS: "Rock'n Me," "Abracadabra," "The Joker," "Gangster of Love," "Fly like an Eagle," "Jungle Love," "Mercury Blues," "Buffalo Serenade," "Macho City," "Jet Airliner," "Take the Money and Run," "Living in the U.S.A."

Steve Miller has demonstrated an admittedly brilliant gift for catchy radio pop over the years, with many of the best examples here: "Living in the U.S.A.," "Rock'n Me," "Fly like an Eagle," "Jungle Love," "The Joker," "Take the Money and Run," "Jet Airliner." It's pretty mindless stuff, and you just *know* it's derivative as hell even though Miller's a tad too clever to make it easy to guess what it's derivative of—yet it's nearly impossible to resist, and for many people the body of work contained here no doubt constitutes a hefty chunk of the soundtracks of their lives. And if any of them are really, *really,* REALLY big fans of Steve Miller, maybe they could stand to sit through this straightforward concert video. But Lord, is it dull. The problem is that the Steve Miller Band is not exciting to watch onstage, and the indifferent simplicity of the shoot only makes it more boring. But the music *is* catchy as hell. You might as well just get the audio album and stare at the photos on the sleeve—it would generate just about the same level of excitement as you'll find here.

□ STEPHANIE MILLS
TELEVISION MEDICINE
★★★

Sony, 1985, 14 minutes
PRODUCED BY: Len Epand
DIRECTED BY: Claude Borenzweig, others
MUSIC FROM: I've Got the Cure (Polygram, 1985); *Merciless* (Polygram, 1984); *Tantalizingly Hot!* (Polygram, 1983).
SELECTIONS: "The Medicine Song," "Pilot Error," "Last Night."
Also available on Pioneer 8-inch Stereo Laser videodisc.

Stephanie Mills, the big-voiced singer who first gained fame as the original Dorothy in the Broadway production of *The Wiz,* is featured in three promotional video clips that generally make for pleasant if unspectacular viewing—just as her three danceable funk-pop tunes make for pleasant, if unspectacular, listening. "The Medicine Song" (directed by Jonathan Seay) is the best song and video in the program: Mills plays a mini-skirted nurse in a sexy hospital scenario that explodes into a colorful festival of lovely, slickly executed special effects and choreography; there are also cute references to *The Wiz* and the Three Stooges. "Pilot Error" (directed by Don Letts) casts Mills as a stewardess in a silly burlesque of airline travel that doesn't really work. "Last Night" finds Stephanie, who's *definitely* not in Kansas anymore, wearing a leopard-print bikini and writhing around her pool in sunny L.A., recalling last night's great party and its romantic aftermath. Mainly for Mills fans, but those seeking serviceable visuals with a good beat might want to check it out, too.

□ RONNIE MILSAP
GOLDEN VIDEO HITS

★

RCA/Columbia, 1985, 28 minutes
PRODUCED BY: David Hogan
DIRECTED BY: David Hogan, uncredited others
MUSIC FROM: Various Ronnie Milsap albums.
SELECTIONS: "She Loves My Car," "It's All I Can Do," "Any Day Now," "I Wouldn't Have Missed It for the World," "Stranger in My House," "(There's) No Gettin' over Me," "Lost in the Fifties."

Milsap's a likeable enough countrypolitan entertainer, but he's liable to suffer some serious guilt-by-association from this compilation of promos, which alternates highly produced rock video–style conceptual clips directed by David Hogan with concert shots from the Aladdin Hotel in Las Vegas ("Produced and Directed by XXXXXXXXXX" it says in the credits). Each of Hogan's lush concept clips suffers from the same disgusting sexist portrayals of women and macho neuroses endemic to too much rock video: women are always ravishingly beautiful, lingerie-clad, and ready, willing, and able to use sexual allure as a weapon of sadistic conquest (it's as bad as pornography if you think about it, and besides, this kind of swill gives rock video as a whole a terrible name). It's even in the ostensibly sweet nostalgia number "Lost in the Fifties," where a bizarre trade-partners sexual gambit pops up out of nowhere on prom night, and of course it's those fickle gals who start it all off. "She Loves My Car" does have a nice cameo by John Doe and Exene Cervenka of L.A. punk rockers X (then again, it's also got gratuitous breakdancing); and in a twisted way, the scheming-slut portrayal of the woman in "Any Day Now" *does* match the lyric's paranoid pessimism. But "Stranger in My House" (and, if you think about it, all these videos) seems like a cruel joke on Milsap's blindness, as the lyric "There's somebody here that I can't see" is literally illustrated. Meanwhile, it's no wonder nobody took credit for the live-in-Vegas stuff, it's so bland and static. I can't believe anybody out there would happily swallow these clips just because Milsap is such a popular singer.

□ MINOR DETAIL
MINOR DETAIL VIDEO 45

★★

Sony, 1985, 11 minutes
PRODUCED BY: Billy Whelan
MUSIC FROM: Minor Detail (Polydor, 1983).
SELECTIONS: "Canvas of Life," "Hold On," "Take It Again."

"Canvas of Life" is clever and nicely done, with tasteful special effects, despite the overweening cuteness of its mime-who-takes-you-by-the-hand-to-lead-you-to-spiritual-enlightenment motif. Overall, however, this pair of Irish brothers lives down to its name with bland-out shlock-rock, like an MTVersion of Air Supply. Overall, the visuals aren't nearly enough to make this worth the trouble, "Canvas of Life" marginally excepted on the level of video craft alone.

□ MISSING PERSONS
SURRENDER YOUR HEART
★★

Sony, 1985, 20 minutes
DIRECTED BY: Peter Heath, Simon Milne, Peter Max
MUSIC FROM: Missing Persons (Capitol, 1982); *Mental Hopscotch* (Capitol, 1984).
SELECTIONS: "Right Now," "Give," "Destination Unknown," "Surrender Your Heart."

No less a musical authority than Miles Davis claims to like Missing Persons, who I always found a particularly annoying and affected synth-pop band. Either they deserve another listen, or Miles is senile. Another listen later, and Miles is a magnificent jazzman, but perhaps senile when it comes to synth-pop. Still, Peter Heath's "Right Now" is a marvelous music video, gorgeous with the lush textures and sensuous wit of European TV commercials. Peter Max—yes, *the* Peter Max, of cosmically cute '60s posters fame—directed the title cut, and with its ultimately trivial, layered psychedelic solarizations and color-splashed computer graphics, it looks it. Both clips are enjoyable on a surface-sensory level, Heath's much more so; Heath's "Give" is less impressive, and Simon Milne's "Destination Unknown" is a darkly turgid life-on-the-road metaphor that's even more of a drag. "Right Now" deserves to be seen, all right, but if you really want to pay for what is basically a long, tiresome affair with singer Dale Bozzio's mug . . . it's up to you.

□ JONI MITCHELL
SHADOWS AND LIGHT
★★★

Warner Home Video, 1982, 60 minutes
PRODUCED BY: L. A. Johnson
DIRECTED BY: Joni Mitchell
MUSIC FROM: Shadows and Light (Warner Bros., 1980), *Court and Spark* (Asylum, 1974); *The Hissing of Summer Lawns* (Asylum, 1975); *Hejira* (Asylum, 1976).
SELECTIONS: "In France They Kiss on Main Street," "Edith and the King Pin," "Coyote," "Free Man in Paris," "Goodbye Pork Pie Hat," "Jaco's Solo," "Dry Cleaner from Des Moines," "Amelia," "Pat's Solo," "Black Crow," "Furry Sings the Blues," "Raised on Robbery," "Why Do Fools Fall in Love."
Also available on Pioneer Stereo Laser videodisc.

It's no news that, musically, Joni—here in her dressed-up jazz-mama mode, circa 1979, onstage outdoors at the Santa Barbara Bowl—is a singular artist. But it might surprise some to find that she's a pretty competent director, too. Her use of artsy special effects and cut-ins of film clips (from *Rebel Without a Cause,* among others) and "conceptual" footage to complement the fine concert shots is, for the most part, as tasteful as the music. And, with a band of jazz-fusion all-stars like Pat Metheny, Jaco Pastorius, and Michael Brecker (not to mention the Persuasions on background vocals), the music is *very* tasteful. Only in "Coyote" and "Amelia" (as in Earhart) is the added footage so literal-minded as to become superfluous.

□ THELONIOUS MONK, OTHERS
MUSIC IN MONK TIME
★★★★

Video and the Arts, 1986, 60 minutes
PRODUCED BY: Paul Matthews and Stephen Rice
DIRECTED BY: John Goodhue

MUSIC FROM: Various Thelonious Monk albums.

SELECTIONS: Thelonious Monk: "Crepescule with Nellie," "Coming on the Hudson"; Thelonious Monk Quartet: "Blue Monk," " 'Round Midnight"; Dizzy Gillespie, Charlie Rouse, Milt Jackson, Walter Davis, Jr., Larry Gales, Ben Riley: "52nd Street Theme"; Rouse, Davis, Gales, Riley: "Rhythm-a-Ning," "Light Blue"; Gillespie, T. S. Monk with student orchestra: "Little Rootie Tootie"; Carmen McRae with Gillespie Sextet: " 'Round Midnight"; Jon Hendricks, other vocalists with Gillespie Sextet: "In Walked Bud"; Gillespie Sextet: "Blue Monk."

Music in Monk Time is as recommendable for its subject as for its execution in putting that subject into perspective. Thelonious Sphere Monk, the thoroughly original pianist and composer whose spidery, off-kilter lyricism made him a bebop innovator and an immortal, influential giant of modern jazz, was a mysterious, misunderstood genius. Even many of those who adored him and/or his music couldn't help but regard him as something of an eccentric. And while longtime Monk sidemen such as tenor saxophonist Charlie Rouse, bassist Larry Gales, and drummer Ben Riley, and contemporaries such as Dizzy Gillespie and Carmen McRae provide affectionate *and* unsentimental reminiscences, they come up short on genuine insights—figuratively shrugging and smiling at what a curious character he was and how lucky they were to have known him. Which is fine, as far as it goes, and gets no argument from me. Then Monk's son, T. S. Monk (who's proven himself a successful R&B recording star, and sits in here on drums with a student big band for "Little Rootie Tootie," a song his father wrote for him), talks about what a regular guy Monk could be around the house and how he always took pains to shield his family from the vicissitudes of the innovator's life-style. Interesting and admirable, for sure—but it still doesn't reconcile the other side of Monk that we know better from music and legend. Veteran jazz scat singer Jon Hendricks's narration (which is accompanied by some great archival photos) comes closest, at times, to manifesting the elusive essence of Monk—but then he indulges in some painfully cute rhyming couplets that shatter the intimate atmosphere.

The music, of course, speaks a bit more eloquently. The bulk of it consists of '80s versions of Monk classics played by various permutations of the aforementioned sidemen and contemporaries, the student orchestra's so-so reading of Hall Overton's big-band arrangement of "Little Rootie Tootie," and some footage of Monk, solo and with his quartet, performing on Norwegian and French TV. And yet, what footage there is of Monk himself in action leaves us wanting more, much more—especially since the program, despite its classy execution and commendable intentions, has failed to shed enough light on his character through its "witnesses" and Hendricks's narration.

Music in Monk Time makes the most of what resources it has, and is certainly worth seeing if you're a Monk fan, or, especially, if you're not. But one can't help but feel it could or at least *should* have been even better. However, the main reason for that is its very profound and peculiar subject. And, for making such a nice attempt at illuminating Monk, it fully earns its four stars.

□ THE MONKEES
MONKEEMANIA, VOLUME ONE
★★★★

RCA/Columbia, 1986, 50 minutes

PRODUCED BY: Robert Rafelson and Bert Schneider

DIRECTED BY: Robert Rafelson
MUSIC FROM: The Monkees (Colgems, 1966); episodes 3 and 8 of *The Monkees* TV show (NBC, 1966).
SELECTIONS: "Last Train to Clarksville," "Papa Jean's Blues," "All the King's Horses," "Saturday's Child."

□ THE MONKEES
MONKEEMANIA, VOLUME TWO
★★★½

RCA/Columbia, 1986, 50 minutes
PRODUCED BY: Robert Rafelson and Bert Schneider
DIRECTED BY: James Frawley
MUSIC FROM: More of the Monkees (Colgems, 1967); *The Birds, the Bees and the Monkees* (Colgems, 1968).
SELECTIONS: "I'm a Believer," "Daydream Believer," "Star Collector," "I'll Be Back Upon My Feet."

Boy oh boy, did the Monkees ever get a bad rap when they first appeared in 1966: decried as a prefab rip-off by the self-consciously hip in an age when things had to be "organic, ma-a-an" to be cool, they were actually twenty years ahead of their time. Think about it: they were in essence the world's first video rock band, hired to act in a TV show which would then promote their records. Now how many acts are there in the '80s who can't or don't play their own instruments and/or write their own music, seem to be as concerned with their visual image as with their music, and rely on music videos to sell their records? Of course, there are plenty of them, and while they shall remain nameless here so yours truly doesn't get slapped with any lawsuits, the point is that while these '80s acts are uniformly dull, stultifying, and/or even scrofulously crass and mercenary, the Monkees were adorable and cool. *Really.* If you felt compelled by peer pressure to hate Davy, Micky, Peter, and Mike back in the '60s, look again: the TV show holds up magnificently as a pre–*Laugh In* example of post–Ernie Kovacs irreverence and hellzapoppin' vaude-video surrealism. And repeated viewings of those old episodes give me, for one, the distinct feeling that the longevity of their appeal is *not* just a matter of the general decline in quality of *everything* from the '60s to the '80s. The '80s revival of Monkeemania, which MTV ingeniously sparked by owning up to its heritage and rerunning every original episode of *The Monkees*, is an indication of that, methinks. It was MTV's "Pleasant Valley Sunday"—an all-day marathon of *Monkees* episodes—that ultimately inspired the release of this videocassette series.

Each *Monkeemania* cassette contains two complete episodes of the original *Monkees* TV show—including, of course, those protean rock video segments in which the prefab four lip-synched their tunes. Volume One starts off with episode number 3 of *The Monkees*, "Monkees vs. Machine," in which the kindhearted boys disguise themselves as kids to save the job of a kindly old toy designer whose job is threatened by automation; renowned anti–rock 'n' roll adman Stan Freberg is given a felicitous guest-starring role as the toy factory's nebbishy computer freak; and Davy, Micky, Peter, and Mike lip-synch to the magnificent "Last Train to Clarksville," certainly one of their three or four greatest numbers ever. Volume One also includes "Gift Horse," episode number 8 from that same fab first season of *The Monkees*: it's got a slightly limp story line, in which the Monkees help a little boy save his old horse, but the musical end is especially intriguing—there are two very fine Mike Nesmith songs, "Papa Gene's Blues" and "All the King's Men," the latter of which was never released on record.

Volume Two kicks in with one of the funniest *Monkees* episodes ever, "Dance, Monkees, Dance" (show number 14 from the first season), in which the boys become ersatz dance instructors in order to escape a lifetime contract for dance lessons they've been suckered into; the featured song is the divine "I'm a Believer," probably their most popular song ever and certainly among their very best. The other episode, "Hitting the High Seas" (show number 44, from the second and last season), finds the Monkees signing on as seamen (don't ask why or how—this *was* a sitcom, remember) only to learn that their demented captain plans to sink the *Queen Elizabeth.* The featured tune is another all-time classic, "Daydream Believer"—one of the surprisingly few Monkees songs that Davy Jones, "the singer," actually *did* sing. As hardy Monkeephiles and those who caught MTV's *Monkees* revival know, the supremely versatile Micky Dolenz—master mimic, and a piano- and guitar-playing singer who took up the drums to be a Monkee—sang lead vocals on the lion's share of the Monkees songs.

Indeed, those who not only watched but videotaped MTV's rebroadcast of *The Monkees* must feel that the *Monkeemania* videocassette series is a waste of time. But what about all those people with VCRs who don't have cable TV? What about all those people who have cable and just may have somehow missed it? Folks, the *Monkeemania* videocassette series is a wonderful idea, and anyone who even *thinks* they're in any way serious about rock video owes it to himself to display these tapes proudly on their shelves.

□ THE MONKEES
MONKEES A LA CARTE/THE PRINCE AND THE PAUPER
★★★½

RCA/Columbia, 1986, 50 minutes
PRODUCED BY: Bert Schneider, Bob Rafelson
DIRECTED BY: Jim Frawley, James Komack
MUSIC FROM: More of the Monkees (Colgems, 1967).
SELECTIONS: "(I'm Not Your) Steppin' Stone)," "She," "Mary, Mary."

□ THE MONKEES
HERE COME THE MONKEES/I WAS A TEENAGE MONSTER
★★★½

RCA/Columbia, 1986, 50 minutes
PRODUCED BY: Bert Schneider, Bob Rafelson
DIRECTED BY: Mike Elliot, Sidney Miller
MUSIC FROM: The Monkees (Colgems, 1966); *More of the Monkees* (Colgems, 1967).
SELECTIONS: "I Wanna Be Free," "Let's Dance On," "Your Auntie Grizelda."

Monkees A La Carte/The Prince and the Pauper and *Here Come the Monkees/I Was a Teenage Monster,* the next two volumes in the series begun with *Monkeemania,* are named after the titles of the episodes they contain. In *A La Carte* (episode 11, first season), the boys play good samaritans by disguising themselves as the notorious "Purple Flower Gang" in order to save Pop's Restaurant from an uptown crime syndicate. Micky gets to do his patented Cagney-style gangster impression in not one but two roles—as Micky-the-fake-gangster, and as the real tough-as-nails leader of the Purple Flower Gang. The featured songs are the real draw here, though: "Steppin' Stone (I'm Not Your)," a riff so timelessly potent even the Sex Pistols couldn't resist covering it, and the beautiful, steadily building and very underrated "She." In *Prince* (episode 21, first season), based on the classic tale, Davy impersonates a bashful prince to help the real prince save his throne; Rodney Bingenheimer, L.A.'s veteran reigning pop DJ, cameos as the prince for whom Davy doubles. "Mary, Mary," an okay stop-start rocker, is the featured song.

Here Come the Monkees is a more noteworthy episode than usual: it was actually the series pilot, though it was shown during the first season as the tenth episode; it features a cameo by Paul Mazursky, the future film *auteur* who co-wrote this and several other *Monkees* episodes; and it closes with the black-and-white screen tests of Mike Nesmith (who comes off like an arrogantly obnoxious jerk) and Davy Jones (who's a little bit cocksure but still cute as ever). The storyline is classic *Monkees* show fodder: Davy falls in love with a girl and gets the whole band of Monkees into hot water. In this case, he falls for the lovely blonde hostess of a Sweet 16 party. Mazursky cameos in the midst of the frantic party go-go dancing, as a flustered and very square TV reporter trying to come to grips with the crazy scene before his eyes. The party scene also features a wonderful, typically irreverent pre–*Laugh-In* bit: the camera focuses on one frenetically frugging lady; the frame freezes on her, and a drawn-in caption appears above her, asking, "A typical American teenager?"; the action unfreezes a few seconds, freezes again, and the answering caption appears—"No, a friend of the producers!" *I Was a Teenage Monster* is perhaps the weakest of all the episodes available on these cassettes: the boys meet a mad scientist and the *Mod* monster he's created; the mad prof wants to transfer the Monkees' musical brains into his monster. It's cute and all, and any *Monkees* episode is always better than *no Monkees* episode, but it's still not one of their best. Same goes for the featured song, Peter Tork's inane, fuzz-toned feature "Your Auntie Grizelda."

□ THE MONKEES
HEAD

★★★★

RCA/Columbia, 1986, 86 minutes

PRODUCED BY: Bob Rafelson, Jack Nicholson, and Bert Schneider

DIRECTED BY: Bob Rafelson

MUSIC FROM: Head motion picture soundtrack (Colgems, 1969); (Rhino, 1986).

SELECTIONS: The Monkees: "Porpoise Song (Theme from *Head*)," "Ditty Diego—War Chant," "Circle Sky," "Can You Dig It," "As We Go Along," "Daddy's Song," "Long Title: Do I Have to Do This All Over Again"; orchestral soundtrack selections composed and arranged by Ken Thorne: "Opening Ceremony," "Supplicio," "Gravy," "Superstitious," "Dandruff," "Poll," "Swami—Plus Strings, etc."

Head is something else again—and will most likely be a jaw-dropping surprise for both original Monkeemaniacs and those who rediscovered the show twenty years later through MTV's revival and the subsequent Dolenz/Tork/Jones sold-out U.S. tour in the summer of '86. At the time of its 1968 release, *Head* died a quick and horrible box-office death, not only because Monkeemania had pretty much run its course by then but because *Head* is a particularly black and vicious form of conceptual suicide by the Monkees—an acknowledgement of, and a wallow in, all the negative things critics of the "organic" radical left leveled at the Monkees for being a "plastic," pre-fab commercial commodity. *Head* is at least as aggressively disjointed and surreal as the Monkees' TV show, but with willfully little of the show's it's-only-a-joke levity for leavening.

Head opens with Micky Dolenz disrupting a pompous bridge-opening ceremony—by jumping off the bridge. He then experiences a psychedelically solarized underwater interlude with a pair of mermaids to the tune of the lovely, appropriately floating and liturgical "Porpoise Song," with its haunting "Goodbye, goodbye, goodbye" refrain hammering home the fact that with this film, the Monkees were kissing off both their collective image and individual personae. Then comes a near-Brechtian, frantically spoke-sung, sardonic remake of the original TV-show-opening "Monkees Theme" that billboards *Head* 's virulence: "Hey hey we are the Monkees,/You know we aim to please,/A manufactured image,/With no philosophies . . . You say we're manufactured,/To that we all agree,/So make your choice and we'll rejoice in never being free!"

There follows a ninety-minute series of nightmares-within-nightmares, many based on Hollywood clichés (e.g., an in-the-trenches war sequence, a man-lost-in-the-parched-desert sequence featuring Micky and an empty Coke machine, a Western mini-saga, and on and on), and featuring cameos by football player Ray Nitschke, boxer Sonny Liston, former teen idol and Mouseketeer Annette Funicello, Hollywood character actor Timothy Carey, Frank Zappa (who, in his scene, tells Davy Jones to spend more time on his music "because the youth of America depends on you to lead the way," while his talking cow exclaims in a stagey Sigmund Freud accent, "Monkees iss der craziest pipples!"), stripper Carol Doda, a young Teri Garr, and, most notably, Victor Mature, who keeps reappearing throughout *Head* 's last half as a figure of callous God-like power—e.g., the Monkees are ordered by an off-camera voice (director Bob Rafelson's in all probability) to cavort through what turns out to be Mature's hair, but then the camera pulls back to see the mini-Monkees being vacuumed back out; he later inadvertantly swipes them with his golf club; and so on. Along the way, some vintage Hollywood film clips—specifically from Bela Lugosi's *Dracula* and Rita Hayworth's *Gilda*—are used to comment on the action in *Head.* The bad-dreams-within-bad-dreams motif intensifies its Chinese-box effect as the movie draws to a close, with surreal nonsequitur sequences moving in and out of each other with accelerating frenzy, culminating in an abrupt return to that opening bridge-jumping scene—only this time, all four of them "take the plunge" and symbolically kill the Monkees. But as they hit the water in an ostensible *Incident at Owl Creek Bridge* finale, the camera pulls back . . . see it for yourself.

It's not hard to see the meaning of that whole Victor Mature riff: that the Monkees had been chewed up, spat out, and left for dead by the values and machinations of the "old Hollywood" Mature personifies; and that no matter how obviously lame those old Hollywood values were, they still vanquished the hip-generation Monkees with ease. There's a similarly cynical anti-pop metaphor in an early concert-performance scene, where the Monkees are attacked by screaming hordes of teenage girls at the conclusion of their song—and then instantly transform into mannequins, which are literally ripped limb from limb by the teenyboppers. *Head* does have its occasional funny moments, but with such a relentlessly virulent and dark tone, it's nearly impossible for much of the Monkees' telegenic happy-go-lucky irreverence to bloom. Surely much of this is due to the screenplay by Rafelson and Jack Nicholson (who are seen briefly on the set during a Pirandellian movie-within-a-movie sequence midway through), but just as obviously the Monkees themselves must have been all too ready, willing, and able to dance on their collective graves by the time *Head* was shot. Watching it, I felt more sadness than anything else, as the enormity and inescapability of the torment the Monkees were suffering kept overtaking me. It's easy to imagine teenyboppers at the time of the movie's release sitting shell-shocked through *Head* 's first ten minutes or so before quietly shuffling out of the theater, wondering to themselves "What the hell was *that?!?* "

But of course, they missed the point, because *Head* was fifteen or twenty years ahead of its time. Made a year before Altamont happened, and two years before *Gimme Shelter* was released, *Head* and its bitterly bleak, cynical critique of the whole pop process anticipated post-punk rock flicks like *The Great Rock & Roll Swindle, D.O.A.,* and even *This Is Spinal Tap.* While its sober-minded version of the Monkees' TV show's vaude-video surrealism is intriguing on its own, *Head* is most recommendable for its poignant, piercing perspicacity in showing up the exigencies of Hollywood's image-making machinery, and in showing what it could do to the real people who get ground up in it.

☐ **THE DIVINYLS**
MONKEY GRIP
★★★★

Embassy, 1985, 117 minutes
PRODUCED BY: Patricia Lovell
DIRECTED BY: Ken Cameron
MUSIC FROM: Desperate (Chrysalis, 1983); *Monkey Grip* motion picture soundtrack (Pavilion Films, 1983).
SELECTIONS: "Gonna Get You," "Boys in Town," "Only Lonely," "Girlfriends," "Only U," "Elsie."

First and foremost, this Australian film is a penetrating, powerful, and very adult character study of a single mother—breathtakingly portrayed by the very attractive and talented Noni Hazelhurst—who, against her better judgment, finds herself in a potentially dangerous love affair with a mysterious and unpredictable casual acquaintance (Colin Friels). The film's title, which has absolutely *nothing* to do with the Bill Wyman solo album of the same name, refers to the bond of sexual attraction that keeps Hazelhurst involved in her ominous liaison.

Monkey Grip is also a music film; during the course of it Hazelhurst makes the rounds of the local club scene and starts hanging out with the members of the superb Australian rock band the Divinyls, who all play themselves with alacrity—especially lead singer Christina Amphlett, whose striking countenance can only be described as that of a runty ingenue and who turns in a vivid screen debut as a highly charged, emotionally vulnerable waif-at-heart with a tough-as-nails exterior. Since most of the Divinyls songs share the same subject matter as *Monkey Grip* itself—love and lust and the ways they bring us together and tear us apart—director Ken Cameron made an especially felicitous choice in featuring them in the film. "Boys in Town" (heard here as the band shoots an artsy-fartsy video for it) and "Girlfriends" synch in especially powerfully with the story, but all the songs work well and without contrivance. Divinyls fans should take note that "Girlfriends" and "Gonna Get You" are, at this writing, not available on the band's U.S. albums.

☐ **VARIOUS ARTISTS (JIMI HENDRIX, THE WHO, JANIS JOPLIN, OTIS REDDING, ET AL.)**
MONTEREY POP
★★★½

Sony, 1985, 88 minutes
PRODUCED BY: John Phillips and Lou Adler
DIRECTED BY: D. A. Pennebaker
MUSIC FROM: Various albums by various artists; motion picture soundtrack Monterey *Pop* (Pennebaker, 1968).
SELECTIONS: Big Brother and the Holding Company: "Combination of the

Two"; Scott McKenzie: "San Francisco (Be Sure to Wear Flowers in Your Hair)"; the Mamas and the Papas: "California Dreamin'," "Creeque Alley," "Get a Feelin' "; Canned Heat: "Rollin' and Tumblin' "; Simon and Garfunkel: "59th Street Bridge Song (Feelin' Groovy)"; Jefferson Airplane: "High Flying Bird," "Today"; Hugh Masekela: "Healing Song"; Janis Joplin: "Ball and Chain"; the Who: "My Generation"; Country Joe and the Fish: "Section 43"; Eric Burdon and the Animals: "Paint It, Black"; Otis Redding: "Shake," "I've Been Loving You Too Long"; the Jimi Hendrix Experience: "Wild Thing"; Ravi Shankar: "Raga Bhimpalasi."

The seminal concert rockumentary film was shot at the seminal, 1967 outdoor rock festival. And while it was shot and edited together very crudely, it's got more good performances than bad and lots of hippie-era historical value, not to mention a few memorable moments (like Mama Cass mouthing an enthusiastic "Wow!" during Janis Joplin's "Ball and Chain") amidst the seemingly endless audience shots. Mainly, it's got the Who's "My Generation," Jefferson Airplane's "Today," the critically underrated Mamas and Papas, Country Joe and the Fish (whose instrumental "Section 43" is a gorgeous classic of space-surfing San Francisco psychedelia), a smoking Otis Redding, and a literally incendiary Jimi Hendrix in his U.S. stage debut. Also noteworthy: Hugh Masekela and Eric Burdon and the Animals (with a bizarre "Paint It, Black").

□ THE MOTELS
MOTELS VIDEO 45
★★★

Sony, 1984, 14 minutes

PRODUCED BY: Picture Music International

DIRECTED BY: Russell Mulcahy and Val Garay

MUSIC FROM: All Four One (Capitol, 1982); *Little Robbers* (Capitol, 1983).

SELECTIONS: "Suddenly Last Summer," "Only the Lonely," "Take the L," "Remember the Nights."

Also available on Pioneer 8-inch Stereo Laser videodisc.

With the two Russell Mulcahy–directed rock video classics here, "Only the Lonely" and "Take the L," the Motels' statuesque lead singer Martha Davis successfully suggested a chicly decadent, romantically saturated femme fatale persona. Davis is a luxurious leftover the morning after an extravagant, *perhaps* real party in the lavish "Only the Lonely" (which also pays homage to Stanley Kubrick's *The Shining*), and a *True Romance* comic-book character come to pre-*Dynasty* jet-set life in the visually imaginative "Take the L." These clips gave the band its only real big hits. Val Garay, their record producer, also shot the other two, much less successful, videos: "Suddenly Last Summer" tries to recapture the dreamy atmosphere of romance remembered from "Only the Lonely," using a *Summer of '42* setting; "Remember the Nights" is chiefly noteworthy for a direct homage to David Bowie's "China Girl" video, when the screen goes to black-and-white and a man tosses a bowl of rice over his head—and an on-screen title reads "See Bowie 'China Girl' video." Cute, but not nearly enough to dispel the notion that unless you're a Motels fan their music becomes unbearably pompous.

□ MOTORHEAD
DEAF NOT BLIND
★★★

JEM/Passport, 1986, 60 minutes

PRODUCED BY: Keefco

DIRECTED BY: Keith "Keef" MacMillan, Jon Roseman, Bill Long, Rod Swenson

MUSIC FROM: Overkill (Bronze, 1979); *Bomber* (Bronze, 1979); *Ace of Spades* (Mercury, 1980); *Iron Fist* (Mercury, 1982);

Another Perfect Day (Bronze, 1983).
SELECTIONS: "Overkill," "Stay Clean," "No Class," "Capricorn," "Bomber," "Poison," "Dead Men Tell No Tales," "Ace of Spades," "Chase Is Better Than the Catch," "Iron Fist," "Motorhead," "Killed by Death."

Led by Ian "Lemmy" Kilmister, onetime bassist with British space-cadets Hawkwind, Motorhead race back and forth across the tightrope between heavy metal and hardcore punk—in other words, they're very loud, very hard, very fast, and quite intriguing and even significant. They're also very ugly—yet, Lemmy's snaggletoothed antiglamour is, in a way, refreshingly, poignantly honest and human compared to such loathsomely puffed-up cocks-of-the-walk as, say, Mötley Crüe. Motorhead's no-nonsense music is similarly far tougher, nastier, and more *serious* than the run-of-the-metal-mill; so much so that it stands up to a ridiculous presentation like this. The 1983 edition of the band (with ex–Thin Lizzy guitarist Brian Robertson and Philthy Animal Taylor on drums) lip-synch on a horribly overlit stage to an empty hall, with post-dubbed audience noise between tunes (the amusingly gonzo 1985 conceptual clip of "Killed by Death" is tacked on at the end). Lemmy's so brutally frank and winningly candid he even acknowledges the farcical set-up by getting on his knees at one point to blow kisses to the nonexistent audience!

□ MOTORHEAD
LIVE IN TORONTO
★★★

JEM/Passport, 1986, 65 minutes
PRODUCED BY: John Martin
DIRECTED BY: John Martin
MUSIC FROM: Various albums by Motorhead.
SELECTIONS: "Overkill," "Heart of Stone," "Stone You in the Back," "The Hammer," "Jailbait," "America," "Religion," "Capricorn," "Grind Ya Down," "Road Crew," "No Class," "Bite the Bullet," "Iron Fist," "Bomber."

Live in Toronto was shot before a *real* audience at the Toronto Collosseum (*sic*) in 1982, just before guitarist "Fast Eddie" Clarke left to form Fastway. This program is as unadorned and unapologetically straight-ahead as Motorhead and their music: the lighting's not the greatest, and the direction is the usual competent, not-overly-inspired mix of short-, medium-, and long-range shots, with all three band members getting their fair share of on-camera close-ups. But Motorhead blast through their set with a relentless, damn-the-torpedos vengeance, and their fans ought to be mighty satisfied with this. Non-fans who are getting tired of the same old breast-beating heavy metal plod may get a real jolt out of the band as well. Just remember: Motorhead may be refreshingly free of pretense, but to neophytes they may at first seem disconcertingly free of charisma as well. It just takes a bit of time to realize that Motorhead's lack of charisma *is* its charisma. Note also that *Live in Toronto* closes with a brief interview segment with members of the band, in which they complain that Toronto's bars close too early, discuss their embodiment of the punk-metal connection, and generally put up with some lame questions from a self-consciously hip interviewer (who *has* to be a radio DJ from the way he talks)—like three nice, regular chaps.

□ VARIOUS ARTISTS
MOTOWN TIME CAPSULE: THE 60'S
★★★★

MCA, 1986, 50 minutes
PRODUCED BY: Gino Tanasescu
DIRECTED BY: Gino Tanasescu

MUSIC FROM: Various albums by various artists (Motown, 1960–69); *Motown Time Capsule: The 60's* (Motown, 1986).

SELECTIONS: Smokey Robinson and the Miracles: "Shop Around," "What's So Good About Goodbye," "I Second That Emotion"; Mary Wells: "You Beat Me to the Punch"; Marvin Gaye: "Pride and Joy"; the Temptations: "The Way You Do the Things You Do"; the Four Tops: "I Can't Help Myself"; the Supremes: "You Keep Me Hangin' On"; Stevie Wonder: "For Once in My Life"; Edwin Starr: "Twenty-five Miles."

☐ **VARIOUS ARTISTS**

MOTOWN TIME CAPSULE: THE 70's

★★★½

MCA, 1986, 50 minutes

PRODUCED BY: Gino Tanasescu

DIRECTED BY: Gino Tanasescu

MUSIC FROM: Various albums by various artists (Motown, 1971–79); *Motown Time Capsule: The 70's* (Motown, 1986).

SELECTIONS: Edwin Starr: "War"; Marvin Gaye: "What's Going On"; Stevie Wonder: "Superstition," "Living for the City," "Boogie On Reggae Woman"; Jackson Five: "Dancing Machine"; Diana Ross: "Love Hangover"; Commodores: "Easy"; Rick James: "You and I"; Smokey Robinson: "Cruisin'."

☐ **VARIOUS ARTISTS**

MOTOWN'S MUSTANG

★★½

MCA, 1986, 43 minutes

PRODUCED BY: John B. Caldwell and Mark Robinson

DIRECTED BY: Mark Robinson

MUSIC FROM: Various albums by various artists (Motown); *Motown's Mustang* soundtrack (Motown, 1986).

SELECTIONS: Barrett Strong: "Money (That's What I Want)"; Martha and the Vandellas: "Quicksand"; Smokey Robinson and the Miracles: "Mickey's Monkey"; the Four Tops: "Baby, I Need Your Lovin'," "The Same Old Song"; Marvin Gaye: "Can I Get a Witness"; Junior Walker and the All Stars: "(I'm a) Road Runner"; the Temptations: "Psychedelic Shack," "Beauty Is Only Skin Deep"; Stevie Wonder: "I Wish"; the Jackson Five: "ABC."

☐ **VARIOUS ARTISTS**

THE LAST RADIO STATION

★★½

MCA, 1986, 60 minutes

PRODUCED BY: Alexis Omeltchenko

DIRECTED BY: Dominic Orlando

MUSIC FROM: Various albums by various artists (Motown); *The Last Radio Station* soundtrack (Motown, 1986).

SELECTIONS: The Supremes: "Reflections"; the Jackson Five: "Never Can Say Goodbye"; Marvin Gaye: "How Sweet It Is (To Be Loved By You)," "Let's Get It On"; Martha and the Vandellas: "Nowhere to Run," "Dancing in the Street"; the Four Tops: "Standing in the Shadows of Love"; Gladys Knight and the Pips: "If I Were Your Woman"; the Temptations: "I Can't Get Next to You"; Stevie Wonder: "Uptight (Everything's Alright)."

With these four "Video Originals," Motown Productions made an interesting, partly successful foray into the made-for-home-video sweepstakes with two narrative "mini-movies" (*Motown's Mustang* and *The Last Radio Station*) and two collections of decade-spanning nostalgic newsreels (the *Time Capsules*), all set to the unbeatable sound of classic Motown tracks. On the plus side, these programs mark some distinct advances for Motown Productions itself: the mini-movies have classy production values, whereas Motown's endlessly bloated TV specials had always marked it as one of the tackiest of prime-time programming purveyors, and both the mini-movies and *Time Capsule* tapes rate as genuine, if rather modest, innovations in the home music video area.

Indeed, there's little in the way of a downside to the *Time Capsule* programs: between the music and the time-traveling imagery of the newsreels and other archival clips, they both provide solid-to-outstanding nostalgia in its simple, remember-*that?* essence, matching memorable sights and sounds with nothing getting in the way. Both programs are arranged so that one song for each year of the decade in question accompanies clips of the year's events and trends in history, politics, sports, entertainment, and fashion. Neither program ever misses a chance to go for the bludgeoningly obvious, literal-minded sound-and-vision matchup—from the silly animated openings of time capsules being launched into space and played on the planets where they land, accompanied by Martha and the Vandellas' "Come and Get These Memories," to footage of JFK and Martin Luther King, Jr., for Marvin Gaye's "Pride and Joy" in the *'60s* tape and Vietnam battle scenes for Edwin Starr's "War" in the *'70s* tape. But that's not so much a complaint as an observation; after all, these programs don't claim to be any more than entertaining nostalgia, and that's just what they are. They would also seem to be tailor-made for the role of first-rate party videos (with the bonus that a roomful of dancing partygoers won't make a videocassette skip).

Motown's Mustang and *The Last Radio Station* are a bit more problematic, because they both go the ambitious, innovative but dangerous route of stringing together plots to accompany songs. *Mustang* follows a vintage red '64 model from the assembly line (where a young black auto worker sets his sights on it as *his* car) through a tangled twenty years in which it's stolen, lost, found, restored, and—through the inevitable incredible twist of fate—returned to its original owner. It opens with the young auto worker watching an actual period black-and-white Ford commercial featuring the first wave of Mustangs, which cues Barrett Strong's "Money." That's one of the *least* contrived song setups in either program. Director Mark Robinson (who's also made a passel of narrative video clips, such as the Pretenders' "Brass in Pocket" and Pat Benatar's "Shadows in the Night") does yeoman work with an attractive and capable young cast, getting more emotional pith out of his compacted subplots than one should rightfully expect. But it's not enough, as a sort of conceptual double-bind winds up sinking the program: on one hand, the plot sequences themselves are just too obviously contrived to cue the songs, and never really convince us otherwise; on the other hand, when the plots evolve into music video sequences, they're too often rendered unsatisfying as well, by fading the songs out too early to make way for trumped-up dialogue furthering the weak plot line. Let's credit *Motown's Mustang* as an intriguing idea that unfortunately backs itself into a *Little Chill* corner.

The Last Radio Station is set in the 1990s, with the last radio station left in America, XRDO, about to surrender to the onslaught of music video programs and channels and become video station KVDO. Like *Mustang,* it's got a slick look (director/coscenarist Dominic Orlando has shot his share of MTV-style clips as well, such as Kansas's "Fight Fire with Fire" and Carly Simon's "You Know What to Do"). But also like *Mustang,* it boils down to a specious series of setups for soundtrack songs accompanied by generally annoying videos, as listeners to the last radio station's last DJ phone in stories about themselves that cue the songs and dumbly literal-minded videos. Smokey Robinson and Thelma Houston make brief cameos—as does Hollywood bodybuilder Jake Steinfeld, whose presence is a vivid reminder of Motown's usual tack-ola TV production values. And as for the irony of a home video program about an audio-only medium fighting off video encroachment: intriguing and courageous as the idea of this program may be, its execution—especially its unbelievably sappy, slap-in-the-face happy ending—leaves so much to be desired that radio can rest easy for now. As the last DJ himself wonders aloud on the air: "Whatever happened to imagination?" Indeed.

☐ **VARIOUS ARTISTS**

MOTOWN 25: YESTERDAY, TODAY, FOREVER

★★★★

MGM/UA, 1985, 127 minutes

PRODUCED BY: Don Mischer and Buz Kohan

DIRECTED BY: Don Mischer

MUSIC FROM: The television special "Motown 25" (NBC, 1983), with added nonbroadcast footage.

SELECTIONS: Smokey Robinson and the Miracles: "Shop Around"/"You Really Got a Hold on Me"/"Tears of a Clown"/"Going to a Go-Go"; Stevie Wonder: "Uptight"/"Signed, Sealed, Delivered (I'm Yours)"/"My Cheri Amour"/"Sir Duke"/"You Are the Sunshine of My Life"; the Four Tops and the Temptations: "Reach Out"/"Get Ready"/"It's the Same Old Song"/"Ain't Too Proud to Beg"/"Baby, I Need Your Loving"/"My Girl"/"Can't Get Next to You"/"I Can't Help Myself"/"(I Know) I'm Losing You"; Marvin Gaye: "Yesterday, Today, Forever," "What's Goin' On"; Martha Reeves: "Heat Wave"; Mary Wells: "My Guy"; Junior Walker: "Shotgun"; T. G. Sheppard: "Devil in the Bottle"; Jose Feliciano: "Lonely Teardrops"; the Commodores: "Brick House"; Adam Ant: "Where Did Our Love Go"; Lionel Richie: "You"; the Jacksons: "I Want You Back"/"The Love You Save"/"Never Can Say Goodbye"/"I'll Be There"; Michael Jackson: "Billie Jean"; DeBarge: "The Way of Love"; High Energy: "Pretender"; Smokey Robinson and Linda Ronstadt: "Ooh, Baby Baby"/"The Tracks of My Tears"; Smokey Robinson: "Being with You"/"Cruisin' Together"; Diana Ross and the Supremes: "Ain't No Mountain High Enough"/"Someday We'll Be Together (with full cast)"/"Reach Out and Touch (Somebody's Hand)."

The only thing that keeps this from getting a full five-star rating is the fact that it *is* a prime-time TV special celebrating the twenty-fifth anniversary of one of the most important and productive record labels in pop music history, and suffers a lot of the crass glitziness endemic to the genre. The added twenty-five minutes of footage is just a bunch of Motown songwriters and producers shooting the breeze about the old days with disappointing superficiality. Especially grating is the short shrift given such performers as Martha Reeves, Mary Wells, and Junior Walker (all sandwiched in a snippet-of-one-song-apiece medley hosted by obnoxious cast members of TV's *WKRP in Cincinnati,* which had been canceled years before this special even aired) and Rick James (who gets only a fifteen-second video montage right before what would've been a station break). One also has to wonder what country crooner T. G. Sheppard and British new wave fop Adam Ant (who is utterly embarrassing as he destroys "Where Did Our Love Go") are even doing here in the first place. And it's strange to note the unacknowledged tension that must have been created by the fact that, except for Stevie Wonder and Smokey Robinson, the biggest stars present—Michael Jackson, Diana Ross, Marvin Gaye—had all left Motown long before.

On the other hand, Smokey and Stevie are as brilliant as ever; the battle-of-the-vocal-groups medley between the Four Tops and Temptations is a genuine gas; and there are many snippets of great vintage footage (Martha and the Vandellas in an early music video set on a Detroit assembly line; movies of the Jackson 5 auditioning for Motown). But two moments in particular make the tape worth owning. Michael Jackson breaks away from a Jackson 5 medley with his brothers, saying, "Yeah, I love those old songs . . . but I also love—the *new* songs," as he breaks into an absolutely electrifying "Billie Jean"; especially with the very audible and spontaneous shrieks of the crowd, it's probably the single best memento of Michaelmania. But even better, for me, is the late Marvin Gaye's transfixed, transfixing set: as he swings from the slightly spacey poetic ruminations of "Yesterday, Today, Forever" into the glorious "What's Goin' On," it's pretty hard not to feel shivers down the spine; anger and sadness at the loss of such a talent merge with sheer wonderment and joy at his angelic voice and magnificent music. It's *this* moment that never fails to bring me to tears.

☐ **VARIOUS ARTISTS**

MTV'S CLOSET CLASSICS

★★★

Vestron, 1986, 60 minutes

PRODUCED BY: Robert Odell, Michael Lekebusch

DIRECTED BY: Robert Odell, Michael Lekebusch

MUSIC FROM: Various albums by various artists; Radio Bremen German TV show *Beat Club.*

SELECTIONS: Beach Boys: "Surfin' USA"; the Who: "Magic Bus"; Cream: "I Feel Free"; Ike and Tina Turner: "Proud Mary"; Moody Blues: "Nights in White Satin"; Steppenwolf: "Born to Be Wild"; Yes: "All Good People"; Black Sabbath: "Paranoid"; the Byrds: "So You Want to Be a Rock 'n' Roll Star"; the Grateful Dead: "One More Saturday Night"; Santana: "Black Magic Woman"; Jimi Hendrix Experience: "Wild Thing"; Free: "All Right Now"; Mungo Jerry: "In the Summertime."

The slightly misleading title of this program refers to the clips from German TV's late-'60s/early-'70s rock showcase *Beat Club,* to which MTV acquired the rights—but not until after USA Cable Network's *Night Flight* had already shown most of the *Beat Club* library to death (making the failure to mention *Beat Club* anywhere in the title doubly questionable, in a way). These clips are a somewhat mixed proposition. On one hand, they do offer some genuine vintage glimpses (some are even in black and white) of a solid array of period artists. On the other hand, they do get to be an enervating drag to watch after a while: the performances are invariably lip-synchs, many of them sloppy and obvious (the Who get almost subversive about messing theirs up), and *Beat Club* director Michael Lekebusch inevitably shot them rather clumsily (you keep sitting there biting your lip and clenching your fists, hoping he'll get back to a nice close-up already). Worse, he loved to saturate the artists in a psychedelic soup of eyesore special effects such as solarization and video feedback (shooting into a monitor to get an infinitely repeating multi-image prism effect). After a while it looks like everyone's swimming inside a lava lamp, and it takes a hardy disposition toward rock history and/or hippie-era nostalgia to be able to put up with it for very long. But it *does* have a strong musical lineup and historical/nostalgia value. (Especially given this program's title, these are a unique break from the ahistorical slickness of most MTV clips.) And it's always kinda cool to see how artists who, at this writing, are still at it looked way back when (like the Beach Boys, Tina Turner, the Moody Blues, Yes, Black Sabbath and Ozzy Osbourne, the Grateful Dead, Santana, and especially Paul Rogers of Free and later—*much* later—the Firm). Ike and

Tina Turner's very live—not to mention nice 'n' rough—"Proud Mary" is the highlight.

☐ GERRY MULLIGAN
JAZZ IN AMERICA (Long Version)
★★★★

Embassy, 1984, 60 minutes
PRODUCED BY: Gary Keys
DIRECTED BY: Stanley Dorfman
MUSIC FROM: Various Gerry Mulligan albums.
SELECTIONS: "17 Mile Drive," " 'Round About Sundown," "For an Unfinished Woman," "Walk on the Water," "North Atlantic Run," "Song for Strayhorn," "K-4 Pacific."

☐ GERRY MULLIGAN
JAZZ IN AMERICA (Short Version)
★★★

Sony, 1984, 18 minutes
PRODUCED BY: Gary Keys
DIRECTED BY: Stanley Dorfman
MUSIC FROM: Various Gerry Mulligan albums; the video program *Gerry Mulligan: Jazz in America* (Embassy, 1984).
SELECTIONS: "K-4 Pacific," "North Atlantic Run."

Baritone saxmeister Gerry Mulligan is caught during a 1981 club date fronting a quartet at Eric's, a jazz club on Manhattan's Upper East Side, for these two programs. The band includes the capable Harold Danko on piano and Frank Luther on bass, and the excellent Billy Hart on drums, and they play good ol' acoustic jazz, straight up. As with other Jazz in America programs (such as Dizzy Gillespie's), the music is solidly swinging and often better than that, and the direction and production are tastefully apt, with unobtrusive close-ups and smooth edits.

The shorter Sony program includes only two upbeat numbers, "K-4 Pacific" (named for, and according to Mulligan's intro depicting, a steam locomotive) and "North Atlantic Run" (dedicated to 747 pilots—one might call this a "traveling music" tape). While both are fine showcases for Mulligan's songful, effortless mastery of the big horn, their comparatively limited scope pales next to the greater breadth of tempo and color in Embassy's longer version, which also includes tender ballads such as "Round About Sundown," which as its title indicates is a sort of lighter, brighter inversion of Thelonious Monk's classic " 'Round Midnight." "For an Unfinished Woman," meanwhile, manages to maintain its urgency while effectively evoking a bittersweet, ruminative mood. Mulligan does something rare in "Walk on the Water"—he plays *soprano* sax, and nicely, too. His full-bodied baritone rhapsodizing on the lovely "Song for Strayhorn" is perhaps the highest of many musical highlights.

☐ THE MUPPETS, VARIOUS GUEST ARTISTS
ROCK MUSIC WITH THE MUPPETS
★★★½

CBS/Fox Playhouse, 1985, 54 minutes
PRODUCED BY: Jim Henson
DIRECTED BY: Peter Harris and Philip Casson
MUSIC FROM: Various albums by various artists; various episodes of the TV show *The Muppets.*
SELECTIONS: Deborah Harry: "Call Me," "One Way or Another"; Linda Ronstadt: "Shoop Shoop Song (It's in His Kiss)"; Alice Cooper: "Welcome to My Nightmare," "School's Out"; Ben Vereen with the Muppets: "Jump, Shout, Knock Yourself Out"; Gonzo Muppet: "Workin' at the Car Wash Blues"; Animal Muppet: "Drum Solo," "Wild Thing"; Helen Reddy: "How Can You Be Happy"; Leo Sayer: "When I Need You," "You Make Me Feel Like Dancin' "; the Geriatrics (Muppets): "Who Put the Bomp?"; Muppet Angels and Muppet Devil: "You're No Good"; Loretta Swit: "I Feel the Earth Move"; Floyd and

Scooter Muppet: "Hey Mr. Bassman"; Dr. Teeth and the Muppets: "Don't Blame the Dynamite"; Muppet Rats: "Rock Around the Clock"; Muppet Cavepigs: "Yakety Yak"; Kermit and the Muppet Frogs: "Disco Frog"; Paul Simon: "Love Me like a Rock"; Muppet Birdies: "Rockin' Robin."

Dr. Teeth is your DJ, and the bumbling Beaker is his engineer, for this series of musical excerpts from the popular TV show *The Muppets* featuring the show's guests (not *all* of whom are from the field of rock music), as well as several Muppet performances. Not all of the rock singers are lip-synching to familiar recordings, as the program's best moments illustrate: Deborah Harry sashays out for Blondie's "One Way or Another," spots her Muppet accompanists, and says, "Hey, this ain't my normal band!" before rolling her eyes and sighing, "Ah, what's so normal about a *band,* anyway?"; Muppet Animal does a hysterical caveman rave-up drum solo before Helen Reddy's spot—then he disrupts her song with more bumptious bashing. In other highlights, Leo Sayer is chased up a tree by a Muppet raccoon to croon "When I Need You"; Linda Ronstadt cradles a picture of Kermit the Frog as she wails, "It's in his kiss"; and Loretta Swit's "I Feel the Earth Move" is funny in more ways than one, as a Muppet monster stomping Kong-like around her vies for comic laurels with Swit's hapless warbling. Just as cute and child-approved as anything from Disney, while a whole lot more irreverent and less saccharine, *Rock Music with the Muppets* is kid's programming any adult can enjoy.

N

☐ NAKED EYES
NAKED EYES VIDEO 45

★½

Sony, 1984, 14 minutes
MUSIC FROM: Naked Eyes (EMI-America, 1983).
SELECTIONS: "When the Lights Go Out," "Promises, Promises," "Always Something There to Remind Me," "Voices in My Head."
Also available on Pioneer 8-inch Stereo Laser videodisc.

There may be some fans of this British synth-pop duo—they did have a hit with their flatulent version of Burt Bacharach's "Always Something There to Remind Me"—but it's hard to imagine anyone giving a darn about this collection of completely unremarkable videos for four completely unremarkable songs by a completely unremarkable band.

☐ NAZARETH
LIVE

★½

Media, 1984, 58 minutes
PRODUCED BY: Irving Rappaport
DIRECTED BY: Stuart Orme
MUSIC FROM: Razamanaz (A&M, 1973); *Hair of the Dog* (A&M, 1975); *Expect No Mercy* (A&M, 1977); *Malice in Wonderland* (A&M, 1980); *Fool Circle* (A&M, 1981).
SELECTIONS: "Telegram Suite," "Razamanaz," "I Want to Do Everything for You," "Holiday (Mama Mama Please)," "Heart's Grown Cold," "Cocaine," "Let Me Be Your Leader," "Dressed to Kill," "Pop the Silo," "Love Hurts," "Hair of the Dog," "Expect No Mercy," "Shapes of Things to Come."

The few Stateside fans this veteran, nondescript Scottish heavy-metal band might have will probably go for this adequate document of their 1982 U.K. tour, which includes interviews as well as concert footage. All others are advised to ignore its existence altogether.

☐ RICK NELSON
IN CONCERT

★★★

MCA, 1986, 21 minutes
PRODUCED BY: T. V. Grasso, Jeff Kranzdorf
DIRECTED BY: T. V. Grasso
MUSIC FROM: Various Ricky Nelson albums.
SELECTIONS: "Stood Up," "Waitin' in School," "I Got a Feeling," "Travelin' Man," "Hello Mary Lou," "Garden Party," "You Known What I Mean," "Believe What You Say."

Shot several months before Nelson's death in a Texas plane crash—and tastelessly rushed into syndicated TV broadcast just a few weeks after—*In Concert* provides a nice little memento of an underrated rocker whose credibility was never fully recognized until after his death. Nelson and his country-rock backup band are caught, in standard no-fuss TV style, live at L.A.'s Universal Amphitheater in the summer of 1985. The first teen idol of the rock/TV age covers both his earliest rockabilly and pop hits ("Hello, Mary Lou," "Stood Up," "Travelin' Man") and the thoughtful, mature, hard-bitten countryish hits he penned and sang ten years later in the late '60s ("Garden Party," "Believe What You Say"). I certainly don't mean to offend, but Nelson hardly performs as if, say, this were his last show; but he looks and sounds okay throughout, and as of this writing, this was the sole video program available of Nelson in action later in his career.

☐ WILLIE NELSON, OTHERS
HONEYSUCKLE ROSE

★★★

Warner Home Video, 1983, 120 minutes
PRODUCED BY: Gene Taft

DIRECTED BY: Jerry Schatzberg
MUSIC FROM: Honeysuckle Rose motion picture soundtrack (Warner Bros., 1980).
SELECTIONS: "Loving Her Was Easier," "Yesterday's Wine," "Angel Eyes," "Honeysuckle Rose," "Singing the Yodelling Blues," "Eighth of January," "Under the 'X' in Texas," "Til I Gain Control Again," "I Didn't Write the Music," "Pick Up the Tempo," "Fiddlin' Around," "Working Man Blues," "Blue Eyes Crying in the Rain," "Bloody Mary Morning," "I Don't Do Windows," "Uncloudy Day," "Two Sides to Every Story," "Angel Playing Too Close to the Ground," "If You Want Me to Love You I Will," "It's Not Supposed to Be That Way."

Willie Nelson's effortless personal charm and inimitable way with a song easily carry the soapy but entertaining *Honeysuckle Rose.* Willie plays a country singer whose whole life is a never-ending series of one-night stands on the road—yet he has a gorgeous wife (played by Dyan Cannon) back home who remains loyal to him. But there's a dramatic crux when she refuses to go out on the road with him again. While on tour without her, Willie falls into a relationship with his best pal Slim Pickens's daughter, a young guitarist in Willie's band played by Amy Irving. Cannon learns of it and threatens divorce, but Pickens helps reunite them and smooth everything out for a happy in-concert ending. One thing that makes *Honeysuckle Rose* so easy to take is that whenever the drama starts to falter, up pops another of its abundant Willie Nelson performance sequences. In the supporting roles, Cannon and Pickens are as solid as usual, and Irving is as awkward as ever, though in this role that makes her a bit more appealing and credible than usual. Emmylou Harris makes a cameo appearance, as does Austin, Texas, Tex-Mex organ whiz Augie Meyers (who played that pumping organ on the Sir Douglas Quintet's "She's About a Mover") as a stage manager in one concert sequence.

□ WILLIE NELSON AND FAMILY
IN CONCERT
★★★★

CBS/Fox, 1983, 89 minutes
PRODUCED BY: Terry Lickona
DIRECTED BY: Allan Muír
MUSIC FROM: Various Willie Nelson albums.
SELECTIONS: "Tougher than Leather," "Good Old-Fashioned Karma," "Somewhere in Texas," "Leaves of Autumn," "Innocent Cowboy," "Changing Skies," "I'll Always Be with You," "Nobody Slides," "Tenderly" (by Jackie King), "There Will Never Be Another You," "Nightlife," "Blue Eyes Crying in the Rain," "Blue Skies," "Georgia on My Mind," "All of Me," "Stardust," "Mamas, Don't Let Your Babies Grow Up to Be Cowboys," "Angel Flying Too Close to the Ground," "On the Road Again," "Always on My Mind," "Will the Circle Be Unbroken."

Willie's voice is a touch of pure heaven on earth, everybody knows that—and if they don't, they ought to learn about it firsthand right away. This is not a bad way to be introduced, and it should satisfy the Redheaded Stranger's diehard fans as well. What's most surprising about this competently shot concert, from 1983 at Austin's Opry House, isn't just Willie's voice, but his guitar playing. In the long and winding medley that opens the show, Willie pulls all sorts of eyebrow-raising, tasty licks out of that beat-up old acoustic of his—from bluegrass to shades of Django Reinhardt, the great gypsy jazz guitarist (come to think of it, Willie and Django are probably kindred spirits). Then, after a short break, Willie brings out jazz guitarist Jackie King, who essays a nice "Tenderly" and backs Willie on "There Will Never

Be Another You." Highlights include Willie's magnificent, poignantly understated readings of the standards "Blue Skies," "All of Me," and "Stardust." You've gotta love a guy like Willie, and on video, this is probably the best way to do it.

☐ WILLIE NELSON AND KRIS KRISTOFFERSON

SONGWRITER

★★★

RCA/Columbia, 1984, 94 minutes
PRODUCED BY: Sydney Pollock
DIRECTED BY: Alan Rudolph
MUSIC FROM: Songwriter motion picture soundtrack (Columbia, 1984).
SELECTIONS: "Forever in Your Love," "Songwriter," "How Do You Feel About Foolin' Around," "Night to Remember," "Under the Gun," "Who Am I," "Cajun Hideaway," "Nobody Said It Was Going to Be Easy."

You've gotta work real hard not to like Willie Nelson, especially here in the role of a would-be music-business entrepreneur, songwriter, and all-around rascal with a heart of gold. Doc Jenkins (Nelson) and his ex-partner Blackie Buck (Kristofferson) stick by each other through thick and thin to overcome the Nashville music mogul who's ripping Doc off. Of course they hatch a brilliant plan, and in the end justice and good prevail. In between are lots of cute one-liners, good singin' and playin', and everything any Willie or Kris fan could want. Though the direction is a little slow in places and costar Lesley Ann Warren is not the most convincing country singer we've seen on film, it's amazing that this film didn't receive more exposure. Despite its occasional drawbacks, it's a charming and mildly satirical look at the country music business, life on the road, friendship, and love, and deserves a wider audience.—P.R.

☐ MICHAEL NESMITH

ELEPHANT PARTS

★★★½

Pacific Arts, 1981, 60 minutes
PRODUCED BY: Michael Nesmith
DIRECTED BY: William Dear
SELECTIONS: "Magic," "Cruisin'," "Light," "Tonight," "Rio."

☐ MICHAEL NESMITH

RIO AND CRUISIN'

★★★½

Sony, 1983, 11 minutes
PRODUCED BY: Michael Nesmith
DIRECTED BY: William Dear
MUSIC FROM: Elephant Parts (Pacific Arts, 1981).
SELECTIONS: "Rio," "Cruisin'."

As a former Monkee, Nesmith has a legitimate claim to rock video pioneer status—a claim he substantiated by taking some of the millions his mom (who invented Liquid Paper) left him and founding Pacific Arts Video, then producing *Elephant Parts,* an early long-form music video and the first such program to ever win a Grammy. Actually, *Elephant Parts* is, quantitatively, much more comedy than music—overall, in fact, it seems to follow the format of the TV variety shows that were still prevalent when *The Monkees* was a revolutionary TV show, albeit with faster pace, hipper attitude, and better production values. Many of the comedy skits as much in the manner of *Saturday Night Live,* not to mention Nesmith's sadly short-lived 1984–85 NBC series *Television Parts.* And, while Nesmith found very able collaborators in director William Dear and head writer/cast member William Martin, a lot of the post-'60s drug humor—the "Name That Drug" game-show parody, the commercial for "Elvis Drugs" (e.g., "Blue Suede Ludes," "All Shook Uppers")—though clever and chucklesome, also dates with each passing hour. Still, most of it is good-humored, witty, and entertaining, and certainly far funnier than most other home rock video programs made before or since.

Nesmith's music videos, also directed by Dear, were ahead of their time in terms of production values and conceptual sophistication, especially considering the general ignorance of music video at the time they were made (some date back to the mid-'70s). Dear illustrates Nesmith's likable, laconic country-rock-pop in stylish, whimsical fashion, whether skateboarding along the sun-drenched streets of L.A. (as in "Cruisin' ") or lovingly re-creating an Astaire-Rogers/Busby Berkeley dance routine in a dreamily darkened studio (in "Rio," an affectionate swipe at the escapist fantasies of L.A.'s idle bourgeoisie).

☐ VARIOUS ARTISTS
NEW DEAL RHYTHM
★★½

Video Yesteryear, 1985, 51 minutes

MUSIC FROM: Panoram Soundies and other short musical films (1930–37).

SELECTIONS: Charles "Buddy" Rogers: "New Deal Rhythm"; Ruth Etting: "Roseland"; Red Nichols: "Story of the Dixieland Band"; Emery Deutsch: "When a Gypsy Makes His Violin Cry"; Ferde Grofe: "Mardi Gras Suite"; the Cabin Kids with Buddy Page and Alice Dawn: "Rhythm Saves the Day"; Ina Ray Hutton: "I'm 100% for You"; and others.

One of many compilations of Panoram Soundies distributed by Video Yesteryear, many of whose tapes are serviced only to the largest stores, otherwise available only by mail order. These are mainly of interest to nostalgia freaks and those sufficiently history-minded to care to learn about Soundies.

Panoram Soundies were short musical films made in the '30s and '40s, mainly to be played on "Soundie" machines, which were in essence the first video, or film, jukeboxes. Soundies were also played in movie houses as pre-feature trailers, along with newsreels, cartoons, and previews of coming attractions. While many Soundies were crude, corny performance setups, some did essay ahead-of-their-time conceptual storylines and special effects. Highlights of this reel include: "Roseland," a "Vitaphone Variety" short film circa 1930 starring Ruth Etting, an extremely underrated jazz singer, here cast as a hopeful singer waiting for a shot at the famous ballroom's big time, and "The Star Reporter," a cavalacade-of-stars short from 1937 featuring Ina Ray Hutton, "the pretty little spitfire of syncopation," leading her all-girl orchestra. In another number demonstrating the casual surrealism of the post-Depression/WW II era, Ms. Hutton dances on a floor full of inflated balloons! Talk about "pop" music!

☐ NEW ORDER
TARAS SHEVCHENKO
★★★★

Factory/Ikon, 1983, 53 minutes

PRODUCED BY: Michael Shamberg and Barry Rebo

DIRECTED BY: Michael Shamberg and Barry Rebo

MUSIC FROM: Taras Shevchenko (Factory UK, 1982).

SELECTIONS: "ICB," "Dreams Never End," "Everything's Gone Green," "Truth," "Senses," "Procession," "Ceremony," "Little Dead," "Temptation."

☐ NEW ORDER
PUMPED FULL OF DRUGS

Factory/Ikon, 1985, 54 minutes

PRODUCED BY: Anthony Wilson

DIRECTED BY: Anthony Wilson

MUSIC FROM: Power, Corruption and Lies (Factory UK, 1983); *Low-Life* (Factory UK, 1985).

SELECTIONS: "Confusion," "Love Vigilantes," "We All Stand," "As It Is When It Was," "Sub-culture," "Face Up,"

"Sunrise," "This Time of Night," "Blue Monday."

Musically and visually, this is the best program released by the waywardly self-conscious/doomy/avant-garde British label Factory. Shot at a November 1981 concert at the Ukrainian National Home in New York City's East Village (the program's title is the name of a Ukrainian patriot; the Ukrainian National Home is on a street named for him), *Taras Shevchenko* captures Factory's most accomplished band at the peak of their powers. New Order grew from the ashes of Joy Division when the latter's lead singer, Ian Curtis, eerily bore out the band's depressive lyrics by hanging himself in 1980. With the addition of guitarist Gillian Gilbert, guitarist Bernard Albrecht, bassist Peter Hooke, and drummer Stephen Morris carried on, furthering Joy Division's exploration into the doomy, darkly compelling realms of Velvet Underground–descended drone rock. But by the time of this concert, the members of New Order had begun finding their own unique identity, manifested in more upliftingly anthemic and entrancing tunes—such as the then-recent singles "Everything's Gone Green," "Ceremony," and "Temptation," all among the highlights of this program.

And for once, Factory's production values are better than fifth-rate. No, they're not quite first-rate, but the camera tripods are held steady, as is the focus, and the lighting is adequate enough—all fairly revolutionary advances in technical quality for Factory's productions. Onstage, New Order present very little in the way of conventional entertainment value: they're pretty poker-faced, putting their heads down and solemnly concentrating on what they're doing, showing little or no outward emotion or personality. However, that's not to say their music lacks emotive power. Quite to the contrary: starting about halfway through the show, with "Procession," the members of New Order come together, riding the ever-cresting waves of Hooke's trebly bass throbs and gather an exhileratingly intense momentum that just keeps climbing to the tautly ecstatic finale, "Temptation"—the first real, traditional love song the band ever did. The camera does a decent enough job of capturing the band as they forge this compelling intensity.

Pumped Full of Drugs, from a 1985 Tokyo show, finds New Order having progressed to a more danceable sound with more eclectic music and varied moods. However, it lacks the single-minded force of *Taras Shevchenko*, and the visual quality is back in Factory's usual amateurish vein. *Pumped* has its musical moments, and hard-core New Order fans will want both programs, but *Taras Shevchenko* is imbued with a special quality that makes it easily more recommendable—to hard-core fans, new wave fans in general who may or may not be heavily into New Order, and even non-fans. (Available in stores or by mail order from Factory.)

□ RANDY NEWMAN
LIVE AT THE ODEON
★★★★

RCA/Columbia, 1985, 57 minutes
PRODUCED BY: James Signorelli
DIRECTED BY: Michael Lindsay-Hogg
MUSIC FROM: Various Randy Newman albums (Reprise/Warner Bros. 1968–83).
SELECTIONS: "I Love L.A," "Burn On Big River," "Simon Smith and His Amazing Dancing Bear," "Marie," "Christmas in Cape Town," "Short People," "Texas Girl at the Funeral of Her Father," "Linda," "Real Emotional Girl," "Rednecks," "Baltimore," "Sail Away," "Mama Told Me Not to Come," "Let's Burn Down the Cornfield,"

"Political Science," "God's Song," "My Life Is Good," "Rider in the Rain," "I Think It's Going to Rain Today," "It's Lonely at the Top."

Also available on Pioneer Stereo Laser videodisc.

Newman is hardly the world's most riveting live performer—unless you're already tuned into the intensity of his songs—but at least he seems to be fully conscious of it, and freely admits it during his self-mocking between-songs banter in this decently-enough-shot concert at Lower Manhattan's ritzy watering hole. Then again, "Sail Away," "My Life Is Good," "God's Song" and other songs are fairly riveting, no matter who's doing them. And the flat, ironic diffidence with which Newman shrugs many of his songs off usually does work. Ry Cooder and Linda Ronstadt join Newman for a few numbers; Ronstadt's turn on "Real Emotional Girl" is, fittingly enough, the most disarmingly candid and emotion-charged performance I've ever seen or heard her deliver. That revelation aside, this program is just Randy Newman, straight up—a solid, intimate, unadorned portrait of a most gifted and unique artist.

□ WAYNE NEWTON
AT THE LONDON PALLADIUM

★★★

MGM/UA, 1983, 63 minutes
PRODUCED BY: Scott Sternberg
DIRECTED BY: Scott Sternberg
MUSIC FROM: Various Wayne Newton albums.
SELECTIONS: "Fanfare/Getaway," "C.C. Rider," "Georgia," Medley: "Red Roses for a Blue Lady"/"Danke Schoen"/ "The Hungry Years"/"Daddy, Don't You Walk So Fast," Medley: "Jambalaya"/ "Lonesome Me"/"Goodhearted Woman," "The Impossible Dream," "New York, New York," "MacArthur Park," Medley: "Baby Face"/"Robert E. Lee"/"Orange Blossom Special"/ "When the Saints Go Marching In," "I Made It Through the Rain."

For fans of Mr. Las Vegas, this is it: the biggest draw in Nevada in a rare appearance *outside* the Vegas/Tahoe/ Reno golden triangle. It's all here: the unctuous, self-confident stage demeanor distracting his audience from his disconcerting lack of a good voice, the cannily eclectic song selection, the shlocky arrangements, the multi-instrumental medley in which Wayne accompanies himself on guitar, banjo, fiddle, and trumpet . . . and, for Wayne-haters, there is also of course the built-in camp value of this nicely shot program. Can't miss, can you?

□ OLIVIA NEWTON-JOHN
OLIVIA PHYSICAL

★★★

MCA, 1982, 54 minutes
PRODUCED BY: Scott Millaney
DIRECTED BY: Brian Grant
MUSIC FROM: Physical (MCA, 1982).
SELECTIONS: "Landslide," "Magic," "Physical," "Carried Away," "A Little More Love," "Recovery," "The Promise," "Love Make Me Strong," "Stranger's Touch," "Make a Move on Me," "Falling," "Silvery Rain," "Hopelessly Devoted to You."

Collection of concept and performance clips for the *Physical* album that radically remade ONJ's image from Milquetoast MOR crooner to punky, saucy queen of sassy, funky pop. By far the best video is "Physical" itself, a ribald comic classic set in a workout gym where Olivia trims down some fat guys to more suitable physiques for the kind of bodily pleasures she's singing about—only to find at the end that the guys head for the showers with each other! The kind of all-in-good-fun joke that could now never be made in the post-AIDS age, it also neatly deflates the clip's creeping tendency to portray sweet ol' ONJ as one of those typical rock video Queen Bitch sex amazons. As for the rest of this program, ONJ fans probably already have it and love it, and for the curious it's probably the most recommendable of her many tapes.

□ OLIVIA NEWTON-JOHN
OLIVIA IN CONCERT
★★½

MCA, 1983, 78 minutes
PRODUCED BY: Christine Smith
DIRECTED BY: Brian Grant
MUSIC FROM: Various Olivia Newton-John albums.
SELECTIONS: "Deeper than the Night," "Let Me Be There," "Please Mister Please," "If You Love Me (Let Me Know)," "Jolene," "Sam," "Xanadu," "Magic," "Suddenly," "Silvery Rain," "Falling," "Heart Attack," "Make a Move on Me," "Hopelessly Devoted to You," "You're the One That I Want," "Physical," "I Honestly Love You."
Also available on MCA Stereo Laser videodisc.

Since this 1983 concert was shot (in typical flashy MTV fashion) just after ONJ crossed over from her mellow-yellow early style to her comparatively flaming-punk *Physical* style, there's a certain schizoid quality to it. You get the insufferably demure soft-sells of "If You Love Me (Let Me Know)," "I Honestly Love You," "Xanadu," and you get the sassier stuff like "Physical" and "Make a Move on Me," "Heart Attack," and "You're the One That I Want." ONJ is very lovely, and I love her spunkier recent material; the audience at Utah's Weber State University Hall loves all of it, and if you're a fan, so will you.

□ OLIVIA NEWTON-JOHN
TWIST OF FATE
★★

MCA, 1984, 25 minutes
DIRECTED BY: Brian Grant, David Mallet
MUSIC FROM: Two of a Kind original soundtrack (MCA, 1983); *Olivia's Greatest Hits, Volume Two* (MCA, 1983).
SELECTIONS: "Twist of Fate," "Take a Chance," "Livin' in Desperate Times," "Shaking You," "Heart Attack," "Tied Up."

The first four clips were all shot to promote the box-office bomb *Two of a Kind,* a misbegotten Olivia–John Travolta vehicle. Brian Grant directed all of them except "Take a Chance," which David Mallet shot. Both directors are veterans of MTV-style rock videos, and their clichéd lighting, cutting, camera angles, and imagery don't help an already lame project. Grant also shot the concept clip for "Heart Attack" and the performance clip of "Tied Up," both from *Olivia's Greatest Hits, Volume Two*; the former tries to bring back some of the sassy sexuality of Grant's earlier "Physical" clip, and fails.

□ OLIVIA NEWTON-JOHN
SOUL KISS
★★½

MCA, 1985, 20 minutes
PRODUCED BY: Jacqui Byford
DIRECTED BY: David Mallet
MUSIC FROM: Soul Kiss (MCA, 1985).
SELECTIONS: "Soul Kiss," "Culture Shock," "Emotional Tangle," "Toughen Up," "The Right Moment."

Most of these video clips are straightforward performance shots that ONJ's fans will like and others will find boring. "Culture Shock" has inanely candid lyrics about the threesome lifestyle ("Why can't the three of us live together?" goes the whining chorus), but ONJ or director Mallet chickens out of a potentially provocative illustration of the scenario with more moribund straight performance. "Soul Kiss" has some sultriness to match the song, and harks back to the playfulness of the classic "Physical" in one bathtub scene, but ONJ looks more narcotized than horny lying on her side lip-synching, and Mallet's cut-ins of classic movie kisses ruin the mood. The centerpiece is the funny, kinda gross, and ultimately fascinacting (as a pop-culture artifact dripping with subtexts) "Toughen Up": at what looks like a girls' boarding school, ONJ—in equestrian garb (Mallet lingers tellingly on her boots and riding crop)—teaches her girls how to deal with obnoxious, sexist guys. Yet it's done with a tawdry, sexist-in-itself Benny Hill cartoonishness (e.g., short skirts on all the luscious, pouting "girls") that undercuts the feminist message and black-comic touches.

☐ STEVIE NICKS

STEVIE NICKS IN CONCERT

★★★

CBS/Fox, 1982, 60 minutes

PRODUCED BY: Marty Callner

DIRECTED BY: Marty Callner

MUSIC FROM: Various Stevie Nicks and Fleetwood Mac albums.

SELECTIONS: "Sarah," "The Edge of Seventeen," "Stop Draggin' My Heart Around," "Rhiannon (Will You Ever Win)," "Dreams," "I Need to Know," "Gold Dust Woman."

☐ STEVIE NICKS

I CAN'T WAIT

★★½

RCA/Columbia, 1986, 29 minutes

PRODUCED BY: Marty Callner

DIRECTED BY: Marty Callner

MUSIC FROM: Bella Donna (Modern, 1981); *The Wild Heart* (Modern, 1983); *Rock a Little* (Modern, 1985).

SELECTIONS: "Leather and Lace," "Stop Draggin' My Heart Around," "Stand Back," "If Anyone Falls," "Talk to Me," "I Can't Wait."

In Concert, shot at the end of Nicks's 1982 solo tour, presents rock's white witch and an all-star band doing her greatest hits. From the minute her father introduces her and the band (E Streeter Roy Bittan, Heartbreaker Benmont Tench, Waddy Wachtel, Bobbye Hall, and Russ Kunkel) kicks in, the show just rolls along, with Nicks twirling, screeching, and changing shawls like there's no tomorrow. Steviephiles will love this one, especially the encore version of "Rhiannon"—first sung to Bittan's piano accompaniment, then with the full band—and "Stop Draggin' My Heart Around," a duet with Wachtel in Petty's place. Unfortunately, Nicks suffers from throat problems, and, in places here, you almost wince in sympathy. For someone to write such beautiful songs—vacuous or not—and not be able to really sing them well is sad. But those of us who can appreciate Nicks's talents yet can't stand *her* have a difficult task here. She cries a lot, particularly when the fans load her up with Cabbage Patch dolls, stuffed Snoopys, and flowers, and her so-called dancing (does someone fill those stacked soles with cement, or what?) is distractingly funny. Note, too, that this is the exact program that ran for a while on HBO. If you taped that and the sound is decent, you can skip this.—P.R.

Nicks is up to more of her usual white-witch tricks in *I Can't Wait*, a compilation of promo clips that have almost all had heavy-rotation runs on MTV and all the other music video shows. "Leather and Lace" and "Stop Draggin' My Heart Around," the latter a nice duet with Tom Petty, are both competently shot concert clips. "Stand Back" is a straightforward, dance-oriented studio performance of one of her best songs (featuring an uncredited cameo on the soundtrack by Prince, who plays that high-pitched, sirenlike one-note synthesizer line on the chorus), nicely shot and edited by *Flashdance* choreographer Geoffrey Hornaday. "If Anyone Falls," Nicks's first real concept clip after Fleetwood Mac's "Gypsy," predictably fleshes out her occultist persona with quaintly atmospheric Gothic settings, here shot in black and white, with Fleetwood Mac drummer Mick Fleetwood making a fleeting cameo in an acolyte's hood and robe. "Talk to Me" and "I Can't Wait" are nearly identical Technicolor clips combining the dance-oriented performance of "Stand Back" with the dreamy settings of "Gypsy" and "If Anyone Falls." Nicks pirouettes, incessantly and awkwardly, around sprawling stairways and what look like huge towers or castle turrets—the atmosphere is right, but she still comports herself like a hopelessly self-involved jerk. At the very best, these clips give the impression of a uniquely exotic lunatic who, through sheer good looks and triumph-of-the-will doggedness, has managed to take over the asylum for three or four minutes. If you don't care for Nicks, these won't sway you; if you're already a fan, she could be shown leafing through a phone book in each and every clip and you'd probably still be more than satisfied.

□ NIGHT RANGER
7 WISHES TOUR

MCA, 1986, 80 minutes
PRODUCED BY: John Diaz
DIRECTED BY: Larry Jordan
MUSIC FROM: 7 Wishes (MCA, 1985); *Dawn Patrol* (MCA, 1983); *Midnight Madness* (MCA, 1983).
SELECTIONS: "7 Wishes," "Sing Me Away," "Rumours in the Air," "This Boy Needs to Rock," "Sentimental Street," "When You Close Your Eyes," "Faces," "Eddie's Comin' Out Tonight," "Call My Name," "Four in the Morning," "I Need a Woman," "Night Ranger," "Touch of Madness," "Rock in America (You Can Still)," "Sister Christian," "Don't Tell Me You Love Me," "Goodbye."

This San Francisco Bay–area band went from unknown status to the platinum-sales level in just three years, with a classic, exemplary AOR-rock sound: bombastic, equally derivative of heavy metal and symphonic progressive-rock, emotionally shallow, intellectually empty, and full of macho posing and bravado, from the lyrics to the guitar solos. Here, they're caught live at the New Orleans Superdome on their 1985 tour promoting the *7 Wishes* album—and they and the program itself deliver just about all that any Night Ranger or AOR-rock fan could ever ask. This is a very nicely shot, commendably straight-ahead concert video, and while Night Ranger may have a more or less totally indistinct and uninspired sound, they do work hard for the money and they do show a definite rapport with their rabidly devoted audience. At a suggested thirty-dollar retail (at this writing) for close to ninety solid minutes of concert action, this is a pretty good deal for any fan of the band.

□ HARRY NILSSON (WITH RINGO STARR)
THE POINT
★★★

Vestron, 1986, 74 minutes
PRODUCED BY: Fred Wolf, Harry Nilsson, Jerry Good, Larry Gordon
DIRECTED BY: Fred Wolf
MUSIC FROM: The Point soundtrack album (RCA, 1970); TV animated special (NBC, 1970).
SELECTIONS: "Can You Hear Me," "Town," "Me and My Arrow," "Poli High," "Think About Your Troubles," "Hello," "The Last Time."

This 1970 TV special tells the animated, nonconformist fable of little Oblio, the first round-headed baby ever born in the Land of Point—where everyone and everything has a point. While Fred Wolf's animation does have its own sort of rag-tag charm, *The Point* suffers by occasionally coming across as a low-budget *Yellow Submarine.* Still, it has a timeless and honorable message, and nice narration from Ringo Starr. And then there's Harry Nilsson's soundtrack: a light, airy soufflé of layered, Beatlesque pop motifs, at times a bit *too* sweet and cute, but generally quite tasty. The bright, bouncy "Me and My Arrow" (Arrow being Oblio's dog) was the big hit from this soundtrack, but a delightful, mildly black-humored yet still naïvely wondrous evolutionary-chain joke like "Think About Your Troubles" is at least as good. As is the bizarre (in *this* story) latent-psychedelic hangover song "The Last Time," which is about the only thing making me think twice before recommending this as children's entertainment.

☐ **VARIOUS ARTISTS**

NO NUKES

★★★

CBS/Fox, 1980, 103 minutes

PRODUCED BY: Julian Schlossberg and Danny Goldberg

DIRECTED BY: Barbara Kopple, Haskell Wexler, and Anthony Portenza

MUSIC FROM: No Nukes—The MUSE Concerts for a Non-Nuclear Future (Asylum, 1979).

SELECTIONS: Carly Simon and James Taylor: "Mockingbird"; Bonnie Raitt: "Runaway"; Crosby, Stills and Nash: "Suite: Judy Blue Eyes"; James Taylor, Carly Simon, John Hall, Graham Nash: "The Times They Are A'Changin' "; Jackson Browne: "Running on Empty," "Before the Deluge"; the Doobie Brothers: "What a Fool Believes"; Graham Nash: "Barrel Full of Pain," "Our House"; James Taylor: "Your Smiling Face"; Gil Scott-Heron: "We Almost Lost Detroit"; Avis Davis: "No More Nukes"; Jesse Colin Young: "Get Together"; ensemble: "Takin' It to the Streets," "Power"; Bruce Springsteen and the E Street Band: "Thunder Road," "The River," "Quarter to Three."

MUSE (Musicians United for Safe Energy) made headlines with these shows in 1979, partially because they happened soon after the accident at Three Mile Island and partially because the all-star lineup guaranteed huge crowds. By all accounts, the MUSE concerts were a success. This film, which captures sets from the Madison Square Garden shows and a large afternoon rally at Battery Park in Manhattan soon after, is more than a concert documentary, for it also contains an interesting film documentary on nuclear power that was shown during the shows (parts of which would be familiar to anyone who's seen *Atomic Cafe*). As an educational effort, MUSE worked wonders, and though the musicians as antinuclear spokespeople could sound silly (the lyrics to Graham Nash's "Barrel Full of Pain," fine though the sentiment is, would shame a thinking ten-year-old), some were in fact brilliant. When queried by a skeptical reporter about the group's goal, Jesse Colin Young replied, "Intact genetic human survival."

That's all well and good, but if it's great music you're looking for, *No Nukes* is a truly mixed bag. First, it's very much of its time. The Doobie Brothers, despite their multiplatinum success, aren't much more than footnotes in rock history, and one look at this shows why. In fact, a large portion of the sets are either sort of nostalgia bits (Crosby, Stills and Nash) or a "counterculture" (ha!) *American Bandstand*. Yes, kids, "Mockingbird," "What a Fool Believes," and "Runaway" were big hits. This is the stuff punk and new wave sought to usurp, and on the whole, it just doesn't hold up. Second, as tightly edited as it is, *No Nukes* has a distance that undercuts any sense of intimacy or urgency regarding its purpose.

But despite all this, *No Nukes* does have some truly great moments, and the lack of home video material on

Bruce Springsteen and Jackson Browne gives it added importance. Jackson Browne's set is great, but Bruce Springsteen's is stunning, with the powerful "Thunder Road," a rocking "Quarter to Three," and a moving rendition of one of his most underrated songs, "The River." When Bruce cries, "I'm just a prisoner of rock and roll," you believe it. Also worth watching is Gil Scott-Heron, whose "We Almost Lost Detroit" is one of the amazingly few songs that actually address the issue at hand.—P.R.

□ RED NORVO
JAZZ AT THE SMITHSONIAN
★★★★

Sony, 1985, 58 minutes
PRODUCED BY: Clark and Delia Gravell Santee
DIRECTED BY: Clark and Delia Gravell Santee
SELECTIONS: "All of Me," "Jitterbug Waltz," "Cheek to Cheek," "Fascinating Rhythm," "When You're Smiling," "School Days," "Teach Me Tonight," "The Wave," "Just Friends," "Pennies from Heaven."

Norvo is one of jazz's original masters of the idiophones—you know, vibraphone, xylophone, marimba, etc. His career goes back to the late '20s, when in the post-doo-wacka-doo days he played rollicking xylophone licks with hot-shot young white jazz ensembles. When that instrument became relegated to cartoon soundtracks, Norvo concentrated on vibraphone, with its less intrusive tone and wider, subtler dynamic range. Some of Norvo's best and best-loved work was with the brilliant, reclusive jazz guitarist Tal Farlow, who retired from performing in the late '50s. This 1982 concert at Washington, D.C.'s Smithsonian Institute reunites Norvo and Farlow, and it's a real treat to see them express their mutual delight in such a spirited yet refined, sophisticated but direct musical manner. Singer Mavis Rivers guests on a few numbers, and she does just fine, but the Red 'n' Tal Show is the centerpiece: their delicate, quicksilver improvisations seem telepathically linked, and each keeps outdoing the other in a friendly game in which the audience is the real winner. Brief interview snippets with Norvo talking to Voice of America DJ Willis Conover are interspersed with the concert footage—Norvo's warm, gentle demeanor and the twinkle in his eye echo the ingratiating, low-key lyricism of his playing.

O

☐ MARK O'CONNOR
CONTEST FIDDLING, CHAMPIONSHIP STYLE
★★★★

Homespun, 1985, 60 minutes
PRODUCED BY: Happy Traum
DIRECTED BY: Happy Traum
SELECTIONS: "Wild Fiddler's Rag," "Skater's Waltz," "Soppin' Up the Gravy," and others.

O'Connor is another rising star in the "newgrass" acoustic bluesgrass/country/swing movement (like fellow Homespun instructor Tony Rice), and this tape is more for intermediate-to-accomplished players than the beginning fiddler. O'Connor breaks down several tunes for the viewer, going into fine points of technique and nuances of feel; he's also seen in performance with a band, playing as he would in a genuine Texas-style fiddling contest. Entertaining and informative, with Homespun's usual super-competent but unspectacular production values. (Available by mail order from Homespun Tapes.)

☐ VARIOUS ARTISTS
ONE NIGHT STAND: A KEYBOARD EVENT
★★

CBS/Fox, 1982, 98 minutes
MUSIC FROM: One Night Stand: A Keyboard Event (Columbia, 1981).
SELECTIONS: Eubie Blake: "Sounds of Africa," "Memories of You"; Kenny Barron and Bobby Hutcherson: "Sunshower"; Bob James and Ron Carter: "Winding River"; George Duke and Charles Earland: "When Johnny Comes Marching Home"; Sir Roland Hanna and Arthur Blythe: "A Common Cause"; Herbie Hancock, Rodney Franklin, George Duke, Bob James, Kenny Barron, Sir Roland Hanna, Eubie Blake, Ron Carter, and Buddy Williams: "Hexagon."

One Night Stand is one of those all-star programs that just don't live up to their billing. It tries to cram too many different performers into one rilly big shoe, the disappointing end result being that nobody really has any time to stretch out and do his thing at his best. Those who come closest include: alto saxist Blythe and pianist Hanna with their duet on "A Common Cause"; pianist Barron and vibraphonist Hutcherson on "Sunshower"; and Eubie Blake, then ninety-eight years young. But just when you're starting to enjoy each of them, it's time for someone else. Perhaps the biggest disappointments are the organ duet between Charles Earland and George Duke (Duke was playing an organ for the first time in twenty years—and you can tell) and the grand finale, which epitomizes the program's problems: "Hexagon," a piece composed especially for this "event" by Jay Chattaway, with no less than six grand pianists effectively canceling one another out.

☐ VARIOUS ARTISTS
ONE NIGHT WITH BLUE NOTE PRESERVED, VOLUME ONE
★★★★½

Sony, 1985, 60 minutes
PRODUCED BY: Tammara Wells
DIRECTED BY: John Jopson
MUSIC FROM: One Night with Blue Note, Volumes One and Two (Blue Note, 1985).
SELECTIONS: Bobby Hutcherson, Herbie Hancock, Ron Carter: "Bouquet"; Hancock, Carter, Tony Williams, Joe Henderson, Freddie Hubbard: "Cantaloupe Island"; Stanley Jordan: "When You Wish upon a Star," "Jumpin' Jack"; Art Blakey, Curtis Fuller, Johnny Griffin, Reggie Workman, Walter Davis, Jr., Hubbard: "Moanin' "; Bennie Wallace, Cecil McBee, Jack DeJohnette: "Broadside"; Hutcherson, Hancock, Carter, Williams, James Newton: "Little B's Poem."

Also available on Pioneer Stereo Laser videodisc.

☐ VARIOUS ARTISTS
ONE NIGHT WITH BLUE NOTE PRESERVED, VOLUME TWO
★★★★½

Sony, 1985, 60 minutes
PRODUCED BY: Tammara Wells
DIRECTED BY: John Jopson
MUSIC FROM: One Night with Blue Note, Volumes Three and Four (Blue Note, 1985).
SELECTIONS: Kenny Burrell, Grover Washington, Jr., Reggie Workman, Grady Tate: "Summertime"; McCoy Tyner: "Sweet and Lovely"; Tyner, Jackie McLean, Woody Shaw, Cecil McBee, Jack DeJohnette: "The Blessing"; Charles Lloyd, Michel Petrucciani, McBee, DeJohnette: "Tone Poem," "Lady Day"; Lou Donaldson, Jimmy Smith, Burrell, Tate: "Blues Walk"; Cecil Taylor: "Pontos Cantados."
Also available on Pioneer Stereo Laser videodisc.

Taking these two volumes as a whole, this document of the February 22, 1985, all-star jazz concert at New York's Town Hall, to celebrate the rebirth of the legendary Blue Note label, is probably the best single jazz program—or jazz performance program, at any rate—available on home video. The music and musicians are of uniformly high quality, with a galaxy of modern-jazz stars covering a gamut of styles, from Blue Note's classic straightahead bebop to the volcanic free-form piano eruptions of Cecil Taylor, from Bobby Hutcherson's gossamer vibe meditations to guitar phenom Stanley Jordan's unique, orchestral pointillism. If one were forced to pick between the two, it could be said that Volume One has a slightly heavier lineup. But what really makes both volumes so superb is the direction of John Jopson (not to mention the classy, but never overdone, production of Tammara Wells): he obviously has a deep understanding and appreciation of the players and their music, and it shows in the unobtrusive intimacy of his felicitous camera angles; his cuts between cameras usually follow the musical action so perfectly it's almost as if Jopson is another member of each band onstage. Here, he has established the model for what all jazz-concert videos should be.

☐ YOKO ONO
THEN AND NOW
★★★½

Media, 1984, 56 minutes
PRODUCED BY: Barbara Graustark
DIRECTED BY: Barbara Graustark
MUSIC FROM: Various albums by John Lennon, Yoko Ono, John and Yoko, the Beatles, including *Double Fantasy* (Geffen, 1980); *Season of Glass* (Geffen, 1981); *It's Alright* (Polydor, 1983).
SELECTIONS: "Imagine," "Give Peace a Chance," "Walking on Thin Ice," "Watching the Wheels," "Beautiful Boy," "Starting Over," "Let It Be," "I Want You."
Also available on Pioneer Stereo Laser videodisc.

Even those who've always hated Yoko may find themselves taken aback by the intelligence with which journalist Barbara Graustark states Yoko's case in this enlightening, absorbing documentary. *Then* consists of happenings and bag art performances from Those Fabulous Sixties with John (who seems to have loved Yoko ever more fiercely the more she alienated everyone else). *Now* is Yoko after John's murder. You can't deny that she is a remarkably strong and admirably assured woman, no matter what you think of her art. There are interviews, shots of Yoko and Sean at home and in the studio, and so on. With the references to John reined in, *Then and*

Now forces us to evaluate Yoko on her own terms—and you might be surprised at how you feel when it's over.

☐ ORCHESTRAL MANOEUVRES IN THE DARK
CRUSH—THE MOVIE
★★½

Sony, 1986, 70 minutes
PRODUCED BY: Andy Harries
DIRECTED BY: Andy Harries, Andy Morahan
MUSIC FROM: Crush (Virgin/Epic, 1985).
SELECTIONS: "So In Love," "Hold You," "Bloc Bloc Bloc," "Crush," "Secret," "La Femme Accident," "88 Seconds in Greensboro," "The Native Daughters of the Golden West," "Women III," "The Lights Are Going Out."

This is a nicely shot, attractively produced documentary on the making of the British electro-pop band's *Crush* LP, combining in-studio recordings and performances of some songs with promotional videos for others, and including interviews with OMD principals Andy McCloskey and Paul Humphreys on the subject of how they met, how they compose, each other as a bandmate, how and why they're making *Crush* the way they are, and so on. There are also travelogue scenes in Spain (where they shot videos for "Hold You," "So In Love," "Secret," and "La Femme Accident"), and brief snatches of conversation with their producer and with members of their backing band—whose presence throughout the album, an apparent first in OMD's history, is discussed several times by several people. The music is pleasant, lushly arranged contemporary pop, with nothing as memorably hooky as early classics such as "Electricity" or "Enola Gay," nor as affectingly atmospheric as such subsequent pieces as "Joan of Arc" and "Souvenir." Similarly, in conversation OMD seem like nice enough chaps, but have nothing very compelling to say—except for one moment, when McCloskey discusses the inspiration for "88 Seconds in Greensboro": the TV documentary footage he happened to catch on the horrifying bloodbath at a 1979 anti–Ku Klux Klan rally in Greensboro, North Carolina. That footage, with Klansmen blithely shooting down five protestors in broad daylight, is intercut with the band's performance of the tune. Unfortunately, as honorable as OMD's sentiments may be here, the tune itself is nowhere near powerful enough to avoid trivializing that riveting, overwhelmingly hideous footage. The boys in the band seem too well meaning to have intended such tackiness, so perhaps *Crush* does them as well as us a disservice. At any rate, at seventy endless minutes, *Crush* is strictly for OMD fans.

☐ OZZY OSBOURNE
THE ULTIMATE OZZY
★★★

CBS/Fox, 1986, 85 minutes
PRODUCED BY: John Diaz
DIRECTED BY: Andy Morahan
MUSIC FROM: Various albums by Ozzy Osbourne and Black Sabbath, including Ozzy's *The Ultimate Sin* (CBS, 1986).
SELECTIONS: "Shot in the Dark," "Bark at the Moon," "Suicide Solution," "Never Know Why," "Mr. Crowley," "I Don't Know," "Killer of Giants," "Thank God for the Bomb," "Lightning Strikes," "Flying High Again," "Secret Loser," "Iron Man," "Crazy Train," "Paranoid," "The Ultimate Sin."

Ozzy fans will adore *The Ultimate Ozzy*, which brackets beautifully shot concert footage from Kansas City during Ozzy's 1986 tour with two conceptually connected video clips from the *Ultimate Sin* album Ozzy was promoting at the time. (In an intriguing marketing move, CBS/Fox got this shot early in Ozzy's tour and was able to release it when the tour was only half over—a practice that will probably become much more common in the future.) Both the opening "Shot in the Dark" and the closing "The Ultimate Sin" feature statuesque brunette Julie Gray, a member of the L.A. Rams cheerleaders, the Embraceable Ewes. In "Shot in the Dark" she and her girlfriends drive to an Ozzy concert (Frank Zappa's son Dweezil cameos as one of their boyfriends), where she's transformed via not-so-special effects into the she-demon with glowing red eyes on the *Ultimate Sin* album cover. In "The Ultimate Sin" she's Ozzy's magically endowed nemesis in an extremely silly *Dallas* parody with Ozzy as J.R.: while Ozzy keeps leering and mugging in his own stupid way, apparently lost in his own little world, she keeps materializing, casting withering looks at him and holding her hands to her temples in what one assumes is meant as an attempt to launch telekinetic weapons at Ozzy, but merely looks like she's got a splitting headache (in which case, who can blame her?). It's remarkably akin to what Tanya Roberts did in similar situations in the equally idiotic *Sheena of the Jungle*. It ends with Ozzy pushing her into his backyard pool—after which we see a horse in the nearby corral falling over dead. What *that* is supposed to mean, I don't even want to think about.

Anyway, in between those clips, the concert footage occasionally integrates quick little scenes that further elaborate the Osbourne-Gray relationship: right after "Shot in the Dark" there is a scene where she's whipping Ozzy's band, shackled like a team of dogs, across a field while Ozzy prowls the woods nearby, mugging at the moon as if he were a village idiot; between "Never Know Why" and "Mr. Crowley" (as in Aleister, the late British magician with whom Jimmy Page of Led Zeppelin also has a strange fascination) we cut to a scene in a castle, with Ozzy turning into a vampire and heading upstairs, where Julie tosses and turns in bed; after "Mr. Crowley," we see her in the audience, flashing vampire teeth of her own. But during the show-closing "Crazy Train," the vampire riff is dropped in favor of a Western homage in broad daylight, with Ozzy tying the girl to the tracks, Snidley Whiplash–style, as a locomotive approaches. And while we last see her still tied to the tracks, there's no real payoff—just a moronically vainglorious cop-out, with the screen momentarily filled with a super of Ozzy winking and blowing smoke off his pistol, outlaw-fashion, over concert footage.

Ozzy fans may or may not find this an ultimately entertaining diversion from watching their idol prancing about the stage like the Joan Collins of rock in his caftans and makeup; and I'm just as sure they won't be analyzing this "plot" for deep meaning as I am sure that no deep meaning is intended. Meanwhile, if you're not an Ozzy fan, this won't make you one. The music is a bit more pop-oriented than a lot of heavy metal (most effectively so in "I Don't Know") but still top-heavy with genre clichés. Randy Castillo performs an entertaining drum solo in "Secret Loser," not only displaying the usual flashy physical prowess *behind* his kit but also walking around in front of it, whacking at drum shells and cymbal stands as well as drums and cymbals. "Killer of Giants" is your basic acoustic-style "Stairway to Heaven" nod, until guitarist Jake E. Lee ends it with a solo of endless hammer-ons and pull-offs and other Eddie Van Halen–style technics that are so indulgently calisthenic it becomes another of those real-life heavy metal moments that make you realize just how good a joke *This Is Spinal Tap* really was. Meanwhile, throughout the concert, Ozzy keeps bellowing, "I love you people!" at the crowd with a desperately sincere glee—as if he can't *believe* they're really buying his flatulent, bombastic old circus of a show. And who can blame him?

☐ **VARIOUS ARTISTS**
THE OTHER SIDE OF NASHVILLE
★★★½

MGM/UA, 1984, 118 minutes
PRODUCED BY: Etienne Mirlesse
DIRECTED BY: Etienne Mirlesse
MUSIC FROM: Various LPs by various artists.
SELECTIONS: Kenny Rogers: "The Gambler"; Porter Wagoner: "Y'all Come"; Bobby Bare: "They Call Me the Breeze"; Ricky Skaggs: "Don't Get Above Your Raisin' "; Emmylou Harris: "Two More Bottles of Wine," "Racing in the Streets"; Hank Williams, Sr.: "Hey Good Lookin'," "Your Cheatin' Heart"; Hank Williams, Jr.: "Jesus Just Left Chicago"; Carl Perkins: "Match Box," "Honey Don't," "Blue Suede Shoes"; Bob Dylan and Johnny Cash: "Girl from the North Country," "One Too Many Mornings"; Willie Nelson: "Always on My Mind," "Whiskey River"; Johnny Cash: "Folsom Prison Blues"; Charlie Daniels: "Will the Circle Be Unbroken"; Johnny Cash: "I Walk the Line"; Hank Williams: "Your Cheatin' Heart"; Gail Davies: "Round the Clock Lovin' "; Terri Gibbs: "What'd I Say?"; Rattlesnake Annie: "Blue Flame Cafe"; others.

Entertaining and informative documentary on the capital of commercial country music—more entertaining than informative, really, and a good introduction for the casual listener/viewer seeking a well-rounded home video library. Though it does cover a good deal of history, it doesn't pretend to be comprehensive. Rather, it relaxes, winks, chuckles, and lets intimate style triumph over diffuse content. Despite the title, the program deals v-e-r-y carefully with Nashville's reputation as a bottomless pit of crassly commercial vipers; but there are nice quasi-subversive moments, like Barbara Mandrell lamely claiming that "commercial" is really "a positive label for music." Also, there's a cavalcade of interviews (with Chet Atkins, Kris Kristofferson, Johnny Cash, Carl Perkins, Hank Williams, Jr., Willie Nelson, and others) and performances, plus vintage kinescopes and other historical matter. Highlights include: classic, early TV footage of Hank Williams rocking through "Hey Good Lookin' " and Carl Perkins with a switchblade-sharp "Blue Suede Shoes"; Johnny Cash singing "Folsom Prison Blues" live at Folsom Prison; footage of Bob Dylan recording with Johnny Cash; and Chet Atkins's thoughtful comments on the modernization and inevitable commercialization of country music—a curmudgeonly, but commanding, conservative Greek chorus that runs throughout the program.

☐ **THE OUTLAWS**
OUTLAWS VIDEO LP
★★

Sony, 1983, 81 minutes
PRODUCED BY: Rene Garcia and Marcus Peterzell
DIRECTED BY: Don Roy King
MUSIC FROM: Various Outlaws albums (Arista, 1975–83).
SELECTIONS: "Devil's Road," "Hurry Sundown," "Don't Stop," "Long Gone," "You Are the Show," "Easy Does It," "Goodbye," "Foxtail Lily," "Green Grass . . . and High Tides," "(Ghost) Riders in the Sky," "There Goes Another Love Song."

The Outlaws are so blatantly derivative of both Southern boogie rock (as in the Allman Brothers, Marshall Tucker,

Lynyrd Skynyrd, Charlie Daniels) and a passel of country-rockers (the Byrds, Poco, etc.) that you don't know whether to hate them or congratulate them on getting away with so many connect-the-dots facsimiles of bits and pieces you *know* you've heard somewhere else before. Well, if you *are* a fan of this singularly uninspired cowboy-hatted lot, you'll probably just love this straightforwardly shot 1982 concert, originally shown on MTV. Otherwise, you'd best be movin' on, pardner.

P

□ ROBERT PALMER
RIPTIDE

★★½

RCA/Columbia, 1986, 15 minutes
PRODUCED BY: Terrence Donovan, Andrea Ambados
DIRECTED BY: Terrence Donovan, Ted Bafouloukas
MUSIC FROM: Riptide (Island, 1986).
SELECTIONS: "Riptide," "Addicted to Love," "Discipline of Love," "I Didn't Mean to Turn You On."

After years of nondescript solo efforts, Palmer struck gold in 1986 with "Addicted to Love," a great hard-rock riffer of a radio song, co-written with Duran Duran guitarist Andy Taylor, that bears a startling resemblance to the best of Bad Company (later that same year, Taylor came up with another fine hard-rocking radio classic, "Take It Easy," which blatantly alluded to T. Rex's "Bang a Gong," a number Taylor and Palmer had covered the year before in Power Station). The video helped a lot, no doubt, since it was a naked (pardon the pun) indulgence in sexism so up-front it almost became disarmingly candid: all it was was Palmer and a "band" lip-synching the tune before a dumb Technicolor-sunset backdrop. The "band" consisted of five lovely fashion models all done up in identical Helmut Newton ice-bitch chic, with basic black dresses, severely slicked-down, pulled-back hair, and the sort of fire-engine-red lipstick that's a cosmetic equivalent of the classic "fuck me" pumps. You can almost feel the saliva drooling from director Donovan's camera as it lingers on their breasts. "I Didn't Mean to Turn You On," Palmer's inferior remake of the 1984 Cherelle dance classic, originally written and produced by the outstanding Minneapolis team of former Time members Jimmy Jam and Terry Lewis, goes "Addicted to Love" one better on video, with Palmer and the same sort of sex-object backing band being shot in a clip-within-the-clip by a crew of, you guessed it, similarly done-up female sex objects. The brief snippet of the old standard "Riptide" serves as an atmospheric opening prelude. But the best clip by far is probably the least known of all: "Discipline of Love," shot by Ted Bafouloukas, who earlier directed the reggae film *Rockers*. It's this clip, with its simple and effective semi-plot of Palmer pursuing a girl from a bar through a cemeterylike nighttime setting, that makes the most of his Continental good looks and sartorial smarts and remains the most quirkily intriguing and atmospheric music video here.

□ VARIOUS ARTISTS (LUCKY MILLINDER, MAMIE SMITH)
PARADISE IN HARLEM

★★½

Video Yesteryear, 1980, 83 minutes
MUSIC FROM: The film *Paradise in Harlem,* 1940.
SELECTIONS: Not listed.

Despite the title, this is an especially depressing all-black backstage soap opera, with a plot of involving frustrated showbiz ambitions, tragic death, and ending up on Skid Row. It's intriguing in both its glimpses at actual black performers of the era, and in its racist representation of their supposed "real" lifestyles in Harlem. For jazz and blues buffs, most valuable for some musical numbers which feature Lucky Millinder's Orchestra, a genuinely fine swing band of the late '30s, and blues belter Mamie Smith.

☐ GRAHAM PARKER
GRAHAM PARKER VIDEO LP
★★★

Sony, 1983, 60 minutes
PRODUCED BY: Jay Dubin
DIRECTED BY: Jay Dubin
MUSIC FROM: Howlin' Wind (Mercury, 1976); *Heat Treatment* (Mercury, 1976); *Stick to Me* (Mercury, 1977); *Squeezing out Sparks* (Arista, 1979); *The Up Escalator* (Arista, 1980); *Another Grey Area* (Arista, 1982).
SELECTIONS: "Jolie Jolie," "Fear Not," "Black Honey," "Thankless Task," "Howlin' Wind," "Stick to Me," "Passion Is No Ordinary Word," "Can't Waste a Minute," "No More Excuses," "Heat Treatment," "Dark Side of the Bright Lights," "You Hit the Spot," "Empty Lives," "Nobody Hurts You."

Critics' favorite Parker never found the commercial success some thought his hard-edged, rootsy, bitterly poetic soul-rock deserved, and by the time this June 1982 show at Chicago's Park West Club was shot for an MTV concert, his career was in decline. He had followed up his best album ever, *Squeezing out Sparks,* with the lame *The Up Escalator,* and his superb backing band, the Rumour, fragmented. Here, Parker was promoting his worst album yet, *Another Grey Area,* with guitarist Brinsley Schwarz the only original Rumour left. Even so, his raspy voice is in fine form, and he still stalks the stage in the aviator shades he *always* seems to wear, while performing with conviction. And when the trouper's classy effort meets his best material, we get the flashes of flinty brilliance his earlier albums (through *Squeezing out Sparks*) displayed. That material comprises about half of this concert: "Black Honey," "Howlin' Wind," "Stick to Me," "Passion Is No Ordinary Word," "Heat Treatment," and "Nobody Hurts You." Still, as good as this show is at times, it would have been better to have caught Parker and the original Rumour a few years earlier.

☐ DOLLY PARTON
DOLLY IN LONDON
★★★★

RCA/Columbia, 1984, 79 minutes
PRODUCED BY: Stan Harris
DIRECTED BY: Stan Harris
MUSIC FROM: Various Dolly Parton albums (RCA, 1970–84); cable TV special (HBO, 1983).
SELECTIONS: "Baby I'm Burning," "Jolene," "Two Doors Down," "Coat of Many Colors," "Appalachian Memories," "Apple Jack," "Do I Ever Cross Your Mind?," "Gospel Medley: Brother Love's Traveling Salvation Show"/"I'll Fly Away"/ "When the Saints Go Marching In"/"Old Time Religion," "Dueling Banjos"/"Orange Blossom Special," "Rhumba Girl," "All Shook Up," "Me and Little Andy," "Down from Denver," "Here You Come Again," "9 to 5," "Great Balls of Fire," "I Will Always Love You."

As *Real Love*—the program she shares with Kenny Rogers—may indicate to some, and as *Dolly in London* proves, Dolly could wipe any stage with Kenny Rogers, who's hardly fit to lick the high heels of her shoes as a singer, songwriter, or all-round entertainer. *Dolly in London* provides a generous helping of the inimitable Dolly serving up a solid and wide-ranging selection of songs, most of them her own, for an extremely adoring British throng. As if the fine, nicely shot show itself weren't enough, there are also some funny and/ or eyebrow-raising scenes surrounding it: Dolly arrives at Heathrow Airport, where a customs official asks her her business in England—to which she replies, "I sing"; at a hotel press conference, Dolly tells the media, "If I'd been born a man, I probably would've been a drag queen!"; and most remarkably of all, the crush of fans outside the Dominion Theater in London for Dolly's show contains an amazing number of punk rockers in pink hair—which may not be so strange after all, considering the sorts of hairdos Dolly and so many other country stars have been known to sport.

□ JACO PASTORIUS
MODERN ELECTRIC BASS
★★★★

DCI, 1985, 90 minutes
PRODUCED BY: Rob Wallis and Paul Siegel
DIRECTED BY: Rob Wallis and Paul Siegel
MUSIC FROM: Various albums by Jaco Pastorius and Weather Report.
SELECTIONS: "Naima," "Birdland," "If I Only Had a Heart," "Donna Lee," "Funky Broadway," "Alfie," plus twenty minutes of untitled improvisation with trio.

Onetime Weather Report bassist Jaco Pastorius is one of the most respected—actually idolized—fusion-jazz bassists. Recently, he's also become quite notorious for his sullenly egomaniacal mood-swings. So it's especially gratifying that Drummers Collective caught him on a really good day for this excellent personal portrait/instructional cassette, in which Jaco is prompted by fellow bassist Jerry Jemmott, who's no slouch himself, having been house bassist on Atlantic Records' classic '60s soul sessions. In fact, it could be the presence of another bassist, one whom Jaco at one point identifies as one of his influences, that inspired him to be so cooperative and coherent.

This tape covers Jaco's roots and influences, how he developed his technique, fretless vs. fretted electric bass, right- and left-hand technique, harmonics and arpeggios, practice routines, and so on. Jaco solos and improvises for twenty minutes with a trio including outstanding jazz guitarist John Scofield and drummer Kenwood Dennard. As with most DCI tapes, there's also an accompanying instruction booklet notating Jaco's exercises and dauntingly fast runs; one great feature of the tape is that at certain moments as Jaco demonstrates an exercise or technique a title will flash on-screen saying "See Exercise Seven in accompanying booklet," and so on. Beginners and experienced players can learn from this tape—and will probably want to keep it for years, reaping different benefits from it as time goes by. (Available by mail order from DCI.)

□ TEDDY PENDERGRASS
LIVE IN LONDON
★★½

CBS/Fox, 1982, 75 minutes
PRODUCED BY: Mike Mansfield
DIRECTED BY: Mike Mansfield
MUSIC FROM: Various Teddy Pendergrass albums.
SELECTIONS: "Just Can't Get Enough," "I Can't Live Without Your Love," "Love TKO," "Lady," "My Latest, Greatest Inspiration," "Keep on Lifting Me Higher," "Where Did All the Loving Go," "The Whole Town's Laughing at Me," "Come On Over to My Place," "Close the Door," "Turn off the Lights," "Tell Me What You Want to Do," "You Got What I Want," "Reach Out and Touch (Somebody's Hand)."

Onetime lead singer with Harold Melvin and the Blue Notes, Pendergrass began a successful solo career as a smoochy R&B ladies' man crooner in the late '70s. This concert at London's Hammersmith Odeon was recorded shortly before his tragic 1982 auto accident, which has since left him wheelchair-bound. Unless you're a fan of the man his fans affectionately call "Teddy Bear" (in New York once they had a ladies-only Pendergrass show and gave away chocolate "Teddy Bear" lollipops to every lady in the house!), his boudoir-baritone antics may seem like sub–Barry White camp. But fans will revel in this decently shot chance to catch Teddy in prime form delivering the seductive goods.

☐ **VARIOUS ARTISTS**
PERFORMANCE
★★★½

Warner Home Video, 1980, 102 minutes
PRODUCED BY: Sanford Lieberson
DIRECTED BY: Donald Cammell and Nicolas Roeg
MUSIC FROM: Performance motion picture soundtrack (Warner Bros., 1970).
SELECTIONS: Randy Newman: "Gone Dead Train"; Merry Clayton: "Poor White Hound Dog"; Mick Jagger with Ry Cooder: "Memo from Turner"; incidental soundtrack music by Randy Newman and Jack Nitzsche.

In this seminal post-countercultural example of self-consciously arty cinema, directors Cammell and Roeg dress up what is basically a gangster-on-the-lam story (*à la* the Bogart classic *Petrified Forest*) in decadent, drug-addled, androgynous drag, creating a disturbingly fragmented and provocatively surreal scenario that obliquely anticipates much of rock video's luridly dreamlike, sexually flamboyant arrogance. The creepy strangeness is set in motion when James Fox, a gangster running from both the cops and the crooks he's betrayed, hides out in the home of retired rock star Turner—"played" by Mick Jagger, whose powerfully perverse presence plays blatantly on his real-life image as a satanic shaman, thus indicating what the film's title really means. Hint: it has to do with identity and morality, as well as loss of identity and amorality. It's also noteworthy that Roeg's *à clef* use of Jagger here presaged his apposite casting of David Bowie in *The Man Who Fell to Earth*. Also worth mentioning: Anita Pallenberg (before she lost her bewitching good looks) and Michele Breton (daughter of poet André, founder of Surrealism) as amoral coquettes cavorting in Turner's richly appointed town house. The rock soundtrack, mainly featuring Randy Newman and Jack Nitzsche, is very strong throughout, with Newman's "Gone Dead Train"—one of his few and most successful stabs at genuine hard rock—a highlight. But by far the most stunning scene, and very much a protean music video interlude, is the self-contained sequence in which Jagger sneers "Memo from Turner" over Ry Cooder's breathtaking slide guitar swoops and in the face of a boardroom full of flabbergasted businessmen. A most memorable moment in a film that once seen, is impossible to forget.

☐ **CARL PERKINS, VARIOUS GUESTS**
BLUE SUEDE SHOES
★★★½

MCA, 1986, 60 minutes
PRODUCED BY: Stephanie Bennett
DIRECTED BY: Tom Gutteridge
MUSIC FROM: Various albums by Carl Perkins and Rosanne Cash; cable TV special (Cinemax, 1986).
SELECTIONS: Carl Perkins with Dave Edmunds and others: "Boppin' the Blues," "Cat Clothes," "Turn Around," "The World Is Waiting for the Sunrise"; Perkins with Eric Clapton: "Match Box," "Mean Woman Blues"; Perkins with Rosanne Cash: "Jackson"; Perkins with George Harrison: "Your True Love"; Ringo Starr: "Honey, Don't"; Rosanne Cash: "What Kinda Girl"; George Harrison: "Everybody's Trying to Be My Baby"; Perkins, Edmunds, Harrison, Clapton, Cash, Starr, Earl Slick, others: "That's Alright," "Blue Moon of Kentucky," "Night Train to Memphis," "Glad All Over," "Whole Lotta Shakin' Goin' On," "Gone, Gone, Gone," "Blue Suede Shoes."

Carl Perkins has always been overshadowed by Elvis Presley and Jerry Lee Lewis in rock and rockabilly history, thanks in part to a tragic twist of fate. Perkins recorded "Blue Suede Shoes" in 1955, about a year before Elvis Presley did, but soon after recording it Perkins was involved in an auto accident en route to a taping of the Perry Como TV show. His brother Jay was killed, and it took nine months for Perkins to recover from the injuries he sustained, during which time Presley recorded "Blue Suede Shoes" and had a big national hit.

Here, he gets some of what's due him in the way of affectionate respect and tribute from an appropriate all-star cast: some members of British rock royalty whom Perkins decisively influenced, such as Dave Edmunds, George Harrison (Perkins befriended the Beatles on a 1963 U.K. tour and later oversaw their recordings of some of his rockabilly classics), Eric Clapton, and Ringo Starr, as well as young neorockabilly guns Lee Rocker and Slim Jim Phantom of the Stray Cats, both of whom at the time of this taping were playing in a new band with onetime David Bowie guitarist Earl Slick, who's also present.

The music is solid throughout, with Edmunds guiding the backup band in his usual authentic, authoritative way and Perkins looking and sounding great. And while the music is never really revelatory, it does have its outstanding moments—especially Clapton's solos in "Match Box," "Mean Woman Blues," and "Blue Moon of Kentucky," in which old Slowhand, as Eric is known, comes out smoking and just burns hotter and hotter as the show goes on. Clapton is obviously inspired by the sense of occasion here to some of the finest performances of his career—and it's that sense of occasion and inspiration, as well as tribute and respect, that really elevates *Blue Suede Shoes* and lets it modestly transcend mere music-oriented critique, as well as nostalgia. There's a near-palpable love passing back and forth onstage between elder statesmen Perkins and his two or three generations of disciples, and the cameras capture it without making a big deal out of it—it's there in the way Edmunds, Harrison, and Clapton gaze at Perkins when he's not looking, with a mixture of tremulous awe and incredulity at his presence and vitality. And it's *really* there in Perkins's benevolent, enthusiastic, humble-yet-proud way of presiding over things: shouting encouragement to a rather tentative Harrison for their duets, frequently noting how happy he is to be there, and *always* seeming to be sincerely overjoyed.

As the closing "Blue Suede Shoes" ends—it's already been played a second time, Edmunds leading it, after Perkins had done it once—Ringo and Slim Jim Phantom keep bashing at their drums, and nobody seems to want to end it. Perkins comes to the mike and says he thinks the cameras have been turned off, and then, with a tear or two rolling down his cheek, tells the crowd onstage and the crowd in the seats before him, "I wrote that song thirty years ago this month, and I never—*never*—had such a good time playing it as I have here tonight with you people." It requires no effort at all to believe him completely, and his statement provides a marvelous close to a very nice program.

□ **VARIOUS ARTISTS**
PERSONAL PROPERTY
★½

Sony, 1985, 20 minutes

PRODUCED BY: Don Oriolo and Jurgen S. Korduletsch

DIRECTED BY: Don Oriolo and Jurgen S. Korduletsch

MUSIC FROM: Various albums by various artists (Personal, 1983–85).

SELECTIONS: George Kranz: "Trommeltanz (Din Daa Daa)"; Boytronic:

"You"; Malibu: "Goin' Cruisin' "; Psychodrama: "I'm Not Your Doormat"; Tarracco: "Sultana"; Bobby Orlando and the Flirts: "Danger."

This compilation of promo clips by artists on the independent Personal Records label at first comes on like Sony's *Danspak* tapes, like cheap video art. Since the *Danspak* programs themselves are highly erratic at best, that's not necessarily a good thing. George Kranz's verbal/percussive dadaistic/atavistic assault "Trommeltanz" is invigorating, funky fun, shot with spartan straightforwardness. It's the class of the lot by a million miles. Psychodrama's "I'm Not Your Doormat" sets up the male singer, who whines misogynistic bluster over wheezy synth-pop for a trapdoor fall. Tarracco's "Sultana" is an abstract tone-and-image poem full of sounds and sights of high-speed travel and clattering percussion. That's the rest of the good stuff. Boytronic, Malibu, and Bobby Orlando and the Flirts are all insultingly dumb, sleazoid attempts at assembly-line '80s dance-pop. It says "Dance Mix" on the cassette cover, but only "Trommeltanz" really cuts it on the dance floor, and except for Tarracco's cerebral interlude, none of the rest of this forgettable stuff is worth a look or a listen.

□ TOM PETTY AND THE HEARTBREAKERS
PACK UP THE PLANTATION LIVE!
★★★

MCA, 1986, 96 minutes
PRODUCED BY: Kim Dempster and Kathleen Dougherty
DIRECTED BY: Jeff Stein
MUSIC FROM: Tom Petty and the Heartbreakers (Shelter, 1976); *You're Gonna Get It!* (Shelter, 1978); *Damn the Torpedoes* (Backstreet, 1979); *Hard Promises* (Backstreet, 1981): *Long After Dark* (Backstreet, 1982); *Southern Accents* (MCA, 1985).
SELECTIONS: "American Girl," "You Got Lucky," "It Ain't Nothin' to Me," "Don't Do Me like That," "The Waiting," "I Need to Know," "Don't Come Around Here No More," "Spike," "Southern Accents," "Rebels," "Breakdown," "Refugee," "Little Bit O' Soul," "So You Wanna Be a Rock and Roll Star," "Make It Better," "Route 66."

This document of Petty's summer '85 *Southern Accents* tour is splendidly directed by Jeff Stein, who uses an army of cameras and cranes to keep things moving visually—but Stein does it with unobtrusive grace instead of the usual edit-happy clumsiness endemic to far too many rock concert videos. That, and the fact that overall Petty and band do a good job covering a wide range of their very popular and very derivative '60s/country/folk-inflected pop-rock, make this a modestly recommendable program. Petty fans will undoubtedly find an epiphany, or at least a highlight, in "Breakdown," where Petty lets the audience sing the entire first verse of the song for him. Even if you're not a Petty fan, that's a pretty remarkable scene. However, Petty and the Heartbreakers have their erratic moments: for instance, an extremely lame cover of the '60s bubblegum classic "Little Bit O' Soul" is followed by a very solid cover of the Byrds' folk-rock classic "So You Wanna Be a Rock and Roll Star." One more thing: if you don't cotton to the romanticizing of the redneck that Petty indulged on this tour—with a Tara-styled plantation set behind him, and draping himself in the Confederate flag, and so on—this program is not for you.

□ VARIOUS ARTISTS (PROFESSOR LONGHAIR, TUTS WASHINGTON, ALLEN TOUSSAINT)
PIANO PLAYERS RARELY EVER PLAY TOGETHER
★★★★½

Stevenson Productions, 1986, 60 and 76 minutes

PRODUCED BY: Stevenson J. Palfi
DIRECTED BY: Stevenson J. Palfi
MUSIC FROM: Various albums by various artists; Mississippi Educational TV special.
SELECTIONS: Professor Longhair, Allen Toussaint, Tuts Washington: "Variation on Pinetop's Boogie Woogie"; Washington: "Arkansas Blues," "Mr. Freddie's Blues," "Sunny Side of the Street," "Russian Lullabye," "Swanee River," "Tico Tico," "Variation on Yancey Special"; Professor Longhair: "Tipitina," "Mardi Gras in New Orleans," "Whola Lotta Lovin'," "Willie Fugal's Blues," "Gone So Long"; Allen Toussaint: "Southern Nights," "Yes We Can Can," "What Is Success," "Java," "Whipped Cream," "Workin' in a Coal Mine," "Fortune Teller," "Holy Cow," "Ain't It the Truth," "Mother-In-Law," "The Old Professor"; Earl Turbinton and Willie Tee: "Variation on Swanee River"; Olympia and Tuxedo Brass bands: "Battle Hymn of the Republic"; and others.

Outstanding, oft-awarded documentary that looks at the continuity of New Orleans musical tradition through three of the Crescent City's greatest pianists: the seminal Isidore "Tuts" Washington; roots rock 'n' roller (and acknowledged founder of "the New Orleans Sound") Professor Longhair (born Henry Byrd); and modern-day renaissance man (hit-making songwriter/producer/performer in his own right) Allen Toussaint. In their own ways, all three are brilliant performers and wonderful personalities. This trio of keyboard giants was caught playing together for the first time while rehearsing for their first joint concert. Longhair died two days before that scheduled performance, and having a visual record of this astounding musical figure makes this tape worthwhile all by itself. We also get a rare look at Longhair's jazz wake and traditional New Orleans funeral procession, followed by an appropriate coda—the originally planned concert, which Washington and Toussaint turn into a tribute to the late, great Professor Longhair. (NOTE: This tape is available in both sixty- and seventy-six-minute versions, the longer version adding mostly a few more Toussaint songs; available by mail order from Stevenson Productions, Inc.).

□ VARIOUS ARTISTS
PICTURE MUSIC
★★½

Vestron, 1983, 60 minutes
PRODUCED BY: Picture Music International
MUSIC FROM: Various albums by various artists.
SELECTIONS: Kim Carnes: "Bette Davis Eyes"; Strange Advance: "She Controls Me"; Naked Eyes: "Always Something There to Remind Me"; America: "The Border"; J. Geils Band: "Freeze-Frame"; Kim Wilde: "Kids in America"; Red Rider: "Light in the Tunnel"; Talk Talk: "Talk Talk"; Thomas Dolby: "She Blinded Me with Science"; George Thorogood: "Bad to the Bone"; Steve Miller: "Abracadabra"; Eddie Jobson: "Turn It Over"; Billy Squier: "Everybody Wants You"; Burning Sensations: "Belly of the Whale."
Also available on Pioneer Stereo Laser Videodisc.

The first big various-artists clips compilation, *Picture Music* ended up proving one thing: these kinds of programs just don't sell too well, for whatever reason (trying to please everyone all the time and inevitably failing, perhaps). Still, for those in a K-Tel frame of mind, *Picture Music* offers a pretty good sampling of the state-of-the-art of MTV-style rock video circa 1983. Of course, the state of the art at that time was as generally erratic as it's ever been in music video. The good clips include: Kim Carnes's "Bette Davis Eyes," with its immortal face-slapping dance scene, one of the first triumphs for rock video *auteur* Russell Mulcahy; Thomas Dolby's silent-movie-styled slapstick lampoon of institutional science, "She Blinded Me with Science"; and Burning Sensations' "Belly of the Whale," a bouncy calypsoid tune with a colorfully inventive, good-humored, action-packed video.

The low points are: Strange Advance's self-conscious surrealism and garden-variety sexism in "She Controls Me"; Naked Eyes' "Always Something There to Remind Me," a flatulent synth-pop assault on the Bacharach-David classic with a deadly dull video; America's "The Border," simply because it's America and America is a pretty lame band, period (unless they're giving Bill Murray fodder like "Horse with No Name" for his lounge-singer routines); George Thorogood's "Bad to the Bone," in which the slavishly derivative roots-rock revivalist shows highly questionable respect for those roots, by striding into a poolroom in a tough part of town and beating no less than Bo Diddley (I don't care if Bo went along with it willingly—the day Thorogood creates an original tune one-fiftieth as powerful, memorable, and influential as, say, "Bo Diddley" is the day he earns the right to indulge in such Uncle Tomfoolery); and the J. Geils Band's "Freeze-Frame," a pleasant enough tune with an inane, lazy video that's an intelligence-insulting mix of paintbrush shenanigans, irrelevant silent-movie clips, and low-budget "special effects." Somewhere in between are: Kim Wilde's "Kids in America," with rock video *auteur* Brian Grant shooting the pretty, pouting blonde chanteuse in vintage provocatively vacuous, chicly sexist, attitude-copping rock video fashion; Red Rider's "Light in the Tunnel" with its somewhat thoughtful but ultimately turgid biological-humanist philosophizing; Talk Talk's "Talk Talk," meant to be a chaotic parody of stage-performance but not wholly successful; Steve Miller's "Abracadabra," oozing with irrelevant but "oh wow"-evoking special effects; Eddie Jobson's undistinguished "Turn It Over"; and Billy Squier's "Everybody Wants You," a so-so performance ("enhanced" with Andy Warhol post-production treatments) video for one of Squier's better hard-rock pop tunes.

□ PINK FLOYD
PINK FLOYD AT POMPEII
★★★½

Vestron, 1981, 85 minutes
PRODUCED BY: Michele Arnaud
DIRECTED BY: Adrian Maben
MUSIC FROM: Ummagumma (EMI/Harvest, 1970); *Dark Side of the Moon* (EMI, 1972); *Meddle* (EMI/Harvest, 1971).
SELECTIONS: "One of These Days I'm Going to Cut You into Little Pieces," "Careful with That Axe, Eugene," "Saucerful of Secrets," "Set the Controls for the Heart of the Sun," "Mademoiselle Nobs," "Echoes, Parts I and II," "Us and Them," "Eclipse."

This 1971 French film is a fascinating moment in rock and rock-video history, in some ways. It captures Pink Floyd just as they were leaving their early psychedelic cult-band period and were about to enter a whole new commercially successful existential art-rock phase. Their past is represented by the performance sequences, shot by director Adrian Maben in a Pompeii amphitheater with no audience (appropriate, since the band projects zero personality as they perform, and the music is very cerebral, anyway). Floyd's future is depicted in a few tantalizing in-studio shots of guitarist David Gilmour, bassist Roger Waters, and keyboardist Richard Wright working on a few songs-in-progress to be released on *Dark Side of the Moon,* their commercial breakthrough album (which has remained on the charts longer than any other album in history). Maben's performance shots in the amphitheater are ahead of their time: awesomely beautiful, thoughtful, and considered, with s-l-o-w panoramic tracking shots and dollies in and out that not only play perceptual tricks on the viewer, but also intrinsically elevate the value of what's being shot (not to mention showing an apposite *2001* techno-awe influence). In these ways the film best anticipates the later course of rock video; the hamfisted cutaways to band members stumbling about bubbling lava pools aren't so much proto-conceptual as post-psychedelic. The interminably dull interview sequences are another bummer—scan city. But the good points far outweigh the bad; this is a movie of historical value that stands the test of time at its best to remain visually and musically entertaining (especially those space-surfing psychedelic classics, featuring Wright's Egyptian Farfisa organ snakecharming).

□ PINK FLOYD, BOB GELDOF
THE WALL

★

MGM/UA, 1983, 95 minutes
PRODUCED BY: Alan Marshall
DIRECTED BY: Alan Parker
MUSIC FROM: Pink Floyd The Wall (Columbia, 1982).

SELECTIONS: "The Tigers Broke Free, Part One," "Another Brick in the Wall, Part One," "The Tigers Broke Free, Part Two," "The Happiest Days of Our Lives," "Empty Spaces," "One of My Turns," "Don't Leave Me Now," "Another Brick in the Wall, Part Three," "Goodbye Cruel World," "Is There Anybody Out There," "Nobody Home," "Vera," "Waiting for the Worms," "Outside the Wall," "In the Flesh," "In the Flesh, Part Two," "Stop," "Thin Ice," "Another Brick in the Wall, Part Two," "Mother," "Goodbye Blue Sky," "Bring the Boys Back Home," "Young Lust," "Comfortably Numb," "Run like Hell," "The Trial."

Also available in MGM/UA Stereo Laser videodisc.

If you're a maniacal Pink Floyd fan—or simply the kind of alienated teenager who thinks the whole world revolves around your petty manic depressions; sulks; does a lot of drugs; and then goes on some sort of murderous or self-destructive bender—you probably adore *The Wall.* Otherwise, this endlessly self-indulgent, solipsistic, misanthropic, and misogynistic poison-pen letter to the human race is to be avoided like the plague. Some devil's advocates maintain that *The Wall* is actually commendable in bringing modern neuroses out in the open, rather than gilding or hiding or smoothing over them. But in fact *The Wall* wallows in and glorifies such neuroses as much as it attacks them inferentially—and this is especially, and most regrettably, true for the maniacally bilious sexism in Gerald Scarfe's scrofulous animation sequences, in which every twelve-year-old male virgin's typical *vagina dentorum* paranoias are brought to life. Hard to believe Mr. Feed the World himself, Bob Geldof, actually starred in this slop as the hyper-anomic rock star whose steadily loosening grip on reality constitutes *The Wall*'s flimsy excuse for a "plot" (there's no dialogue, either—the music and the occasionally striking music video–style *mise en scène* of director Alan Parker tell the tale).

□ JOE PISCOPO
THE JOE PISCOPO VIDEO

★★½

Vestron, 1984, 60 minutes
PRODUCED BY: Rocco Urbisci
DIRECTED BY: Jay Dubin
MUSIC FROM: Cable TV special (HBO, 1984)

SELECTIONS: "Come Fly with Me," "Witchcraft," "Rappin' Rooney," "The DaNono Song," "Quarter to Three," "Thriller."

Nominally a comedy video, but about half of this program is musical or music-related. Piscopo does his superb Sinatra impression for "Come Fly with Me," "Quarter to Three," and "Witchcraft"—the latter done as the Chairman of the Board's first heavy-metal video, and good for a few chuckles, though what really makes it work is its musical substance and acuity (kudos to Ralph Shuckett, who worked on all the music with Piscopo). Also funny is "Rappin' Rooney," as in Andy of *60 Minutes,* in which Joe-as-Andy castigates just about everything on the tube and thus manages to interpolate quick appearances as David Hartman, Phil Donahue, Lee Iacocca, Ed McMahon, David Letterman, Joan Rivers, and Ted Koppel into the rap and the video. "The DaNono Song" is a doo-wop parody sung by the hapless "Del-Tones" (which was actually the name of surf-rock pioneer Dick Dale's band) at a party for a mafioso named "Mr. DaNono." There's also a meant-to-be-poignant-as-well-as-funny bit where Piscopo is a bum who magically turns into a rock drummer—who proceeds to snort his life away and end up back in the gutter. Tying the whole program together is footage of Piscopo being interviewed by a pretty young woman; eventually, it leads to a parody of Michael Jackson's "Thriller" in which Joe and the interviewer walk through the dusky darkness, having just wrapped up the interview after his show, and Joe tells her he's not like other guys . . . and before her horrified eyes, metamorphoses into—Jerry Lewis! As he stalks her, hordes of undead Jerrys, also with buck teeth and glasses askew and spastic walks, etc., rise from their graves. It's pretty funny, but it gets *very* laborious when the Jerrys do a spastic dance in unison and you realize Piscopo's gonna parody *the whole thing.* Meanwhile, in non-music-related comedy news, special guest (and Piscopo's close pal) Eddie Murphy is very funny as Carl Lewis in one sketch. Overall, there's laughter and cleverness here—and yet *The Joe Piscopo Video* falls victim to that old comedy-album bugaboo, and one has to seriously question just how *repeatable* it is.

☐ **VARIOUS ARTISTS**

PLAYBOY JAZZ FESTIVAL, VOLUME ONE

★★½

RCA/Columbia, 1982, 91 minutes
PRODUCED BY: Joseph Ruffalo
DIRECTED BY: Dwight Hemion
MUSIC FROM: Various albums by various artists.

SELECTIONS: Red Norvo/Tal Farlow Trio: "Everywhere Calypso"; Art Farmer, Benny Golson, Nancy Wilson: "I'll Remember April," "I Want You to Save Your Love for Me," "I Thought About You"; Grover Washington, Jr., with Pieces of a Dream: "Just the Two of Us"; plus various others by Willie Bobo, McCoy Tyner's "Great Quartet," Maynard Ferguson Orchestra, and Lionel Hampton's All Star Jam Session.

☐ **VARIOUS ARTISTS**

PLAYBOY JAZZ FESTIVAL VOLUME TWO

★★½

RCA/Columbia, 1982, 91 minutes
PRODUCED BY: Joseph Ruffalo
DIRECTED BY: Dwight Hemion
MUSIC FROM: Various albums by various artists.

SELECTIONS: Weather Report with Manhattan Transfer: "Birdland"; Sarah Vaughan: "Send in the Clowns"; Dave Brubeck: "Take Five"; Dexter Gordon with Milt Jackson: "Bag's Groove"; Gordon, Jackson with O. C. Smith: "I'm Trying a Woman Who Wants to Grow Old with Me"; plus various others by Ornette Coleman and Prime Time, Wild Bill Davison, Maynard Ferguson Orchestra and Free Flight.

Both of these tapes—shot at the fourth annual Playboy Jazz Festival at the Hollywood Bowl in 1982—suffer from some very glaring faults. They try to cram far too many acts into far too little time, and purists or fans of particular acts can't help but be annoyed. And they cut much, much, *much* too frequently both between and *during* performances to shots of Hugh Hefner at his groaning-board of a table, surrounded by gorgeous dames, a smugly self-satisfied grin on his face. Seeing an ingenious musical maverick with the innately humble nobility of Ornette Coleman leading his electric funk-jazz band Prime Time in such surroundings is surreal, to say the least. Still, each volume has its highlights (McCoy Tyner's "Great Quartet," which includes Freddie Hubbard, Ron Carter and Elvin Jones, on Volume One; Ornette Coleman, Sarah Vaughan, and Dexter Gordon with Milt Jackson on Volume Two) as well as its lowlights (Maynard Ferguson's screeching blasphemy of big-band jazz on both volumes; Art Farmer and Benny Golson reunited after twenty years on Volume One—only to back up Nancy Wilson). Unfortunately, the high points end up getting short shrift—especially. Still, both could be seen as serviceable surveys of recent jazz, one supposes—while desperately hoping that there *must* be something else a *little* better out there.

□ POINTER SISTERS
SO EXCITED

★★

RCA/Columbia, 1986, 30 minutes
PRODUCED BY: Various
DIRECTED BY: Various
MUSIC FROM: Break Out (RCA/Planet, 1983); *Contact* (RCA/Planet, 1985).
SELECTIONS: "I'm So Excited," "Jump (for My Love)," "Dare Me," "Freedom," "Baby Come and Get It," "Back in My Arms," "Twist My Arm."

Together with producer Richard Perry, the Pointer Sisters have fashioned some stunning, soulful pop-funk hits. However, only two of them—"I'm So Excited" and "Jump (for My Love)"—are here, and the best of their mid-'80s streak, "Automatic," is missing. Furthermore, as good as the Pointers sound on record, that's how awful they are in their videos (several of which Perry codirected)—jumping around in tasteless costumes, often amidst tacky sets, with an idiotic abandon and stultifying clumsiness that are embarrassing. Only once do they transcend their vast visual defects: in Kenny Ortega's "I'm So Excited," in which some sexy opening scenes of the girls in their boudoirs preparing for a party (sexy because they're cut quick, so you find yourself looking for things like flashes of pubic hair in a bathtub scene) lead to the colorful, exuberantly choreographed party with a spirit and energy perfectly befitting the music. It also helps that Ortega keeps a helluva lot of stuff happening around the Pointers throughout the clip.

Otherwise, there are moderately entertaining concepts for "Dare Me" (the Pointers in male drag challenging a boxer in a gym) and "Back in My Arms" (the girls become living portraits in an art gallery and proceed to lip-synch commentary on the amorous pursuits of the gallery's patrons), and precious little else to divert the eye. With such exuberantly danceable music so immaculately produced and performed, these videos would have to be uniformly exceptional to hold up visually, and they haven't a prayer. Forego this video and stick with what the Pointers do best—the records.

□ THE POLICE
SYNCHRONICITY CONCERT

★★★★★

A&M, 1984, 76 minutes
DIRECTED BY: Godley and Creme
MUSIC FROM: Outlandos d'Amour

(A&M, 1978); *Regatta de Blanc* (A&M, 1979); *Zenyatta Mondatta* (A&M, 1980); *Ghost in the Machine* (A&M, 1981); *Synchronicity* (A&M, 1983).

SELECTIONS: "Synchronicity I," "Walking in Your Footsteps," "Message in a Bottle," "Walking on the Moon," "Wrapped Around Your Finger," "Hole in My Life," "Tea in the Sahara," "Oh My God," "King of Pain," "One World," "De Do Do Do De Da Da Da," "Every Breath You Take," "Can't Stand Losing You," "Spirits in the Material World," "So Lonely."

Also available on Pioneer Stereo Laser videodisc.

The Police, one of recent pop music's most accomplished, adventurous, innovative, and important bands, are caught at the peak of their powers at Atlanta's Omni on their 1984 U.S. tour. That in itself would be enough to make this a highly recommendable program. But even more, directors Godley and Creme—who are a music-video equivalent of the Police in terms of accomplishment, innovation, etc.—set new standards for the visual vocabulary of rock concert videos with this masterpiece. Using eleven cameras, including a go-anywhere-do-anything "Hothead" crane, and every high-tech special effect known to man, Godley and Creme provide an action-packed *mise en scène* that's somehow very *musical* (perhaps because they're musicians themselves). Some may carp that they overdo it, but when they cut *right* on the staccato beat back and forth between Sting and an audience member, each singing the syllables of the word "synchronicity" in the opening tune; when they turn an ecstatic girl in the audience into a dancing white silhouette against a black-void background; when a series of supersonically fast cuts between all eleven cameras during a high-velocity instrumental build-up in "Can't Stand Losing You" explodes in time with the band into a panoramic long shot that zooms back breathtakingly . . . it all works wonderfully. There are also frame-saturating color bursts that pop up quickly here and there, in the red/yellow/blue schematic of the *Synchronicity* album cover; "Every Breath You Take" and "Wrapped Around Your Finger" are shot in moodily lit semi-slo-mo that echoes their famous video clip treatments. And at the end we get that amazing moment when Sting chants the title of "So Lonely," his hymn to alienation, over and over to a crowd of thousands who are cheering, singing along, and adoring him the whole time.

□ IGGY POP
LIVE IN SAN FRANCISCO '81

★★★

Target, 1986, 60 minutes
PRODUCED BY: Joe Rees
DIRECTED BY: Joe Rees
MUSIC FROM: The Idiot (RCA, 1976); *Lust for Life* (RCA, 1977); *TV Eye* (RCA, 1978); *New Values* (Arista, 1979); *Soldier* (Arista, 1980); *Party* (Arista, 1981).

SELECTIONS: "Some Weird Sin," "Houston Is Hot Tonight," "Eggs on Plate," "Rock and Roll Party," "Bang Bang," "Lust for Life," "Pumpin' for Jill," "I'm a Conservative," "TV Eye," "1969," "Dum Dum Boys," "I Need More."

Iggy Pop began earning his "Godfather of Punk" title back in the late '60s when, as front man for the crude, abrasively rocking Stooges, he pioneered the confrontational technique of leaping over the stage proscenium into the audience. He also, according to legend, rubbed raw steaks over his naked torso and ground shards of broken glass into his chest. By 1981, of course—following a self-imposed retirement due to increasing drug problems, and a subsequent career-reviving liaison with David Bowie—the Ig had mellowed considerably. But as this show proves, he could still be a commanding presence and one that obviously influenced his benefactor Bowie. Just check out his stage attire: black leather storm-trooper hat, black leather jacket, black tie with no shirt, black bikini briefs, black garter belt, and black nylon stockings. Backed by a solid, punkishly energetic band driven by hyperactive then–Blondie drummer Clem Burke and featuring ex-Blondie Gary Valentine and Bowie band member Carlos Alomar on guitars (Alomar wears a ski mask through the first half of the show), Iggy is impassively intense throughout. But he doesn't really get going with abandon until past the halfway point, and along the way he virtually throws away a version of the Stooges classic "1969." Things start to reach a peak with "I'm a Conservative" and "I Need More"—but then Iggy says good night to the crowd. The intensity holds steady, however, for the encores, a charging version of his classic "Lust for Life" and a powerful rendition of the then-new "Pumpin' for Jill," during which Iggy seems positively possessed. The production by Target Video is rewarding in its up-close, low-budget rawness, though the erratic lighting sometimes detracts. (Available in stores, or by mail order from Target Video or Independent World Video.)

□ THE POWER STATION
THE POWER STATION

★ ½

Sony, 1986, 23 minutes
DIRECTED BY: Peter Heath
MUSIC FROM: The Power Station (Capitol, 1985).
SELECTIONS: "Some Like It Hot," "Get It On (Bang a Gong)," "Communication."

The Power Station was a "temporary supergroup" formed in 1985 by Duran Duran guitarist Andy Taylor and bassist John Taylor, with Chic/David Bowie drummer Tony Thompson and vocalist Robert Palmer, a man of continental good looks but debatable talent who has been around since the late '60s, when he co-led the rather lackluster British white-soul band Vinegar Joe (whose chief musical asset was underrated female singer Elkie Brooks). With such a collective pedigree, of course, the Power Station sold millions of records, even though their sound was a bruisingly bumptious but rather uninspired meld of hard-rock clichés and insignificant post-rap dance-music production effects. "Some Like It Hot" is tolerable but nothing special, throwing ricochet-echo electronic percussion, elephantine funk bass, and sub–James Brown horn charts into a post-modern Cuisinart; still, it was a big hit, as was Power Station's woeful butchering of Marc Bolan's "Get It On (Bang a Gong)," one of T. Rex's most enduring classics. "Communication," which failed to hit, provides more of the same big noise signifying nothing. Ironically, Andy Taylor paid infinitely better hommage to Bolan by recasting the "Get It On" guitar riff in his own "Take It Easy," a very fine radio-rocker from the soundtrack of the abominable 1986 movie *American Anthem*. It was a hit around the same time as Palmer's "Addicted to Love," a super-solid Bad Company–style rocker Taylor and Palmer co-wrote for the singer's *Riptide* LP. Unfortunately, of course, neither "Take It Easy" nor "Addicted to Love" are here, and the music that *is* here is 20,000 leagues lower in quality. The visuals, meanwhile, are even worse than the music, mixing ugly lighting and art direction, crude animation, meaningless antics among models and band members in a loft set, and forgettable lip-synched performance.

□ TONY POWERS

DON'T NOBODY MOVE (THIS IS A HEIST)

★★★½

Sony, 1984, 24 minutes

PRODUCED BY: Tony Powers and Brian Owens

DIRECTED BY: Brian Owens

SELECTIONS: "Don't Nobody Move (This Is a Heist)," "Odyssey," "Midnite Trampoline."

The mysterious Mr. Powers claims to have been a Brill Building songsmith during the early-'60s glory days of Carole King and Gerry Goffin, Ellie Greenwich and Jeff Barry, and Barry Mann and Cynthia Weill. He *has* made some notable acquaintances over the years, some of whom—actors Treat Williams and Peter Riegert, actresses Marcia Strassman and Lois Chiles—cameo here. And onetime Rascals guitarist Gene Cornish coproduced the music with Powers; considering the credentials of those involved, it's a surprisingly uninspired mélange of rock, pop, funk, and jazz, with Powers "singing" in a thick, growly, unintelligible hep-cat's mumble. At first glance, the most intriguing thing about this tape is the fact that Powers never made a record to go with these videos—which leaves us wondering if that was deliberate on Powers's part or a function of the music's mediocrity, but at least indicates his pioneer's faith in music video as an autonomous new form.

Despite the indifferent music and the preponderance of guest-star cameos, which tend to lessen one's opinion of Powers's own charms, this program won the Silver Medal in 1983 at the 25th International Film and Video Festival in New York City. And it deserves the prize, too. There are wit, filmmaking expertise, and a refreshing off-the-wall spirit aplenty here, enough to almost make you stop asking, "Who the hell *is* this Tony Powers guy, anyway, and why can't I understand a *word* he's trying to sing?"

In the title clip, Powers prowls the streets of nocturnal Manhattan like some sort of dazed, dislocated bum, wandering in and out of a variety of surreal non-sequitur encounters and situations; he surprises Treat Williams in his shower, and manages to unsettle Peter Riegert enough to keep him from ever finishing his hot dog at the legendary, now-defunct downtown-Manhattan eatery Dave's Luncheonette (once home to the best egg creams in town). It never ends up making enough rational sense to add up to the *Naked City* parody or whatever that its title implies, but it oozes a cockeyed, deadpan humor all its own, and it's very well-made. "Odyssey" is a more downbeat mood piece, with Powers again meandering around Manhattan; this time, he shadows an alluring mystery woman, played by Lois Chiles, over the fog-shrouded piers of Manhattan's atmospheric West Side waterfront. In keeping with the overall comic tone of the tape, there's a bit of self-mocking sting in this rumination on unrequited desire. In "Midnite Trampoline," Powers and director Brian Owens parody Italian cinema of the '60s, from Fellini to those romantic comedies like *Marriage, Italian Style* and *Divorce, Italian Style;* Powers plays another sleazoid, in this case a gigolo billing himself as a "Professor of Love," trying and failing to seduce assorted wealthy dowagers.

All in all, this is one queer little item, but it shows enough taste, intelligence, and drollery to be well worth a look for those tired of the run-of-the-mill and in the mood for an off-beat fillip.

□ ELVIS PRESLEY

LOVE ME TENDER

★★★

CBS/Fox, 1956, 89 minutes

PRODUCED BY: David Weisbart

DIRECTED BY: Robert D. Webb
MUSIC FROM: Love Me Tender EP (RCA, 1956).
SELECTIONS: "Love Me Tender," "Let Me Be," "Poor Boy," "We're Gonna Move."

LOVING YOU
★★★

Warner Home Video, 1957, 101 minutes
PRODUCED BY: Hal Wallis
DIRECTED BY: Hal Kanter
MUSIC FROM: Loving You (RCA, 1957).
SELECTIONS: "Let Me Be Your Teddy Bear," "Got a Lot of Livin' to Do," "Loving You," "Lonesome Cowboy," "Hot Dog," "Mean Woman Blues," "Party."

JAILHOUSE ROCK
★★★★★

MGM/UA, 1957, 96 minutes
PRODUCED BY: Pandro S. Berman
DIRECTED BY: Richard Thorpe
MUSIC FROM: Jailhouse Rock (RCA, 1957).
SELECTIONS: "Jailhouse Rock," "Young and Beautiful," "I Want to Be Free," "Don't Leave Me Now," "Treat Me Nice," "(You're So Square) Baby I Don't Care," "One More Day."

KING CREOLE
★★★★½

CBS/Fox, 1958, 115 minutes
PRODUCED BY: Hal Wallis
DIRECTED BY: Michael Curtiz
MUSIC FROM: King Creole (RCA, 1958).
SELECTIONS: "King Creole," "As Long As I Have You," "Hard Headed Woman," "Trouble," "Dixieland Rock," "Don't Ask Me Why," "Lover Doll," "Crawfish," "Young Dreams," "Steadfast, Loyal and True," "New Orleans," "Turtles, Berries and Gumbo," "Banana."

G.I. BLUES
★★★½

CBS/Fox, 1960, 104 minutes
PRODUCED BY: Hal Wallis
DIRECTED BY: Norman Taurog
MUSIC FROM: G.I. Blues (RCA, 1960).
SELECTIONS: "G.I. Blues," "Doin' the Best I Can," "Frankfurt Special," "Shoppin' Around," "Wooden Heart," "Pocketful of Rainbows," "Tonight Is So Right for Love," "Didja Ever?," "What's She Really Like," "Big Boots."

FLAMING STAR
★★★

CBS/Fox, 1960, 101 minutes
PRODUCED BY: David Weisbart
DIRECTED BY: Don Siegal
SELECTIONS: "Flaming Star."

WILD IN THE COUNTRY
★★★

CBS/Fox, 1961, 114 minutes
PRODUCED BY: Jerry Wald
DIRECTED BY: Philip Dunne
SCREENPLAY BY: Clifford Odets
SELECTIONS: "Lonely Man," "I Slipped, I Stumbled, I Fell," "In My Way," "Wild in the Country."

BLUE HAWAII
★★★★

CBS/Fox, 1961, 101 minutes
PRODUCED BY: Hal Wallis
DIRECTED BY: Norman Taurog
MUSIC FROM: Blue Hawaii (RCA, 1961).
SELECTIONS: "Blue Hawaii," "Almost Always True," "Aloha Oe," "No More," "Hawaiian Wedding Song," "Can't Help Falling in Love," "Rock-a-Hula Baby," "Ku-u-i-po," "Moonlight Swim," "Ito Eats," "Slicin' Sand," "Hawaiian Sunset," "Beach Boy Blues," "Stepping out of Line," "Island of Love (Kauai)," "Home Is Where the Heart Is," "I Got Lucky," "Whistling Tune."

GIRLS! GIRLS! GIRLS!
★★★

CBS/Fox, 1962, 101 minutes
PRODUCED BY: Hal Wallis
DIRECTED BY: Norman Taurog
MUSIC FROM: Girls! Girls! Girls! (RCA, 1962).
SELECTIONS: "Girls! Girls! Girls!," "I Don't Wanna Be Tied," "Where Do You Come From," "I Don't Want To," "We'll Be Together," "A Boy like Me, a Girl like You," "Earth Boy," "Return to Sender,"

"Thanks to the Rolling Sea," "Song of the Shrimp," "The Walls Have Ears," "We're Coming in Loaded."

IT HAPPENED AT THE WORLD'S FAIR

★★½

MGM/UA, 1963, 105 minutes

PRODUCED BY: Ted Richmond

DIRECTED BY: Norman Taurog

MUSIC FROM: It Happened at the World's Fair (RCA, 1963).

SELECTIONS: "I'm Falling in Love Tonight," "Relax," "How Would You Like to Be," "Beyond the Bend," "One Broken Heart for Sale," "Cotton Candy Land," "A World of Our Own," "Take Me to the Fair," "They Remind Me Too Much of You," "Happy Ending."

FUN IN ACAPULCO

★★★½

CBS/Fox, 1963, 98 minutes

PRODUCED BY: Hal Wallis

DIRECTED BY: Richard Thorpe

MUSIC FROM: Fun in Acapulco (RCA, 1963).

SELECTIONS: "Fun in Acapulco," "Vino, Dinero, y Amor," "Mexico," "El Toro," "Marguerita," "The Bullfighter Was a Lady," "(There's) No Room to Rhumba in a Sports Car," "I Think I'm Gonna Like It Here," "Bossa Nova Baby," "You Can't Say No in Acapulco," "Guadalajara."

VIVA LAS VEGAS

★★★½

MGM/UA, 1964, 86 minutes

PRODUCED BY: Jack Cummings and George Sidney

DIRECTED BY: George Sidney

MUSIC FROM: Viva Las Vegas EP (RCA, 1964).

SELECTIONS: "Viva Las Vegas," "If You Think I Don't Need You," "The Lady Loves Me," "I Need Somebody to Lean On," "C'mon Everybody," "Today, Tomorrow, and Forever," "Santa Lucia."

ROUSTABOUT

★★½

CBS/Fox, 1964, 101 minutes

PRODUCED BY: Hal Wallis

DIRECTED BY: John Rich

MUSIC FROM: Roustabout (RCA, 1964).

SELECTIONS: "Roustabout," "Poison Ivy League," "Wheels on My Heels," "It's a Wonderful World," "It's Carnival Time," "Carny Town," "One Track Heart," "Hard Knocks," "Little Egypt," "Big Love, Big Heartache," "There's a Brand New Day on the Horizon."

TICKLE ME

★★

CBS/Fox, 1965, 90 minutes

PRODUCED BY: Ben Schwalb

DIRECTED BY: Norman Taurog

MUSIC FROM: Tickle Me EP (RCA, 1965).

SELECTIONS: "Night Rider," "I'm Yours," "I Feel I've Known You Forever," "Dirty, Dirty Feeling," "Put the Blame on Me," "(Such an) Easy Question," "Slowly But Surely."

HARUM SCARUM

★½

MGM/UA, 1965, 85 minutes

PRODUCED BY: Sam Katzman

DIRECTED BY: Gene Nelson

MUSIC FROM: Harum Scarum (RCA, 1965).

SELECTIONS: "Desert Serenade," "Go East—Young Man," "Mirage," "Kismet," "Shake the Tambourine," "Golden Coins," "So Close Yet So Far Away (from Paradise)," "Harem Holiday," "Hey Little Girl."

PARADISE—HAWAIIAN STYLE

★★½

CBS/Fox, 1966, 91 minutes

PRODUCED BY: Hal Wallis

DIRECTED BY: Michael Moore

MUSIC FROM: Paradise—Hawaiian Style (RCA, 1966).

SELECTIONS: "Paradise, Hawaiian Style," "House of Sand," "Queenie Wahinie's Papaya," "You Scratch My Back," "Drums of the Islands," "It's a Dog's Life," "Datin'," "Stop Where You Are," "This Is My Heaven."

DOUBLE TROUBLE

★★½

MGM/UA, 1966, 91 minutes

PRODUCED BY: Judd Bernard and Irwin Winkler

DIRECTED BY: Norman Taurog

MUSIC FROM: Double Trouble (RCA, 1966).

SELECTIONS: "Double Trouble," "Baby, If You'll Give Me All Your Love," "Could I Fall in Love," "Long-Legged Girls," "City by Night," "Old MacDonald," "I Love Only One Girl," "There Is So Much World to See."

SPEEDWAY

★★

MGM/UA, 1968, 90 minutes

PRODUCED BY: Douglas Laurence

DIRECTED BY: Norman Taurog

MUSIC FROM: Speedway (RCA, 1968).

SELECTIONS: "Speedway," "Let Yourself Go," "Your Time Hasn't Come Yet Baby," "He's Your Uncle, Not Your Dad," "Your Groovy Self," "There Ain't Nothing Like a Song."

Since—and even before—Elvis Presley's death, the standard evidence offered to prove that his talents were squandered and exploited are the thirty-one feature films, the dreaded Elvis Presley Movies. Your average video store probably doesn't stock more than one or two, and anyone who boasts of having seen them all is surely a true Elvis fan(atic). You, dear reader, are a discriminating viewer and can probably boast that you haven't seen any of them. Think that's cool? Think again.

Yes, yes, yes, the majority of Elvis Movies are everything they've been accused of being—bad, embarrassing, silly, unendurable, poorly written, badly acted, stuffed with execrable Tin Pan Alley creations that barely qualify as songs. In that sense, these films are about on a par with the average Hollywood product of the era, and in some cases superior to the average Hollywood product that tried to "rock." What offends most rock aficionados and intelligent Presley fans is not that these films exist but that Elvis Presley, the King of Rock 'n' Roll (and I'm not being facetious) is in them.

Why? If you're one of those misguided people whose only image of Elvis is as an overweight, drug-addled, confused caricature, you probably don't care. But if you're seriously interested in rock and rock-video history, take note. For Elvis was a pioneer in many ways. Not only did he blaze the trail and define what rock sensibility and style were all about, he was the first rocker that the entertainment establishment took seriously enough to exploit. The impact of Elvis's early appearances on television is widely acknowledged as a prophecy of rock video, in terms of their cultural and commercial impact, but his movies fulfilled the same function, especially in the early years. And in this image-conscious age, we should not overlook how much about Elvis besides his music—his look, his sound, his style—has contributed to his mythological stature in American entertainment history. Consider that Elvis made no television appearances between mid-1960 (when he returned from the army) and the justly famous 1968 "comeback special," made no live appearances between 1961 and 1970, and never performed outside the United States (but for one early tour in Canada), *and* spent two years in the service at his commercial peak, and you can see where the movies—for better or worse—fit in. There were only two ways to have him—on records and in the movies—so why just listen when you could see something as stunning as Elvis?

In 1956 Elvis and rock 'n' roll were still just fads that would die, and not soon enough for some folks' tastes. No other teen idol had survived past the first flush of success without something else to "fall back on" when the hits stopped coming, as everyone, including Elvis, feared they would. Even Sinatra made movies. So when Elvis signed his first movie deal, he was making a sound career move. The fact that he was paid handsomely—his fee in the '60s was a million dollars and fifty percent of the profit on each film—probably had something to do with it too.

Elvis's movies are either good or bad. Seeing the bad ones will make you think what a shame it was that a talent as great as Presley was reduced to this. Even worse, though, is to see the good ones and consider just how Elvis might have fared if he'd been given worthy material, real acting to do, and some training. Though Elvis never spoke often enough for us to know how he really felt about most things, he was proud of his serious roles and the better movies (like *Blue Hawaii*) and saw the other films as a way to give the public—his public—what they wanted. If box-office dollars could be interpreted as votes, at least in one sense Elvis was right.

As a film star, Elvis got off to a decent start. His first four films—*Love Me Tender, Loving You, King Creole,* and *Jailhouse Rock*—are his best and are all worth seeing. *Love Me Tender* had a Western setting, no rock 'n' roll in it (unless you count the title track, a number-one hit), and a tear-jerking death scene ending so dramatic and sad that Elvis's mother couldn't bear to watch it. *Loving You,* which had a slightly autobiographical plot, also featured Elvis in a serious role and is worth seeing for some of the music, particularly "Teddy Bear" and the title song. Neither of these films passed muster with most critics, but fans were wild about them. And while Elvis may have been "acting," he was still Elvis, with a face and a body the cameras loved.

Jailhouse Rock was the first musical and by far the best, a rock classic in every sense, from the predominantly Leiber and Stoller soundtrack to the great performances of "Treat Me Nice," "(You're So Square) Baby I Don't Care," and "Jailhouse Rock," arguably the first rock concept video clip ever. The deservedly famous "Jailhouse Rock" production number, which Elvis choreographed, is one of his, and rock video's, finest moments.

Here, Elvis plays Vince Everett, a nice guy who goes to prison after accidentally killing a man in a barroom fight (defending a woman, of course) only to emerge a short time later as a determined young singer with a chip on his shoulder. Vince finds fame but is haunted by a cellmate who wants a share of the action, and love for the young record promotion girl (Judy Tyler) who's helped him make it. Elvis is perfect as the rebel with a cause and in this role he gave his cocky, sensual singing persona a full-blooded third dimension his pelvic swivels had only hinted at. It's a soap opera but with great lines ("That ain't tactics, honey. That's just the beast in me."), great music—all performed in a believable context—and Elvis's most erotic scene. In 1957 girls were probably just screaming when Elvis got the whip from a prison guard because they thought it hurt. Look again. There's Elvis, shirtless, his hands tied together over his head; the whip snaps, he winces, groans, grimaces, sighs, then . . . rewind it and play it again without the sound.

His next film, *King Creole,* is an American *film noir* classic and a must-see. Directed by Michael Curtiz (*Casablanca*), based, loosely, on Harold Robbins's *A Stone for Danny Fisher,* and costarring Walter Matthau, Vic

Morrow, Dean Jagger, and Carolyn Jones, *King Creole* should have been the turning point in Elvis's film career. Set in New Orleans, the story and theme follow your standard 1950s juvenile delinquency morality tale outline. *King Creole* is all that and much more.

Danny Fisher is driven by the dream to regain for himself and his family the security and status they lost when, following his mother's death, his father fell apart. Seeing his father treated like dirt and unwilling to fight back, Danny quits school to work sweeping up bars in the French Quarter. He briefly falls in with a gang of hoods, led by Vic Morrow, with whom he commits one minor crime. In the Quarter he meets Ronnie (Carolyn Jones), an intelligent, sensitive singer turned whore whose pimp and master is the evil Maxie Fields (Walter Matthau), who of course owns the Quarter and everyone in it. How—and if—Danny survives the nightmarish twists and turns of fate is for you to find out. Shot in black-and-white, the film has the look and feel of a dark, endless nightmare. Only in the next to last scene, where Danny and Ronnie are finally together, safely forever, we hope, is there sunlight, and that is a blinding glare.

The important thing about *King Creole,* Elvis-wise, is that it was the first time Elvis actually got good reviews for his acting. He literally smolders and exudes a sexual charisma that's transfixing. The film also contains some good music: the title song (a Leiber-Stoller composition), "Trouble" (which Elvis used to open his comeback special in 1968), "Hard Headed Woman" (a number-one hit), and the ballad "As Long as I Have You." Of all Elvis's films, this is the one that will make you hate everything that follows.

Two years later, Elvis returned from the service, even more unsure of his place in America's heart than ever. The first post-service film, *G.I. Blues,* presented Elvis as a soldier stationed in Germany (as he had been in real life). This was one of the biggest box-office hits in history and the soundtrack was the longest-charting Elvis album ever, but contemporary viewers will be hard-pressed to figure out why. That's because this was the first Elvis Presley Movie.

To understand the rest of them you need to understand the basic formula: basically nice, charming, extremely good-looking guy, who also often happens to sing, gets in a jam, which may or may not involve a girl. This guy can be a former circus acrobat turned cliff diver *(Fun in Acapulco),* a movie star kidnapped by Arabs *(Harum Scarum),* a pilot *(It Happened at the World's Fair),* a race car driver *(Viva Las Vegas),* but he always gets his girl (Ann-Margret, Shelley Fabares, Joan Blackman, Nancy Sinatra). The curious are advised to stick with movies that contain songs they like (surprisingly, the movies sometimes offer the only visual record of him singing, or synching, complete versions of some of his greatest hits) or stick to the not-so-awful ones: *Acapulco*, *Blue Hawaii*, *Viva Las Vegas*, *Double Trouble*.

So what did these films have that people wanted to see? A few had some great songs—as did the biggest smash of all and Elvis's favorite film, *Blue Hawaii,* "Can't Help Falling in Love"—and a couple even had him acting some more, like *Follow That Dream* and *Flaming Star.* But what they all had, no matter how good or bad they were, was Elvis. In the lesser films (of which there are more), Elvis became the cinematic equivalent of a Barbie doll. You could dress him up in any of a dozen lavish costumes and make believe he was anything in the world. The whole time, though, true believers always knew who he was—not some middling actor sleepwalking through a goofy script and barely mouthing the words to "Song of the Shrimp" or "Yoga Is as Yoga Does"—but Elvis.

That Elvis continued making these things past 1963—and so many of them (at least three and sometimes four a year)—was the career equivalent of Nero fiddling while Rome burned. We all know what happened after the Beatles arrived, and though Elvis released many fine records between 1964 and 1969, he was locked out of the Top Ten. In 1968 there was no such thing as a thirty-year-old rock star, much less one who was thirty-three, and in the wake of the Movies even Presley fans were wondering when or if he would rise to the challenge. Though it was of course unintentional, the Elvis Presley Movies had so lowered public opinion of Elvis as a rocker that the so-called comeback special had to be regarded with skepticism. With everyone believing Elvis dead and buried in the movies, it's no wonder that the comeback special was regarded with all the awe, wonder, and respect of a resurrection. And justly so.—P.R.

□ ELVIS PRESLEY
ELVIS! 68 COMEBACK SPECIAL
★★★★★

Media, 1981, 76 minutes

PRODUCED BY: Steve Binder and Claudia Ravier

DIRECTED BY: Steve Binder

MUSIC FROM: The TV special "Singer Presents Elvis" (NBC, 1968); various Elvis Presley albums.

SELECTIONS: "Lawdy Miss Clawdy," "Baby, What You Want Me to Do," "Heartbreak Hotel," "Hound Dog," "All Shook Up," "I Can't Help Falling in Love," "Jailhouse Rock," "Don't Be Cruel," "Love Me Tender," "Are You Lonesome Tonight," "That's All Right," "Tiger Man," "Little Egypt," "Tryin' to Get to You," "One Night with You," "Memories," Medley: "Motherless Child"/"Up Above My Head (There Is Music in the Air)"/"Where Could I Go?"/"I'm Saved," "I'm Evil," "Let Yourself Go," "Nothingsville," "Big Boss Man," "Someone like You," "If I Can Dream."

□ ELVIS PRESLEY
ONE NIGHT WITH YOU
★★★★★

Media, 1985, 53 minutes

PRODUCED BY: Steve Binder and Claudia Ravier

DIRECTED BY: Steve Binder

MUSIC FROM: 1968 Elvis Presley "comeback" TV special, "Singer Presents Elvis", never-before-seen outtakes from broadcast; songs from various Elvis Presley albums.

SELECTIONS: "That's All Right," "Heartbreak Hotel," "Love Me," "Baby, What You Want Me to Do" (three versions), "Blue Suede Shoes," "Lawdy Miss Clawdy," "Are You Lonesome Tonight?," "When My Blue Moon Turns to Gold Again," "Blue Christmas," "Tryin' to Get to You," "One Night with You" (two versions), "Memories."

Along with Video Yesteryear's *Early Elvis* (and those parts of it that overlap with *This Is Elvis*), these tapes constitute the very best Elvis performances ever captured on video. *68 Comeback Special* contains the full broadcast version of the epochal 1968 prime-time TV special "Singer Presents Elvis"—an unforgettable moment in rock, and rock-on-TV, history. Steve Binder's sensitive, intelligent direction masterfully balances intimate spontaneity with theatrical gesture, and he happens to be catching an Elvis in rare form—loose and irreverent, but urgent and *dangerous,* too, and looking gorgeous. In its time, this show instantly reasserted Elvis's status as the King of Rock 'n' Roll, though much of the rest of the world may have been too busy with psychedelia and the war to notice. Today, it stands as a simply splendid document of an incredible artist, displaying his command of the form he helped invent with casual arrogance and fascinating, self-deprecating humor. There's a delightfully loose jam-session-in-the-round, featuring such Sun Records originals as guitarist Scotty Moore and drummer D. J. Fontana; a nice medley of gospel songs; and the "Guitar Man" mini-rock-opera, intriguing in its apparent autobiographical fatalism.

One Night with You concentrates on the jam session alone, containing not only the set the original TV audience saw as part of the special, but the outtakes and retakes originally considered too time-consuming or risqué for broadcast. There's nothing *really* dirty here, but it is hard to resist analyzing the King's at times near-perverse cutting-up for deeper meanings.

□ ELVIS PRESLEY
EARLY ELVIS
★★★½

Video Yesteryear, 1981, 56 minutes
PRODUCED BY: Reel Images
DIRECTED BY: Various
MUSIC FROM: 1956 Dorsey Brothers, Steve Allen, Ed Sullivan TV shows.
SELECTIONS: "Money Honey," "Heartbreak Hotel," "I Want You, I Need You, I Love You," "Hound Dog" (three versions), "Don't Be Cruel" (two versions), "Love Me Tender" (two versions), "Ready Teddy," "Love Me," "Peace in the Valley," "Too Much," "When My Blue Moon Turns to Gold Again."

A fascinating, but problematic, motherlode for Elvis fans: vintage black-and-white kinescopes of Elvis on three different network-TV variety shows (The Dorsey Brothers' Stage Show, *The Steve Allen Show,* and *The Ed Sullivan Show*) in his breathtaking 1956 prime. Most songs feature the Jordanaires on harmony vocals. Highlights include: one of two versions of "Hound Dog" on *Ed Sullivan* (Elvis says "Friends—as a great philosopher once said," before breaking right into the song); and the entire *Steve Allen* segment, where Elvis wears a monkey suit to belt "Hound Dog" at a top-hatted, pedestal-mounted basset hound (!), and then smiles like a trouper through a hideous hillbilly-baiting skit with Allen, Imogene Coca, and Andy Griffith. That's all fascinating, but the problem is that the kinescopes vary wildly in sound and picture quality, and they're cut together with such crudeness the tape plays like a bobby-soxer's hurriedly thrown-together time capsule. In a way, that adds to the program's charm, but it also docks it a technical demerit. Besides, the best of this stuff is also available on *This Is Elvis*.

□ ELVIS PRESLEY
ELVIS: ALOHA FROM HAWAII
★★★

Media, 1973, 75 minutes
PRODUCED BY: Marty Pasetta
DIRECTED BY: Marty Pasetta
MUSIC FROM: Elvis: Aloha from Hawaii via Satellite (RCA, 1973).
SELECTIONS: "See See Rider," "Burning Love," "Something," "You Gave Me a Mountain," "Early Morning Rain," "My Way," "Steamroller Blues," "Love Me," "Johnny B. Goode," "Blue Suede Shoes," "It's Over," "I Can't Stop Lovin' You," "Hound Dog," "What Now My Love," "Blue Hawaii," "Fever," "Welcome to My World," "Suspicious Minds," "Hawaiian Wedding Song," "Whole Lotta Shakin' Goin' On," "A Big Hunk of Love," "I'm So Lonesome I Could Cry," "Can't Help Falling in Love," "An American Trilogy."

When this television special first aired on January 14, 1973, it was broadcast live around the world via satellite and was seen by an estimated one billion people. American audiences saw it several months later as this television special. Though cluttered with bits of travelogue footage and a few absolutely incomprehensible split-screen filmlets (while Elvis is singing!), *Elvis: Aloha from Hawaii* captures him at the end of his post-comeback prime. He's still reasonably energetic and attentive to his audience, and seems happy to be there. Though several classics—including "Blue Suede Shoes"—get a rushed, perfunctory treatment, other numbers shine: "Something," Hank Williams's "I'm So Lonesome I Could Cry," and a powerfully sensual "Fever" are among the highlights. Every now and then you may get impatient with the TV-special-style quick-cuts, the long shots of the inexplicably sedate audience, and the careless camera angle that reveals how close to being post-prime Elvis really was. Like most Elvis product out—probably like Elvis, period—you look closely for him, but he never reveals anything. Even when he's reasonably sexy, he seems to be laughing at himself. For fans.—P.R.

□ ELVIS PRESLEY
ELVIS ON TOUR
★★★

MGM/UA, 1973, 93 minutes

PRODUCED BY: Pierre Adidge and Robert Abel

DIRECTED BY: Pierre Adidge and Robert Abel

MUSIC FROM: Various Elvis Presley albums.

SELECTIONS: "Johnny B. Goode," "See See Rider," "Polk Salad Annie," "Separate Ways," "Proud Mary," "Never Been to Spain," "Burning Love," "Don't Be Cruel," "Ready Teddy," "Love Me Tender," "That's All Right," "Until It's Time for You to Go," "Bridge over Troubled Water," "Memories," "Ain't It Funny How Time Slips Away," "An American Trilogy," "Mystery Train," "Suspicious Minds," "I Got a Woman," "Amen," "Big Hunk of Love," "Lawdy Miss Clawdy," "You Gave Me a Mountain," "Sweet Sweet Spirit," "Can't Help Falling in Love," "I John," "The Lighthouse," "Lead Me, Guide Me," "Bosom of Abraham."

This was Elvis's thirty-third and last feature-film release, one of two Elvis feature documentaries that he made before his death. (The other, *Elvis—That's the Way It Is,* was released in 1970 and has yet to surface on home video.) Covering a fifteen-day tour in 1972, this film captured Elvis before the novelty of playing live again wore off. Combining old footage (Andrew Solt, who later produced and directed *This Is Elvis,* did the research) with behind-the-scenes footage and some great concert performances, *On Tour* covers much the same ground as *This Is* and other Elvis tapes with one crucial difference. *On Tour*'s narration, what little of it there is, is done by Elvis himself, in his own words. There are priceless scenes of him backstage, seemingly caught off-guard, or relaxing with his entourage. In one beautiful portion, he sings a series of gospel songs with J. D. Summer and the Stamps during a rehearsal; in another scene, he begins recounting the previous night's adventures in bed before he realizes the camera's rolling, then laughs and breaks into another gospel song. With all due respect to Leo and Solt, I'd like to think that *this* was Elvis.

The concert footage is generally good and includes, as all Elvis films do, those crazy fans, screaming, crying, and telling us why they love Elvis, though in this film they seem particularly bizarre. Highlights of the shows include "Mystery Train," "Johnny B. Goode," and "Bridge over Troubled Water." One drawback to seeing this on the television screen is that old home-video pest, the split-screen, which is used here ad nauseam. Still, this is a fine rock documentary and well worth checking out.—P.R.

□ ELVIS PRESLEY
THIS IS ELVIS
★★★★½

Warner Home Video, 1981, 144 minutes
PRODUCED BY: Andrew Solt and Malcolm Leo
DIRECTED BY: Andrew Solt and Malcolm Leo
MUSIC FROM: This Is Elvis soundtrack (RCA, 1981).
SELECTIONS: "That's All Right," "Shake, Rattle and Roll," "Heartbreak Hotel," "I Was the One," "Hound Dog," "Merry Christmas Baby," "Mean Woman Blues," "Ready Teddy," "Teddy Bear," "King Creole," "Jailhouse Rock," "G.I. Blues," "Frankfurt Special," "Stuck on You," "Rock-a-Hula Baby," "I Got a Thing About You Baby," "I Need Your Love Tonight," "Blue Suede Shoes," "If I Can Dream," "Don't Be Cruel," "Viva Las Vegas," "My Baby Left Me," "Moody Blue," "(Marie's the Name) His Latest Flame," "Suspicious Minds," "Promised Land," "Always on My Mind," "Too Much Monkey Business," "Are You Lonesome Tonight," "My Way," "An American Trilogy," "Big Hunk of Love," "Can't Help Falling in Love," "Memories."

If you've never thought much about Elvis Presley, or if you have only the time or inclination to view one Elvis clip, this is the one. Producer/directors Solt and Leo, who were responsible for *The Compleat Beatles,* have assembled an almost flawless, factual, and honest-yet-sympathetic account of Presley's life, drawn from old television and movie clips, press conferences, concerts, and other sources. With the exception of a few remarkable books (the Presley biographies by Jerry Hopkins and Dave Marsh's *Elvis*), this is the clearest, most accurate, and best balanced account of the rise and fall of the King of Rock 'n' Roll.

That said, let's dispense with what is not so great. This film starts off by following Elvis (played by Presley impersonator Ral Donner) into Graceland on his last night on earth. The camera peers over his shoulder as he says hello to assorted relatives, hangers-on, and his daughter Lisa Marie, before retiring for his last night. To say that it's melodramatic would be an understatement. Between our knowing what will happen to Elvis, the strange background music, and Graceland's naturally gruesome decor, it's almost unwatchable. Next, we're on the road with the crew and Colonel Tom Parker getting ready for Elvis's big show in Portland, Maine (they're lining his hotel windows with aluminum foil and wheeling in racks of studded jumpsuits), when Parker gets the word: Elvis is dead. Mercifully, this lasts just a few minutes before we're listening to Donner—as the voice of Elvis—telling us about growing up in Tupelo, then Memphis. We also hear what Mr. and Mrs. Presley "thought" about it all, which may be accurate and is certainly interesting, but still rings false. A regular voiceover narration and a few old stills would have accomplished much the same thing and been more honest. After all, these aren't Elvis's words, or are they? Note here, too, that Colonel Tom Parker was the film's technical adviser, so who knows? The point is, don't let this put you off what follows.

Things start to move once we get out of the docudrama and into history, beginning with "Shake, Rattle and Roll" performed on the Dorsey Brothers' TV show in January 1956. From then on, it's one jaw-dropping performance, clip, or song after another, including the historical "Hound Dog" from Milton Berle's show, a revealing interview with Hy Gardner, "Don't Be Cruel" from Ed Sullivan's show, "Teddy Bear" from his first feature film, *Loving You*, the title production number from *Jailhouse Rock* (in a slightly different mix than the hit single version), and documentary clips of his induction in the army, his release two years later, his marriage, and other important events. Though little docudrama bits surface now and again, they are easily overlooked. Also included are newsreel-type footage of record burnings and a redneck denouncing Presley's music as "nigger-bop," which show how far we've gone and what a phenomenon Elvis was. On the lighter side are clips of Elvis with Liberace, Elvis's dad on *What's My Line,* Groucho Marx posing as the president of a Presley fan club, and so on.

As the film moves into the late '60s, there's more voiceover and ample coverage of Elvis's famous comeback and the concerts that followed. Also here are the signs of his decline: the confused, awkward conversations, the increasing girth, the blinding sweat. And finally, a press conference held by three former friends and employees upon the publication of their tell-all *Elvis—What Happened?*, the first book to reveal the details of Elvis's drug use and personality problems, just days before Elvis's death. The home-video release contains footage that was not included in the feature-film release—such as a look at Elvis's gold Cadillac—but lacks the feature's most poignant scene: Elvis in concert in June 1977 blubbering through "Are You Lonesome Tonight," obviously very confused and disturbed. A representative of Leo's denied that the scene, which in the original version was the very last before the newsreel footage of Elvis's funeral procession, was cut for artistic reasons. Apparently a dispute over the rights to the footage is to blame. If you can see the feature film, do so. Those few excised minutes say more about Elvis's end than most of us could stand to know and represent perhaps the most powerful moments in any rock documentary.—P.R.

☐ **VARIOUS ARTISTS**
PRIME CUTS
★★½

CBS/Fox, 1984, 37 minutes
PRODUCED BY: Various
DIRECTED BY: Various
MUSIC FROM: Various albums by various artists.
SELECTIONS: Journey: "Chain Reaction"; Quiet Riot: "Cum On Feel the Noize"; Romantics: "Talking in Your Sleep"; Toto: "Rosanna"; Cyndi Lauper: "Girls Just Want to Have Fun"; Matthew Wilder: "The Kid's American"; Bonnie Tyler: "Total Eclipse of the Heart"; Men at Work: "Down Under."

Wildly erratic big-hit video clip compilation. The good: Cyndi Lauper's "Girls Just Want to Have Fun," a career-making music video directed with vertiginously affectionate wit by Edd Griles; Quiet Riot's "Cum On Feel the Noize," a classic heavy-metal video scenario by director Mark Rezyka with nary a trace of the genre's usual browbeating macho sexism and violence; and, trailing somewhere further back, Men at Work's cutely and acutely literal-minded "Down Under," and Toto's "Rosanna," an extravagant *West Side Story* cop by director Steve Barron that was one of the first big showbiz breaks for actress/dancer Cynthia Rhodes *(Flashdance, Staying Alive, Runaway)*. The bad: Journey's "Chain Reaction," with vocalist Steve Perry engaging in some of the most hilariously bombastic gritted-teeth/clenched-fist lip-synch overacting ever; and Bonnie Tyler's "Total Eclipse of the Heart," one of the worst, most hilariously overdone video clips of all time. The ugly: The Romantics'

"Talking in Your Sleep," one of rock video's creepiest chauvinist/sexist fantasies ever. Percentage-wise, this collection *barely* makes the grade; but for media mavens, it's as good a quickie sampler as any available of the state of corporate rock video circa 1984.

☐ **VARIOUS ARTISTS**
PRIME CUTS: HEAVY METAL
★★½

CBS/Fox, 1984, 34 minutes
PRODUCED BY: Various
DIRECTED BY: Various
MUSIC FROM: Various albums by various artists.
SELECTIONS: Ozzy Osbourne: "Bark at the Moon," "So Tired"; Slade: "Run Runaway," "My Oh My"; Fastway: "Tell Me," "All Fired Up"; Judas Priest: "You've Got Another Thing Comin'," "Freewheel Burning."

Erratic enough that it may not satisfy the garden-variety metal maniac, yet intermittently interesting enough that it may appeal to people who never thought they could watch heavy-metal videos. Ozzy's clips are both crashing bores, and Slade's "My Oh My" and Fastway's "All Fired Up" devolve into the predictable macho clichés. But Fastway's "Tell Me" has a fun bank-robbing scenario, and both Judas Priest clips are intriguing, if you care to try reading into their subtexts. "You've Got Another Thing Comin' " is similar to "Tell Me" in that metal fights back at a symbol of anti-rock social institutions, here a suit-and-derby banker type; *but* notice the way the banker bites it in the end—Priest's intensity makes his head explode *while his pants drop.* Think about that (and the last word in the song's title) while you check out singer Rob Halford's leather-boy get-up, which is right out of the Village People. And then there's "Freewheel Burning," where a soft, pudgy little boy really gets into playing a Priest video game—and appears to faint or die of ecstasy or exhaustion at the end. Interesting.

☐ **VARIOUS ARTISTS**
PRIME CUTS: JAZZ AND BEYOND
★★½

CBS/Fox, 1985, 50 minutes
PRODUCED BY: Various
DIRECTED BY: Various
MUSIC FROM: Various albums by various artists.
SELECTIONS: Miles Davis: "Decoy"; Herbie Hancock: "Hard Rock"; Chuck Mangione: "Diana 'D' "; Al DiMeola: "Sequencer"; Andreas Vollenweider: "Pace Verde"; Hiroshima: "San Say"; Clarke-Duke Project: "Heroes"; Weather Report: "Swamp Cabbage."

The first-ever various *jazz* artists clips compilation has a cute between-clips continuity device—a scrap-metal beatnik with goatee and beret punching up each clip on a computer—which also gives away its electric-fusion leanings. It contains two instant classics of the nascent jazz-promo genre: Miles Davis's "Decoy," with the trumpet maestro shot by Cucumber Studios of England (who also did such classic rock videos as Donald Fagen's "New Frontier" and Tom Tom Club's "Genius of Love," as well as the opening computer-animation for NBC's *Friday Night Videos*) in glistening hard-lit black-and-white, with full-color abstract-geometric forms spinning out of his horn; and Chuck Mangione's "Diana 'D,' " a horribly limp Barry White update more than saved by the Nam June Paik burlesque/tribute of director Zbigniew Rybczinski. The Clarke-Duke Project's "Heroes" is a neat little Republic Serials takeoff; Hiroshima's "San Say" has a mildly intriguing urban kung-fu scenario that just rolls over and dies at the end. The rest is eye-and-ear candy of varying quality: from the sub-*Koyaanisqatsi* backdrops for Andreas Vollenweider's watercolor-pastel harpings, to the silly *Star Wars* martial-arts bombast of Al DiMeola's "Sequencer," from Weather Report's *feh* straight-performance to Herbie Hancock's obnoxious soft-core porn setup for "Hard Rock." It's worth owning for the Miles and Mangione clips.

□ VARIOUS ARTISTS
PRIME CUTS: RED HOTS
★ ½

CBS/Fox, 1985, 35 minutes
PRODUCED BY: Various
DIRECTED BY: Various
MUSIC FROM: Various albums by various artists.
SELECTIONS: Wham!: "Wake Me Up Before You Go-Go!"; Scandal, featuring Patty Smyth: "The Warrior," "Hands Tied"; John Cafferty and the Beaver Brown Band: "Tender Years"; Survivor: "I Can't Hold Back"; Eurogliders: "Heaven"; REO Speedwagon: "I Can't Fight this Feeling," "I Do'wanna Know."

A collection of big-hit videos, MTV-style, circa 1984–85. Unfortunately, most of the music is formulaic AOR mush, as in Scandal and pathetic Springsteen-wanna-be John Cafferty and Beaver Brown Band, Survivor's three-Kleenex romanticism and REO Speedwagon's milksop banality. The only remotely interesting videos are Andy Morahan's masterfully lively performance piece for Wham!'s obnoxious "Wake Me Up Before You Go-Go" and Kevin Dole's antic slapstick for REO's "I Do'wanna Know" (and the latter tries *so* damned hard it ends up being more obnoxious than effective anyway). Scandal's "The Warrior" is so pretentiously moronic it ends up being one of those so-bad-it's-hysterical anticlassics.

□ PRINCE (WITH THE TIME, APOLLONIA 6)
PURPLE RAIN
★★★★ ½

Warner Home Video, 1984, 113 minutes
PRODUCED BY: Robert Cavallo, Joseph Ruffalo, Steven Fargnoli
DIRECTED BY: Albert Magnoli
MUSIC FROM: Purple Rain original soundtrack album (Warner Bros., 1984); the Time: *Ice Cream Castle* (Warner Bros., 1984); Applolonia 6: *Apollonia 6* (Warner Bros., 1984).
SELECTIONS: Prince and the Revolution: "Let's Go Crazy," "Take Me with U," "The Beautiful Ones," "Computer Blue," "Darling Nikki," "When Doves Cry," "Purple Rain," "I Would Die 4 U," "Baby I'm a Star"; the Time: "Jungle Love," "The Bird"; Apollonia 6: "Sex Shooter"; Dez Dickerson: "Modernaire."

□ PRINCE AND THE REVOLUTION
PRINCE AND THE REVOLUTION LIVE
★★★ ½

Warner Music Video, 1985, 116 minutes
PRODUCED BY: Robert Cavallo, Joseph Ruffalo, Steven Fargnoli
DIRECTED BY: Paul Becher
MUSIC FROM: Controversy (Warner Bros., 1981); *1999* (Warner Bros., 1982); *Purple Rain* (Warner Bros., 1984).
SELECTIONS: "Let's Go Crazy," "Delirious," "1999," "Little Red Corvette," "Take Me with U," "Do Me, Baby," "Irresistible Bitch," "Possessed," "How Come U Don't Call Me Anymore," "Let's Pretend We're Married," "God," "Computer Blue," "Darling Nikki," "The Beautiful Ones," "When Doves Cry," "I Would Die 4 U," "Baby I'm a Star," "Purple Rain."

Purple Rain, the 1984 box-office smash that finally elevated Prince from best-kept funk-rock secret to new-Michael-Jackson superstar, is one of the most provocative and problematic career moves in recent pop history. Despite the rigged trappings of its Hollywood-style sentimental-inspiration screenplay (executive producer and coscenarist William Blinn did, after all, give us *Brian's Song* and *Fame*), the story gains resonance because of its *à clef* slants and autobiographical realism. In real life, Prince was a post-disco one-man funk-rock pop band, with a defiantly androgynous, sexually charged style—who came from, of all places, Minneapolis. With his gradual rise to semi-popularity prior to *Purple Rain,* the pint-sized maverick visionary also became a sort of Howard Hughes of rock, secretively wielding a chilling amount of control over his own career and his local Twin Cities scene. Taking the alias "Jamie Starr," he used his own success to help start careers for his friends and colleagues, like the Time and Vanity 6, whose debut albums Prince composed and produced under the pseudonym. Yet, despite Prince's poignant generosity in doing so under another name, by all accounts it was he who was in complete control of the scene; it's said that many Twin Cities denizens who've worked or dealt with Prince call him "Ayatollah" or "Little Napoleon."

Considering Prince's personal and professional eccentricities, the way he creates a funhouse-mirror image of reality with *Purple Rain* can be seen as a fascinating form of public auto-psychoanalysis, as well an exercise in obliquely gaudy narcissism. First off, consider that just about *everyone* in the movie plays themselves—except for the actors as Prince's parents (Clarence Williams III, Linc in *The Mod Squad,* is excellent as the psychotic father) and Prince himself, who plays "the Kid." By all accounts, in real life Prince came from a broken home; and in *Purple Rain,* his black father and white (but ethnic, as in Greek; she's played by Olga Karlatos, who is given some excruciatingly bad lines of dialogue) mother are constantly having knock-down-drag-out fights ("We don't have any fun anymore!" sobs Mom in one pathetic moment, after Dad's beaten her senseless) which lead the Kid to dismiss them as "a freak show." *But,* where in reality Prince was empowered to create and groom the Time, in *Purple Rain* the Kid is an upstart on Minneapolis's mixed-ethnic funk-rock scene, vying for scene-supremacy with the Time, whose crowd-pleasing good-time dance music is constrasted with the Kid's more ambitious, adventurous, and personal funk-rock fusions in a series of smashing performance sequences at the First Avenue Club (in real life, Minneapolis's top rock showcase and Prince's favorite hometown hangout). Of course, in classic Hollywood fashion things get darkest just before the dawn, both personally (in Prince's relationships with his parents and with Apollonia Kotero) and professionally—but the Kid comes out on top at the end.

Along the way, however, *Purple Rain* delves into some particularly repugnant aspects of misogyny: Prince has this thing about dressing his women in nothing but flimsy, frilly lace camisoles, push-up-bra corsets, garters, and fishnets; he's also got a thing about hurting the one he loves—manifested by smacking Apollonia around a bit—which he obviously inherited from Dad; and, in an early moment that made several friends of mine who *like* Prince and the Time walk out of the movie, the Time's Morris Day orders his valet Jerome Benton to throw a girlfriend who's annoying Morris into a trash dumpster, which Jerome smirkingly does (most sickeningly of all, the girl is seen popping right back up out of the dumpster with an "I can take it!" smile). It's most unsettling because for the rest of the film Morris and Jerome play marvelously comic foils, their neo–Louis Jordan zoot-suited jive contrasting vividly with Prince's sullen, pouting introspection. On one hand, *Purple Rain* is intriguing and perhaps commendable for the warts-and-all way it exposes the nastier sides of its protagonists' personalities. Still, one can't help but feel queasy seeing such virulent sexism paraded in a film that implicitly glorifies its male stars.

But balancing such misgivings are the performance sequences—and the superbly considered and felicitous way in which they're integrated into the plot (making *Purple Rain* a more legitimate and successful heir to '40s movie-musical tradition than, say, Julien Temple's well-intentioned but self-consciously stylized 1986 *Absolute Beginners*). The performances by Prince and the Revolution and the Time are nothing short of sensational (Apollonia 6 is another matter . . .); and especially in the cases of "The Beautiful Ones," "Darling Nikki," "Computer Blue," and "Purple Rain" they crucially advance and focus the plot in ways that mere dramatic exposition could not—and they do it without resorting to movie-musical clichés.

Purple Rain's emotional climax brings its art-life mimesis full-circle: just as in real life *Purple Rain* was the first album in which Prince gave his band credit for composition, arranging, production, and performance, in the film's crux the Kid realizes he must forsake his insular control-freak ways; where once he sneered at band members Lisa and Wendy's offer of a slow groove track for him to use, after his father's failed suicide attempt (how *do* you point a pistol at your head and *miss,* anyway?) sets the stage, the Kid uses their tape as the basis for the gut-wrenching title tune's musical expiation. The song—a moving gospel-folk ballad—and the way it's used in the storyline are enough to move most audiences to tears, and when Prince leans over onstage and kisses Wendy's cheek, it's a sublime gesture that can cancel one's reservations over the misogyny displayed earlier.

Despite its flaws, *Purple Rain*'s value as historical career move and as a mostly thrilling rock musical cannot be denied. And in some ways, its candor indicates that perhaps *Purple Rain* reveals more than its makers realize, which is especially intriguing considering what a reclusive oddball Prince is.

Live is problematic in its own peculiar ways. There's a strange quantity-for-quality tradeoff at work here. Yes, it captures Prince's *Purple Rain* tour extravaganza, with one of rock's hottest figures at the peak of his popularity (if not his powers—but then, that's debatable), and it was all marketed for the low, low price of about thirty dollars. It could be a heck of a deal, except that technically this is one of the *worst* concert videos ever released. Taken directly off the satellite feed that simulcast this March 30, 1985, show at the Syracuse, New York, Carrierdome to Europe, *Live* has lighting so poor, or at least so wrong for video recording purposes, that the onstage action frequently dissolves into a blue-black murk—kinda like watching through a car's windshield spattered with, er, purple rain—that leaves the viewer wondering what he/she may be missing. Becher's gracelessly straightforward direction may or may not make matters worse; depending on your perspective, it could also be refreshingly direct and unadorned.

Also on the minus side, much of what we see—or can't see—is no more than a neurotically faithful rerun of those sizzling performance scenes from the *Purple Rain* movie, and as good as those sequences are in the film, in concert you do wish Prince would give it a rest after a while. Taking matters to a ridiculous extreme, the whole of "When Doves Cry" is presented in that neo-psychedelic mirror-image video effect used at the end of the song's promo clip.

Still, this *is* Prince, and the talent and energy he displays on stage are remarkable, and remarkably generous. The highlight is the extended sequence kicked off by "Do Me, Baby," which covers such tantalizing non-LP single-flipsides as "How Come U Don't Call Me Anymore" and "Irresistible Bitch," as well as the frenzied funk of the yet-to-be-released (as of this writing) "Possessed" (appropriately dedicated to James Brown in the closing credit roll). The musical lowlight comes earlier, with the insultingly short shrift given to three of Prince's greatest songs ever, "1999," "Delirious," and "Little Red Corvette" (the last is especially butchered). Offsetting that are several bizarrely arresting theatrical interludes and "talks with God," which reveal and revel in the twisted narcissism and provocative paradoxes at the heart of this quintessentially American character.

☐ **VARIOUS ARTISTS**

THE PRINCE'S TRUST ROCK GALA

★★½

MGM/UA, 1983, 60 minutes

PRODUCED BY: George Martin, Pete Townshend, and Peter Abbey

DIRECTED BY: Mike Mansfield

MUSIC FROM: Various LPs by various artists.

SELECTIONS: Madness: "Madness," "Baggy Trousers"; Unity: "Crab Race"; Ian Anderson: "Pussy Willow," "Jack in the Green"; Joan Armatrading: "Give Me Love"; Phil Collins: "In the Air Tonight"; Midge Ure: "No Regrets"; Pete Townshend: "Slit Skirts," "Let My Love Open the Door"; Gary Brooker: "Whiter Shade of Pale"; Kate Bush: "Wedding List"; Robert Plant: "I Don't Know"; Townshend, Collins, Plant, Brooker, Ure, and company: "I Want to Take You Higher."

A not-bad, not-great array of Brit-rock performances from the 1982 edition of the annual rockshow for the Prince's Trust charity. Standouts include the wacky, sub–Monty Python high energy and spirits of Madness; Joan Armatrading; Phil Collins's atmospheric "In the Air Tonight"; Gary Brooker revisiting the haunting Procol Harum classic "Whiter Shade of Pale"; and two old guys, Pete Townshend and Robert Plant, rocking out harder than many a young guy with "Slit Skirts" and "I Don't Know," respectively. Oh, one other highlight: Prince Charles himself, *very* awkwardly presenting a best-new-band prize to all-black reggae band Unity. That the traditional stiff upper lip should even try to prevail in such surreal circumstances is downright hilarious.

☐ **VARIOUS ARTISTS**

PRIVATE MUSIC VIDEOS

★★★

Private Music, 1985, 25 minutes

PRODUCED BY: Peter Baumann

DIRECTED BY: Peter Baumann

MUSIC FROM: Jerry Goodman: *On the Future of Aviation* (Private Music, 1985); Patrick O'Hearn: *Ancient Dreams* (Private Music, 1985); Eddie Jobson: *Theme of Secrets* (Private Music, 1985); Sanford Ponder: *Etosha* (Private Music, 1985); Lucia Hwong: *House of Sleeping Beauties* (Private Music, 1985).

SELECTIONS: Jerry Goodman: "On the Future of Aviation"; Patrick O'Hearn: "Ancient Dreams"; Eddie Jobson: "Memories of Vienna"; Sanford Ponder: "Water Garden"; Lucia Hwong: "Dragon Dance."

Peter Baumann, a onetime member of Tangerine Dream, formed the Private Music record and video labels in 1985, as a sort of sophisticated, subtly urbanized counterpart to Windham Hill's "New Age" or "ambient" aesthetics. The subtle urbanization figures mainly in the music—which, while still quiescently meditative and pleasantly amorphous for the most part, is less self-consciously wistful/pastoral and more overtly electronic than Windham Hill's comparatively wimpier musings. At times—as in the selections from violinists Jerry Goodman (formerly of the original Mahavishnu Orchestra) and Lucia Hwong—the music here has interludes that are downright aggressive. This is not to say Private Music's stuff is necessarily better than Windham Hill's, but simply that it's similar yet different, and might be more appealing to a certain sensibility.

On the visual side, there's more similarity here with Windham Hill: the slickly post-modern aural wallpaper is visually complemented by a nonnarrative series of gorgeously photographed (by cameraman Barry Braverman) shots of breathtaking natural vistas, most often edited in soothing slow-dissolve fashion. The Private Music approach is different in some ways: more living creatures are seen—even, in Hwong's and former Jethro Tull/Roxy Music/U.K. violinist/keyboardist Eddie Jobson's pieces, human beings; and producer/director Baumann likes to stretch his slow-dissolve edits so that we often have one superimposed image lingering over another.

But in one major aspect, *Private Music Videos* is very similar to any Windham Hill title or just about any other such "ambient" music-video program: the visuals may be nonnarrative, but they're still so heavily literal that they achieve a simple-minded, though effective, thematic flow. So for Goodman's "On the Future of Aviation" we get all manner of shots of birds in flight, usually in slo-mo of course, as well as high-speed aerial photography of deserts and waterways in which we can see—purposely, I suspect—the birdlike shadow of the camera-carrying jet in the lower right corner of the screen. For onetime Missing Persons keyboardist Patrick O'Hearn's "Ancient Dreams" we get windswept, mist-shrouded, elemental/primeval nature scenes of volcanos, waterfalls, mountains, jungles, glaciers, and the like, with slow-dissolve superimpositions of tribal masks and other primitive-culture artifacts (there's also a stunning little sequence of time-lapse lightning storms). For Jobson's "Memories of Vienna" there's the expected meandering, high-productive-value travelogue of the Old World capital. Keyboardist Sanford Ponder's "Water Garden" is visualized with lots and lots of—what else—water imagery.

This approach does fall flat once—in Hwong's closing "Dragon Dance." It's an okay piece of music, with koto-like plucked violins over tabla-like rapid hand-drumming. But with shots of an Oriental woman dancing around in traditional Geisha-like garb while superimposed over cloud-covered mountains, bamboo forests and cherry-blossom orchards and the like, it's really just an update of the sort of trite, vaguely racist "Orientalia" we've been getting in the forms of Fu Manchu and Charlie Chan movies. It's too bad that an otherwise rather classy program has to close with the clunk of such comparative tackiness.

☐ **VARIOUS ARTISTS**

THE PUNK ROCK MOVIE

★★

Sun Video, 1980, 86 minutes
PRODUCED BY: Peter Clifton
DIRECTED BY: Don Letts
MUSIC FROM: The film (1978).

SELECTIONS: Sex Pistols: "God Save the Queen," "Seventeen," "Liar," "Pretty Vacant," "New York"; the Clash: "White Riot," "Garageland," "1977"; Slaughter and the Dogs: "Right Between the Eyes"; Billy Idol and Generation X: "Walking in the City," "Kleenex"; Subway Sect: "Why Don't You Shoot Me"; Wayne County and the Electric Chairs: "Fuck Off"; Eater: "You"; the Slits: several incomplete songs in rehearsal; Siouxsie and the Banshees: "Bad Shape," "Limbless in Love"; Heartbreakers: "Chinese Rocks," "Born to Lose"; X-Ray Spex: "Oh Bondage Up Yours."

Extremely—or appropriately, depending on your attitude—crude Super 8 documentary of the first flowering of British punk in 1977, shot at the Roxy club and during a Clash/Heartbreakers/Slits/Siouxsie and the Banshees tour. The Sex Pistols, Heartbreakers, and X-Ray Spex come off best; the chance to see a *very* young Billy Idol changing in a filthy, crowded bathroom before singing two way-out-of-tune numbers is also noteworthy. More valuable as a time capsule than for its performances, and the total lack of production values almost negates that. Frustratingly, at one point the camera lingers on Siouxsie of the Banshees getting made up backstage—while onstage and off-camera, the Buzzcocks can faintly be heard ripping through "Boredom," one of the best songs of the era.

Q

□ QUEEN
QUEEN'S GREATEST FLIX
★★★

HBO/Cannon, 1981, 60 minutes
MUSIC FROM: Various Queen albums including *Greatest Hits* (Elektra, 1981).
SELECTIONS: "Bohemian Rhapsody," "You're My Best Friend," "Tie Your Mother Down," "Somebody to Love," "We Are the Champions," "We Will Rock You," "Spread Your Wings," "Bicycle Race," "Fat Bottomed Girls," "Don't Stop Me Now," "Love of My Life," "Crazy Little Thing Called Love," "Save Me," "Play the Game," "Another One Bites the Dust," "Flash."
Also available in Pioneer Stereo Laser videodisc.

Queen's Greatest Flix gives a solid and complete overview of the band's video-clip catalogue through 1980, and if you're a Queen fan, you'll want to check it out. Note, however, that these are pre-1980 clips, as in pre-MTV. As in comparatively primitive and low-budget. The program has another problem, in a way: It peaks with its first clip, "Bohemian Rhapsody," which has been popularly misrepresented as "the first rock video." It wasn't, but it *was* the first rock video to cause a sensation by dramatically spurring a record's sales in the absence of touring. "Bohemian Rhapsody" was shot by pioneering rock video director Bruce Gowers in a single day on a budget of about $7,000 (roughly one-seventh the average budget of a 1985 rock video), and still stands as a monumentally important model in rock video's short history. Most of the hallmarks to which rock videos aspire in the post-MTV age were all there, albeit in cheaper, more rough-hewn form than the '80s would bring. There's the basic stark set-up of the four band members' faces against a black void, based on the album cover art for *Queen II,* a form of product identification (not unlike Z.Z. Top's cherry red hot rod); the use of primitive special effects, like prismatic wipes and multi-image trails, that appear in synch with musical flourishes, is corny but effective in accomplishing the ultimate prime directive of every rock video—to hoodwink viewers with enough razzle-dazzle to make them go "Oh, *wow*." *Then* you throw in the crucial footage of the band in tortured, bombastic lip-synching performance, as "Bohemian Rhapsody" does. It's really rather remarkable when you consider that the vast majority of music video has not progressed an iota beyond the formula Gowers laid out back in 1975.

The rest of the clips, however, plow similar territory to the extent that only a Queen fan could bear. Queen descend to the pits of tastelessness with "Bicycle Race" and "Fat Bottomed Girls," but then taste is not the kind of thing one looks for in a purposefully over-the-top pomp-rock outfit like this. Things actually pick up a wee bit over the last half of the tape, as director Dennis DeVallance (responsible for all clips from "Don't Stop Me Now" through "Flash," Queen's theme for the 1978 *Flash Gordon* remake) alleviates the group's terminal indulgences with the stray bit of animation or primitive computer graphics. Again: *mainly* for Queen fans only, though music video history buffs ought to see "Bohemian Rhapsody."

□ QUEEN
LIVE IN RIO
★★★½

Sony, 1985, 60 minutes
PRODUCED BY: Global Television
DIRECTED BY: Global Television
MUSIC FROM: Various Queen albums (Elektra, 1973–84).
SELECTIONS: "Tie Your Mother

Down," "Seven Seas of Rhye," "Keep Yourself Alive," "Liar," "It's a Hard Life," "Now I'm Here," "Is This the World We Created?," "Love of My Life," "Brighton Rock," "Hammer to Fall," "Bohemian Rhapsody," "Radio Gaga," "I Want to Break Free," "We Will Rock You," "We Are the Champions," "God Save the Queen."

Queen fans seeking a hefty onstage dose of the veteran British band's flamboyantly baroque hard rock and bombastically theatrical pop should be more than satisfied by the straightforwardly shot document from the January 1985 Rock in Rio Festival in Rio de Janeiro, Brazil. There is some historical value in the fact that Queen were officially opening the four-day festival before a crowd of 250,000, the largest crowd ever assembled for a single concert. I say Queen fans *should* enjoy this program, because the band plays just about everything any fan could ever hope to hear—but they cram it all into an hour, so some might feel cheated by the occasional rushed or truncated rendition. Of course, the crowd at Rock in Rio seems to have enjoyed it, but then one has to wonder how much the setting had to do with that.

□ QUEEN
WE WILL ROCK YOU
★★★★

Vestron, 1986, 60 minutes
PRODUCED BY: Saul Swimmer and Jim Beach
DIRECTED BY: Saul Swimmer
MUSIC FROM: Various Queen albums.
SELECTIONS: "We Will Rock You," "Let Me Entertain You," "Play the Game," "Somebody to Love," "Killer Queen," "Save Me," "Get Down, Make Love," "I'm in Love with My Car," "Love of My Life," "Dragon Attack," "Bohemian Rhapsody," "Tie Your Mother Down."

We Will Rock You is yet another Queen concert video, this time from Montreal in 1982. What sets it apart from the rest is its lovely photography and the tightness of the band's show this time out, something indicated by the two opening titles. Indeed, it's rather a surprise to see "We Will Rock You," which normally works beautifully at its sledgehammer-slow recorded pace, played with a punkish (!) velocity. Yet, while anyone can admire the ingenuity and finesse of Brian May's guitar flash, lead singer and stage focus Freddie Mercury remains a taste that can be acquired only by the devout Queen fan—for whom this program, like their others, is mainly intended.

□ QUEENSRYCHE
LIVE IN TOKYO
★★½

Sony, 1985, 50 minutes
PRODUCED BY: Picture Music International
DIRECTED BY: Lindsay Clenell
MUSIC FROM: The Warning (EMI, 1984).
SELECTIONS: "Nightrider," "Prophecy," "Deliverance," "Child of Fire," "En Force," "Blinded," "The Lady Wore Black," "Warning," "Take Hold of the Flame," "Queen of the Reich."

Fans of this Seattle, Washington, '80s band, who play a baroque form of corporate heavy metal a bit faster than usual—as well as fans of this genre (which is related to, though a bit more refined than, the speed-metal of bands like Metallica)—will enjoy this program, nicely shot at a 1984 Tokyo concert. But there's nothing here to recommend *Queensryche Live in Tokyo* to anyone else.

R

☐ THE RACCOONS, OTHERS
LET'S DANCE
★

Embassy, 1984, 23 minutes
PRODUCED BY: Kevin Gillis
DIRECTED BY: Kevin Gillis
MUSIC FROM: Various albums by various artists.
SELECTIONS: John Schneider: "Calling You," "Shining"; Leo Sayer: "You Can Do It," "Takin' My Time"; Rita Coolidge and Leo Sayer: "To Have You"; Dottie West: "Lions and Tigers"; Dottie West and John Schneider: "Friends."

Execrable kiddie-vid from the creators of the Saturday morning *Raccoons* cartoon series, with lame animation, nauseating characters, even lamer and more nauseating countrypolitan-MOR mush for music, and the incredibly awful concept of a concert in the woods attended by all the wee forest beasties. I'd rather have my kids watch Twisted Sister.

☐ JESSE RAE
RUSHA
★★

Sony, 1980, 10 minutes
PRODUCED BY: Jesse Rae
DIRECTED BY: Jesse Rae, Woody Wilson, Bob Lampell
SELECTIONS: "Rusha," "D.E.S.I.R.E."

Upon its 1980 release, this Video 45 had some people calling Rae a pioneer video artist. Well, he did have a flair for video effects (superimpositions, moving video postcards and cut-out silhouettes, digital image manipulation around the screen, etc.), which he shows off to no end here. And he did have such funk heavyweights as synth wizard Bernie Worrell and Average White Band drummer Steve Ferrone fleshing out his slight songs. But these two clips (this author could find no corresponding American-released record) never really add up to any more than the sum of their parts. "Rusha" has a spunky, ugly-duckling ballerina pirouetting with maniacal determination around and through a phalanx of Soviet soldiers; it may be some sort of anti-war/pro-peace statement, but the ballerina has such an obnoxiously fixed smile you end up hoping the Russkies will shoot her down. "D.E.S.I.R.E." applies Rae's fast-moving, effects-heavy video delirium to some barely titillating shots of geisha girls.

☐ RAFFI
A YOUNG CHILDREN'S CONCERT WITH RAFFI
★★★½

A&M, 1986, 50 minutes
PRODUCED BY: David Devine
DIRECTED BY: David Devine
MUSIC FROM: Singable Songs for the Very Young (Shoreline, 1977); *More Singable Songs for the Very Young* (Shoreline, 1978); *The Corner Grocery Store* (Shoreline, 1979); *Baby Beluga* (Shoreline, 1980); *Rise and Shine* (Shoreline, 1982).
SELECTIONS: "The More We Get Together," "Baa Baa Black Sheep," "Wheels on the Bus," "Baby Beluga," "He's Got the Whole World in His Hands," "When the Spirit Says," "Six Little Ducks," "Little Red Wagon," "All I Really Need," "Workin' on the Railroad," "Apples and Bananas," "There's a Rat," "Mr. Sun," "The Corner Grocery Store," "Something in My Shoe," "Thanks a Lot," "Sing My Sillies Out," "Down by the Bay."

Raffi's a pretty engaging and unobjectionable guy, all things considered. Quietly, with little or no media fanfare, this easy-going, good-looking, bearded Canadian who appears to be of Mediterranean extraction has become an internationally acclaimed, best-selling children's entertainer—the Springsteen of the small, if you will. In this competently produced but unflashy concert video, shot in Toronto in 1984, Raffi shows how and why: he simply sits on a stool before a blue-sky backdrop, wearing a loud Hawaiian shirt and playing soft acoustic guitar as he gently croons his kiddie ditties, and effects an effortless and immediate rapport with his young audience. Intriguingly, all the youngsters seem to be accompanied by one or both parents—and the adults seem to be as involved, and enjoying themselves as much, as their kids. The whole audience also appears to understand that audience participation is a cornerstone of Raffi's appeal, and the camera wisely spends as much time on the little kids delightedly singing and clapping along while their parents prompt, help, or just look on in smiling approval, as on Raffi himself. Apparently, Raffi sincerely wants his concerts to be shared family experiences, something which indicates another of the secrets of his appeal: he treats kids and adults the same, approaching them all as an interested, excited, and responsive peer, with no condescension and no fuss. Heck, the guy even hangs around after the show—with cameras running—to chat with and give autographs and even hugs to the adoring kids.

Thankfully, Raffi is also smart enough as a children's entertainer and, let's face it, educator to do nothing *but* perform his innocuous tunes and act as smiling, laid-back camp-counselor for his diminutive charges. So, while one *could* conceivably look for more in a program aimed at such a very young and impressionable audience, one could easily find a lot *less*—not to mention a lot more to be worried about—elsewhere. Then again, considering Raffi's family-shared appeal, if you're the kind of parent who gets a kid video mainly to get your kids out of your hair for a few hours, this tape may backfire on you. By the same token, unless you're a little kid or a parent with one, Raffi himself may prove to be something less than compelling. But since little kids have an instinctive way of taking cues from other little kids when it comes to new learning experiences like this, yours ought to take to this once they catch the enraptured reaction shots of Raffi's 1984 Toronto fans. All in all, *A Young Children's Concert With Raffi* is a very smoothly efficient revival of those old pre-*Sesame Street* educational-TV children's hootenanny shows.

□ CHRIS RAINBOW
BODY MUSIC
★★½

Sony, 1985, 30 minutes
PRODUCED BY: Picture Music International
DIRECTED BY: Brian Aris and Peter Conn
Also available on Pioneer Stereo Laser videodisc.

As soft-core porn music video, *Body Music* isn't half-bad. Brian Aris's tasteful photos of several gorgeous young women lounging nude and semi-nude around Jamaica and Ibiza are treated with computer animation and special effects by Peter Conn, who's worked on such great music videos as George Clinton's "Atomic Dog." Visually, it creates an artsy but delicately erotic atmosphere. Unfortunately, the unlistenable lounge Muzak of Chris Rainbow (who?) sets the teeth on edge. If you're prone (pardon the pun) to checking something like this out, supply your own appropriate mood music.

□ RAINBOW
LIVE BETWEEN THE EYES
★★

RCA/Columbia, 1983, 77 minutes
PRODUCED BY: Aubrey Powell

DIRECTED BY: Nigel Gordon
MUSIC FROM: Various Rainbow and Deep Purple albums, including Rainbow's *Straight Between the Eyes* (Mercury, 1982).
SELECTIONS: "Overture," "Over the Rainbow," "Spotlight Kid," "Miss Mistreated," "Can't Happen Here," "Tearin' out My Heart," "All Night Long," "Stone Cold," "Power," "Blues Interlude," "Difficult to Cure (Beethoven's Ninth)," "Long Live Rock 'n' Roll," "Smoke on the Water."

□ RAINBOW
THE FINAL CUT
★★★

RCA/Columbia, 1986, 60 minutes
PRODUCED BY: Len Epand, Claude Borenzweig, and Don Bernstine
MUSIC FROM: Various Rainbow albums.
SELECTIONS: "Spotlight Kid," "Death Alley Driver," "I Surrender," "All Night Long," "Can't Happen Here," "Difficult to Cure," "Can't Let You Go," "Power," "Since You've Been Gone," "Stone Cold," "Street of Dreams."

Ritchie Blackmore proved himself a more than capable heavy-metal guitarist while with Deep Purple. But he's been coasting ever since with Rainbow, the band he formed in the 1975 after Purple broke up. Indeed, in *Live,* shot at a 1982 San Antonio, Texas, concert, even Blackmore—playing before one of those silly album-promoting stage sets, with a pair of gigantic eyes shooting laser beams into the audience—looks bored silly. Fans will lap up Blackmore's indulgent fretboard flash on his extended solo "Blues Interlude" and the Beethoven references he tosses into "Difficult to Cure," and they'll flip for the revival of Deep Purple's classic "Smoke on the Water." The ladies will be entertained by handsome lead singer Joe Lynn Turner, who sounds most comfortable on more pop-oriented tunes like "Stone Cold." And longtime Blackmore/Purple fans will note that ex-Purple bassist Roger Glover had joined Rainbow here. But all of that still doesn't make *Live* recommendable to anyone but the hardcore Rainbow fan.

Ditto for *Cut,* though its career-covering mix of concert clips and conceptual and performance videos is much more variegated. Included are selections with all three of Rainbow's various vocalists: Ronnie James Dio, Graham Bonnet, and Turner. The high point for fans will probably be the clip capturing, according to the notes on the cassette case, "the one and only time 'Difficult to Cure' was performed with a full concert orchestra." Fair-minded musical eclectics hoping against hope (or fearing the worst), take note: Rainbow's "Spotlight Kid" is *not* the same song as Captain Beefheart's "The Spotlight Kid."

□ VARIOUS ARTISTS (RESIDENTS, RENALDO AND THE LOAF, ET AL.)
RALPH RECORDS VIDEO, VOLUME ONE
★★★★½

Ralph, 1983, 40 minutes
PRODUCED BY: the Cryptic Corp.
DIRECTED BY: Graeme Whifler, the Residents
MUSIC FROM: Various Ralph Records albums.
SELECTIONS: Tuxedomoon: "Jinx"; MX–80 Sound: "Why Are We Here?"; the Residents: "One Minute Movies," "Hello Skinny," "Third Reich & Roll"; Snakefinger: "Man in the Dark Sedan"; Renaldo and the Loaf: "Songs for Swinging Larvae."

And now for something completely different: the *only* various-artists clips compilation that really matters, because (a) director Graeme Whifler (who shot all of it except the Residents' pioneering, self-directed mid-'70s "Third Reich & Roll") offers such bracingly bizarre alternatives to the usual rock video clichés, and (b) it collects the best work of the Residents, San Francisco's mysterious (they always appear in full costume, when they appear, and have carefully guarded their true identities) avant-electronic cult heroes. Their eyeball masks have become fitting symbols, for the Residents have an almost frightening gift for imagery that's not only strange and dreamlike and purposely enigmatic, but *powerful,* too. So piercingly, primevally powerful that, much of the time—and thanks also to Whifler's craftily crazy *mise en scène*—the viewer gets the tingly sense that he is eavesdropping on a provocative, private, and possibly pagan ritual. Their material alone makes this tape a must-have. The best of the rest is Renaldo and the Loaf's creepy trilogy "Songs for Swinging Larvae"—based on an actual California child-napping case (so it may or may not be stranger than the truth). (Available by mail order from Ralph Records.)

□ RATT
RATT: THE VIDEO
★★½

Atlantic, 1985, 37 minutes

PRODUCED BY: Alexis Omeltchenko, Pendulum Productions, Limelight, Inc.

DIRECTED BY: Mark Rezyka, Marshall Berle and Alexis Omeltchenko, Don Letts

MUSIC FROM: Ratt (Atlantic, 1984); *Ratt* (EP) (Atlantic, 1985); *Invasion of Your Privacy* (Atlantic, 1985); *Out of the Cellar* (Atlantic, 1986).

SELECTIONS: "Round and Round," "Back for More," "Wanted Man," "You Think You're Tough," "Lay It Down."

Yet another of those '80s heavy-metal bands from the Los Angeles club scene—*à la* Van Halen, Mötley Crüe, Quiet Riot, et al.—Ratt are actually closer to the poppier side of hard rock than the macho sludgemongering of heavy metal, as their first hit, "Round and Round," demonstrated. But as their *videos* demonstrate, Ratt are given over to plenty of the usual macho posturing, comic-book pirate threads, and bombastic sneering that are *de rigueur* for heavy metal heroes. In fact, it could be that Ratt overindulge such imagery purposely, to make up for the comparative poppiness of their sound. At any rate, don't start thinking Ratt are another Twisted Sister or something—they're not. They just come off visually like any other connect-the-dots metal band. Their videos are all nicely produced but uniformly unexceptional. "Round and Round" is dubiously noteworthy for its casting of Milton Berle (whose nephew Marshall manages Ratt and directed some of their videos, though *not* "Round and Round") in what has to be *the* most gratuitous guest-star cameo in rock video history. Along with the promo clips, there's also some typically dull and inane backstage and on-the-road footage from Ratt's 1985 Japanese tour. For fans.

□ VARIOUS ARTISTS
READY STEADY GO!, VOLUME ONE
★★★★½

HBO/Cannon, 1984, 60 minutes

PRODUCED BY: Francis Hitchings

DIRECTED BY: Robert Fleming, Rollo Gamble, Daphne Shadwell, Michael Lindsay-Hogg

MUSIC FROM: Various albums by various artists; '60s British TV show *Ready Steady Go!*

SELECTIONS: The Beatles: "You Can't Do That," "Can't Buy Me Love"; Dusty Springfield: "Every Time I Have to Cry"; the Animals: "Baby Let Me Take You Home"; Cilla Black: "You're My World"; Billy Fury: "I Will"; Van Morrison and Them: "Baby Please Don't Go"; Lulu: "Shout"; Georgie Fame and the Blue Flames: "Yeh Yeh"; the Searchers: "What Have They Done to the Rain"; Gerry and the Pacemakers: "Ferry Cross the Mersey";

Dave Clark 5: "Do You Love Me," "Glad All Over"; Peter Cook and Dudley Moore: "Goodbye-ee"; the Rolling Stones: "Under My Thumb," "Paint It, Black"; the Who: "Anyway, Anyhow, Anywhere."

☐ **VARIOUS ARTISTS**
READY STEADY GO! VOLUME TWO
★★★★½

HBO/Cannon, 1985, 60 minutes
PRODUCED BY: Francis Hitchings
DIRECTED BY: Robert Fleming, Rollo Gamble, Daphne Shadwell, Michael Lindsay-Hogg
MUSIC FROM: Various albums by various artists; '60s British TV show *Ready Steady Go!*
SELECTIONS: The Beatles: "Twist and Shout," "She Loves You"; the Beach Boys: "I Get Around," "When I Grow Up"; Marvin Gaye: "Can I Get a Witness"; Dusty Springfield: "Losing You"; Gene Pitney: "I'm Gong to Be Strong"; Freddie and the Dreamers: "I Love You Baby"; the Fourmost: "Baby I Need Your Lovin' "; Rufus Thomas: "Walkin' the Dog"; Isley Brothers: "Stagger Lee"; Jerry Lee Lewis: "Whole Lot of Shakin' Goin' On"; the Rolling Stones: "I Got You Babe"; Martha and the Vandellas: "Dancing in the Street"; the Dave Clark 5: "Bits and Pieces," "Can't You See That She's Mine."

☐ **VARIOUS ARTISTS**
READY STEADY GO! VOLUME THREE
★★★★½

HBO/Cannon, 1985, 60 minutes
PRODUCED BY: Francis Hitchings
DIRECTED BY: Robert Fleming, Rollo Gamble, Daphne Shadwell, Michael Lindsay-Hogg
MUSIC FROM: Various albums by various artists; '60s British TV show *Ready Steady Go!*
SELECTIONS: Jerry Lee Lewis: "High Heel Sneakers"; Billy Fury: "Nothin' Shakin' "; Lulu: "Can't Hear You No More"; the Moody Blues: "Lose Your Money"; Dusty Springfield: "Can I Get a Witness"; Marvin Gaye: "How Sweet It Is to Be Loved By You"; Four Pennies: "Juliet"; Martha and the Vandellas: "Heat Wave"; the Rolling Stones: "Off the Hook," "Little Red Rooster"; Kim Weston: "Little More Love"; the Beatles: "She's a Woman," "Baby's in Black," "Kansas City."

Running on Rediffusion TV in the U.K. from 1963 to 1967, *RSG!* may have been Britain's most influential TV pop show ever. It was a sort of hybrid of our own *American Bandstand* and *Shindig!/Hullaballoo*: it had the low-key-host-mingling-with-audience-of-kids of the former, and some of the rec-room party atmosphere of the latter (though more genuine and less showbizzy). But unlike the Yank shows, *RSG!* also featured lots of genuine *live* performances instead of just lip-synchs. All three nicely packaged and produced volumes are of considerable historical/nostalgic value; each contains some great moments that elevate the tapes to a higher level. It's nearly impossible, though, to say which one is the best out of the three.

Volume One's highlights include Van Morrison and Them's sullen Belfast blues, Georgie Fame's ultracool jazz-cop "Yeh Yeh," the very live Stones and Who (the Beatles are lip-synching in this volume, but do have a nice interview segment), and Lulu's "Shout," which is quite revelatory in its surprising intensity.

Volume Two has more such revelatory moments: the Beach Boys (again very live) messing up the a capella intro to "When I Grow Up"; cohostess Cathy McGowan introducing Marvin Gaye by gushing, "Even the Beatles think he's simply *fab*ulous!"; and the Rolling Stones' sardonic, slapstick, lip-synched deconstruction of Sonny and Cher's "I Got You Babe." Also: Dusty Springfield blows her lip-synch on-camera; Paul McCartney is the judge in a sort of proto–*Puttin' on the Hits* segment called "Mime Time" (amazingly, the winning girl accepts her prize from Paulie without batting an eyelash); and Jerry Lee Lewis is in his usual maniacal form.

Volume Three has Jerry Lee coolly dispatching a swaggering "High Heel Sneakers" with the camera right in his face; more surprisingly gritty Lulu; the pre-Mellotron, garage-rockin' Moody Blues (talk about revelatory!); girls aping Ella Fitzgerald's cover of "Can't Buy Me Love" in "Mime Time"; some great Mod-era vintage British TV commercials (one stars a young Benny Hill; the ads for eggs and pears are way, way out); the Stones (lip-synching this time—but boy do they look young!), with Mick Jagger and Brian Jones gawking politely through their quick interviews; and the Beatles lip-synching and giving good interviews at the height of Beatlemania (the Fab Four almost lose their celebrated cool amidst all the screaming).

An ironic footnote:Volumes One and Two both contain non-RSG! footage of the Dave Clark 5 (Volume Two cuts the band's lip-synching with ecstatic audience reactions obviously from elsewhere—*really* pathetic). That same Dave Clark now owns and reissues the *RSG!* archives.

☐ **VARIOUS ARTISTS**

READY STEADY GO! SPECIAL EDITION: SOUNDS OF MOTOWN

★★★★★

Sony, 1985, 50 minutes
PRODUCED BY: Jack Good
DIRECTED BY: Rollo Gamble
MUSIC FROM: Various albums by various artists.

SELECTIONS: Medley: the Supremes: "Baby Love"/Smokey Robinson and the Miracles: "You Really Got a Hold on Me"/ Stevie Wonder: "I Call It Pretty Music"/ Temptations: "The Way You Do the Things You Do"/Martha and the Vandellas: "Heat Wave"/Dusty Springfield: "You Lost the Sweetest Boy"; Smokey Robinson and the Miracles: "Ooh, Baby Baby," "Shop Around"; Martha Reeves and Dusty Springfield: "Wishin' and Hopin' "; the Temptations: "It's Growing," "My Girl"; the Supremes: "Shake," "Stop! In the Name of Love," "Baby Love"; Martha and the Vandellas: "Nowhere to Run," "Dancing in the Street"; Stevie Wonder: "Kiss Me Baby"; Marvin Gaye: "How Sweet It Is to Be Loved by You," "Can I Get a Witness"; Dusty Springfield: "Can't Hear You No More"; Smokey Robinson and the Miracles, the Supremes, et al.: "Mickey's Monkey."

A far, far better record of Motown's glory days than anything you'll find in *Motown 25: Yesterday, Today, Forever*—or anywhere else, for that matter. During the 1965 British tour of the Motortown Revue, a few episodes of England's reigning pop-TV show were shot, and here they are, packaged together along with a three-song insert remembering Marvin Gaye (who was not part of the tour that year) and his *RSG!* appearances. The opening round-robin medley, with snippets of songs presented in revue form amidst some proto–*Solid Gold* Brit-teen dancers, is a bit disconcerting. But then it settles down for the real deal: *very* live performances of Motown classics and more obscure nuggets, all backed by the Earl Van Dyke Sextet. Temptations lead singer David Ruffin is the coolest performer, but there isn't a slouch in the bunch—and that certainly includes the marvelous Dusty Springfield, England's most soulful female singer by far and thus a perfect choice as hostess. Rollo Gamble's direction is fantastic: typical Brit that he must've been at the time, he's so utterly fascinated by these black-skinned foreigners from the colonies with their jumping beat and instantly memorable songs he can't help but *constantly* move in *real* tight for one awesome close-up after another.

Thanks Rollo, and all else (Dave Clark, who controls the *RSG!* archives, and so on) responsible for making this available.

☐ **VARIOUS ARTISTS**
RED HOT ROCK
★½

Vestron, 1985, 46 minutes
PRODUCED BY: Various
DIRECTED BY: Various
MUSIC FROM: Various albums by various artists.
SELECTIONS: The Tubes: "Sports Fans," "Mondo Bondage"; Peter Godwin: "Images of Heaven"; Helix: "Gimme Gimme Good Lovin' "; Queen: "Body Language"; Duran Duran: "The Chauffeur"; O'Bryan: "Breakin' Together," "Lovelite"; Dwight Twilley: "Girls"; SSQ: "Screaming in My Pillow."

Sure to find a prominent place on Tipper Gore's mantel, *Red Hot Rock* collects some of rock's saucier videos from the early-to-mid-'80s. And if you've ever rolled your eyes at the gratuitous smarm and sleaze that infect so many sexist rock clips, you know pretty much what to expect here: lotsa bimbos in lingerie pouting and strutting through all manner of tawdry, turgid, macho-male sex fantasies. *Yawn*. The Tubes' two clips (both also available in *The Tubes Video*) are garishly vulgar, exceptional solely because "Sports Fans" finds lead singer Fee Waybill with the *cojones* to show *his* in full-frontal fashion. Peter Godwin's "Images of Heaven" is a comparatively early *Penthouse* lesbian-lust sexcapade with some startlingly good special effects considering its reportedly microscopic budget. The flashes of nudity in O'Bryan's two unspectacular R&B/funk workouts are totally gratuitous. So too with electro-poppers SSQ's "Screaming in My Pillow," which also features the band's exceptionally nauseating blonde New Wave Hooker vocalist writhing around in her satin sheets. Duran Duran's "The Chauffeur" is a *Penthouse* (*European* edition!) kiss-my-whip lesbo/bondage scenario shot *à la* Helmut Newton. Helix's clip gratuitously has the Canadian metal band posturing pathetically while assorted bimbettes parade semi-nude in a hard-rock beauty pageant. The *only* clip here with even a shred of wit is Dwight Twilley's affectionate *Porky's* homage "Girls"—but, of course, a *Porky's* homage is hardly the sort of thing to make this tape recommendable.

☐ **OTIS REDDING** (WITH OTHERS)
READY, STEADY, GO! SPECIAL EDITION
★★★★★

Sony, 1985, 25 minutes
PRODUCED BY: Francis Hitching
DIRECTED BY: Peter Croft
MUSIC FROM: Various albums by Otis Redding, Eric Burdon, and Chris Farlowe; September 16, 1966, British TV show *Ready, Steady, Go!*
SELECTIONS: Otis Redding: "Satisfaction," "My Girl," "Respect," "Pain in My Heart," "I Can't Turn You Loose"; Eric Burdon: "Hold On, I'm Coming"; Chris Farlowe: "This Is a Man's World"; Redding, Burdon, and Farlowe: "Shake," "Land of 1,000 Dances."

Here's another of those rock-archives programs that proves music video's historical value. This great soul singer's death at twenty-six in a December 1967 plane crash and his posthumous #1 hit "(Sittin' on) the Dock of the Bay" made him a legend. But as this September 16, 1966, episode of the British pop program convincingly demonstrates, he would have gained legendary status had he lived. He really was *that good*—though it takes until late in the second number, "My Girl," for Otis to hit his gritty, sweaty, soul-deep stride. After Otis and his crack backing band (who, though not identified, look and sound like the Bar-Kays, his usual band) swing from the smoldering "My Girl" right into a sizzling "Respect," you suspect an unfortunate, pace-rupturing letdown when Otis introduces Animal Eric Burdon and then Chris Farlowe. But perhaps inspired by their company, both of these lads turn in pretty good work, particularly Farlowe. Then Otis returns to show how it's *really* done; his "I Can't Turn You Loose" defines the term "to cook." On the last two tunes, Otis effortlessly cuts Burdon and Farlowe, who wisely defer to him most of the way through. Meanwhile, the camerawork throughout is swooningly good, with loads of breathtaking close-ups, and some extreme high- and low-angle shots that reflexively demonstrate the appropriate awe evoked in Britons by performers as distinctly, powerfully American and universally appealing as Redding.

□ LOU REED
A NIGHT WITH LOU REED
★★★

RCA/Columbia, 1983, 56 minutes
PRODUCED BY: Bill Boggs and Richard Baker
DIRECTED BY: Clark Santee
MUSIC FROM: Various Lou Reed and Velvet Underground albums.
SELECTIONS: "Sweet Jane," "I'm Waiting for My Man," "Martial Law," "Don't Talk to Me About Work," "Women," "Waves of Fear," "Walk on the Wild Side," "Turn Out the Lights," "New Age," "Kill Your Sons," "Satellite of Love," "White Light/White Heat," "Rock 'n' Roll."

A certified master of rock, in fact one of the most influential figures in the music's history, Reed is definitely not for everybody. He doesn't compromise, he's usually given to brutally frank takes on often sordid subjects, and his clenched stage manner projects as much of the usual "presence" and "personality" of a "rock entertainer" as his flat, nasal, deadpan voice. Sometimes, he gets downright perverse, as here when he seems to willfully rush or lag his vocals, or push his capable backing trio (highlighted by Robert Quine's gonzo guitar and Fernando Saunders's fabulously melodic bass) into bulldozing this career-spanning repertoire. But that's Lou—an acquired taste for sure, but if you've acquired it, this ought to satisfy. Clark Santee's direction is as flat and straightforward as Lou's singing, and in both cases, that's just fine. As the credits roll, the cameras linger in the dressing room; Lou tells coproducer Bill Boggs (a New York TV talk show host; what he's doing coproducing a Lou Reed concert video is beyond me) how pleased he is that such an intense performance has been captured and preserved. Well, it may not be quite as brilliant as Lou makes out, but hey, it *is* Lou, and it is good.

□ VARIOUS ARTISTS
REGGAE GOT SOUL
★★★½

Import, 1983, 52 minutes
MUSIC FROM: Various albums by various artists.
SELECTIONS: Bob Marley and the Wailers: "Jamming," "Could You Be Loved," "Buffalo Soldiers," "Redemption Song"; Burning Spear: "Jah Is My Driver," "Foggy Road," "Jah No Dead"; Toots and the Maytals: "Reggae Got Soul"; Peter Tosh: "Get Up, Stand Up," "Irie Ites"; the Abyssinians: "Satta Ammassaganna"; Black Uhuru: "Guess Who's Coming to Dinner," "Push Push," "Abortion," "Happiness," "World Is Africa"; Third World: "Try Jah Love."

Solid compilation of reggae performance clips, with the exception of Bob Marley and the Wailers' "Buffalo Soldiers," the only real concept clip here, which was produced after Marley's death. Though the visuals are uneven, the music is relentlessly strong; the only real disappointment is the Marley and the Wailers material, taken from Marley's later years, when his strength as a stage performer was waning due to his declining health. Burning Spear's entranced and entrancing hard-core reggae is the highlight, with the ebullient Toots and the Maytals and the dead-serious Black Uhuru close behind.

□ REO SPEEDWAGON
LIVE INFIDELITY
★★

CBS/Fox, 1981/84, 88 minutes
PRODUCED BY: Richard Namm
DIRECTED BY: Richard Namm
MUSIC FROM: 1981 McNichols Arena concert in Denver; various REO Speedwagon albums.
SELECTIONS: "Don't Let Him Go," "Like You Do," "Keep Pushin'," "Only the Strong Survive," "Tough Guys," "Time for Me to Fly," "Take It on the Run," "Keep On Loving You," "Roll with the Changes," "Flying Turkey Trot," "Say You Love Me or Say Goodnight," "Back on the Road Again," "Ridin' the Storm Out," "157 Riverside Avenue," "Shakin' It Loose."

□ REO SPEEDWAGON
WHEELS ARE TURNIN'
★★½

CBS/Fox, 1986, 80 minutes
PRODUCED BY: John Weaver
DIRECTED BY: Kim Paul Friedman
MUSIC FROM: Ridin' the Storm Out (Epic, 1973); *A Decade of Rock 'n' Roll* (Epic, 1980); *Hi-Infidelity* (Epic, 1980); *Good Trouble* (Epic, 1982); *Wheels Are Turnin'* (Epic, 1984).
SELECTIONS: "Don't Let 'Em Go," "Thru the Window," "I Do'wanna Know," "One Lonely Night," "Gotta Feel More," "Take It on the Run," "Can't Fight This Feeling," "Tough Guys," "Live Every Moment," "Shakin' It Loose," "Keep On Loving You," "Keep Pushin'," "Roll with the Changes," "Ridin' the Storm Out," "Time for Me to Fly."

Also available on CBS/Fox Stereo Laser videodisc.

The title of *Live Infidelity* refers to the *Hi-Infidelity* LP REO was supporting on the tour captured in this program—the album that finally broke them to multi-platinum status after years of slogging it out on the road. But that title could just as easily be read as an indictment of REO's anonymous, blandly formulaic, totally trivial music, which is "rock 'n' roll" only in the most superficial sense—and which is a graphic illustration of the betrayal of genuine rock 'n' roll roots epitomized by the AOR formula rock of bands like this. To be blunt: their whitebread sludge is dull, dull, dull, and their stage presence in concert is nothing to write home about either. Of course, the audiences at the *Live Infidelity* show and the 1984 Kansas City concert shot for *Wheels Are Turnin'* didn't feel that way, and if you're an REO fan, you won't either. However, you REO fans should note that many songs overlap between these two programs. *Wheels* is the better of the two, if only because it's shot a bit better, and includes offstage scenes in which the band members come across as genuinely nice guys.

□ THE RESIDENTS
MOLESHOW/WHATEVER HAPPENED TO VILENESS FATS
★★★½

Ralph, 1985, 60 minutes
PRODUCED BY: The Cryptic Corp.
DIRECTED BY: The Residents
MUSIC FROM: Mark of the Mole (Ralph, 1981); *Tunes of Two Cities* (Ralph, 1982); *Vileness Fats* (made 1972–76; never released).

The first half of this tape provides a rare glance at San Francisco's mysterioso mutant-music quartet onstage (they've only toured two or three times in their fifteen-year career), circa 1982–83, doing their very involved and typically cryptic "Mole Show" (a metaphorical epic about subterranean culture clashes). The staging and costumes are as bizarrely inventive and striking as one might expect from a band who've adopted enormous eyeball masks as icons of stylized anonymity; the stage performances are intercut with intriguing, *faux*-primitive computer graphics. The last half is a blitheringly bizarre descent into the recut remainder of the Residents' long-abandoned (made between 1972 and 1976) "video movie," *Vileness Fats.* Again, the sets, costumes, lighting, and camerawork (not to mention the soundtrack) are stupendously strange and imaginative—stunning enough, in fact, that it hardly matters that *Vileness Fats* makes absolutely no sense at all. For those who dare, here's musical-visual synergy of unparalleled originality and integrity. (Available by mail order from Ralph Records.)

□ TONY RICE

AN INTIMATE LESSON

★★★★

Homespun, 1985, 60 minutes
PRODUCED BY: Happy Traum
DIRECTED BY: Happy Traum
MUSIC FROM: Various Tony Rice albums.
SELECTIONS: "Church Street Blues," "Cold on the Shoulder," "Georgia on My Mind," "Gold Rush," "Blackberry Blossom," "Mule Skinner Blues."

Rice is a leading proponent of "newgrass" music, an acoustic-swing resurgence building on elements of bluegrass, country swing, and traditional jazz that also includes performers like David Grisman and Mark O'Connor (who's also made a Homespun instructional cassette). He's also a master of flatpicking, using a complex right-handed picking technique to do things most other players would probably do with fingerstyle playing or fingerpicking. Here, in a natural progression from Happy Traum's more beginner-oriented Homespun *Learning to Flatpick* tape, Rice covers techniques like hammer-ons and pull-offs (no, heavy-metal guitarists like Eddie Van Halen didn't invent 'em), cross-picking, alternate strokes, little-finger barre-chording, position playing, and block-chording—and he covers them eloquently and in detail, with a mellow, personable, easy going style. Interestingly, Rice also demonstrates some fiddle tunes that he's transcribed to guitar. As with all Homespun Tapes, the camerawork is excellent and split-screens are used whenever appropriate. There's also an accompanying booklet. (Available by mail order from Homespun Tapes.)

□ BUDDY RICH AND HIS BAND

MR. DRUMS (LIVE ON KING STREET, SAN FRANCISCO—THE "CHANNEL ONE" SET)

★★★½

Sony, 1985, 55 minutes
PRODUCED BY: Gary Reber
DIRECTED BY: Scott Ross
MUSIC FROM: Various Buddy Rich albums.
SELECTIONS: "Machine," "Best Coast," "One O'clock Jump," "Sophisticated Lady," "Norwegian Wood," "Love for Sale," "No Exit," "Channel One Suite."
Also available on Pioneer Stereo Laser videodisc.

A fine, no-nonsense concert recording of superdrummer Rich and his brassy big band in San Francisco in 1985. At times Rich's band does give the impression of just riffing and blaring along between the leader's furious drum solos. But Rich himself is more than just a show-off: he always swings like a demon, he's a very musical drummer, and if you just listen to his ride cymbal alone when the band is cooking at fast tempos, you'll hear an amazingly ferocious force at work, which seems all the more remarkable considering Rich's age. Likewise, his band is more musical and refined than many observers might admit at first, and featured soloist Steve Marcus shines throughout on tenor and soprano saxes. The program is sonically rich and varied enough to attract a wide variety of viewers; the band handles itself with crisp efficiency, and Buddy Rich remains a wondrous force.

□ LIONEL RICHIE
ALL NIGHT LONG

★★½

RCA/Columbia, 1985, 34 minutes

PRODUCED BY: Michael Nesmith, Joe Layton

DIRECTED BY: Bob Rafelson, Bob Giraldi

MUSIC FROM: Can't Slow Down (Motown, 1984).

SELECTIONS: "All Night Long," "Running with the Night," "Hello," "Penny Lover," "Running with the Night" (live), "All Night Long" (live).

Lionel's legions of fans ought to like this collection of clips and concert footage just fine. Others will either be bored to death, develop diabetes, or suffer some other dreadful illness as it runs its beamingly vain, smugly sugarcoated course. Lionel sits at his piano introducing video clips and concert footage. At one remarkable point, he looks into the lens with all the sincere humility he can muster and says, "I just want to thank Bob Giraldi for making three of the greatest videos ever"—meaning, of course, the three he did for Lionel, which are actually vacuous and offensively slick ("Running with the Night"), clichéd and treacly ("Hello"), and pathetically overdone ("Penny Lover"). So, Lionel, what's Bob Rafelson—chopped liver? Especially when his "All Night Long"—though no great shakes overall in the music video scheme of things—is, compared to Giraldi's endeavors, positively refreshing in its high-spirited, colorful variation on the big ol' production-number theme.

□ LEE RITENOUR
LIVE RIT SPECIAL

★★½

Sony, 1986, 75 minutes

DIRECTED BY: Stanley Dorfman

MUSIC FROM: Various Lee Ritenour albums.

SELECTIONS: "Heavenly Bodies," "Mr. Briefcase," "Voices," "Dolphin Dreams," "Operator (Thief on the Line)," "Other Love," "Sunset Drivers," "Mandela," "Amaretto," "Rio Funk," "Is It You?," "RIT Variations II," "I'm Not Responsible."

Jazz-fusion guitarist Lee "Rit" Ritenour is also known as "Captain Fingers" because of his dexterity. His version of jazz fusion is poppier than many, with vocals (sung in forgettable fashion by one Phil Perry) on many of the tunes. His crack backup band at this 1984 concert at California's Concord Pavilion includes such respected players as saxophonist Ernie Watts (who's played with the Rolling Stones and Frank Zappa as well as the *Tonight Show* orchestra) and drummer Carlos Vega, who's right at home on Latin-inflected numbers like "Rio Funk." The concert is nicely shot, but neither the visuals nor the music are exceptional or exciting enough to keep anyone but a Ritenour fan, or a fusion aficionado, from getting more than a bit bored by all the slickly competent, innocuous noodling. However, fans of Ritenour or the fusion genre should enjoy it.

□ MAX ROACH
IN SESSION

★★★

DCI, 1982, 40 minutes

PRODUCED BY: Kenny Klompus and Steve Apicella
DIRECTED BY: Kenny Klompus and Steve Apicella
MUSIC FROM: *Chattahoochie Red* (CBS, 1982).
SELECTIONS: "Chattahoochie Red," "Living Room," "Lonesome Lover," "Wefe," "Don't Weep for the Lady," "The Dream"/"It's Time."

□ MAX ROACH
IN CONCERT
★★★★

DCI, 1982, 50 minutes
PRODUCED BY: Max Roach and Axis Video
DIRECTED BY: Kenny Klompus and Steve Apicella
MUSIC FROM: New York Kool Jazz Festival, 1982.
SELECTIONS: "The Smoke That Thunders," "African Butterfly," "Odd Meter Medley"/"The Drum Also Waltzes," "Where's the Wind," "Drums Unlimited," "Hi-Hat Solo."

□ MAX ROACH QUARTET
MAX ROACH VIDEO EP
★★★½

Sony, 1981, 19 minutes
MUSIC FROM: Performance at Blues Alley, Washington, D.C., 1981.
SELECTIONS: "Effie," "Six Bits Blues."

Roach is a towering figure in jazz history, an intelligent and dignified presence whose forty-year career spans several stylistic developments, in which he's always been in the forefront. DCI Video's two "Percussion Profiles" (see also their *Bruford and the Beat*) capture Max *In Session* as he records his *Chattahoochie Red* LP along with Odean Pope (sax, oboe), Cecil Bridgewater (trumpet), Walter Bishop, Jr. (piano), Calvin Hill (bass), Matilda Haywood (vocals), and his daughter Maxine (viola); Max's voiceovers and on-camera commentary link the footage of him and the band arranging, rehearsing, and recording the material; in-studio documentary footage alternates with cheesy, Leroy Neiman–style paintings of the players in action. *In Concert* has him all alone onstage, dazzling us with nothing but his drums and his genius in a series of imaginative solos. Sony's Video EP captures the same core ensemble seen recording on *In Session,* minus pianist Bishop, blowing their way through two recent examples of Roach's own refined, post-bop jazz, and is good enough to leave the viewer wanting more (though it's also recommended to dilettantes who'd like to impress visitors with the titles on their shelves). (*In Session* and *In Concert* are available by mail order from DCI Music Video.)

□ MAX ROACH
IN WASHINGTON, D.C.—JAZZ IN AMERICA
★★★★

Embassy, 1986, 60 minutes
PRODUCED BY: Gary Keys
DIRECTED BY: Stanley Dorfman
MUSIC FROM: Various Max Roach albums.
SELECTIONS: "Big Sid," "Six Bit Blues," "Back to Basics," "Mr. Hi Hat (Papa Jo)," "It's Time," "Nommo," "Five for Paul," "Effie."

This is the long version of Sony's two-cut Jazz Video EP, and so those of you who loved the shorter version and/or found it *too* short should definitely spring for this one. Roach and his quartet play superbly throughout this eight-song set at the Washington, D.C., Blues Alley club. Particular highlights of this version include tributes to two of Roach's percussive forebears: "Big Sid," a ferociously swinging piece in memory of the great swing drummer Sid Catlett, and "Mr. Hi Hat (Papa Jo)," a stupendously brilliant hi-hat solo by Roach in honor of the drummer who pioneered the integral use of hi-hat in swing rhythm and laid the foundations for modern rhythm-section drumming, the late great "Papa Jo" Jones.

☐ **VARIOUS ARTISTS**
ROCK & ROLL DISCIPLES
★½

Monticello Productions, 1984, 30 minutes
PRODUCED BY: Thomas Corboy
DIRECTED BY: Thomas Corboy
SELECTIONS: Chris Marshon: "God Called Elvis Home"; Thomas Wayne: "The King Lives On Forever"; the Hanson Brothers: "My Friend Elvis"; Artie Mentz: "Battle Hymn of the Republic"; Leon Everette: "Goodbye King of Rock and Roll."

Sordid documentary that gapes and gawks at the most pathetic Elvis Presley worshipers and imitators it can find, without shedding any insightful light onto this perverse phenomenon of modern-day Americana. *Possibly* useful only as a camp exercise, and even that is stretching it mightily.

☐ **VARIOUS ARTISTS (THE RAMONES, OTHERS)**
ROCK 'N' ROLL HIGH SCHOOL
★★★

Warner Home Video, 1981, 94 minutes
PRODUCED BY: Michael Finnell
DIRECTED BY: Allan Arkush
MUSIC FROM: Rock 'n' Roll High School motion picture soundtrack (Sire/WB, 1979); various albums by various artists.
SELECTIONS: The Ramones: "Rock 'n' Roll High School," "Sheena Is a Punk Rocker," "I Wanna Be Sedated," "Teenage Lobotomy," "I Just Want to Have Something to Do," "I Want You Around," "Blitzkrieg Bop," "California Sun," "DUMB," "I Wanna Be Your Boyfriend," "Do You Wanna Dance?," "Questioningly," "She's the One," "Pinhead"; Paul McCartney and Wings: "Did We Meet Somewhere Before?"; Brownsville Station: "Smokin' in the Boys Room"; Velvet Underground: "Rock and Roll"; Chuck Berry: "School Days"; Nick Lowe: "So It Goes"; Alice Cooper: "School's Out"; Bent Fabric: "Alley Cat"; Devo: "Come Back Jonee"; Fleetwood Mac: "Albatross," "Jigsaw Puzzle Blues"; MC5: "High School"; the Paley Brothers: "C'mon Let's Go," "You're the Best"; Eddie and the Hot Rods: "Teenage Depression"; Todd Rundgren: "A Dream Goes On Forever"; Brian Eno: "Spirits Drifting," "Alternative 3," "Energy Fools the Magician"; Bobby Freeman: "Do You Want to Dance?"

As a seriocomic (more comic than serious), post-punk revision of classic '50s jukebox rock musicals, *Rock 'n' Roll High School* succeeds as much despite the ham-fisted direction of Roger Corman grad Allan Arkush (whose subsequent *Get Crazy* functions in a similar way) as because of it. Its salutary plot—the eagerly energetic P. J. Soles (who was also in *Stripes* and appeared briefly in *Sweet Dreams*) is a student at Vince Lombardi High School whose undying devotion to the Ramones kicks off a revolutionary movement among the student body, which will stop at nothing to be able to see the Ramones in person—is mainly there to set up a series of set-pieces that satirize those wholesome '50s rock flicks and '70s suburban lifestyles. The satire is uneven, to say the least, mainly because Arkush's sledgehammer touch too often produces a premise-deflating slapstick overkill. But there are some fine moments along the way, particularly the early scenes in which the distraught Soles imagines that she sees various members of the Ramones lurking around her house. For a self-consciously dumb rock comedy such as this, it's incredible that such scenes achieve a genuinely haunting poignancy; perhaps they do because they're such fleetingly ephemeral moments that Arkush doesn't have a chance to beat them into the ground. Mary Woronov, a hardy perennial in such trashy efforts, once again rises above her material with a killer performance as demonic

Principal Togar. And there's plenty of solid rock soundtrack music all over the place, by the original Noo Yawk punk rockers, the Ramones, as well as by a host of appropriately chosen others.

But there are two things that really earn *Rock 'n' Roll High School* its three stars. One is the fact that it unabashedly idolizes the Ramones—who, despite an intense cult following, are still perceived by the vast majority of Americans as ugly, incompetent scum—and still got made, thus providing a fairly congenial forum for the band's masterfully taut and surprisingly (if you think they're incompetent scum) tuneful buzz-saw reduction of rock history. And there's its finale, in which the students of Vince Lombardi High, charged up by the Ramones, burn their prison-of-a-school to the ground. Coming at the end of a late-'70s lowbrow "youth comedy," such a literally incendiary and subversive climax made all the hit-or-miss shenanigans that preceded it worthwhile. Twisted Sister, to cite one rock band that seems to have at least partially inherited the *Rock 'n' Roll High School* spirit, has yet at this writing to come up with such a memorably profound antiadult image in their videos.

Rock 'n' Roll High School is mainly for Ramones fans and trash-flick aficionados and at the very least is fairly good, dumb fun. But since its entire premise is based on the vastly misunderstood and underappreciated Ramones and since it has that flamingly seditious coda, it gets extra recommendability points.

☐ **VARIOUS ARTISTS**

ROCK AND ROLL: THE EARLY DAYS

★★★★

RCA/Columbia, 1985, 59 minutes

PRODUCED BY: Patrick Montgomery

DIRECTED BY: Patrick Montgomery and Pamela Page

MUSIC FROM: Various albums by various artists.

SELECTIONS: Elvis Presley: "Hound Dog"; Chuck Berry: "Sweet Little 16"; Little Richard: "Tutti-Frutti"; Buddy Holly: "Peggy Sue"; Jerry Lee Lewis: "Great Balls of Fire"; Bill Haley: "Rock Around the Clock"; Pat Boone: "Tutti-Frutti"; plus many more.

Another rockumentary winner from the folks who brought you *The Compleat Beatles.* There are oodles of fantastic archival film clips: gray-flanneled '50s adults trying to decipher rock's jungle-telegraph message to their kids; middle-aged newsmen bemused and befuddled by ardent teenage hepsters; proto-conservative denunciations of the devil's music by terrifyingly square-looking authorities; and of course spine-tingling performance clips pulled from feature films and Golden Age of TV kinescopes. More impressive even than the rich source material is the way it's put together—not just in entertaining and informative fashion (John Heard's understated narration helps), but also with underplayed wit and an ever-vigilant socially conscious eye. For instance, one point the tape stresses is the way white, establishment middle America virulently decried rock 'n' roll on one hand, and on the other did all it could to co-opt black R&B hits with appallingly innocuous cover versions by sanctioned Caucasian artists. I mean, you haven't been really sickened until you've seen Pat Boone, his tie loosened to signal "naughtiness," desecrating "Tutti-Frutti" with his namby-pamby uptight reading.

☐ **VARIOUS ARTISTS**

ROCK & RULE

★★

MGM/UA, 1986, 79 minutes

PRODUCED BY: Patrick Loubert and Michael Hirsh
DIRECTED BY: Clive A. Smith
MUSIC FROM: Rock & Rule motion picture soundtrack (United Artists, 1983).
SELECTIONS: Deborah Harry: "Angel's Song," "Invocation Song," "Send Love Through"; Deborah Harry and Robin Zander: "Send Love Through—Finale"; Iggy Pop: "Pain and Suffering"; Lou Reed: "My Name Is Mok," "Triumph"; Cheap Trick: "Born to Raise Hell," "I'm the Man," "Ohm Sweet Ohm"; Earth, Wind and Fire: "Dance, Dance, Dance"; Melleny Brown: "Hot Dogs and Sushi."

This post–Ralph Bakshi (*Heavy Metal*) animated fantasy feature film with rock soundtrack never really got much of a theatrical release. And seeing it on home video, one realizes why—the good points are easily eclipsed by the bad.

Rock & Rule is set in a distant-future, postapocalypse world, but its story also contains the arcane epic fantasy elements prescribed by the *Star Wars* formula (in this case, an evil magician whose demon-invocation plans provide the dramatic tension). The plot is essentially as pat and predictable as any fairy-tale (or as the occasional visual references to *Star Wars* and *Bladerunner*)—yet it's also larded down with pointless obscurities and complexities, no doubt added to make it seem "deeper," but which ultimately confuse. The filmmakers *should* have overcome plot predictability with character likability, but *Rock & Rule* features characters of mutant human/canine/feline/rodent extraction who, being for the most part quite unappealing both physically and personality-wise, are the film's crucial flaw. We are never made to care a jot about what's happening. The animation is okay, but not nearly exceptional enough to salvage the film. Same goes for the extremely erratic soundtrack, much of which is empty, anonymous bombast or simply lightweight and undistinguished.

There are a *few* good points: some cute character voices are dubbed by former *SCTV* star Catherine O'Hara; the idea of using Lou Reed's songs to personify the evil magician Mok is the only show of wit in the whole film, and "My Name Is Mok" is actually one of the best songs on the soundtrack ("Triumph," which sounds like it could be good, is given short shrift); Deborah Harry's numbers as heroine Angel are nice in a sub-Blondie pop-rock mode (her boyfriend and Blondie guitarist Chris Stein produced them and most of the rest of the soundtrack); and best of all is a number called "Hot Dogs and Sushi," a loony inspired, effervescent blend of punk, funk, Latin, and electropop sung in the movie by one of the evil magician's overweight, disused harem girls, but actually sung by someone named Melleny Brown. Her chirpy, eccentric vocals, along with the spry, dislocated music which features Patricia Cullen (synthesizers), Katherine Moses (sax), and Toby Swann (guitar), make "Hot Dogs and Sushi" an inspired delight.

If *Rock & Rule* had only concentrated on the kind of off-the-wall ebullience embodied by "Hot Dogs and Sushi," it would have been a whole lot more interesting and unusual—not to mention watchable. As is, it's recommendable mainly to diehard fans of the soundtrack artists, or fanatics of the animated-rock-feature genre.

☐ **VARIOUS ARTISTS**
ROCKERS
★★★½

Import, 1979, 100 minutes
PRODUCED BY: Patrick Hulsey
DIRECTED BY: Theodoras Bafoloukas
MUSIC FROM: Various albums by various artists; *Rockers* motion picture soundtrack (Island/Mango, 1979).
SELECTIONS: Inner Circle: "We A

Rockers"; the Maytones: "Money Worries"; Junior Murvin: "Police and Thieves"; the Heptones: "Book of Rules"; Peter Tosh: "Stepping Razor"; Jacob Miller: "Tenement Yard"; Junior Byles: "Fade Away"; Bunny Wailer: "Rockers"; Gregory Isaacs: "Slavemaster"; Ras Michael and the Sons of Negus: untitled Rasta hymn; Rockers All Stars: "Man in the Street"; Kiddus I: "Graduation in Zion"; Burning Spear: "Jah No Dead"; Third World: "Satta Amassaganna"; Justin Hines and the Dominoes: "Natty Take Over."

As a movie, *Rockers* achieves mixed success: its sub–*Harder They Come* plot, in which a crime syndicate is making things very difficult for struggling reggae musicians and real-life reggae drummer Leroy "Horsemouth" Wallace leads the fight to topple their hegemony, is pretty predictable. But as a travelogue through the world of Jamaican reggae, it presents many sights any reggae fan would want to see, and the soundtrack is consistently outstanding. The film's highlight comes about midway through, when the seemingly down-and-out Wallace goes to seek solace from Winston "Burning Spear" Rodney, leader of one of reggae's greatest bands, Burning Spear. Rodney sits Wallace down on a little bridge over a creek and in the tropical dusk serenades Wallace with a moving a cappella "Jah No Dead." Also seen in brief snatches, either performing or just hanging around, are such fine reggae performers as Big Youth, the Mighty Diamonds, Dillinger, Jack Ruby, and Prince Hammer. The soundtrack's highlights, aside from Rodney's goosebump-raising interlude, include Peter Tosh's defiantly funky "Stepping Razor" and the Heptones' rapturous, doo-wop–derived "Book of Rules."

☐ **VARIOUS ARTISTS**

ROCK! ROCK! ROCK!

★★½

Media, 1985 (1956), 83 minutes

PRODUCED BY: Max J. Rosenberg and Milton Subotsy

DIRECTED BY: Will Price

MUSIC FROM: Rock! Rock! Rock! soundtrack (Chess, 1956/1986).

SELECTIONS: Chuck Berry: "You Can't Catch Me"; Frankie Lymon and the Teenagers: "I Am Not a Juvenile Delinquent," "Baby Baby"; the Moonglows: "I Knew from the Start," "Over and Over Again"; Connie Francis: "It's Never Happened to Me"; the Flamingos: "Would I Be Crying"; Johnny Burnette: "Lonesome Train"; La Vern Baker: "Tra La La"; Alan Freed and His Rock 'n' Roll Band with Freddie Mitchell on sax: "Rock 'n' Roll Boogie."

One of the first so-called rock movies, *Rock! Rock! Rock!* was one of several '50s films to star disc jockey Alan Freed and a cast of early rock and R&B performers. What there is of a plot revolves around Dori (Tuesday Weld in her film debut) and her various typically teenage problems—falling in love, losing her boyfriend Tommy (the very wooden Teddy Randazzo from the Three Chuckles), and getting him back, all while Tommy sings his way through two of Freed's talent shows. Meanwhile Dori occasionally breaks into song—mid-conversation at the malt shop or while walking in the woods—and through a miracle of technology, Connie Francis's voice comes out (!). While some of the performances are classics (Chuck Berry, Frankie Lymon and the Teenagers) and others offer rare glimpses of great but almost forgotten performers (Johnny Burnette, La Vern Baker, the Moonglows, and the Flamingos; also worth noting is sax man Freddie Mitchell), the majority are laughably old-fashioned, offering convincing evidence that rock 'n' roll *had* to happen. One look at the Chuckles, Jimmy Cavallo and His House Rockers (a quintet with two saxes?), or Cirino and the Bowties and you know why kids thanked God for Elvis. Not surprisingly, many of the lesser-knowns were signed to Coral Records, a label Freed was involved with, so you know they weren't included here because they were in any way important.—P.R.

☐ VARIOUS ARTISTS
THE ROCKY HORROR PICTURE SHOW
★★★★½

Mail order only, originally released 1975, 101 minutes

PRODUCED BY: Michael White

DIRECTED BY: Jim Sharman

MUSIC FROM: The Rocky Horror Picture Show motion picture soundtrack (Ode, 1975).

SELECTIONS: "Science Fiction/Double Feature," "Dammit Janet," "Over at the Frankenstein Place," "The Time Warp," "Sweet Transvestite," "I Can Make You a Man," "The Sword of Damocles," "Hot Patootie—Bless My Soul," "I Can Make You a Man: Reprise," "Touch-a, Touch-a, Touch Me," "Eddie," "Rose Tint My World," "Floor Show," "Fanfare/Don't Dream It," "Wild and Untamed Thing," "I'm Going Home," "Super Heroes," "Science Fiction/Double Feature: Reprise."

In the years since its theatrical release, *The Rocky Horror Picture Show* has become the top-grossing and most popular cult film of all time. Over a decade after its inauspicious first showings, *Rocky Horror* still plays to packed houses of Transylvanians—diehard Rocky fans who dress up like the film's main characters, hop into the aisles to do the Time Warp, mouth off to the screen, and shower one another with everything from rice to toilet paper on cue. Sadly, those of us who love *Rocky Horror* and are old enough to vote have suffered—unjustly, I think—for having what could be described as either very catholic, or simply no, taste. Being a real *Rocky Horror* fan is probably like having been to est—you just have to get it.

Rocky's availability on home video, limited as it is, gives the faint of heart, the misguided, and the uninitiated a chance to really see—and hear all the lines of—the film in the privacy of their own homes. It also allows you to look at the film as a film rather than as a cult phenom. And, contrary to what you might think, *Rocky Horror* has much to recommend it as a film.

Your first clue is in the film's overture, "Science Fiction/Double Feature," a loving ode to such sci-fi film classics as *The Day the Earth Stood Still, The Invisible Man,* and *It Came from Outer Space.* The story involves Brad Majors (Barry Bostwick) and Janet Weiss (Susan Sarandon), two straight, uptight kids from Denton who stumble upon the castle of Dr. Frank 'n' Furter (Tim Curry), a mad, sex-crazed scientist from the planet Transexual. Once inside the castle, Brad and Janet meet Riff Raff (Richard O'Brien, who wrote the original musical play, music, and lyrics), his sister Magenta (Patricia Quinn), Frank's ex-lover, Columbia (Little Nell Campbell), and Frank's new creation, Rocky, a muscle man, and witness the gruesome murder of Columbia's current boyfriend, Eddie (Meat Loaf). And they both become the objects of Frank's seemingly insatiable lust. But, like all mad doctors, Frank has overreached, and so Riff and Magenta stage a coup, kill Frank, Rock, and Columbia, and return to Transylvania.

It only sounds dumb—honest. Curry's Frank is a wild campy cross between Judy Garland, Mick Jagger, and Basil Rathbone, and Meat Loaf's Eddie is the consummate dumb biker punk. Everyone else is appropriately decadent, except for Brad, Janet, and Dr. Scott, their high-school science teacher who is hip to Frank's experiments. And the three "innocents" get theirs in the end, in more ways than one. In a wonderful twist on science fiction and horror films, *Rocky Horror* celebrates the good in evil, self-knowledge through sex, and hedonism as religion and sport, and does it with a lot more panache and intelligent good humor than *Dallas.* Plus, some scenes—"The Time Warp," Frank's entrance to "Sweet Transvestite," and Meat Loaf's "Hot Patootie"—are so visually arresting, for an assortment of reasons ranging from the sublime to the ridiculous, and the music is so good that you won't forget them for a long time. And, if you find that you really love it, you might even notice little things, like Riff biting the biscuit before the Time Warp, that might make you begin thinking that this really is deeper than it looks. And it is. (Available by mail order only from Playings Hard To Get.)—P.R.

□ KENNY ROGERS AND DOLLY PARTON
REAL LOVE

★★★

RCA/Columbia, 1985, 90 minutes
PRODUCED BY: Ken Yates
DIRECTED BY: Stan Harris
MUSIC FROM: Concert special (HBO, 1985).
SELECTIONS: "Real Love," "Here You Come Again," "Jolene," "Applejack," "Coat of Many Colors," "Lady," "We've Got Tonight," "Island in the Stream," "Baby I'm Burnin'," "Two Doors Down," "9 to 5," "Appalachian Memories," and others.

Two of countrypolitan's most charismatic superstars in one lavish program, with footage from both separate and duet shows all cut together. Interestingly, the program openly acknowledges its divergent source material, with the recurrent motif of a director's video console which shows the Dolly concert, the Kenny concert, the Kenny-and-Dolly concert, and the backstage interviews with them playing on different monitors. Onstage and off, despite the banality of much of the contemporary crossover-pop music, Dolly is incandescent and impossible not to love. Smooth as Rogers is, he's a wet blanket next to her. Hard-core Parton fans will be disappointed to see many of her great early country hits, like "Jolene," given short shrift to make room for the slicker Rogers duets. But for fans of the more current hit material, this ought to satisfy.

□ THE ROLLING STONES, OTHERS
GIMME SHELTER

★★★★★

RCA/Columbia, 1981, 92 minutes
PRODUCED BY: Maysles Films, Inc.
DIRECTED BY: David Maysles, Albert Maysles, Charlotte Zwerin
MUSIC FROM: Various Rolling Stones albums, and other albums by other artists; *Gimme Shelter* motion picture soundtrack (Maysles Films, 1970).
SELECTIONS: Flying Burrito Brothers: "Six Days on the Road"; Jefferson Airplane: "The Other Side of this Life"; Tina Turner: "I've Been Loving You Too Long"; Rolling Stones: "Jumping Jack Flash," "(I Can't Get No) Satisfaction," "You Gotta Move," "Wild Horses," "Brown Sugar," "Love in Vain," "Honky Tonk Women," "Street Fighting Man," "Sympathy for the Devil," "Under My Thumb," "Street Fighting Man (reprise)," "Gimme Shelter."

Perhaps the most chilling rock documentary yet, *Gimme Shelter* captures the Rolling Stones' December 1969 concert at Altamont Speedway, near San Francisco. Occurring as it did just a few months after the Utopian dream-come-true that was Woodstock, Altamont marked the beginning of the end of the '60s. For during the Stones' set—while they were singing "Sympathy for the Devil," no less—a young black man was stabbed to death by several members of the Hell's Angels, a scene the Maysles unknowingly filmed. Yet despite the tension and violence, *Gimme Shelter* is one of the most beautifully made rockumentaries ever (don't be fooled by the occasionally chaotic camerawork or the muddied sound), and "a manual for cliché-avoidance in rock filmmaking," as David Ehrenstein and Bill Reed wrote in *Rock on Film. Gimme Shelter* also contains a wealth of excellent concert footage of the Stones at the *Get Yer Ya-Ya's Out* peak, from both their 1969 tour-opening show at New York's Madison Square Garden (the scene of the earlier portion's live footage) and Altamont, their tour-closing thank-you and farewell. The inclusion of the Garden footage is far from gratuitous: the callow, ostensibly innocuous satanism the Stones paraded onstage, and the hysteria it provoked even under the best of circumstances, come back to haunt Altamont even more vividly because of the juxtaposition of the two shows here.

The film shows the heated and harried last-minute planning that guaranteed from the start that Altamont would be a disaster. Then there are the performances—a mediocre set from the Flying Burrito Brothers, a torrid one from Tina Turner, and a so-so performance by the Jefferson Airplane. It's during the Airplane's set that we get the first glimpse of what's to come, when Marty Balin is punched out by a Hell's Angel when he jumps offstage to help a black man who's being beaten. Why didn't security come and haul the Angels out, any rational person might ask. Because the Hell's Angels *were* the security. As the evening wears on, you can almost feel the tension, and while it may have been morally questionable for the Maysles to have included slow-motion footage of Meredith Hunter's murder in the finished film it is undeniably a powerful and riveting moment.

It is also an ironic experience that makes you squirm to see the Stones—rock's self-styled shamans of satanic decadence and anarchy—flummoxed and finally terrified when confronted with the reality of the situation. The moment Jagger begins singing "Sympathy for the Devil," a group of Angels causes some commotion. "We always have something very funny happen when we start that number . . ." Jagger weakly jokes, but nobody's laughing. Soon an Angel is up in Jagger's face telling him something, then Jagger is lamely, pathetically pleading with the crowd to "cool out." Only Keith Richards makes any attempt to address the situation, but it's clearly too late. The Angels are in control. A few minutes later Jagger leans forward and gets the message from people standing around Hunter that they need a doctor. As if to demonstrate how badly hurt Hunter is, they hold up their blood-soaked hands. A few songs later and the Stones were whisked away—along with anyone else who could crowd aboard—by helicopter.

Just as hideously memorable, however, is the moment when Jerry Garcia of the Grateful Dead alights outside the Altamont site halfway through the show. When he's apprised of the havoc the Angels are wreaking, he replies in a Marin County nasal twang that's almost self-parody, "Oh, wow, maaan . . . like what a bummer, maaaan," and not for a second does his stupid beatific smile leave his face.

The beauty of this film lies in the Maysles Brothers' ability to perfectly capture the scene's craziness, tension, and desperation. It was a cold night, the show ran late, there was neither sufficient food nor facilities for the crowd (estimated between 300,000 and 400,000). There were bad vibes all around, which not even the Stones could allay (indeed, which they could only exacerbate). The group had hired their "security" on the mistaken notion that California's Hell's Angels were as harmless as the English Hell's Angels they had used for their Hyde Park concert several months before. The Grateful Dead had recommended them; they were hired and paid in beer.

Altamont raised many issues—for example, the responsibility of performers and promoters to ensure crowd safety—which the movie drove home like no rock film before or since. Hunter's death wasn't the only one; two people were run over by a car as they slept on the ground, and another drowned in a ditch, while untold others were beaten by Angels with pool cues, chains, and fists. "Sympathy for the Devil"? Hardly. Altamont was a classic example of greed, poor planning, carelessness, and stupidity. After an in-depth investigation *Rolling Stone* magazine lay the blame where many (including Bill Graham, whose suggestions had been ignored) still believe it belonged—on the Rolling Stones. The film ends with Charlie Watts and Jagger viewing the footage of the murder. Only Watts seems genuinely disturbed, and even his expression of concern strikes one as oddly cold and somehow insufficient. In his icy rock-star pose, however, Jagger just looks like a jerk, or something more unspeakable. Altamont proved to latter-day hippies and ignorant idealists that Woodstock didn't just happen, that the machinery of bigtime rock 'n' roll can be as crass and indifferent to people's needs as any other money-making industry, that things weren't so groovy after all. And *Gimme Shelter* shows you all that, in a remarkably complete and commendably dispassionate, objective manner.—P.R./M.S.

□ ROLLING STONES
VIDEO REWIND
★★★★

Vestron, 1984, 60 minutes

DIRECTED BY: Julien Temple, various others

MUSIC FROM: Sticky Fingers (Rolling Stones, 1971); *Goat's Head Soup* (Rolling Stones, 1973); *It's Only Rock 'n' Roll* (Rolling Stones, 1974); *Emotional Rescue* (Rolling Stones, 1980); *Tatoo You* (Rolling Stones, 1981); *Undercover* (Rolling Stones, 1983).

SELECTIONS: "Emotional Rescue," "She's So Cold," "Too Much Blood," "She Was Hot," "Undercover of the Night," "Waiting on a Friend," "Neighbors," "Brown Sugar," "Angie," "It's Only Rock 'n' Roll."

Bill Wyman plays a museum security guard. After hours, he surreptitiously enters the Withdrawn Exhibits room, wherein he finds encased skinheads, mohawked punks, a Teddy Boy—and Mick Jagger, frozen in classic rooster-on-acid pose. Wyman unlocks Mick, they reminisce, and "rewind" through Stones video history. There's plenty of good archival footage, and not just the "Angie" and "It's Only Rock 'n' Roll" promo clips and black-and-white onstage "Brown Sugar" (circa Mick Taylor) either. There are also such marvelous moments as Keith Richards's withering retorts to a classically unhip interviewer, and a screamingly hilarious coda in which a worked-up British twit interviewer appears to be simply thrilled to bits at being snubbed backstage by Jagger. The collected videos themselves are erratic, many falling into the Stones' earlier we-couldn't-care-less-about-the-cameras vein of slovenliness ("Emotional Rescue," "She's So Cold," the contrived street bonhomie of "Waiting on a Friend"). Michael Lindsay-Hogg's "Neighbors," here in its uncensored version, is a bloody gloss on Hitchcock's *Rear Window;* Temple's "Too Much Blood" is a hamfisted comment on such gore-fests, most interesting as one of his very few slip-ups. But Temple's "Undercover of the Night," a swirlingly subversive comment on Central American revolutions, and "She Was Hot," a hilarious burlesque of rock video sexism, are both pinnacles of the genre. And as in David Bowie's *Jazzin' for Blue Jean,* Temple coaxes a delightfully self-mocking performance out of Jagger.

□ THE ROLLING STONES
LET'S SPEND THE NIGHT TOGETHER
★★★½

Embassy, 1984, 94 minutes
PRODUCED BY: Ronald L. Schwary
DIRECTED BY: Hal Ashby
MUSIC FROM: Various Rolling Stones albums; *Let's Spend the Night Together* motion picture soundtrack (Raindrops Films, 1982).
SELECTIONS: "Black Limousine," "All Down the Line," "Brown Sugar," "You Can't Always Get What You Want," "Honky Tonk Women," "Jumpin' Jack Flash," "Let It Bleed," "Let's Spend the Night Together," "(I Can't Get No) Satisfaction," "Under My Thumb," "Going to a Go-Go," "Just My Imagination (Running Away with Me)," "Time Is on My Side," "Twenty Flight Rock," "She's So Cold," "Little T & A," "Neighbors."

You can't always get what you want—nor, sometimes, can you avoid resorting to clichés—and if you couldn't get a ticket to the Stones' 1981 tour, or if you did go and would like a remembrance, *Let's Spend the Night Together* ought to do nicely. It was directed by Hal Ashby, one of the most erratic directors in recent cinema history—I mean, here's a guy who goes from wonderful flicks like *Shampoo* and *Bound for Glory* to utterly inexcusable *dreck* like *Harold and Maude*. Here, however, Ashby's apparent awe of the living myth that is (or was) the Stones reins in his tendencies toward mush-minded sentimentality (except for one asinine instance, when he can't resist revisiting *Coming Home* territory to insert a grievously heavy-handed Vietnam-newsreel montage into "Time Is on My Side"). And except for an abrupt clip of Mick Jagger horsing around in a corral for no apparent reason, there are no intrusive, unnecessary shots to get in the way of the spectacle of the concert itself (or rather the concerts themselves, since this film was shot at a number of stops along the U.S. tour). Directors of photography Caleb Deschanel and Gerald Fiel supply awesome camera angles and movements aplenty—such as slo-mo aerial pans over the enormous sports stadia in which the shows took place (before what looks like *millions* of fans at each venue)—which are more than enough to convince someone like me, who didn't get a ticket to the tour itself, that actually being there must've been a lot worse than seeing this film. It's a more convenient and more visually variegated experience than any sporting-event mega-concert could ever be in person. There are a few moments—with "She's So Cold" and "(I Can't Get No) Satisfaction" the most notable—in which the whole pathetic/wonderful/tired/ageless spectacle that is a Stones concert inspires Ashby to sublime, pure-cinema flights of editing and montage as balletic as any of Jagger's prancing stage moves, as pyrotechnical as any of Keith Richards's classic post–Chuck Berry guitar riffs. Meanwhile, the much-ballyhooed Dolby stereo sound is as erratically balanced and occasionally muddy and distorted as any arena sound system's—which adds to the documentary feel of this sometimes-arty concert film. For those who care to know, "Neighbors" and "Little T & A" are the cookingest tunes, and the only moment when Jagger's liver-lipped smile seems unforced and joyously sincere is during his stomping dance with Richards to open "Hang Fire." Meanwhile, there are clips of the '60s Stones intercut with "Time Is on My

Side" that make you understand why they decided *not* to name this film after *that* song. But no matter what one thinks of the Stones in this late period of their career, *Let's Spend the Night Together* is as well done a rock concert movie as any other (including 1975's *Ladies and Gentlemen: the Rolling Stones*, which happened to have caught them during a much hotter phase of their career but which at this writing has yet to make it to home video).

□ THE ROLLING STONES
IN THE PARK
★★★½

Import, 1985, 58 minutes

MUSIC FROM: Various Rolling Stones albums.

SELECTIONS: "(I Can't Get No) Satisfaction," "Jumpin' Jack Flash," "I'm Yours, She's Mine," "I'm Free," "Sympathy for the Devil," "Love in Vain," "Midnight Rambler," "Honky Tonk Women," "I'm Free."

This is a rough-edged recording of the legendary Stones show in London's Hyde Park in July 1969—just a few days after Brian Jones was found dead at the bottom of his swimming pool. Jones's already announced replacement, former John Mayall Bluesbreaker Mick Taylor, makes his performing debut on guitar; the set includes "Honky Tonk Women," which would be officially released a few days after the show. And yes, it opens with Mick Jagger reading an excerpt from Shelley's poem "Adonais" and releasing hundreds of butterflies in tribute to Jones to kick off the show. "I'm Free" is played a second time to close the show as another homage to the dear departed. It should be made clear that as great as the historical-occasion value of this tape may be, the recording *is* rough and so are the Stones: Taylor, obviously, was inexperienced and more than a bit nervous, especially under *these* circumstances, and the rest of the band understandably appear more than a little shaken as well. (Available by mail order from Playings Hard to Get.)

□ SONNY ROLLINS
SONNY ROLLINS LIVE AT LOREN
★★★★

Rhapsody, 1986, 36 minutes

MUSIC FROM: Various Sonny Rollins albums; Dutch concert performance, 1973.

SELECTIONS: "There Is No Greater Love," "Don't Stop the Carnival," "Alfie," "St. Thomas."

□ SONNY ROLLINS
SONNY ROLLINS
★★★★½

Tokei Japan/Instant Replay, 1986, 58 minutes

DIRECTED BY: Pierre Lacombe

MUSIC FROM: Various Sonny Rollins albums.

SELECTIONS: "My One and Only Love," "Don't Stop the Carnival," "I'll Be Seeing You," three others not identified.

Available on Tokei Stereo Laser videodisc only.

Sonny Rollins is the man almost universally regarded as *the* preeminent tenor saxophonist in all of contemporary jazz. In both of these programs, he shows why as he performs in concert before live audiences. Both programs are straightforwardly shot, commendably avoid the opportunity to needlessly trick up the visuals, and let the performers and performances speak for themselves. There are, however, some noteworthy differences between these two mail-order-only programs.

Live, while shorter than *Sonny Rollins* by almost half, was shot earlier—at a 1973 concert in Holland. While the quintet backing Rollins features electric guitarist Yoshiaki Masuo, in this period the leader was playing in a style closer to his bebop roots than to the electrified jazz-funk fusion mode he would adopt as the '70s progressed (the rest of the band includes Walter Davis, Jr., on piano, Bob Cranshaw on bass, and David Lee on drums). Thus, this program might appeal more to the jazz purist who abhors what some see as the crass, restrictive commercialization of jazz fusion.

Sonny Rollins, shot at a 1982 Montreal jazz festival, has two guitarists behind Rollins, Bobby Broom and Masuo, with a rhythm section of Cranshaw and drummer Jack DeJohnette (who's a far superior drummer, with all due respect to Lee). Here, the music is very much in the funk-fusion groove, with enough amplified rhythmic punch to perhaps appeal to those who first became aware of Rollins through his beautiful work on the Rolling Stones' *Tattoo You* album (especially on "Waiting on a Friend"). However, those bebop roots are still evident in the ample soloing time given the players, and along with the fact that this *is*, after all, the "Saxophone Colossus" himself; that should help keep those hard-line purists interested as well. Meanwhile, the visuals are a bit more colorful and excitingly cut than in the earlier program, thanks partially to the more demonstrative audience; and there's just more music and much better stereo sound on the Japanese laser disc than on the cassette (at this writing, the disc sells for thirty dollars, the tape for forty!), which is why the disc gets the extra half-star (*Sonny Rollins Live at Loren* available by mail order from Rhapsody Films; *Sonny Rollins* available by mail order from Instant Replay.)

☐ LINDA RONSTADT (WITH NELSON RIDDLE AND HIS ORCHESTRA) WHAT'S NEW

★★★

Vestron, 1984, 60 minutes

PRODUCED BY: Robert Lombard

DIRECTED BY: David Lewis

MUSIC FROM: What's New (Asylum, 1983); *Lush Life* (Asylum, 1983).

SELECTIONS: "I've Got a Crush on You," "What's New," "Keepin' Out of Mischief Now," "Guess I'll Hang My Tears Out to Dry," "Falling in Love Again," "Someone to Watch Over Me," "Hey Daddy," "Mr. Sandman," "Kalamazoo," "Dream," "Take Me Right Back to the Track," "Ghost of a Chance with You," "Lover Man," "Good-bye."

Also available on Vestron Stereo Laser videodisc.

Ronstadt shocked everyone with her career turnabout in the mid-'80s. Having seemingly mastered country and soft-rock only to flop with lame attempts at new wave, her covers of '40s big-band standards produced the best-selling *What's New* and *Lush Life* LPs. She especially shocked critics, who correctly noted that despite her technically magnificent voice, the '40s hairdo and gowns she wore to get "in the mood," and her collaboration with Nelson Riddle (who originally scored many of these for singers like Sinatra and Sarah Vaughan and who gives Ronstadt the apposite nonpareil settings all over again), Ronstadt hasn't a clue to what these songs mean, and her stiffly superficial delivery is a million miles off the stylistic mark. Too bad—she's real pretty and does have a good voice, and she seems like a sweet, sincerely well-intentioned lady. Still, for all those fans who gobbled up her albums, this video companion should be just what the doctor ordered. Linda's in the hairdo and vintage gown again, she gets to sing while suspended on a movie-musical crescent moon, she essays an Andrews Sisters takeoff, and it's all shot with elegant consideration, lit to get that movie-musical Technicolor look to enhance the mood her clumsiness keeps shattering.

☐ **DIANA ROSS, OTHERS**
MAHOGANY
★★

Paramount, 1976, 109 minutes
PRODUCED BY: Rob Cohen and Jack Ballard
DIRECTED BY: Berry Gordy, Jr.
MUSIC FROM: Mahogany motion picture soundtrack (Motown, 1975).
SELECTIONS: Diana Ross: "The Theme from *Mahogany* (Do You Know Where You're Going To)"; the Temptations: "Shakey Ground"; T. G. Sheppard: "Devil in the Bottle."

This, Ross's second feature film, was a critical disaster and a great disappointment, coming as it did after Ross's auspicious film debut as Billie Holiday in *Lady Sings the Blues*. The story line—a spunky young ghetto girl's rise from department store gofer to top fashion model to top designer—has its parallels in Ross's own life story, and she handles the role as well as one could. After all, Ross is very good at wearing clothes. Costarring is Billy Dee Williams as Brian, a neighborhood activist turned politician who tries to get Tracy (Ross) to see that personal success brings with it an obligation to help other blacks, not just escape from them. It's an issue worth considering, but too weighty for this flimsy golden-age-of-Hollywood rags-to-riches yarn. The most interesting thing about *Mahogany* is Anthony Perkins as the impotent, neurotic, woman-hating, gun-loving fashion photographer who discovers Tracy and makes her Mahogany. His relationship with Mahogany is a cliché, of course, but his character is so fascinating you wish he would kill off Brian so you could see just how sick his thing with Mahogany could get. Alas, those rich possibilities are never explored. Instead, she returns to Chicago and to Brian, to what is "real." Boring! Well, at least the film ends there, thankfully.

While the plot is predictable and the twists are unbelievable, *Mahogany* is no shallower than other *Rocky*-style salutes to self-determination and not nearly as hackneyed as a season of *Dallas*. What is irredeemable is Berry Gordy's direction. In a mere hour and half, *Mahogany* demonstrates—in fact, seems to celebrate—every directorial faux pas in the book. It also contains the most contrived nude-breast shot in history (watch closely; you'll need your slo-mo scan for this one). This tape is recommendable to Ross fanatics *and* to those who absolutely loathe her.—P.R.

☐ **DIANA ROSS**
IN CONCERT
★★

RCA/Columbia, 1980, 80 minutes
PRODUCED BY: Marty Callner
DIRECTED BY: Marty Callner
MUSIC FROM: Various Diana Ross albums.
SELECTIONS: "Ain't No Mountain High Enough," "Too Shy to Say," "Touch Me in the Morning," "I Wanna Be Bad," "I Ain't Been Licked," "Home," "It's My House," "No One Gets the Prize," "Love Hangover," "Reach Out and Touch (Somebody's Hand)," "Baby Love," "Remember Me," "Lady Sings the Blues," "T'ain't Nobody's Bizness If I Do," "God Bless the Child," "My Man," "The Boss," "Do You Know Where You're Going To," "Ain't No Mountain High Enough (Reprise)," "All for One."
Also available on Pioneer Stereo Laser videodisc.

☐ **DIANA ROSS**
VISIONS OF DIANA ROSS
★½

RCA/Columbia, 1985, 28 minutes
PRODUCED BY: ANAID Film/RCA Video
DIRECTED BY: Dominic Orlando, Bob Giraldi, Marty Callner, Paul Justman
MUSIC FROM: Various Diana Ross albums.
SELECTIONS: "Missing You," "All of You," "Swept Away," "Muscles," "Pieces of Ice," "Why Do Fools Fall in Love."

By the time both of these programs were made, Miss Ross had long since become a grotesque caricature of her classic '60s stylistic elegance. *In Concert* is a typical Vegas glitz-fest from Caesar's Palace, notable solely for the presence of Marvin Gaye in the audience; Diana's energetic and looks great, but this soulless pro-forma career retrospective of a set has little to make anyone really care, unless they're Ross fans. *Visions* is a compilation of similarly lame video clips, just about all of which use excessive glitz to intimidate the viewer into thinking that something exciting really *is* going on. Diana's nauseatingly sterile cover of the classic "Why Do Fools Fall in Love" finds her back in Vegas again, grinning like an idiot as she inexplicably runs around the neon-lit streets waving at jes-folks passersby. "All of You" is her sopping-wet duet with Julio Iglesias, who certainly, you know, "looks mmmmmah-velous." Bob Giraldi's "Pieces of Ice" may be the worst video ever made by the man who has never lived up to his auspicious debut with Michael Jackson's "Beat It": it'd be laughable if it weren't so pretentiously turgid and absurdly dumb. The only moment of grace is provided by Dominic Orlando's straightforward shoot of the surprisingly tasteful valentine to the late Marvin Gaye and other deceased Ross associates, including Florence Ballard, "Missing You." But that hardly makes up for all the rest of the garbage contained herein. For fanatic Ross fans (or very intrepid camp fanatics—or is that a redundancy) only.

□ ARLEN ROTH
LEARNING ROCK AND HEAVY METAL GUITAR

★★★★

Hot Licks, 1984, 60 minutes
PRODUCED BY: Arlen Roth
DIRECTED BY: Mark Kaplan
MUSIC FROM: Various demonstrations and performances by Arlen Roth.
SELECTIONS: Proper string bending, vibrato, whammy bar style, right-hand hammer-ons, hammer-ons and pull-offs, "flash" tricks, various harmonic techniques, various scales and licks.

□ ARLEN ROTH
ADVANCED ROCK AND LEAD GUITAR

★★★★

Hot Licks, 1984, 60 minutes
PRODUCED BY: Arlen Roth
DIRECTED BY: Mark Kaplan
MUSIC FROM: Various demonstrations and performances by Arlen Roth.
SELECTIONS: Chromatic style rock leads, volume control effects, advanced single-note bends, advanced double-note bends, harmonic hammer-ons, advanced scales, "trick licks."

□ ARLEN ROTH
HOT COUNTRY LEAD GUITAR

★★★★

Hot Licks, 1985, 60 minutes
PRODUCED BY: Arlen Roth
DIRECTED BY: Mark Kaplan
MUSIC FROM: Various demonstrations and performances by Arlen Roth.
SELECTIONS: Country string bending, "pedal steel" licks, pick and finger techniques, "chicken pickin'," false harmonics, double-note bends, rapid-fire picking, "rockability," "claw style," volume swells.

□ ARLEN ROTH
SLIDE GUITAR

★★★★

Hot Licks, 1985, 60 minutes
PRODUCED BY: Arlen Roth
DIRECTED BY: Mark Kaplan
MUSIC FROM: Various demonstrations and performances by Arlen Roth.
SELECTIONS: Proper slide technique, "box" patterns, blues slide style, country slide style, rock slide style, open E and G tunings, standard-tuning slide, right- and left-hand damping, slide tilting, hammer-ons and pull-offs, harmonics, vibrato, Duane Allman slide style, Elmore James slide style,

Robert Johnson slide style, Muddy Waters slide style.

□ ARLEN ROTH
CHICAGO BLUES GUITAR
★★★★

Hot Licks, 1985, 60 minutes
PRODUCED BY: Arlen Roth
DIRECTED BY: Mark Kaplan
MUSIC FROM: Various demonstrations and performances by Arlen Roth.
SELECTIONS: Blues string bending, vibrato, improvisational skills, rhythm work, ninth chord licks, B. B. King–style, Buddy Guy–style, Otis Rush–style, Eric–Clapton style, Mike Bloomfield–style, blues licks and scales.

Arlen Roth, the New York area studio guitarist and teacher who showed Ralph Macchio how to play blues and slide guitar for the 1986 film *Crossroads*, makes instructional home videos that are at least as good as anyone else's. All Hot Licks tapes are nicely shot, with cameras clearly showing what both right and left hands are doing; split-screens are often employed to good effect, and musical notation appears right on-screen as the notes are being played, an exceptionally convenient touch that eliminates having to look away from the screen at an accompanying booklet. And Roth himself is an authoritative but easygoing and ingratiating presence—just a plain old good instructor. Roth's selections of licks and tricks in his rock guitar tapes may not seem like the latest in ultrahip flash to beginning players weaned on Eddie Van Halen and his ilk, but they certainly offer a solid, expansive foundation from which to start. Rock guitarists should note that *Learning Rock and Heavy Metal Guitar* is for beginning to intermediate guitarists, while *Advanced Rock and Lead Guitar* is for just who it says, more advanced players. (Available by mail order from Hot Licks Productions, Inc.)

□ ROXY MUSIC
THE HIGH ROAD
★★★

RCA/Columbia, 1983, 76 minutes
PRODUCED BY: Robin Nash
MUSIC FROM: Various Roxy Music albums (Atlantic, Warner Bros., 1972–83).
SELECTIONS: "The Main Thing," "Out of the Blue," "Both Ends Burning," "A Song for Europe," "Can't Let Go," "While My Heart Is Still Beating," "Avalon," "My Only Love," "Dance Away," "Love Is the Drug," "Like a Hurricane," "Editions of You," "Do the Strand," "Jealous Guy."
Also available on Pioneer Stereo Laser videodisc.

Shot at Frejus, France, on Roxy's 1983 world tour (probably their last), this has to be one of *the* most basic, straightforward concert videos of all time. There's not a single special effect used anywhere; there's no fancy cutting of any sort; there's just the band going through its silken-smooth *Avalon*-era paces, caught from the minimum-requirement of camera angles and long/medium/close shots, and with gratifyingly few of the obligatory crowd-reaction shots. In a way, it's no wonder no director is credited. But that's not to say *The High Road* seems *un*directed: it's as easy on the eyes as this version of Roxy's music is on the ears, and as smoothly professional as the studio-session heavies (drummer Andy Newmark, percussionist Jimmy Maelen, bassist Neil Hubbard, among others) who back remaining Roxys Bryan Ferry, Phil Manzanera, and Andy Mackay. On one hand, this no-frills approach is right in keeping with Ferry's rather surprisingly dressed-down approach on this tour, as well as with Roxy's more subdued, introspectively romantic music. On the other hand, this is hardly the world's most visually exciting rock show, and by letting the band and its music stand or fall on its own merits, *The High Road* ensures that its appeal is limited to Roxy fans—or those seeking a classy break from MTV-style image-overload. Others will be bored silly. And maybe, like me, you'll be left wishing they made more concert videos back in the early and mid-'70s, when Roxy Music were as delightfully outrageous visually as they were adventurous musically.

□ RUBBER RODEO
SCENIC VIEWS

★★★★

Sony, 1984, 18 minutes
PRODUCED BY: David Brownstein
DIRECTED BY: David Greenberg
MUSIC FROM: Rubber Rodeo (Polygram, 1984).
SELECTIONS: "Anywhere with You," "The Hardest Thing," "How the West Was Won."

A gang of cowboy-wanna-bes from Rhode Island, Rubber Rodeo give country & western a new-wave edge. While their music has never been enough on its own to distinguish them, Davids Greenberg and Brownstein of low-budget Second Story Television Productions have here come up with a wonderfully romantic video mini-masterpiece that deserves wider exposure. The theme of long-distance love and longing between singers Bob Holmes and Trish Milliken is illustrated with footage of Holmes as a trucker on the road, Milliken back home in the trailer park, and a special-effects video postcard that flies between the two of them. "How the West Was Won" is the affectionately flip payoff to their courtship—silent-Western footage cut with shots of Holmes and Milliken in banal trailer-park middle age. Simultaneously poignant, haunting, and funny, this is one of Sony's few Video 45s or Video EPs to hold together with conceptual integrity. And Trish Milliken is *dynamite*—she could be a gen-yoo-wine Hollywood actress any ol' time she pleases.

□ TODD RUNDGREN
VIDEOSYNCRACY

★★½

Sony, 1983, 12 minutes
PRODUCED BY: Todd Rundgren
DIRECTED BY: Todd Rundgren
MUSIC FROM: Hermit of Mink Hollow (Bearsville, 1978); *Healing* (Bearsville, 1981); *The Ever Popular Tortured Artist Effect* (Bearsville, 1983).
SELECTIONS: "Hideaway," "Can We Still Be Friends," "Time Heals."

□ TODD RUNDGREN
THE EVER POPULAR TORTURED ARTIST EFFECT

★

JEM/Passport, 1986, 82 minutes
PRODUCED BY: Todd Rundgren
DIRECTED BY: Todd Rundgren
MUSIC FROM: Various Todd Rundgren albums and Todd Rundgren and Utopia albums.
SELECTIONS: "Stepping Out," "Too Far Gone," "Hello, It's Me," "I Saw the Light," "An LP's Worth of Tunes," "Sometimes I Don't Know," "Eastern Intrigue," "Heaven and Hell," "Compassion," "Black and White," "Don't Break Down on Me," "The Dream Goes on Forever," "Please Come Home," "Born to Synthesize," "Ra," "Real Man," "Healing," "Listen to Your Heart," "Just One Victory," and others.

Videosyncracy collects three very uneven video clips from various Rundgren solo albums. Since all were made with high-tech digital video equipment prior to MTV's prompting of the rock-video revolution, the clips do have a pioneering historical value, which easily overshadows their questionable artistic accomplishments. In "Hideaway" a tiny Todd crawls all over a woman's nude body (avoiding the nasty bits) in between keying scenes into the frames of his shades; in "Can

We Still Be Friends" Todd's at an onstage piano, a post-produced tiny ballet dancer pirouetting on the piano lid (the guy's got a thing about size). "Time Heals" is by far the best of the three clips, with Rundgren using special effects to key himself into a series of classic Surrealist canvases by Dali and Magritte—which is either quite a feat, or a hell of a lot of nerve, or both. The music is all in Todd's bouncy pop vein, which is always a lot easier to take than his plodding progressive-rock indulgences with Utopia.

Tortured Artist is a "video autobiography" Rundgren wrote, produced, and directed in conjunction with England's Channel 4, who were the first to show it. A dubious distinction for them, as this happens to be one of the most insufferably self-indulgent, pretentious, and bilious music videos ever released. Rundgren, looking coldly conceited and calculating, takes part in a blandly trumped-up interview with an off-screen interlocutor; it serves to cue music videos spanning his solo career as well as some material with Utopia, from 1972 to 1983. With the exception of such typically Todd pop classics as "I Saw the Light" and "Hello, It's Me" (both heard in too-brief snippets), and the marginally chucklesome "An LP's Worth of Tunes," it's all embarrassing and dull, low on budget and bereft of ideas. It becomes painfully obvious after a while that Todd sees himself as an artist tortured by an uncomprehending and unappreciative public. So what does he do? He tortures *us* with *this.* Confidential to T.R.: if you're going to make something *this* awful, at least make it so awful it's *funny.*

□ RUSH
EXIT . . . STAGE LEFT
★★½

RCA/Columbia, 1982, 60 minutes
PRODUCED BY: Grant Lough
DIRECTED BY: Martin Kahan
MUSIC FROM: Exit . . . Stage Left (Polygram, 1981) and other Rush albums.
SELECTIONS: "Limelight," "Tom Sawyer," "The Trees," "Instrumental," "Xanadu," "Red Barchetta," "Free Will," "Closer to the Heart," "YYZ," Medley: "By-Tor and the Snow Dogs"/"In the End"/"In the Mood"/"2112 Finale," "YYZ (Instrumental Reprise)."

Also available on Pioneer Stereo Laser videodisc.

The reference in the title to cartoon character Snagglepuss is virtually the sole vestige of humor evidenced anywhere by this unbelievably self-conscious, pretentiously pedantic Canadian power trio, who've garnered hordes of idolatrous fans by relentlessly reconstituting old Led Zeppelin and Yes progressive/hard-rock riffs to frame drummer Neil Peart's obtuse, Ayn Rand–derived lyrics. Bassist/vocalist Geddy Lee, he of the gargoyle visage and banshee-wail voice, is the star of the show, which Rush fans will adore and all others will find incomprehensibly dull and stultifying. Though this 1981 Montreal Forum show is severely underlit, director Martin Kahan does at times transcend such limitations. Rush's use of video, for example the video-game graphics shown during the band's frantically churning odd-meter runs in "Red Barchetta," earns them a few points. Other video clips used in concert showed computer imagery or *SCTV*'s Count Floyd introducing a song (the other vestige of humor evidenced here).

□ RUSH
THROUGH THE CAMERA EYE
★★★

RCA/Columbia, 1985, 44 minutes
PRODUCED BY: Dan Schwarzbaum
DIRECTED BY: LeAnne Sawyers
MUSIC FROM: Various Rush albums (Polygram, 1975–84).

SELECTIONS: "Distant Early Warning," "Vital Signs," "The Body Electric," "Afterimage," "Subdivisions," "Tom Sawyer," "The Enemy Within," "Countdown."

Through the Camera Eye is different from *Exit . . . Stage Left* and *Grace Under Pressure Tour* in that it's mainly a clips compilation, featuring such MTV familiarities as "Distant Early Warning" and "Vital Signs." The former is actually a fairly felicitous illustration of Rush drummer Neil Peart's grandiloquent lyrics, as a young boy rides a cruise missile over the globe in a heavy-handed but effectively provocative metaphor for global nuclear paranoia. Most of the rest are either performance-based or mix performance with similarly silly but apposite imagery. And, just to make sure this program still *does* overlap with the almost-interchangeable *Exit* and *Grace* concert videos, "Tom Sawyer" is included from the former and "Afterimage" from the latter. Which may mean that this is the best choice for the budget-minded Rush fan.

□ RUSH
GRACE UNDER PRESSURE TOUR
★★★

RCA/Columbia, 1986, 69 minutes
DIRECTED BY: David Mallet; Rob Quartly
MUSIC FROM: Power Windows (Polygram, 1986) and other Rush albums.
SELECTIONS: "The Spirit of Radio," "The Enemy Within," "The Weapon," "Witch Hunt," "New World Man," "Distant Early Warning," "Red Sector A," "Closer to the Heart," Medley: "YYZ"/"Temples of Syrinx"/"Tom Sawyer," Medley: "Vital Signs"/"Finding My Way"/"In the Mood."

At this writing, *Grace Under Pressure Tour* was the latest of a trio of very similar Rush concert videos, this time featuring the razzle-dazzle concert direction of longtime Bowie collaborator David Mallet (who did a similar job, under vastly different musical circumstances, with Tina Turner's *Live Private Dancer Tour*) and, after the concert, the slick 1986 conceptual-performance video for "The Big Money," shot by Rob Quartly. Sometimes I watch this program and think maybe *this* is the one to recommend to those unfamiliar with Rush who maybe wanna check 'em out. Then I think: *naaah*.

□ THE RUTLES
THE RUTLES (ALL YOU NEED IS CASH)
★★★★★

Pacific Arts, 1980, 90 minutes
PRODUCED BY: Lorne Michaels
DIRECTED BY: Gary Weis
MUSIC FROM: The Rutles (Warner Bros., 1978).
SELECTIONS: "Hold My Hand," "Number One," "With a Girl Like You," "I Must Be in Love," "OUCH!," "Living in Hope," "Love Life," "Nevertheless," "Good Times Roll," "Doubleback Alley," "Cheese and Onions," "Another Day," "Piggy in the Middle," "Let's Be Natural," "Get Up and Go."

Before there was *This Is Spinal Tap*, the standard for rock parody was the TV special *The Rutles*, a hilarious sendup of the myth and reality—mostly the myth—of the Beatles. It was produced by *Saturday Night Live* creator Lorne Michaels—which accounts for the presences of director Gary Weis (who shot oodles of neat little filmlets for *SNL*) and Not Ready for Prime Time Players Bill Murray, John Belushi, Dan Aykroyd, and Gilda Radner. Eric Idle of Monty Python's Flying Circus wrote it, and Neil Innes of the Bonzo Dog Band (for a time, the aural counterpart to Python's inspired post-'60s dadaistic and very British irreverence) scored it—which accounts for its hilarity. Here is a fictitious

British TV look back at the Rutles and their legacy titled *All You Need Is Cash* (believe me, it's a *lot* funnier than that subtitle might indicate). It starts off with Idle, as a typically Pythonesque twit of a teabag news commentator, revisiting Rutland, home of the Rutles and birthplace of Rutlemania (nobody who has seen this program could ever forget the sight of Idle looking back over his shoulder as he smugly addresses the camera while walking the streets of Rutland—then slowly accelerating to a trot, and then a desperate run for his life as the camera truck keeps accelerating). With incredible irony, *The Rutles* not only presaged *Spinal Tap* but formally amounts to a virtual blueprint of the entirely serious *Compleat Beatles,* which it predated by four years.

The Rutles themselves are portrayed by Idle, as the incessantly eyelash-batting, McCartneyesque Dirk McQuigley; Innes as Lennon-like smart-ass Ron Nasty; John Halsey (in real life, a superb British rock drummer—check out his work on the undeservedly obscure, self-titled 1970 album by British band Patto, if you can find it) as the buffoonishly lovable Ringo Starr–style drummer, Barry Wom; and onetime Beach Boys sideman Rikki Fataar as the George Harrison type. Fataar's casting, while probably the least-remarked aspect of *The Rutles*, might also be its conceptual masterstroke. Think about it: Harrison—prior to becoming known as a devotee of mystical gobbledygook, at least—was the odd man out in the Fab Four, a token nondescript "normal" amidst three exceptionally vivid personalities; Fataar, with his dark-skinned Indo-Arabic appearance (which in itself could be construed as a joke on Harrison's Maharishi fetish), is a "token" presence of another sort, yet at the same time he, too, is "colorless," in that he virtually never has anything to say. Showing great good humor, Harrison himself appears in a cameo (he's a longtime friend and backer of various Python and Python-related projects); Mick Jagger, Ron Wood, and Paul Simon also cameo, as themselves.

The Rutles misses few tricks as it holds a funhouse mirror up to the well-known history of the Beatles: clothes, haircuts, poses, attitudes, TV and movie setups, interview and press conference banter, and so on are all lovingly but bitingly mocked. Perhaps most awesome of all is Innes's music, which for the most part takes some of the best-known and best-loved songs in recent pop music history, puts them in a blender, and pours them back out in coherent, *almost* recognizable form—but with subtle, tantalizing dislocations that will provide endless hours of amusement for Beatle fans or anyone familiar with the music (which includes just about everyone, anyway) as they try to decipher what riffs, chord progressions, solos, choruses, and so on Innes has switched around, recombined, or turned upside down and/or inside out to achieve such an effortlessly convincing parallel-universe sound. While a few of the tunes have obvious sources for their parody—"Piggy in the Middle" is "I Am the Walrus," "Let It Rot" is "Let It Be," "Hold My Hand" is, well, *you know*—overall, Innes has done an absolutely unbelievable job here, covering the Fab Four's sound from Merseybeat through psychedelia to sophisto-pop ("I Must Be in Love" is my favorite). What may be most remarkable about his feat is that he did it by taking off on the world's best-known song catalog—a catalog by a single, very distinctive, and readily identifiable *band*. Mandatory viewing for anyone who takes their music seriously enough to enjoy seeing it lampooned so brilliantly.

S

☐ VARIOUS ARTISTS
THE SACRED MUSIC OF DUKE ELLINGTON
★★★

MGM/UA, 1982, 90 minutes
PRODUCED BY: Charles Thompson
DIRECTED BY: Terry Henbery
MUSIC FROM: Various Duke Ellington albums; three concerts of Duke Ellington's sacred music.
SELECTIONS: Phyllis Hyman: "Lord's Prayer," "Tell Me It's the Truth": McHenry Boatwright: "In the Beginning, God," "God"; the New Swingle Singers: "Praise God," "Rocks of the Bible"; Jacques Loussier: "Meditations"; Tony Bennett: "Almighty God," "Somebody Cares," "Just One"; Will Gaines: "David Danced" (tap dance); Adelaide Hall: "Come Sunday"; Kenny Baker with Orchestra: "The Shepherd"; Rod Steiger: "Fire and Brimstone" (reading).

In the last decade of his life, Ellington wrote three concerts of sacred music, mixing big-band jazz, pop, and devotional song forms, choral and orchestral music, and narrative into a new, swinging liturgical music. This 1982 concert at St. Paul's Cathedral in London presents various pieces from all three sacred concerts, with the Alan Cohen Orchestra doing a fine job playing the beautiful charts (pianist Stan Tracy and baritone saxist John Surman stand out). Tony Bennett and Phyllis Hyman both sing wonderfully, and Will Gaines delivers a properly joyous tap dance for "David Danced." But host Rod Steiger and narrator Douglas Fairbanks, Jr., *really* turn up the unctuous portentousness for the blueblood crowd, marring an otherwise swell program. Still, it *is* the only place to find this stuff presented on video.

☐ SADE
DIAMOND LIFE VIDEO
★★½

CBS/Fox, 1985, 30 minutes
PRODUCED BY: Various
DIRECTED BY: Various
MUSIC FROM: Diamond Life (Portrait, 1985).
SELECTIONS: "Hang on to Your Love," "Smooth Operator," "Your Love Is King," "When Am I Going to Make a Living?"
Also available on CBS/Fox Stereo Laser videodisc.

With her high-fashion Afro-Eurasian looks, Sade is not hard to look at. And her band's swah-vay, jazz-inflected sophisto-pop (let's call her Steely Danielle) is very easy on the ears. But of the clips here, only Julien Temple's elaborately Hitchcockian "Smooth Operator" (here in a longer, even more elaborately Hitchcockian version than the one familiar to MTV viewers) offers more than campy '50s-revisited nightclub sets, lovely looks, and soothing sounds. Indeed, it could be argued that Sade's music is *so* atmospherically suggestive and seductive that, in a way, visuals really do it a disservice. Certainly, the between-clips interview segments do Sade herself a disservice: she has absolutely nothing of interest to say, and can't help but come across as the stereotypically vacuous, self-centered fashion-model-turned-starlet some folks are convinced she really is.

☐ ROLY SALLY
LEARNING ELECTRIC BASS
★★★★

Homespun, 1984, 90 minutes
PRODUCED BY: Happy Traum
DIRECTED BY: Happy Traum

Sally, who plays bass with critically acclaimed neo-rockabilly Chris Isaak, proves himself not only an excellent bassist but an excellent teacher, with a relaxed, easy going, and ingratiating manner that makes learning practically painless. Here, he covers right- and left-hand technique, scales and theory, and runs through a variety of sample bass lines. He also discusses at length the philosophy of the player in backing a singer and blending in with the rhythm section of a band, vital things for any bassist to learn, and relates it all to country, blues, bluegrass, and rock playing. (Available by mail order from Homespun Tapes.)

☐ **VARIOUS ARTISTS**
SAN FRANCISCO BLUES FESTIVAL
★★★½

Sony, 1984, 60 minutes
PRODUCED BY: Vincent Casalaina and Judy Underhill
DIRECTED BY: Vincent Casalaina
MUSIC FROM: 1983 San Francisco Blues Festival.
SELECTIONS: Clifton Chenier: "Louisiana Two Step," "What I Say," "Calinda"; Charles Ford Band: "Tell Me Mama," "40 Days and 40 Nights"; John Littlejohn: "Hoochie Coochie Man," "Bloody Tears"; John Hammond: "Drifting Blues," "Look on Yonder Wall"; Albert Collins: "Cold, Cold Feeling," "Frosty"; Robert Cray: "Too Many Cooks," "Let's Have a Natural Ball"; Clarence "Gatemouth" Brown: "Sometimes I Slip," "Six Levels Below Plant Life."

Though it's a bit disconcerting to see and hear the blues performed at a sunny outdoor show with palm trees visible in the background, authoritative performances and straightforward shooting overcome the incongruity. Standouts include Clifton Chenier's jumping Cajun zydeco (a blend of blues, jazz, and accordion two-step usually sung in bastardized French), John Littlejohn's no-nonsense Chicago blues, Albert Collins's show-stealing guitar mastery, young gun Robert Cray's rejuvenation of the classic form, and Clarence "Gatemouth" Brown's virtuosic eclecticism (how can you not love a song with a title like "Six Levels Below Plant Life"?). There are also off-the-cuff comments on the blues from performers and fans.

☐ **DAVID SANBORN**
LOVE & HAPPINESS
★★★½

Warner Reprise, 1986, 37 minutes
PRODUCED BY: Heidi Nolting
DIRECTED BY: Jean-Marie Perier
MUSIC FROM: Love & Happiness (Warner-Reprise, 1986) and other David Sanborn albums.
SELECTIONS: "Love & Happiness," "Run for Cover," "Lisa," "Straight to the Heart," "Smile," "Hideaway."

The saxophone playing of David Sanborn, a highly regarded New York studio whiz, should be more familiar than his name to most people through his soulful wailing in the *Saturday Night Live* house band. He's also sat in numerous times with Paul Shaffer's band on *Late Night with David Letterman*, and the former guitarist with that house band, Hiram Bullock, is one of the other topflight NYC sessioneers joining Sanborn for this set of expertly rendered jazz-funk fusion grooves performed before a live audience at the SIR rehearsal studio in Manhattan. Also present are bassist Marcus Miller (who's also played with the Letterman band on occasion), *SNL* house band drummer Buddy Williams, keyboardist Don Grolnick, and, on Al Green's "Love & Happiness," onetime Average White Band vocalist Hamish Stuart.

This set is shot with stylish beauty in hard-lit black and white, and more visual interest is added—where, to be honest, virtually none existed before—by frequently shooting the image of the band performing from a slight distance, as it's played on three vertically arranged screens with the top and bottom screens substantially cut off. The music, of course, could be no less than immaculate in these highly skilled hands. In fact, if there's a problem with this program, it's the usual bugaboo that afflicts studio-sessioneer efforts like this (or bands like Stuff, or any number of the groups these guys play in all the time led by other fusion artists): sterility. Yes, the grooves do get heated at times, but these guys are *so* proficient their technique usually overshadows whatever scant trace of genuine emotion might manifest itself. Of course, if you're a fan of this stuff, you'll love it.

☐ **VARIOUS ARTISTS**
SGT. PEPPER'S LONELY HEARTS CLUB BAND
½

MCA, 1978, 111 minutes
PRODUCED BY: Robert Stigwood
DIRECTED BY: Michael Schultz
MUSIC FROM: Sgt. Pepper's Lonely Hearts Club Band motion picture soundtrack (RSO, 1978).
SELECTIONS: Peter Frampton: "The Long and Winding Road," "Golden Slumbers"; Peter Frampton and the Bee Gees: "She Came in Through the Bathroom Window," "Sgt. Pepper's Lonely Hearts Club Band (reprise)," "Getting Better," "A Little Help from My Friends"; Peter Frampton, Maurice Gibb, George Burns, and the Bee Gees: "Being for the Benefit of Mr. Kite"; Peter Frampton, Paul Nicholas, and the Bee Gees: "Good Morning, Good Morning"; Barry Gibb and the Bee Gees: "A Day in the Life"; the Bee Gees: "Carry That Weight," "Nowhere Man," "Polythene Pam"; Paul Nicholas and the Bee Gees: "Sgt. Pepper's Lonely Hearts Club Band"; Jay McIntosh, John Wheeler, and the Bee Gees: "She's Leaving Home"; Alice Cooper and the Bee Gees: "Because"; Earth Wind and Fire: "Got to Get You into My Life"; Steve Martin: "Maxwell's Silver Hammer"; Billy Preston: "Get Back"; Robin Gibb: "Oh, Darling"; George Burns: "Fixing a Hole"; Aerosmith: "Come Together"; Sandy Farina: "Here Comes the Sun," "Strawberry Fields Forever"; Dianne Steinberg, Paul Nicholas, Donald Pleasance, Stargard, and the Bee Gees: "I Want You (She's So Heavy)"; Frankie Howerd: "Mean Mr. Mustard"; Dianne Steinberg and Stargard: "Lucy in the Sky with Diamonds"; Frankie Howerd and Sandy Farina: "When I'm Sixty-four"; Dianne Steinberg and Paul Nicholas: "You Never Give Me Your Money."

This is one of the all-time turkeys, a grade-A mother of a butterball if ever there was one. It was based on the Robin Wagner/Tom (*Hair*) O'Horgan musical play, which turned a host of Beatles tunes from *Sgt. Pepper* onward (and, in a few cases like "Nowhere Man," even earlier albums) into a boring, infantile fairy tale. Nobody ever asked for this movie to be made, and there was never any need or desire for it to exist. Fortunately, very few people actually went and suffered through it, and it died an ignominious death as one of the major box-office bombs of the '70s. It's just plain *awful*—not even so bad that it's good. There are precious few half-decent musical moments—Earth Wind and Fire's "Got to Get You into My Life," Billy Preston's gospel rave-up on "Get Back," and Aerosmith's grungy romp through "Come Together"—but they're hardly worth sitting through the interminable garbage surrounding them.

☐ **RUDY SARZO**
BASS GUITAR MASTER CLASS
★★★★

Hot Licks, 1986, 60 minutes
PRODUCED BY: Arlen Roth
DIRECTED BY: Mark Kaplan
MUSIC FROM: Various demonstrations and performances by Rudy Sarzo.
SELECTIONS: Warming up, equipment, rhythmic patterns, special scales, harmonics, octaves, slapping and popping, right-hand

Flamenco tremolo, soloing, locking in with a drummer.

Bassist Rudy Sarzo (formerly of Quiet Riot, and with Ozzy Osbourne at this writing), like Twisted Sister guitarist Jay Jay French in his *Heavy Metal Primer*, uses his Hot Licks instructional video to show that there's a bit more to heavy metal musicians—and to playing heavy metal music—than a lot of people might think. Sarzo also surprises with the breadth of his knowledge and technique, e.g., his demonstrations of funk-based slap-and-pop tricks and his right-handed "flamenco tremolo." His sections on equipment and locking in with drummers are also helpful above and beyond the norm. And as with all Hot Licks tapes, excellent production values (including split-screens to show what both right and left hands are doing simultaneously) and the use of on-screen musical notation of what's being played make the tape even better. (Available by mail order from Hot Licks.)

☐ **VARIOUS ARTISTS**

SATURDAY NIGHT FEVER

★★★★

Paramount, 1977, 118 minutes
PRODUCED BY: Robert Stigwood
DIRECTED BY: John Badham
MUSIC FROM: Saturday Night Fever motion picture soundtrack (RSO, 1977).
SELECTIONS: The Bee Gees: "Night Fever," "You Should Be Dancing," "Stayin' Alive," "How Deep Is Your Love"; Yvonne Elliman: "If I Can't Have You"; Walter Murphy and the Big Apple Band: "A Fifth of Beethoven"; Tavares: "More than a Woman"; Kool and the Gang: "Open Sesame—Part 1"; Trammps: "Disco Inferno"; K. C. and the Sunshine Band: "Boogie Shoes."

It's hard to look at this and not see the Muppets during the famous disco dance scene, or John Belushi's disco samurai in the dinner scene, but try. A bit overlooked in the antidisco backlash at the time of its release, a decade later *Saturday Night Fever* holds up remarkably well and has a great soundtrack (boasting seven number-one songs). Forget the dancing-as-self-realization tripe that followed: this one was the first, and even if it had been the hundred and first its treatment of the subject of youth subculture is so complete, incisive, and realistic that it would still be the best of the lot. Ironically, the ballyhooed dancing is actually kind of blah.

John Travolta plays Tony Manero, a working-class Italian Brooklynite who toils in a paint store and lives for the weekend nights he spends in the local disco, the only place where he can really be somebody. Tony's life is a textbook example of mid- to late-'70s trash culture: his walls are covered with Farrah Fawcett, Sylvester Stallone, and Bruce Li posters; he wears gold chains, high-waisted polyester pants, and Hukapoo shirts; he loves disco. And, like all young heroes, he's got an attitude. When his boss offers some fatherly advice about planning ahead, Tony snaps, "Fuck the future." His boss replies, "You can't fuck the future; the future fucks you." Indeed.

Tony has problems: Mom and Dad worship the brother who's a priest; Dad is unemployed; the girl Tony loves thinks she's too good for him; he thinks the girl who loves him isn't good enough; one friend's stupidity leads to a rumble with a rival gang; another, who's forced to marry a pregnant girlfriend, kills himself. Tony's daily life is filled with empty macho talk, pointless violence, insensitivity, and mindless behavior. But unlike the dancin' heroes of similar films, Tony eventually dismisses the disco scene—and, we think, dancing—as an unsatisfying escape, another cliquey scene rife with its own phoney standards and prejudices. Bit by bit,

Tony sees the limitations of his surroundings and makes what we presume is his first big step away from home. We also assume that Tony will be all right. Unfortunately, in 1983, Sylvester Stallone (Tony's hero!) helped cook up the film's "sequel," *Staying Alive*, but that's another story (and another review).

When it was first released, *Saturday Night Fever* struck most critics as a vehicle for teen idol Travolta and a career saver for the Bee Gees. And it was both, but there's so much more. As for the soundtrack, the album sold more than fifteen million copies and was the number-one album for six months. Whether you want to see a very good movie or hear some great music, you can't lose here.—P.R.

☐ **VARIOUS ARTISTS**

SAY AMEN SOMEBODY

★★★★★

Pacific Arts, 1984, 100 minutes

PRODUCED BY: George T. Nierenberg

DIRECTED BY: George T. Nierenberg

MUSIC FROM: Say Amen Somebody soundtrack album (DRG, 1983).

SELECTIONS: Willie Mae Ford Smith: "That's All Right," "What Manner of Man," "Singing in My Soul," "Never Turn Back," "Is Your All on the Altar?," "Canaan"; Thomas Dorsey: "Take My Hand, Precious Lord," "When I've Done My Best," "If You See My Savior," "How About You?"; the O'Neal Twins: "He Chose Me," "Jesus Dropped the Charges"; the Barrett Sisters: "The Storm Is Passing Over," "No Ways Tired," "He Brought Us."

Superb, valuable gospel documentary that captures on film some of the people most responsible for the creation and perpetuation of vital American roots music. The Reverend Thomas A. Dorsey, for instance, who composed many great gospel tunes (including, for instance, Elvis Presley's two faves, "Peace in the Valley" and "Precious Lord") by pioneering, back in the '20s, the fusion of unholy blues and holy hymns that forged gospel music—as audacious, significant, and classically American a synthesis as anyone in music has ever attempted. Dorsey was a frail, bent, and crippled eighty-three-year-old when this film was shot, but his indomitable spirit and wiliness shine through. Of his pioneering synthesis Dorsey says, with a mixture of pride and ruefulness, "I was kicked out of some of the finest churches." Later, he demonstrates the proper way to sing gospel; his ghostly, croaking whisper soars to a gorgeous, lyric tenor, and the hair stands up on your neck. Mother Willie Mae Ford Smith, the great gospel singer, is another revelation; at one point the camera's tight on her as she belts out a hair-raising "That's All Right" (*not* the Arthur Crudup tune Elvis Presley recorded); then the camera pulls back, and she's supporting herself all the while on the same sort of aluminum walker Dorsey uses. Then there's the O'Neal Twins; how can you resist a song like "Jesus Dropped the Charges"? Beyond the performances, there are also interviews and footage of a gospel convention honoring the magnificent Reverend Dorsey.

☐ JOHN SCOFIELD

ON IMPROVISATION

★★★★

DCI, 1984, 60 minutes

PRODUCED BY: Rob Wallis and Paul Siegel

DIRECTED BY: Rob Wallis and Paul Siegel

Scofield, a superb jazz and fusion guitarist most recently in Miles Davis's band, gets into a wealth of good info for *serious* guitar players: the use of seventeen different major modes and scales in improvisation; chromatics, passing tones, melodic devices, picking techniques, even nuances of different types of equipment. And it's all geared, as the title indicates, toward using this information in the heady waters of heated jazz improvisation. (Available by mail order from DCI Music Video.)

□ SCORPIONS
FIRST STING
★★

Sony, 1985, 17 minutes
PRODUCED BY: Len Epand, Claude Borenzweig
DIRECTED BY: David Mallet, Hart Perry, and Martin Kahan
MUSIC FROM: Love at First Sting (Mercury, 1984); *Blackout* (Mercury, 1982).
SELECTIONS: "Rock You like a Hurricane," "No One like You," "I'm Leaving You," "Still Loving You."

This tired old German heavy metal band finally figured out in the early '80s how to walk the fine line between posturing hard rock and poppier AOR pomp-romantic shlock right into the hearts and wallets of millions of American teenagers. And unless you're already a fan of theirs, these promo clips won't give you a clue as to how they did it. "Rock You like a Hurricane" (directed by David Mallet) is a sickening exercise in bombastic macho-fantasy clichés, including amazons in ripped black spandex and fishnets, and the cagelike "tribal"/"primitive"/"futuristic" sets and all that other nonsense. That's about the worst of the lot. "No One like You," with Hart Perry directing a fantasy jailbreak sequence with surprising taste and assurance, is by far the best. Overall, though, strictly for fans.

□ SCORPIONS
WORLD WIDE LIVE
★½

RCA/Columbia, 1985, 60 minutes
PRODUCED BY: Hart Perry
DIRECTED BY: Hart Perry
MUSIC FROM: Lovedrive (Mercury, 1979); Blackout (Mercury, 1982); *Love at First Sting* (Mercury, 1984).
SELECTIONS: "Coming Home," "Blackout," "Big City Nights," "Loving You Sunday Morning," "No One like You," "Holiday," "Bad Boys Running Wild," "Still Loving You," "Rock You like a Hurricane," "Dynamite," "I'm Leaving You."

Scorpions are a German heavy-metal band who hung around for years and years before finally hitting on a hard-rock-with-corporate-pop-veneer formula that helped them strike it rich in the MTV age. This all-too-typical documentary of their 1984–85 world tour follows them through rehearsals and soundchecks, catches them autographing countless young female cleavages during in-store promotional appearances, shows them horsing and lollygagging about offstage and at home in der Fatherland, and so on ad nauseam. They seem like a pleasant enough lot except for the rather loutish drummer, Herman "Ze German" Rarebell. But they, like their pompous assembly-line music, are boring, boring, boring. And, despite their apparent nice-guys-behind-it-all attitudes and the less-foreboding-than-most-metal AOR melodicism of some of their songs, there are a few scenes that display a particularly venal condescension toward their audience on the part of the band, the filmmaker, or both—like the one where some fat goon guards the band's backstage door while dozens of drunk/luded-out/whatever fans mill about, hollering and acting like metalhead morons while the goon sneers to the camera, "Yeah, they're a *niiiiice* buncha fans, all right." Maybe it's just brutal candor rather than condescension after all. Anyway, this is still for metalheads *only*.

□ GIL SCOTT-HERON AND THE MIDNIGHT BAND
BLACK WAX
★★★★½

Sony, 1986, 80 minutes

PRODUCED BY: Robert Mugge
DIRECTED BY: Robert Mugge
MUSIC FROM: Various albums by Gil Scott-Heron and the Midnight Band (Flying Dutchman, Arista, 1972–84).
SELECTIONS: "Storm Music," "Washington, D.C.," "Paint It Black," "Waiting for the Axe to Fall," "Billy Green Is Dead," "Angel Dust," "Gun," "Winter in America," "Whitey on the Moon," "Alien," "Black History," "Johannesburg," " 'B' Movie."

Gil Scott-Heron's long-standing political committment and protean influence on rap sing-speech are finally given their due in this outstanding documentary. *Black Wax* was made by independent documentarian Robert Mugge, who shot the equally fine Sun Ra documentary *A Joyful Noise,* and he uses a similar technique here: mixing powerful performance sequences with equally potent, intimate footage of Scott-Heron in his home environs, which happen to be our nation's capital. The phrase "local color" takes on an entirely new meaning as we see Scott-Heron walking the streets of Washington while rapping his unflinchingly relevant protest sing-songs. As in *A Joyful Noise,* Mugge also comes up with some inspired set-pieces: he places Scott-Heron in a wax museum, where he makes some serious fun of the likenesses of various political/historical figures; and he has Scott-Heron recite his unforgettable "Whitey on the Moon" to a wax astronaut dangling over his head. Such Scott-Heron classics as "The Bottle," his unremitting and poignant antialcohol plaint, and the sharply observed Reagan putdown " 'B' Movie" are included, and the only one missing is Scott-Heron's radical '60s anti-anthem "The Revolution Will Not Be Televised." Throughout, the music of the Midnight Band is a supple, seductive fusion of soul, funk, jazz, pop, and Afro-ethnic roots. Scott-Heron himself fairly glows with passion and sincerity, coming across as not only an exceptionally caring, committed, and driven artist, but also as an unusually warm, witty, and likable human being.

□ SCREAMERS
LIVE IN SAN FRANCISCO
★★★

Target, 1986, 30 minutes
PRODUCED BY: Joe Rees
DIRECTED BY: Joe Rees
MUSIC FROM: Various Screamers singles; September 2, 1978, live performance in San Francisco.
SELECTIONS: "Vertigo," "Beat Goes On," "Punish or Be Damned," "122 Hours of Fear," "Another World," "Last 4 Digits," "Magazine Love."

For a couple of years in the late '70s, the Screamers were one of the West Coast's first and best electro-punk bands. Here, in a typically up-close and unfussy Target Video production, they're caught in vintage form before an appreciative San Francisco crowd in a tiny club. Lead singer Tomata du Plenty is a skinny runt who's very animated and rather charismatic in his own offbeat, playfully assaultive way, and his ranting, top-of-his-lungs vocals show exactly how the band got its name. Most of the band's arrangements are fairly powerful and musically attractive, though in a deliberately crude and abrasive way—overall, not bad at all considering the Screamers consisted of only two keyboardists, a drummer, and du Plenty. First-generation punk fans with VCRs will love this program, and it could very well appeal to others with somewhat adventurous tastes. (Available in stores or by mail order from Target Video or Independent World Video.)

☐ VARIOUS ARTISTS
THE SECRET POLICEMAN'S OTHER BALL
★★★½

MGM/UA, 1982, 101 minutes
PRODUCED BY: Martin Lewis and Peter Walker
DIRECTED BY: Roger Graef and Julien Temple
MUSIC FROM: The Secret Policeman's Other Ball (Island, 1982).
SELECTIONS: Pete Townshend: "Won't Get Fooled Again," "Pinball Wizard"; Sting: "Roxanne," "Message in a Bottle"; Jeff Beck and Eric Clapton: "Further On Up the Road"; Donovan: "Catch the Wind"; Phil Collins: "In the Air Tonight"; Clapton, Sting, et al.: "Anyday."

☐ VARIOUS ARTISTS
THE SECRET POLICEMAN'S PRIVATE PARTS
★★★

Media, 1984, 77 minutes
PRODUCED BY: Martin Lewis
DIRECTED BY: Roger Graef and Julien Temple
MUSIC FROM: The Secret Policeman's Private Parts (Island, 1983).
SELECTIONS: Pete Townshend: "Drowning in Love"; Donovan: "Sunshine Superman"; Phil Collins: "The Roof Is Leaking"; Bob Geldof: "I Don't Like Mondays"; Neil Innes: "Down with Everything."

Documents of the annual London comedy-and-rock benefits for Amnesty International (first brought to America in the theatrical release *The Secret Policeman's Other Ball*), featuring members of the Monty Python troupe and other Brit-laffs luminaries (Peter Cook and punk standup comic Alexei Sayle turn up in *Private Parts,* cast members of *Not the Nine O'Clock News* in *Other Ball*). Given the well-known irreverence of such classic Python bits as "the dead parrot" and "The Lumberjack Song" (both in *Private Parts*), it's fitting that these shows were carried off with such refreshing good spirits and lack of piousness. Between the laughs, the musical bits are generally quite strong, especially the solo turns (Sting, Townshend, Donovan, Geldof, Collins), which are quite literally solos and which, in Townshend's (on Volume One) and Sting's cases especially, produce felicitous, revelatory versions of well-known tunes.

☐ VARIOUS ARTISTS
THE SECRET POLICEMAN'S OTHER BALL: THE MUSIC
★★★★

MGM/UA, 1982, 60 minutes
PRODUCED BY: Martin Lewis
DIRECTED BY: Martin Lewis
MUSIC FROM: The Secret Policeman's Ball: The Music (Island, 1980); *The Secret Policeman's Other Ball* (Island, 1982).
SELECTIONS: Sting: "Roxanne," "Message in a Bottle"; Eric Clapton and Jeff Beck: "Further On Up the Road," "Cause We've Ended as Lovers"; Phil Collins: "The Roof Is Leaking," "In the Air Tonight"; Donovan: "Sunshine Superman," "Catch the Wind," "Colours"; Bob Geldof: "I Don't Like Mondays"; Tom Robinson: "Glad to Be Gay"; Pete Townshend: "Won't Get Fooled Again," "Drowned"; Ensemble: "I Shall Be Released."

For those who don't want to bother with the comedy bits (so what's *your* problem?), *The Music* is just that, the music (pulled together from both other programs) and nothing but, and thus the height of convenience. It also happens to work as a most enjoyable concert program, with a couple of generations of British rock royalty on parade.

☐ SEX PISTOLS, OTHERS
THE GREAT ROCK 'N' ROLL SWINDLE
★★★★★

Rough Trade, 1982, 105 minutes

PRODUCED BY: Jeremy Thomas and Don Boyd

DIRECTED BY: Julien Temple

MUSIC FROM: Great Rock 'n' Roll Swindle soundtrack album (Virgin, 1979); *Never Mind the Bollocks, Here's the Sex Pistols* (Warner Bros., 1977).

SELECTIONS: The Sex Pistols: "God Save the Queen," "Anarchy in the U.K.," "No Feelings," "Pretty Vacant," "Holidays in the Sun," "Rock 'n' Roll Swindle," "Johnny B. Goode," "Bodies," "No Fun"; Sid Vicious: "My Way," "Somethin' Else," "C'mon Everybody"; Malcolm McLaren: "You Need Hands"; Tommy Tenpole: "Who Killed Bambi?," "Rock Around the Clock"; the Black Arabs: "Sex Pistols Disco Medley"; Steve Jones: "I'm a Lonely Boy"; Steve Jones with Ronnie Biggs: "Great Train Robbery," "Oh, Dear," "Friggin' in the Riggin'."

One of the funniest, pithiest rock films ever made, combining the best elements of both *A Hard Day's Night* and *This Is Spinal Tap* with its own particular brand of a seriocomic chaos, *The Great Rock 'n' Roll Swindle* managed to turn certain disaster into memorable triumph. Originally, the Sex Pistols were to shoot *Who Killed Bambi?,* directed by sexploitation master Russ Meyer, as their movie debut. Pistols singer Johnny Rotten balked after a few scenes were shot, however; Pistols impressario Malcolm McLaren hired first-time director Julien Temple to shoot grainy footage of Pistols club gigs, documentary footage of the British punk era, and black-humored half-joking dramatic sequences recounting McLaren's behind-the-scenes scheming. Along the way, Pistols bassist Sid Vicious was first arrested for allegedly killing his girlfriend Nancy Spungen, then died of a heroin overdose.

Somehow, future rock video *auteur* Temple, who made this literally fantastic film as his film school senior thesis (!), turned what he had to work with into a mock-Machiavellian mock-rockumentary masterpiece, with McLaren turning the history of the Pistols phenomenon into a series of lessons on fomenting a subversive cultural hoax (the caper of the film's title). Because McLaren revels in, rather than disguises, his own manipulative nature, *Swindle* actually becomes the most candid rock film ever, and while its tongue is planted firmly in cheek, it still manages to raise some serious, even frightening questions about the interrelationships of music, media, and money.

Pistols guitarist Steve Jones turns in a remarkably affecting performance as a Pirandellian gumshoe trying to nail McLaren (a fascinating art-imitates-life motif, as the band's breakup and subsequent litigation have kept the film from U.S. theatrical release); Sid Vicious's bang-up version of Paul Anka's "My Way" is a proto–rock video epiphany; and there are plenty of bellylaughs, the best being Tommy Tenpole's wildly eccentric performance of "Who Killed Bambi?," one of the most hysterically funny moments in film history (I'm quite serious, you know). There's also some fine concert and interview footage of the Sex Pistols in action. But above all, there is a devastating critique of the entire pop process that is highly disturbing in its implications for anyone who considers him- or herself a "music lover." (NOTE: As of this writing, *The Great Rock 'n' Roll Swindle* was available only via mail order from Rough Trade, or Playings Hard to Get. Also note that this is a *Japanese import,* with Japanese subtitles on-screen. However, the film's distribution setup was likely to change at this writing, since in early 1986 the suit between Malcolm McLaren and the Sex Pistols was finally settled in the band's favor, allowing *Swindle,* among other artifacts, to finally be distributed through regular channels.)

☐ HUGH SHANNON
SALOON SINGER

★★★½

VIEW, 1986, 55 minutes

PRODUCED BY: Ralph Mole and Lou Tyrell

DIRECTED BY: Lou Tyrell

MUSIC FROM: Various albums by Hugh Shannon.

SELECTIONS: "Piano Man," "I Can't Get Started," "One Hundred Years from Today," "It Never Entered My Mind," "I Wish I Were in Love Again," "You Fascinate Me So," "I Love My Wife," "Down in the Depths," "As Time Goes By," "If They Could See Me Now," "My Funny Valentine" (with Patrice Munsell), "I Love a Piano," "I Wish You Love," "Good Morning Heartache," "You've Changed," "They Can't Take That Away from Me," "A Room with a View," "Makin' Whoopie," "Baltimore Oriole," "Just Disgustingly Rich," "Send in the Clowns," "You'd Better Go Now."

From the VIEW Video catalog entry on *Hugh Shannon: Saloon Singer:* "When Billie Holiday heard Hugh Shannon for the first time, she said to him, 'Man, you don't sing like nobody. You gotta sing.' It was John Wilson of the *New York Times,* however, who dubbed him 'saloon singer.' From New York, to Paris, Capri, Spain, and the French Riviera, Hugh Shannon has entertained the world. Counts, countesses, and movie stars, millionaires and musicians have all cried for more as he played on to the wee hours of the morning."

Well, I had never heard of the guy, and I don't think I'm alone. But in the interview snippets that pop up from time to time, as well as his nicely shot performance at David K's Aquarian Lounge in New York City, the late Shannon comports himself with distinguished, continental class and poise. *Saloon Singer* opens with him discussing the differences between a saloon and, say, any old bar or lounge: the secret is "coziness . . . it's like a comfortable chair." In performance, Shannon's a man of his word, with an easygoing, jauntily intimate delivery that—with his fine voice and competent piano playing—ultimately proves too dignified and accomplished to mark him as the model for Bill Murray's *Saturday Night Live* skits as lounge singer "Nick." He dispatches the obligatory "Send in the Clowns" with a minimum of bathetic fuss, and carries off Hoagy Carmichael's "Baltimore Oriole" (great choice) with aplomb. He proves himself quite worthy of such redoubtable standards as Cole Porter's "Down in the Depths," Noel Coward's "A Room with a View," and Cy Coleman's "You Fascinate Me So," and his evocation of Billie Holiday in "Good Morning Heartache," which she made famous, is uncanny. Opera-turned-pop singer Patrice Munsell, one of several dear old pals in the music biz and café society that Shannon chats about, sits in for "My Funny Valentine," but she's a momentary diversion. Shannon seems to get better—and more Holidayesque—as the show goes on (in marked contrast to Bobby Short, who in his VIEW Video program, *At the Cafe Carlyle,* gets more painfully and embarrassingly raspy as the show goes on, and on, and on). If you want to transform your living room into a toney Manhattan bistro, you could do a lot worse than this.

☐ VARIOUS ARTISTS
SHINDIG!

★★½

Import, 24 minutes

PRODUCED BY: Jack Good

DIRECTED BY: David Mallet

MUSIC FROM: Various albums by various artists; December 23, 1965, episode of ABC-TV show *Shindig!*

SELECTIONS: Dave Clark 5: "Zip-a-Dee-Doo-Dah," "Can't You See That She's Mine"; Gerry and the Pacemakers:

"Jambalaya"; Billy J. Kramer and the Dakotas: "Trains and Boats and Planes"; Ian Whitcomb: "High Blood Pressure"; Anne Sydney: "The Boy with the Woolly Sweater"; Moody Blues: "I Go Crazy"; Yardbirds: "Early in the Morning"; the Wellingtons: "Go Ahead and Cry"; Lulu and the Luvvers: "Shout."

The December 23, 1965, episode of America's first post–British Invasion prime-time network TV pop music show (*Hullabaloo* was NBC's subsequent response) is a virtual all-English special (the Wellingtons, a lame neo–Four Freshmen vocal group, are obvious Yank ringers and stick out like sore thumbs). While the lineup is a bit erratic, the tape has built-in nostalgia value. Even better, there are a few truly notable moments: the Yardbirds, with a very young and gawky Jeff Beck on guitar, launch an intense rave-up in the midst of their typically tough blues reading of "Early in the Morning"; the Moody Blues, with Denny Laine on guitar and vocals and *definitely* way before they got ponderous with Mellotrons, cover James Brown(!); Lulu, dressed in a genuinely fab-gear mid-era outfit, surprises with the grittiness of her "Shout" just as she does in the *Ready, Steady, Go!* cassettes (a fitting connection, since *RSG!* producer Jack Good was also responsible for *Shindig!*); and the Dave Clark 5 do all right. Meanwhile, Miss World 1965 Anne Sydney delivers a lightweight, adult-sanctioned lesson in the etiquette of innocuous romance—as much an obvious ringer as the Wellingtons and square host Jimmy O'Neill. Indeed, though *Shindig!* was the original model in the States, *Hullabaloo* holds up better after all that time; in trying to outdo *Shindig!* it became a more active, frenziedly trendy show and so has more time capsule value. (Available by mail order from Playings Hard to Get.)

☐ **VARIOUS ARTISTS (JOHN CANDY AND EUGENE LEVY, OTHERS)**

THE SHMENGES: THE LAST POLKA

★★★

Vestron, 1985, 60 minutes

PRODUCED BY: Jamie Paul Rock

DIRECTED BY: John Blanchard

MUSIC FROM: Cable-TV special (HBO, 1985).

SELECTIONS: Yosh and Stan Shmenge with the Happy Wanderers: "Happy Wanderers Theme," "Cabbage Rolls and Coffee Polka," "Strikes, Spares and Shmenges Theme," "Beat It," "The Last Polka"; the Lemon Twins: "I Can Begin Again," "Arabian Nights"; Linsk Mynyk with the Shmenges: "From the Road Again"/"Kansas City Here I Come"/"Chicago"/"Galveston," "Touch Me."

Somewhat slight, but very enjoyable *Spinal Tap*–styled parody of *The Last Waltz,* chronicling the fictitious history of Yosh and Stan Shmenge, the polka-playing brothers created by John Candy and Eugene Levy of Canada's wonderful *SCTV* comedy show. The film traces them from their start, playing *geltkes* (jars) in their native Lutonia ("On the dark side of the Balkans," as they cryptically explain); through their first break on super-manager Colonel Tom Cohen's radio show *Foreigners on Parade;* their first TV show, *Strikes, Spares and Shmenges;* their controversial personal and professional liaison with the Lemon Twins (all *three* of them, played by *SCTV* 's Catherine O'Hara, her sister Mary Margaret, and onetime *SCTV* and *Saturday Night Live* cast member Robin Duke); the infamous "Plattsburgh Disaster," a career-ending salute-to-Michael Jackson concert that failed miserably; and their farewell show. *SCTV* 's Rick Moranis makes a hilarious appearance along the way as smarmy Lutonian crooner Linsk Mynyk; during a reflective interview snippet, he muses, "You ask me why the Shmenges broke up when they did, I tell you . . . I haven't a clue." Unfortunately, this program does not include such vintage *SCTV* Shmenge bits as their nifty covers of Michael Jackson's "Billie Jean" and Flock of Seagulls' "Wishing," and the great "Power to the Punk People Polka" parody video.

□ VARIOUS ARTISTS
SHOCK TREATMENT
★

Key, 1981, 95 minutes
PRODUCED BY: John Goldstone
DIRECTED BY: Jim Sharman

Though touted as something of a sequel to *The Rocky Horror Picture Show, Shock Treatment* is sure to disappoint all but the most rabid midnight-show Transylvanians. Both were written by *Rocky Horror*'s creator, Richard O'Brien (Riff Raff), they share a few cast members (Patricia Quinn, again cast as O'Brien's sister; Charles "No Neck" Gray; and Nell Campbell), and they begin in Denton, the Home of Happiness. Brad and Janet Majors, the two uptight straight American kids we assume Dr. Frank 'n' Furter "liberated" before the big house returned to the planet Transexual, are also back. We find them (played by Cliff DeYoung and Jessica Harper) living unhappily in Denton, where all the townspeople's lives are controlled by shows on the local TV station, which is owned by Farley Flavors, a frozen-food magnate ("Farley fast foods feed and fortify America's families for a fabulous future"), also played by DeYoung. From here on, though, the story gets muddled and, unlike *Rocky Horror,* it's not interesting enough to make you want to sit through it a couple of times until you get it.

The basic concept has countless possibilities, especially when Flavors decides to promote mental health as a product and brainwashes the whole town into committing themselves to Dentonvale, the local loony bin. *Rocky* fans will love O'Brien and Quinn in this later incarnation as Cosmo and Nation McKinley, sibling psychiatrists from someplace else, who, like Magenta and Riff, are also in love. But the story is otherwise incomprehensible, the soundtrack is lame, and the film lacks *Rocky*'s visual panache or characters as flamboyant as, say, Tim Curry's. Talk about being lost in time, lost in space and meaning.—P.R.

□ BOBBY SHORT
FROM THE CAFE CARLYLE
★★★★

V.I.E.W., 1986, 65 minutes
PRODUCED BY: Leah Jay
DIRECTED BY: Lou Tyrrell
MUSIC FROM: Various Bobby Short albums.
SELECTIONS: "Four Walls and One Dirty Window Blues," "Samantha," "Honeysuckle Rose," "You're Just Too Much (Too Marvelous for Words)," "Bojangles of Harlem," "Duke Ellington Medley: "Tall, Tan and Terrific"/"Posin' "/"Truckin' "/"Breakfast in Harlem"/"Old Man Harlem," "Why Shouldn't I?" "The Best Is Yet to Come," "New York Is My Personal Property," "How's Your Romance," "I'm Satisfied," "When in Rome," "On the Amazon," "At the Moving Picture Ball," "Say It Isn't So," "Losing My Mind," "Pilot Me," "Cuba."

I never liked Bobby Short, the long-reigning toast-of-cafe-society Manhattan saloon singer. That is, until I sat through this program purely for review purposes. It was then that I realized that what I'd really hated was practically everyone I'd ever met who adored Short. You know—snooty, waspy *New Yorker* types, and, even worse, would-be *New Yorker* types. *From the Cafe Carlyle*, an intimate and straightforwardly shot 1979 performance at Short's perennial roost, is intercut with quietly revealing interview footage and shows Short to be commandingly assured—if still a very acquired taste—in performance and charmingly candid and classy in conversation. In the interview bits that appear after virtually every song, Short discusses his love for New York City and such fellow jazz-pop-cabaret saloon-singing standard-bearers as Mabel Mercer and Hugh Shannon, how his life has affected his music and vice versa, and, in the most telling moment, how he always adored Cole Porter's songs but would never perform them until he had the "conviction and intelligence" to bring to them to do them justice. It's not just an articulate statement on his part, it's also accurate. Yes, Short's style is effete, affected, and arch, and at times his near-operatic trilling high tenor sounds like Dudley Doright as a pre-jazz '20s crooner; but he's also got a suave confidence and easygoing authority, and, while he's too often stiff and hoity-toity, he can and does swing. You may not like what he does, but you've got to admit he's darned good at it.

Intriguingly, for all his apparent courtly modesty, Short does and yet doesn't quite recognize his own limitations. At one point he confesses that he can't sing the blues, though he does admire blues singers; but then we cut to him proving how right he is by performing the opening "Four Walls and One Dirty Window Blues" in a style that can best be described as "dicty," to use the '20s colloquialism for stiff, soulless, well-to-do whitebread culture. Short courageously sings without a microphone, but in trying to fill this good-sized hotel bar he runs his rather delicate voice ragged, and halfway into the show he's hoarse and weak and missing some notes. Still, he somehow maintains a chin-up sort of dignity, and he does have his moments, including highlights such as a rhythmically acute "The Best Is Yet to Come" and a bossa nova "When in Rome." The rhythm section includes the great swing-era original Beverly Peer on bass, and Short's facile, sometimes mercurial piano keeps the music interesting even when his vocals falter. My one complaint is that there are too many jarring and/or needless cuts to swells in the audience looking either self-consciously appreciative of a Manhattan institution or rudely unappreciative and interested only in chatting and being seen.

All in all, however, the music and conversation by Short is enough to blow any of his fans away. And maybe make a few converts.

☐ VARIOUS ARTISTS
SHORTS
★★

Factory/Ikon, 1985, 60 minutes
PRODUCED BY: Various
DIRECTED BY: Various
MUSIC FROM: Various albums and singles by various artists (Factory UK, 1983–85).
SELECTIONS: Durutti Column: "Prayer"; Stockholm Monsters: "The Longing"; the Wake: "Talk About the Past"; Cabaret Voltaire: "Yashar"; Royal Family: "British Empire"; Section 25: "Back to Wonder," "Looking from a Hilltop"; Kalima: "Smiling Hour"; Jazz Defektors: "Hanki Panki"; Quando Quango: "Tingle"; 52nd Street: "Can't Afford"; New Order: "Blue Monday."

Another of Factory Records' extremely erratic, patience-trying collections of mostly amateurish video clips for self-consciously downcast post-punk British fringe-rock bands. *Shorts* is framed by its two best moments: Durutti Column's appropriately static, straight-performance reading of "Prayer," one of their typically quiescent and mesmerizing repetitive-drone guitar tapestries, and New Order's "Blue Monday," a rare and successful attempt at danceable funk-rock by Factory's best and most dourly serious band. In between is a lot of aural and visual artsy-fartsy noodling around that goes no place and often gets stuck in a rut of pre-novice technical ineptitude. Only Cabaret Voltaire's "Yashar," a jarring visual montage/collage set to equally assaultive electronic *musique concrete*, and Quando Quango's performance of the lively, ethnic-flavored hip-hop "Tingle" arouse any interest. (Available in stores or by mail order from Factory.)

☐ **VARIOUS ARTISTS**
SHOWTIME AT THE APOLLO, VOLUME ONE
★★★

Video Yesteryear, 1980, 79 minutes
MUSIC FROM: 1954 syndicated TV series *Harlem Variety Review.*
SELECTIONS: Titles not listed, but performers include: Duke Ellington Orchestra, Sarah Vaughan, Herb Jeffries, Lionel Hampton and His Orchestra, the Larks, the Nat King Cole Trio, Delta Rhythm Boys, Nipsy Russell, Mantan Moreland.

☐ **VARIOUS ARTISTS**
SHOWTIME AT THE APOLLO, VOLUME TWO
★★★

Video Yesteryear, 1980, 84 minutes
MUSIC FROM: 1954 syndicated TV series *Harlem Variety Review.*
SELECTIONS: Titles not listed, but performers include: Duke Ellington Orchestra, Larry Darnell, the Clovers, Dinah Washington, Amos Milburn, the Count Basie Orchestra, the Lionel Hampton Orchestra, Big Joe Turner, Nat "King" Cole, Faye, Adams, Nipsy Russell, and others.

☐ **VARIOUS ARTISTS**
SHOWTIME AT THE APOLLO, VOLUME THREE
★★★

Video Yesteryear, 1980, 80 minutes
MUSIC FROM: 1954 syndicated TV series *Harlem Variety Review.*
SELECTIONS: Titles not listed, but performers include: Lionel Hampton Orchestra, Lulu Brown, Larry Darnell, the Clovers, Herb Jeffries, Dinah Washington, Joe Turner, Cab Calloway, Sarah Vaughan, Jonah Jones, Amos Milburn, and others.

Series of quick, single-song early-to-mid-'50s performances at Harlem's legendary Apollo Theater, all introduced by swing-era jivester and self-styled "Mayor of Harlem" Willie Bryant. All tapes feature a few comedy routines by the likes of a very young Nipsy Russell, Mantan Moreland, and others. And they all feature nice melanges of swinging jazz (Duke, Hamp, Basie, Jonah Jones), sophisticated black pop (Nat "King" Cole), rare peeks at seminal boogie-woogie/blues (Amos Milburn, Big Joe Turner), and protean R&B (Delta Rhythm Boys, Coasters, Larks, Larry Darnell, Dinah Washington). Sound and picture quality is uniformly good on all three programs, excerpts of which have been shown on the USA Cable Network's *Night Flight.*

☐ **PAUL SIMON**
PAUL SIMON IN CONCERT
★★★½

Warner Home Video, 1982, 54 minutes
PRODUCED BY: Michael Tannen and Phil Ramone
DIRECTED BY: Marty Callner
MUSIC FROM: Various Paul Simon and Simon and Garfunkel albums.
SELECTIONS: "Me and Julio Down by the Schoolyard," "Still Crazy After All These Years," "Ace in the Hole," "Something So Right," "One-Trick Pony," "Jonah," "50 Ways to Leave Your Lover,"

"Late in the Evening," "American Tune," "The Boxer," "The Sound of Silence."

Also available on Pioneer Stereo Laser videodisc.

Musically speaking, this is probably solo-Simon's most satisfying program yet. Caught at the Tower Theater in Philadelphia in October 1980, Simon fronts a band composed of such sterling New York studio-sessioneers as guitarist Eric Gale, pianist Richard Tee, bassist Tony Levin (also a member of the '80s version of King Crimson as well as Peter Gabriel's backing band), and drummer Steve Gadd, plus a horn section featuring respected New York jazzmen such as reed/brass virtuoso Howard Johnson and saxophonist J. D. Parran. When these musicians' musicians back up a glorified lounge act like fuzak saxophonist Grover Washington, Jr., or play for their own amusement in a smugly accomplished but enervating unit like Stuff, they can bore you to tears. But here, they're able to sink their finely honed chops into a solid array of some of Simon's best-known and most popular tunes, and it makes for a nice musical match (though some old-folkie purist types may still be turned off by his perceived sellout).

Simon is his usual ingratiatingly low-key self, and there are no real lows in the program. One high point for this viewer—who, being an amateur drummer, is admittedly biased—is Gadd's awesomely dexterous work on "50 Ways to Leave Your Lover" and "Late in the Evening" (on the latter, he executes a complex, polyrhythmic Latin pattern with *four* sticks, two in each hand). The show is shot in straightforward, unspectacular fashion, which is really all that's needed considering how nice the music is. Fans of Simon's post-folkie solo work should love it and even those who may have admired some of his work but always considered him insufferably cute, wimpy, or bland may find themselves surprised at just how entertained they are.

□ PAUL SIMON, OTHERS
THE PAUL SIMON SPECIAL
★★

Pacific Arts, 1984, 50 minutes

PRODUCED BY: Lorne Michaels

DIRECTED BY: Dave Wilson

MUSIC FROM: Various albums by Paul Simon and Simon and Garfunkel; 1977 NBC-TV special.

SELECTIONS: Paul Simon: "Still Crazy After All These Years," "Something So Right," "Slip Slidin' Away"; Simon with Art Garfunkel: "Bridge over Troubled Water," "Still Crazy After All These Years," "Old Friends"; Simon with the Jessy Dixon Singers: "Loves Me Like a Rock"; Simon with Toots Thielemans: "I Do It for Your Love".

This 1977 television special came only two years after Lorne Michaels and the Not Ready for Prime Time Players had revolutionized TV with *Saturday Night Live.* So it's easy to believe that someone somewhere thought it might be brilliant to have Lorne produce a special for his good buddy Paul Simon. Only problem is, the special is *not* funny and has aged about as well as Lorne Michaels himself—who, after failing with both *The New Show* and his own revamping of *SNL* in the mid-'80s, sported a head of white hair that he earned the hard way. This program takes the form of a sort of "Murphy's Law" making-of-the-special, featuring Charles Grodin as the bumbling, pretentious producer who subjects Simon to all manner of idiotic indignities. Grodin does his usual solid job but can't help the fact that the aforementioned indignities are nowhere near as humorous as they are dumb. When Lily Tomlin appears in a couple of dressing-room interludes that prove completely unmemorable and a Chevy Chase skit (as medieval talk show host Johnny Casanova, whose guests include Shelley Duvall as Joan of Arc) is the comedic highlight, you know you're in deep, deep trouble. Considering all that, it's all the more miraculous that Simon and his music still manage to come up smelling like a rose. Then again, maybe it's not so remarkable: true talent will out, after all, and when a rose sits in a garbage dump its beauty is all the more apparent. For Simon fans—and those who find *anything* that Lorne Michaels and his cronies do to be funny—only.

□ SIMON AND GARFUNKEL
THE CONCERT IN CENTRAL PARK
★★★★

CBS/Fox, 1984, 87 minutes
DIRECTED BY: Michael Lindsay-Hogg
MUSIC FROM: Various Simon & Garfunkel, Paul Simon, and Art Garfunkel albums, including *The Concert in Central Park* (Columbia, 1982).
SELECTIONS: "Mrs. Robinson," "Homeward Bound," "America," "Me and Julio Down by the Schoolyard," "Scarborough Fair," "April Come She Will," "Wake Up, Little Susie," "Still Crazy After All These Years," "Kodachrome"/ "Maybellene," "Bridge over Troubled Water," "50 Ways to Leave Your Lover," "A Heart in New York" "American Tune," "The Late Great Johnny Ace," "Slip Slidin' Away," "Late in the Evening," "The Boxer," "Old Friends," "59th Street Bridge Song (Feelin' Groovy)," "The Sounds of Silence."
Also available on CBS/Fox Stereo Laser videodisc.

Superb looking and sounding document of the great pop-folk duo's spring 1982 concert in New York City's Central Park, where some half-million fans saw them play together for the first time in eleven years as they launched their reunion tour. Director Michael Lindsay-Hogg does a good job capturing the grandeur of the occasion, with several cherry-picker-mounted cameras providing impressive crowd panoramas. The atmospherically designed city-skyline stage (water towers, the works), the generous and eclectic repertoire of Paul and Art's duo and respective solo works, the super-slick backing band (featuring Steve Gadd *and* Grady Tate on drums, Richard Tee on piano, and Howard Johnson on brass), and the audience all combine to make this a special package, which was first shown on HBO.

□ NINA SIMONE
AT RONNIE SCOTT'S LONDON
★★★★½

JEM/Passport, 1986, 55 minutes
PRODUCED BY: RSVP/Wadham Films
MUSIC FROM: Various Nina Simone albums.
SELECTIONS: "God, God, God," "If You Knew," "Mr. Smith," "Fodder in Her Wings," "Be My Husband," "I Loves You, Porgy," "The Other Woman," "Mississippi Goddam," "Moon over Alabama," "For a While," "See-Line Woman," "I Sing Just to Know I'm Alive," "My Baby Just Cares for Me."

The fiercely talented, tempestuously temperamental Simone is an awesomely gifted songstress whose provocative intensity easily transcends her usual "jazz" labeling. An intimate record of her performing live such as this program is mandatory for those with the taste and gumption to get to her level (believe me, she won't come down to anyone *else's*). Nina's own "God, God, God," "Fodder in Her Wings," "Mississippi Goddam," and "I Sing Just to Know I'm Alive" are as wrenchingly intense as her harrowing covers of Brecht-Weill's "Mr. Smith" and "Moon over Alabama" (a.k.a. "Alabama Song" or "Whisky Bar"), not to mention her piercing take on Gershwin's "I Loves You, Porgy." And as a bonus, there's also a pretty fine interview with the lady herself, in which Nina is a lot friendlier and more forthcoming than those long acquainted with her work would ever expect.

□ FRANK SINATRA (WITH GEORGE BENSON, LIONEL HAMPTON, QUINCY JONES AND HIS ORCHESTRA)
PORTRAIT OF AN ALBUM
★★½

MGM/UA, 1986, 65 minutes
PRODUCED BY: Quincy Jones and Emil G. Davidson
DIRECTED BY: Gary Weis
MUSIC FROM: L.A. Is My Lady (Qwest/Warner, 1985).
SELECTIONS: "The Best of Everything," "Until the Real Thing Comes Along," "It's All Right with Me," "How Do You Keep the Music Playing," "A Hundred Years from Today," "After You've Gone," "Teach Me Tonight," "If I Should Lose You," "Stormy Weather," "Mack the Knife," "L.A. Is My Lady."

Warning: this documentary on the making of Sinatra's *L.A. Is My Lady* album is so unctuous it's liable to squirt right out of your hand and leave grease stains on the upholstery. Between shots of Mr. S recording with bandleader Quincy Jones and guest musicians Lionel Hampton and George Benson, there are interview segments. Jones, Hampton, heavyweight producer Phil Ramone, and songwriters Alan and Marilyn Bergman all provide a lot of gushing chin music, mostly stating the obvious or ladling on the adoring blandishments. Jones is nicely articulate on the significance of Michael Jackson's surprise visit to the recording studio, though—but what a shame that we only get a minute or two of montage, covered by Michael's stilted voiceover, and are left starving for much, much more of this meeting of the pop titans. Still, Sinatra fans will revel in the intimate glimpses of the man at work in such a star-studded setting—even as they note that Sinatra himself is conspicuously absent from the interviews.

□ SIOUXSIE AND THE BANSHEES
NOCTURNE
★★½

Media, 1984, 60 minutes
PRODUCED BY: RPM Productions
MUSIC FROM: Nocturne (Polygram, 1983).
SELECTIONS: "Israel," "Cascade," "Melt!," "Pulled to Bits," "Nightshift," "Sin in My Heart," "Painted Bird," "Switch," "Eve White/Eve Black," "Voodoo Dolly," "Spellbound," "Helter Skelter."

Nocturne, the concert counterpart to the *Once Upon a Time* clips compilation, does a decent job of capturing the band and its Brit-punk fans during a three-night stand at London's Royal Albert Hall. Fans will appreciate it all, as Siouxsie twirls about in her black garb on a mostly darkened stage, while the Banshees pound out their deliberately crude, convincingly dark nightmarish odes (drummer Budgie is the instrumental standout). *Nocturne* includes only "Israel" and "Spellbound" from the band's exceptional string of underground hit singles. And the generally so-so selection won't help win any new converts.

□ SIOUXSIE AND THE BANSHEES
ONCE UPON A TIME
★★½

Sony, 1985, 30 minutes
PRODUCED BY: Clive Richardson
DIRECTED BY: Clive Richardson
MUSIC FROM: Once Upon a Time/The Singles (JEM/PVC, 1985).
SELECTIONS: "Hong Kong Garden," "Staircase," "Playground Twist," "Happy House," "Christine," "Red Light," "Israel," "Spellbound," "Arabian Knights."

Solid compilation of greatest-hits video clips by one of British punk's most hauntingly pop-inflected bands. None of the videos is very exceptional (except perhaps "Spellbound"), but many of the tunes—"Hong Kong Garden," "Christine," "Israel," "Spellbound"—are. And as far as the visuals go, Siouxsie's got to be one of the most strikingly stylish punkettes ever.

□ **VARIOUS ARTISTS**
SIX SHORT FILMS OF LES BLANK 1960–1985
★★★½

Flower Films, 1985, 83 minutes
PRODUCED BY: Les Blank
DIRECTED BY: Les Blank, Alan Govenar, Skip Gerson
MUSIC FROM: Cigarette Blues (Flower Films, 1985); *The Sun's Gonna Shine* (Flower Films, 1969); *Dizzy Gillespie* (Flower Films, 1964); *God Respects Us When We Work, But Loves Us When We Dance* (Flower Films, 1968).
SELECTIONS: Sonny Rhodes and His Texas Twisters: "Cigarette Blues"; Lightnin' Hopkins: "Trouble in Mind"; unidentified artist: untitled original instrumental for *God Respects Us When We Work, But Loves Us When We Dance.*

This eclectic compendium spans quixotic ethnocultural documentarian Blank's career, from his first student film (*Running Around like a Chicken with Its Head Cut Off,* a bizarre homage to Ingmar Bergman's *The Seventh Seal*), to *Chicken Real,* a 1970 documentary commissioned by an automated chicken-growing company, right up to 1985's *Cigarette Blues,* six minutes of existential musings by Oakland, California, bluesman Sonny Rhodes, on life, death, cigarette smoking, and the blues, who also performs the darkly cautionary title song. Indeed, except for those two filmlets with *Chicken* in the title, all of the titles here could be seen as music titles in one way or another. *God Respects Us When We Work, But Loves Us When We Dance* is a document of the 1967 Easter Sunday Love-in in Los Angeles that finds Blank's distinctive style already formed, as he captures classic hippie-isms (open marijuana smoking, meditation, free love, all that stuff) in unobtrusively respectful fashion. It's also got a nice, appropriate original rock-music score. But the real musical meat here is *The Sun's Gonna Shine,* a lovely little companion piece to *The Blues Accordin' to Lightnin' Hopkins,* which re-creates the late great bluesman's decision at age eight to stop chopping cotton and sing for a living; and *Dizzy,* Blank's first music film, an affectionate 1964 portrait of the bebop trumpet giant, focusing more on the man himself than his music. (Available by mail order from Flower Films.)

□ **RICKY SKAGGS**
LIVE IN LONDON
★★½

CBS/Fox, 1986, 39 minutes
PRODUCED BY: Deborah Newman, Madeleine French, Lennie Grodin, Bob Jason
DIRECTED BY: Sandi F. Fullerton and Martin Kahan
MUSIC FROM: Waiting for the Sun to Shine (Epic, 1981); *Highways and Heartaches* (Epic, 1982); *Country Boy* (Epic, 1984).
SELECTIONS: "Uncle Pen," "Heartache," "Heartbroke," "Cajun Moon," "Highway 40 Blues," "Waitin' for the Sun to Shine," "Don't Get Above Your Raising," "Honey (Open That Door)," "Country Boy."

Two sweetly amusing Martin Kahan–directed video clips (Clarence Clemons of Bruce Springsteen's E Street Band guests in "Honey," bluegrass giant Bill Monroe and New York City Mayor Ed Koch in "Country Boy") are tacked onto a half hour from a pleasant, if rather perfunctory, concert in London's Dominion Theater. Award-winning singer/songwriter/guitarist/mandolinist Skaggs is talented and appealing, and integrates bluegrass nicely into his countrypolitan blend. But he's a tad too blandly ingratiating for comfort, and so is a lot of his material. Elvis Costello turns in an uninspired guest shot on a rocking version of the Flatt and Scruggs bluegrass chestnut "Don't Get Above Your Raising."

☐ VARIOUS ARTISTS
SMITHEREENS
★★★

Media, 1984, 90 minutes
PRODUCED BY: Susan Seidelman
DIRECTED BY: Susan Seidelman
MUSIC FROM: The film *Smithereens* (1982).
SELECTIONS: Richard Hell and the Voidoids: "The Kid with the Replaceable Head," "Another World"; the Raybeats: "Guitar Beat"; the Nitecaps: "I Never Felt"; the Feelies: "Loveless Love," "Original Love."

Remarkably good feature-film debut by *Desperately Seeking Susan* director Susan Seidelman, especially considering this film's microscopic $100,000 budget. Interestingly, *Smithereens* also presages—in much darker form—some key elements of *Susan*: the suburban roots of its streetwise antiheroine, and the marked similarities between *Susan* star Madonna's supposed real-life story and that of *Smithereens* antiheroine Wren, a smart, ambitious, determined nobody desperately trying to be a somebody on Manhattan's new-wave rock scene. Susan Berman is stupendous as Wren, a young lady *so* jaded and self-centered that even Manhattan's ultra-jaded new-wave narcissists can't stand her; Brad Rinn is very affecting as the Montana hick she takes advantage of; and new-wave rock star Richard Hell is fine as the, well, new wave rock star of whom Wren tries and fails to take advantage. The rock soundtrack is minimal but well chosen—especially the nervously driving, but never peaking, repetitive rock of the Feelies, which perfectly reflects the existential malaise and all-punked-out-with-nowhere-to-go ennui of the film's milieu.

☐ SOFT CELL
NON-STOP EXOTIC VIDEO SHOW
★

HBO/Cannon, 1982, 58 minutes
PRODUCED BY: Gordon Lewis
DIRECTED BY: Tim Pope
MUSIC FROM: *Non-Stop Erotic Cabaret* (Sire, 1982); *Non-Stop Ecstatic Dancing* (Sire, 1982).
SELECTIONS: "Tainted Love," "Bedsitter," "Seedy Films," "Memorabilia," "Entertain Me," "Sex Dwarf," "Frustration," "Torch," "Secret Life," "Youth," "What," "Say Hello, Wave Goodbye."

Tim Pope, who shot this, developed into quite a good music video maker with clips like Neil Young's "Wonderin' " and several Cure videos. But that was a few years after he made this, his first major music video undertaking, and it is the absolute pits of unwatchability. It's not just Pope's fault, however—although the barely existent lighting and bleeding-all-over colors do mark this as a very amateurish production. No, the real culprit is Soft Cell lead singer Marc Almond (no relation to the Marc Almond of '60s U.K. Jazz-rock fame) an unappealing little runt in heavy mascara who fondles snakes and moans and groans and preens and pouts and vamps like a would-be queen and otherwise indulges in all manner of off-putting, self-consciously "perverse," soporific antics. Meanwhile, Soft Cell's electro-pop (with the music provided by Almond's counterpart David Ball on synths and rhythm machines) drones on and on just as dully, with only their club-hit remake of the obscure '60s soul hit "Tainted Love" and the modestly affecting, bittersweet "Wave Hello, Say Goodbye" (featuring, of all things, a hauntingly melancholy clarinet solo) proving listenable. Even those who consider (or considered) themselves fans of Soft Cell's music or Tim Pope's videos may find it exceedingly rough going.

☐ **SORCERY**
STUNT ROCK
★

Monterey/IVE, 1978, 90 minutes
PRODUCED BY: Martin Fink
DIRECTED BY: Brian Trenchard-Smith
MUSIC FROM: 1978 film.
SELECTIONS: "Stunt Rocker," "Wicked City," "Woman," "Talk with the Devil," "Sacrifice," "Survive the Sword," and others.

One of the strangest rock musicals ever, *Stunt Rock* is about "an internationally famous stunt man, Grant Page, and his cousin's band Sorcery," according to the copy on the back of this cassette's storage case. There's no plot, per se—it's just *about* them, without being a documentary or a docudrama. Actually, judging by the shoddy way it's shot, edited, and acted, it seems more like a porn film with the sex scenes edited out, if you can imagine that. Anyway, Grant Page, who appears to be British or Australian, is a likeable enough guy and a good stunt man and all. But his cousin's L.A. band is another matter: they play pompous, grindingly dull hard-rock sludge with Satanic/Magickal motifs that are brought to, er, life in their Doug Henning-meets-Ozzy Osbourne stage show. *Wow* this stuff is awful! Appropriately, the copy I viewed simply turned to static in the midst of a scene three-quarters of the way through the film; I couldn't have come up with a better ending myself.

☐ **VARIOUS ARTISTS**
SPARKLE
★★½

Warner Home Video, 1981, 98 minutes
PRODUCED BY: Howard Rosenman
DIRECTED BY: Sam O'Steen
MUSIC FROM: The movie *Sparkle* original soundtrack album (Warner Bros., 1976).
SELECTIONS: "Look into Your Heart," "Loving You Baby," "Jump," "This Love Is Real," "Giving Him Something He Can Feel," "Sparkle," "Hooked on Your Love," "Rock with Me."

A lot of soon-to-be-famous talents were involved in this slick, clichéd blacksploitation flick, which details the against-all-odds rise to fame of a Supremes-like vocal trio. The screenplay is by Joel Schumacher, who would go on to direct *D.C. Cab, Car Wash,* and *St. Elmo's Fire.* The title character and leader of the girl group is the pre-*Fame* Irene Cara; one of her cohorts in the group is the pre–*Cotton Club* Lonette McKee, a dusky beauty who gives the best performance here. Sparkle's boyfriend, who risks his life to push her budding career, is played by the pre–*Miami Vice* Philip Michael Thomas, billed here as "Philip M. Thomas." But the best thing about *Sparkle* is the music soundtrack, by the by-then already famous Curtis Mayfield.

☐ **VARIOUS ARTISTS**
SPEND IT ALL
★★★★

Flower Films, 1981, 41 minutes
PRODUCED BY: Les Blank with Skip Gerson
DIRECTED BY: Les Blank with Skip Gerson
MUSIC FROM: Various Balfa Brothers albums; *Spend It All* motion picture

soundtrack (Flower Films, 1971).

SELECTIONS: The Balfa Brothers: "Eunice Two-Step," "J'ai Passe Devant Ta Porte," "Cher Tout-Toute," "La Valse de Balfa," "J'etais du Balfas," "La Valse de Grand Bois," "Kaplan Waltz," "Acadian Two-Step"; Adam and Cyprieu Landreau: "Prairie Ronde," "La Talle de Rances"; Marc Savoy: "Zydeco Est Pas Sale," "Les Flammes d'Enfer"; Nathan Abshire: "The Negresse," "Calcasieu Waltz," "New Iberia Polka," "Traditional Instrumental"; Pee Wee Broussard: "Tolan Raltz"; Pee Wee Broussard and Marc Savoy: "Cher Tout-Toute."

Yet another of Les Blank's small, unprepossessing documentaries on Louisiana's Bayou culture, and yet another casually revelatory winner. Where the Mardi Gras–oriented *Always for Pleasure* and the Clifton Chenier profile *Hot Pepper* will strike more chimes of recognition with the general public, *Spend It All,* along with Blank's *Dry Wood,* delves deeper into the backwoods swamps, providing an altogether more exotic trip through the salt bogs and mangroves. Where *Dry Wood* focuses on the black Cajun experience, *Spend It All* homes in on the white Cajuns, who still maintain even closer cultural ties to the old-world spirit of their French-speaking Acadian forebears. Blank, in his typically low-key way, captures the *joie de vivre* of these earthy people, through their cooking (and coffee-roasting), sporting activities (quarter-horse racing), and music (there's also some fascinating footage on how accordions are built). The Balfa Brothers, Nathan Abshire, and others are never less than marvelous, filling your ears with a hearty, joyously danceable sound, half ancient Gallic courtly sentiment and half New World hoedown-stomp. The music coalesces with the sometimes mystical scenery and the earthy, outgoing Cajuns to form a whole that's classic, surreal Americana as only Les Blank can bring it to you. (Available by mail order from Flower Films.)

□ SPINAL TAP, OTHERS
THIS IS SPINAL TAP

★★★★★

Embassy, 1984, 82 minutes
PRODUCED BY: Karen Murphy
DIRECTED BY: Rob Reiner
MUSIC FROM: Motion picture soundtrack album (Polydor, 1984).

SELECTIONS: "Gimme Some Money," "(Listen to the) Flower People," "Hell Hole," "Tonight I'm Gonna Rock You Tonight," "Heavy Duty," "Rock and Roll Creation," "Big Bottom," "Cups and Cakes," "Sex Farm," "Stonehenge."

Also available on Embassy Stereo Laser videodisc.

A screamingly funny mock rockumentary, featuring dead-on satire of the seemingly beyond-parody school of heavy-metal rock, via the fictitious Spinal Tap—"Britain's loudest band"—who are seen here in their fifteenth year, enduring a U.S. tour that goes from bad to worse to downright pathetic to *even worse* before a surprise happy ending. No turn is left unstoned in making fun of the bigtime rock-biz, yet much in the manner of *SCTV,* this is more than just satire, and the people doing it are more than mere comics: they're comic *actors,* and the characters they create are ultimately as *em*pathetic as they are pathetic (and boy, are they pathetic).

Writer/director Rob Reiner stars in the film as the maker of the film, Marty DiBergi, a veteran commercial-maker ("Remember the wagon train going into the cabinet under the sink? That was mine," he says with a smug grin) finally indulging his old rocker's urges by documenting Spinal Tap's tour. Spinal Tap themselves are: Michael McKean as guitarist David St. Hubbins (yes, he was once Lenny, of Lenny and Squiggy, on *Laverne and Shirley*), Christopher Guest as guitarist Nigel Tufnel (formerly with *National Lampoon*, later to be a cast member of *Saturday Night Live* in 1984–85), Harry Shearer as bassist Derek Smalls (a veteran of improvisational troupes, comedy records, and the occasional film and TV appearance who's never gotten the recognition his vast talents deserve), R. J. Parnell as Mick Shrimpton (the latest in Tap's long, long line of ever-changing drummers, who all seem to die in mysterious accidents), and David Kaff as keyboardist Viv Savage.

They not only turn in astonishing performances, they also wrote and played all the Tap tunes themselves—and the mimetic songs, like the characterizations, are poignantly, almost frighteningly credible, which is what really makes *Spinal Tap* work so brilliantly. "Gimme Some Money" (from Tap's early days, seen in a black-and-white mock kinescope) is a genuinely ace Merseybeat garage-rocker, inane lyrics and all; "(Listen to the) Flower People" (seen in another mock kinescope, filled with the "oh wow man" eye-straining prism effects of the psychedelic period) is a perfectly believable bit of ersatz-psychedelic pablum; "Stonehenge" sounds exactly like the silliest Olde English Epick Jethro Tull never quite got around to recording; "Rock and Roll Creation" has progressive-rock instrumental passages that would sound right at home in anything by Yes, Rush, Kansas, or Styx along with a stage set not unlike one the group Angel used; the Kiss-like "Tonight I'm Gonna Rock You Tonight" is a legitimately propulsive hard-rock riffer; and even as you gasp in disbelief at Tap's ode to the female form, "Big Bottom" ("How could I leave this behind?" goes part of the chorus), you just may find yourself subconsciously digging its persuasively plodding, almost funky bass line. Such spine-tingling accuracy attests to the filmmakers' affection for the foibles of the form that lies at the heart of their ultimately good-natured (well, mostly) satire.

Then there are all the delightful cameos, by Billy Crystal and Howard Hesseman and Patrick MacNee and Fred Willard and many many more; most hysterical of all, perhaps, is Paul Shaffer as hapless regional promo-man Artie Fufkin (and how about *National Lampoon* alumnus Tony Hendra as Tap manager Ian Faith?). There's so much more . . . but I don't want to spoil it for you. In fact, *This Is Spinal Tap* is *so* densely packed with ingenious jokes that it's probably better seen at home on TV than in a movie theater—with everyone else laughing so much, you'll inevitably miss many of the gags. Then again, *Spinal Tap* is so richly comic you'll probably want to view it again and again anyway—and believe me, it'll hold up. Kudos to Reiner, McKean, Guest, Shearer, and company, for what is truly one of the great American movies of the '80s. It's a mandatory purchase for anyone who takes rock seriously enough to appreciate it being so brilliantly trashed. Also, tacked onto the home-video release are the commercial for the K-tel *Metal Memories* LP and the Tap rock video for "Hell Hole."

☐ **VARIOUS ARTISTS**
SPLASHIN' THE PALACE 84
★★★★

Passport, 1985, 60 minutes
PRODUCED BY: Tony Johnson
DIRECTED BY: Don Coutts
MUSIC FROM: U.K. Reggae Sunsplash Tour, Crystal Palace Football Stadium, London, 1984 Capitol Music Festival.
SELECTIONS: Prince Buster: "Al Capone"; Skatalites: "Latin Goes Ska"; Leroy Sibbles: "Rock 'n' Come On," "Rock

Steady Party"; King Sunny Adé and His Africa Beats: "Synchro System"; Musical Youth: "Pass the Dutchie"; Black Uhuru: "General Penitentiary," "Guess Who's Coming to Dinner"; Lloyd Parkes and We the People: "Sunsplashin'," "Redemption Song"; Aswad: "Roots Rockin' "; Dennis Brown: "Revolution," "I Can't Stand It," "Promised Land."

Perhaps the single finest various-artists reggae tape available at this writing, with uniformly fine performances from a strong and diversified lineup, all of it shot with tasteful, straightforward savvy and no nonsense. Especially noteworthy because of its pleasantly surprising inclusion of such outstanding but commercially overlooked artists as: the Skatalites, elder-statesmen Rastas who still swing as joyously and expertly as they did twenty years before, when they laid reggae's foundations with their more upbeat ska; the legendary Prince Buster, whose "Al Capone" was lifted whole by the Specials as "Gangsters" for Britain's late '70s "two-tone" movement; reggae crooners Leroy Sibbles and Dennis Brown; and Nigeria's King Sunny Adé, whose entrancing, multileveled "juju music" ain't reggae, but sure is good (besides, Adé *was* critically rated as a probable successor to reggae giant Bob Marley's Third World Ambassador throne—evidence of this program's smarts). Of the rest, Black Uhuru, backed by Sly and Robbie, stand out with a crunchingly powerful ten-minute mini-set.

□ SPLIT ENZ
SPLIT ENZ VIDEO LP
★★★

Sony, 1983, 54 minutes
PRODUCED BY: Simon Fields
DIRECTED BY: Bruce Gowers
MUSIC FROM: True Colours (A&M, 1980); *Beginning of the Enz* (A&M, 1980); *Waiata* (A&M, 1981); *Time and Tide* (A&M, 1982).

SELECTIONS: "Fire Drill," "One Step Ahead," "Giant Heartbeat," "Lost for Words," "Hello Sandy Allen," "Nobody Takes Me Seriously," "Six Months in a Leaky Boat," "Small World," "Never Ceases to Amaze Me," "Dirty Creature," "I Got You," "Shark Attack," "Haul Away," "History Never Repeats."

New Zealanders Split Enz disbanded about a year after this concert was shot for MTV in Ontario, Canada, in 1982. They had begun in the mid-'70s as a Roxy Music–inspired, wildly eclectic art-rock band, who were rarely taken seriously because of their bizarre clownish makeup and elaborate hairdos. But by the time of this show, their personnel had changed, as had their sound and image: this Split Enz is dressed-down, straightforward, ungimmicky, and plays a more accessible brand of pop rock that balances drolly intelligent lyrics with charming, winsome tunes. It's reminiscent of such clever British art-pop bands as 10cc and Squeeze, and in terms of quality it tends to fall right in the middle between the former's sometimes-annoying preciousness and the latter's underappreciated thoughtfulness. The best tunes here include Split Enz's only real U.S. hits, both minor ones in the early '80s, "Six Months in a Leaky Boat" and "I Got You." With their unpretentious stage presence and earnest pop craft, and Bruce Gowers's no-frills, no-fuss direction, the *Split Enz Video LP* is a pause that can refresh the pop fan seeking respite from the razzle-dazzle bombast of most rock concert videos. But the comparative unspectacular subtlety of the proceedings may make this program for fans of the band only.

□ RICK SPRINGFIELD
HARD TO HOLD
★★

MCA, 1984, 93 minutes

PRODUCED BY: D. Constantine Conte
DIRECTED BY: Larry Peerce
MUSIC FROM: Hard to Hold motion picture soundtrack (RCA, 1984).
SELECTIONS: Rick Springfield: "Stand Up," "Great Lost Art of Conversation," "Bop til You Drop," "Don't Walk Away," "S.F.O.," "Love Somebody"; Rick Springfield and Randy Crawford: "Taxi Dancing"; Nona Hendryx: "The Heart of a Woman"; Graham Parker: "When the Lights Go Down"; Peter Gabriel: "I Go Swimming."

Admittedly, Rick Springfield offers little to the serious rock fan; but since there's still the other 95 percent of the world outside that category, he has his fans, and they've made him huge. In his feature-film debut Springfield is Jamie Roberts, a multimillionaire rock star torn between his spoiled-brat co-writer and ex-lover (played by Mrs. Keith Richards, Patti Hansen) and a very straight Tony Bennett–loving child therapist (Janet Eilber) who drives poor Jamie wild. The story, like the music, is lightweight and at times downright silly; and while Springfield can act, the movie might be better retitled *Hard to Believe.* Fans may like the concert sequences, since they're about the only part of the movie that seems real. If you adore Springfield, laugh at herpes jokes, or desire several good close-ups of Rick's bare buns, this is your ticket.—P.R.

□ RICK SPRINGFIELD
THE BEAT OF THE LIVE DRUM
★★

RCA/Columbia, 1985, 75 minutes
PRODUCED BY: Carol A. Stewart
DIRECTED BY: David Fincher
MUSIC FROM: The Beat of the Live Drum (RCA, 1985) and other Rick Springfield albums (RCA, 1981–84).
SELECTIONS: "Don't Walk Away," "Alyson," "Living in Oz," "Affair of the Heart," "Celebrate Youth," "Human Touch," "My Father's Chair," "Jessie's Girl," "State of the Heart," "Bop 'til You Drop," "Don't Talk to Strangers," "Love Somebody," "Souls," "Dance This World Away," "Stand Up."

□ RICK SPRINGFIELD
PLATINUM VIDEOS
★★

RCA/Columbia, 1984, 25 minutes
PRODUCED BY: Various
DIRECTED BY: Rick Springfield, Paul Justman, Doug Dowdle
MUSIC FROM: Various Rick Springfield albums.
SELECTIONS: "Jessie's Girl," "Don't Talk to Strangers," "What Kind of Fool Am I," "Affair of the Heart," "Human Touch," "Souls."

Springfield's certainly good-looking, and appears to be well intentioned; and in "Jessie's Girl," "Don't Talk to Strangers," "Affair of the Heart," and "Love Somebody" he's got some pretty good mainstream-rock tunes. But the concert video, *The Beat of the Live Drum,* suffers from such an indigestible overload of souped-up production design and high-tech post-production effects (as well as the inclusion of scenes from several video clips) that you have to wonder what they're trying to hide. There's a *Bladerunner* stage set, a blimp that passes through flashing messages and lyrics and what-have-you now and then (another reference to *Bladerunner,* what with the latter's floating urban billboards), and more. But it can't camouflage the fact that Rick, though he might mean well, is basically one dull dude onstage; nor does it hide the fact that his repertoire is way too short on decent songs. Rick himself sings it at one point: "We all need it—the human touch." What we *don't* need is more coldly intimidating and inhuman mega-shows disguising the hollowness at the center of the showman in question.

Platinum Videos isn't much better. Most of these clips are too overconceptualized and overproduced, while having little or nothing to say. "Jessie's Girl" (which Springfield produced and directed himself) is inoffensively low-budget and innocuous, and it's a great song so it's easy to take; most interesting of all is Paul Justman's "Don't Talk to Strangers," in which Rick keeps getting embarrassingly cuckolded by his bitch of a girl—one of those rock-video classics that reveal the macho neuroses the stars may not even realize they're putting on display.

□ BILLY SQUIER
LIVE IN THE DARK

★★½

HBO/Cannon, 1982, 60 minutes
PRODUCED BY: Keefco
DIRECTED BY: Keith "Keef" MacMillan
MUSIC FROM: The Tale of the Tape (Capitol, 1980); *Don't Say No* (Capitol, 1981); *Emotions in Motion* (Capitol, 1982); *Live in the Dark* (Capitol, 1982).
SELECTIONS: "In the Dark," "Rich Kid," "My Kinda Lover," "Whadda You Want from Me," "Lonely Is the Night," "Young Girls," "I Need You," "The Stroke," "You Should Be High Love," "Too Daze Gone," "The Big Beat," "You Know What I Like."
Also available on Pioneer Stereo Laser videodisc.

Billy Squier was a thirty-two-year-old Boston-based rock veteran when he hit the big time in the early '80s. Thankfully for him, he still had his boyish good looks and wiry body, which drove millions of young girls crazy for a while. And though he sometimes comports himself on stage in the typical hard-rock macho manner, in this 1981 concert at the Santa Monica, California, Civic Theater Squier also shows that he could cook up a decent little melodic hard-rock song now and then, "My Kinda Lover" and "The Stroke," for instance. Unfortunately, Squier's best song to date, the 1982 hit "Everybody Wants You," was yet to come when this was shot. Meanwhile, Squier's stage show is pretty uneventful unless you're taken with his looks, and veteran director Keef, an old hand at such concert shoots, turns in a competent but uninspired job. All in all, mainly for Squier fans.

□ MICHAEL STANLEY BAND
MICHAEL STANLEY BAND VIDEO LP

★★½

Sony, 1983, 72 minutes
PRODUCED BY: Mike Belkin
DIRECTED BY: Chuck Statler, Mark Robinson, Michael Collins
MUSIC FROM: You Break It . . . You Bought It (Epic, 1975); *Greatest Hits* (Epic, 1979); *Heartland* (EMI-America, 1980); *North Coast* (EMI-America, 1981); *You Can't Fight the Fashion* (EMI-America, 1983).
SELECTIONS: "He Can't Love You," "Take the Time," "My Town," "In the Heartland," "I'll Never Need Anyone More than I Need You Tonight," "Working Again," "We Can Make It," "When Your Heart Says It's Right," "Heaven and Hell," "Don't You Do That to Me," "Lover," "Somewhere in the Night," "Don't Stop the Music," "Play a Little Rock and Roll (Cut the B.S.)."

A solid if unspectacular working-class rock group, the Michael Stanley Band never found much success outside of their native Cleveland, except for the minor MTV-era hit "He Can't Love You." But as the 1982 show at the Blossom Music Festival in Cleveland included here testifies, their hometown fans love their no-frills, bar-band rock to death. Indeed, MSB do come off as hard-working, honest crowd pleasers in the concert, shot with felicitous straightforwardness by director Chuck Statler. There are also three video clips added at the start of the tape, the best being the 1983 all-American anthem "My Town," a sort of rah-rah precursor to Bruce Springsteen's much more subtle and somber "My Hometown"; it's surprising that this one wasn't more of a hit than it was. At any rate, already converted MSB fans probably own this already, and if they don't they should; others seeking a no-nonsense, middle-American alternative to self-consciously decadent chic may also find satisfaction here. But the band's shoulda-been-contenders legacy of long and fruitless local struggle also suggests that they may be a tad *too* rank-and-file for many.

☐ **VARIOUS ARTISTS**
STARS OF JAZZ, VOLUME ONE
★★½

Video Yesteryear, 1980, 51 minutes
MUSIC FROM: 1958 ABC TV specials.
SELECTIONS: Titles not listed, but performers include: Charlie Barnet Orchestra, Mel Torme, Juan Tizol, Andre Previn, Shelly Manne, Red Mitchell.

☐ **VARIOUS ARTISTS**
STARS OF JAZZ, VOLUME TWO
★★½

Video Yesteryear, 1980, 82 minutes
MUSIC FROM: 1958 ABC TV specials.
SELECTIONS: Firehouse Five Plus Two Plus One: "The Devil and the Deep Blue Sea"; other titles not listed, but performers include: Howard Rumsey's Lighthouse All Stars, Julie London, June Christy, Barbara Dane.

Bobby Troup (remember that lousy TV show *Emergency*? He also co-wrote "Route 66"—not the TV show, the song the Rolling Stones covered) hosted both of these for-real-music-fans 1958 ABC TV specials, which brought live jazz jams to prime-time network TV. To quote Video Yesteryear's catalogue: "Jazz and only jazz on this outstanding series. Not for the general viewer. These shows were for the jazz lover and are well worth a listen and a look today." Volume One is especially noteworthy for the presence of Ellington trombonist Juan Tizol (author of "Caravan"), Red Mitchell, and Shelly Manne; Volume Two for the luscious torch singer Julie London (Video Yesteryear's catalogue raves about the "creative lighting" for her segment), West Coast cool-jazz doyens Shorty Rogers and Bud Shank playing with the Lighthouse All Stars, and—again according to VY's catalogue—Troup reviewing and "panning unmercifully" a book about jazz.

☐ **STARS ON 45**
STARS ON 45
★

MCA, 1983, 71 minutes
PRODUCED BY: Ken Ehrlich
DIRECTED BY: Ken Ehrlich
MUSIC FROM: Stars on 45 (MCA, 1983).
SELECTIONS: "Rock Around the Clock," "Shake, Rattle and Roll," "Jailhouse Rock," "Love Me Tender," "Where the Boys Are," "Blowin' in the Wind," "Sounds of Silence," "Drive My Car," "Hey Jude," "Foxey Lady," "Somebody to Love," "Papa's Got a Brand New Bag," "Macho Man," "Whip It."
Also available on MCA Stereo Laser videodisc.

You know those assembly-line nostalgia records—now avoid the video at all costs. A gaggle of relentlessly smiling and energetic spandexed young singer/dancers race through a Vegas-style revue, churning out classics—sometimes for barely recognizable seconds at a time—from the early rock and doo-wop, teen idol, British invasion, psychedelic, disco, and new wave eras. A few of the vocal simulations are uncannily accurate, most are forgettable, while a few (Jimi Hendrix and Elvis, especially) are downright insulting. The apparently serious set-piece for "Blowin' in the Wind" is ultimately surreal in its horrific hilarity. Recommended as camp only, but surely you can find better camp than *this*.

☐ STARSHIP
VIDEO HOOPLA
★

RCA/Columbia, 1986, 14 minutes
DIRECTED BY: Francis Delia
MUSIC FROM: Knee Deep in the Hoopla (RCA, 1985).
SELECTIONS: "We Built This City," "Sarah," "Tomorrow Doesn't Matter Tonight."

Hoopla—defined in the dictionary as "utterances designed to bewilder or confuse"—is dead on and shockingly accurate for a corporate-rock enterprise as cynically calculated as this one. Oh, how far Jefferson Airplane/Starship had come before devolving to this point: from revolutionary psychedelic fervor all the way to crass, airheaded, commercial pablum. And, typical of the business-conglomerate rock of the '80s, the group didn't even write their biggest hit, "We Built This City." It became something of an anthem for millions—not one of whom, I'd bet, suspects or even cares what the song means. If anything, it's a celebration of rock as corporate-capital-intensive-business—rock as a big dollar sign with a guitar neck stuck on top. More specifically, it's the band's way of saying, "We sold out—and we're glad we did!" In a way, one has to respect Starship's marketing savvy in meeting the crying need for such a Yuppie cheerleading song head-on. But one doesn't have to *like* such naked venality. And the video, with the band lip-synching around dumb cityscape sets against a black void, doesn't help any.

"Sarah" is even worse, if that's possible. A sopping wet lost-love ballad is illustrated with singer Mickey Thomas's *Grapes of Wrath*–style black-and-white flashback, the attractive production of which is nullified and then some by continual color inserts of "actress" Rebecca de Mornay acting like a literally incredible caricature of an impossibly scatterbrained and whimsically cute teenage waif.

"Tomorrow Doesn't Matter Tonight" is more completely uninspired, fourth-hand, connect-the-dots Journey/Triumph/Survivor AOR crap, with a stupid and overdone video, setting the band's lame lip-synch in a vaguely *Bladerunner*-ish futuristic nightclub set. Director Francis Delia has made some fine music videos in the past, such as Wall of Voodoo's "Mexican Radio" and the Ramones' "Psychotherapy," but you'd never know it from this hideosity. Similarly, it seems almost inconceivable that this Starship Enterprise is in any way related to that psychedelic-era band that came up with such rock classics as "Somebody to Love," "White Rabbit," "The Ballad of You and Me and Pooneil," and others. About the only thing that hasn't changed in all that time (Paul Kantner and Marty Balin have both been long gone by this time) is Grace Slick's annoying-as-ever tendency to mouth lyrics exuberantly whenever Mickey Thomas is singing them. Yeah, they've come a long way—*down.* Think of it this way: back when this band's ancestral parent, Jefferson Airplane, was making its best and most meaningful music, Frank Zappa was only half-kidding when he titled an album *We're Only in It for the Money*; the Starship of *Video Hoopla* take Zappa's title completely to heart, but it seems extremely doubtful that they'd ever have the integrity and/or guts to title an album after their apparent motto. Unless you're a fan of such pap, *Video Hoopla* is a nauseating experience.

☐ VARIOUS ARTISTS
STARSTRUCK
★★★½

Embassy, 1983, 95 minutes
PRODUCED BY: David Elfick and

Richard Brennan
DIRECTED BY: Gillian Armstrong
MUSIC FROM: Starstruck motion picture soundtrack (Oz/A&M, 1982).
SELECTIONS: The Swingers: "Starstruck," "Gimme Love"; Jo Kennedy: "Temper Temper," "Surfside Tango," "Body and Soul," "My Belief in You," "It's Not Enough," "Monkey in Me"; Ross O'Donovan: "I Want to Live in a House"; Jo Kennedy and John O'May: "Tough"; Turnaround: "Turnaround."

Starstruck is a delightful rock musical directed by Gillian Armstrong, who previously made the acclaimed *My Brilliant Career* and would go on to shoot the beautiful Bob Dylan/Tom Petty concert video *Hard to Handle.* One of the most appealing things about it is its easy, breezy mix of movie-musical tradition with punk-era modernity. In fact, it's essentially a vintage MGM "Hey-kids-we-can-put-on-the-show-right-here!" musical in new-wave drag. Adorably respectful of musical-cinema verities, *Starstruck* has a vivacious teen-punkette *chanteuse* (Jo Kennedy) and her homely fourteen-year-old cousin/lyricist/manager (Ross O'Donovan) winning an amateur talent contest through luck, pluck, and the aid of a local celebrity VJ, so they can save their lovable family's hotel-bar with the prize money. There are sprawling, punkish production numbers all over the place (the one early on in a punk disco, set to the Swingers' "Gimme Love," is most memorable), and even though *Starstruck* often violates a rather crucial musical-cinema norm—intelligible lyrics—the songs work through sheer energy and scruffy charm, as does the entire film.

Like its hero and heroine, *Starstruck* isn't too heavy or serious, but it is winningly feisty and human, and while it's often adorable it never crosses the line into the cloying. The music is solid, if not outstanding, throughout. Kennedy is delightful, but O'Donovan is even better and really steals the show. Armstrong's coda—post-victory parallel shots of Kennedy onstage and O'Donovan offstage revolving in twin spirals of ecstasy—is nothing short of sublime, ensuring that the fireworks that accompany the end credits of this sadly overlooked rock film don't seem misplaced.

□ THE STATLER BROTHERS
BROTHERS IN SONG
★★

RCA/Columbia, 1986, 19 minutes
PRODUCED BY: Len Epand, Claude Borenzweig, others
DIRECTED BY: Jim Owens, Marc Ball, Steve Womack
MUSIC FROM: Atlanta Blue (Mercury, 1984); *The Legend Goes On* (Mercury, 1983); *Today* (Mercury, 1983); *Pardners in Rhyme,* (Mercury, 1985).
SELECTIONS: "Sweeter and Sweeter," "My Only Love," "Whatever," "Elizabeth," "Atlanta Blue," "Guilty."

By the time *Brothers in Song* was released, some twenty years had passed since the Statler Brothers first hit the charts with "Flowers on the Wall" in 1965. And they've aged . . . well, they've aged. Here they amble through a series of romantic concept videos as soft-focus and predictable as their extremely square, middle-of-the-road countrypolitan music. Some of the conceptual stuff is intercut with static performance shots of the Statlers in "action." In "Sweeter and Sweeter," the Statlers are made up as elderly men sitting on a park bench, nostalgically recalling youthful romances and setting the tone for the whole program. "My Only Love" strains belief a bit with its wedding day scenario in which Harold Statler, the brother with the triple-chinned jowly mug and Rodney-Dangerfield eyes, gets hitched to a nubile blonde. "Whatever," an old-time jazz-era country swing throwback with corny double-entendre lyrics, has the brothers doing "whatever" it takes—buying a new house, flowers, ritzy dinners, furs—to please their ladies. "Elizabeth" spans the Civil War to the present in time-traveling with a lovely tease—the only real instance of rock-video-style sexism in the program. "Atlanta Blue" plops Gay '90s fantasy into modern-day reality to dumbly surreal effect. "Guilty" is a lot of stage performance, but with inserts illustrating a domestic quarrel leading to a sweet making-up conclusion; it's the simplest, most effective, and easiest to take clip here. All in all, mainly for Statler fans, or those who like their country *very* middle of the road—or their middle of the road a little bit country.

☐ STATUS QUO
END OF THE ROAD '84
★★★

JEM/Passport, 1986, 59 minutes
PRODUCED BY: Keith "Keef" MacMillan
DIRECTED BY: Keef
MUSIC FROM: Various albums by Status Quo (1968–81).
SELECTIONS: "Caroline," "Roll Over Lay Down," "Whatever You Want," Medley: "Mystery Song"/"Railroad"/"Most of the Time"/"Wild Side of Life"/"Slow Train," "Rockin' All Over the World," "Dirty Water," "Roadhouse Blues," "What You're Proposing," "Down Down," "Bye Bye Johnny."

Status Quo have always been a largely British phenomenon, and in some ways it seems sad that they're virtually unknown in the U.S.; Quo guitarists Rick Parfitt and Francis Rossi were those two long-haired gents in the Band-Aid "Do They Know It's Christmas?" video that *nobody* in America recognized. For some twenty years, since they got started in 1966 with the psychedelic hit "Pictures of Matchstick Men" (their only release to make any sort of impression here), Quo's specialty—indeed, their only riff—has been energetic, heads-down, stomping boogie-rock. Their simplicity, chumminess, and lack of pretense made them a hugely popular "people's band" in the U.K. The American equivalent would probably—some might say *definitely*—be Creedence Clearwater Revival, which makes Quo's joyous cover version of John Fogerty's "Rockin' All Over the World" (with which Quo kicked off the July 1985 Live Aid concert) all the more appropriate.

This tape documents their 1984 farewell concert, an open-air affair at Britain's enormous Milton Keynes Bowl. Of course, since Quo *was* the first band to perform at Live Aid, this "farewell" was obviously premature (in fact, the band—with a slightly different lineup—re-formed on an allegedly permanent basis shortly before this tape was released). This program is no work of art, but it does efficiently portray some solid, clodlike rockabooogie played damn hard by a band of vets who still have a good time doing it—as their fans do watching and listening to it. It's enjoyable, if a tad numbing after a while. All in all, a good chance to catch up on a worthwhile band many Yanks have probably missed out on all along.

☐ VARIOUS ARTISTS
STAYING ALIVE
★

Paramount, 1983, 96 minutes
PRODUCED BY: Robert Stigwood
DIRECTED BY: Sylvester Stallone
MUSIC FROM: *Staying Alive* motion picture soundtrack (RSO, 1983).
SELECTIONS: The Bee Gees: "Stayin' Alive," "I Love You Too Much," "Breakout," "Someone Belonging to

Someone," "Woman in You," "Life Goes On"; Gary Wright: "Devils and Seducers"; Frank Stallone: "Far from Over," "Moody Girl"; Frank Stallone: "Waking Up"; Leroy Faragher: "Look Out for Number One"; Tommy Faragher: "(We Dance) So Close to the Fire."

In this, the sequel to *Saturday Night Fever,* John Travolta unwisely revives Tony Manero, now a young dance teacher living in a scummy single-residence hotel who longs to make it on Broadway. When we left him at the end of the first movie, he had transcended the disco scene and was on his way to growing up. Now, he's there and, as he says, "Since I moved to Manhattan I got a new mature outlook on life." You'd never know it. Five or six years later, Tony has regressed from a fairly promising guy to a total dope. He cheats on his faithful girlfriend (decently played by Cynthia Rhodes) to play stud for one night with the tempestuous leading lady, Laura (Finola Hughes), who, of course, dumps him.

All the action revolves around the production of *Satan's Alley*—an all-dancing Broadway play that makes the Solid Gold Dancers look like the Bolshoi—and the sexual tension between Tony (the young chorus boy who emerges the star, of course) and Laura. Really trite stuff, which would be bad enough, but which becomes intolerable with Sylvester Stallone's rock 'em sock 'em direction. The dance scenes look just like the fight scenes in *Rocky,* with lots of shots right into the lights and a million quick-cuts that make no sense at all. The soundtrack is no better, really, not even the Bee Gees stuff. Except maybe for the title track.—P.R.

□ ROD STEWART
LIVE AT THE L.A. FORUM
★★½

Warner Home Video, 1979, 60 minutes

PRODUCED BY: Len Epand

DIRECTED BY: Bruce Gowers

MUSIC FROM: Various Rod Stewart albums.

SELECTIONS: "Hot Legs," "Tonight's the Night," "Da Ya Think I'm Sexy," "I Just Wanna Make Love to You," "Blondes Have More Fun," "Maggie May," "If Loving You Is Wrong," "The Wild Side of Life," "You're in My Heart," "Sweet Little Rock 'n' Roller," "Stay with Me," "Twistin' the Night Away," "Every Picture Tells a Story."

□ ROD STEWART (WITH TINA TURNER)
TONIGHT HE'S YOURS (Long Version)
★★★

Embassy, 1981, 90 minutes

PRODUCED BY: Simon Fields and Paul Flattery

DIRECTED BY: Bruce Gowers

MUSIC FROM: Various Rod Stewart albums.

SELECTIONS: "Give Me Wings," "Sweet Little Rock 'n' Roller," "Tear It Up," "Passion," "She Won't Dance with Me," "You're in My Heart," "Rock My Plimsoul," "Young Turks," "Tora, Tora, Tora," "If Loving You Is Wrong," "Maggie May," "Da Ya Think I'm Sexy," "I Was Only Joking," "You Wear It Well," "The Wild Side of Life"; with Tina Turner: "Hot Legs," "Get Back."

Also available on Embassy Stereo Laser videodisc.

□ ROD STEWART
TONIGHT HE'S YOURS (Short Version)
★★½

Sony/Embassy, 1983, 16 minutes

PRODUCED BY: Simon Fields and Paul Flattery

DIRECTED BY: Bruce Gowers

MUSIC FROM: Various Rod Stewart albums.

SELECTIONS: "Da Ya Think I'm Sexy," "Young Turks," "Passion."

☐ ROD STEWART

THE ROD STEWART CONCERT VIDEO

★★½

Karl/Lorimar, 1986, 83 minutes

PRODUCED BY: Toby Martin and Carolyn Raskin

DIRECTED BY: Carolyn Raskin

MUSIC FROM: Various Rod Stewart and Rod Stewart and the Faces albums.

SELECTIONS: "Infatuation," "Bad for You," "Tonight's the Night," "Listen to My Heart," "Dance with Me," "Hot Legs," "You're in My Heart," "Baby Jane," "(Sitting on) The Dock of the Bay," "Young Turks," "Passion," "Da Ya Think I'm Sexy," "Maggie May," "Some Guys Have All the Luck," "Stay with Me."

If you've never experienced Rod live but have heard about it, and you have video gear and want to check it out, or if you *adore* Rod, *especially* in concert, you'll want to examine one of these. After noting that the Sony/Embassy Video 45 takes a few tunes out of the long-form Embassy program, it must also be pointed out that both the Warner and Embassy programs look and sound very similar—both shot by the same director at the L.A. Forum, with substantially the same repertoire. Also, observe that the Embassy program is longer, features a nice guest appearance by Tina Turner, and contrasts a more contemporary dance-groove band sound with the rougher-edged booze-and-blooze sound of the Warners tape. From there, it's your move, depending on the intensity of your fanaticism. None of these is especially outstanding as an example of rock concert video, but they each do a fine job of capturing one of rock's inveterate lads in action; the Sony and Embassy programs each cut bits of Rod's ambitious, Russell Mulcahy–directed "Young Turks" video clip into the concert rendition.

What makes *The Rod Stewart Concert Video* different from all the other Rod Stewart Concert Videos? Not much, except: it was shot on his 1984 U.S. tour, at the San Diego Sports Arena instead of the usual L.A. Forum; and it opens with a nice little video bio of Rod, complete with family photos and tantalizing archival footage (Rod with the Jeff Beck Group and the Faces) accompanied by Rod's voiceover. Otherwise, it's the usual tired old arena rock entertainment, complete with endless wardrobe changes, endlessly protracted songs, the ol' soccer ball shtick, and endlessly annoying direction straight out of that condescending, they-have-no-attention-spans-anyway-so-keep-the-damn-thing-moving school of unwatchable concert videos. You know: all jar and no jam.

☐ STING

BRING ON THE NIGHT

★★★

Karl-Lorimar, 1986, 90 minutes

PRODUCED BY: David Manson

DIRECTED BY: Michael Apted

MUSIC FROM: Sting: *The Dream of the Blue Turtles* (A&M, 1985); the Police: *Synchronicity* (A&M, 1983); *Ghost in the Machine* (A&M, 1981); *Zenyatta Mondatta* (A&M, 1980); *Outlandos d'Amour* (A&M, 1979); *Brimstone and Treacle* motion picture soundtrack (Island/A&M, 1982).

SELECTIONS: "Bring on the Night"/ "When the World Is Running Down," "Set Them Free," "Low Life," "Fortress around Your Heart," "Love Is the Seventh Wave," "Shadows in the Rain," "Consider Me Gone," "Driven to Tears," "We Work the Black Seam," "I Burn for You," "Children's Crusade," "Need Your Love So Bad," "Roxanne," "Russians," "Been Down So Long," "Demolition Man," "Message in a Bottle."

In 1985 Sting, bassist/vocalist of the Police, enlisted four accomplished and respected jazz and jazz-rock musicians—saxophonist Branford Marsalis, keyboardist Kenny Kirkland, Miles Davis bassist Darryl Jones, and

Weather Report drummer Omar Hakim—plus the equally respected backing vocalists Dolette McDonald and Janice Pendarvis, to record his solo debut, *The Dream of the Blue Turtles.* *Bring on the Night* documents Sting and band rehearsing for their first stage show, in Paris, purportedly before the album was recorded. And it gets three stars not only because it affords any fan a classy-looking, up-close-and-personal document of their idol in action, but also because, whether he knows it or not, director Michael (*Coal Miner's Daughter, Gorky Park*) Apted has captured, as no other rock movie ever has except perhaps *This Is Spinal Tap,* a major rock star's laughable pretentiousness. (It doesn't get any more than three stars, however, because I doubt that this was Apted's intention.) *Bring on the Night* was probably conceived simply as a vanity project, a promotional documentary. But the vanity is the movie's monster, consuming all the good aspects, and leaving any sensible viewer more than a bit repulsed.

At the time of its theatrical release, much of the publicity bluster concerned how documentaries on rock bands were always made near the end of a band's career, not at the beginning, a theme that Sting, some of his band members, and other associates also spout off in the film. Not once does anyone stop to ponder why this is so. Did it ever occur to them that these movies are made after we all know that the band's work will be worthy of such attention? Obviously not. And this miscalculation—that this band would be great, and interesting—gives the film a lot to live up to.

Sting's band members talk a lot about "knocking down walls" between jazz and rock, black and white, and so on. Sure, it's a honorable idea; but the way they all blather on about it, you wonder if they know that many other artists and bands—including the Police, Talking Heads, Miles Davis, and Weather Report (all of whom someone in this band has played with)—have taken this same "daring" step. In a rare moment of good-humored candor, Sting blithely acknowledges the charade, saying—during one of his carefully posed, moodily lit interview segments—that "the record label, the management, even the general public were perturbed to hear the word 'jazz' . . . but really our music has nothing to do with jazz." And he's right: this music is sophisticated, refined, vaguely funk/jazz/reggae-inflected pop rock.

The film is well-turned and has its moments, to be sure, especially "I Burn for You," from *Brimstone and Treacle*'s soundtrack, with a simmering, slow-building climax in which Hakim becomes an awesome dervish of whirling polyrhythms and draws a deserved standing ovation from the Parisian audience. There are also some wonderful moments: a French guide ushering a group of elderly tourists through the Château Courson, where Sting and the band are rehearsing, and having to yell over the music about this settee and that painting; Sting's tour manager, Miles Copeland, engaged in an argument that pits his Yankee-boorish obsession with the bottom line against a set designer's refined set of esthetics, and it looks like it came straight out of *Spinal Tap.* Still, none of it adds up to make this the earth-shattering film it pretends to be.

What *Bring on the Night* does succeed at is giving us a fairly illustrative look at the supporting musicians, all of whom come across as much more down-to-earth and fun than their leader. Most notable are Jones, who sounds the sole note of muted discord when he tries to tactfully explain to an off-camera interviewer how he had hoped the band might have been more democratic, "a real band," and Marsalis, whose every appearance comes like a gust of fresh air. At one point, he tries to loosen Sting up by getting him to join in an impromptu version of the Flintstones theme; instead, Sting looks more uncomfortable than ever.

Ironically, especially considering that this should be a film that reveals something about its subject, *Bring On the Night* captures few moments of humor or candor with Sting. He comes off as one extremely serious, contained, stiff-upper-lip Brit. At one point, his companion Trudy Styler observes that working with this band has "lightened îStingï up" but we never see it. Even in the film's most powerful sequence, when Apted's camera is perched right over Trudy's shoulder as she gives birth to Sting's son Jake with Sting at her side, Sting remains coolly detached. He blinks back a few tears and that's it. An incredibly gripping scene, Jake's birth is also much better than *Bring on the Night* deserves. Talk about going from the ridiculous to the sublime: little Jake's arrival is one "new release" that really puts the rest of this film's hype and careermanship into the proper perspective.

The film closes with Sting singing "Message in a Bottle" solo to his hushed Parisian audience, and it's a moving plea for understanding and communication. But while the movie shows Sting doing lots of different things, it never really penetrates the fortress around his heart.

□ STRAY CATS

STRAY CATS VIDEO 45

★★★½

Sony, 1984, 13 minutes

PRODUCED BY: Picture Music International

DIRECTED BY: Julien Temple, Ian Leech, and Peter Heath

MUSIC FROM: Stray Cats (Arista U.K., 1983); *Gonna Ball* (EMI-America, 1982); *Built for Speed* (EMI-America, 1982).

SELECTIONS: "(She's) Sexy & 17," "Stray Cat Strut," "I Won't Stand in Your Way," "Rock this Town."

Also available on Pioneer 8-inch Stereo Laser videodisc.

The Stray Cats, in an ironic twist on classic British Invasion teen-idoldom, had to leave their native Long Island, New York, and go to London to make it big—both over there and back here—with their rockabilly act. And while some derided them as mere nostalgists, leader/guitarist/vocalist Brian Setzer showed more than a little talent and stylish flair in updating the rockabilly sound. Two of the clips here, "Stray Cat Strut" and "(She's) Sexy & 17," are classics that helped the band a lot in their time. The former, directed by Julien Temple, has enough of the dramatically compressed stylization of classic movie musicals to mark it as a very early forebear of Temple's 1986 musical feature *Absolute Beginners,* down to the back-alley '50s-rebel jazzbo-hipster milieu. Ian Leech's "(She's) Sexy & 17" is a fast-paced, colorful romp that takes off from a *Blackboard Jungle*–influenced premise and features a delightfully choreographed scene with teachers and students slamming each other against lockers that predates Twisted Sister's use of the same device two years later in "I Wanna Rock." Temple's "Rock this Town" is also fun, especially its bowling alley scene, where Setzer rolls a huge strike right over a bunch of discophiles making fun of his pompadour. Peter Heath's "I Won't Stand in Your Way" is nicely produced, but this rather limp ballad needs more than atmosphere to click. It's the only real slow spot in what is otherwise a solid little program.

☐ **VARIOUS ARTISTS**
STREETS OF FIRE
★½

MCA, 1984, 93 minutes
PRODUCED BY: Lawrence Gordon and Joel Silver
DIRECTED BY: Walter Hill
MUSIC FROM: Streets of Fire motion picture soundtrack LP (MCA, 1984).
SELECTIONS: Dan Hartman: "I Can Dream About You," "Countdown to Love"; Jim Steinman and Diane Lane: "Tonight Is What It Means to Be Young," "Nowhere Fast," "Never Be You," "Sorcerer"; Ry Cooder: "Get out of Denver," "Hold That Snake," "You Got What You Wanted," "Rumble," "First Love, First Tears"; the Fixx: "Deeper and Deeper"; the Blasters: "Blue Shadows," "One Bad Stud."

This bombastically silly "rock fable" from action director Walter (*48 Hours, The Warriors*) Hill bombed out in a big way at the box office. Set in some indeterminate, allegedly mythical big city that exists only on Hollywood backlots and on MTV, it's got Diane Lane being absolutely unbelievable as a rock singer stolen by a big bad wolf of a motorcycle gang leader (the fine Willem Dafoe), and Michael Pare (*Eddie and the Cruisers*) as the sullenly Mitchum-esque hunk who rescues her. Why anyone would ever bother to rescue dead weight like Lane, or even listen to her supposed "rock" music, is a mystery the film never even tries to explain. In fact, probably the best and only way to enjoy a movie like *Streets of Fire* is as witting or unwitting self-parody, in the campy so-awful-it's-funny sense. At times, *Streets of Fire* seems, in fact, to be a self-parody that really does know how ridiculous it is; especially when Rick Moranis of *SCTV* fame is on-screen as Lane's pushy manager, an ultra-nerd so aggressively obnoxious he's utterly hysterical in a totally incongruous way. Ry Cooder falls below his usual standards with his soundtrack contributions (but in a project like this, who can blame him?). The Blasters actually make a couple of quick, inconsequential appearances in the film; the occasional background tunes from the likes of the Fixx, Tom Petty, and Stevie Nicks are also inconsequential; and Jim Steinman creates his usual breast-beating mountain of nonsense for Lane to "sing" through (*ugh!*). Only Dan Hartman rises above it all with the sublime "I Can Dream About You," the *only* reason—along with Rick Moranis (and Amy Madigan in another supporting role)—to bother seeing this.

☐ **VARIOUS ARTISTS (DAN HARTMAN, DIANE LANE)**
MUSIC VIDEO FROM STREETS OF FIRE
★½

MCA, 1984, 30 minutes
PRODUCED BY: Lawrence Gordon and Joel Silver
DIRECTED BY: Walter Hill
MUSIC FROM: The film *Streets of Fire* (Universal, 1984).
SELECTIONS: Dan Hartman/"The Sorrells": "I Can Dream About You;" Diane Lane/"Ellen Aim": "Tonight Is What It Means to Be Young," "Nowhere Fast."

As with the movie itself, the *only* reason this gets any star-rating at all is because it includes Dan Hartman's heavenly "I Can Dream About You," one of the very best pop songs of the '80s. Unfortunately, it also includes the awful Diane Lane lip-synching to the bombastic sub-Springsteenisms of Meat Loaf/Bonnie Tyler producer Jim Steinman—something that does about as good a job of killing rock 'n' roll as anything that's come down the pike since 1956. The blunt-instrument recutting of action scenes from the movie *Streets of Fire* doesn't help, nor does the eight-minute "Making of

Streets of Fire" filmlet, which is really just an elongated ad for the movie. Whether you liked the movie or not (and not many people did), that is something to avoid, unless you somehow have absolutely *no* other way of experiencing the marvelous "I Can Dream About You."

□ BARBRA STREISAND
MY NAME IS BARBRA
★★★★½

CBS/Fox, 1986, 60 minutes
DIRECTED BY: Joe Layton
MUSIC FROM: My Name Is Barbra original soundtrack album (Columbia, 1965) and other Barbra Streisand LPs (Columbia, 1963–65).
SELECTIONS: "My Name Is Barbra," "I'm Late," "Make Believe," "How Does the Wine Taste," "Kid Again/I'm Five," "Sweet Zoo," "Where Is the Wonder," "People," "Second Hand Rose," "Give Me the Simple Life," "I Got Plenty of Nothin'," "Brother, Can You Spare a Dime," "Nobody Knows You When You're Down and Out," "The Best Things in Life Are Free," "When the Sun Comes Out," "Why Did I Choose You," "Lover Where Can You Be," "You Are Woman," "Don't Rain on My Parade," "Music That Makes Me Dance," "My Man," "Happy Days Are Here Again."

□ BARBRA STREISAND
COLOR ME BARBRA
★★★★½

CBS/Fox, 1986, 60 minutes
DIRECTED BY: Joe Layton
MUSIC FROM: Color Me Barbra original soundtrack album (Columbia, 1966).
SELECTIONS: "Draw Me a Circle," "Yesterdays," "One Kiss," "Minute Waltz," "Gotta Move," "Non C'est Rien," "Where or When," "Animal Crackers in My Soup," "Funny Face," "That Face," "I've Grown Accustomed to Her Face," "Sam You Made the Pants Too Long," "What's New Pussycat," "Who's Afraid of the Big Bad Wolf," "We Have So Much in Common," "Try to Remember," "Spring Again," "Have I Stayed Too Long at the Fair," "Look at That Face, Look at That Fabulous Face," "Any Place I Hang My Hat Is Home," "It Had to Be You," "C'est Si Bon," "Where Am I Going," "Starting Here, Starting Now."

My Name Is Barbra and *Color Me Barbra,* Streisand's first two prime-time CBS TV specials, were epochal television events in the mid-'60s. Now that they're on home video, those who missed them when they were first broadcast can see why. Of course, those who saw them first time around will never forget them, but will most likely have to own these anyway. Both of them are great television, and great *musical* television—the concepts, staging, and direction perfectly complement Streisand's own imposing self-possession and sheer star power, as well as her awesome voice. *My Name Is Barbra,* broadcast April 28, 1965, at 10 P.M., gave the American public its first extended, up-close dose of La Streisand: rushing in a frenzy from one set to another, trailing a long, flowing evening gown in "I'm Late"; playing in an oversize playground for "Kid Again/I'm Five" (a setup that seems to have provided the mold for Lily Tomlin's *Laugh-In* character "Edith Ann"); cracking up her audience in a monolog about a lady called "Pearl from Istanbul"; dancing through the toney Bergdorf Goodman department store in a variety of chi-chi getups for "Second Hand Rose"; and finally delivering a stunning straight-concert performance to wind it up. Classics include "People," "Don't Rain on My Parade," and "My Man."

The following year, Streisand triumphed again with *Color Me Barbra,* which expanded the skits/locations motif of the first TV special: she's Marie Antoinette frantically trying to complete the "Minute Waltz" while a guillotine blade dangles ominously above; she visits a circus for a spree of humorously selected tunes, from "Animal Crackers in My Soup" through "Who's Afraid of the Big Bad Wolf," during which she shows just how self-possessed she really *was* by comparing profiles with an anteater; in another segment, she wanders through the Philadelphia Museum taking song cues from Egyptian artifacts and Modigliani portraits. Once again, Streisand's own charisma and talent were enough to make this, like *My Name Is . . .*, powerful and influential enough that subsequent TV generations got to know the style set here mainly through parodies and inherently campy adulterated imitations by later variety shows and specials. The bona fide original is really worth checking out—and for you younger post–Baby Boomers out there, either or both of these would make a fabulous gift for your parents. Just check to make sure they haven't already run out and bought them themselves.

□ BARBRA STREISAND
"PUTTING IT TOGETHER"—THE MAKING OF THE BROADWAY ALBUM

★★½

CBS/Fox, 1986, 40 minutes
PRODUCED BY: Joni Rosen
MUSIC FROM: The Broadway Album (Columbia, 1985).
SELECTIONS: "Something's Coming," "Putting It Together," "Can't Help Lovin' Dat Man," "If I Loved You," "Somewhere."

Streisand fans who only need to see her in action—be it performing or simply being Barbra—ought to be plenty satisfied with this document of the album Ms. Streisand calls "a return to my roots." There's no denying that she's a magnificent vocalist, with stunning command. And here, she looks just as marvelous as she sounds.

However, Ms. Streisand is also a *star* of the first magnitude. She knows it, everyone around her knows it, we all know it, and this program never lets you forget it. Not only is her charisma frequently on fascinating display, but included are some despicably fatuous, glaringly contrived interviews between Ms. Streisand and moviemaker William Friedkin, shot as a "casual chat." On the basis of the chatty segments alone, "*Putting It Together*" suffers from that most insidious of programmatic diseases: rampant egomania and self-indulgence—in other words, "Vanity Projectitis." Next to a fawning Friedkin, Barbra seems humble. And you may well wonder how responsible she was for that.

Early in the chat between Barbra and "Billy," as she calls him, the pretension of this whole set-up is revealed, though the principals seem not to realize it. First, there's in-studio documentation of the recording of what Streisand calls the "art-versus-commerce dialogue" that opens the song "Putting It Together." It's really a dramatization of the way Streisand must see her own self-determined career, as filmmaker Sydney Pollack, *Broadway Album* producer Richard Baskin, and Barbra's longtime friend and Geffen Records chief David Geffen all play crass execs bickering in the background about the singer's audacity in choosing a "dangerous" career move like *The Broadway Album.* The lyrics that composer Stephen Sondheim rewrote for the song fulfill the same spunky self-aggrandizing function. Sure, the idea of such supposed hemming and hawing and agonizing is a sham, given the very star-power and self-determined careerwomanship dramatized here and evident throughout Streisand's career. But as reflexive artifice-imitating-life, it's fascinating. Then, however, we cut to Barbra and Billy back in the theater seats. "I never understood the opposition to this album," she muses.

"I still don't." "Of *course* you don't," one can't help but think, "the very *idea* of *The Broadway Album* being some sort of daring artistic risk for you is to *laugh, dahlink.*" Who is she kidding?

It's not until the end of the program, in fact, that the absolute vanity of the project is finally acknowledged. Friedkin quotes the album's liner notes by songwriters Alan and Marilyn Bergman in reference to "Somewhere": "They say 'there's a glimpse of infinity in it,' " says Friedkin, with creepy resonance, ". . . like this album." Streisand looks at him, poised precariously between pleasure and embarrassment; she giggles nervously, says "Infinity, inschminity" in classic Barbra-ese, gets serious a second to clasp his hand and murmur, "Thank you, Billy," then looks around in nervous distraction before asking the camera, "How do we end this thing?"

Moments like those are enough to make you forget the good parts of "*Putting It Together,*" but they exist. There's an opening prelude montage spanning her career, accompanying "Something's Coming," and featuring her first-ever TV appearance (introduced on a talk show by host Orson Bean) and some truly fab '60s footage; and Friedkin's beautifully produced video for "Somewhere," which in its own way is as fascinating and revealing of Streisand's personal and artistic power as the whole "Putting It Together" sequence. With strident felicity—since Streisand has just told Friedkin that it was the "universality" of "Somewhere" that inspired her to select it for video accompaniment—Friedkin opens it with shots of planets in outer space before zooming into earth and, finally, to a theater stage where Barbra is singing the song. In another tribute to his subject as the real *auteur* of the video, Friedkin uses loving pans of Barbra's ethnically polyglot audience with montages of Ellis Island–style footage to create a mini-*Yentl* hymn to America as the Land of the Free—the "Somewhere" that's a Place for Us.

☐ THE STYLE COUNCIL
FAR EAST AND FAR OUT—COUNCIL MEETING IN JAPAN
★★

Media, 1984, 60 minutes

PRODUCED BY: Hiroki Shirahama, Shinichi Majima

SELECTIONS: "Intro," "My Ship Came In," "The Big Boss Groove," "Here's One That Got Away," "You're the Best Thing," "It Just Came to Pieces in My Hands," "Mick's Up," "Dropping Bombs on the White House," "Long Hot Summer," "My Ever Changing Moods" "Le Depart," "The Whole Point of No Return," "Money-Go-Round" "Headstart for Happiness," "Speak Like a Child," "Reprise—Le Depart."

After breaking up the furious Who-derived punk band the Jam in 1982, Paul Weller made an about-face by forming Style Council with keyboardist Mick Talbot. Here, the music is mellow and moody, jazzy and soul-inflected if not quite actually soulful. Therein lies the problem: the music's well written and atmospherically arranged, but Weller and his fellow white Brits just don't have the stuff to re-*create* classic R&B; they can only *refer* to it. Impressive as it sometimes can be, it's ultimately inconsequential; a real disappointment considering the Jam's driven, pointed intensity. This 1985 Tokyo concert is competently shot, however, and for fans of Weller this may be worth a look.

☐ STYX
CAUGHT IN THE ACT
★★

A&M, 1983, 87 minutes

DIRECTED BY: Jerry Kramer, Brian Gibson

MUSIC FROM: Kilroy Was Here (A&M,

1983) and other Styx albums.

SELECTIONS: "Kilroy Was Here," "Mr. Roboto," "Rockin' the Paradise," "Blue Collar Man," "Snowblind," "Too Much Time on My Hands," "Don't Let It End," "Heavy Metal Poisoning," "Cold War," "Best of Times," "Come Sail Away," "Renegade," "Haven't We Been Here Before?" "Don't Let It End (reprise)."

Also available on Pioneer Stereo Laser videodisc.

Styx play state-of-the-art AOR corporate pomp-rock—in other words, execrably formulaic sludge, tepidly mingling heavy metal overtones with progressive/symphonic rock pretentions. This 1983 concert, from their *Kilroy Was Here* album-promoting tour, brings to turgid life that LP's half-baked *1984*-based concept of a futuristic world where rock is outlawed, borrowing heavily from Devo for its high-tech stage sets and ambience. Director Jerry Kramer does a beautiful job shooting it all, so Styx fans will revel in it. But I cannot in good conscience recommend this to anyone else.

☐ VARIOUS ARTISTS
SUBURBIA

★★½

Vestron, 1985, 96 minutes
PRODUCED BY: Bert Dragin
DIRECTED BY: Penelope Spheeris
MUSIC FROM: Various albums by various artists; soundtrack of *Suburbia* (New World, 1984).

SELECTIONS: D.I.: "Richard Hung Himself"; T.S.O.L.: "Wash Away," "Darker My Love"; the Vandals: "The Legend of Pat Brown," "Urban Struggle"; Steve Berlin: "Suzann's Theme"; the Germs: "No God."

What happens when Penelope Spheeris, creator of the bluntly honest L.A. punk rock documentary *Decline and Fall . . . of Western Civilization,* makes her first narrative feature film under the aegis of trashmonger Roger Corman's New World Pictures? You get a generally predictable and schematic outlaw melodrama that is to hardcore punks what *Psych-Out* was to hippies: not The Truth, but a campy refraction of same that should live on for some time in pop-culture annals. Spheeris does manage to create a few very powerful scenes—like the vicious opening prologue, and the brutally protracted symbolic rape of an uptight girl in a crowded punk rock club, which ends hilariously when the club owner, trying to avert an apparent riot, pulls the plug on the live band (the fine T.S.O.L.) and, in order to evacuate the crowd, orders his soundman, "Okay—give 'em the Muzak!" On comes the sound of Percy Faith's 1001 Strings, and out file the punkers. Spheeris also gets strong performances from skinhead Timothy Eric O'Brien and Michael Bayer (now better known as Flea of punk-funk band the Red Hot Chili Peppers) as Razzle, the punk whose constant companion is his pet rat.

☐ DONNA SUMMER
A HOT SUMMER NIGHT . . . WITH DONNA

★½

RCA/Columbia, 1983, 79 minutes
PRODUCED BY: Christine Smith
DIRECTED BY: Brian Grant
MUSIC FROM: Various Donna Summer albums (Oasis, Casablanca, Geffen, Mercury, 1975–83) and pay-cable TV concert special (HBO, 1983).

SELECTIONS: "MacArthur Park," "Love Is In Control (Finger on the Trigger)," "Unconditional Love," "Romeo," "Don't Cry for Me, Argentina," "On the Radio" "Forgive Me," "Woman in Me," Medley: "Dim All the Lights"/"Sunset People"/"Bad Girls"/"Hot Stuff," "Last Dance," "She Works Hard for the Money," "State of Independence."

Also available on Pioneer Stereo Laser videodisc.

Vegasitis strikes, and you know what that means: needlessly slick and vulgar production numbers, with some of Summer's best tunes—like "Bad Girls" and "Hot Stuff"—getting crammed into throwaway medleys, while others, like "I Feel Love," aren't here at all. As she instead essays camp pap like "Don't Cry for Me, Argentina." Besides which, amidst all the highly produced onstage hubbub, the ultra-wooden Summer looks as lost as ever.

□ SUN RA
A JOYFUL NOISE
★★★★½

Rhapsody, 1982, 60 minutes
PRODUCED BY: Robert Mugge
DIRECTED BY: Robert Mugge
MUSIC FROM: 1980 film; various Sun Ra albums.
SELECTIONS: "Astro Black," "Along Came Ra/The Living Myth," "Mister Ra/ Mystery," "Discipline 27," "Discipline 27–11," "Calling Planet Earth," "Space Loneliness Blues," "Requiem for Trevor Johnson," " 'Round Midnight," "Ankh," "Ancient Egyptian Infinity Lightning Drum," "Rock-Si-Chord Solo" "Organ Solo," "Spaceship Earth (Destination Unknown)," "We Travel the Spaceways."

Sun Ra is a venerable titan of the jazz avant-garde, a bandleader/keyboardist/ composer/arranger/philosopher/shaman of considerable talents, accomplishments, and self-determination. The flamboyantly unique Ra has, since the mid-'50s, led a kaleidescopically eclectic Afro-psychedelic jazz "Arkestra" that pioneered free improvisation and African polyrhythms; Ra was among the very first in any kind of music to use electronic keyboards; and he transduced ancient Egyptian mythology and ahead-of-its-time space-age philosophy into an outlook all his own, dead serious and deadpan-funny at the same time.

According to what Earthly records there are of this mysterious genius, Ra arrived on this planet in Alabama around 1915, though you'd never know it to see the energy of this roly-poly little old man in performance; Ra himself claims to be an ambassador sent here against his will from outer space by the Creator of what he calls "the Omniverse," and that he was born millennia ago on Saturn. Considering all he's done over the years through thin and thin, as well as the inarguable, innate dignity he projects through his glittery rainbow-hued dime-store-psychedelic garb, I'm not about to argue.

Trying to cover all there is to say about this most flamboyantly unique artist is a daunting task, especially in an hour, but Robert Mugge's *A Joyful Noise* does a darned good job. More personal portrait than actual comprehensive musical documentary, it presents a good range of Ra's many musical moods, from heraldic horn fanfares ("Discipline 27") to funky seriocomic chants and jingles ("Astro Black," "We Travel the Spaceways"), from free-form outbursts and African-inflected tone poems to more traditional fare (" 'Round Midnight"). There are also revealing interviews with some of Ra's longest-standing sidemen/acolytes, including John Gilmore, another noble and dignified warrior/musician who happens to be right up there with Sonny Rollins among the best tenor saxophonists in all of jazz—though, because he's remained with Ra, few know it. But *A Joyful Noise* is best at showing Ra's whimsical yet stern personality, his playful gifts for phonetic/syntactic/philosophical punning; it shows Ra leading his band in a variety of indoor and outdoor locations, catches Ra rehearsing the band for a while, and lets him sermonize outside the White House and, most felicitously, in the Egyptian Antiquities wing of a museum in

Philadelphia (where Ra has resided since the early '70s). "They say history repeats itself," says Ra in his beguiling cat's-purr of a drawl, "but that's *his* story, not *my* story. My story is endless. *My* story is more a *mys*tery." Indeed. What a guy. What a movie.

☐ SUPERTRAMP
BROTHER WHERE YOU BOUND
★★★½

A&M, 1985, 29 minutes
PRODUCED BY: Steve Barron, Rene Daalder
MUSIC FROM: Brother Where You Bound (A&M, 1985).
SELECTIONS: "Brother Where You Bound," "Cannonball," "Better Days."

Very intriguing, ambitious program, with the visuals really lifting Supertramp's competent but bland post–progressive-rock pop to a higher level. The program opens with two video clips, "Cannonball" and "Better Days," each employing disruptive time-traveling motifs to make interesting, but ultimately inconclusive comments on modern-day anomie: in the former, *Quest for Fire* cavemen abruptly encounter the mechanized present (in which, of course, Supertramp is seen performing); in the latter, a kid is ripped from Depression-soupline newsreel footage to be shown the sterility of the future—our present—by two obnoxious mimes. Rene Daalder's extended visual accompaniment to "Brother Where You Bound" is a disturbing, atmospheric, highly produced, and quite tendentious antiwar statement, involving the "Star Wars" outer-space defense plan, a rebel defense technician, creepy mutants, shell-shocked masses, and a *Bladerunner/Road Warrior* post-apocalyptic look and feel. Again, it just drifts to a disappointingly inconclusive end, but it too offers enough food for thought prior to petering out to be more than worth a look.

☐ VARIOUS ARTISTS (JAN AND DEAN, THE BEACH BOYS, OTHERS)
SURFING BEACH PARTY
★

Media, 1984, 56 minutes
DIRECTED BY: Ted Mather
MUSIC FROM: Various Jan and Dean and Beach Boys albums.
SELECTIONS: "Little Deuce Coupe," "Dead Man's Curve," "Drag City," "Little Old Lady from Pasadena," "Fun, Fun, Fun," "Jennie Lee," "New Girl in School," "Barbara Ann," "Surf City," "Surf with Me," "Surfin' Safari," "Ride the Wild Surf," "Baby Talk," "Sidewalk Surfing," "Surfer Girl," "Pipeline," "Wipe Out."

Dean Torrence, of Jan and Dean fame, somehow got suckered into hosting this pathetic compendium of surf-rock vocal classics, which director Ted Mather has set to stupefyingly dull modern-day videos, starring team after team of smiling, dancing, lip-synching dancers. Who would ever buy something like this? Certainly not surf-rock fans—and probably not you either.

☐ VARIOUS ARTISTS
SWEET DREAMS
★★★★

HBO/Cannon, 1985, approximately 120 minutes
PRODUCED BY: Bernard Schwartz
DIRECTED BY: Karel Reisz
MUSIC FROM: Sweet Dreams motion picture soundtrack (MCA, 1985).
SELECTIONS: Patsy Cline: "Blue Moon of Kentucky," "Your Cheatin' Heart," "Walking after Midnight," "Foolin' Around," "Sweet Dreams," "Crazy," "San Antonio Rose," "Seven Lonely Days," "Lovesick Blues," "She's Got You," "I Fall to Pieces"; Sam Cooke: "You Send Me"; Gene Vincent: "Be-Bop-a-Lula"; Buddy Holly: "That'll Be the Day."

Sweet Dreams is a gracefully shot, wonderfully acted film biography of the late country great Patsy Cline that presents her music beautifully (Jessica Lange lip-synched the performance sections to Cline's original recordings) and Cline rather sweetly. Lange and Ed Harris, as Patsy's husband, Charlie Dick, have a special chemistry that's fascinating, and there's never a dull moment.

Music historians and Cline fans might quibble with the general candy coating of the story and the film's portrayal of Cline's music and success as if they had occurred in a vacuum. In fact, as stridently profeminist as *Sweet Dreams* is, Patsy Cline was apparently far tougher and more independent than Lange's character. And Lange's constant charm gets tedious even if you don't know that the real Cline never cared too much what anyone thought about anything she did. Historically, there are other flaws, for as rapid as Cline's ascent was, it wasn't quite the Cinderella story *Sweet Dreams* describes. While this movie begins to verge on the melodramatic in the last half, Cline's real life was worse yet, complicated by drink and men (including her manager Randy Hughes, here depicted as just a close friend). Also excluded are facts and characters of interest to fans; for example, the two barely identified men who died in the March 1963 plane crash that killed Cline were country stars Cowboy Copas and Hawkshaw Hawkins. Nor do we get a real sense of the richness of the music community she lived in. She seems to go to gigs the way other women would go to work at the local cannery. Her spunkiness, well known to other country performers, is apparent only in her volatile relationship with husband Dick.

Sweet Dreams wasn't a great box-office smash, but its availability on home video should foster a greater knowledge and appreciation of Cline's work. In just over six years, Cline singlehandedly changed contemporary country music with a classic sound and style which can be heard today in the work of Linda Ronstadt and others, and which, on Cline's own recordings, sound as fresh as if they were made only yesterday. Cline's records also pioneered the use of strings and other pop-production elements in country music, presaging the countrypolitan school by a good fifteen to twenty years. Her songs, especially the hauntingly beautiful "Sweet Dreams," are lyrically rich and complex, qualities enhanced by her readings, which provide a classically American paradox by seamlessly and organically melding guts, craft, and dignity. Many critics agree that Cline was one of America's best singers in any genre, and her magnificent voice and interpretive prowess on classics such as "I Fall to Pieces" and Willie Nelson's "Crazy" are simply stunning no matter what your musical taste. It's easy to forgive *Sweet Dreams* its flaws merely for demonstrating Cline's enduring talents. But Jessica Lange's so-credible-it's-*in*credible lip-synching job is grand enough to make *Sweet Dreams* even more admirable—and yet, at the same time, even more frustrating for failing to adequately contextualize Cline's musical significance (which is not necessarily the same as her talent and appeal). As a *music* movie, *Sweet Dreams* has both good and bad points; but as a *movie* movie, at the very least, it's well worth seeing.—P.R.

□ SWEET HONEY IN THE ROCK
GOTTA MAKE THIS JOURNEY

★★★★

PBS, 1983, approximately 60 minutes
PRODUCED BY: Michelle Parkerson

DIRECTED BY: Joseph Camp
SELECTIONS: include "Seven Day Kiss" and "Down by the Riverside."

This hour-long documentary commemorating the ninth anniversary of this famous black female a cappella quintet was originally produced for the Public Broadcasting System and so is not generally available. And the price—$350—almost precludes ownership by all but the most dedicated and well-heeled fans. But your local public library, music school, or college music department may well have a copy on hand, and for anyone with an interest in black music, gospel, music in politics, or the feminist movement in the arts, this is a must-see.

Like all PBS productions, this has a clean look and sound. Combining powerful concert sequences with interviews, *Gotta Make This Journey* presents an engrossing, informative, and entertaining look at this unique and awesomely talented group. As the current five members—Yaseem Williams, Evelyn Harris, Aisha Kahill, Ysaye Barnwell, and Bernice Johnson Reagon—discuss their pasts, their families, their politics, their responsibilities to their music and the audience, you can't help but be impressed by their intelligence and determination. Though all rock fans like to talk about how direct, honest, and uncompromised their music is, compared to these women ninety-nine percent of other performers are, if not frauds, at least less than totally committed. It's one thing to sing about people needing education, justice, and freedom—lots of performers do that. It's something else again to see performers whose art is a product of their lives, not vice versa. Barnwell, for example, directs a program for abused children, while Johnson Reagon, whose work in the civil rights movement dates back to its roots, compiles and studies black music for the Smithsonian. I'd also be less than honest if I didn't admit that I found them amazing just for being so forthright. Whether that says more about me or music video—or popular music in general—I don't know. Sweet Honey in the Rock's polish is the product of skill and passion, not shtick. You could almost say that they don't have an act, and that would probably be all right with them, since they don't want to be pop stars anyway.

Of course, the final proof is in the music, and here their stunning harmonies and intense lyrics shine. Their political songs—particularly one about South Africa and another about Stephen Biko—are simply compelling, and as powerful, honest, and direct as anything rock 'n' roll has produced. Unfortunately, the song's titles appear nowhere in the credits, so they cannot be accurately identified. There is one song, however, that almost celebrates the growing universal impatience with racism, and one particularly rousing line, "Here comes Stephen Biko walking down the street," is a chilling threat, prayer, and prophecy all in one. But Sweet Honey is about much more. Their "Seven Day Kiss" is as sexy—sexier, really—than anything even Prince could dream up, largely because these women are real people, not pop-image creations. And their gospel songs exemplify the literal meaning of the word "inspiration."

Through their first nine years, Sweet Honey has had eighteen members (and this version technically has six, if you count Shirley Johnson, who translates their lyrics onstage through sign language for the deaf). After seeing this, I really feel like I missed something by not following them more closely early on. See this—or them—as soon as you can. Sweet Honey in the Rock is truly a national treasure.—P.R.

T

☐ MASAYOSHI TAKANAKA
RAINBOW GOBLINS STORY—LIVE AT BUDOKAN
★½

Paramount, 1985, 60 minutes
PRODUCED BY: Yutaka Tanaka
DIRECTED BY: Takeshi Shimizu
SELECTIONS: "Prologue," "Once upon a Song," "Seven Goblins," "The Sunset Valley," "The Moon Rose," "Soon," "Thunderstorm," "Rising Arch," "Plumed Bird," "You Can Never Come to This Place."
Also available on Pioneer Imports Stereo Laser videodisc.

☐ MASAYOSHI TAKANAKA
TAKANAKA WORLD
★½

Paramount, 1985, 60 minutes
PRODUCED BY: Takeshi Shimuzu
SELECTIONS: "Ready to Fly," "Oh! Tengo Suerte," "The Fairy of the Coral Reef," "Radio Rio," "Blue Lagoon," "Le Premier Mars," "Early Bird," "I Remember You."
Also available on Pioneer Imports Stereo Laser videodisc.

Japanese guitarist Masayoshi Takanaka is a fluid player in the style of Carlos Santana and Larry Carlton, and his jazz-rock fusion music is as competent and tunefully pretty as just about anyone's. Unfortunately, however, it also lacks spark and personality and easily fits the label "fuzak" (as in fusion Muzak, a term coined by writer Peter Occhiogrosso). Still, millions of people enjoy other sorts of critically derided fuzak, so fusion fans will certainly want to check Takanaka out.

In *Rainbow Goblins Story,* Takanaka sets out to do what his music cannot: provide an appropriate soundtrack for a fairy tale about how the flora and fauna of Rainbow Valley band together to keep a gang of rainbow-eating goblins at bay. As the fairy tale moves from innocence to the introduction of evil, from danger to hope and then happily-ever-after, the music seems to keep churning, oblivious of changes in mood or sound. Ultimately, it epitomizes the assembly-line blandness that infects so much fusion music and ensures that the story and the soundtrack have nothing to do with each other. The fact that the story is illustrated in the most salutary fashion—with occasional picture-book drawings of goblins and rainbows dissolving quickly in and out of what is basically straightforward Takanaka concert footage; the cheap-looking production values don't help either. But if you're a fusion-loving parent seeking safe entertainment for your offspring, here you go.

You *may,* however, want to keep the kids away from *Takanaka World.* It contains plenty of soft-core nudity, mostly of the topless-female variety. While *Rainbow Goblins Story* gets pretty boring all in all, *Takanaka World* is boredom of a different sort—it's "boredom," as in "ambient" or "environmental" video. Actually, since Takanaka's music is basically aural wallpaper, that's a much better idea than juxtaposing it with a fairy tale. Here, the visuals consist mainly of sunny, splashy—but ultimately cheap-looking and dull (those old *Rainbow Goblins* bugaboos)—travelogue footage, much of it shot on the nude beaches of Rio de Janeiro. For contrast, "Blue Lagoon" is virtually nothing but a long shot of Takanaka on a sand dune, spelling out the title with his footprints in huge letters; later, we get to see him at a hotel's poolside bar under the stars, being served a tropical drink in a coconut, with a lit sparkler in it—and in slo-mo, yet; later still, there's a hamfisted stab at sustained erotica as two attractive young ladies skinny-dip in someone's backyard pool. Pretty inspired, huh? Well, if the *idea* of *Takanaka World* was better than that of *Rainbow Goblins,* the reality is just as banal.

Though jazz-fusion lovers may enjoy Takanaka's music, there's no reason for them to pay the higher price of a videocassette or disc to get it, when hundreds of domestic record albums sound just like Takanaka, and Takanaka's visuals aren't worth seeing.

□ TALK TALK
TALK TALK VIDEO 45
★★½

Sony, 1984, 16 minutes
PRODUCED BY: MGMM and GLO
DIRECTED BY: Russell Mulcahy and Tim Pope
MUSIC FROM: Party's Over (EMI-America, 1984); *It's My Life* (EMI-America, 1984).
SELECTIONS: "Talk Talk," "It's My Life," "Such a Shame," "Dum Dum Girl."

A thoughtful if unexceptional British new-music band of the early to mid-'80s, Talk Talk doesn't have nearly enough musical or visual spark to make this cassette recommendable to all. Their fans, of course, will be interested in it, and those who are generally partial to this sort of thing—let's call it *tasteful* MTV-rock—might want to check it out. The last three videos, all by the idiosyncratic Tim Pope, are more intriguing in their offbeat concepts and use of mixed media than Russell Mulcahy's off-handed, enervating opening performance clip. The best of the lot is "It's My Life," in which Pope inventively superimposes all manner of wildlife footage over and around the performing band. At one point, he even tips his hat cleverly to Luis Buñuel's surrealist classic *Un Chien Andalou* (a motherlode of startling imagery often raided by rock video directors) by having the singer's mouth turn into a mass of crawling black ants.

□ TALKING HEADS
STOP MAKING SENSE
★★★★★

RCA/Columbia, 1985, 98 minutes
PRODUCED BY: Gary Kurfirst and Jonathan Demme
DIRECTED BY: Jonathan Demme
MUSIC FROM: Various Talking Heads and other LPs, including *Tom Tom Club* (Sire/Warner Bros., 1981); *The Name of This Band Is Talking Heads* (Sire/Warner Bros., 1982); *Stop Making Sense* motion picture soundtrack (Sire/Warner Bros., 1984); *The Catherine Wheel* (Sire/Warner Bros., 1981).
SELECTIONS: "Psycho Killer," "Heaven," "Thank You for Sending Me an Angel," "Found a Job," "Slippery People," "Cities," "Burning Down the House," "Life during Wartime," "Making Flippy Floppy," "Swamp," "What a Day That Was," "This Must Be the Place," "Once in a Lifetime," "I Zimbra," "Genius of Love," "Girlfriend Is Better," "Take Me to the River," "Crosseyed and Painless."

Talking Heads in the best American rock band of the past decade or so, and this tape captures them at the peak of their form at L.A.'s Pantages Theater during their 1984 U.S. tour. Their awesome set was shot with more elegant care and beauty than we'd seen in any rock film since Martin Scorcese's *The Last Waltz*. In fact, some people thought Jonathan Demme's photography was *too* beautiful—as in sterile—especially given the sweaty catharsis of the expanded lineup's Afro-polyrhythmic funk rock.

The show builds incrementally, starting with David Byrne's smashing solo-acoustic-with-boom-box-rhythm "Psycho Killer"; one by one, the other band members come on, as the band works its way through its career, culminating in the full nine-piece ensemble's extended orgy of multifarious jungle-rhythm ecstasy. Along the way, they give rather short shrift to their earlier work (for me, anyway), but that's carping. However, they also essay some multimedia theatrical gambits (like slide shows and a living-room set) that smack of superfluous preciousness; gaunt, nervous David Byrne, the Norman Bates of rock (as someone once aptly called him), is more than enough rock theater all by himself.

Still, on the whole this is one heck of a band playing one heck of a show, and it's all captured magnificently. Take special note of the bizarrely evocative facial tics and grimaces of keyboard whiz Bernie Worrell as he draws unearthly sounds from his synthesizers. Also note that the home video release contains some numbers not in the film's original theatrical release.

□ TEARS FOR FEARS
TEARS FOR FEARS VIDEO 45
★★

Sony, 1984, 12 minutes

PRODUCED BY: Tony Hazell and Siobhan Barron

DIRECTED BY: Clive Richardson and Steve Barron

MUSIC FROM: The Hurting (Mercury, 1983).

SELECTIONS: "Mad World," "Change," "Pale Shelter."

Also available on Pioneer 8-inch Stereo Laser Videodisc.

These three clips were made before Tears for Fears became an international pop phenomenon with 1984's *Songs from the Big Chair.* As videos, that may be the most interesting thing about them. "Change" and "Pale Shelter" are fine musical works, with the band's typical lapidary arrangements applied to cinematic melds of minimalist trance-music (e.g., the marimba ostinatos in "Change") and cerebral art-pop. But the videos are all totally dispensable: "Mad World" is a dumbly literal illustration of its postmodern anomie theme; "Change" and "Pale Shelter" are annoyingly irrelevant mélanges of meaningless imagery (not unlike the later "Everybody Wants to Rule the World"). But then, the songs aren't really *about* anything aside from Tears for Fears principals Curt Smith and Roland Orzabal's own maundering auto-analysis. Perhaps directors Clive Richardson and Steve Barron (who have both done outstanding work elsewhere) should have been inspired to flights of complementary abstract imagery of a breadth and power commensurate with the admittedly fine music (music as opposed to lyrics, that is). But it didn't happen. Ignore this and stick with the records; even Tears for Fears fans would have to find these clips totally forgettable.

□ TEARS FOR FEARS
SCENES FROM THE BIG CHAIR
★★½

RCA/Columbia, 1985, 78 minutes

PRODUCED BY: Nigel Dick and Sarah de V. Wills

DIRECTED BY: Nigel Dick

MUSIC FROM: Songs from the Big Chair (Polygram, 1985).

SELECTIONS: "Broken" (two versions), "Everybody Wants to Rule the World" (two versions), "Shout" (two versions), "Head Over Heels," "Listen," "Memories Fade," "The Hurting," "Mothers Talk," "I Believe," "The Working Hour."

It's really just a reward-for-record-sales vanity production, but this mix of conceptual video clips and concert footage from America and Europe (their biggest hits, "Shout" and "Everybody Wants to Rule the World," appear in both live and concept-clip versions), interviews, and on-the-road documentary is nicely produced. Bandleaders Curt Smith and Roland Orzabal (with a few other band members chiming in from time to time) discuss the band's formation and how they write songs. But they come across as smug, self-involved eggheads, devoid of personality—fitting, given their unexciting stage show and (except for the affecting romantic comedy of "Head Over Heels") vapid videos. Still, their dullness is surprising, given the professed roots of their lushly orchestrated art-rock in the emotional catharsis of Jungian therapy. For fans only.

□ RICHARD TEE
CONTEMPORARY PIANO
★★★★

DCI, 1983, 60 minutes
PRODUCED BY: Rob Wallis and Paul Siegel
DIRECTED BY: Rob Wallis and Paul Siegel
MUSIC FROM: Various albums by various artists, and various jams and demonstrations by Richard Tee.
SELECTIONS: "Nothing from Nothing," "Deep Purple," "Happy Birthday," "Take the 'A' Train," "My Little Brother."

Tee is one of the world's busiest session pianists, and has backed artists from Aretha Franklin to Paul Simon since the early '60s. Here, he demonstrates and discusses practice techniques, chord substitutions, left-hand technique, how to back a vocalist, how to play in studio sessions (keep your head up and your eyes on the other players as well as on the charts); he jams on "Take the 'A' Train" and "My Little Brother" with super-drummer Steve Gadd, and does "Happy Birthday" in both a Ray Charles funky-blues vein *and* in perfect boogie-woogie time. As with just about every DCI instructional video, Tee comes across not as a paranoid pro zealously guarding his tricks of the trade, but as a wonderfully open guy who's a natural teacher, only too happy to share his knowledge and insights. (Available by mail order from DCI Music Video.)

□ 10CC
LIVE IN CONCERT
★ ½

Media, 1985, 60 minutes
DIRECTED BY: Bruce Gowers
MUSIC FROM: Various 10cc albums, including *Greatest Hits, 1972–78* (Mercury, 1979).
SELECTIONS: "Wall Street Shuffle," "Good Morning Judge, " "The Things We Do for Love," "Feel the Benefit," "People in Love," "So Long," "Rendezvous," "I'm Not in Love," "She's Gone," "She's Gone (reprise)."

From 1973 to 1976, the British pop band 10cc was known for extremely precious, archly black-humored songs like "Rubber Bullets," a sick joke about a prison riot in the U.K. (Speaking of sick humor, the band's name was a joking reference to the 9 cc of semen ejaculated by the average male.) When their self-consciously clever half, Kevin Godley and Lol Creme, left to become a recording and video-directing duo, the other original members, Eric Stewart and Graham Gouldman, took over—and from its earlier smart-ass annoyances, 10cc turned around to become insufferably cloying and fatuous. This before-and-after difference is on dramatic display here. Just compare their two biggest hits, the Godley-Creme era "I'm Not in Love" and the Stewart-Gouldman "The Things We Do for Love": the former is devastatingly ironic in its analysis of our emotional defense mechanisms. and ingenious in its use of studio technology; the latter is puppy-eyed fluff. The rest of the tunes in this 1977 show at London's Hammersmith Odeon are even less inspiring; the one other Godley-Creme-era song, "Wall Street Shuffle," seems like sheer genius by comparison to Stewart-Gouldman's twee sludge. The band's playing and stage presence, as well as Bruce Gowers's direction, are bland, and the concert itself is underlit and washed-out looking (fitting, that). Of historical interest: snippets of 10cc's early music videos for "Good Morning Judge," "Feel the Benefit," and "I'm Not in Love" are intercut with their live renderings.

□ TEST DEPT.
PROGRAM FOR PROGRESS
★★½

Sony, 1986, 43 minutes
PRODUCED BY: Test Dept.
DIRECTED BY: Brett Turnbull, Barclay/Delaney Productions, Angle/O'Toole Productions
MUSIC FROM: Various Test Dept. records and videos (Some Bizarre, 1984-86).
SELECTIONS: "Cold Witness," "Shockwork," "Compulsion," "The Fall from Light," "Total State Machine," "Mirbach," "Inheritance," "V.F.M."

Test Dept. isn't so much a "band" as a collective of six British avant-garde performance artists who "explore past and future rhythms—testing the bounds of endurance, creating new strength—through the use of percussion, voice, bugle, film, still photography, and video," as the cassette liner notes put it (the notes also ask, "Is it progress if a cannibal uses a knife and fork?"). Their "music" consists of stray noises, simple tribal drumming, clanging "industrial" percussion (as in what sounds like the banging of pipes, sheet metal, and the like), hoarse collective and individual chanting, and tape/electronic effects. The visuals range from very seriously provocative and discomfiting bondage/S&M footage edited together in a most artful semi-abstract way (in "Compulsion") to very "industrial" stuff, whether urban/factory photos or ominous Devo-like shots of androgynous young men working heavy machinery with blank industriousness ("Cold Witness," "Shockwork"), to media-guerilla video collages. This stuff is very weird, very disturbing—cryptic it may be, and perhaps to an unbearably self-conscious degree, yet much of it (especially "The Fall from Light" and "Total State Machine") is potent enough that it stays with you. Heck, this is bizarre even for *me.* Proceed with caution, folks.

□ VARIOUS ARTISTS
THANK GOD IT'S FRIDAY
★½

RCA/Columbia, 1979, 90 minutes
PRODUCED BY: Rob Cohen
DIRECTED BY: Robert Klane
MUSIC FROM: Thank God It's Friday original soundtrack album (Casablanca, 1978).
SELECTIONS: Donna Summer: "Love to Love You Baby," "Try with Your Love," "Last Dance," "Je T'aime"; Commodores: "Brick House," "Easy," "Too Hot ta Trot"; Cameo: "Find My Way," "It's Serious"; Fifth Dimension: "You're the Person I Feel Like Dancing With"; Thelma Houston: "Love Masterpiece," "I'm Here Again"; Paul Jabara: "Disco Queen," "Trapped in a Stairway"; Love and Kisses: "Thank God It's Friday."

This one-night-in-the-life-of-Hollywood's-least-inhibited-fictional-disco epic was a box-office flop that was also universally dismissed by critics as a piece of garbage. Why? Because it is a piece of garbage, plain and simple, as monotonously ground-out as the assembly-line dance music that made reactionary rock fans start the "Disco Sucks" movement. It is of some historical value, though, for its pre–greater fame glimpses of the Commodores with Lionel Richie, and stars Debra Winger, Jeff Goldblum (later to appear in *The Big Chill* and *The Fly*), and Terri Nunn (a soap opera refugee who would go on to form the execrable synth-pop band Berlin). Donna Summer, who was already a disco diva at the time, is still as wooden as always.

☐ VARIOUS ARTISTS
THAT WAS ROCK
★★★★★

Media, 1984, 90 minutes
PRODUCED BY: Lee Savin and Phil Spector
DIRECTED BY: Steve Binder and Larry Peerce
MUSIC FROM: The T.A.M.I. Show (1964); *The Big T.N.T. Show* (1965).
SELECTIONS: Chuck Berry: "Maybellene," "Sweet Little Sixteen," "Nadine"; James Brown: "Out of Sight," "Night Train"; Ray Charles: "Georgia on My Mind," "Let the Good Times Roll"; Bo Diddley: "Hey Bo Diddley," "The Beat"; Marvin Gaye: "Stubborn Kind of Fellow," "Pride and Joy," "Can I Get a Witness," "Hitch Hike"; Smokey Robinson and the Miracles: "That's What Love Is Made Of," "You Really Got a Hold on Me," "Mickey's Monkey"; the Rolling Stones: "Around and Around," "Off the Hook," "Time Is on My Side," "It's All Over Now," "I'm Alright"; the Ronettes: "Be My Baby," "Shout"; the Supremes: "Baby Love," "Where Did Our Love Go"; Ike and Tina Turner: "A Fool in Love," "Please, Please, Please," "Goodbye, So Long"; Lesley Gore: "Maybe I Know," "You Don't Own Me"; Jan and Dean: "Sidewalk Surfin' "; Gerry and the Pacemakers: "Maybellene."

An awesome compendium of great performances, culled from two mid-'60s rock-and-soul cavalcade-of-stars teen-flicks, *The T.A.M.I. Show* and *The Big T.N.T. Show.* You get Chuck Berry, James Brown, Ray Charles, Bo Diddley, Marvin Gaye, Smokey Robinson and the Miracles, the baby-faced Rolling Stones, the Ronettes, the Supremes, and Ike and Tina Turner, all in vintage form before live audiences of screaming kids who probably didn't even know just how lucky they were. It's virtually all highlights; even Lesley Gore provides a proto-feminist revelation with "You Don't Own Me." The only valleys among these peaks are Gerry and the Pacemakers and Jan and Dean—so why, oh why, did they have to drop James Brown's incredible cape-routine "Please, Please, Please" from *The T.A.M.I. Show* for this tape? That's the only complaint.

☐ ED THIGPEN
ON JAZZ DRUMMING
★★★★

DCI, 1983, 60 minutes
PRODUCED BY: Rob Wallis and Paul Siegel
DIRECTED BY: Rob Wallis and Paul Siegel

Thigpen's an outstanding, New York–based veteran jazz drummer who's long been accomplished in a wide variety of musical settings. Here, he takes you from the very basics of jazz drumming to the importance of the bass drum in jazz (something very easy to overlook for rock drummers who think "jazz" drumming is no more than bebop hi-hat/ride cymbal triplets), from jazz ride cymbal patterns to how to phrase fills both in time and against the rhythm. He also covers melodic approaches to creating fills and accompaniments, and gets very deeply into brush technique. And he covers everything very well indeed. (Available by mail order from DCI Music Video.)

☐ .38 SPECIAL
WILD-EYED AND LIVE
★★½

A&M, 1984, 75 minutes
PRODUCED BY: Picture Music International
DIRECTED BY: Jim Yukich
MUSIC FROM: Rockin' into the Night (A&M, 1979); *Wild-Eyed Southern Boys* (A&M, 1981); *Special Forces* (A&M, 1982); and other .38 Special albums.

SELECTIONS: "Take 'Em Out," "Back on the Track," "Rough-Housin'," "Stone Cold Believer," "Caught Up in You," "Wild-Eyed Southern Boys," "Chain Lightnin'," "Undercover Lover," "Back Where You Belong," "If I'd Been the One," "Twentieth Century Fox," "Hold On Loosely," "I Been a Mover," "Rockin' into the Night."

Standard concert-shoot of modern-day Southern boogie-rock band (modern means they have *three* guitars instead of two for those sweet sustained harmonies, and are capable of corporate-pop as well as the usual yee-haw rifferama) led by Donnie Van Zandt, brother of Lynyrd Skynyrd's late Ronnie. Caught on their 1984 U.S. tour at Nassau Coliseum on Long Island, New York, .38 Special are competent at what they do—especially their recent, more melodic, hit-bound numbers, like "Hold On Loosely," "If I'd Been the One," "Caught Up in You," and "Back Where You Belong"—although their double drummers are so redundant it gets kind of hilarious after a while. But there's nothing here to appeal to anyone but a .38 Special fan.

□ RICHARD THOMPSON
ACROSS A CROWDED ROOM

★★★★½

Sony, 1985, 84 minutes
PRODUCED BY: Steven J. Swartz
DIRECTED BY: Larry Jordan
MUSIC FROM: I Want to See the Bright Lights Tonight (Island, 1974); *Pour Down Like Silver* (Island, 1975); *Shoot Out the Lights* (Hannibal, 1982); *Hand of Kindness* (Hannibal, 1983); *Across a Crowded Room* (Polydor, 1985).
SELECTIONS: "Fire in the Engine Room," "She Twists the Knife Again," "Shoot Out the Lights," "You Don't Say," "Wall of Death," "Little Blue Number," "When the Spell Is Broken," "Did She Jump or Was She Pushed," "Wrong Heartbeat," "Summer Rain," "For Shame of Doing Wrong," "Bright Lights Tonight," "Nearly in Love," "Love in a Faithless Country," "I Ain't Gonna Drag My Feet No More," "Tear Stained Letter," "Living with a Skull and Cross Bone," "Withered and Died."

For years, Thompson has been the object of rabid critical adulation, and one of the best things about this outstanding concert program is that it so clearly, thoroughly, and powerfully documents why. Larry Jordan's tastefully apt direction indicates he's studied Thompson's music closely—and the payoff is, it's music well worth repeated listenings, which of course strengthens the repeatability of this program. As the amazingly wide selection of his songs proves, Thompson is a unique, gifted, and accomplished artist, crafting a taut, elegant fusion of English folk and rock to carry his bitter, penetratingly fatalistic observations on life, love, and spirituality. He's also one *hell* of a brilliant guitarist, *and* a quietly intense, intelligent figure onstage, as intriguing as his music is gripping. Thompson acknowledges the harrowing emotional intensity of his songs only occasionally, and with small, subtle gestures—which Jordan's cameras always catch.

□ THOMPSON TWINS
SIDEKICKS THE MOVIE: LIVE IN LIVERPOOL

★½

HBO/Cannon, 1983, 60 minutes
DIRECTED BY: Derek Burbidge
MUSIC FROM: In the Name of Love (Arista, 1982); *Side Kicks* (Arista, 1983).
SELECTIONS: "Kamikaze," "Love Lies Bleeding," "Judy Do," "Tears," "Watching," "If You Were Here," "All Fall Out," "Lucky Day," "Lies," "Detectives," "In the Name of Love," "Beach Culture," "Love on Your Side."

This concert video was recorded at the Royal Court Theater in Liverpool, England, in 1983, before the Thompson Twins became an international success with the album *Into the Gap* and its hit single "Hold Me Now." For those unfamiliar with the band's pre-celebrity sound, here it is: much more jagged, percussive, and funk-oriented than their subsequent ultrasmooth pop. Thompson Twins fans converted by the hits may be interested in checking out this straightforwardly shot program; come to think of it, those who *hate* the band's hit-making sound might also find this earlier material worthy of a look-hear. Then again, they might not; I don't much care for *any* of their music, yet I love "In the Name of Love," an early single that remains a solid chunk of polyrhythmically funky new-wave dance rock. However, only a confirmed fan could put up with much of the band's stage presence—or, in the cases of tiresomely poker-faced leader Tom Bailey and dreadlocked-and-dour Joe Leeway (who left the band in the spring of 1986), lack thereof. Percussionist Alannah Currie, on the other hand, is simply strident to the point of being obnoxious.

□ THOMPSON TWINS
INTO THE GAP LIVE

★

RCA/Columbia, 1985, 80 minutes
PRODUCED BY: Scott Millaney and Frank Hilton
DIRECTED BY: Dee Trattmann
MUSIC FROM: Into the Gap (Arista, 1984) and other Thompson Twins albums.
SELECTIONS: "The Gap," "Hold Me Now," "Doctor, Doctor," "Love on Your Side."

Even Thompson Twins fans may find this hard to endure. From the first few minutes of on-the-road documentary-style footage, you get the idea that life for the group is hell. They're making tons of money and seem to have a good enough time onstage, but Tom is complaining about how journalists don't really have lots of creative ideas (some songwriters have the same problem, Tom), and then there's Alannah crying her eyes out because being on the bus all the time is such a drag. Boo-hoo. Too bad they didn't just stay home. If this California show is any indication of how boring this trio is onstage (you may feel differently if watching three hideously dressed ragamuffins aerobicize while kinda playing some instruments is your idea of fun), and if the crowd's rabid reactions say anything about how dearly they love the Twins, well, they deserve each other. You may have seen this on MTV, where it has aired in the past.—P.R.

□ THROBBING GRISTLE
LIVE AT KEZAR

★★½

Target, 1983, 60 minutes
PRODUCED BY: Joe Rees
DIRECTED BY: Joe Rees
MUSIC FROM: Mission of Dead Souls (Fetish UK, 1981).
SELECTIONS: "Dead Dog," "Freelink," "Stadium of Dead Souls," "Persuasion," "Discipline."

□ THROBBING GRISTLE
RECORDING HEATHEN EARTH/ LIVE AT OUNDLE SCHOOL

★★

Factory/Doublevision, 1984, 120 minutes
MUSIC FROM: Heathen Earth (Industrial UK, 1980).

Throbbing Gristle, a British punk-era performance-art ensemble *cum* avant-rock band, had gained an imposing reputation for experimental provocation by the time they made this, their only U.S. performance (and their final performance period), in 1981 at Kezar Stadium (!), home to San Francisco's football 49ers. Before a crowd of more than fifteen hundred, Throbbing Gristle—Genesis P-Orridge (bass, vocals), Peter Christopher (drum machines and tapes), Chris Carter (synthesizer), and a woman called Cosey Fanny Tutti (inaudible slide guitar)—stand about in more or less static diffidence, producing a blurping, buzzing sludge of rhythmic, atonal noise comprised of drum-machine patterns, synth-blips and whizzes, live percussion, and other instrumental sounds that are electronically modified virtually beyond recognition, as well as an assortment of vocal sounds (screams, moans, mumbled recitations, even the occasional attempt at "singing") that are also echoed and distorted, much in the manner of vocalist/performance artist Diamanda Galas, who does a more artfully controlled job of it on her Target Video cassette *The Litanies of Satan.* While the crowd seems suitably entranced throughout, it's not until the halfway mark that we get anything remotely resembling actual "music": "Persuasion," an ostensible diatribe against the manipulative fascism of advertising and politics, has P-Orridge talk-singing effectively over a single loud, recurring bass note, and "Discipline," which works the crowd into a swaying, chanting frenzy, finds P-Orridge finally leaving his impassive position behind the microphone to prowl the front of the stage screaming, "I want discipline!" over and over and over above a relentless, compelling electro-pulse, kneeling and then writhing at the front of the stage, letting audience members grab the microphone and "play" his bass, and at one point kissing what appears to be a balding clone on the top of his head, and then on the mouth.

That is by far the highlight of what amounts to a rather disappointing show, given the expectations (not to mention the fact that according to the Target Video catalogue, Throbbing Gristle call this their best live show ever). Not much else happens, really, and the sound through the first half of the program is extremely erratic. Since Throbbing Gristle's motto was "entertainment through pain," they may well have meant to bore, distract, and so on. Still, those who happened to be there, and anyone else who simply *has* to see what a Throbbing Gristle performance looked and sounded like (not to mention those who have only the soundtrack LP), will have to check out this tape. Certainly, Diamanda Galas aside, there's no other concert tape like it, and, sound problems aside, it does a good job of documenting the event. (Available in stores, or by mail order from Target Video or Independent World Video.)

Heathen Earth/Live is pretty much more of the same, albeit in two different locales, the recording studio and an English boys' school. Again, Throbbing Gristle's semi-legendary act appears to consist of doing little or nothing, which may be their more-radical-than-thou way of subverting expectations of radical "happenings" or something. Who knows? Maybe their philosophy is to use boredom as an assaultive weapon. Interesting in theory, perhaps, but not very enjoyable to experience—though the sight of Throbbing Gristle performing their anti-act before a bored/apprehensive/bemused audience of young Limey poofters-to-be does have its perversely intriguing aspects. Still, once more recommendable only to diehards and/or those who simply *must* check out Throbbing Gristle's notorious rep. (Available in stores or by mail order from Factory.)

□ JOHNNY THUNDERS AND THE HEARTBREAKERS

DEAD OR ALIVE

★★½

JEM/Passport, 1986, 45 minutes
PRODUCED BY: Eddie Babbage
DIRECTED BY: Don Letts, Eddie Babbage, Torquil Dearden

MUSIC FROM: New York Dolls (Mercury, 1973); the Heartbreakers: *L.A.M.F.* (Track, 1977); Johnny Thunders: *So Alone* (Real, 1980); Johnny Thunders: *Too Much Junkie Business* (ROIR cassette, 1985).

SELECTIONS: "Chinese Rocks," "Pipeline," "Personality Crisis," "One Track Mind," "Too Much Junkie Business," "Born to Lose," "Hurt Me," "You Can't Put Your Arms Around a Memory," "Eve of Destruction," "Like a Rolling Stone," "In Cold Blood," "Seven Day Weekend," "So Alone," "Just Because I'm White," "Baby Talk," "Do You Love Me," "Sad Vacation."

Led by ex–New York Dolls guitarist Johnny Thunders and drummer Jerry Nolan, the Heartbreakers began with an exhilarating, post–Rolling Stones raunch 'n' roll that helped shape the sound and style of punk. However, by the late '70s they'd become tired failures, a decline Thunders personified with his notorious stumblebum antics of the period (falling offstage or appearing to nod out mid-song, not showing up for gigs, and so on). What a waste. Even worse, this tape captures the band several years after *that,* in a 1984 London show reuniting the original members (guitarist Walter Lure and bassist Billy Rath fill out the band). Sadly, they look and sound much like the has-beens they in fact were at the time, playing their still-great material with barely any spark or energy; Thunders is still wasted and clumsy. This tragic document is intercut with bits of meaningless interviews with Thunders, equally irrelevant footage of Johnny and his blonde European girlfriend, and too little of Don Letts's intriguing Super 8 footage from the fabled 1976 U.K. punk-rock "Anarchy" tour. The Heartbreakers deserved a better memento than this—but then, they deserved a better *career* than the one they had, too. Still, disappointing as it is, it's probably the only document we'll ever get of an important and once-superb band.

☐ VARIOUS ARTISTS
TIMES SQUARE
★

HBO/Cannon, 1981, 111 minutes

PRODUCED BY: Robert Stigwood and Jacob Brackman

DIRECTED BY: Alan Moyle

MUSIC FROM: Times Square motion picture soundtrack (RSO, 1980); and various albums by various artists.

SELECTIONS: The Cars; "Dangerous Type"; Joe Jackson: "Pretty Boys"; Garland Jeffreys: "Innocent, Not Guilty"; Gary Numan: "Down in the Park"; the Pretenders: "Talk of the Town"; the Ramones: "I Wanna Be Sedated"; Lou Reed: "Walk on the Wild Side"; Roxy Music: "Same Old Scene"; Patti Smith: "Pissing in the River"; Talking Heads: "Life during Wartime"; XTC: "Take this Town."

Stupid, ineptly directed bomb which, along with the even worse *Sgt. Pepper's Lonely Hearts Club Band,* finally did us all the great service of halting the latter phase of rock mogul Robert Stigwood's movie-producing career. Trini Alvarado is modestly effective as a middle-class girl with emotional problems, but Robin Johnson is forcibily obnoxious as the streetwise free spirit with whom she runs away from a hospital. Together, they get by living day-to-day in Manhattan's Times Square, which seems so hospitable here it's downright mind-boggling for anyone who's ever actually been there. Eventually, the duo become a punk rock band called the Sleaze Sisters, and Tim Curry (of *Rocky Horror Picture Show* fame) comes along as a DJ trying to get publicity by rescuing Alvarado from her plight . . . and, well, it just seems endless and never makes any sense and it's just a piece of garbage, basically. There are a lot of good songs, each and every one is sullied a bit by its association with this misbegotten fiasco.

☐ **VARIOUS ARTISTS**
TIMEX ALL STAR JAZZ SHOW
★★½

Video Yesteryear, 1980, 60 minutes
MUSIC FROM: TV special (CBS, 1958).
SELECTIONS: Louis Armstrong: "Tiger Rag"; other titles not listed, but performers include: Duke Ellington Orchestra, Dizzy Gillespie, George Shearing, Gene Krupa, Jo Jones, Roy Eldridge, Bobby Hackett, Coleman Hawkins, Vic Dickenson, Milt Hinton.

Jazz-jam spectacular, circa 1958, hosted by Jackie Gleason and with John Cameron Swayze announcing. While details are few and Video Yesteryear refuses to provide review copies, their catalogue promises a duet between Louis Armstrong and Dizzy Gillespie, and a no-holds-barred extended closing jam—which, with names like Jo Jones, Milt Hinton, Vic Dickenson, Coleman Hawkins, and Roy Eldridge listed, could be seriously worth a look by any self-respecting jazz fan. Video Yesteryear does, however, warn that the visual quality of the kinescope leaves something to be desired.

☐ MEL TORME
THE MEL TORME SPECIAL
★★★

Sony, 1983, 53 minutes
PRODUCED BY: Steve Michelson
DIRECTED BY: Norm Levy
MUSIC FROM: Various Mel Torme albums.
SELECTIONS: "New York State of Mind," "Here's That Rainy Day," "Bluesette," "Born to Be Blue," "Blues in the Night," "Oh, Lady Be Good," "When Sunny Gets Blue," "Down for Double."

The Velvet Fog in concert, backed by the Mel Lewis jazz orchestra, at the 1982 San Francisco Kool Jazz Festival. There are a few brief interview segments, and for the closing "Down for Double," Mel brings out Jon Hendricks, of the famed jazz vocal group Lambert, Hendricks and Ross, for an extended scat duel. Mel's fans should love this smoothly delivered set of old ("Blues in the Night") and new ("New York State of Mind") standards.

☐ PETER TOSH
PETER TOSH LIVE
★★★½

Sony, 1986, 60 minutes
PRODUCED BY: Michael C. Collins
DIRECTED BY: Michael C. Collins
MUSIC FROM: Equal Rights (Columbia, 1977); *Wanted Dread and Alive* (Rolling Stones, 1981); *Mama Africa* (EMI-America, 1983).
SELECTIONS: "Intro," "Start All Over," "African," "Coming in Hot," "Not Gonna Give It Up," "Rastafari Is," "Where You Gonna Run," "Glass House," "Equal Rights/Downpressor Man," "Johnny B. Goode," "Get Up, Stand Up."

A very nicely shot, admirably straightforward document of reggae star and original Wailer (with Bob Marley) Peter Tosh onstage in Los Angeles in 1983. (A note about this program: It was originally announced and promoted as *Peter Tosh Live in Africa,* and that title appears at the opening of the program—with a large-type "LIVE" superimposed over the small-type "In Africa" on the lower third of the screen.) Tosh enters, to the reggaefied strains of "Hallelujah Chorus," garbed in a hot-pink, patterned burnoose, blinding yellow robe, and shades, a gold scepter in one hand and an enormous spliff billowing marijuana smoke in the other. But even when he doffs the exotic raiments and puts down those other props (well, the spliff never really leaves his hand for too long), Tosh presents an imposing, sometimes even foreboding charisma—forceful, to say the least, but also compelling, at times even commanding.

Here, Tosh may not be playing all of his best material (where, for instance, are "Legalize It" and "Stepping Razor" and "Keep On Walkin' and Don't Look Back" and the juju-reggae fusion of "Mama Africa"?), but he performs with enough conviction to be at or near his best most of the time, and to make much of the material that *is* here sound better than it originally did on record. Though, to be fair, even at their worst Tosh's songs are never less than competent and serviceable, with a unique and pronounced gospel-soul feel (especially in "Start All Over," "Not Gonna Give It Up," and "Glass House"), which adds a welcome flair and distinction to his politicized anthems of Rasta rant 'n' cant, and harks back to the sound and the roots of the original Wailers. Meanwhile, Tosh's Word, Sound and Power band, featuring Donald Kinsey on guitar and Carlton "Santa" Davis on drums, plays like a very well-oiled reggae machine throughout.

The highlight is "Rastafari Is," a beatific reggae rhapsody that combines Afro-polyrhythmic percussion with an affectingly folksy hymnal feel, much in the manner of those comparatively obscure roots-reggae Rastafarian spiritual sects from Jamaica's mysterious hills, Count Ossie and the Mystic Revelations of Rastafari, and Ras Michael and the Sons of Negus. It's strikingly beautiful music, and performing it, the exceedingly tough-looking Tosh takes on a genuinely sweet, gentle humility. Sure, that spliff he's still puffing must make him feel plenty beatific and spiritual all right, but the fact is that he delivers an intense rendering of a moving piece of music. His version of "Johnny B. Goode" is a nice one, but after "Rastafari Is," it's anticlimactic.

□ PETE TOWNSHEND
PETE TOWNSHEND VIDEO EP
★★

Sony, 1983, 30 minutes

PRODUCED BY: Genevieve Daley

DIRECTED BY: Chalkie Davies and Carol Starr

MUSIC FROM: All the Best Cowboys Have Chinese Eyes (Atco, 1982).

SELECTIONS: "Prelude," "Face Dances, Part Two, " "Communication," "Stardom in Action," "Exquisitely Bored," "Slit Skirts," "Uniforms."

Townshend is not only one of rock's most accomplished artists, but also one of its most articulate and intelligent. But sometimes even the most intelligent people can *think too much* and get lost up their own arseholes, as the British would say. That's just what happens to Townshend in this half-hour interview-and-video-clips special, originally produced for MTV to promote *All the Best Cowboys Have Chinese Eyes.* Unfortunately, this mostly manic-depressive series of musings on the themes of aging, alienation, and the exigencies of rock's star-making machinery was one of Townshend's weaker efforts. "Slit Skirts," the LP's only (minor) hit, is by far the best song, and that isn't saying much for a guy who has composed more classics than many. The videos, by and large, are as unspectacular as the music. "Uniforms" is a heavy-handed commentary on Britain's social class system, with Townshend as a harried waiter in a country club, serving a dining room full of richly attired mannequins. "Stardom in Action" may be the best of this mediocre lot, as the man who once wrote, "Hope I die before I get old" is seen as an old (old*er,* at least) man encountering some young punks on the streets of London (Townshend seems obsessed with this theme; it cropped up again later in his "Rough Boys" clip). All in all, the songs and their accompanying videos really have little to say, at least little that isn't self-consciously depressing on Pete's part.

The same goes for Townshend's interviews, in which he rambles on darkly about his recent heavy bout with alcoholism and its untoward effects on himself and his family (he might have added his music, judging by the songs here). You can't ridicule a man for surviving such an ordeal, of course. But you *can* be put off by a program that appears to use such a human-interest angle to promote a record album that sounds uninspired and overdone (surprisingly so, given Townshend's life at the time). Unless, that is, you're *such* a Who/Townshend fan you simply *have* to have this. If so, then here you are. Others will want to reach into the TV screen, shake Pete a bit, and tell him things aren't *that* bad.

□ PETE TOWNSHEND
WHITE CITY
★★½

Vestron, 1985, 60 minutes
PRODUCED BY: Michael Hamlyn and Walter Donohue
DIRECTED BY: Richard Lowenstein
MUSIC FROM: White City (Atco, 1985).
SELECTIONS: "Give Blood," "Face the Face," "Secondhand Love," "Crashing by Design," "I Am Secure," "Night School."

Townshend's one of the smartest guys in rock, but he can also be among the most pretentious—as in this ambitious but flawed attempt at neo–kitchen-sink realism, which also hamfistedly tries to be no less than a revisionist critique of kitchen-sink realism. Townshend revisits the pre–WWII low-income-housing ghetto of the title, near which he was raised; observations of some of its present-day denizens (nicely played by Andrew Wilde and Frances Barber) are mixed with flashbacks into their childhoods. Despite Richard Lowenstein's accomplished if arty direction, and Townshend's obviously good intentions, it ends up going nowhere, and is more pretentious than substantial (Townshend subtitled the equally slight accompanying album—which does *not* match the video tune-for-tune—"a novel"). In fact, it's so muddled Townshend apparently felt compelled to tack on a quick interview after the program itself, attempting to explain it. Also added on is a video clip of "Night School" (not on the LP either) being recorded in the studio.

□ PETE TOWNSHEND
PETE TOWNSHEND'S DEEP END
★★★★

Atlantic, 1986, 86 minutes
PRODUCED BY: Harvey Weinstein and Bill Curbishley
DIRECTED BY: Keith "Keef" MacMillan
MUSIC FROM: Various albums by Pete Townshend, the Who, and others.
SELECTIONS: "Won't Get Fooled Again," "Little Is Enough," "Secondhand Love," "Behind Blue Eyes," "Barefootin'," "After the Fire," "Love on the Air," "I Put a Spell on You," "I'm One," "Magic Bus," "Save It for Later," "Eyesight to the Blind," "Walkin'," "Stop Hurting People," "The Sea Refuses No River," "Face the Face," "Pinball Wizard," "Give Blood."

□ PETE TOWNSHEND
PETE TOWNSHEND'S DEEP END MINI CONCERT
★★★½

Atlantic, 1986, 29 minutes
PRODUCED BY: Harvey Weinstein and Bill Curbishley
DIRECTED BY: Keith "Keef" MacMillan
MUSIC FROM: Various albums by Pete Townshend and the Who.
SELECTIONS: "Won't Get Fooled Again," "Little Is Enough," "Stop Hurting People," "Face the Face," "Give Blood."

As uneven as *White City* is, and as depressing as the *Video EP* can be, that's how strong *Deep End* is. Shot at an early 1986 concert (shortly after the release of the *White City* album) in London's depressed Brixton area, Townshend and a sixteen-piece band deliver a strong set of Townshend and Who tunes, and intriguingly chosen, well-executed covers, with super-slick competence tempered by red-hot urgency. And it's all captured with perfectly placed cameras and perfectly paced edits by rock video pioneer Keith "Keef" MacMillan, who turns in what may be the best work of his long career. Townshend plays acoustic guitar throughout; his band features Pink Floyd's David Gilmour on guitar, and fusion ace Simon Phillips on drums, as well as a female percussionist, two female and three male backing singers, a five-piece horn section, bass, and keyboards. The set kicks off with an excellent version of the Who classic "Won't Get Fooled Again," with the first half folkishly rearranged in solo-acoustic fashion. From there, Townshend's eclectic mix of cosmopolitan pop rock and passionate bluesiness rarely lets up (and consistently sounds far better live than on record). One forgivable mistake is playing "Behind Blue Eyes" *à la* the *Who's Next* original, for despite Phillips's ambidexterous, clean-machine flash, it misses Keith Moon's careening explosions.

The first half of the concert—through Gilmour's "Love on the Air," which he sings, and including "After the Fire," which Roger Daltrey recorded and which Townshend introduces as being written for Live Aid—is merely fine. But starting with a nicely restrained "I Put a Spell on You" that takes the camp out of the Screamin' Jay Hawkins original and replaces it with classy blues power, it becomes irresistibly intense. Townshend's solo acoustic "I'm One" and "Magic Bus" (with the crowd responding to Townshend's calls on the latter, while he does those classic windmill-strums on his amplified acoustic), and the mostly solo acoustic cover of the English Beat's "Save It for Later," are all sublime. An authentic, tough Chicago blues recasting of *Tommy*'s "Eyesight to the Blind" is introduced marvelously by Townshend, who apes Bruce Springsteen's overdone onstage intros of Clarence Clemons by screaming, "Ladies and gentlemen, the master of the universe—the *Little Man!*" and grabbing his diminutive, skinheaded harmonica player. Towshend is in such unusually good humor he even does some loose-limbed jive dancing while the band cruises assuredly through Miles Davis's "Walkin'." "Stop Hurting People" is a particular highlight, as Townshend talk-sings compellingly over an inexorable Latin-jazz-rock vamp. And the pounding "Face the Face," solo acoustic "Pinball Wizard" (the crowd again answering "I don't know" to Townshend's "How do you think he does it?"), and ringingly authentic breakneck "Give Blood" make for an appropriately rousing finale. The *Mini Concert* version is fine, too, but leaves out too much great material.

□ HAPPY TRAUM
LEARNING TO FINGERPICK

★★★★

Homespun, 1984, 60 minutes
PRODUCED BY: Happy Traum
DIRECTED BY: Happy Traum
SELECTIONS: "Buffalo Gals," "Spike Driver's Blues," "Nine Pound Hammer," and others.

□ HAPPY TRAUM
LEARNING TO FLATPICK

★★★★

Homespun, 1984, 60 minutes
PRODUCED BY: Happy Traum
DIRECTED BY: Happy Traum

SELECTIONS: "All the Good Times," "Wildwood Flower," "East Virginia," and others.

Traum, a highly respected acoustic folk guitarist, has been residing in Woodstock, New York, for some time now, where he performs and records with his brother Artie and others. He also runs the aptly named Homespun Tapes—which, along with Hot Licks, Star Licks, and Drummer's Collective's DCI Video, has been responsible for some very fine work in that most obviously functional area of home music video, instructional programs. Homespun Tapes are low-key, warm, intimate, friendly, unpretentious, kinda laid-back . . . you know, homespun. And very good, too, with learned players providing articulate insight into the sorts of folk-music techniques one might not expect to be documented in this new medium. In these programs with Happy himself, what you see in the title is exactly what you get—and though the production values are so homey they almost seem low budget, Traum always takes care to use close-ups and split-screens perfectly, not just supplementing but focusing and amplifying his easy-going show-and-tell teaching. *Learning to Fingerpick* focuses on coordinating the right hand to play steady bass with the thumb while picking out a syncopated melody with the fingers. *Learning to Flatpick* is a great introduction to country and bluegrass styles for the beginner, dealing in detail with bass runs and hammer-ons as well as complete melodies, scalar runs, and pick-holding techniques.

☐ PAT TRAVERS
JUST ANOTHER KILLER DAY
★½

RCA/Columbia, 1984, 30 minutes
PRODUCED BY: Len Epand
DIRECTED BY: Various
MUSIC FROM: Hot Shot (Polydor, 1984).
SELECTIONS: "Killer," "Women on the Edge of Love," "Louise," "Hot Shot."

Journeyman heavy-metal guitarist/singer Travers finds himself in the middle of an all-too-typical hard-rock daydream of a narrative concept here: "sex sirens" from outer space have come to Earth in search of rock, since music cannot be heard in public on their planet. Of course, the "sex sirens" are as coldly, arrogantly sexy and ominously Amazonian as your typical heavy-metal video babes, and the concept is as dumb, dumb, dumb as in any such heavy-metal clip. But even worse, the execution of the moronic concept is incompetent in terms of acting and scripting, it's hard to figure out just what the heck is going on most of the time, and even harder to care. Perhaps worst of all—since only those who are fans of Travers's music are likely to be drawn to this swill anyway—the concept goes nowhere, except right in the way of the music most of the time.

☐ VARIOUS ARTISTS
A TRIBUTE TO BILLIE HOLIDAY
★★★

Media, 1980, 57 minutes
PRODUCED BY: Don St. James
DIRECTED BY: Don St. James
MUSIC FROM: Various albums by various artists; TV concert special (1979).
SELECTIONS: Morgana King: "As Time Goes By," "Easy Livin' "; Carmen McRae: "Good Morning, Heartache," "Miss Brown to You"; Esther Phillips: "Lover Man," "I Ain't Good Lookin' "; Nina Simone: "I Loves You, Porgy," "Glad to Be Unhappy," "I Can't Face the Music"; Maxine Weldon: "Sometimes I'm Happy," "When the Sun Comes Out"; King, McRae, Phillips, Simone, Weldon: "God Bless the

Child"; Billie Holiday: "Lost Man Blues," "God Bless the Child."

Despite the usual so-so TV-special production values, the bland backing of the Ray Ellis Orchestra, and a comparatively slow start with Maxine Weldon and Morgana King, this program isn't half-bad. Sure, none of the five admittedly fine-or-better singers on hand at this 1979 Hollywood Bowl concert is truly comparable to Billie—and the too-brief snippets of Billie singing in movies from 1935 and 1950 hammer the point home—but then who is? Nina Simone stands out with her usual commanding intensity, Esther Phillips turns in an at times hair-raising impression of the real thing, and Carmen McRae is just plain good. Put all that—which is really more a solid display of good jazz singing than an actual tribute—together with those cherishable clips of Lady Day herself, and you've got a program that's more than worth it.

□ TRIUMPH
LIVE AT THE US FESTIVAL
★★½

MCA, 1986, 67 minutes
PRODUCED BY: Steve Sterling
DIRECTED BY: Ed Acita, Don Allen, and Mark Rezyka
MUSIC FROM: Rock 'n' Roll Machine (RCA, 1979); *Just a Game* (RCA, 1979); *Allied Forces* (RCA, 1980); and other Triumph albums.
SELECTIONS: "Allied Forces," "Lay It on the Line," "Never Surrender," "Magic Power," "World of Fantasy," "Rock and Roll Machine," "When the Lights Go Down," "Fight the Good Fight," "Spellbound," "Follow Your Heart."

Triumph is one of those Canadian AOR-rock bands—in this case a power trio—whose breast-beating, militaristic (check their album titles again) lyrical motifs really *do* flesh out the macho bombast suggested by their silly name (my favorite in this Canucklehead genre has to be Saga—I mean, who's next, Argosy?). But they do have their fans and those hordes ought to enjoy this program, which consists mainly of Triumph blasting out some representative selections under the hot California sun at the 1983 edition of Apple Computers whiz kid Steve Wozniak's US Festival. In concert, guitarist Rik Emmett tends to dominate proceedings with his ultrafacile flash, throwing in all manner of Spanish-classical licks and other fleet-fingered tricks amidst the hard-rock riffs. Emmett and drummer Gil Moore share the vocal duties, and while Moore has the more tolerable voice, neither could be called a genuinely good singer.

The concert portion features loads of quick cutaways to interview comments by band members and US Festival audience members saying whatever comes into their besotted heads. The concert is competently shot (by Ed Acita) in the usual arena-style mix of long-, medium-, and close-up shots and with no fancy edits. Following the concert are two slickly produced video clips: "Follow Your Heart" (directed by Don Allen) captures the band in concert on film and with some special-effects treatments; "Spellbound," with a guest appearance by former *Fridays* noodnik Mark Blankfield, is director Mark Rezyka's ham-fisted attempt at burlesquing the typical sexist femme fatale rock concept video scenario. It ends up every bit as noxiously, predictably misogynist as what it's attempting to parody.

□ THE TUBES
LIVE AT THE GREEK
★★½

Monterey/IVE, 1980, 60 minutes
PRODUCED BY: Jerry Kramer and Gary Rocklen
DIRECTED BY: Jerry Kramer

MUSIC FROM: Remote Control (Capitol, 1979) and other Tubes albums.
SELECTIONS: "Turn Me On," "TV Is King," "Don't Touch Me There," "Love's a Mystery," "What Do You Want from Life," "No Way Out," "Telecide," "White Punks on Dope," "Shout," "Baba O'Riley," "The Kids Are Alright," "Stand Up and Shout."

San Francisco's multimedia rockers are caught live at L.A.'s Greek Theater, promoting their 1979 *Remote Control* album, a rather flaccidly didactic attack on television's control over our lives. Lead singer Fee Waybill, whose demeanor walks the tenuous tightrope between hardworking eager-to-please sincerity and unnerving smarm, rides a Harley with leather-clad singer/dancer Re Styles for the Phil Spector parody "Don't Touch Me There"; gets a TV set stuck on his head for "No Way Out"; and trots out his old glitter-rock caricature Quay Lewd (as in Quaalude, the drug) for an extended encore that includes some Who covers. Meanwhile, the Tubes' music is complex, super-competent, processed-sounding techno-flash generally lacking in any personality or real distinction. For fans only, for the most part.

□ THE TUBES
THE TUBES VIDEO
★★

HBO/Cannon, 1982, 53 minutes
PRODUCED BY: Christine Smyth
DIRECTED BY: Russell Mulcahy
MUSIC FROM: The Completion Backwards Principal (Capitol, 1981).
SELECTIONS: "Sports Fans," "Mr. Hate," "Weebee Dance," "Sushi Girl," "Amnesia," "Talk to Ya Later," "Mondo Bondage," "White Punks on Dope," and others.
Also available on Pioneer Stereo Laser videodisc.

Though ambitious for its time, this album-length series of conceptual videos suffers from crass, vulgar "humor," bland corporate-rock songs (epitomized by the hit "Talk to Ya Later"), a hollow sham of a connecting concept (the "completion backwards principal," whatever that double-talk is supposed to mean), and pioneering rock video *auteur* Russell Mulcahy's garish, overwrought direction. Still, some people really enjoy this kind of stuff. Two genuine points of interest: singer Fee Waybill has the balls to show his during "Sports Fans"; and the tacked-on "White Punks on Dope," from the band's early, semi-subversive media-guerrilla days—a clip that shows just how low the Tubes had sunk by the time of *The Tubes Video.*

□ IKE AND TINA TURNER
THE IKE AND TINA TURNER SHOW
★★★½

Vestron, 1986, 21 minutes
PRODUCED BY: Skip Taylor and John Hartman
DIRECTED BY: Jack Tellander
MUSIC FROM: Various Ike and Tina Turner albums.
SELECTIONS: "Sweet Soul Music," "I Wanna Take You Higher," "Honky Tonk Women," "Everyday People," "I've Been Loving You Too Long," "A Love like Yours," "Proud Mary."

One of the legendary hardworking '60s soul revues caught in 1971 at Caesar's Palace, Las Vegas, before a typically ofay middle-aged crowd that politely applauds after Ike and Tina burn through such smoldering classics as "Proud Mary." Despite such a setting and the extremely crude production values (off-kilter camera angles, erratic focus, clumsy edits—and most songs presented in incomplete versions), this is a fairly invaluable time capsule if only by default, since it is at this writing the sole document of a great, long-gone exemplar of a grand tradition that has all but disappeared today (but for James Brown, *the* hardest-working soul revue around).

What makes this little program so interesting is that along with the performances are some fascinating dressing-room interviews. Onstage, Ike lurks in the background, coolly directing the show, while out front Tina and the three Ikettes, all clad in glittery miniskirts, twirl and frug and shimmy in classic, frenetic '60s dance routines. Ike's wah-wah guitar solo in "I Wanna Take You Higher" isn't the only thing dating the ITT Revue's sound, but they're still undeniably hot, greasy, nasty, and deliciously satisfying.

Offstage, things are rather similar: aside from one jive rap about the "young generation," Ike mostly sits there quietly, imperiously, appearing to patiently indulge Tina as she talks to her makeup mirror with such unpretentious candor she's nearly banal, though disarmingly so. Occasionally, Ike narrows his eyes or raises his eyebrows at her remarks—and, knowing what has since been revealed and/or insinuated about Ike and Tina's tempestuous offstage relationship, it chills the blood a bit. Especially when the program cuts from one such backstage chat to Tina onstage, singing "I've Been Loving You Too Long," already in progress. Tina sings, "I've been loving you too long, I don't wanna stop now"—and, from off-camera, Ike answers in his ominous baritone, "Cos you don't wanna die," lingering over that last word, elongating and rolling it around in his mouth.

Still, the simply awesome "Proud Mary" is almost enough to vanquish the memory of such creepiness, even though the legendary "nice 'n' rough" opening rap is missing (!); during the smoking, upbeat second half, Ike thrillingly interpolates a snatch of "Johnny B. Goode," Tina and the Ikettes whirl about with their hands in the air, and that baritone sax honks and grunts transcendently while the brass shout joyfully. It's wonderful, it's marvelous—it's pure bedrock rock 'n' soul.

□ TINA TURNER
QUEEN OF ROCK 'N' ROLL
★★★

Media, 1982, 60 minutes
PRODUCED BY: Annie Rowe
DIRECTED BY: Steve Turner
MUSIC FROM: Various Tina Turner and Ike and Tina Turner albums.
SELECTIONS: "Nutbush City Limits," "River Deep, Mountain High," "Hot Legs," "Acid Queen," "Fever," "Proud Mary," "The Bitch Is Back," "I Can't Turn You Loose," "Music Keeps Me Dancing," "Don't Leave Me This Way," "Honky Tonk Woman," "Le Freak," "It's Gonna Work Out Fine," "Sometimes When We Touch," "You Don't Bring Me Flowers," "Rock 'n' Roller," "Every 1's a Winner," "Help Me Make It Through the Night," "I Want to Take You Higher," "Disco Fever."

A strange one, this. As a document of post-Ike, pre-comeback Tina, this may rate a slight edge over *Nice 'n' Rough*; where the latter is an intimate, down-and-dirty club date, this an ultraslick, at times nearly tacky, 1982 concert in London—*not* Harlem's legendary Apollo Theater, as it says on the outside jacket. Still, Tina's band and repertoire here are a little sharper and hotter, her dancing a little better too, than in *Nice 'n' Rough,* and it's fascinating fun to see her tackle shlock like "You Don't Bring Me Flowers" and "Sometimes When We Touch" (yes, she almost makes them sound genuinely gritty and urgent!). During a hot medley of "Fever" and the Trammps' classic "Disco Inferno" ("Disco Fever"), Tina strips down from deep-cleavage tiger-striped disco top and gold spandex pants to a black negligee, without missing a beat of her dance routine. She works hard for the money, all right.

□ TINA TURNER
LIVE: NICE 'N' ROUGH
★★★

Thorn–EMI, 1982, 55 minutes
PRODUCED BY: Jacqui Byford
DIRECTED BY: David Mallet
MUSIC FROM: Various Tina Turner albums.
SELECTIONS: "Kill His Wife (Foolish Behavior)," "Tonight's the Night," "Honky Tonk Woman," "Crazy in the Night," "River Deep, Mountain High," "Nutbush City Limits," "Giving It Up for Your Love," "Jumpin' Jack Flash," "It's Only Rock 'n' Roll," "Acid Queen," "Proud Mary," "Hollywood Nights."

This is the pre-comeback Tina, captured on a U.S. tour in 1982: no punked-out wig, a glittery retro gown (and two retro revue-style female dancers) instead of her '80s designer suits, and a repertoire consisting mostly of old covers. But, her gratifying resurgence aside, there's no need to feel bad for "the old Tina" in this program: she was as indomitably proud and smolderingly sexy then as she always has been and still is, and even then she danced and pranced as if she were stamping on cockroaches during an earthquake. Besides, this program opens with a genuine vengeance—the vicious pathology of "Kill His Wife" (especially intriguing given Tina's reportedly tempestuous life with Ike Turner), and a "Honky Tonk Woman" in which Tina role-reverses the lyrics with relish. It doesn't maintain such intensity throughout—things get a bit strange when she takes the classic "River Deep, Mountain High" at half-tempo—but Tina herself sure does. What a trouper (and how nice to see that it all really paid off for her).

□ TINA TURNER
PRIVATE DANCER
★½

Sony, 1985, 17 minutes
PRODUCED BY: Picture Music International
DIRECTED BY: Mark Robinson, Brian Grant, David Mallet
MUSIC FROM: Private Dancer (Capitol, 1984).
SELECTIONS: "What's Love Got to Do with It," "Better Be Good to Me," "Let's Stay Together," "Private Dancer."
Also available on Pioneer 8-inch Stereo Laser videodisc.

□ TINA TURNER
LIVE PRIVATE DANCER TOUR
★★★★

Sony, 1985, 55 minutes
PRODUCED BY: Jacqui Byford
DIRECTED BY: David Mallet
MUSIC FROM: Private Dancer (Capitol, 1984); David Bowie: *Let's Dance* (EMI-America, 1983); *Tonight* (EMI-America, 1985); the Beatles: *Help!* (Capitol, 1965).
SELECTIONS: "Intro," "Show Some Respect," "I Might Have Been Queen," "What's Love Got to Do with It," "I Can't Stand the Rain," "Better Be Good to Me," "Private Dancer," "Let's Stay Together," "Help!," "It's Only Love," "Tonight," "Let's Dance—Versions 1 and 2."
Also available on Pioneer Stereo Laser videodisc.

Private Dancer's four cuts from the comeback album of the same name represent some thrillingly good work by Tina—a pop-soul high priestess at a new peak of power—and her assorted British producers. But the videos themselves are another matter. None is very inspired, one is downright horrible, and all of them suggest that Tina's very persona and hard-earned personal power intimidate the living hell out of video directors. Or, at least, that *something* goes terribly wrong when Tina makes a video. Here you have an extraordinarily strong and beautiful woman of proven, time-tested talents, with an amazing roller-coaster art-and-life story behind her, and she's delivering profound, urgent performances of intense material—what more could you need?

At any rate, Mark Robinson's "What's Love Got to Do with It" plops Tina on the streets of New York, where she observes lovers at play and the like; it skirts the general area of, but ultimately misses the point of, the song's bitterly cynical lyric. Brian Grant's "Better Be Good to Me" is a straightforward performance clip shot in a nightclub, featuring an awkward cameo by guest vocalist Cy Curnin of the Fixx; the performance-clip idea is a good one for Tina, since just showing her in action ought to be enough, but even here Grant stumbles with annoyingly jarring edits and self-consciously "odd" camera angles. David Mallet's "Let's Stay Together" works better as straight-performance: an atomospherically lit Tina performs the slow-burning torch song in front of a whole bunch of what appear to be tuxedoed young upper-class British pretty boys banging on big jungle drums that light up behind her. It's ultimately stiff and silly, but comes just close enough to the moody mark that, combined with the sheer power of the song, it works.

Grant's "Private Dancer," on the other hand, is an unmitigated disaster. Here Tina delivers a transcendently gritty and dignified performance of Mark Knopfler's curiously sensitive gender-fucking lyric, in which a call girl takes stock of herself—and what does Grant do with it? He sets it in Rock Video Cliché Land, with oafishly stilted choreography and moronically tasteless costumes in an attics-of-the-mind "fantasy" set that looks like it was used for a hundred other such embarrassments. Worst of all, it makes Tina look silly, clumsy, and lost. A textbook example of how a music video can ruin a great performance of a good song.

Yes, Tina deserves *much* better—and that goes for all the videos here. Maybe it's her own fault. After all, Tina and/or her management *do,* one supposes, ultimately have to approve these travesties. If so, she's her own worst enemy. Still, *Private Dancer* gets one and a half stars instead of just one because it does show her performing some of her finest music.

Live Private Dancer Tour is the concert video to stick with: it catches Tina in her full glory, and it was shot in England, where one can always count on finding a rapt white audience responding ecstatically to a black American performer. And it's got a couple of big bonuses: Tina duets with Bryan Adams, her opening act on the *Private Dancer* tour, on his composition "It's Only Love," and she duets with David Bowie—a Royal Rock Seal of Approval if ever there was one—on Iggy Pop's dark ballad "Tonight," and on two versions of "Let's Dance," the first Bowie's 1983 chunk of crunching blues-funk, the second Chris Montez's bopping early-'60s classic. Tina is in superb, strutting and snarling form, her band is super tight, and it's directed by David Mallet, whose heavy-handedly spectacular touch here is just right. Anyone viewing this program would almost have to be aware of its significance, to both Tina and the pop world in general; given that, Mallet's constantly swooping cameras and frantically abrupt edits aren't so much jarring as reflective of the excitement spectators at an arena rock show like this must feel. It's not almost like being there, it's better. And when Bowie emerges through dry-ice fog from the back of the stage to join Tina, and the crowd roars, it's an unforgettable moment that's captured beautifully.

□ TUXEDOMOON
FOUR MAJOR EVENTS
★★

Target, 1984, approximately 50 minutes
PRODUCED BY: Joe Rees
DIRECTED BY: Joe Rees
MUSIC FROM: Half-Mute (Ralph, 1980) and other Tuxedomoon singles, EPs and albums.
SELECTIONS: "Jinx," "Stranger," "What Use," "59 to 1," "Desire," and several others not identified.

San Francisco's cerebral post–new wave art-rock band Tuxedomoon is captured here in excerpts from performances in Paris, Rotterdam, and San Francisco. Their music is a decidedly avant-garde and at times atonal and arhythmic mélange of electronics, violin, saxophone, vaguely recognizable electronically modified guitars and keyboards, and Winston Tong's vocals, which alternate between the tormented and the expressionless. Most of the time, Target Video's Joe Rees mixes static, underlit, electronically treated performance footage, including a lot of slow-motion and slightly out-of-focus extreme close-ups, with computer graphics and various superimposition and solarization effects to form an abstract visual montage. It's offbeat, but not too inviting or very exciting. Very definitely an acquired taste, and a program that should appeal only to those who've already acquired it. (Available in stores, or by mail order from Target Video or Independent World Video.)

□ 23 SKIDOO
SEVEN SONGS/TRANQUILISER
★★½

Factory/Doublevision, 1983, 60 minutes
PRODUCED BY: Richard Helsop
DIRECTED BY: Richard Helsop
MUSIC FROM: Seven Songs (Fetish/UK, 1981).
SELECTIONS: "Kundalini," "Vegas El Bandito," "Mary's Operation," "Lock Grove," "New Testament," "Porno Base," "Quiet Pillage," "Tranquiliser."

One of the more intriguing offerings in Factory's catalog of poker-faced post-punk experimental amateurism, this tape consists of seven video clips to accompany 23 Skidoo's offbeat avant-garde sound collages, plus an experimental film collage called "Tranquiliser." Director Richard Helsop uses jarring, heavy edits and searingly bright, supersaturated colors to treat his montages of found footage and sundry other imagery, rendering the whole most unusual, as hard to ignore as it is to watch after a while. The musical highlight, meanwhile, is probably "Quiet Pillage," a witty sendup of Martin Denny's '50s ethnoimperialist novelty hit "Quiet Village." Not for everyone, but then it doesn't try to be—and it's a bit more accomplished and provocative than the run of Factory's often-trying mill. (Available in stores or by mail order from Factory.)

□ TWISTED SISTER
STAY HUNGRY
★★★

Embassy, 1984, 60 minutes
PRODUCED BY: Marty Callner
DIRECTED BY: Marty Callner, Arthur Ellis
MUSIC FROM: You Can't Stop Rock 'n' Roll (Atlantic, 1983); *Stay Hungry* (Atlantic, 1984); *Under the Blade* (Atlantic, 1985).
SELECTIONS: "The Kids Are Back," "We're Not Gonna Take It," "Under the Blade," "You Can't Stop Rock 'n' Roll," "The Price," "Stay Hungry," "Burn in Hell," "SMF."

Also available on Pioneer Stereo Laser videodisc.

Stay Hungry, a mix of 1984 concert footage from San Bernardino, California, video clips, and interviews with Dee Snider (there are no "party outtakes" and "animated sequences" as promised on the sleeve), has absolute fan appeal. But for interested outsiders, it's an up-and-down affair with only a few really recommendable portions: Arthur Ellis's wonderful promo clip for "You Can't Stop Rock 'n' Roll," circa 1983—the seminal video in the band's ongoing antiauthority vid-clip saga, and funnier, more action-packed, and more substantial plot-wise than any of the clips that followed it (including Callner's "We're Not Gonna Take It," the other clip here); and a too-brief post-concert interview with Snider, in what looks like a homey suburban kitchen. He reveals himself as intelligent, articulate, funny, and intensely committed to his populist-rock-maverick ideology. He's a man of the people: "When I'm on tour *nothing* gets in the way of my performance; there's no drugs, no parties after the show—people are paying good money to see us, and if I go out the night before and get wasted and don't sleep, they're not gonna get 100 percent, and that's a rip-off." His analysis of the audience-performer relationship, and especially the "distance" between a "star band" like Mötley Crüe (whom he likes) and their fans, is interesting and insightful. Unfortunately, unless you're a fan, sitting through their concert—which is shot nicely and treated with the occasional razzle-dazzle high-tech video effect—is a trying experience that mainly shows just how crucial those video clips are in diverting attention from Twisted Sister's rather pedestrian crunch 'n' thud stomps. In his ranting intro to the show-closing "SMF" (which stands for "Stupid MotherFucker," though Dee explains his profanity nicely in his interview), Snider even belies the smarts he proves he has a few minutes later: after dedicating the upcoming tune to the band's longtime fans, who stuck with them through a decade on their local Long Island, New York, grind without a record label, Snider starts half-jokingly cussing out the Johnnies-come-lately in the crowd. "Y'know, some of you people," he bellows at professional-wrestler pitch, "I was kickin' ass with Twisted Sister while you were still in your bedrooms jerkin' off!" Think hard, Dee: Is that really something to be bragging about?

□ TWISTED SISTER
COME OUT AND PLAY
★★★★

Atlantic, 1985, 30 minutes
PRODUCED BY: Rabia Dockray
DIRECTED BY: Marty Callner
MUSIC FROM: Come Out and Play (Atlantic, 1985).
SELECTIONS: "Come Out and Play," "We're Not Gonna Take It," "Leader of the Pack," "I Wanna Rock," "Be Chrool to Your Scuel," "You Want What We Got."

Twisted Sister, the heavy metal band from Long Island, New York, is one of rock's ultimate video bands—not because they're so good-looking that video can disguise their lack of musical ability, like Duran Duran. Rather, like Texan hard-rockers Z.Z. Top, Twisted Sister have used rock video with canny alacrity to not only maximize their exposure, but also to totemize their own coded symbolism as a way of (a) solidifying the ties with the audience video exposure has maximized, and (b) sharing their worldview with that audience.

Twisted Sister's worldview, and the message of all their videos, is that rude, nasty, dirty, loud heavy metal rock 'n' roll is not just the right of kids everywhere, but also their rallying point in the ongoing battle against Adult Authority. Twisted Sister's earliest video, "You Can't Stop Rock 'n' Roll," established the motif; since that one was directed by Britisher Arthur Ellis, while all the later clips collected on *Come Out and Play* were directed by American Marty Callner, and since Twisted Sister's mascaraed lead singer Dee Snider is credited as scenarist on all the clips on *Come Out and Play,* it's obvious that Snider is the real rock video *auteur* here. However, the later, Callner-directed clips do represent a quantum leap of sorts, and not only in terms of production values: they also introduced and continued Twisted Sister's totemism, specifically in the brilliant casting of Mark Metcalf—who played the ragingly uptight militarist Niedermeyer in *Animal House*—as the surly symbol of authority. He's the father of the average kid in "We're Not Gonna Take It," and he's the drill sergeant of a teacher who tortures the fat slob teenager in "I Wanna Rock." In another *Animal House* reference, Stephen Furst—who played the fat nerd Flounder in *Animal House,* and who went on to join the cast of NBC's *St. Elsewhere*—cameos at the end of "I Wanna Rock," spritzing Niedermeyer with a seltzer bottle as he utters his *Animal House* catch-phrase, "Oh boy, is this *great!*"

Come Out and Play does a fine, no-nonsense job of compiling Twisted Sister's better-known clips, and in fact amplifies the ongoing symbolism of those clips by joining them with quick little scenes in which the troubled teens in the videos find the bank lurking in what appears to be a postapocalyptic junkyard. Guest star and gonzo comic Bob Goldthwaite describes it best when he pulls up, looks around, and shrieks, "What is this, Mel Gibson's house?" The kid from "We're Not Gonna Take It" walks up to the junkyard dejectedly, holding a classified ad offering the band's services; he looks up at Dee and company, mutters," "It's my father," and Dee and company sagely reply "We know," cueing the video. The fat slob from "I Wanna Rock" sighs, "It's that teacher," cueing *that* clip. And so on. In the closing clip, "Be Chrool to Your Scuel," Snider tips his hat affectionately to his own roots in past rock outrages with the guest appearance of rock's original master of the no-redeeming-social-value-gross-out, Alice Cooper (appropriate, given the clip's students-as-zombies motif).

Most of the way through, Twisted Sister's call to rock 'n' roll arms is played out with serio-comic, purposely overdone charm, all slapstick-cartoon violence and the aforementioned apposite casting (note that Niedermeyer is a cartoon himself anyway). It's *so* cartoonish that, the band's relentlessness aside, you've got to wonder how the PMRC could seriously attack them. But if you look closely there *is* something a bit pernicious going on here: note that when the kids approach Twisted Sister at "Mel Gibson's house," the band is always on high looking down on those pathetic cases seeking their help; and note especially that when that fat slob approaches them, Dee first sniffs around with a scowl on his face and gets the slob to admit that he's soiled his pants on the way over. It's one thing to separate yourself from your audience even as you're trying to establish a bond with them—but this is a bit much.

U

☐ UB40

LABOUR OF LOVE

★★★★

Import, 1984, 31 minutes
DIRECTED BY: Bernard Rose
MUSIC FROM: Labour of Love (A&M, 1983).
SELECTIONS: "Version Girl," "Sweet Sensation," "Cherry Oh Baby," "Red Red Wine," "Guilty," "Please Don't Make Me Cry," "She Caught the Train," "Johnny Too Bad," "Many Rivers to Cross."
Also available on Monaural Laserdisc.

Hailing from grimy, industrial Birmingham, England, UB40 (who take their name from the code numbers of a British unemployment form) is probably the best reggae band in the world outside of Jamaica. *Labour of Love,* a superb collection of their covers of early '60s reggae and "rock-steady" (a slightly faster Jamaican precursor to reggae) classics, was the most popular of their undeservedly obscure albums in the U.S. But tragically the accompanying home video is, at this writing, available here only as an import. It's a beautiful piece of work, merging classic British "kitchen sink" realism with a credible love story, featuring lead singer Ali Campbell and starring the rest of the band as well as some supporting players. Director Bernard Rose, shooting in atmospheric black-and-white, which lends the program a fitting feel of bittersweet nostalgic recollection, makes great use of slow-motion in barroom scenes to indicate inebriation, and the performances he draws from the band and everyone else strike just the right notes. "Red Red Wine," the video clip pulled from this program for airing on MTV, is the only piece of *Labour of Love* that Americans have seen. It's a great little video that gives you an excellent idea of how good the rest of the tape is. (Available by mail order only from Playings Hard to Get).

☐ VARIOUS ARTISTS

URGH! A MUSIC WAR

★★★★½

CBS/Fox, 1981, 124 minutes
PRODUCED BY: Michael White
DIRECTED BY: Derek Burbidge
MUSIC FROM: Various albums by various artists; *Urgh! A Music War* soundtrack (A&M, 1981).
SELECTIONS: The Police: "Driven to Tears," "Roxanne"; Wall of Voodoo: "Back in Flesh"; Toyah Wilcox: "Dance"; John Cooper-Clark: "Health Fanatic"; Orchestral Manoeuvres in the Dark: "Enola Gay"; Chelsea: "I'm On Fire"; Oingo Boingo: "Ain't This the Life"; Echo and the Bunnymen: "All Along"; Jools Holland: "Only for You"; XTC: "Respectable Street"; Klaus Nomi: "Total Eclipse"; Athletico Spizz '80: "Where's Captain Kirk"; the Go-Go's: "We Got the Beat"; Dead Kennedys: "Bleed"; Steel Pulse: "Ku Klux Klan"; Gary Numan: "Down in the Park"; Joan Jett and the Blackhearts: "Bad Reputation"; Magazine: "Model Worker"; Surf Punks: "Come On"; Members: "Offshore Banking Business"; Au Pairs: "Come Again"; Cramps: "Tear It Up"; Invisible Sex: "Valium"; Pere Ubu: "The Art of Walking"; Devo: "Uncontrollable Urge"; Alleycats: "Child"; John Otway: "Cheryl's Going Home"; Gang of Four: "Cheeseburger"; 999: "Homicide"; Fleshtones: "Shadow-line"; X: "Beyond and Back"; Skafish: "Sign of the Cross"; Splodgenessabounds: "Two Little Boys"; UB40: "One in Ten"; the Police, UB 40, Skafish, XTC, et al.: "So Lonely."

For those who missed the punk/new wave explosion of the late-'70s/early '80s, and for those who just want to remember it vividly, go no further than this. This super-eclectic concert documentary has been playing the midnight-movie circuit for so long now that it's in danger of being taken for granted, which would be a tragedy.

Urgh! is outstanding. Derek Burbidge's direction is commendably straightforward and unobtrusive, with just enough audience shots to deepen the context as well as provide visual variety. And the selection of U.S. and U.K. bands, shot in London, Holland, New York, Los Angeles, and San Diego, is first-rate. Highlights include: the demented psycho-rockabilly of the Cramps; Devo in all their flower-pot-hatted glory; Orchestral Manoeuvres in the Dark with the gorgeous electro-pop of "Enola Gay"; the savagely kinetic and visceral Dead Kennedys; the Police; John Otway's endearingly energetic and loopy, way-over-the-top fractured folk-rock; the critically underrated Magazine; and especially the brilliant, sadly overlooked Au Pairs, whose riveting "Come Again" sets a political analysis of male-female sexual relationships to slashing Gang of Four–style punk-funk. Meanwhile, Skafish, Gary Numan, and the late Klaus Nomi redefine camp for the '80s, and the lulls (the inconsequential Toyah Wilcox, Oingo Boingo, and Splodgenessabounds; the insulting Surf Punks) are comparatively very few. All in all, a magnificent memento of new wave before it devolved into "new music."

□ USA FOR AFRICA

WE ARE THE WORLD—THE VIDEO EVENT

★★★½

RCA/Columbia, 1985, 30 minutes

PRODUCED BY: Craig Golin, Howard Malley

DIRECTED BY: Tom Trbovich

MUSIC FROM: We Are the World (Columbia, 1985).

SELECTIONS: "We Are the World."

Also available on Pioneer Stereo Laser videodisc.

This document on the making of one of pop's most auspicious allstar get-togethers in recent memory is full of privileged up-close-among-the-stars moments: Cyndi Lauper's clanking jewelry ruining some vocal takes; Stevie Wonder imitating Bob Dylan to show Dylan (who looks like a basket case in such stellar company) how to sing his part; etc. Unfortunately, Jane Fonda's pretentious, ponderous narration only gets in the way, and ultimately serves to fuel the accusations of self-serving hype that cynics immediately began leveling at USA for Africa. The one-hour HBO special from which this is taken has even more good stuff, and if you have HBO and they ever rerun it, you'd be better off taping that than owning this. Still, this *does* have quite a lineup, quite a song, quite a gesture, and quite a moment in pop history covered fairly well.

□ UTOPIA

AN EVENING WITH UTOPIA

★★½

MCA, 1983, 85 minutes

PRODUCED BY: Marcus Peterzell

DIRECTED BY: Joshua White

MUSIC FROM: Deface the Music (Bearsville, 1980); *Swing to the Right* (Bearsville, 1982); *Healing* (Bearsville, 1981); *Utopia* (Network, 1982); *Hermit of Mink Hollow* (Bearsville, 1978).

SELECTIONS: "Infrared and Ultraviolet," "Libertine," "Couldn't I Just Tell You," "Set Me Free," "I'm Looking at You But I'm Talking to Myself," "Princess of the Universe," "Hammer in My Heart," "Call It What You Will," "You Make Me Crazy," "Rock Love," "Love Alone," "Feet Don't Fail Me Now," "Say Yeah," "Only Human," "The Very Last Time," "The Road to Utopia," "Caravan," "Love in Action," "One World," "Love Is the Answer," "Just One Victory."

□ UTOPIA

THE UTOPIA SAMPLER

★★

Sony, 1983, 11 minutes

PRODUCED BY: Todd Rundgren
DIRECTED BY: Todd Rundgren
MUSIC FROM: *Utopia* (Network, 1982); *Swing to the Right* (Bearsville, 1982); *Adventures in Utopia* (Bearsville, 1979).
SELECTIONS: "Hammer in My Heart," "You Make Me Crazy," "Feet Don't Fail Me Now."

□ TODD RUNDGREN AND UTOPIA
UTOPIA: A RETROSPECTIVE 1977–1984
★★

JEM/Passport, 1985, 70 minutes
PRODUCED BY: Eric Gardner
DIRECTED BY: Todd Rundgren, Bob Lampel
MUSIC FROM: Various Utopia albums, (Bearsville, 1974–84).
SELECTIONS: "Ra," "Magic Dragon Theater," "Love of the Common Man," "Wouldn't Have Made Any Difference," "Set Me Free," "You Make Me Crazy," "Rock Love," "Trapped," "Emergency Splashdown," "I Just Want to Touch You," "Love in Action," "Just One Victory," "Feet Don't Fail Me Now," "Crybaby," "Utopia Theme."

□ TODD RUNDGREN AND UTOPIA
LIVE AT THE ROYAL OAK
★★

JEM/Passport, 1985, 60 minutes
PRODUCED BY: Eric Gardner
DIRECTED BY: Bob Lampel
MUSIC FROM: *Swing to the Right* (Bearsville, 1982); *Adventures in Utopia* (Bearsville, 1979); *Healing* (Bearsville, 1981).
SELECTIONS: "One World," "Road to Utopia," "Back on the Street," "Caravan," "Time Heals," "The Wheel," "The Very Last Time," "Lysistrada," "Love in Action," "Couldn't I Just Tell You," "Love Is the Answer," "Just One Victory."

Utopia is the crucial wrong turn that Todd Rundgren took to sink his already-accomplished and still-promising career in the mid-'70s. They were a lousy progressive-rock band, and not much better at more straightforward pop-rock either. It's hard to believe a band so utterly mediocre (and that's at their *best*) is so well represented on home video.

An Evening With catches them at L.A.'s Rismiller's club, running through a wider variety of styles than usual: from the Beatles-mockeries of the *Deface the Music* LP, through the more typically Utopian electronics-dominated progressive-rock, to the straightforward, romantic pop tunes at which Rundgren has always been most adept. It's decently shot overall, and is occasionally treated with snazzy post-production effects. All Utopia home videos are primarily for Todd fans only; this one comes close to being recommendable to others who are curious.

But then, so does *Sampler*—if only because it's so short. Rundgren was considered a music video pioneer because he was one of the very first people to spend big bucks on high-tech video equipment—but he has so little to *say* in the new synergistic medium. "Hammer in My Heart" treats concert footage with post-production effects to mildly intriguing ends; "You Make Me Crazy" is stridently obnoxious slapstick trying, and failing, to comment incisively on contemporary neuroses; and "Feet Don't Fail Me Now," with its stupidly cute centipede-costume antics (geddit?), is the most endearing, if only by default. All in all, it adds up to a yawn—but a *little* yawn.

A Retrospective is one enormous, torturously prolonged yawn, covering many more of Todd's terribly self-indulgent video clip bases. Todd fans will be delighted; others, beware.

Royal Oak is a competent, uninspired shoot (occasionally tricked up with video effects) of a competent, uninspiring set by Rundgren and band, who are dressed in combat-camouflage outfits ostensibly because they were promoting the *Swing to the Right* LP. Once again as usual, they sound best on Rundgren's poppier material (like "Road to Utopia," "Time Heals," and "Couldn't I Just Tell You"), and overall this is for Rundgren fans only.

☐ **U2**
LIVE AT RED ROCKS: UNDER A BLOOD RED SKY
★★★★½

RCA/Columbia, 1983, 55 minutes
PRODUCED BY: Rick Wurpel, Doug Stewart
DIRECTED BY: Gavin Taylor
MUSIC FROM: Boy (Island, 1980); *October* (Island, 1981); *War* (Island, 1982); *Under a Blood Red Sky* (Island, 1983).
SELECTIONS: "Surrender," "Seconds," "Sunday Bloody Sunday," "October," "New Years Day," "I Threw a Brick," "A Day without Me," "Gloria," "Party Girl," "11 O'Clock Tick Tock," "I Will Follow," "40."

Outstanding concert documentary catching the important, innovative Irish band on their 1983 U.S. tour at the Red Rocks Amphitheater outside of Denver, Colorado. The amphitheater, carved right out of the red granite Rockies, makes a dramatic backdrop of U2's urgent antiwar, Christian anthems, which merge hard arena rock with new wave minimalism and edge (not to mention *the* Edge, né Dave Evans, their guitarist, one of the most creative and influential new players in rock). So what you've got here is a pretty darned good band, playing a strong set to an intensely into-it audience, all within a literally awesome setting—and it so happens this show was on an abnormally raw June day, with whipping wind and rain that perfectly compliment vocalist Bono's plaintively chanting Biblical intensity. All director Gavin Taylor had to do was aim and shoot to guarantee a great video, and that's pretty much what he did. No fancy pre- or post-production was needed to enhance this particular union of sound and vision—and thankfully, none was used. Recommended.

☐ **U2**
THE UNFORGETTABLE FIRE COLLECTION
★★½

RCA/Columbia, 1985, 51 minutes
PRODUCED BY: Various
DIRECTED BY: Various
MUSIC FROM: The Unforgettable Fire (Island, 1985).
SELECTIONS: "The Unforgettable Fire," "Bad," "Pride," "A Sort of Homecoming," "The Making of *The Unforgettable Fire.*"

This collection of video clips also includes a half-hour documentary on the making of the album whence they all came. The clips are rather uneven; by far the best is Donald Cammell's "Pride," with strong black-and-white imagery matching the superb song. The documentary shows the band recording the dramatic environs of Ireland's Slane Castle; their interactions with producer Brian Eno are pretty much the usual uneventful rock-band-at-work stuff. Where *Under a Blood Red Sky* has a universal starkness and urgency, this is strictly for fans only.

V

☐ FRANKIE VALLI AND THE FOUR SEASONS
LIVE FROM PARK WEST CHICAGO
★★★

Prism, 1982, 60 minutes
PRODUCED BY: Jose Pretlow
DIRECTED BY: Dick Carter
SELECTIONS: "Dawn," "Who Loves You," "Grease," "Our Day Will Come," "My Eyes Adored You," Medley: "Working My Way Back to You"/"Will You Love Me Tomorrow"/"Opus 17 (Don' Worry 'bout Me)"/"I've Got You Under My Skin," "Sunday Kind of Love," "Can't Take My Eyes Off of You," Medley: "Sherry"/"Walk Like a Man"/"Big Girls Don't Cry"/"Bye Bye Baby," Medley: "Save It for Me"/ "Candy Girl"/"Big Man in Town"/ "Ronnie"/"Rag Doll," Medley: "Silence Is Golden"/"Tell It to the Rain," "Stay," "Let's Hang On."

This 1982 concert took place just one year after the Four Seasons were reunited, following a years-long hiatus during which Frankie Valli vowed he'd never work with the Seasons again. These guys aren't really the original Seasons, either, but a group of fine rock musicians who, musically and vocally, do justice to the group's biggest hits. This crowd obviously loves it, and if you are a Valli and Seasons fan, you will too. At forty-five, Valli sounds better than ever, and hearing the hits one right after the other makes you wonder why this group is so often overlooked in rock history. As always in live concert situations, you must endure the audience singing along in spots, and, regrettably, the band is never introduced, so who knows who's up there with Frankie. Still, a solid tape for fans.—P.R.

☐ GINO VANNELLI
GINO VANNELLI
★★

Warner Home Video, 1982, 56 minutes
PRODUCED BY: Henry Less and Wolfhound Productions
DIRECTED BY: Bruce Gowers, Henry Less, and Wolfhound Productions
MUSIC FROM: Various albums by Gino Vannelli.
SELECTIONS: "Powerful People," "The Evil Eye," "Appaloosa," "Omens of Love," "I Just Wanna Stop," "Brother to Brother," "People Gotta Move," "Where Am I Going," "One Night with You," "Wheels of Life," "Living inside Myself," "Nightwalker."

With his long, thick mane of black curls Vannelli's a superstar in his native Canada. Outside of the Great White North, though, he's rightly considered a numbingly pompous joke. And with his repertoire of clumsy sub–Jim Morrison (sudden spastic jerks and bends at the waist), sub–Rod Stewart (mike-stand twirling) stage moves, capable but undistinguished voice, overarranged vacuous pop bombast, it's a wonder he ever became a star anywhere. Still, fans will probably enjoy this program, which primarily consists of adequately photographed concert footage from New Orleans, Detroit, Chicago, and Toronto, shot between 1977 and 1981. There are also two mediocre music videos of the dry-ice-shrouded performance variety, for "Living inside Myself" and "Nightwalker." And there are frequent glimpses of Gino backstage, Gino rehearsing at sound checks, Gino in his limo on the road with his brother Joe (credited on the cassette package as "narrator," though he's hardly very evident as such), and so on. Progressive-rock fans may care to note (with dismay) that Vannelli's band here includes guitarist Daryl Steurmer (who would go on to join

Genesis) and drummer Mark Craney (who would join Jethro Tull); hard-rock fans should know that one of Vannelli's later bands included drummer Greg Bissonette, who in 1986 joined David Lee Roth's post–Van Halen band.

□ VENOM
THE 7TH DATE OF HELL—LIVE
★/★★★

Sony, 1985, 57 minutes
PRODUCED BY: Michael Rodd
DIRECTED BY: Bob Harvey
MUSIC FROM: Various Venom albums.
SELECTIONS: "Leave Me in Hell," "Countess Bathory," "Die Hard," "7 Gates of Hell," "Buried Alive," "Don't Burn the Witch," "In Nominie Satanus," "Welcome to Hell," "Warhead," "Stand Up and Be Counted," "Bloodlust."

Here's another one of those split-ratings reviews, which means the program is either horrible (one star) or it's so awful it's actually funny (three stars). Since Venom are a kinda funny joke, they get only three stars here on the ironic-appreciation meter. As a glance at their song titles reveals, Venom specializes in the kind of caricatured-macabre satanism that could conceivably give the PMRC's Washington Wives fits of apoplexy. Their "music" is basically anonymous, formulaic, head-banging heavy-metal sludge—a tad too fast to be typically plodding classic metal yet a tad too slow and clichéd to be true "speed metal." Onstage in 1984 at London's Hammersmith Odeon in this indifferently shot concert program, Venom demonstrate a rather, er, unique presence: The guitarist (known as "Mantas"; the drummer is "Abaddon," the bassist/singer "Cronos"; cute, eh?) doesn't *talk* to the audience between songs, he *screams* at them at the top of his lungs, like a professional wrestler. "You're gonna get one hour of pure fuckin' mayhem tonight" he shouts at one point—but Venom never deliver anything remotely threatening. During "7 Gates of Hell," the roar of the onstage pyrotechnics (which look like a bunch of big sparklers, really) nearly drowns out the band (unfortunately, *only* nearly). *The 7th Date of Hell—Live* opens with a deep, hoarse voice croaking over the sound system, "Ladies and gentlemen, from the very depths of Hell—Venom!" If that's where they really came from, then maybe they ought to go right back there as soon as possible.

□ VENOM
ALIVE IN 85
★★½

Embassy, 1986, 60 minutes
PRODUCED BY: Philip Goodhand-Tait
DIRECTED BY: Maddy French
MUSIC FROM: Various Venom albums.
SELECTIONS: "Too Loud," "Black Metal," "Nightmare," "Countess Bathory," "7 Gates of Hell," "Buried Alive," "Don't Burn the Witch," "In Nomine Satanus," "Welcome to Hell," "Warhead," "Schitzo," "Satanachist," "Bloodlust," "Witching Hour."

A year after *7 Gates of Hell* was shot, Venom were back onstage at Hammersmith Odeon in London spewing their bilious, blazingly Beelzebubian bombast for *Alive in 85,* which is virtually identical in every way to the earlier program. The differences: "7 Gates of Hell" is played as an excruciating bass solo by Cronos; "Warhead" is played as a similarly excruciating guitar solo (incredibly like a certain scene in *This Is Spinal Tap* featuring Christopher Guest as Nigel Tufnel playing speed-licks-for-speed's-sake) by Mantas, and there are some extra tunes here, such as "Too Loud" (I'll say!), "Black Metal," and "Schitzo." If you can call them tunes, that is.

☐ **THE VENTURES**
LIVE IN L.A.
★★★½

Import, 1981, 51 minutes
MUSIC FROM: Various albums by the Ventures (Liberty, 1960–70).
SELECTIONS: "Walk—Don't Run," "Telstar," "Penetration," "Apache," "Surfin' and Spyin'," "House of the Rising Sun," "Wipe Out," "Pipeline," "Hawaii Five-O," "Ghost Riders in the Sky," "Perfidia," "Diamond Head," "I Walk the Line," "Ram-Bunk-Shush."
Also available on Stereo Laser videodisc.

☐ **THE VENTURES**
ORIGINAL MEMBERS—LIVE IN JAPAN
★★★★

Import, 1984, 56 minutes
MUSIC FROM: Various albums by the Ventures (Liberty, 1960–70).
SELECTIONS: "Apache," "Walk—Don't Run," "Slaughter on Tenth Avenue," "Tequila," "Let's Go," "Hawaii Five-O," "Pipeline," "Wipeout," "Yesterday," "Surfin' and Spyin'," "Telstar," "Penetration," "Lullaby of the Leaves," "Diamond Head," "The 2,000 Pound Bee (Part 2)," "Secret Agent Man," "Guitar Boogie Shuffle," "Out of Limits."

Though fondly recalled by many as the original surf-rock instrumental guitar band, the Ventures actually predated the surf-rock explosion of 1962–64 with their first single, the 1960 classic "Walk—Don't Run." And, as both of these nicely shot concert programs prove, the Ventures maintained their popularity and distinctive appeal long after surf rock had become a memory. However, while one of them is titled *Original Members,* it's really only three-quarters true: guitarists Don Wilson and Nokie Edwards and bassist Bob Bogle were originals, but drummer Mel Taylor—who reunited with the other three, first in 1981 and then in '84 for the two "comeback" tours documented here—replaced original drummer Howie Johnston in 1963. But that's just a technicality. That timeless, trademark sound—guitars twanging out catchy melodies over throbbing tom-tom tattoos—is still there, and sounds as great as ever. Of course, the Ventures' stage presence is nothing to write home about—they're as faceless as they are voiceless. But that probably won't matter to Ventures fans. Each program is in large part interchangeable with the other, but the more recent Japanese program gets a slightly higher rating because it's got more songs and slightly better visual and aural quality. (Available by mail order from Playings Hard to Get.)

☐ **VARIOUS ARTISTS**
VIDEO A GO-GO, VOLUME ONE
★★

RCA/Columbia, 1985, 25 minutes
PRODUCED BY: Len Epand and Claude Borenzweig
DIRECTED BY: Various
MUSIC FROM: Various albums by various artists.
SELECTIONS: Animotion: "Obsession"; Kool and the Gang: "Fresh"; the Vels: "Look My Way"; Stephanie Mills: "Medicine Song"; Bananarama: "Cruel Summer"; Bar-Kays: "Freakshow on the Dance Floor."

Mediocre dance-music video compilation, generally indicating the various ways in which video-makers can fail to create visual counterparts anywhere near as compelling as the music they're working from. Classic example: Kool and the Gang's "Fresh," an outrageously good tune with a pleasantly dull straightforward video; and especially Animotion's "Obsession," a classic track with an insultingly lame Fellini-by-the-pool video accompaniment. While the solid dance grooves keep coming, so do the ineffectual videos, which reach another nadir with Bananarama's airheaded antics in "Cruel Summer."

☐ **VARIOUS ARTISTS**

VIDEO A GO-GO, VOLUME TWO

★★½

RCA/Columbia, 1986, 27 minutes

PRODUCED BY: Len Epand and Claude Borenzweig

DIRECTED BY: Mark Robinson, Don Letts, Marius Penczner David Hodge, Felix Limardo, Michael Oblowitz

MUSIC FROM: Various albums by various artists.

SELECTIONS: Ashford and Simpson: "Solid"; Gap Band: "Party Train"; the Bar-Kays: "Your Place or Mine"; Al Corley: "Cold Dresses"; Kool and the Gang: "Misled"; Kurtis Blow: "Basketball."

Volume Two starts out very promising, but ends up extremely erratic. Ashford and Simpson's "Solid" (directed by Mark Robinson) finds them under a walking bridge in Central Park, finding refuge from the rain, and rediscovering their love—and making their typical icky goo-goo eyes at each other. An ominous-looking gang of city kids joins them in the tunnel, but Nick and Val's music and intense love vibes merely provoke joyous dancing and jamming. This romantic, mini–"Beat It" is an almost laughably silly concept, but the song is so irresistible we can forgive it. The Gap Band's "Party Train" (directed by Don Letts) has a similar theme of turning potential negative energy (violence) into positive energy (dancing), with a comical seaside boxing match turning into a dance fest as the band plays on. In the Bar-Kays' "Your Place or Mine" (directed by Marius Penczner), the Rick James–lookalike vocalist sings the lyric to a cutie in the club audience where the band performs; sweetly comical conceptual cut-ins illustrate the romantic fantasies of the young lady, who desires the singer and not all the other cads and nerds in the club. So far, so good: three solidly danceable tunes, three basically positive and humanistic videos.

But from this refreshing peak *Video A-Go-Go, Volume Two* nosedives straight to the pits with Al Corley's "Cold Dresses," a bad video with a bad concept in which the ex-*Dynasty* star sings a bad song in a bad voice, while dancing badly in bad clothes. Kool and the Gang's "Misled" is yet another of their admirably crafted funk-pop gems, but the video—in which singer J. T. Taylor hallucinates a mysterious temptress, while *Raiders of the Lost Ark*-style inserts show us her origins—is ultimately a silly, irrelevant extravagance, left unredeemed by its cloying finale, a rather lame nod to Michael Jackson's "Thriller." Kurtis Blow's "Basketball" is a dumb rap song illustrated in silly, slapdash, barely likable fashion, with sloppy choreography of a gaggle of white cheerleaders (a bid for MTV airplay?) and dull slo-mo basketball footage intercut with Kurtis's cheerful lip-synch (which takes place amidst a choreographed basketball game in a schoolyard). All in all, would that the second half were as good as the first—but the first half is good enough to make this a shade better than most various-artists compilations.

W

☐ JOHN WAITE
NO BRAKES LIVE
★★½

RCA/Columbia, 1985, 50 minutes
PRODUCED BY: Tammara Wells
DIRECTED BY: Jim Yukich
MUSIC FROM: *Ignition* (Chrysalis, 1983); *No Brakes* (EMI-America, 1984); *Mask of Smiles* (EMI-America, 1985).
SELECTIONS: "Saturday Night," "Tears," "Dark Side of the Sun," "The Choice," "Dreamtime/Shake It Up," "Missing You," "Change," "Euroshima," "For Your Love," "Midnight Rendezvous," "Head First."

"As founder and lead vocalist of the Babys in the late '70s," reads the copy on the back of this cassette's cover, "John Waite became one of rock and roll's major voices." That's about right, but it neglects to mention that between then and his '80s solo career, Waite was also Pope for awhile. A "major voice"? Hardly. The Babys were a sub-Raspberries hard-pop band, and Waite solo is a good-looking guy with little to say. Every now and then he comes up with a good song, like "Change," which was composed by Holly Knight (author of "Better Be Good to Me" and Heart's "Never"). In "Missing You," he has come up with a *great* song, by far his best to date. In this 1985 concert, originally shot for MTV, Waite proves he is hardly the world's most exciting stage performer (unless you swoon just looking at him). His band is anonymously competent, just like Jim Yukich's direction.

☐ GROVER WASHINGTON, JR.
IN CONCERT
★★★

Warner Home Video, 1982, 60 minutes
PRODUCED BY: Bruce Buschel and Gary Delfiner
DIRECTED BY: Donny Osmond
MUSIC FROM: Various Grover Washington, Jr., albums.
SELECTIONS: "Winelight," "Let It Flow (for Dr. J.)," "Come Morning," "Make Me a Memory (Sad Samba)," "Just the Two of Us," "Mister Magic."
Also available on Pioneer Stereo Laser videodisc.

Saxophonist Grover Washington, Jr., gained a big audience in the mid- to late-'70s with a funky, silky smooth but all-consumingly vapid blend of jazz-fusion and Muzak that epitomizes the kind of somnolent groovemongering critics like to deride as "fuzak." Here, he's caught in June 1981 at the Shubert Theater in Philadelphia fronting a band that includes percussionist Ralph McDonald (composer of Washington's two biggest hits, "Mister Magic" and "Just the Two of Us"), guitarist Eric Gale, keyboardist Richard Tee, bassist Anthony Jackson, and drummer Steve Gadd—all very highly regarded studio-session whizzes who can play this stuff in their sleep. In fact, that's exactly the problem with this music for non-fans: it *sounds* like they're all playing in their sleep. Vocalist Zack Sanders sits in for a few numbers, including "Just the Two of Us," a pleasant little pop tune that widened Washington's audience even further to include the AOR/MOR crowd. While the visuals are completely unexciting, it's all shot with straightforward competence and some degree of intimacy, and if you are a fan of this stuff, you should enjoy this. If not, however, pop it in the player only if you've been suffering from insomnia.

☐ BILL WATROUS REFUGE WEST BAND
WATROUS LIVE
★★★

Sony, 1983, 24 minutes

PRODUCED BY: Wesley Ruggles, Jr. and Gary Reber

DIRECTED BY: Ric Trader

MUSIC FROM: Watrous Live (Dig-It, 1981).

SELECTIONS: "Space Available," "Samantha," "The Slauson Cutoff," "Birdland."

Watrous is an outstanding jazz trombonist who has been winning critics' and readers' polls in jazz magazines for years. Here he leads a very able, young, 18-piece big band in a 1981 concert at the Concerts by the Sea, the Southern California jazz club owned by onetime Stan Kenton Orchestra bassist Howard Rumsey. In his long hair, blue jeans, and casually open-necked shirt, Watrous appears laid-back and mellowed-out, but he's a physically emphatic bandleader, frequently breaking out in spontaneous little dances to the music, evoking a sense of outgoing enjoyment that belies the band's obvious discipline and accomplished efficiency. With the exception of Joe Zawinul's "Birdland," a latter-day standard made familiar by Weather Report and Manhattan Transfer, all the songs are comparatively unknown, but all are very good, with crisp readings of sharp, colorful charts. "Slauson" by Tom Kubis is the best of the lot, with intriguing, unusual voicings, and the reed and brass sections taking turns playing whole passages by themselves. Drummer Chad Wackerman, who's also played with Frank Zappa and Men at Work, drives the band along neatly. Throughout, Watrous himself towers over his band's solid work, making it pale in comparison to his solos, which are mini-masterpieces of inspiration, imagination, and stunningly precise control. The camera work is fine, and the digitally recorded sound is excellent, especially with a hi-fi deck.

□ WEATHER REPORT
THE EVOLUTIONARY SPIRAL
★ ½

Sony, 1984, 15 minutes

PRODUCED BY: Mark L. Mawrence and Larry Lachman

DIRECTED BY: Larry Lachman

MUSIC FROM: Procession (Columbia, 1983).

SELECTIONS: "Procession," "Plaza Real," "Two Lines."

From the cassette cover copy: "Travel from the birth of the universe, through ancient cultures and the high tech world of today, then on to a vision of art in the future . . ." Well, you can probably guess that this is really just latter-day psychedelia: a rapid succession of uninspired abstract and representational images, run through a high-tech video-effects wringer. Weather Report's jazz-funk fusion music is competent, but not much more inspired than Lachman's visuals. Still, the idea of non-narrative "video art" abstraction set to contemporary music isn't necessarily a bad one, and besides, some latter-day hippies may actually *like* this flotsam-and-jetsam as ambient party entertainment.

□ THE WEAVERS
WASN'T THAT A TIME!
★★★★

MGM/UA, 1983, 78 minutes

PRODUCED BY: Jim Brown, Harold Leventhal, and George Stoney

DIRECTED BY: Jim Brown

MUSIC FROM: The film *Wasn't That a Time!* (1981).

SELECTIONS: "On Top of Old Smokey," "When the Saints Go Marching In," "Tzena, Tzena, Tzena," "Goodnight, Irene," "Wasn't That a Time," "If I Had a Hammer," "Banjo Breakdown," "Kisses Sweeter than Wine," "Darling Corey," "Allelujah," "Guantanamera," "Tomorrow Lies in the Cradle," "Woody's Rag," "Miner's Life," "Venga Jaleo," "Einstein

Theme Song," "Victor Jara," "Nobody Knows You When You're Down and Out," "Hay Una Mujer," "Wimoweh," "Get Up and Go," "We Wish You a Merry Christmas."

Excellent documentary movie on the seminal modern-era folk music group the Weavers (Pete Seeger, Lee Hays, Ronnie Gilbert, and Fred Hellerman), who as Studs Terkel says here, "Introduced, for the first time, authentic folk songs to the mainstream of American culture." Lots of other big names—from Peter, Paul and Mary to Arlo Guthrie, Don McLean to Harry Reasoner—appear to acknowledge the importance and influence of the Weavers, whose up-and-down career is well covered, from the early million-selling days to their blacklisting in the early '50s, from their 1955 Carnegie Hall comeback-reunion show to the 1981 Carnegie reunion show staged for this film. Educational and entertaining, and the Weavers come across like lovely folks.

□ PETE WERNICK
BEGINNING BLUEGRASS BANJO
★★★★

Homespun, 1985, 90 minutes
PRODUCED BY: Happy Traum
DIRECTED BY: Happy Traum
SELECTIONS: Nine bluegrass songs, no titles listed.

A bit more oriented to the beginner than Bela Fleck's Homespun cassette *Banjo Picking Styles,* as Pete "Dr. Banjo" Wernick, of the highly regarded bluegrass revival band Hot Rize, shows you three-finger bluegrass banjo from scratch, covering basic rolls, left-hand fingering, melodies and a whole lot more. Along the way Wernick demonstrates nine all-time bluegrass classics. (Available by mail order from Homespun Tapes.)

□ WHAM!
WHAM! THE VIDEO
★★★

CBS/Fox, 1985, 30 minutes
PRODUCED BY: Various
DIRECTED BY: Various
MUSIC FROM: Fantastic (Columbia, 1983); *Make It Big* (Columbia, 1984).
SELECTIONS: "Wham Rap," "Bad Boys," "Club Tropicana," "Wake Me Up Before You Go-Go," "Careless Whisper," "Last Christmas," "Everything She Wants."

Yeah, I know: unless you're a teenybopper or can weed through all their nauseating trappings to appreciate George Michael's undeniable gift for disposable pop tunes, it's hard not to find Wham! icky and plastic and oh-so-derivative and all that. But there *is* a subtext running through *Wham! The Video* that pop pundits and media mavens may sink their teeth into if they so desire. This chronological clips compilation goes back to the halcyon days of Wham UK!—back when George Michael had black hair, and it seemed that Andrew Ridgely maybe actually *did* something to contribute to their sound, and Tim Pope directed spunky, inventive, and repeatable clips such as "Wham Rap" and "Bad Boys" for them. With the hopelessly naïve literalness of "Club Tropicana," the boys make their move for jet-set allure (George and Andy play vacationing pilots, y'see), and with "Wake Me Up Before You Go-Go," they, er, Make It Big. And, after umpteen million airings, Andy Morahan's "Wake Me Up" video remains a brilliantly staged and shot piece of work that still virtually leaps out of the TV screen (though I still say George Michael looks less like a man than a mannequin). Having reached this heady plateau, they kick back and relax a while with two easily digestible, gossamer-light pop confections, "Careless Whisper" and "Last

Christmas," by which time Wham! has already begun to seem like a pathetically obvious George Michael solo vehicle under an old, ever-more-obsolescent name. The real payoff comes with the closing "Everything She Wants": a wounded-looking Michael sullenly lip-synchs the bitter you-hurt-me lyric, superimposed over shots of screaming teenybopper audiences and paper money flying through space. One can't help but sense that Wham! deeply resented not only the exigencies of massive success but also the audience that brought them that success. Talk about hopelessly naïve—what'd they expect?

The real question is: would pop pundits and media mavens care to wade through all the icky oh-so-derivative plastic in order to chew on this meat by-product? I don't know. But I *do* know that for diehard Wham! fans, there *is* no question: this is a must-have.

☐ WHAM!
WHAM! IN CHINA—FOREIGN SKIES
★★½

CBS/Fox, 1986, 62 minutes
PRODUCED BY: Jazz Summers and Martin Lewis
DIRECTED BY: Lindsay Anderson
MUSIC FROM: Fantastic (Columbia, 1983); *Make It Big* (Columbia, 1984).
SELECTIONS: "Everything She Wants (incomplete)," "Bad Boys," "Blue," "Club Tropicana," "Ray of Sunshine," "Young Guns (Go for It)," "Wake Me Up Before You Go-Go," "Careless Whisper," "Everything She Wants," "Like a Baby," "If You Were There," "Runaway," "Love Machine."

Foreign Skies documents Wham!'s historic tour of the People's Republic of China in 1985, the first by an English-speaking Western pop band. However, aside from the rare opportunity to see something like everyday life in China, this is a fairly typical, though nicely produced, tour documentary. It starts with the finale of "Everything She Wants" on a U.K. stage, George Michael telling his fans, "See you when we get back from China!" Cut to footage of China: a woman in traditional garb and makeup plucks a koto; kung fu cults work out in the hills; a jet lands and an on-screen title reads "Peking"; we see George and Andrew Ridgely in the airport, in their limo, in their hotel . . . at the Great Wall . . . you get the picture. There's one clever little bit early on, when a montage of Beijing life set to "Bad Boys" leads to a crowd of people standing around in an appliance store—someone flicks a switch and the song stops dead. Along with concert footage (nicely shot) from Beijing and Canton, there are on-the-street interviews with Chinese teens and young adults about Wham! and their arrival there, and footage of a soccer game between Wham! and their crew and a team of locals.

Surprisingly, as interesting as it is for a group like Wham! to be playing in a place like China for the first time, the on-the-street interviews are mundane, yielding very little in the way of insight into a rather fascinating subject. Perhaps the Chinese were just too freaked by the whole Wham! tour phenomenon, and there was some sort of insurmountable gap created by the culture shock. Anyway, Wham! are less than compelling onstage unless you're a fan, and they seem to get a literally mixed reaction from the Chinese crowds—most of them seem to be exuberant Wham!-maniacs all right, but the camera also captures whole sections of seats where people sit stock still, blank and uncomprehending. As the camera trails George and Andy, they reveal themselves to be true male bimbos—two pretty, vacant, giggly boys with neither a thing of interest to say nor an apparent care in the world. Boring. At one point they have a tiff in the back of a limo over what to say between songs, and it's so staged-to-seem-spontaneous it's pathetic. Of course, if it really *was* spontaneous, it's *still* pathetic. As for the music, well, unless you're a Wham! fan you'll have to agree with me that the best stuff here by far is the tantalizingly few moments of an ensemble of Beijing natives getting down with some *baaad* traditional music on the street. They play koto, bamboo flute, and things that look and/or sound like violins, cellos, mandolins, and oboes—and boy, do they swing, albeit in a most unusual way. If it weren't for them, I might give this an even lower rating.

□ LENNY WHITE
IN CLINIC

★★★★

DCI, 1983, 60 minutes
PRODUCED BY: Rob Wallis and Paul Siegel
DIRECTED BY: Rob Wallis and Paul Siegel
MUSIC FROM: Lenny White drum clinic, jam session with trio.

The star jazz-fusion drummer, a onetime member of Return to Forever as well as leader of his own units, discusses and demonstrates his approach to playing, equipment, and practice techniques; gets in-depth on the nuances of drumming in jazz-rock fusion music, on which he is certainly an expert; and, most fascinatingly, gets into his own concepts of "internal time-keeping" and relaxation while playing. He also plays some improvisational jams with a trio featuring onetime Mahavishnu Orchestra bassist Rick Laird. (Available by mail order from DCI Music Video.)

□ WHITESNAKE
FOURPLAY

★½

Sony, 1984, 16 minutes
PRODUCED BY: Picture Music International
DIRECTED BY: Lindsey Clenell and Maurice Philips
MUSIC FROM: *Fourplay* (EMI-America, 1983).
SELECTIONS: "Fool for Your Loving," "Don't Break My Heart Again," "Here I Go Again," "Guilty of Love."

Four completely forgettable videos from a completely forgettable British metal band whose singer, David Cloverdale, was once a member of Deep Purple in the mid-'70s. For diehard heavy metal completists only.

□ ROGER WHITTAKER
ROGER WHITTAKER IN KENYA—A MUSICAL SAFARI

★★★

Sony, 1984, 53 minutes
PRODUCED BY: Tom Ingle
DIRECTED BY: Tom Ingle
MUSIC FROM: *Roger Whittaker in Kenya* (Tembo, 1983).
SELECTIONS: "I'm Back," "Come with Me," "My Land Is Kenya," "Shimoni," "Good Old E.A.R. & H.," "Did You Really Have To?," "High," "Make Way for Man," "Come Back Again," "Yangarara," "Chenjalep (Nandi Folk Song)."

Whittaker is an internationally popular, middle of the road singer/songwriter whose music falls into a folksy, vaguely countrypolitan vein and who is possessed of a distinctive and strong baritone voice. He's bound to be intolerably lame and mushy for any rock fan, but Whittaker does have his legions of fans, and they'll probably enjoy this tape of a 1982 TV special in which the singer leaves England to revisit Kenya, the land of his birth, for the first time in some twenty years. Whittaker promises at the start of the program to show the viewer all the splendor of "my beautiful, beloved Kenya," though he later tells the camera he's sorry he has only "a few minutes" in which to try to pack all that splendor. But there is plenty of nice Kenyan travelogue footage, much of which is used for *Wild Kingdom*-styled music videos for the songs on the soundtrack.

Early in the show, Whittaker joins some natives in a percussion jam and generally lives up (or down, as the case may be) to all those racial stereotypes about who's got rhythm and who hasn't. It starts getting a bit queasy—but then, suddenly, Whittaker's talking with the natives in their own language, and they're responding, and he's lovingly describing to the camera the complex relationships between the drums and the dancers . . . and it's here that it slowly starts dawning on a rock-weaned viewer like me that Kenya really *does* mean a lot to Roger Whittaker. His sincerity and enthusiasm are genuinely touching. And as the program goes on, it keeps coming at you: in his eloquent descriptions of the country's peculiar natural attractions; when he jams with some Nandi tribesmen on "Chenjalep," a native folk song he learned as a child, he coaxes the natives along like a hardy, excited camp counselor, and just as you start thinking, "His music may be lame, but this guy is practically *adorable,*" he apologizes to you for the audible hum of the electrical generator—but, as he explains, "We *are* literally *right* in the *middle* of the African *forest* here . . ." And then you think, "He *is* adorable!" Whittaker goes on to an informative tour of Shimoni, a slave port in the days of Arab rule over Kenya, occasioning a protest song that's, well, at least well meaning. And then comes a real jaw-dropper: following a sequence of Whittaker and his wife in a Jeep checking out peaceful elephants, rhinos, and hippos, comes the music video for "Make Way for Man"—which consists of fairly riveting footage of elephants charging the camera, being shot, staggering, and collapsing *right in front of you.* The existential-ecological intensity of it is surprisingly intense, until a clichéd ending with quick-cuts to famine-struck African children and then an atom bomb's mushroom cloud.

It's because of such moments that, however you feel about Whittaker's music, one realizes that at least his mission here is a whole heck of a lot better-intended than Stewart Copeland's jaunt to shoot *The Rhythmatist* was. And, I might add, *A Musical Safari* is, on its own terms, a better program than *The Rhythmatist.*

□ THE WHO
THE KIDS ARE ALRIGHT
★★★★★

HBO/Cannon, 1979, 96 minutes

PRODUCED BY: Bill Curbishley and Tony Klinger

DIRECTED BY: Jeff Stein

MUSIC FROM: Various Who albums.

SELECTIONS: "My Generation," "I Can't Explain," "Shout and Shimmy," "Young Man Blues," "Substitute," "Anyway, Anyhow, Anywhere," "Magic Bus," "Pictures of Lily," "See Me, Feel Me," "Pinball Wizard," "Happy Jack," "A Quick One While He's Away," "Baba O'Riley," "Won't Get Fooled Again," "Road Runner," "Barbara Ann," "Who Are You."

□ THE WHO
THE WHO ROCKS AMERICA
★★½

CBS/Fox, 1983, 114 minutes

DIRECTED BY: Richard Namm

MUSIC FROM: Various Who albums; 1982 "last show" in Toronto, Canada.

SELECTIONS: "My Generation," "I Can't Explain," "Dangerous," "Sister Disco," "The Quiet One," "It's Hard," "Eminence Front," "Baba O'Reilly," "Boris the Spider," "Drowned," "Love Ain't for Keeping," "Pinball Wizard"/"See Me, Feel Me," "Squeezebox," "Who Are You," "Love Reign O'er Me," "Long Live Rock," "Won't Get Fooled Again," "Naked Eye," "Young Man Blues," "Twist and Shout."

Also available on CBS/Fox Stereo Laser videodisc.

The Kids Are Alright's director, Jeff Stein, is obviously an ardent Who fan—and that's good, because only such a fan would've and could've gathered such a diverse range of great footage (from concerts to TV appearances, from interviews to rare vintage music videos like "Happy Jack" and "Tommy Can You Hear Me?") to paint such a fitting portrait of one of rock's grandest bands. Though Stein avoids strict chronology, he never lets anything get in the way of the various facets of the Who's energetic, anarchic, *and* constructive essence. His free-floating, more abstract approach takes the fan's familiarity with the basics about the band for granted—providing an intriguing and instructive contrast to the far more methodical approach of, say, *The Compleat Beatles.*

It starts fittingly, with the Who destroying the set of the Smothers Brothers TV show in a vintage '60s appearance doing "My Generation." It ends with the aging quartet, not long before Keith Moon's tragic death, manfully giving "Won't Get Fooled Again" a go in what appears to be a specially staged mini-concert. In between, we see them as young Mods blazing through classics like "I Can't Explain" and "Anyway, Anyhow, Anywhere"; we get a tantalizing peak at their first mini–rock opera "A Quick One While He's Away," from the legendary, never-released *Rolling Stones Great Rock and Roll Circus*; we see Pete Townshend look on with indulgent, fatherly bemusement as Keith Moon's antics destroy a BBC-TV interview with straightlaced host Russell Harty; and so on.

Because the Who were such a grand and crucial band in rock history, *The Kids Are Alright* is recommended to all. But because, as I said, it presumes the viewer's more-than-passing familiarity with the Who, it's really really *really* for Who fans, who will find it an orgasmic experience.

Stein shot his film before Moon's death (it was released afterward, though), so he didn't have to bother with the travesty of the Who continuing with ex-Faces drummer Kenney Jones—a very competent drummer, and probably a nice guy, but no Keith Moon. Only Keith Moon was Keith Moon, and his spirit as well as his revolutionary technique were both integral and irreplaceable. The Who should have done the honorable thing and just called it quits right there (at least Led Zeppelin had the sense to do so when John Bonham died). But they didn't begin calling it quits until the supposed swan song from the stage (the Who *always* seem to be threatening to reunite one last time, and in fact they did it *again* at the 1985 Live Aid benefit concert in London) captured in *Rocks America.* The band's "last show" was simulcast live via satellite all over the United States from Toronto's Maple Leaf Gardens on December 17, 1982.

Visually speaking, this program is a perfect illustration of the chilling similarities between arena rock and arena sports: in both cases, you're *much* better off watching on TV than from any seat in the house. Especially here, as the hall was purposely lit for video cameras more than for the live audience, and because director Richard Namm had cameras all over the place and cut between them pretty smartly. *BUT,* for all of you too young to have experienced the Who in their most memorable glory (see *The Kids Are*

Alright for that, among other programs), don't get fooled again—this is *not* the Who, but "The Who," a gang of tired old men desperately grabbing for as many pension dollars as they can get before expiring. They try to rise to the occasion and all, but it's a pitiful end to a mostly marvelous legacy—a tarnishing made all the more unseemly because it wasn't really necessary. Yeah, *Rocks America* is well shot, it's an historic moment, and it *is* "The Who," but it's really got about as much to do with the Who's true legacy as those beer commercials they did around the same time as the farewell show.

□ THE WHO
QUADROPHENIA
★★★★½

RCA/Columbia, 1979, 120 minutes
PRODUCED BY: The Who, Roy Baird, Bill Curbishley
DIRECTED BY: Franc Roddam
MUSIC FROM: Quadrophenia motion picture soundtrack (Polydor, 1979).
SELECTIONS: The Who: "I Am the Sea," "The Real Me," "I'm One," "5:15," "Love, Reign O'er Me," "Bell Boy," "I've Had Enough," "Helpless Dancer," "Doctor Jimmy," "Get Out and Stay Out," "Four Faces," "Joker James," "The Punk and the Godfather"; James Brown: "Night Train"; the Kingsmen: "Louie Louie"; Booker T. and the MGs: "Green Onions"; the Cascades: "Rhythm of the Rain"; the Chiffons: "He's So Fine"; the Ronettes: "Be My Baby"; the Crystals: "Da Doo Ron Ron (When He Walked Me Home)."

This feature film based on the Who's *Quadrophenia* tells the story of Jimmy, an early-'60s Mod whose sense of self is wholly defined by the rebellious youth culture scene. Unlike the other Mods, Jimmy's commitment to his cause—whatever it is—is so intense yet unfocused that he nearly self-destructs before running his hero Ace's (the king Mod whom Jimmy discovers is only a scraping bellhop) scooter off the white cliffs of Brighton in the film's climactic end. His pals seem to see the limits of their rebellion and to appreciate it as a good though occasionally violent time. Jimmy, on the other hand, quits his job, leaves his family, wrecks his bike, and wanders about in a pill-induced stupor, essentially a faithless, cowardly, stupid boy.

What makes this film so powerful and great is the acting, especially Phil Daniels as Jimmy, and the Who's soundtrack. This music—especially "Love Reign O'er Me," "I'm One," and "The Real Me"—has a sweeping power on record that has been beautifully matched by the story and the cinematography. In fact, it's so grand that the small screen doesn't do it full justice, and so seeing it at least once in a theater is recommended.—P.R.

□ THE WHO, OTHERS
TOMMY
★★★

Columbia, 1982 (originally released in 1975), 111 minutes
PRODUCED BY: Robert Stigwood and Ken Russell
DIRECTED BY: Ken Russell
MUSIC FROM: Tommy soundtrack (Polydor, 1975).
SELECTIONS: The Who: "Amazing Journey," "Sensation," "Welcome," "Sally Simpson," "We're Not Gonna Take It"; Keith Moon: "Fiddle About," "Tommy's Holiday Camp"; Eric Clapton: "Eyesight to the Blind"; Tina Turner: "The Acid Queen", Elton John: "Pinball Wizard"; Ann-Margret and Oliver Reed: "Bernie's Holiday Camp," "You Didn't Hear It," "Christmas," "Do You Think It's Alright," "There's a Doctor I've Found"; Ann-Margret: "Tommy Can You Hear Me," "Smash the Mirror"; Ann-Margret, Oliver Reed, Jack Nicholson: "Go to the Mirror Boy"; Paul Nicholas: "Cousin Kevin."

You might scan the musical selections and say, "What's Ann-Margret/Oliver

Reed/Jack Nicholson doing singing Who songs?" Rest assured that many, many Who fans were asking the same questions when this came out; and if you're a Who purist, you might just want to skip this one. However, if you did like *Tommy* the album (by the Who), enjoy bombastic, flamboyant-bordering-on-obscene visual displays, and can stomach a good cartoon rendition of a pseudo-Christian morality tale, this may be for you. By now everyone probably knows the story of Townshend's deaf, dumb, and blind pinball wizard-cum-savior who is ultimately crushed under the weight of his own popularity. If you could understand all that from the record, you don't need this. But if you're like the rest of us, or if you can appreciate and treasure the wonderful moments here (Tina Turner's Acid Queen, Keith Moon's lech *de luxe* Uncle Ernie, Elton John's Pinball Wizard), *Tommy* is worth a look. And Roger Daltrey never looked better.

The music, despite some of the performances, is good, and even those who cannot sing (like Oliver Reed as Tommy's disgusting step-father) sound like their characters, which is fine. Visually, Russell's work here is interesting if overdone and has the simple clarity and hyperkinetic punch of a good, campy cartoon, which seems somehow appropriate. The unabashed grossness and excess of Ann-Margret's infamous baked beans and chocolate scene is bizarrely fascinating, a little like watching someone upchuck in public. How good or bad this is all depends on the viewer. You could say that *Tommy* works despite and maybe because of its flaws. Generally recommendable, though parents of young kids should know that "Fiddle About"—which seemed a lot funnier before sex crimes against children became front-page news—clearly presents Uncle Ernie as a homosexual pedophile with enema bags, soiled undies, and all, and Tommy as the victim. It seems strange to describe a scene in a movie so obviously unrealistic as graphic or potentially harmful, but it is.—P.R.

□ WHODINI
BACK IN BLACK
★★★

RCA/Columbia, 1986, 18 minutes
PRODUCED BY: Ricardo Siciliano, Philip Meese
DIRECTED BY: Melvin Van Peebles, Adam Friedman
MUSIC FROM: Back in Black (Jive/Arista, 1986); *Escape* (Jive/Arista, 1985).
SELECTIONS: "Funky Beat," "Freaks Come Out at Night," "Big Mouth," "Escape (I Need a Break)."

This is a solid if unspectacular video clip showcase for one of hip-hop/rap's most promising mid-'80s acts, an act that has already shown a surprising ability to cross over to a larger pop audience—surprising considering the raw, minimally melodic street-beat sound in which this trio is rooted. The tape kicks off appropriately with "Funky Beat," a prime example of their original lean, mean, starkly powerful big-beat sound. The video was directed by Melvin Van Peebles, whose ribald antiblacksploitation movie *Sweet Sweetback's Baadasssss Song* (1971) was a reverse-racist classic that marked him as one of the more unique and wayward new cinematic talents of his generation. He never followed up on that promise, however. "Funky Beat" is an okay video that starts out with a quick onslaught of imagery that whets the appetite for better things: in the first thirty seconds, Malcolm-Jamal Warner of TV's *Cosby Show* is seen on a podium, stuttering out the opening of a lecture on "the funk," when he's interrupted by jumping, dancing newsboys shouting "Extra!" and flashing papers headlined "Whodini's Funky Beat!"; one such front page spins out at the viewer as the funky beat kicks in *hard,* and then a little clown puppet appears on-screen, squeaking, "Rap to that funky beat!"; cut to Whodini themselves, dancing at the camera from the far end of a long, dark, misty tunnel. From there, it's into a steadily cross-cut montage of Whodini stage performance, plenty of dancing/clapping/bouncing-in-their-seats audience shots, and lyric-illustrating silent-film clips and shots of Whodini in various locales and situations (strutting the ghetto streets, flipping burgers, in jail, etc.) with assorted other guest stars (boxer Mark Breland and fellow rappers Run-D.M.C. and Kurtis Blow). For all its kineticism, it still doesn't go anywhere special, though the music is forceful enough to make it something more than merely ordinary.

"Big Mouth," which is in New York's Museum of Modern Art music video collection, is similar musically and in some ways visually to "Funky Beat." There are some non sequitur shots, markedly similar to scenes in Power Station's "Bang a Gong" clip, in which a starkly lit guy or girl dances in a doorway next to a dramatically angled big screen that flashes lyric-illustrating imagery pulled from a variety of archival sources (cartoons, science filmstrips). And there are lots of on-the-beat cuts between scenes of a Whodini rapping at the camera and telling off the girl of the title—who, at the end, drives the group away in a big black limo. It takes place mostly in an office set placed on a huge pier for no apparent reason. Again, the clip (directed by Adam Friedman) is, well, *okay*—but they put *this* in MOMA?

"Escape (I Need a Break)" and "Freaks Come Out at Night" are both high-spirited, competently produced mini-documentaries of the 1985 Fresh Fest Tour, in which Whodini joined Kurtis Blow, Run-D.M.C., and others in a package tour harking back to the golden age of '50s and '60s rock and soul revues. While Whodini's energetic stage performance dominates, there are also affectionate, home-movie-style shots of the other performers on the tour demonstrating their camaraderie, as well as a few brief special-effects-treated shots of breakdancers.

And so, despite my quibbles with some of the individual clips, *Back in Black* gives Whodini fans, or anyone else interested in checking them out, a decent enough chance to dig 'em in action.

□ BOB WILBER

JAZZ AT THE SMITHSONIAN: A TRIBUTE TO SIDNEY BECHET

★★★

Sony, 1983, 59 minutes

PRODUCED BY: Clark and Delia Gravelle Santee

DIRECTED BY: Clark and Delia Gravelle Santee

MUSIC FROM: Various Bob Wilber albums.

SELECTIONS: "Down in Honky Tonky Town," "Si Tu Vois Ma Mere," "Dans les Rues d'Antibes," "Summertime," "Coal Cart Blues," "China Boy," "Kansas City Man Blues," "Lady Be Good," "Polka Dot Stomp," "Petite Fleur."

The idea of jazz repertory is a good one, especially with as accomplished a soprano saxophonist as Wilber at the helm, preserving the legacy of a musician as great as Bechet—who, along with Louis Armstrong and Coleman Hawkins, practically invented swing back in the 1920s. Perhaps the most obvious example of Bechet's imperial boudoir lyricism here is the simmering "Summertime," but everything is handled with proper care and feeling (the Smithsonian Jazz

Repertory Ensemble also features trumpeter Glenn Zottola and guitarist Chris Florey). Of course, if you think Dixieland jazz is incapable of such smashingly florid sensuality, you'll find all this a real bore, but those with the ears to hear will certainly enjoy what is probably the only chance we'll ever get to experience Bechet's music on video (despite the apparent incongruity of seeing it performed by a tuxedoed, all-white ensemble before a sit-down audience of bluebloods).

□ HANK WILLIAMS, JR., AND OTHERS
A STAR-SPANGLED COUNTRY PARTY
★★★

Pacific Arts, 1986, 60 minutes
DIRECTED BY: Marty Pasetta
MUSIC FROM: Various albums by Hank Williams, Jr., Waylon Jennings, Earl Thomas Conley, and Gus Hardin.
SELECTIONS: Hank Williams, Jr.: "Honky Tonkin'," "Texas Women," "Dixie on My Mind," "The Conversation," "Women I've Never Had," "Gonna Go Hunting Tonight," "Man of Steel," "Family Tradition," "A Country Boy Can Survive," "La Grange"; Earl Thomas Conley: "Your Love's on the Line"; Gus Hardin: "I'll Pass"; Waylon Jennings with Hank Williams, Jr.: "Are You Sure Hank Done It This Way?," "Love Sick Blues"; Waylon Jennings: "Luckenbach, Texas," "Good-Hearted Woman"; Waylon Jennings with Jessi Colter: "Storms Never Last."

There's a fine, heapin' helpin' of solid, entertaining country and country-rock music here from Hank, Jr., Waylon (who duets with Hank, Jr., and with Mrs. Waylon, Jessi Colter), Earl Thomas Conley, and up-and-comer (at the time this was shot in late 1984, at least) Gus Hardin. But to enjoy it, you've got to endure the typical-TV-special direction of Pasetta, with its constant banal cutaways and occasional blatantly bad edits and generally uninspired camerawork. Since this show was taped on board the American naval flagship U.S.S. *Constellation*—and there's a forty-foot-tall red, white, and blue American eagle as a backdrop that really lays the patriotic rah-rah on a little thick—the cutaways are to sailors raisin' hell, and the jarring edits include one with Hank, Jr., purportedly jumping into an F-14 fighter jet that's laugh-out-loud bogus. There's also a tour of the vessel and some mundane chin music between Hank, Jr., and the ship's captain. When it sticks to the performers, this is a good tape, and fortunately it does that about seventy-five percent of the time. If it did it even more, it'd get a higher rating.

□ JOE WILLIAMS
JAZZ AT THE SMITHSONIAN
★★★

Sony, 1983, 58 minutes
PRODUCED BY: Clark and Delia Gravelle Santee
DIRECTED BY: Clark and Delia Gravelle Santee
MUSIC FROM: Various albums by Joe Williams.
SELECTIONS: "Everyday I Have the Blues," "The Comback," "Once in a While," "If It's the Last Thing I Do," "Same Old Story," "Everything Must Change," "Who She Do," "Well, Alright, OK, You Win," "Stella By Starlight," "But Not for Me," "I Had Someone Else Before I Had You," "Save That Time for Me," "Joe's Blues."

Joe Williams first came to fame when he recorded "Everyday I Have the Blues" with Count Basie's Orchestra in the '50s; it became his theme song and epitomizes his classy fusion of urbane bluesiness and a distinctive, full-bodied crooner's voice. However, most contemporary TV viewers probably know Williams from his frequent *Tonight Show* appearances, where he inevitably belts it out along with the house big band. Here, he's backed by a trio (Kirk Stuart on piano, Keeter Best on bass, and Steve Williams on drums) and gets to show a wider and substantially different range of moods and approaches than some folks might expect. On slow, soft ballads such as "Once in a While" he goes from an intimate purr to soaring, near-operatic declamations, and then back to low-key lyricism, seamlessly maintaining his dignity all the while. As expected, he handles the up-tempo tunes with unflagging authority, but with more delicate shadings than are possible in a big-band setting. As usual in Jazz at the Smithsonian programs, the photography is excellent, intimate without being intrusive or forced, the direction is always tastefully complementary to the performance, and there are too-brief interview snippets with the performer. All in all, a unique opportunity to glimpse what a most estimable mainstream jazz-pop vocalist has to offer.

□ WILLIE AND THE POOR BOYS

WILLIE AND THE POOR BOYS

★★½

JEM/Passport, 1985, 30 minutes

DIRECTED BY: Eddie Arno and Mark Innocenti

MUSIC FROM: Willie and the Poor Boys (JEM, 1985).

SELECTIONS: "Poor Boy Boogie," "You Never Can Tell," "Chicken Shack Boogie," "Let's Talk It Over," "All Night Long," "Saturday Night," "Baby Please Don't Go."

Rolling Stones Bill Wyman and Charlie Watts, along with guests like fellow Stone Ron Wood (here seen honking a baritone sax rather than playing guitar) and Who drummer Kenney Jones, get back to their boogie-woogie/R&B roots with a selection of classic cover tunes, presented in an affectionately nostalgic sock-hop setting. Ringo Starr cameos at the end as a janitor cleaning up after the hop. Pleasant, innocuous fun, but ultimately a bit disappointing considering the talent lineup.

□ NANCY WILSON AND BAND

A VERY SPECIAL CONCERT

★★★

Sony, 1983, 60 minutes

PRODUCED BY: Michael M. Galer

DIRECTED BY: Gary Legon

MUSIC FROM: Echoes of an Era (Electra Musician, 1981); *The Griffith Park Collection* (Electra Musician, 1982).

SELECTIONS: "I Want to Be Happy," "I Get a Kick Out of You," "Round Midnight," "But Not for Me," "Yesterday," "Them There Eyes," "Take the 'A' Train."

In this, the second, vocal half of the same 1982 California concert whose opening instrumental portion is available on Sony's *Chick Corea Video LP,* middle-of-the-road jazz singer Nancy Wilson fronts a fine, straight-ahead modern acoustic jazz quartet comprised of pianist Corea, bassist Stanley Clarke, drummer Lenny White, and tenor saxophonist Joe Henderson. Wilson sings live what Chaka Khan sang on the band's *Echoes of an Era* album. The comparison between the two vocalists is interesting: Wilson is nowhere near as distinctively powerful and mercurial a singer as Khan and lacks the latter's gospel-rooted fire, but her more traditional, scat-based approach, in which she frequently phrases with a horn-like growl, could be seen as a more natural fit with the quartet's neoclassic post-bop swing. However, she's outshone by the *real* horn onstage—Henderson, whose playing is impeccably poised between control and abandon throughout.

□ VARIOUS ARTISTS

WINDHAM HILL: AUTUMN PORTRAIT

★★★½

Paramount, 1985, 55 minutes

PRODUCED BY: Dann Moss
DIRECTED BY: Stanley Dorfman
MUSIC FROM: Various albums by various artists (Windham Hill).
SELECTIONS: William Ackerman: "Bricklayer's Beautiful Daughter," "Synopsis 2," "The Impending Death of the Virgin Spirit"; Alex De Grassi: "Turning," "Clockwork"; Daniel Hecht: "Afternoon Postlude Soliloquy"; Shadowfax: "Move the Clouds"; Philip Aaberg: "Lou Ann"; Mark Isham: "When Things Dream"; Scott Cossu: "Almost like Heaven"; Michael O'Domhnaill and Bill Oskay: "Bridges"; Bill Quist: "3 Gymnopedies #2," "3 Gymnopedies #3."
Also available on Pioneer Stereo Laser videodisc.

☐ **VARIOUS ARTISTS**
WINDHAM HILL: WATER'S PATH
★★★½

Paramount, 1985, 53 minutes
PRODUCED BY: Dann Moss
DIRECTED BY: Stanley Dorfman
MUSIC FROM: Various albums by various artists (Windham Hill).
SELECTIONS: William Ackerman: "Visiting," "3 Observations of One Ocean;" Scott Cossu: "Purple Mountain"; Daniel Hecht: "Confluence of the Rivers"; Michael Hedges: "Aerial Boundaries"; Bill Quist: "3 Gnossienne #1," "3 Gnossienne #2"; Shadowfax: "Kindred Spirits," "Big Song"; Ira Stein and Russell Walder: "Elements"; George Winston: "Colors/Dance."
Also available on Pioneer Stereo Laser videodisc.

☐ **VARIOUS ARTISTS**
WINDHAM HILL: WESTERN LIGHT
★★★½

Paramount, 1985, 55 minutes
PRODUCED BY: Dann Moss
DIRECTED BY: Stephen Verona
MUSIC FROM: Various albums by various artists (Windham Hill).
SELECTIONS: William Ackerman: "Ventana," "Remedios," "Hawk Circle," "Processional"; Alex De Grassi: "Blue and White," "Western," "36"; Mark Isham: "On the Threshold of Liberty," "In the Blue Distance"; Shadowfax: "The Dreams of Children," "Vajra"; Liz Story: "Water Caves."
Also available on Pioneer Stereo Laser videodisc.

☐ **VARIOUS ARTISTS**
WINDHAM HILL: WINTER
★★★½

Paramount, 1985, 53 minutes
PRODUCED BY: Dann Moss
DIRECTED BY: Sterling Johnson
MUSIC FROM: Various albums by various artists (Windham Hill).
SELECTIONS: Mark Isham: "Winter," "Interlude 1," "Interlude 2," "Men Before the Mirror," "Interlude 3"; Alex De Grassi: "Empty Room"; Shadowfax: "Snowline"; Darol Anger with the Barbara Higbie Quintet: "Duet"; William Ackerman: "Threes"; Paul Dondero: "Out to Play"; Cyrille Verdeaux: "Messenger of the Sun"; Bill Oskay and Michael O. Domhnaill: "The 19-A"; Liz Story: "Wedding Rain"; Michael Manring: "Welcoming."
Also available on Pioneer Stereo Laser videodisc.

Windham Hill Records is the brainchild of Northern Californian guitarist William Ackerman. It began in the mid-'70s as a cottage industry with a cult following who appreciated the label's quixotic philosophy of quiescent, immaculately recorded, spare, and atmospheric mood music that, while generally pretty in sound, gentle in tone, relaxed in tempo, and often warmly pastoral, made few ostensible concessions to pop. Seemingly against all odds, by the early '80s Windham Hill had become a highly successful, mass-cult phenomenon, making major sellers out of such retiring musical artisans as synthesist/trumpeter Mark Isham, guitarist Alex De Grassi, pianist George Winston, and Ackerman himself. Cynics may deride Windham Hill music as "Yuppie Muzak," but there's no denying that an awful lot of people think it's the hippest aural wallpaper, and/or the greatest sensory escape around.

The Windham Hill videos are logical extensions of the label's distinctive aural identity into the visual realm. As the music is pretty and relaxed and pastoral, so are the visuals—consisting of beautifully photographed, scenic natural vistas, with slow-dissolve edits to match the way the music slowly uncoils in a vast, reverberant space. Where the music is meditative and instrumental, avoiding song structure in favor of an enveloping drone, the images are also presented in an "abstract," as in nonnarrative, fashion. The visuals undeniably complement the music well, and vice versa, though it's strictly a matter of personal taste whether any synergistic epiphanies exist here. *Autumn Portrait* features the kaleidoscopic forest palette of New England in the fall (it's the most colorful of these four); *Water's Path* goes to Ackerman's home turf (from the Sierras to Big Sur, Carmel to Monterey) to take its title literally, following water's path from clouds to mountain lakes, from brooks to ponds, from streams to lakes, from rivers to the sea (it's the most hypnotic, and could be seen as erotic in spots); *Western Light* focuses on such imposing natural wonders of the American West as Monument Valley and the Grand Canyon (it's the most awe-inspiring); and *Winter* features the snow-covered high country of California, Colorado, Nevada, and Utah (it's the coolest).

The jaded will probably dismiss Windham Hill video as a sub-*Koyaanisqatsi* audio-visual narcotic. But those who like or love Windham Hill music, or think they might, will probably respond to the videos, too, maybe even for the same reasons cynics hate them. And they're certainly the most impressively produced and immediately functional entries yet in that fringe genre known as "ambient/environmental/alternative" video, which was previously the domain of video fireplaces, video fishtanks, and pretentious twaddle like Brian Eno's *Thursday Afternoon.*

□ JOHNNY WINTER
LIVE

★★★

Media, 1984, 45 minutes

DIRECTED BY: Stan Jacobsen

MUSIC FROM: Various Johnny Winter albums.

SELECTIONS: "Jumpin' Jack Flash," "Rock and Roll Hoochie Koo," "Stranger," "Unseen Eye," "Sweet Papa John," "Highway 61 Revisited," "Mean Town Blues," "Johnny B. Goode," "It's All Over Now."

The veteran Texas albino blues guitar whiz, live at Toronto's Massey Hall in 1983. The straight-shootin' set—Winter fronts a bass-and-drums rhythm section and that's it, and the material's all down and dirty and played straight, no chaser—is shot straightforwardly. There's nothing here to appeal to the non-aficionado either musically or visually (even for fans, Johnny's white skin and hair, Gibson Firebird guitar, and black cowboy hat get a little wearing on the eyes—speaking of which, the cowboy hat covers Johnny's pink eyes, which may not be such a bad thing). Still, Winter's in good form, and handles his fleet-fingered guitar solos and gutbucket vocals with authority. There's a brief interview midway through, where Winter talks about maybe making "a more commercial album, 'cos straight blues ain't gonna get much airplay." Just as you're thinking how sad that is, we're back onstage and Winter's ripping through a torrid blues reading of Dylan's "Highway 61 Revisited," the highlight of the tape.

☐ **PAUL WINTER CONSORT**
CANYON CONSORT
★★★½

A&M/Windham Hill, 1986, 60 minutes
PRODUCED BY: David Vassar and John Lyddon
DIRECTED BY: David Vassar
MUSIC FROM: Canyon (Living Music/A&M, 1985).
SELECTIONS: "Grand Canyon Sunrise," "Morning Echoes," "Bright Angel," "Raven Dance," "Bedrock Cathedral," "River Run," "Elves' Chasm," "Sockdolager," "Air," "Grand Canyon Sunset."

The Paul Winter Consort makes the sort of quiescent, meditative, pastel-shaded music that comes under Windham Hill's "New Age" banner, but Winter comes by the label more honestly than most. Along with Oregon—with whom he's played, and some of whose members have played with him—he's been making this sort of music since the late '60s. And, along with Oregon, Winter puts a bit more bracing atonality and world-music ethnic substance into his version of post-hippie mantra-music than most of the more one-dimensional Windham Hill crowd. It's gratifying to see that someone stuck at his thing long enough for a real audience to come around to him.

Like Windham Hill's other "ambient" videos, especially the desert-oriented *Western Light, Canyon Consort* matches the muted music with lovely, awesome-majesty nature photography—in this case, we follow the Consort (including reedman Winter, cellist Eugene Friesen, Glen Velez on assorted ethnic percussion instruments, and organist Paul Halley) down the Colorado River as they raft through the Grand Canyon. It's a particularly felicitous match in this case, for back in the "organic, man" '60s Winter's music was often known as "Earth music" for its mystical/romantic/pantheistic way of trying to merge and harmonize with nature itself. Furthermore, if you have the original audio album you know the liner notes provide a sort of visual play-by-play evoking Canyon sights to go with each selection (for instance, "Raven soars out from rim . . . swoops down over Bright Angel Trail, cavorting, barrel-rolling . . . plays with updrafts, flies into the depths . . ."), so it's really not much of a leap from that to this. Indeed, seeing the players drifting along the golden, sun-dappled waters or running the white-water rapids on their raft, and individually improvising plaintive solos at various breathtaking stops along the way, not only conveys something of the immediacy of their contact with Mother Nature, but also captures something of the mystical power of their experience as well.

☐ **VARIOUS ARTISTS**
WOODSTOCK I
★★★★

Warner Home Video, 1970, 90 minutes
PRODUCED BY: Bob Maurice
DIRECTED BY: Michael Wadleigh
MUSIC FROM: Woodstock motion picture soundtrack (Cotillion, 1970).
SELECTIONS: Canned Heat: "Going Up the Country"; Crosby, Stills, Nash and Young: "Long Time Gone," "Wooden Ships," "Woodstock"; Richie Havens: "Handsome Johnny," "Sometimes I Feel Like a Motherless Child"/"Freedom"; Joan Baez: "Joe Hill," "Swing Low, Sweet Chariot"; the Who: "We're Not Gonna Take It," "Summertime Blues," "Young Man Blues"; Sha Na Na: "At the Hop"; Joe Cocker: "With a Little Help from My Friends."

☐ **VARIOUS ARTISTS**
WOODSTOCK II
★★★★

Warner Home Video, 1970, 90 minutes

PRODUCED BY: Bob Maurice
DIRECTED BY: Michael Wadleigh
MUSIC FROM: Woodstock motion picture soundtrack (Cotillion, 1970).
SELECTIONS: Country Joe and the Fish: "Rock & Soul Music," "The 'Fish' Cheer," "I-Feel-Like-I'm-Fix'n-to Die Rag"; Arlo Guthrie: "Coming into Los Angeles"; Crosby, Stills and Nash: "Suite: Judy Blue Eyes"; Ten Years After: "I'm Going Home"; John Sebastian: "Younger Generation"; Santana: "Soul Sacrifice"; Sly and the Family Stone: "I Want to Take You Higher"; Jimi Hendrix: "The Star Spangled Banner," "Purple Haze."

In the years since Woodstock happened over three days in August 1969, the festival has become the symbol of the more positive aspects of the generation that still bears its name, and rightfully so. Given the generally dark history of the rock festival—starting with Altamont just a few months after this—it's hard to imagine that there were half a million people living together fairly happily despite rains, mud, crowding, and a dearth of food and water (cynics might argue that adversity forced people to behave), but it did happen that way—and if it sounds like one of those things you'd have to see to believe, here's your chance.

Of course, what Woodstock was known for above all else was the music, here beautifully presented with sound that is amazingly good even without stereo. It was at Woodstock that several acts, including Santana, Joe Cocker, and Crosby, Stills and Nash, really launched their careers, and all but the latter never sounded better. Other highlights include the Who's set (before which Pete Townshend had unwittingly been slipped some acid), Sly and the Family Stone's "I Want to Take You Higher," Joan Baez's performance, and Jimi Hendrix's "Star Spangled Banner." There's also all the stuff that doesn't really hold up, but was so typical of the day and the time that—well, you can always fast-forward through Arlo Guthrie and John Sebastian—they just seem to belong. Of note to young guitar maniacs: Alvin Lee's flying fingers on "I'm Going Home" never fail to dazzle, though it's sixteen years since I first saw this and I still don't know why. As good as these sets are, you can't help but wonder what you're missing; among the acts not included in the film were Creedence Clearwater Revival, the Band, Janis Joplin, Mountain, and Paul Butterfield (though some of these performances are on the soundtrack albums; there was a *Woodstock Two* in 1971).

What really sets this film apart, though, is its quality as a film. It's a documentary that captures not only the event but the time, through short interviews with the promoters, local residents of the upstate New York area near Bethel, fans—even the Port-o-San maintenance guy. Tracing the festival from the first arrivals—riding horses through a field—to the last stragglers surveying a mud field of trash, *Woodstock* shows you not just what happened but how. But watching today, you can't help but giggle at the warnings about the brown acid and the interview with a young couple who seem proud that they're free enough to let each other sleep around; it's also sad to realize that as misdirected as we might think these kids were, at least there was some kind of hope there. The treatment seems pretty evenhanded—people on drugs look really stupid, one young girl almost has a nervous breakdown on camera, Bill Graham characteristically argues to close off the festival site to people without tickets, and things do go wrong. The key to really enjoying this is *not* to try to guess which multinational corporation which naked kid is now running, but to really appreciate it for the miracle it was.

So as film and a history lesson for the kids—maybe everybody—*Woodstock* is highly recommended. One thing about it that eluded me for many years is that it doesn't present the acts in the order they actually appeared, a small quibble. It's not really clear, for example, that when Hendrix plays he's the last act and only thirty thousand people are still there. But as a cassette, it leaves something more to be desired: first, the first *Woodstock* soundtrack contains music on both of these tapes. Second, it's not clear that it takes two cassettes to make up the one film, since they are titled I and II, *à la* a sequel, not part I, part II. If you're renting it, be sure you get both parts. Finally, the film was made at the height of split-screen mania and on an average television screen, you lose so much of, say, a triple screen that you may think your TV or VCR is on the blink. But look on the bright side—you don't have to sit in the mud.—P.R.

□ BILL WYMAN
BILL WYMAN VIDEO 45

★½

Sony, 1983, 10 minutes
PRODUCED BY: Bill Wyman
MUSIC FROM: Various Bill Wyman singles (Rolling Stones, 1981).
SELECTIONS: "(Si Si) Je Suis Un Rock Star," "A New Fashion," "Come Back Suzanne."

Stones bassist Wyman exhibits his famous droll, deadpan demeanor in three unspectacular video clips based on some time-killing 1981 solo singles. "Come Back Suzanne" is both the best video and best song of an uninspired lot—the music's agreeable honky-tonk rockarama, and the clip aspires to slapstick comedy, with Bill messing up his kitchen because his girl's gone away. For maniacal Stones fans only.

□ BILL WYMAN
DIGITAL DREAMS

★½

Media, 1985, 70 minutes
PRODUCED BY: Bill and Astrid Wyman
DIRECTED BY: Robert Dornhelm
MUSIC FROM: Digital Dreams motion picture soundtrack (Ripple Prod., 1983).
SELECTIONS: Terry Taylor and Mike Batt: "Teardrop Waltz"; Patrick Moore: "Penguin Parade"; the Rolling Stones: "Miss You," "(I Can't Get No) Satisfaction," "Street Fighting Man," "The Last Time," "Have You Seen Your Mother, Baby," "Jumpin' Jack Flash," "Around and Around."

Digital Dreams, which says at its outset that it was "adapted from the computerized diaries of Bill Wyman," was made in 1983 but never released theatrically in America. It's not hard to see why. Subtitled "The Life and Dreams of Bill Wyman" and apparently meant to be a freewheelingly fanciful semidocumentary, *Digital Dreams* is indulgent and self-consciously arty enough to make you care even less than you thought you might about how Bill and Astrid Wyman met and what they think of each other. (For those who do care, it appears their relationship was dissolving as this film was being shot.) Nothing personal, Bill, but if This Is Your Life, it is *dull.* In fact, Wyman takes his trademark deadpan cool to another, more curious level at one point in *Digital Dreams,* when he comes right out and verbally acknowledges the contrived boredom of the proceedings. Aside from seemingly endless shots of the Wymans at home, with Bill absorbed by his computer and ignoring Astrid's attempts at starting conversations—the kind of scenes that make *Digital Dreams* seem several times longer than it is—there are stupid, ham-fisted "surreal" interludes starring James Coburn, of all people (whose presence is never really explained—the only *legitimately* surreal thing about it), and some striking but ultimately pointless animation by Gerald Scarfe, who is better known for his contributions to *Pink Floyd The Wall.* Richard O'Brien, of *Rocky Horror Picture Show* fame, is a funny scene-stealer as the Wyman's wacko butler, and there are a few, far-too-brief glimpses of some fabulous archival Stones footage, including quick concert snippets and a tantalizing peek at the pie-fight staged for the original cover of the *Beggars Banquet* album—and those are the only real highlights of the whole film. Wyman and Mike Batt, a veteran British pop-pablum producer, co-wrote the light-classical original music score, which is tastefully rendered by the London Symphony Orchestra; snatches of some Stones classics and other incidental bits pop up on the soundtrack briefly here and there. All in all, I don't care if Wyman *is* a Rolling Stone, and *is* cool enough to acknowledge the waste of time that this movie is: it's a waste of time, pure and simple, and there can be no excuses for it. For *maniacal* Stones cultists only.

X

☐ VARIOUS ARTISTS
XANADU
★ ½

MCA, 96 minutes, 1980
PRODUCED BY: Lawrence Gordon
DIRECTED BY: Robert Greenwald
MUSIC FROM: Xanadu motion picture soundtrack (MCA, 1980).
SELECTIONS: Olivia Newton-John: "Magic"; Olivia Newton-John and Cliff Richard: "Suddenly"; Olivia Newton-John and the Tubes: "Dancin' "; Olivia Newton-John and Gene Kelly: "Whenever You're Away from Me"; Electric Light Orchestra: "I'm Alive," "All Over the World," "The Fall," "Don't Walk Away," "Xanadu."

Only a few seconds into this you may find yourself saying, "God, this is dopey," but whether you're a fan of Olivia Newton-John, bad Busby Berkley–style dance numbers, ridiculous costumes, wooden acting, Gene Kelly, ELO, roller-skating, or camp, chances are you will watch it. The visuals are so obscenely rich and stunning and the plot so vacuous that morbid fascination alone could get you through it. Wheels start turning when Newton-John, as the mythical Muse Terpsichore, awakens and comes to life from a mural in Venice, California. She decides to use her powers to help a young painter (Michael Beck) and an old big-band musician turned multimillionaire (Gene Kelly!) open a sumptuous-looking roller disco. Of course, Beck falls in love with her, but—of course—he is a mere mortal, and in the one well-written scene, he must ask Zeus before he takes the god's daughter to Xanadu's opening. It probably wouldn't surprise you to know that Terpsichore was also in love with Kelly, in an earlier life, of course. Sounds like a '40s movie, huh? It was (*Down to Earth*).

As hard as *Xanadu* tries, it leaves you thinking about how they don't make 'em like they used to. Although there are a couple of wonderful pieces, such as the Tubes' "Dancin'," presented imaginatively as an '80s/'40s battle of the bands, and Kelly and Olivia's "Whenever You're Away from Me," it's easy to see why this bombed at the box office, despite the then-big ELO hits included. Still, it is very innocent (even including some very Disney-like animation sequences and neat special effects) and younger viewers could enjoy it a great deal. Put it this way: as long as you've got a fast-forward button, you're safe.—P.R.

Y

□ Y&T

LIVE AT THE SAN FRANCISCO CIVIC

★½

A&M, 1984, 60 minutes
DIRECTED BY: Michael Miner
MUSIC FROM: Various Y&T albums (A&M).

Very typical concert shoot of the Bay Area metalmongers in a 1984 homecoming show. Legendary San Francisco rock promoter Bill Graham introduces the hometown boys as "kick-ass rock 'n' roll," and that's about as close to distinction as Y&T get. Y&T stands for "Yesterday & Tomorrow," but based on their thoroughly standard grind-it-out boogie, it could just as easily stand for "Yawning & Trite."

□ WEIRD AL YANKOVIC

THE COMPLEAT AL

★★★

CBS/Fox, 1985, 100 minutes
DIRECTED BY: Jay Levey and Robert K. Weiss
MUSIC FROM: Weird Al Yankovic (Epic, 1982); *In 3–D* (Epic, 1985).
SELECTIONS: "Ricky," "I Love Rocky Road," "Eat It," "I Lost on Jeopardy," "This Is the Life," "Like a Surgeon," "One More Minute," "Dare to Be Stupid."
Also available on CBS/Fox Stereo Laser videodisc.

Yankovic's parodies of rock videos are generally very good, but after a while one begins to notice that they suffer from that dreaded comedy-album sickness: once you've gone through once and gotten the joke, you seldom if ever feel the need to go back to it again. Especially when all of Al's comic ingenuity in clips like "Eat It" and "Like a Surgeon" is merely in the service of simply aping other videos scene for scene and then tossing in the yocks like spanners in the works. Better are the clips like "Ricky," "I Love Rocky Road," and "I Lost on Jeopardy," where Al goes much further in creating his *own* comic scenarios, which have laugh-lives of their own and don't rely so totally on mocking a better-known video by a bigger artist. Best of all, though, is "Dare to Be Stupid," a Devo parody that so adroitly and completely mocks the spud boys' entire video catalogue (not to mention how the music approximates their cartoonish electro-rock) it's nothing less than awesome, and easily the best parody clip Al's done to date (after all, the guy *is* parodying an entire *oeuvre* with this one). However, "This Is the Life" (from the film *Johnny Dangerously*) bombs out completely, and the "original" music video "One More Minute" is a cornball sick joke that peters out pretty quickly. The between-clips material is, for the most part, vastly unfunny and, even worse, seemingly goes on forever—the dead giveaway that the people who made it thought it was screamingly brilliant. It ain't. Still, for its great moments and general distinction as a rock video comedy package, *The Compleat Al* is worth a look. And you can't *totally* dismiss anyone who so single-mindedly lampoons a form so deserving of satire.

□ YES

YESSONGS

★★★

VidAmerica, 1985, 70 minutes
PRODUCED BY: Brian Lane
DIRECTED BY: Peter Neal
MUSIC FROM: The Yes Album (Atlantic, 1970); *Fragile* (Atlantic, 1971); *Close to the Edge* (Atlantic, 1972); *Yessongs* (Atlantic, 1973).
SELECTIONS: "All Good People," "The Clap," "And You and I," "Close to the Edge," "Excerpts from *Six Wives of Henry*

VIII," "Roundabout," "Yours Is No Disgrace," "Wurm (Starship Trooper, Part III)."

□ YES
9012LIVE
★★★

Atlantic, 1985, 67 minutes
PRODUCED BY: Yes and Tony Dimitriades
DIRECTED BY: Steven Soderbergh
MUSIC FROM: The Yes Album (Atlantic, 1970); *90125* (Atlantic, 1984); *9012Live* (Atlantic, 1985).
SELECTIONS: "Introduction," "Cinema," "Leave It," "Hold On," "All Good People," "Changes," "Owner of a Lonely Heart," "It Can Happen," "City of Love," "Starship Trooper."

These two programs by the veteran British progressive-rock band should make for an interesting split in the band's audience. Fans of the original band and entrenched classical-rock purists will most likely opt for the nicely photographed—albeit muddled with silly "psychedelic" indulgences (zoo-plankton footage, extreme close-ups of mirror-balls, etc.)—1973 concert film *Yessongs.* It captures Yes in a more vintage period, long before they "sold out" in the eyes of prog-rock fanatics with *90125*'s "Owner of a Lonely Heart." Back in 1972, when Yes was caught at London's Rainbow Theater for *Yessongs,* they had art-rock heroes Steve Howe on guitar (later with Asia and GTR) and Rick Wakeman on keyboards (who had replaced Tony Kaye—later to rejoin for the *9012Live* edition). It is unfortunately that Yes were not shot a year *earlier* when they had another giant of the genre, their inventively agile and cracklingly precise original drummer, Bill Bruford (later with King Crimson and, briefly, Genesis). His tracks on the not-completely-corresponding *Yessongs* album ("Perpetual Change" and "Long Distance Runaround/The Fish") are not included here, and on the rest he's replaced by the plodding, out-of-place Alan White, formerly of John Lennon's Plastic Ono Band.

White never did adapt very well to Yes's intricate, suitelike symphonic-rock extravaganzas. Instead, the band adapted to *his* simple, straightforward timekeeping (*Yessongs* contains an intriguing early instance of this in the extended, funkily rearranged "Yours Is No Disgrace"). By the time of *9012Live,* shot on a 1985 tour in Edmonton, Alberta, Canada, Yes sounded much less fussy and much more commercial and direct, and White sounded right at home on the taut, funk-inflected "Owner of a Lonely Heart." But, except for new guitarist Trevor Rabin (who doesn't acquit himself too badly at all on Howe's demanding parts, inveterate Howe fans to the contrary), Yes *look* rather decrepit—especially Tony Kaye, who looks like his own grandfather, and puffy overweight bassist Chris Squire, who looks simply ghastly.

In an ostensible effort to divert attention from the unsightly spectacle Yes had become, Steve Soderbergh's gorgeously shot concert footage was subsequently treated with special-effects and all manner of other visual material by Charlex, the accomplished New York City production house whose instantly identifiable high-tech style can be seen in the Cars' classic "You Might Think," and any number of mid-'80s soft drink, bubblegum, and candy commercials. For some unexplained reason, Charlex chose to intercut Yes onstage with a motherlode of '50s footage of cornball suburban utopias, the wonders of technology, and so on. It's all very eye-catching and the '50s stuff is pleasing, I suppose, it is also completely irrelevant to Yes and their music. So much so that it just becomes annoying and bizarre. The added footage, and the dazzling way it's manipulated around the concert clips, also overshadows Yes quite easily.

Then again, Charlex's extended '50s footage opening for *9012Live* is strangely, perhaps subversively appropriate, given Yes's status as one of the first and biggest symphonic-rock bands. Consider this: a teenaged guy, a gal, and her dad are in her living room, which could easily be down the street a bit from the Cleaver household; while the gal looks on with a bored frown, the guy's waxing ecstatic to Dad about the wonders of technology—"Why, sir, sometimes the hum of turbines sounds like *music* to me!" The girl suddenly gets interested, convinces the guy to put on a record, and gets up, ready to start dancing, but the guy puts a *symphony* on the hi-fi. She draws the sign for "square" in the air with her fingers, exasperatedly rolling her eyes—and as Charlex paint the outline of the square, it becomes a video postcard, flying through a high-tech steeplechase, from outer space eventually zooming through a pair of columns to find Yes onstage before their audience.

To read that subversively, think about it this way: the '50s stuff equals the roots-of-rock 'n' roll milieu, and the "square" symphony equals Yes's own Euro-classical denaturing of rock's folkish, straightforward roots. The girl's frown symbolizes all the rock critics who ever despised Yes. And the way the "square" sign zooms through that high-tech maze and eventually leads us to Yes performing before a big, happy audience is probably the band's way of saying to all those critics, "Screw you!" Then again . . .

□ NEIL YOUNG
RUST NEVER SLEEPS
★★★★

Vestron, 1980, 111 minutes

PRODUCED BY: L. A. Johnson

DIRECTED BY: "Bernard Shakey" (a.k.a. Neil Young)

MUSIC FROM: Decade (Reprise, 1978); *Rust Never Sleeps* (Reprise, 1979); and various other Neil Young albums.

SELECTIONS: "Sugar Mountain," "I Am a Child," "Comes a Time," "After the Gold Rush," "My My, Hey Hey," "The Loner," "Welfare Mothers," "The Needle and the Damage Done," "A Lotta Love," "Powderfinger," "Sedan Delivery," "Cortez the Killer," "Ride My Llama," "Cinnamon Girl," "Like a Hurricane," "My My, Hey Hey," "Tonight's the Night."

□ NEIL YOUNG
IN BERLIN

VidAmerica, 1986, 60 minutes

PRODUCED BY: Lorne Michaels

DIRECTED BY: Michael Lindsay-Hogg

MUSIC FROM: Trans (Geffen, 1982); *Rust Never Sleeps* (Reprise, 1979); *American Stars 'n' Bars* (Reprise, 1977); *Harvest* (Reprise, 1972); *After the Gold Rush* (Reprise, 1970); *Everybody Knows This Is Nowhere* (Reprise, 1969).

SELECTIONS: "Cinnamon Girl," "Computer Age," "Little Thing Called Love," "Old Man," "Needle and the Damage Done," "After the Gold Rush," "Transformer Man," "Sample and Hold," "Hurricane," "Hey Hey My My (into the Black)," "Berlin."

□ NEIL YOUNG
SOLO TRANS
★★½

Pioneer Artists, 1986, 60 minutes

DIRECTED BY: Hal Ashby

MUSIC FROM: Trans (Geffen, 1982) and other Neil Young albums.

SELECTIONS: "Sample and Hold," "Computer Age," "Hold On to Your Love," "We R in Control," "Transformer," "Mr. Soul," "Ohio," "Payola Blues," "Get Gone," and others.

Also available in Pioneer Stereo Laser videodisc.

In 1979, the quixotic folk-rocker Neil Young made one of the most unusual concert films ever—*Rust Never Sleeps,* which he directed under the pseudonym "Bernard Shakey." It's very strange, but then anyone who knows Young's work well—or who got a good look at his eyes during his guest shot in the Band's *The Last Waltz*—should not be surprised. Young performs a solo acoustic set and an electric set (with Crazy Horse, his wonderfully raw backup band of the period) while dwarfed by hyperbolically huge amplifier and microphone props; frequently scurrying about the stage are "Road-Eyes," roadies with hooded shawls and glowing penlight eyes apparently inspired by the then-recent *Star Wars.* Some regard all that stuff as a needless distraction from Young's performance; personally, I feel the oversize props make a nicely gonzo comment on arena rock, but the real point is this—how could you be distracted from *this* music? Young goes through a veritable greatest-hits catalogue of sensitive, soulful acoustic folk and biting electric rock numbers, and is in fine form throughout. And the new material he introduced here—the punk rock requiem "My My, Hey Hey" ("The king is gone but he's not forgotten / This is the story of Johnny Rotten"), in both elegiac acoustic and buzzsaw electric versions; "Powderfinger" and "Sedan Delivery," more marvelously searing rockers—was pretty much brilliant through-and-through. Overall, the whole show is imbued with Neil's own cockeyed, different-drummer persona; if you don't like *Rust Never Sleeps,* you just don't like Neil Young.

On the other hand, if you really *are* a Neil Young fan, you may want to *avoid* both *In Berlin* and *Solo Trans,* which are from Young's *Trans* tour—his most disappointingly specious, dilettantish period to date, in which he used synthesizers, rhythm sequencers, and vocoders to create droning, metronomic, monotonic machine-age music. Shooting this concert in Berlin, home of Kraftwerk, the original machine-musicians, may have seemed like a good idea at the time. But the electronic material is a drag, plain and simple, and not even the energetic presence of Neil's longtime second guitarist Nils Lofgren can relieve the tedium. Michael Lindsay-Hogg's direction, which ranges from strangely slack to downright annoying in its disregard for what's going on onstage and with the music, doesn't help a bit. The more traditional classics still sound okay, though; I'd tell you to see and hear 'em on *Rust* except "Old Man" is here, as well as a never-released-elsewhere song, "Berlin." So, for the diehard devotee . . .

With Hal Ashby directing, *Solo Trans* fares a bit better. Shot at a Dayton, Ohio, concert, it's put together as a TV show, hosted by the smarmily bland "Don Clear," who bugs people backstage and in the audience for their reactions to Neil's latest career move. Neil performs his *Trans* tunes solo, with backing tapes, which makes sense since the music sounds totally canned anyway. The computer blues are alleviated by video montages for "Mr. Soul" (a retrospective of Neil's career in quick archival flashes) and "Ohio" (newsreel footage), and by the appearance late in the show of the Shocking Pinks, who join Neil for a few of the cheerily ragged rockabilly numbers they were about to record for the *Everybody's Rockin'* LP, including the great "Payola Blues." *Rust Never Sleeps* remains the definitive Neil Young on video to date.

□ PAUL YOUNG
THE VIDEO SINGLES

★★½

CBS/Fox, 1986, 25 minutes

PRODUCED BY: Various
DIRECTED BY: Various
MUSIC FROM: No Parlez (Columbia, 1984); *The Secret of Assocation* (Columbia, 1985).
SELECTIONS: "Come Back and Stay," "Everytime You Go Away," "I'm Gonna Tear Your Playhouse Down," "Tomb of Memories," "Everything Must Change."

Young is a more than competent British blue-eyed soul singer, and Laurie Latham provides him with marvelous arrangements and production. Furthermore—at least according to just about every woman I know—Young's a certified hunk. So, despite the fact that none of these video clips for his hit tunes is particularly outstanding *as a video* (Godley and Creme's "Everything Must Change" comes closest), they all feature plenty of pretty Paulie. Combine that with the enveloping lushness of Latham's production and the penetrating warmth of Young's voice, and maybe you can understand why I'll risk being branded a hideous male chauvinist pig, and suggest that this tape might make an outstanding video fireplace for some of you ladies out there.

Z

☐ **VARIOUS ARTISTS**
ZABRISKIE POINT
★★½

MGM/UA, 1982, 112 minutes
PRODUCED BY: Carlo Ponti
DIRECTED BY: Michelangelo Antonioni
MUSIC FROM: Zabriskie Point motion picture soundtrack album (MGM, 1969).
SELECTIONS: Pink Floyd: "Heart Beat, Pig Meat," "Crumbling Land," "Come In Number 51, Your Time Is Up"; Grateful Dead: "Dark Star (excerpt)"; Jerry Garcia with the Grateful Dead: "Love Scene"; Kaleidoscope: "Brother Mary," "Mickey's Tune"; the Youngbloods: "Sugar Babe"; Roscoe Holcomb: "I Wish I Was a Single Girl Again"; John Fahey: "Dance of Death"; Patti Page: "The Tennessee Waltz."

Antonioni's self-consciously psychedelic/surreal analysis of the existential/metaphysical gestalt of the hippie movement almost suffocates from a surfeit of cryptic artiness, a nonstory scripted in part by Sam Shepard, and the enervating antipresences of its two non-actor leads, Mark Frechette and Daria Halprin. Here's what happens: radical student Frechette, accused of killing a cop, flees by stealing a small plane; he lands in Death Valley, where he encounters blanked-out waif Halprin, who's driving aimlessly to Phoenix; they have a dreamlike, seemingly endless love scene on the sands of Zabriskie Point, in the middle of the desert; he flies back to L.A., where he's ambushed and killed by the cops; she drives to her land-developer boss's desert home, hears of Mark's death over the radio, and calmly plants a bomb in her employer's house; it explodes, over and over, in solarized slow-motion while Pink Floyd's spacy acid-rock wails on the soundtrack. The End. As dumb, dull, and dated as it can often be, however, *Zabriskie Point* makes fairly good use of a whole lot of rock music on its soundtrack, and some of its sequences—in which there's nothing except music and (only at times stunning) abstracted, representational imagery—can be seen as protean music videos, so it has its historical significance. And if you don't try to think too hard, it can be enjoyed superficially as a bizarro sensual treat of sorts. Of course, some may find quite a bit of nostalgia value here, too.

☐ **VARIOUS ARTISTS**
ZACHARIAH
★★½

CBS/Fox, 1980, 93 minutes
PRODUCED BY: George Englund
DIRECTED BY: George Englund
MUSIC FROM: Zachariah motion picture soundtrack (ABC/Dunhill, 1971).
SELECTIONS: Country Joe and the Fish: "We're the Crackers," "One More Mount," "I Wanna Wash in a Bathtub of Gold"; Doug Kershaw: "Zachariah"; New York Rock and Roll Ensemble: "I Really Had to Set Her Free"; Elvin Jones: untitled drum solo.

Billed at the time of its 1971 release as "the first electric western," this psychedelic artifact has a cracked screenplay by the Firesign Theater, which consists mostly of surreal reversals of Western-movie clichés contrived to set the stage for the occasional hippie-era antiviolence platitude or the you've-gotta-be-stoned-to-get-it laugh. It's definitely got its gonzo-camp aspects: the cast includes John Rubinstein—yes, the same nice-Jewish-boy son of classical pianist Arthur Rubinstein who managed to survive this experience and star in TV's *Crazy Like a Fox* some fifteen years later—as the title character. And in the most galvanically surreal touch of all, the great jazz drummer Elvin Jones is cast as quick-draw artist and saloon keeper Cain. In the musical high point, Jones plays a typically stupendous, roilingly polyrhythmic drum solo in his Apache Wells saloon. Elsewhere, Country Joe and the Fish appear in cowboy drag as "the Crackers" to perform a few numbers, and the hard-to-take New York Rock and Roll Ensemble perform the turgidly classical-influenced "I Really Had to Set Her Free" in the nude in a brothel boudoir. Mainly recommendable as nostalgia for '60s survivors.

□ FRANK ZAPPA

DOES HUMOR BELONG IN MUSIC?

★½

MPI, 1986, 60 minutes
PRODUCED BY: Frank Zappa
DIRECTED BY: Frank Zappa
MUSIC FROM: Various albums by Frank Zappa and Frank Zappa and the Mothers of Invention.
SELECTIONS: "Zoot Allures," "Tinsel Town Rebellion," "Trouble Every Day," "Hot Plate Heaven at the Green Hotel," "The Dangerous Kitchen," "He's So Gay," "Bobby Brown," "Keep It Greasy," "Honey, Don't You Want a Man Like Me?," "Dinah-Moe Hum," "Cosmik Debris," "Be in My Video," "Dancin' Fool," "Whipping Post."

Since he first emerged from the Los Angeles "freak scene" in 1966 leading the Mothers of Invention, Frank Zappa has proved himself an accomplished guitarist, composer, arranger, and social satirist. He has even been called a genius—as he himself will be the first to tell you. Twenty years later he became a sort of counterculture hero all over again with his determined, high-visibility opposition to the PMRC's (Parents Music Resource Center) record-rating campaign. Unfortunately, that side of Frank Zappa is barely evident throughout *Does Humor Belong in Music?,* mix of concert footage (shot in August 1984 at New York City's Westside Pier) and various interview and press conference snippets. Instead, we get Zappa the smug. And the tape reveals what his albums have been suggesting for a while now—Frank's just not that funny or sharp anymore.

The bad news begins a few minutes into the program, when "Tinsel Town Rebellion"—a decent satire of record biz trendmongering—is interrupted in midperformance by interview footage. This keeps happening throughout the program. Then there's a terrible, sloppy jazz-funk version of "Trouble Every Day," which on the 1966 Mothers of Invention debut album *Freak Out!* was one of the most searingly powerful protest songs in the history of rock. "The Dangerous Kitchen" is sadly typical of the latter-day ruination of Zappa's once-challenging body of music: it's a dumb, trivial attempt at social-satire comedy that's not very funny, and it's set to "music" that's really just a jerry-rigged assemblage of riffs and rhythms that are metrically odd and complex purely for the sake of being odd and complex.

With "He's So Gay," a doo-wop (one of Zappa's favorite devices) tune, you have what those who are unfamiliar with Zappa's style might read as a vicious pandering to knee-jerk antigay reactionaries. Where "Tinsel Town Rebellion" features a modestly amusing direct reference to Culture Club, "He's So Gay" ends with Zappa's band crooning, "Do you really want to hurt me?" and answering with "We sure do!" "Bobby Brown" is more of the same, and "Keep It Greasy" is still *more* of it (the title here refers to anal sex). Even giving Zappa the most generous benefit of the doubt, the humor is so lame that these songs actually do seem to work better as attacks on their subjects than as attacks on their subjects' critics. At this point one can't help but wonder, Why does he bother, and what, exactly, is served by these "satires"? Yes, it's a free country and no group merits special consideration under those First Amendment protections right-wing groups like the PMRC are so wrongly attacking. At the same time, though, I found these songs simply offensive, and while Zappa can—and certainly should—say whatever he wants, I reserve the right not to have to listen to it.

Finally, in "Be in My Video," we get the first decent bit of satire, though here Zappa is making fun of one of the easiest and most obvious targets known to modern man. The show ends with a solid, apparently sincere, and thus rather dumbfounding, version of the Allman Brothers' encore classic "Whipping Post." After the credits, a business-suited Zappa appears for a moment to deliver a solemn plea to viewers to register to vote. That's a nice little touch, but it does nothing to remove the awful taste left by what's preceded it.

□ Z'EV
SIX EXAMPLES
★★★½

Target, 1984, 60 minutes
PRODUCED BY: Joe Rees
DIRECTED BY: Joe Rees
MUSIC FROM: Six live percussion performances in San Francisco and London (1978–80).
SELECTIONS: Six untitled percussion "sound performances."

Z'ev (real name Stephen Weisser) is a most unusual San Francisco–based percussionist who came to prominence on the post-punk scene of the late '70s and early '80s, and who anticipated the mid-'80s avant-rock trend toward industrial "noise" music (e.g., the German group Einsterzende Neubauten, Britain's SPK and Test Dept., and so on). Here, he's captured nicely with Target Video's usual gritty, low-budget intimacy in several San Francisco performances and one from London, between 1978 and 1980. He's got quite an act: Z'ev doesn't "play" "percussion" in the traditional sense at all; rather, he strips off his shirt, puts on his hockey-style knee guards, and proceeds to kick, clang together, hit, or drag around strung-together pots and pans, trashcans and trashcan lids of both metal and plastic, various pipes and fittings, plastic tubes, glass bottles and plastic or metal jugs, metal sheets, steel bars, and so on—creating not only a spontaneous, dadaistic form of theatrical performance art, but also some mighty hair-raising and often surprisingly musical sounds and rhythmic noises, all of which is strategically altered and amplified through the use of microphones and echo and reverb effects as well as natural room acoustics. About the closest Z'ev comes to "traditional" concepts of percussion is when he taps on a huge steel industrial spring with thin metal sticks, producing a wild tintinnabulation. He's not for everybody—but then, he doesn't try to be. For those who dare, Z'ev should prove a fascinating, eye-and-ear-opening experience, and despite the barely existent production values, Target Video's Joe Rees does a fine job of capturing this uniquely post-industrial spectacle. (Available in stores, or by mail order from Target Video or Independent World Video.)

□ WARREN ZEVON
WARREN ZEVON VIDEO LP
★★★

Sony, 1982, 68 minutes
PRODUCED BY: John Scher, Amy Polan, Jonathan Strathakis
DIRECTED BY: Len Dell'Amico
MUSIC FROM: Warren Zevon (Asylum, 1976); *Excitable Boy* (Asylum, 1978); *Bad*

Luck Streak in Dancing School (Asylum, 1980); *Stand in the Fire* (Asylum, 1980); *The Envoy* (Asylum, 1982).

SELECTIONS: Johnny Strikes Up the Band," "A Certain Girl," "Jeannie Needs a Shooter," "Excitable Boy," "Mohammed's Radio," "Werewolves of London," "Poor Poor Pitiful Me," "The Envoy," "Ain't That Pretty at All," "The Overdraft," "Jungle Work," "Accidentally like a Martyr," "Roland the Headless Thompson Gunner."

Zevon fans will find much to enjoy in this 1982 concert film shot at the Capital Theater in New Jersey. Zevon covers most of his best-known songs and gets absolutely crazy on a few, like "Ain't That Pretty at All" and "A Certain Girl." Unfortunately, this band is not the same one used on 1980's live album *Stand in the Fire,* which was widely acclaimed for its instensity and passion. The performances are fine, though nonfans may soon tire of Zevon's constant references to his good buddy Bruce. Sadly, Zevon gets the biggest rise out of this crowd when he does the Boss's "Cadillac Ranch."

Maybe it wasn't Zevon's night, and that might explain some of the show's problems. The tape, however, suffers most from being a straightforward, no-frills MTV concert shoot that probably missed as many great moments as it captured. And when, oh when, will directors get it through their thick heads that turning the brights on a crowd in search of those transcendent audience reaction shots only manages to capture a bunch of slack-jawed stares and goofy faces?—P.R.

Home Video Distributors and Mail Order Sources

A&M Video
c/o A&M Records
1416 North LaBrea Avenue
Hollywood, California 90028

Carmine Appice Enterprises, Inc.
Post Office Box 69780
Los Angeles, California 90069

Atlantic Video
75 Rockefeller Plaza
New York, New York 10019

Blackhawk Films
One Old Eagle Brewery
Post Office Box 3990
Davenport, Iowa 52808

CBS/Fox Home Video
1211 Avenue of the Americas
New York, New York 10036

Continental Video
2320 Cotner
Los Angeles, California 90064

DCI Music Video
541 Avenue of the Americas
New York, New York 10011
1-800-924-6624

Walt Disney Home Video
500 South Buena Vista Street
Burbank, California 91521

Elektra Video
75 Rockefeller Plaza
New York, New York 10019

Embassy Home Entertainment
1901 Avenue of the Stars
Los Angeles, California 90067

Factory
325 Spring Street
Room 233
New York, New York 10013

Flower Films
10341 San Pablo Avenue
El Cerrito, California 94530

HBO/Cannon Video
1370 Avenue of the Americas
New York, New York 10019

Homespun Tapes
Post Office Box 694
Woodstock, New York 12498

Hot Licks Productions, Inc.
Post Office Box 337
Pound Ridge, New York 10576

Independent World Video
Post Office Box 38357
Hollywood, California 90038

Instant Replay
479 Winter Street
Waltham, Massachusetts
02154-1216

International Video Entertainment
(I.V.E.)
Suite 300
21800 Burbank Boulevard
Post Office Box 4062
Woodland Hills, California
91365-4062

JEM/Passport Video
c/o JEM Records
3619 Kennedy Road
South Plainfield, New Jersey 07080

Karl/Lorimar Home Video
17942 Cowan Avenue
Irvine, California 92714

MCA Home Video
100 Universal City Plaza
Universal City, California 91608

Media Home Entertainment
/Music Media
5730 Buckingham Parkway
Culver City, California 90230

MGM/UA Home Video
1350 Avenue of the Americas
New York, New York 10019

MPI (Maljack Productions, Inc.)
15825 Rob Roy Drive
Oak Forest, Illinois 60452

Pacific Arts Video Records
Post Office Box 22770
Carmel, California 93922

Paramount Home Video
5555 Melrose Avenue
Hollywood, California 90038

Pioneer Artists
200 West Grand Avenue
Montvale, New Jersey 07645

Playings Hard to Get
580 Old Mine Office
Madrid, New Mexico 87010

Private Music
220 East 23rd Street
New York, New York 10010

Ralph Records Video
566 Folsom Street
San Francisco, California 94105

RCA/Columbia Pictures
Home Video
3500 West Olive Avenue
Burbank, California 91505

Republic Pictures Home Video
Post Office Box 66930
Los Angeles, California 90066-0930

Rhapsody Films
30 Charlton Street
New York, New York 10014

Rough Trade
326 Sixth Street
San Francisco, California 94103

Sony Video Software
1700 Broadway
New York, New York 10019

Spotlite Video
(see Blackhawk Films)

Star Licks
2210 Wilshire Boulevard
Suite 124
Santa Monica, California 90403

Stevenson Productions, Inc.
3227 Banks Street
New Orleans, Louisiana 70119
1-405-822-7678

Target Video
678 South Van Noss
San Francisco, California 94110

Thorn-EMI Home Video
(see HBO/Cannon Video)

University of Chicago at Illinois
Instructional Research Lab
m/c 210
Box 4348
Chicago, Illinois 60680

Vestron Video
Post Office Box 4000
Stamford, Connecticut 06907

VidAmerica
235 East 55th Street
New York, New York 10022

Video Yesteryear
Box C
Sandy Hook, Connecticut 06482

V.I.E.W. Video
34 East 23rd Street
New York, New York 10010

Warner Home Video
4000 Warner Boulevard
Burbank, California 91522

Warner Music Video
(see Warner-Reprise Video)

Warner-Reprise Video
3300 Warner Boulevard
Burbank, California 91505

INDEX

About the Author

Michael Shore has been writing about popular music and music video for over ten years and is the author of the widely acclaimed *Rolling Stone Book of Rock Video,* the first serious critical and historical study of the music video phenomenon, and *The History of American Bandstand* (with Dick Clark). His articles have appeared in *The Soho Weekly News, Village Voice, Musician, Music-Sound Output, Rolling Stone, Billboard, Hit Parader, The Record, International Musician and Recording World,* and *America Illustrated,* and he was a major contributor to the reference works *The Rolling Stone Encyclopedia of Rock & Roll* and *The Rolling Stone Rock Almanac.* He has been a featured speaker at video and music business conventions in the United States and Canada and a judge and awards presenter at *Billboard* 's Fifth International Video Music Awards Conference. He is currently a news and feature writer for MTV, for which he has written specials on Prince as well as the network's "New Video Hour." Shore wrote the home video program *British Rock: The First Wave.*

Patricia Romanowski (P.R.) is an editor and writer who specializes in popular culture and rock. While an editor at Rolling Stone Press, she conceived and edited Michael Shore's *Rolling Stone Book of Rock Video* and was the editor of the *Rolling Stone Encyclopedia of Rock & Roll* and *The Rolling Stone Rock Almanac.* More recently she edited *Heavy Metal Thunder* by Philip Bashe and *Where Did Our Love Go* by Nelson George, and co-wrote, with Mary Wilson, *Dreamgirl: My Life As a Supreme.*